Solr in Action

TREY GRAINGER
TIMOTHY POTTER

MANNING

SHELTER ISLAND

For online information and ordering of this and other Manning books, please visit
www.manning.com. The publisher offers discounts on this book when ordered in quantity.
For more information, please contact

Special Sales Department
Manning Publications Co.
20 Baldwin Road
PO Box 261
Shelter Island, NY 11964
Email: orders@manning.com

Photographs in this book were created by Martin Evans and Jordan Hochenbaum, unless
otherwise noted. Illustrations were created by Martin Evans, Joshua Noble, and Jordan
Hochenbaum. Fritzing (fritzing.org) was used to create some of the circuit diagrams.

Many of the designations used by manufacturers and sellers to distinguish their products are
claimed as trademarks. Where those designations appear in the book, and Manning
Publications was aware of a trademark claim, the designations have been printed in initial caps
or all caps.

⊗ Recognizing the importance of preserving what has been written, it is Manning's policy to have
the books we publish printed on acid-free paper, and we exert our best efforts to that end.
Recognizing also our responsibility to conserve the resources of our planet, Manning books
are printed on paper that is at least 15 percent recycled and processed without the use of
elemental chlorine.

Manning Publications Co.
20 Baldwin Road
PO Box 261
Shelter Island, NY 11964

Development editors: Elizabeth Lexleigh, Susan Conant
Copyeditor: Melinda Rankin
Proofreader: Elizabeth Martin
Typesetter: Dennis Dalinnik
Cover designer: Marija Tudor

ISBN: 9781617291029
Printed in the United States of America
1 2 3 4 5 6 7 8 9 10 – MAL – 19 18 17 16 15 14

brief contents

contents

foreword

Solr has had a long and successful history, but a major new chapter began recently with the advent of Solr 4 and SolrCloud. This is the perfect time for *Solr in Action*. With clear examples, enlightening diagrams, and coverage from key concepts through the newest features, *Solr in Action* will have you successfully using Solr in no time!

Solr was born out of necessity in 2004, at CNET Networks (now CBS Interactive), to replace a commercial search engine being discontinued by the vendor. Even though I had no formal search background when I started writing Solr, it felt like a very natural fit, because I have always enjoyed making software "go fast." I viewed Solr more as an alternate type of datastore designed around an inverted index than as a full-text search engine, and that has helped Solr extend beyond the legacy enterprise search market.

By the end of 2005, Solr was powering the search and faceted navigation of a number of CNET sites, and soon it was made open source. Solr was contributed to the Apache Software Foundation in January 2006 and became a subproject of the Lucene PMC (with Lucene Java as its sibling). There had always been a large degree of overlap with Lucene (the core full-text search library used by Solr) committers, and in 2010 the projects were merged. Separate Lucene and Solr downloads would still be available, but they would be developed by a single unified team. Solr's version number jumped to match that of Lucene, and the releases have since been synchronized.

The recent Solr 4 release is a major milestone, adding SolrCloud—the set of highly scalable features including distributed indexing with no single points of failure. The NoSQL feature set was also expanded to include transaction logs, update durability, optimistic concurrency, and atomic updates. *Solr in Action*, written by longtime Solr power users and community members, Trey and Timothy, covers these important recent Solr features and provides an excellent starting point for those new to Solr.

Solr is now used in more places than I could ever have imagined—from integrated library systems to e-commerce platforms, analytics and business intelligence products, content-management systems, internet searches, and more. It's been rewarding to see Solr grow from a few early adopters to a huge global community of helpful users and active volunteers cooperatively pushing development forward.

Solr in Action gives you the knowledge and techniques you need to use Solr's features that have been under development since 2004. With *Solr in Action* in hand, you too are now well equipped to join the global community and help take Solr to new heights!

YONIK SEELEY
CREATOR OF SOLR

preface

In 2008, I was asked to take over leadership of CareerBuilder's search technology team. We were using the Microsoft FAST search platform at the time, but realized that search was too important to the success of our business for us to continue relying on a commercial vendor instead of developing the domain expertise internally. I immediately began investigating open source alternatives such as Solr, which seemed to provide most of the key features needed for our products. By the summer of 2009, we decided that we were ready to bring our search expertise in-house and convert our systems to Solr.

The timing was great. Lucene, the open source search library upon which Solr is built, had become a full top-level Apache project in February 2005, and Solr, which had been contributed to the Apache Software Foundation in 2006, had become a top-level Apache project in January of 2007. Both technologies were reaching critical mass and would soon be merged (in March 2010) into a unified project.

By the summer of 2010, our entire platform was converted to Solr. In the process, we increased the speed of our searches, significantly reduced the number of servers necessary to support our search infrastructure, dropped expensive licensing fees, increased platform stability, and in-sourced much of the search expertise for which we had previously been dependent on a commercial vendor.

Little did we know at that time how much additional value we would gain by bringing search in-house. We have been able to build entirely new suites of search-based products—from traditional keyword and semantic search, to big data analytics products, to real-time recommendation engines—utilizing Solr as a scalable search architecture to handle billions of documents and millions of queries an hour across hundreds of servers. We have entered the era of cloud services, elastic scalability, and an explosion of data that we strive to make meaningful for society, and with Solr we are able to tackle each of these challenges head-on.

When Manning approached me about writing *Solr in Action*, I was hesitant because I knew it would be a large undertaking. My one requirement was that I needed a strong coauthor, and that is exactly what I found in Timothy Potter. Tim also has years of experience developing search-based solutions with Lucene and Solr. He has a wealth of expertise building text analysis systems for social data and architecting real-time analytics solutions using Solr and other cutting-edge big data technologies. With both of us having received so much help from the Solr community over the years and with such a clear need for an example-driven guide to Solr, Tim and I are excited to be able to provide *Solr in Action* to help the next generation of search engineers. It's the book we wish we'd had five years ago when we started with Solr, and we hope that you find it to be useful, whether you are just getting introduced to Solr or are looking to take your knowledge to the next level.

TREY GRAINGER

acknowledgments

Much like Solr, this book would not have been possible without the support of a large community of dedicated people:

- Lucene/Solr committers who not only write amazing code but also provide invaluable expertise and advice, all the while demonstrating patience with new members of the community
- Active Lucene/Solr community members who contribute code, update the wiki and other documentation, and answer questions on the Lucene and Solr mailing lists
- Yonik Seeley, original creator of Solr, who contributed the foreword to our book
- Our Manning Early Access Program (MEAP) readers who posted comments in the Author Online forum
- The reviewers who provided valuable feedback throughout the development process: Alexandre Madurell, Ammar Alrashed, Brandon Harper, Chris Nauroth, Craig Smith, Edward Welker, Gregor Zurowski, John Viviano, Leo Cassarani, Robert Petersen, Scott Anthony, Sopan Shewale, and Uma Maheshwar Rao Gunuganti
- Ivan Todorović and John Guthrie who provided a detailed technical proofread of the manuscript shortly before it went into production
- Our Manning editors, Elizabeth Lexleigh, Susan Conant, Melinda Rankin, Elizabeth Martin, and Janet Vail

- Bert Bates at Manning for helping us improve the instructional quality of our writing
- Family and friends who supported us through the many hours of research and writing

TREY GRAINGER

First and foremost, I would like to thank my amazing wife, Lindsay, for her support and patience during the many long days and nights it took to write this book. Without her understanding and help throughout the journey, this book would have never been possible (especially with the birth of our daughter midway through the project).

I would also like to thank Paula and Steven Woolf for the countless hours they spent watching Melodie so that I could push this project to completion. Finally, I would like to thank the team at CareerBuilder—both the company leadership and my Search team—for giving me the opportunity to work with such great people and to build a cutting-edge search platform that benefits society in such a clear way.

TIMOTHY POTTER

I would like to thank Sharon Russom, my mother, for instilling a love of learning and books early in my childhood, and David Potter, my father, for all of his support throughout college and my career. This book would not have been possible without the help of Lori Joy. Thank you for your support and for being understanding during the late evenings and missed weekends, and for being a sounding board early in the writing process.

I also thank my former team at the Dachis Group. I could not have done this without their insightful questions about Solr and their giving me the opportunity to build a large-scale search solution using Solr.

about this book

Whether handling big data, building cloud-based services, or developing multitenant web applications, it's vital to have a fast, reliable search solution. Apache Solr is a scalable and ready-to-deploy open source full-text search engine powered by Lucene. It offers key features like multilingual keyword searching, faceted search, intelligent matching, content clustering, and relevancy weighting right out of the box.

Solr in Action is the definitive guide to implementing fast and scalable search using Apache Solr. It uses well-documented examples ranging from basic keyword searching to scaling a system for billions of documents and queries. With this book, you'll gain a deep understanding of how to implement core Solr capabilities such as faceted navigation through search results, matched snippet highlighting, field collapsing and search results grouping, spell-checking, query autocomplete, querying by functions, and more. You'll also see how to take Solr to the next level, with deep coverage of large-scale production use cases, sophisticated multilingual search, complex query operations, and advanced relevancy tuning strategies.

Roadmap

Solr in Action is divided into three parts: "Meet Solr," "Core Solr capabilities," and "Taking Solr to the next level." If you are new to Solr and to search in general, we strongly recommend that you read the chapters in part 1 in order, as many of the concepts presented in these chapters build on each other.

The concepts covered in part 2 were chosen because they are common features of most search applications. You can safely skip any chapter in part 2 that may not apply to your current needs. For example, result grouping is a common feature in many search engines, but if your data doesn't require grouping, then you can safely skip chapter 11.

The four chapters (13–16) in part 3 are the most challenging as they introduce advanced topics, including multilingual search, running Solr in a large-scale cluster environment, advanced data operations, and relevancy tuning.

Most of the chapters use hands-on activities to help you work through the material. Our goal for each example was that it be easy to use but cover the chapter topic thoroughly. In many examples, we used data from real-world datasets so that you would get exposure to working with realistic use cases.

Chapter 1 introduces the type of data and use cases Solr was designed to handle. You'll learn about the kinds of problems you can solve with Solr and gain an overview of its key features. Solr 4 is a significant milestone for the Lucene/Solr project, so even if you're an expert on previous versions of Solr, we encourage you to read chapter 1 to get a sense for all the new and exciting features in Solr 4.

Chapter 2 shows how to install and run Solr on your local workstation. After starting Solr, we demonstrate how to index and query a set of example documents that ship with Solr. We also take a brief tour of Solr's web-based administration console.

Chapter 3 introduces general search theory and how Solr implements that theory in practice. Most interestingly, this chapter covers the inverted search index and how relevancy scoring works to present the most relevant documents at the top of search results. Even if you have worked with Solr in the past, we recommend reading this chapter to refresh your understanding of the fundamental operations in a search engine.

Chapter 4 shows the basics of Solr's configuration, primarily focused on Solr's main configuration file: *solrconfig.xml*. Our aim in this chapter is to introduce the most important configuration settings for Solr, particularly those that impact how Solr processes requests from client applications. The knowledge you gain in this chapter will be applied throughout the rest of the book.

Chapter 5 teaches how Solr indexes documents, starting with a discussion of another important configuration file: *schema.xml*. You'll learn how to define fields to represent structured data like numbers, dates, prices, and unique identifiers. We also cover how update requests are processed and configured using *solrconfig.xml*.

Chapter 6 builds on the material in chapter 5 by showing how to index text fields using text analysis. Solr was designed to efficiently search and rank documents requiring full-text search. Text analysis is an important part of the search process in that it removes the linguistic variations between indexed text and queries.

At this point in the book, you'll have a solid foundation and will be ready to put Solr to work on your own search needs. As your knowledge of search and Solr grows, so too will your need to go beyond basic keyword searching and implement common search features such as advanced query parsing, hit highlighting, spellchecking, autosuggest, faceting, and result grouping.

In chapter 7, we cover how to construct queries and how they are executed. You'll learn about Solr's many query parsers, as well as how to sort, format, return, and debug search results.

In chapter 8, you'll learn about one of the most powerful and popular features of Solr—faceting. Solr's faceting provides tools to refine search criteria and helps users discover more information by categorizing search results into subgroups.

Chapter 9 explains how to highlight query terms in search results in order to improve the user experience with your search solution.

In chapter 10, we cover spell-checking and autosuggestions. Solr's autosuggest features allow a user to start typing a few characters and receive a list of suggested queries as they type.

Chapter 11 explores Solr's result grouping and field collapsing support to help you return an optimal mix of search results when your index includes many similar documents, such as multiple locations of the same restaurant in a city.

Chapter 12 helps you prepare to deploy Solr in a production environment. This chapter will help you plan your hardware and resource needs, as well as whether you need to consider sharding and replication to handle a large number of documents and query requests.

Chapter 13 covers a set of distributed features known as SolrCloud. You'll learn how to run Solr in cloud mode so that you can scale your search application to support a large volume of users and documents. You'll come away from this chapter having a solid understanding of how Solr achieves scalability and fault tolerance by distributing indexes across multiple servers.

Chapter 14 builds upon the text analysis concepts covered in chapter 6 by teaching you how to handle multilingual text in your search engine. If you need to work with non-English text or support multiple languages in the same index, this chapter is a must-read.

Chapter 15 explores advanced query features, including function queries, geospatial search, multilevel faceting, and cross-document and cross-index joins.

In chapter 16, you'll learn techniques for improving the relevancy of your results, such as boosting, scoring based upon functions, alternate similarity algorithms, and debugging relevancy scores. In addition, we provide an in-depth discussion of using Solr for personalized search and recommendations.

There are three appendixes, which cover a number of subtopics from earlier chapters in greater depth. Appendix A focuses on working with the Solr codebase and how you can create your own custom Solr distribution if you need features or bug fixes not available in an official release. This is an extension of some of the material from the beginning of chapter 12.

Appendix B lists, in table format, out-of-the box configurations for many of the languages Solr supports. This material is an extended version of the language configurations covered in chapter 14.

Appendix C highlights the Data Import Handler (DIH) in more detail (extending coverage from chapters 10 and 12), demonstrating the steps necessary for importing a number of large, publicly available datasets.

How to use this book

Solr in Action is designed to be accessible for any software engineer—no previous experience working with search engines is assumed. The topics covered rise in expertise level throughout the book, and even the most seasoned Solr professionals are likely to learn something from the last few chapters. The scope of the book is massive—coming in at over 600 pages—but the engaging and practical real-world examples and careful balance between theory and practice make the book a real asset to anyone using Solr —whether you are just getting started or have years of experience.

As mentioned above, the chapters in part 1 provide the foundation upon which the rest of the book will be built, and they will be critical for anyone new to Solr. These chapters should be read in sequence to give you the best overview of Solr and search in general. If you are new to Solr, chapter 2 will show you how to start and use Solr for the first time, and chapter 3 will provide the key search theory that the rest of the book builds upon. Configuring your Solr server and setting up field types to properly analyze your content round out the search topics needed to understand Solr's fundamentals.

Many of the chapters in part 2 can be skipped if your work does not include the features discussed. In particular, chapters 9, 10, and 11 are largely standalone topics that are not important for understanding later chapters, so you can skip them if you are not planning on implementing hit highlighting, query suggestions, or result grouping/field collapsing any time soon. Chapters 7 and 8 cover some of the most commonly used features of many search applications, so you will want to at least skim through them before putting the book away.

The remaining chapters cover some of the advanced topics surrounding Solr. Tough challenges will be tackled, including scaling a cluster of servers, multilingual search, complex query operations, and advanced relevancy techniques. While all chapters in parts 2 and 3 build on part 1, chapter 13 ("SolrCloud") additionally builds on chapter 12 ("Taking Solr to production"), chapter 15 ("Complex query operations") builds on chapters 7 ("Performing queries and handling results") and 8 ("Faceted search"), and chapter 16 ("Mastering relevancy") further builds on chapter 15. In order to get the most benefit out of the book, be mindful not to skip any earlier chapters that provide the necessary background for your understanding of these more advanced topics.

Many of the chapters include executable examples that you can run as you read along. These examples demonstrate new topics and provide you with the opportunity for hands-on exploration of Solr's capabilities—often through just hitting a running Solr server from your web browser. While you do not have to run all of the examples and can simply use them as reference configurations in many cases, running the examples will provide you with hands-on experience that may help some of the more challenging topics sink in.

Whether you plan to work your way through the whole book—going from first-time Solr user to Solr expert—is up to you. If not, you can always refer to the book over time as your interest and need for more advanced Solr capabilities continue to grow.

Code conventions and downloads

Java code, configuration snippets, executable commands, contents of files, and server requests/responses (subsequently referred to as "source code") in this book are in a `fixed-width` font, which sets them apart from the surrounding text. In many listings, the source code is annotated to point out the key concepts. In some cases, source code is in **`bold fixed-width font`** for emphasis. We have tried to format the source code so it fits within the available page space in the book by adding line breaks and using indentation carefully. Sometimes, however, very long lines include line-continuation markers like this: ➥.

Throughout the book you will find references to files that are included with Solr or with the examples that come with the book. File names will typically be in *italics*, except when they are referenced within source code, where they will still use a `fixed-width` font.

Source code examples appear throughout this book, with longer listings appearing under clear listing headers and shorter listings appearing between lines of text. Source code for all the working examples in the book is available for download from the publisher's website at www.manning.com/SolrinAction or www.manning.com/grainger.

A *README.txt* file is provided in the root folder of the accompanying source code, providing details on how to compile and run the examples. We chose to use Java as the development language for this book because it is the language used within the Lucene/Solr project, and we thought it would be easiest for readers to deal with one, consistent programming language.

After you download Solr in chapter 2, we will refer to the folder in which you installed Solr as *$SOLR_INSTALL* in the rest of the book. Similarly, we will refer to the folder into which you download and extract the source code accompanying this book as *$SOLR_IN_ACTION*. Wherever you see either of these, you should substitute the actual folder name on your system.

Author Online

Purchase of *Solr in Action* includes free access to a private web forum run by Manning Publications where you can make comments about the book, ask technical questions, and receive help from the authors and from other users. To access the forum and subscribe to it, point your browser to www.manning.com/SolrinAction or www.manning.com/grainger. The page provides information on how to get on the forum once you're registered, what kind of help is available, and the rules of conduct on the forum.

Manning's commitment to our readers is to provide a venue where a meaningful dialog between individual readers and between readers and the authors can take place. It's not a commitment to any specific amount of participation on the part of the authors, whose contribution to the forum remains voluntary (and unpaid). We suggest you ask the authors challenging questions lest their interest stray!

The Author Online forum and the archives of previous discussions will be accessible from the publisher's website as long as the book is in print.

About the cover illustration

The figure on the cover of *Solr in Action* is captioned "A Gothscheer woman," or a woman from a Gothic tribe. The Goths were a northern people that came from Scandinavia to Europe 2000 years ago, and originally settled around the Baltic Sea. They played an important role in the fall of the Roman Empire and the emergence of Medieval Europe. They eventually separated into two branches, with the Visigoths becoming federates of the Romans and then moving west to France and Spain, and the Ostrogoths moving to northern Italy, the Balkans, and as far east as the Black Sea. Over time, their language and culture disappeared as they assimilated in the regions where they had settled.

This illustration is taken from a recent reprint of Balthasar Hacquet's *Images and Descriptions of Southwestern and Eastern Wenda, Illyrians, and Slavs* published by the Ethnographic Museum in Split, Croatia, in 2008. Hacquet (1739–1815) was an Austrian physician and scientist who spent many years studying the botany, geology, and ethnography of many parts of the Austrian Empire, as well as the Veneto, the Julian Alps, and the western Balkans, inhabited in the past by peoples of many different tribes and nationalities. Hand-drawn illustrations accompany the many scientific papers and books that Hacquet published.

The rich diversity of the drawings in Hacquet's publications speaks vividly of the uniqueness and individuality of Alpine and Balkan regions just 200 years ago. This was a time when the dress codes of two villages separated by a few miles identified people uniquely as belonging to one or the other, and when members of an ethnic tribe, social class, or trade could be easily distinguished by what they were wearing. Dress codes have changed since then and the diversity by region, so rich at the time, has faded away. It is now often hard to tell the inhabitant of one continent from another, and today's inhabitants of the towns and villages on the shores of the Baltic or Mediterranean or Black Seas are not readily distinguishable from residents of other parts of Europe.

We at Manning celebrate the inventiveness, the initiative, and the fun of the computer business with book covers based on costumes from two centuries ago brought back to life by illustrations such as this one.

Part 1

Meet Solr

Our primary focus in these first six chapters will be to explore Solr's two most important functions: indexing data and executing queries. After reading part 1, you should have a solid understanding of Solr's query and indexing capabilities, including how to perform analysis of text and other data types, and how to execute searches across that data.

As with every new subject, first we must start with the basics—learning how to install Solr and run it locally.

If you are new to the full-text search space, some of the terminology may be unfamiliar, so consider chapter 3 a dictionary of sorts. What are the key differentiators between a search engine and a database? What is an inverted index? What is relevancy ranking and how does Solr implement it?

With the basics out of the way, starting with chapter 4, we begin looking under the hood of the Solr engine to see how requests are executed and to get an idea of the configuration settings that govern request processing. The main configuration file in Solr, *solrconfig.xml*, contains numerous settings, some of which (such as cache management settings) are useful when just starting out, while others are intended for advanced users.

A search engine is not very interesting until it has some documents indexed. In chapters 5 and 6, we focus on how documents get indexed, covering document schema design, field types, and text analysis. Understanding these core aspects of indexing will help you throughout the rest of the book.

Introduction to Solr

With fast-growing technologies such as social media, cloud computing, mobile applications, and big data, these are exciting, and challenging, times to be in computing. One of the main challenges facing software architects is handling the massive volume of data consumed and produced by a huge, global user base. In addition, users expect online applications to always be available and responsive. To address the scalability and availability needs of modern web applications, we've seen a growing interest in specialized, nonrelational data storage and processing technologies, collectively known as NoSQL (Not only SQL). These systems share a common design pattern of matching storage and processing engines to specific types of data rather than forcing all data into the once-standard relational model. In other words, NoSQL technologies are optimized to solve a specific class of problems for specific types of data. The need to scale has led to hybrid architectures composed of a variety of NoSQL and relational databases; gone are the days of the one-size-fits-all data-processing solution.

This book is about Apache Solr, a specific NoSQL technology. Solr, just as its nonrelational brethren, is optimized for a unique class of problems. Specifically, Solr is a scalable, ready-to-deploy enterprise search engine that's optimized to search large volumes of text-centric data and return results sorted by relevance. That was a bit of a mouthful, so let's break that statement down into its basic parts:

- *Scalable*—Solr scales by distributing work (indexing and query processing) to multiple servers in a cluster.
- *Ready to deploy*—Solr is open source, is easy to install and configure, and provides a preconfigured example to help you get started.
- *Optimized for search*—Solr is fast and can execute complex queries in subsecond speed, often only tens of milliseconds.
- *Large volumes of documents*—Solr is designed to deal with indexes containing many millions of documents.
- *Text-centric*—Solr is optimized for searching natural-language text, like emails, web pages, resumes, PDF documents, and social messages such as tweets or blogs.
- *Results sorted by relevance*—Solr returns documents in ranked order based on how relevant each document is to the user's query.

In this book, you'll learn how to use Solr to design and implement scalable search solutions. You'll begin by learning about the types of data and use cases Solr supports. This will help you understand where Solr fits into the big picture of modern application architectures and which problems Solr is designed to solve.

1.1   Why do I need a search engine?

Because you're looking at this book, we suspect that you already have an idea about why you need a search engine. Rather than speculate on why you're considering Solr, we'll get right down to the hard questions you need to answer about your data and use cases in order to decide if a search engine is right for you. In the end, it comes down to understanding your data and users and picking a technology that works for both. Let's start by looking at the properties of data that a search engine is optimized to handle.

1.1.1   Managing text-centric data

A hallmark of modern application architectures is matching the storage and processing engine to your data. If you're a programmer, you know to select the best data structure based on how you use the data in an algorithm; that is, you don't use a linked list when you need fast random lookups. The same principle applies with search engines. Search engines like Solr are optimized to handle data exhibiting four main characteristics:

1 Text-centric
2 Read-dominant
3 Document-oriented
4 Flexible schema

A possible fifth characteristic is having a large volume of data to deal with; that is, "big data," but our focus is on what makes a search engine special among other NoSQL technologies. It goes without saying that Solr can deal with large volumes of data.

Although these are the four main characteristics of data that search engines like Solr handle efficiently, you should think of them as rough guidelines, not strict rules. Let's dig into each to see why they're important for search. For now, we'll focus on the high-level concepts; we'll get into the "how" in later chapters.

TEXT-CENTRIC

You'll undoubtedly encounter the term *unstructured* used to describe the type of data that's handled by a search engine. We think unstructured is a little ambiguous because any text document based on human language has implicit structure. You can think of unstructured as being from the perspective of a computer, which sees text as a stream of characters. The character stream must be parsed using language-specific rules to extract the structure and make it searchable, which is exactly what search engines do.

We think *text-centric* is more appropriate for describing the type of data Solr handles, because a search engine is specifically designed to extract the implicit structure of text into its index to improve searching. Text-centric data implies that the text of a document contains information that users are interested in finding. Of course, a search engine also supports nontext data such as dates and numbers, but its primary strength is handling text data based on natural language.

The *centric* part is important because if users aren't interested in the information in the text, a search engine may not be the best solution for your problem. Consider an application in which employees create travel expense reports. Each report contains a number of structured data fields such as date, expense type, currency, and amount. In addition, each expense may include a notes field in which employees can provide a brief description of the expense. This would be an example of data that contains text but isn't text-centric, in that it's unlikely that the accounting department needs to search the notes field when generating monthly expense reports. Just because data contains text fields doesn't mean that data is a natural fit for a search engine.

Think about whether your data is text-centric. The main consideration is whether or not the text fields in your data contain information that users will want to query. If yes, then a search engine is probably a good choice. You'll see how to unlock the structure in text by using Solr's text analysis capabilities in chapters 5 and 6.

READ-DOMINANT

Another key aspect of data that search engines handle effectively is that data is read-dominant and therefore intended to be accessed efficiently, as opposed to updated frequently. Let's be clear that Solr does allow you to update existing documents in your index. Think of *read-dominant* as meaning that documents are read far more often than they're created or updated. But don't take this to mean that you can't write a lot of data or that you have limits on how frequently you can write new data. In fact, one of the key features in Solr 4 is *near real-time* (NRT) search, which allows you to index thousands of documents per second and have them be searchable almost immediately.

The key point behind read-dominant data is that when you write data to Solr, it's intended to be read and reread myriad times over its lifetime. Think of a search engine as being optimized for executing queries (a read operation), for example, as opposed to storing data (a write operation). Also, if you must update existing data in a search engine often, that could be an indication that a search engine might not be the best solution for your needs. Another NoSQL technology, like Cassandra, might be a better choice when you need fast random writes to existing data.

DOCUMENT-ORIENTED

Until now, we've talked about data, but in reality, search engines work with documents. In a search engine, a *document* is a self-contained collection of fields, in which each field only holds data and doesn't contain nested fields. In other words, a document in a search engine like Solr has a flat structure and doesn't depend on other documents. The flat concept is slightly relaxed in Solr, in that a field can have multiple values, but fields don't contain subfields. You can store multiple values in a single field, but you can't nest fields inside of other fields.

The flat, document-oriented approach in Solr works well with data that's already in document format, such as a web page, blog, or PDF document, but what about modeling normalized data stored in a relational database? In this case, you need to denormalize data spread across multiple tables into a flat, self-contained document structure. We'll learn how to approach problems like this in chapter 3.

You also want to consider which fields in your documents must be stored in Solr and which should be stored in another system, such as a database. A search engine isn't the place to store data unless it's useful for search or displaying results; for example, if you have a search index for online videos, you don't want to store the binary video files in Solr. Rather, large binary fields should be stored in another system, such as a content-distribution network (CDN). In general, you should store the minimal set of information for each document needed to satisfy search requirements. This is a clear example of not treating Solr as a general data-storage technology; Solr's job is to find videos of interest, not to manage large binary files.

FLEXIBLE SCHEMA

The last main characteristic of search-engine data is that it has a *flexible schema*. This means that documents in a search index don't need to have a uniform structure. In a relational database, every row in a table has the same structure. In Solr, documents can have different fields. Of course, there should be some overlap between the fields in documents in the same index, but they don't have to be identical.

Imagine a search application for finding homes for rent or sale. Listings will obviously share fields like location, number of bedrooms, and number of bathrooms, but they'll also have different fields based on the listing type. A home for sale would have fields for listing price and annual property taxes, whereas a home for rent would have a field for monthly rent and pet policy.

To summarize, search engines in general and Solr in particular are optimized to handle data having four specific characteristics: text-centric, read-dominant, document-oriented, and flexible schema. Overall, this implies that Solr is *not* a general-purpose data-storage and processing technology.

The whole point of having such a variety of options for storing and processing data is that you don't have to find a one-size-fits-all technology. Search engines are good at certain things and quite horrible at others. This means, in most cases, you're going to find that Solr complements relational and NoSQL databases more than it replaces them.

Now that we've talked about the type of data Solr is optimized to handle, let's think about the primary use cases a search engine like Solr is designed for. These use cases are intended to help you understand how a search engine is different than other data-processing technologies.

1.1.2 Common search-engine use cases

In this section, we look at things you can do with a search engine like Solr. As with our discussion of the types of data in section 1.1.1, use these as guidelines, not as strict rules. Before we get into specifics, we should remind you to keep in mind that the bar for excellence in search is high. Modern users are accustomed to web search engines like Google and Bing being fast and effective at serving modern web-information needs. Moreover, most popular websites have powerful search solutions to help people find information quickly. When you're evaluating a search engine like Solr and designing your search solution, make sure you put user experience as a high priority.

BASIC KEYWORD SEARCH

It's almost too obvious to point out that a search engine supports keyword search, as that's its main purpose, but it's worth mentioning, because keyword search is the most typical way users will begin working with your search solution. It would be rare for a user to want to fill out a complex search form initially. Given that basic keyword search will be the most common way users will interact with your search engine, it stands to reason that this feature must provide a great user experience.

In general, users want to type in a few simple keywords and get back great results. This may sound like a simple task of matching query terms to documents, but consider a few of the issues that must be addressed to provide a great user experience:

- Relevant results must be returned quickly, within a second or less in most cases.
- Spelling correction is needed in case the user misspells some of the query terms.
- Autosuggestions save keystrokes, particularly for mobile applications.
- Synonyms of query terms must be recognized.

- Documents containing linguistic variations of query terms must be matched.
- Phrase handling is needed; that is, does the user want documents matching all words or any of the words in a phrase.
- Queries with common words like "a," "an," "of," and "the" must be handled properly.
- The user must have a way to see more results if the top results aren't satisfactory.

As you can see, a number of issues exist that make a seemingly basic feature hard to implement without a specialized approach. But with a search engine like Solr, these features come out of the box and are easy to implement. Once you give users a powerful tool to execute keyword searches, you need to consider how to display the results. This brings us to our next use case: ranking results based on their relevance to the user's query.

RANKED RETRIEVAL

A search engine stands alone as a way to return "top" documents for a query. In an SQL query to a relational database, a row either matches a query or it doesn't, and results are sorted based on one or more of the columns. A search engine returns documents sorted in descending order by a score that indicates the strength of the match of the document to the query. How the strength of the match is calculated depends on a number of factors, but in general a higher score means the document is more relevant to the query.

Ranking documents by relevancy is important for a couple of reasons:

- Modern search engines typically store a large volume of documents, often millions or billions of documents. Without ranking documents by relevance to the query, users can become overloaded with results with no clear way to navigate them.
- Users are more comfortable with and accustomed to getting results from other search engines using only a few keywords. Users are impatient and expect the search engine to "do what I mean, not what I say." This is true of search solutions backing mobile applications in which users on the go will enter short queries with potential misspellings and expect it to simply work.

To influence ranking, you can assign more weight to, or boost, certain documents, fields, or specific terms. You can boost results by their age to help push newer documents toward the top of search results. You'll learn about ranking documents in chapter 3.

BEYOND KEYWORD SEARCH

With a search engine like Solr, users can type in a few keywords and get back results. For many users, though, this is only the first step in a more interactive session in which the search results give them the ability to keep exploring. One of the primary use cases of a search engine is to drive an information-discovery session. Frequently, your users won't know exactly what they're looking for and typically don't have any idea what information is contained in your system. A good search engine helps users narrow in on their information needs.

The central idea here is to return documents from an initial query, as well as tools to help users refine their search. In other words, in addition to returning matching documents, you also return tools that give your users an idea of what to do next. You can, for example, categorize search results using document features to allow users to narrow down their results. This is known as *faceted search*, and it's one of the main strengths of Solr. You'll see an example of a faceted search for real estate in section 1.2. Facets are covered in depth in chapter 8.

DON'T USE A SEARCH ENGINE TO ...

Let's consider a few use cases in which a search engine wouldn't be useful. First, search engines are designed to return a small set of documents per query, usually 10 to 100. More documents for the same query can be retrieved using Solr's built-in paging support. Consider a query that matches a million documents; if you request all of those documents back at once, you should be prepared to wait a long time. The query itself will likely execute quickly, but reconstructing a million documents from the underlying index structure will be extremely slow, as engines like Solr store fields on disk in a format from which it's easy to create a few documents, but from which it takes a long time to reconstruct many documents when generating results.

Another use case in which you shouldn't use a search engine is deep analytic tasks that require access to a large subset of the index (unless you have a lot of memory). Even if you avoid the previous issue by paging through results, the underlying data structure of a search index isn't designed for retrieving large portions of the index at once.

We've touched on this previously, but we'll reiterate that search engines aren't the place for querying across relationships between documents. Solr does support querying using a parent-child relationship, but doesn't provide support for navigating complex relational structures as is possible with SQL. In chapter 3, you'll learn techniques to adapt relational data to work with Solr's flat document structure.

Also, there's no direct support in most search engines for document-level security, at least not in Solr. If you need fine-grained permissions on documents, then you'll have to handle that outside of the search engine.

Now that we've seen the types of data and use cases for which a search engine is the right (or wrong) solution, it's time to dig into what Solr does and how it does it on a high level. In the next section, you'll learn what capabilities Solr provides and how it approaches important software-design principles such as integration with external systems, scalability, and high availability.

1.2 *What is Solr?*

In this section, we introduce the key components of Solr by designing a search application from the ground up. This will help you understand what specific features Solr provides and the motivation for their existence. But before we get into the specifics of what Solr *is*, let's make sure you know what Solr *isn't*.

- Solr isn't a web search engine like Google or Bing.
- Solr has nothing to do with search engine optimization (SEO) for a website.

Now imagine we need to design a real estate search web application for potential homebuyers. The central use case for this application will be searching for homes for sale using a web browser. Figure 1.1 depicts a screenshot from this fictitious web application. Don't focus too much on the layout or design of the UI; it's only a mock-up to give visual context. What's important is the type of experience that Solr can support.

Let's tour the screenshot in figure 1.1 to illustrate some of Solr's key features. Starting at the top-left corner, working clockwise, Solr provides powerful features to support a keyword search box. As we discussed in section 1.1.2, providing a great user experience with basic keyword search requires complex infrastructure that Solr provides out of the box. Specifically, Solr provides spell-checking (suggesting as the user types), synonym handling, phrase queries, and text-analysis tools to deal with linguistic variations in query terms, such as buying a house or purchase a home.

Solr also provides a powerful solution for implementing geospatial queries. In figure 1.1, matching home listings are displayed on a map based on their distance from the latitude/longitude of the center of our fictitious neighborhood. With Solr's geospatial support, you can sort documents by geo distance, limit documents to those within a particular geo distance, or even return the geo distance per document from any location. It's also important that geospatial searches are fast and efficient, to support a UI that allows users to zoom in and out and move around on a map.

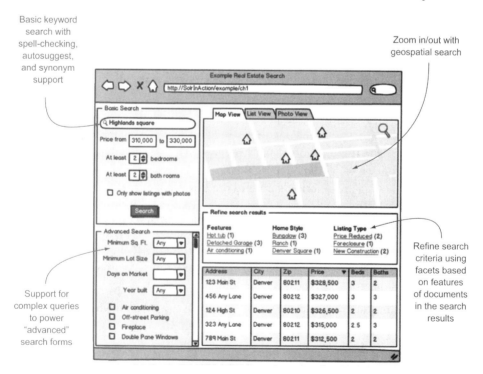

Figure 1.1 Mock-up screenshot of a fictitious search application to depict Solr features

Once the user performs a query, the results can be further categorized using Solr's faceting support to show features of the documents in the result set. Facets are a way to categorize the documents in a result set in order to drive discovery and query refinement. In figure 1.1, search results are categorized into facets for features, home style, and listing type.

Now that we have a basic idea of the type of functionality we need to support our real estate search application, let's see how we can implement these features with Solr. To begin, we need to know how Solr matches home listings in the index to queries entered by users, as this is the basis for all search applications.

1.2.1 *Information retrieval engine*

Solr is built on Apache Lucene, a popular, Java-based, open source, information retrieval library. We'll save a detailed discussion of what information retrieval is for chapter 3. For now, we'll touch on the key concepts behind information retrieval, starting with the formal definition taken from one of the prominent academic texts on modern search concepts:

> Information retrieval (IR) is finding material (usually documents) of an unstructured nature (usually text) that satisfies an information need from within large collections (usually stored on computers).[1]

In our example real estate application, the user's primary need is finding a home to purchase based on location, home style, features, and price. Our search index will contain home listings from across the United States, which definitely qualifies as a "large collection." In a nutshell, Solr uses Lucene to provide the core data structures for indexing documents and executing searches to find documents.

Lucene is a Java-based library for building and managing an *inverted index*, a specialized data structure for matching query terms to text-based documents. Figure 1.2 provides a simplified depiction of a Lucene inverted index for our example real estate search application.

You'll learn all about how an inverted index works in chapter 3. For now, it's sufficient to review figure 1.2 to get a feel for what happens when a new document (#44 in the diagram) is added to the index and how documents are matched to query terms using the inverted index.

You might be thinking that a relational database could easily return the same results using an SQL query, which is true for this simple example. But one key difference between a Lucene query and a database query is that in Lucene results are ranked by their relevance to a query, and database results can only be sorted by one or more of the table columns. In other words, ranking documents by relevance is a key aspect of information retrieval and helps differentiate it from other types of queries.

---

[1] Christopher D. Manning, Prabhakar Raghavan, and Hinrich Schütze, *Introduction to Information Retrieval* (Cambridge University Press, 2008).

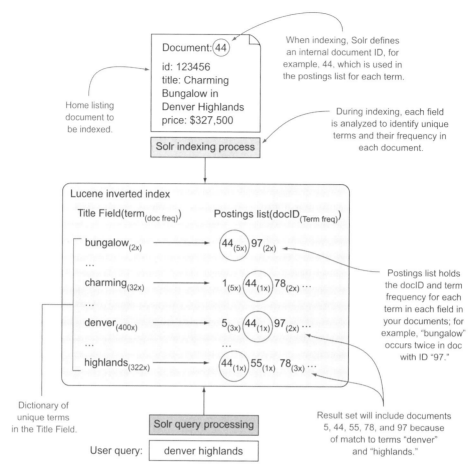

Figure 1.2 **The key data structure supporting information retrieval is the inverted index.**

Building a web-scale inverted index

It might surprise you that search engines like Google also use an inverted index for searching the web. In fact, the need to build a web-scale inverted index led to the invention of MapReduce.

MapReduce is a programming model that distributes large-scale data-processing operations across a cluster of commodity servers by formulating an algorithm into two phases: map and reduce. With its roots in functional programming, MapReduce was adapted by Google for building its massive inverted index to power web search. Using MapReduce, the map phase produces a unique term and document ID where the term occurs. In the reduce phase, terms are sorted so that all term/docID pairs are sent to the same reducer process for each unique term. The reducer sums up all term frequencies for each term to generate the inverted index.

(continued)

Apache Hadoop provides an open source implementation of MapReduce, and it's used by the Apache Nutch open source project to build a Lucene inverted index for web-scale search using Solr. A thorough discussion of Hadoop and Nutch is beyond the scope of this book, but we encourage you to investigate these projects if you need to build a web-scale search index.

Now that we know that Lucene provides the core infrastructure to support search, let's look at what value Solr adds on top of Lucene, starting with how you define your index structure using Solr's flexible *schema.xml* configuration document.

1.2.2 Flexible schema management

Although Lucene provides the library for indexing documents and executing queries, what's missing is an easy way to configure how you want your index to be structured. With Lucene, you need to write Java code to define fields and how to analyze those fields. Solr adds a simple, declarative way to define the structure of your index and how you want fields to be represented and analyzed: an XML-configuration document named *schema.xml*. Under the covers, Solr uses *schema.xml* to represent all of the possible fields and data types necessary to map documents into a Lucene index. This saves programming time and makes your index structure easier to understand and communicate to others. A Solr-built index is 100% compatible with a programmatically built Lucene index.

Solr also adds nice constructs on top of the core Lucene indexing functionality. Specifically, Solr provides copy and dynamic fields. *Copy fields* provide a way to take the raw text contents of one or more fields and have them applied to a different field. *Dynamic fields* allow you to apply the same field type to many different fields without explicitly declaring them in *schema.xml*. This is useful for modeling documents that have many fields. We cover *schema.xml* in depth in chapters 5 and 6.

In terms of our example real estate application, it might surprise you that we can use the Solr example server out of the box without making any changes to *schema.xml*. This shows how flexible Solr's schema support is; the example Solr server is designed to support product search, but it works fine for our real estate search example.

At this point, we know that Lucene provides a powerful library for indexing documents, executing queries, and ranking results. And, with *schema.xml*, you have a flexible way to define the index structure using an XML-configuration document instead of having to program to the Lucene API. Now you need a way to access these services from the web. In the next section, we learn how Solr runs as a Java web application and integrates with other technologies, using proven standards such as XML, JSON, and HTTP.

1.2.3 Java web application

Solr is a Java web application that runs in any modern Java Servlet engine, such as Jetty or Tomcat, or a full J2EE application server like JBoss or Oracle AS. Figure 1.3 depicts the major software components of a Solr server.

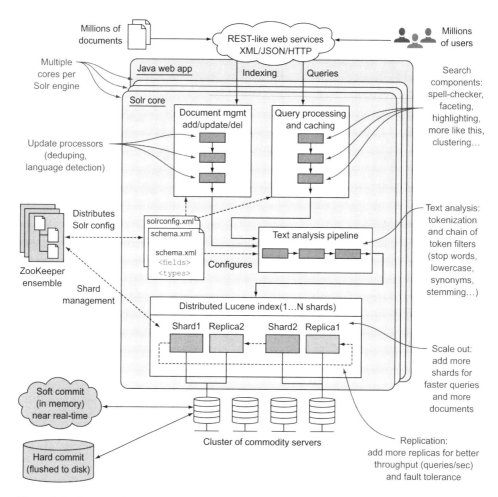

Figure 1.3   Diagram of the main components of Solr 4

Admittedly, figure 1.3 is a little overwhelming at first glance. Take a moment to scan the diagram and get a feel for the terminology; don't worry if you're not familiar with all of the terms and concepts represented in it. After reading this book, you should have a strong understanding of all the concepts presented in figure 1.3.

As we mentioned in the introduction to this chapter, the Solr designers recognized that Solr is best as a complementary technology that works within existing architectures. In fact, you'll be hard put to find an environment in which Solr doesn't drop right in. As you'll see in chapter 2, you can start the example Solr server in a couple of minutes after you finish the download.

To achieve the goal of easy integration, Solr's core services need to be accessible from many different applications and languages. Solr provides simple REST-like services based on the proven standards of XML, JSON, and HTTP. As a brief aside, we avoid the RESTful label for Solr's HTTP-based API, as it doesn't strictly adhere to all

REST (Representational State Transfer) principles. For instance, in Solr, you use HTTP POST to delete documents instead of HTTP DELETE.

A REST-like interface is nice as a foundation, but often developers like to have access to a client library in their language of choice to abstract away some of the boilerplate machinery of invoking a web service and processing the response. The good news here is that most of the popular languages, including Python, PHP, Java, .NET, and Ruby, have a Solr client library.

1.2.4 Multiple indexes in one server

One hallmark of modern application architectures is the need for flexibility in the face of rapidly changing requirements. One of the ways Solr helps in this situation is that you don't have to do all things in Solr with one index, because Solr supports running multiple cores in a single engine. In figure 1.3, we've depicted multiple cores as separate layers, all running in the same Java web-application environment.

Think of each core as a separate index and configuration, and there can be many cores in a single Solr instance. This allows you to manage multiple cores from one server so that you can share server resources and administration tasks such as monitoring and maintenance. Solr provides an API for creating and managing multiple cores, which will be covered in chapter 12.

One use of Solr's multicore support is data partitioning, such as having one core for recent documents and another core for older documents, known as chronological sharding. Another use of Solr's multicore support is to support multitenant applications.

In our real estate application, we might use multiple cores to manage different types of listings that are different enough to justify having different indexes for each. Consider real estate listings for rural land instead of homes. Buying rural land is a different process than buying a home in a city, so it stands to reason that we might want to manage our land listings in a separate core.

1.2.5 Extendable (plugins)

Figure 1.3 depicted three main subsystems in Solr: document management, query processing, and text analysis. Of course, these are high-level abstractions for complex subsystems in Solr; we'll learn about each one later in the book. Each system is composed of a modular "pipeline" that allows you to plug in new functionality. This means that instead of overriding the entire query-processing engine in Solr, you plug a new search component into an existing pipeline. This makes the core Solr functionality easy to extend and customize to meet your specific application needs.

1.2.6 Scalable

Lucene is an extremely fast search library, and Solr takes full advantage of Lucene's speed. But regardless of how fast Lucene is, a single server will reach its limits in terms of how many concurrent queries from different users it can handle due to CPU and I/O constraints.

As a first step to achieving scalability, Solr provides flexible cache-management features that help your server reuse computationally expensive data structures. Specifically, Solr comes preconfigured with a number of caches to save expensive recomputations, such as caching the results of a query filter. We'll learn about Solr's cache-management features in chapter 4.

Caching gets you only so far, and at some point you're going to need to scale out your capacity to handle more documents and higher query throughput by adding more servers. For now, let's focus on the two most common dimensions of scalability in Solr—query throughput and the number of documents indexed. Query throughput is the number of queries your engine can support per second. Even though Lucene can execute each query quickly, it's limited in terms of how many concurrent requests a single server can handle. For higher query throughput, you add replicas of your index so that more servers can handle more requests. This means that if your index is replicated across three servers, you can handle roughly three times the number of queries per second, because each server handles one-third of the query traffic. In practice, it's rare to achieve perfect linear scalability, so adding three servers may only allow you to handle two and a half times the query volume of one server.

The other dimension of scalability is the number of documents indexed. If you're dealing with large volumes, then you'll likely reach a point at which you have too many documents in a single instance, and query performance will suffer. To handle more documents, you split the index into smaller chunks called shards, then distribute the searches across the shards.

Scaling out with virtualized commodity hardware
One trend in modern computing is building software architectures that can scale horizontally using virtualized commodity hardware. Add more commodity servers to handle more traffic. Fueling this trend toward using virtualized commodity hardware are cloud-computing providers such as Amazon EC2. Although Solr will run on virtualized hardware, you should be aware that search is I/O and memory intensive. Therefore, if search performance is a top priority for your organization, you should consider deploying Solr on higher-end hardware with high-performance disks, ideally solid-state drives (SSDs). Hardware considerations for deploying Solr are discussed in chapter 12.

Scalability is important, but ability to survive failures is also important for a modern system. In the next section, we discuss how Solr handles software and hardware failures.

1.2.7   *Fault-tolerant*

Beyond scalability, you need to consider what happens if one or more of your servers fails, particularly if you're planning to deploy Solr on virtualized hardware or commodity hardware. The bottom line is that *you must plan for failures*. Even the best architectures and the most high-end hardware will experience failures.

Let's assume you have four shards for your index, and the server hosting shard2 loses power. At this point, Solr can't continue indexing documents and can't service queries, so your search engine is effectively down. To avoid this situation, you can add replicas of each shard. In this case, when shard2 fails, Solr reroutes indexing and query traffic to the replica, and your Solr cluster remains online. The result of this failure is that indexing and queries can still be processed, but they may not be as fast because you have one less server to handle requests. We'll discuss failover scenarios in chapters 12 and 13.

At this point, you've seen that Solr has a modern, well-designed architecture that's scalable and fault-tolerant. Although these are important aspects to consider if you've already decided to use Solr, you still might not be convinced that Solr is the right choice for your needs. In the next section, we describe the benefits of Solr from the perspective of different stakeholders, such as the software architect, system administrator, and CEO.

1.3 Why Solr?

In this section, we provide key information to help you decide if Solr is the right technology for your organization. Let's begin by addressing why Solr is attractive to software architects.

1.3.1 Solr for the software architect

When evaluating new technology, software architects must consider a number of factors including stability, scalability, and fault tolerance. Solr scores high marks in all three categories.

In terms of stability, Solr is a mature technology supported by a vibrant community and seasoned committers. One thing that shocks new users to Solr and Lucene is that it isn't unheard of to deploy from source code pulled directly from the trunk, rather than waiting for an official release. We won't advise you either way on whether this is acceptable for your organization. We only point this out because it's a testament to the depth and breadth of automated testing in Lucene and Solr. If you have a nightly build off trunk in which all the automated tests pass, then you can be fairly confident that the core functionality is solid.

We've touched on Solr's approach to scalability and fault tolerance in sections 1.2.6 and 1.2.7. As an architect, you're probably most curious about the limitations of Solr's approach to scalability and fault tolerance. First, you should realize that the sharding and replication features in Solr have been improved in Solr 4 to be robust and easier to manage. The new approach to scaling is called SolrCloud. Under the covers, SolrCloud uses Apache ZooKeeper to distribute configurations across a cluster of Solr servers and to keep track of cluster state. Here are highlights of the new SolrCloud features:

- Centralized configuration.
- Distributed indexing with no single point of failure (SPoF).

- Automated failover to a new shard leader.
- Queries can be sent to any node in a cluster to trigger a full, distributed search across all shards, with failover and load-balancing support built in.

This isn't to say that Solr scaling doesn't have room for improvement. SolrCloud still requires manual interaction when modifying the size of your search indexes (merging or splitting indexes), and not all Solr features work in a distributed mode. We'll get into all of the specifics of scaling Solr in chapter 12, and the new SolrCloud features in particular in chapter 13, but we want to make sure architects are aware that Solr scaling has come a long way in the past few years and now enables robust scaling with no SPoF.

1.3.2   *Solr for the system administrator*

As a system administrator, high among your questions about adopting a new technology like Solr is whether it fits into your existing infrastructure. The easy answer is: yes it does. As Solr is Java-based, it runs on any OS platform that has a J2SE 6.x/7.x JVM. Out of the box, Solr embeds Jetty, the open source Java servlet engine provided by Oracle. Otherwise, Solr is a standard Java web application that deploys easily to any Java web application server such as JBoss or Apache Tomcat.

All access to Solr can be done via HTTP, and Solr is designed to work with caching HTTP reverse proxies like Squid and Varnish. Solr also works with JMX, so you can hook it up to your favorite monitoring application, such as Nagios.

Also, Solr provides a nice administration console for checking configuration settings, viewing statistics, issuing test queries, and monitoring the health of SolrCloud. Figure 1.4 is a screenshot of the Solr 4 administration console. We'll learn more about that in chapter 2.

Figure 1.4   A screenshot of the Solr 4 administration console, in which you can send test queries, ping the server, view configuration settings, and see how your shards and replicas are distributed in a cluster.

1.3.3 *Solr for the CEO*

Although it's unlikely that many CEOs will be reading this book, here are some key talking points about Solr in case your CEO stops you in the hall.

- Executives like to know that an investment in a technology today is going to pay off in the long term. You can emphasize that many companies are still running on Solr 1.4, which was released in 2009; this means that Solr has a successful track record and is constantly being improved.
- CEOs like technologies that are predictable. As you'll see in the next chapter, Solr "just works," and you can have it up and running in minutes.
- Solr has a large support community. What happens if the Solr guy walks out the door; will business come to a halt? It's true that Solr is complex technology, but having a vibrant community behind it means that you have help when you need it. You also have access to the source code, which means that if something is broken and needs fixing, you can do it yourself. Many commercial service providers can also help you plan, implement, and maintain your Solr installation, and many offer training courses for Solr.
- Solr doesn't require much initial investment to get started. (This one may be an argument of more interest to the CFO.) Without knowing the size and scale of your environment, we're confident in saying that you can start up a Solr server in a few minutes and be indexing documents quickly. A modest server running in the cloud can handle millions of documents and many queries with subsecond response times.

1.4 *Features overview*

Finally, let's do a quick rundown of Solr's main features, organized around the following categories:

- User experience
- Data modeling
- New features in Solr 4

Providing a great user experience with your search solution will be a common theme throughout this book, so let's start by seeing how Solr helps make your users happy.

1.4.1 *User-experience features*

Solr provides a number of important features that help you deliver a search solution that's easy to use, intuitive, and powerful. You should note, however, that Solr only exposes a REST-like HTTP API and doesn't provide search-related UI components in any language or framework. You'll have to roll up your sleeves and develop your own search UI components that take advantage of some of the following user-experience features:

- Pagination and sorting
- Faceting

- Autosuggest
- Spell-checking
- Hit highlighting
- Geospatial search

PAGINATION AND SORTING

Rather than returning all matching documents, Solr is optimized to serve paginated requests, in which only the top N documents are returned on the first page. If users don't find what they're looking for on the first page, you can request subsequent pages using simple API request parameters. Pagination helps with two key outcomes: (1) results are returned more quickly, because each request only returns a small subset of the entire search results; and (2) it helps you track how many queries result in requests for more pages, which may be an indication of a relevance-scoring problem. You'll learn about paging and sorting in chapter 7.

FACETING

Faceting provides users with tools to refine their search criteria and discover more information by categorizing search results into subgroups using facets. In our real estate example (figure 1.1), we saw how search results from a basic keyword search were organized into three facets: features, home style, and listing type. Faceting is one of the more popular and powerful features in Solr; we cover it in depth in chapter 8.

AUTOSUGGEST

Most users will expect your search application to "do the right thing," even if they provide incomplete information. Autosuggest allows users to see a list of suggested terms and phrases based on documents in your index. Solr's autosuggest features allow a user to start typing a few characters and receive a list of suggested queries with each keystroke. This reduces the number of incorrect queries, particularly because many users may be searching from a mobile device with a small keyboard.

Autosuggest gives users examples of terms and phrases available in the index. Referring to our real estate example, as a user types hig... Solr's autosuggestion feature can return suggestions like "highlands neighborhood" or "highlands ranch." We cover autosuggest in chapter 10.

SPELL-CHECKER

In the age of mobile devices and people on the go, spelling correction support is essential. Again, users expect the search engine to handle misspellings gracefully. Solr's spell-checker supports two basic modes:

- *Autocorrect*—Solr can make the spell correction automatically, based on whether the misspelled term exists in the index.
- *Did you mean*—Solr can return a suggested query that might produce better results so that you can display a hint to your users, such as "Did you mean *highlands*?" if your user typed in hilands.

Spelling correction was revamped in Solr 4 to be easier to manage and maintain; we'll see how this works in chapter 10.

HIT HIGHLIGHTING

When searching documents that have a significant amount of text, you can display specific sections of each document using Solr's hit-highlighting feature. Most useful for longer format documents, hit highlighting helps users find relevant documents by highlighting sections of search results that match the user's query. Sections are generated dynamically based on their similarity to the query. We cover hit highlighting in chapter 9.

GEOSPATIAL SEARCH

Geographical location is a first-class concept in Solr 4, in that it has built-in support for indexing latitude and longitude values as well as sorting or ranking documents by geographical distance. Solr can find and sort documents by distance from a geo location (latitude and longitude). In the real estate example, matching listings are displayed on an interactive map in which users, using geospatial search, can zoom in/out and move the map's center point to find nearby listings.

Another exciting addition to Solr 4 is that you can index geographical shapes such as polygons, which allows you to find documents that intersect geographical regions. This might be useful for finding home listings in specific neighborhoods using a precise geographical representation of a neighborhood. We cover Solr's geospatial search features in chapter 15.

1.4.2 Data-modeling features

As we discussed in section 1.1, Solr is optimized to work with specific types of data. In this section, we provide an overview of key features that help you model data for search:

- Result grouping/field collapsing
- Flexible query support
- Joins
- Document clustering
- Importing rich document formats such as PDF and Word
- Importing data from relational databases
- Multilingual support

RESULT GROUPING/FIELD COLLAPSING

Although Solr requires a flat, denormalized document, Solr allows you to treat multiple documents as a group based on some common property shared by all documents in the group. Result grouping, also referred to as field collapsing, allows you to return unique groups instead of individual documents in the results.

The classic example of field collapsing is threaded email discussions, in which emails matching a specific query can be grouped under the original email message that started the conversation. You'll learn about result grouping/field collapsing in chapter 11.

FLEXIBLE QUERY SUPPORT

Solr provides a number of powerful query features, including

- Conditional logic using AND, OR, and NOT
- Wildcard matching
- Range queries for dates and numbers
- Phrase queries with slop to allow for some distance between terms
- Fuzzy string matching
- Regular expression matching
- Function queries

We'll cover these terms in chapter 7.

JOINS

In SQL, you use a *join* to create a relation by pulling data from two or more tables together using a common property such as a foreign key. In Solr, joins are more like SQL subqueries, in that you don't build documents by joining data from other documents. With Solr joins, you can return child documents of parents that match your search criteria. One example in which Solr joins are useful is returning all retweets of a Twitter message into a single response. We discuss joins in chapter 15.

DOCUMENT CLUSTERING

Document clustering allows you to identify groups of documents that are similar, based on the terms present in each document. This is helpful to avoid returning many documents containing the same information in search results. For example, if your search engine is based on news articles pulled from multiple RSS feeds, it's likely that you'll have many documents for the same news story. Rather than returning multiple results for the same story, you can use clustering to pick a single representative story. Clustering techniques are discussed briefly in chapter 16.

IMPORTING RICH DOCUMENT FORMATS SUCH AS PDF AND WORD

In some cases, you may want to take a bunch of existing documents in common formats like PDF and Word and make them searchable. With Solr this is easy, because it integrates with the Apache Tika project that supports most popular document formats. Importing rich format documents is covered briefly in chapter 12.

IMPORTING DATA FROM RELATIONAL DATABASES

If the data you want to search with Solr is in a relational database, you can configure Solr to create documents using an SQL query. We cover Solr's Data Import Handler (DIH) in chapter 12.

MULTILINGUAL SUPPORT

Solr and Lucene have a long history of working with multiple languages. Solr has language detection built in and provides language-specific text-analysis solutions for many languages. We'll see Solr's language detection and multilingual text analysis in action in chapter 14.

1.4.3 New features in Solr 4

Before we wrap up this chapter, let's look at a few of the exciting new features in Solr 4. In general, Solr 4 is a huge milestone for the Apache Solr community, as it addresses many of the major pain points discovered by real users over the past several years. We selected a few of the main features to highlight here, but we'll also point out new features in Solr 4 throughout the book.

- Near real-time search
- Atomic updates with optimistic concurrency
- Real-time get
- Write durability using a transaction log
- Easy sharding and replication using ZooKeeper

NEAR REAL-TIME SEARCH

Solr's near real-time (NRT) search feature supports applications that have a high velocity of documents that need to be searchable within seconds of being added to the index. With NRT, you can use Solr to search rapidly changing content sources such as breaking news and social networks. We cover NRT in chapter 13.

ATOMIC UPDATES WITH OPTIMISTIC CONCURRENCY

The atomic update feature allows a client application to add, update, delete, and increment fields on an existing document without having to resend the entire document. If the price of a home in our example real estate application from section 1.2 changes, we can send an atomic update to Solr to change the price field specifically.

You might be wondering what happens if two different users attempt to change the same document concurrently. Solr guards against incompatible updates using *optimistic concurrency*. In a nutshell, Solr uses a special version field named _version_ to enforce safe update semantics for documents. In the case of two different users trying to update the same document concurrently, the user that submits updates last will have a stale version field, so their update will fail. Atomic updates and optimistic concurrency are covered in chapter 5.

REAL-TIME GET

At the beginning of this chapter, we stated that Solr is a NoSQL technology. Solr's real-time get feature definitely fits within the NoSQL approach by allowing you to retrieve the latest version of a document using its unique identifier, regardless of whether that document has been committed to the index. This is similar to using a key-value store such as Cassandra to retrieve data using a row key.

Prior to Solr 4, a document wasn't retrievable until it was committed to the Lucene index. With the real-time get feature in Solr 4, you can safely decouple the need to retrieve a document by its unique ID from the commit process. This can be useful if you need to update an existing document after it's sent to Solr without having to do a commit first. As we'll learn in chapter 5, commits can be expensive and can impact query performance.

WRITE DURABILITY USING A TRANSACTION LOG

When a document is sent to Solr for indexing, it's written to a transaction log to prevent data loss in the event of server failure. Solr's transaction log sits between the client application and the Lucene index. It also plays a role in servicing real-time get requests, as documents are retrievable by their unique identifier regardless of whether they're committed to Lucene.

The transaction log allows Solr to decouple update durability from update visibility. This means that documents can be on durable storage but not visible in search results yet. This gives your application control over when to commit documents to make them visible in search results without risking data loss if a server fails before you commit. We'll discuss durable writes and commit strategies in chapter 5.

EASY SHARDING AND REPLICATION USING ZOOKEEPER

If you're new to Solr, you may not be aware that scaling previous versions of Solr was a manual and often cumbersome process. With SolrCloud, scaling is simple and automated because Solr uses Apache ZooKeeper to distribute configurations and manage shard leaders and replicas. The Apache website (http://zookeeper.apache.org) describes Zoo-Keeper as a "centralized service for maintaining configuration information, naming, providing distributed synchronization, and providing group services."

In Solr, ZooKeeper is responsible for assigning shard leaders and replicas and keeping track of which servers are available to service requests. SolrCloud bundles ZooKeeper, so you don't need to do any additional configuration or setup to get started with SolrCloud. We'll dig into the details of SolrCloud in chapter 13.

1.5   Summary

We hope you now have a good sense for what types of data and use cases Solr supports. As you learned in section 1.1, Solr is optimized to handle data that's text-centric, read-dominant, document-oriented, and has a flexible schema. We also learned that search engines like Solr aren't general-purpose data-storage and processing solutions, but are instead intended to power keyword search, ranked retrieval, and information discovery. Using the example of a fictitious real estate search application, we saw how Solr builds upon Lucene to add declarative index configuration and web services based on HTTP, XML, and JSON. Solr 4 can be scaled in two dimensions to support millions of documents and high-query traffic using sharding and replication. Solr 4 has no SPoF when used in a distributed SolrCloud configuration.

We also touched on reasons to choose Solr based on the perspective of key stake-holders. We saw how Solr addresses the concerns of software architects, system administrators, and even the CEO. Lastly, we covered some of Solr's main features and gave you pointers to where to go to learn more about each feature in this book.

We hope you're excited to continue learning about Solr; now it's time to download the software and run it on your local system, which is what we'll do in chapter 2.

Getting to know Solr

This chapter covers

- Downloading and installing Apache Solr 4.7
- Starting the example Solr server
- Sorting, paging, and results formatting
- Exploring the Solritas example search UI

It's natural to have a sense of unease when you start using an unfamiliar technology, but you can put your mind at ease with Solr, because it is designed to be easy to install and use out of the box. In the spirit of being agile, you can start out with the basics and incrementally add complexity to your Solr configuration. For example, Solr allows you to split a large index into smaller subsets, called shards, and add replicas to increase your capacity to serve queries. But you don't need to worry about index sharding or replication until you run into scale issues.

By the end of this chapter, you'll have Solr running on your computer, know how to start and stop Solr, know your way around the web-based administration console, and have a basic understanding of key Solr terminology such as Solr home, core, and collection.

> **What's in a name? Solr 4 vs. SolrCloud**
>
> You may have heard of SolrCloud and wondered what the difference is between Solr 4 and SolrCloud. Technically, SolrCloud is the code name for a subset of features in Solr 4 that makes it easier to configure and run a scalable, fault-tolerant cluster of Solr servers. Think of SolrCloud as a way to configure a distributed installation of Solr 4.
>
> Also, SolrCloud doesn't have anything to do with running Solr in a cloud-computing environment like Amazon EC2, although you can run Solr in the cloud. We presume that the "cloud" part of the name reflects the underlying goal of the SolrCloud feature set to enable elastic scalability, high availability, and the ease of use we've all come to expect from cloud-based services. We cover SolrCloud in depth in chapter 13.

Let's get started by downloading Solr from the Apache website and installing it on your computer.

2.1 Getting started

Before you can get to know Solr, you have to get it running on your local computer. This starts with downloading the binary distribution of Solr 4.7 from Apache and extracting the downloaded archive. Once it's installed, we'll show you how to start the example Solr server and verify that it's running by visiting the Solr administration console from your web browser. Throughout this process, we assume you're comfortable executing simple commands from the command line of your chosen OS. There is no GUI installer for Solr, but you'll soon see that the process is so simple that you won't need one.

2.1.1 Installing Solr

Installing Solr is a bit of a misnomer in that all you need to do is download the binary distribution (*.zip* or *.tgz*) and extract it. Before you do that, let's make sure you have the necessary prerequisite Java 1.6 or greater (also known as J2SE 6) installed. To verify you have the correct version of Java, open a command line on your computer and enter

```
java -version
```

You should see output that looks similar to the following:

```
java version "1.6.0_24"
Java™ SE Runtime Environment (build 1.6.0_24-b07)
Java HotSpot™ 64-Bit Server VM (build 19.1-b02, mixed mode)
```

If you don't have Java installed, we recommend you use Oracle's JVM (www.oracle.com/technetwork/java/javase/downloads/index.html). Even though the Solr server requires Java, that doesn't mean you have to use Java in your application to interact with Solr. Client interaction with Solr happens over HTTP, so you can use any language that provides an HTTP client library. In addition, a number of open source client libraries are available for Solr for popular languages like .NET, Python, Ruby, PHP, and Java.

Assuming you've got Java installed, you're ready to install Solr. Apache provides source and binary distributions of Solr; for now, we'll focus on the installation steps using the binary distribution. We cover building Solr from source in chapter 12.

To download the most recent version of Solr, go to the Solr home page at http://lucene.apache.org/solr and click the Download button for Apache Solr on the right. This will direct you to a mirror site for Apache downloads. (It's advisable to download the current version from a mirror site to avoid overloading the main Apache site.) If you're on Windows, download *solr-4.7.0.zip*. If you're on Unix, Linux, or Mac OS X, download *solr-4.7.0.tgz*. All of the examples in this book will be based upon Solr 4.7.0, so if Solr 4.7.0 is no longer available from the homepage and you want to follow the examples as you read, then you can always find Solr 4.7.0 in the Apache Software Foundation archives at http://archive.apache.org/dist/lucene/solr/4.7.0/.

After downloading, move the downloaded file to a permanent location on your computer. On Windows, you could move it to the *C:\root* directory, or on Linux, choose a location like */opt/solr/*. For Windows users, we highly recommend that you extract Solr to a directory that doesn't have spaces in the name; that is, avoid extracting Solr into directories like *C:\Documents and Settings* or *C:\Program Files*. Your mileage may vary on this, but as Solr is Java-based software, you're likely to run into issues with paths that contain a space.

No formal installer is needed because Solr is self-contained in a single archive file; all you need to do is extract it. When you extract the archive, all files will be created under the *solr-4.7.0/* directory. On Windows, you can use the built-in ZIP extraction support or a tool like WinZip. On Unix, Linux, or Mac, run `tar zxf solr-4.7.0.tgz`. This will create the directory structure shown in figure 2.1.

We refer to the location where you extracted the Solr archive (*.zip* or *.tgz*) as *$SOLR_INSTALL/* throughout the rest of the book. We use this name because, as you'll see shortly, Solr home will be a different path, so we didn't want to use *$SOLR_HOME/* as the alias for the top-level directory in which you extracted Solr. Now that Solr is installed, you're ready to start it up.

2.1.2   *Starting the Solr example server*

To start Solr, open a command line, and enter the following:

```
cd $SOLR_INSTALL/example
java -jar start.jar
```

Remember that *$SOLR_INSTALL/* is the alias we're using to represent the directory into which you extracted the Solr download archive, such as *C:\solr-4.7.0* on Windows. That's all there is to starting Solr.

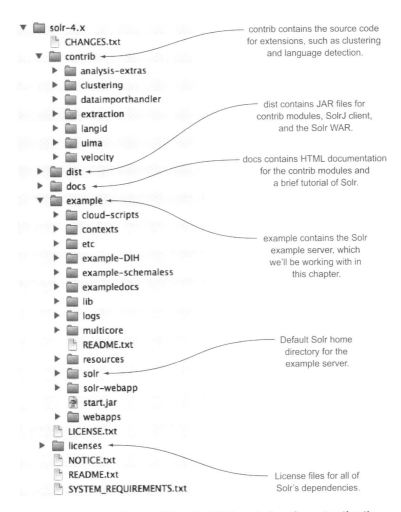

Figure 2.1 Directory listing of the solr-4.7.0 installation after extracting the downloaded archive on your computer. We'll refer to the top-level directory as *$SOLR_INSTALL/* throughout the rest of the book.

During initialization, you'll see some log messages printed to the console. If all goes well, you should see the following log message at or near the bottom:

```
3504 [main] INFO  org.eclipse.jetty.server.AbstractConnector  - Started
    SocketConnector@0.0.0.0:8983
```

WHAT HAPPENED?

That was so easy that you might be wondering what was accomplished. To be clear, you now have a running version of Solr 4.7 on your computer. You can verify that Solr started correctly by directing your web browser to the Solr administration page at http://localhost:8983/solr. Figure 2.2 is a screenshot of the Solr administration

Main navigation
toolbar.

Initial Dashboard page shows high-level
system settings for your server.

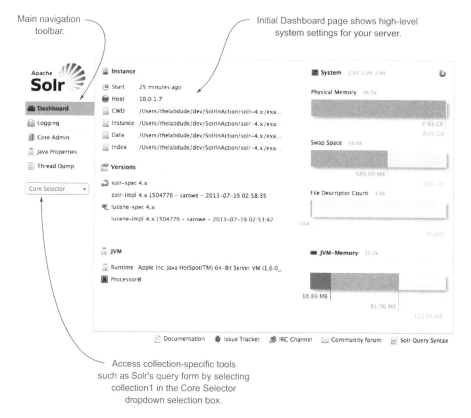

Access collection-specific tools
such as Solr's query form by selecting
collection1 in the Core Selector
dropdown selection box.

Figure 2.2   The Solr 4.7 administration console, which provides a wealth of tools for working with your new Solr instance. Click the `collection1` link to access more tools, including the query form.

console; please take a minute to get acquainted with the layout and navigational tools in the console.

Behind the scenes, *start.jar* launched a Java web server named Jetty, listening on port 8983. Solr is a web application running in Jetty. Figure 2.3 illustrates what is now running on your computer.

TROUBLESHOOTING
Not much can go wrong when starting the example server. The most common issue if the server doesn't start correctly is that the default port 8983 is already in use by another process. If this is the case, you'll see an error that looks like `java.net.Bind-Exception: Address already in use`. This is easy to resolve by changing the port Solr binds to. Change your start command to specify a different port for Jetty to bind to using `java -Djetty.port=8080 -jar start.jar`. Using this command, Jetty will bind to port 8080 instead of 8983.

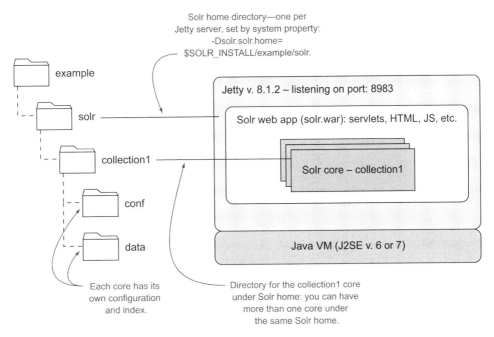

Figure 2.3 **Solr from a systems perspective showing the Solr web application (*solr.war*) running in Jetty on top of Java. There is one Solr home directory set per Jetty server, using Java system property** `solr.solr.home`. **Solr can host multiple cores per server, and each core has a separate directory (for example, *collection1*) containing a core-specific configuration and index (*data*) under Solr home.**

Jetty vs. Tomcat

We recommend staying with Jetty when first learning Solr. If your organization uses Tomcat or some other Java web-application server, such as Resin, you can deploy the Solr WAR file. Because we're getting to know Solr in this chapter, we'll refer you to chapter 12 to learn how to deploy the Solr WAR file.

Solr uses Jetty to make the initial setup and configuration process a no-brainer. But this doesn't mean that Jetty is a bad choice for production deployment. If your organization already has a standard Java web-application platform, then Solr will work with it. But if you have some choice, then we recommend you try out Jetty. It's fast, stable, mature, and easy to administer and customize. In fact, Google uses Jetty for its App Engine—see www.infoq.com/news/2009/08/google-chose-jetty/—which gives great credibility to Jetty as a solid platform for running Solr in even the most demanding environments!

STOPPING SOLR

For local operation, you can kill the Solr server by pressing Ctrl-c in the console window in which you started Solr. Typically, this is safe enough for development and testing. Jetty does provide a safer mechanism for stopping the server, which will be discussed in chapter 12.

Now that we have a running server, let's take a minute to understand where Solr gets its configuration information and where it manages its Lucene index. Understanding how the example server you started is configured will help you when you're ready to start configuring a Solr server for your application.

2.1.3 *Understanding Solr home*

In Solr, a *core* is composed of a set of configuration files, Lucene index files, and Solr's transaction log. One Solr server running in Jetty can host multiple cores. Recall that in chapter 1 we designed a real estate search application that had a core for houses and a separate core for land listings. We used two separate cores because the indexed data was different enough to justify having two different index structures. The Solr example server you started in section 2.1.2 has a single core named collection1.

As a brief aside, Solr also uses the term *collection*, which only has meaning in the context of a Solr cluster in which a single index is distributed across multiple servers. Consequently, we feel it's easier to focus on understanding what a Solr core is for now. We'll return to the distinction between core and collection in chapter 13 when we discuss SolrCloud.

Solr home is a directory structure that encapsulates one or more cores, which historically were configured by a configuration file named *solr.xml.* But as of Solr 4.4, cores can be autodiscovered and do not need to be defined in *solr.xml.* Consequently, you can ignore the *solr.xml* file provided with the example server for now, as it contains advanced options that only apply to running Solr in cloud mode. Solr also provides a Core Admin API that allows you to create, update, and delete cores programmatically from your application. We cover the Core Admin API in more detail in chapter 12.

For now, what's important is to understand that each Solr server has one and only one Solr home directory that contains all cores. The global Java system property solr.solr.home sets the location of the Solr home directory. Figure 2.4 shows a directory listing of the default Solr home, solr, for the example server.

We'll learn more about the main Solr configuration file for a core, named *solrconfig.xml*, in chapter 4. Also, *schema.xml* is the main configuration file that governs index structure and text analysis for documents and queries; you'll learn all about *schema.xml* in chapter 5. For now, scan figure 2.4 so that you have a sense for the basic structure of a Solr home directory.

The example directory contains two other Solr home directories for exploring advanced functionality. Specifically, the *example/example-DIH/* directory provides a Solr core for learning about the DIH feature in Solr. Also, the *example/multicore/* directory provides an example of a multicore configuration. We'll learn more about these features later in the book. For now, let's continue with the simple example by adding documents to the index, which you'll need to work through the examples in section 2.2.

Figure 2.4   Directory listing of the default Solr home directory for the Solr examples. It contains a single core named collection1, **which is configured in** *solr.xml.* **The** *collection1* **directory corresponds to the core named** collection1 **and contains core-specific configuration files, the Lucene index, and a transaction log.**

2.1.4   Indexing the example documents

When you first start Solr, there are no documents in the index. It's an empty server waiting to be filled with data to search. We cover indexing in more detail in chapter 5. For now, we'll gloss over the details in order to get example data into the Solr index so that we can try out some queries. Open a new command-line interface and enter the following:

```
cd $SOLR_INSTALL/example/exampledocs
java -jar post.jar *.xml
```

You should see output that looks like the following:

```
SimplePostTool version 1.5
Posting files to base url http://localhost:8983/solr/update using content-
     type application/xml..
POSTing file gb18030-example.xml
POSTing file hd.xml
POSTing file ipod_other.xml
POSTing file ipod_video.xml
POSTing file manufacturers.xml
POSTing file mem.xml
POSTing file money.xml
POSTing file monitor.xml
POSTing file monitor2.xml
POSTing file mp500.xml
POSTing file sd500.xml
POSTing file solr.xml
POSTing file utf8-example.xml
POSTing file vidcard.xml
14 files indexed.
COMMITting Solr index changes to http://localhost:8983/solr/update..
```

The *post.jar* file sends XML documents to Solr using HTTP POST. After all the documents are sent to Solr, the *post.jar* application issues a commit, which makes the example documents findable in Solr. To verify that the example documents were added successfully, go to the Query page in the Solr administration console (http://localhost:8983/solr) and execute the find all documents query (*:*). You need to select collection1 in the dropdown box on the left to access the Query page. Figure 2.5 shows what you should see after executing the find all documents query.

At this point, we have a running Solr instance with some example documents loaded.

2.2　*Searching is what it's all about*

Now it's time to see Solr shine. Without a doubt, Solr's main strength is powerful query processing. Think about it this way; who cares how scalable or fast a search engine is if the results it returns aren't useful or accurate? In this section, you'll see Solr query processing in action, which we think will help you see why Solr is such a powerful search technology.

Throughout this section, pay close attention to the link between each query we execute and the documents that Solr returns, and particularly the order of the documents in the results. This will help you start thinking like a search engine, which will come in handy in chapter 3 when we cover core search concepts.

2.2.1　*Exploring Solr's query form*

You've already used Solr's query form to execute the find all documents query. Let's take a quick tour of the other features in this form so you get a sense for the types of queries Solr supports. Figure 2.6 provides some annotations of key sections of this form. Take a minute to read through each annotation in the diagram.

The find all documents
query in Solr is *:*

Search results from executing
the find all documents query.

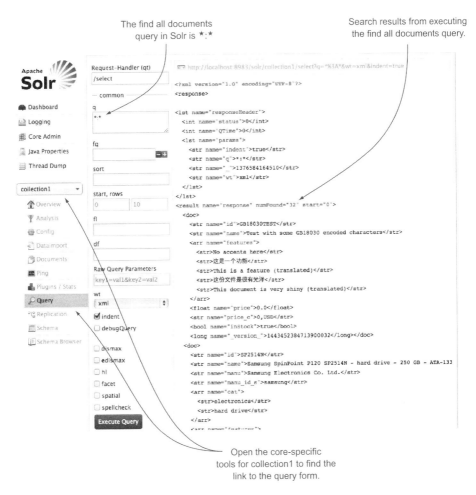

Open the core-specific
tools for collection1 to find the
link to the query form.

Figure 2.5   A screenshot of the query form on the Solr administration console. You can verify that the example documents were indexed correctly by executing the find all documents query.

In figure 2.6, we formulate a query that returns two of the example documents we added in section 2.1.4. Fill out the form and execute the query in your own environment. Do the two documents that Solr returned make sense? Table 2.1 provides an overview of the form fields we're using for this example.

As we discussed in chapter 1 (section 1.2.3), all interaction with Solr's core services, such as query processing, is performed with HTTP requests. When you fill out the query form, an HTTP GET request is created and sent to Solr. The form field names shown in table 2.1 correspond to parameters passed to Solr in the HTTP GET request. Listing 2.1 shows the HTTP GET request sent to Solr when you execute the query depicted in figure 2.6. Note that the request doesn't include line breaks between the parameters, which we've included here to make it easier to see the separate parameters.

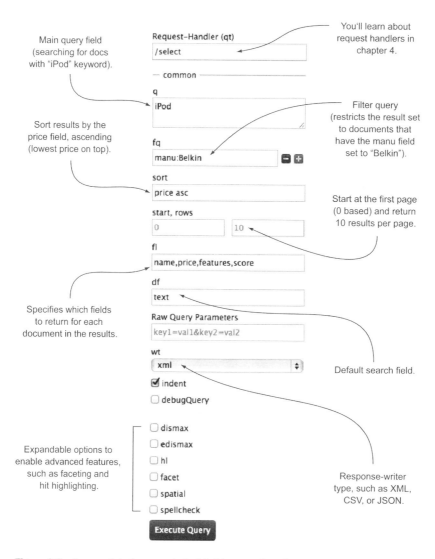

Main query field (searching for docs with "iPod" keyword).

You'll learn about request handlers in chapter 4.

Sort results by the price field, ascending (lowest price on top).

Filter query (restricts the result set to documents that have the manu field set to "Belkin").

Start at the first page (0 based) and return 10 results per page.

Specifies which fields to return for each document in the results.

Default search field.

Expandable options to enable advanced features, such as faceting and hit highlighting.

Response-writer type, such as XML, CSV, or JSON.

Figure 2.6   An annotated screenshot of Solr's query form illustrating the main features of Solr query processing, such as filters, results format, sorting, paging, and search components

Table 2.1   Overview of query parameters from figure 2.6

Form field	Value	Description
q	iPod	Main query parameter; documents are scored by their similarity to terms in this parameter.
fq	manu:Belkin	Filter query; restricts the result set to documents matching this filter but doesn't affect scoring. In this example, we filter results that have manufacturer field manu equal to Belkin.

Table 2.1 Overview of query parameters from figure 2.6 (continued)

Form field	Value	Description
sort	price asc	Specifies the sort field and sort order; in this case, we want results sorted by the price field in ascending order (asc) so that documents with the lowest price are listed first.
start	0	Specifies the starting page for results; because this is our first request, we want the first page to use 0-based indexing. Start should be incremented by the page size to advance to the next page.
rows	10	Page size; restricts the number of results returned per page, in this case 10.
fl	name,price, features, score	List of fields to return for each document in the result set. The score field is a built-in field that holds each document's relevancy score for the query. You have to request the score field explicitly for it to be returned, as is done in this example.
df	text	Default search field for any query terms that don't specify which field to search on; text is the catch-all field for the example server.
wt	xml	Response-writer type; governs the format of the response.

Listing 2.1 Breakdown of the HTTP GET request sent by the query form

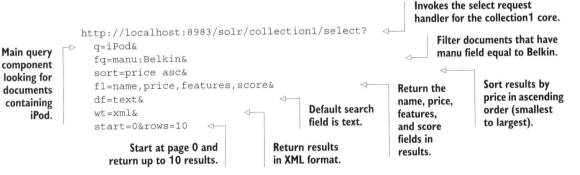

Looking for more example queries?
We cover queries in more depth in chapter 7. But if you don't want to wait that long and want to see more queries in action, we recommend looking at the tutorial provided with Solr. Open *$SOLR_INSTALL/docs/tutorial.html* in your web browser and you'll find additional queries for the example documents you loaded in section 2.1.4.

We probably don't have to tell you that this form isn't designed for end users; Solr provides the query form so that developers and administrators have a way to send queries without having to formulate HTTP requests manually or develop a client application to send a query to Solr. But let's be clear that with Solr-based applications, you're responsible for developing the UI. As we'll see in section 2.2.5, Solr provides a customizable example search UI, called Solritas, to help you prototype your own awesome search application.

2.2.2   *What comes back from Solr when you search*

We've seen what gets sent to Solr, so now let's learn about what comes back in the results. The key point in this section is that Solr returns documents that match the query, as well as additional information that can be processed by your Solr client to deliver a quality search experience. The operative phrase being *by your Solr client!* Solr returns the raw data and features that you need to create a quality search experience for your users.

Figure 2.7 shows what comes back from the example query we used in section 2.2.1. As you can see, the results are in XML format and are sorted from lowest to highest price. Each document contains the term `iPod`. Paging doesn't come into play with this result set because there are only two results total.

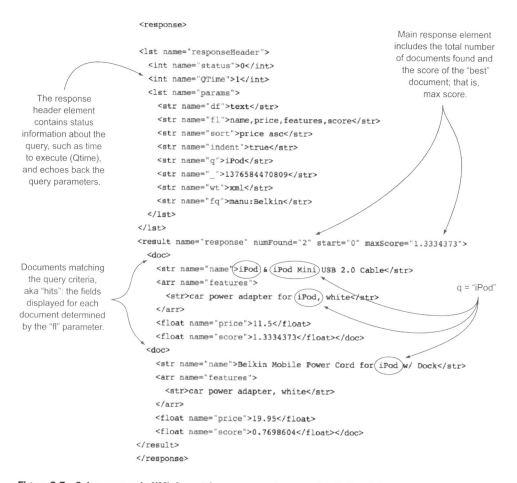

Figure 2.7   Solr response in XML format from our sample request in listing 2.1

So far, we've only seen results returned as XML, but Solr also supports other formats such as CSV (comma-separated values), JavaScript Object Notation (JSON), and language-specific formats for popular languages. For instance, Solr can return a Python-specific format that allows the response to be safely parsed into a Python object tree using the `eval` function.

2.2.3 *Ranked retrieval*

As we touched upon in chapter 1, the key differentiator between Solr's query processing and that of a database or other NoSQL data store is ranked retrieval: the process of sorting documents by their relevance to a query, in which the most relevant documents are listed first.

Let's see ranked retrieval at work with some of the example documents you indexed in section 2.1.4. To begin, enter `iPod` in the q text box and `name,features,score` in the `fl` text field, and click Execute. This should return three documents sorted in descending order by score. Take a moment to scan the results and decide if you agree with the ranking for this simple query.

Intuitively, the ordering makes sense because the query term `iPod` occurs three times in the first document listed, twice in the name and once in the features; it occurs only once in the other documents. The numeric value of the score field isn't inherently meaningful; it's only used internally by Lucene to do relative ranking and is not comparable across different queries. The key takeaway is that every document that matches a query is assigned a relevance score for that specific query, and results are returned in descending order by score; the higher the score, the more relevant the document is to the query.

Next, change your query to `iPod power` and you'll see that the same three documents are returned and are in the same order. This is because all three documents contain both query terms in either their name or features field. But the scores of the top two documents are much closer: 1.521 and 1.398 for the second query versus 1.333 and 0.770 (rounded) for the first query. This makes sense because `power` occurs twice in the second document, so its relevance to the `iPod power` query is much higher than its relevance to the `iPod` query.

Now, change your query to `iPod power^2`, which boosts the power query term by 2. In a nutshell, this means that the `power` term is twice as important to this query as the `iPod` term, which has an implicit boost of 1. Again, the same three documents are returned but in a different order. Now the top document in the results is `Belkin Mobile Power Cord for iPod w/ Dock`, because it contains the term `power` in the `name` and `features` fields, and we told Solr that `power` is twice as important as `iPod` for this query.

Now you have a taste of what ranked retrieval looks like. You'll learn more about ranked retrieval and boosting in chapters 3, 7, and 16. Let's move on and see some other features of query processing, starting with how to work with queries that return more than three documents using paging and sorting.

2.2.4   *Paging and sorting*

Our example Solr index contains only 32 documents, but a production Solr instance typically has millions of documents. You can imagine that in a Solr instance for an electronics superstore, a query for iPod would probably match thousands of products and accessories. To ensure results are returned quickly, particularly on bandwidth-constrained mobile devices, you don't want to return thousands of results at once, even if the most relevant are listed first.

PAGING

The solution is to return a small subset of results called a *page*, along with navigational tools to allow the user to request more pages if needed. *Paging* is a first-class concept in Solr query processing, in that every query includes parameters that control the page size (rows) and starting position (start). If not specified in the request, Solr uses a default page size of 10, but you can control that using the rows parameter in the query request. To request the next page in the results, you increment the start parameter by the page size. For example, if you're on the first page of results (start=0), then to get the next page, you increment the start parameter by the page size: for example, start=10.

It's important to use as small a page size as possible to satisfy your requirements, because the underlying Lucene index isn't optimized for returning many documents at once. Rather, Lucene is optimized for query processing, so the underlying data structures are designed to maximize matching and scoring documents. Once the search results are identified, Solr must reconstruct each document, in most cases by reading data off the disk. It uses intelligent caching to be as efficient as possible, but in comparison to query execution, results construction is a slow process, particularly for large page sizes. Consequently, you'll get much better performance from Solr using small page sizes.

SORTING

As you learned in section 2.2.3, results are sorted by relevance score, in descending order (highest to lowest). But you can request Solr to sort results by other fields in your documents. You saw an example of this in section 2.2.1 in which you sorted results by the price field in ascending order, producing the lowest-priced products at the top.

Sorting and paging go hand in hand because the sort order determines the page position for results. To help get you thinking about sorting and paging, consider the question of whether Solr will return deterministic results when paging without specifying a sort order. On the surface, this seems obvious because the results are sorted in descending order by score if you don't specify a sort parameter. But what if all documents in a query have the same score? For example, if your query is inStock:true, then all matching documents will have the same score; you can verify this yourself using the query form.

It turns out that Solr is able to return all documents in a deterministic order when you page through the results even though the score is the same. This works because

Solr finds all documents that match a query and then applies the sorting and paging offsets to the entire set of documents. Solr keeps track of the entire set of documents that match a query independently of the sorting and paging offsets. Incidentally, if all documents have the same score, then they are returned in index order, which is based on an internal document ID managed by Lucene. The internal document ID roughly equates to the order in which documents were indexed, but you should not rely on this value for sorting, as it can change as your index changes.

2.2.5 Expanded search features

The query form contains a list of check boxes that enable advanced functionality during query processing. As shown in figure 2.6, the form contains check boxes that reveal additional form fields to activate the following search features:

- `dismax`—Disjunction Max query parser (see chapter 7)
- `edismax`—Extended Disjunction Max query parser (see chapter 7)
- `hl`—Hit highlighting (see chapter 9)
- `facet`—Faceting (see chapter 8)
- `spatial`—Geospatial search, such as sorting by geo distance (see chapter 15)
- `spellcheck`—Spell-checking on query terms (see chapter 10)

If you click any of these check boxes, you'll see that it's not clear what to do when you look at the form. That's because using these search components from the query form requires additional knowledge that we can't cover quickly in this getting started chapter. Rest assured that we'll cover each of these components in depth later in the book.

For now, we can see some of these search features in action using Solritas, Solr's example search interface available in your local Solr instance at http://localhost:8983/solr/collection1/browse. Navigate to this URL in your web browser and you'll see a screen that looks like figure 2.8.

As shown at the top of figure 2.8, Solr provides three examples to choose from: Simple, Spatial, and Group By. We'll briefly cover the key aspects of the Simple example here and encourage you to explore the other two examples on your own.

Scan figure 2.8 to identify the various search components at work. One of the more interesting search components in this example is facet, shown on the left side of the page, starting with the header Field Facets. The facet component categorizes field values in the search results into useful subsets to help the user refine their queries and discover new information. For instance, when we search for `video`, Solr returns three example documents, and the facet component categorizes the `cat` field of these documents into three subsets: electronics (3), graphics card (2), and music (1). Click the music facet link, and you'll see the results are filtered from three documents down to only one. The idea here is that in addition to search results, you can help users refine their search criteria by categorizing the results with different filters. We'll cover facets in detail in chapter 8.

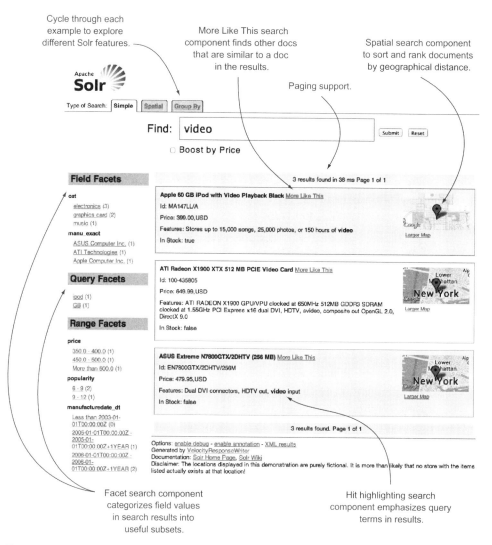

Figure 2.8 The Solritas Simple example, which illustrates how to use various search components, such as faceting, More Like This, hit highlighting, and spatial, to provide a rich search experience for your users.

Next, let's look at another search component that isn't immediately obvious from figure 2.8: namely, the spellcheck component. To see how spell-checking works, type vydeoh in the search box instead of video. No results are found, as shown in figure 2.9, but Solr does return a link that effectively asks the user if they meant video; if so, they can re-execute the search using the link.

There's a lot of powerful functionality packed into the three Solritas examples, and we encourage you to spend time with each. For now, let's move on and tour the rest of the administration console.

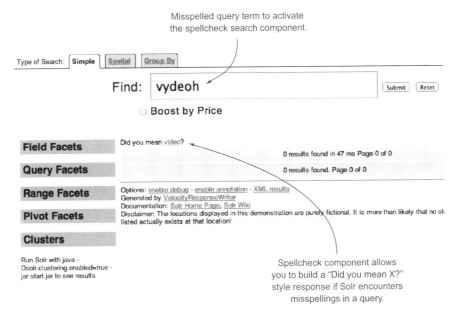

Figure 2.9 Example of how the spellcheck component allows your search UI to prompt the user to re-execute the search using the correct spelling of a query term; in this case, Solr found `video` as the closest match for `vydeoh`.

2.3 Tour of the Solr administration console

At this point, you should have a good feel for the query form, so let's take a quick tour of the rest of the administration console (shown in figure 2.10).

Figure 2.10 The Solr administration console: explore each page using the toolbar on the left.

Rather than spending your time reading about the administration panel, we think it's better to start clicking through some of the pages yourself. Thus, we leave it as an exercise for you to visit all the links in the administration console to get a sense for what is available on each page. Here are some highlights of what the administration console provides:

- See how your Solr instance is configured from Dashboard.
- View recent log messages from Logging.
- Temporarily change log verbosity settings from Level under Logging.
- Add and manage multiple cores from Core Admin.
- View Java system properties from Java Properties.
- Get a dump of all active threads in your JVM from Thread Dump.

In addition to these main pages, there are a number of core-specific pages for each core in your server. Recall that the example server we've been working with has only one core, named `collection1`. The core-specific pages allow you to do the following:

- View core-specific properties such as the number of Lucene segments from the main core page (for example, `collection1`).
- Send a quick request to a core to make sure it's healthy and responding using Ping.
- Execute queries against the core's index using Query.
- View the currently active *schema.xml* for the core from Schema; you'll learn all about *schema.xml* in chapters 5 and 6.
- View the currently active *solrconfig.xml* for the core from Config; you'll learn more about *solrconfig.xml* in chapter 4.
- See how your index is replicated to other servers from Replication. You'll learn how to set up replication in chapters 12 and 13.
- Analyze text from Analysis; you'll learn all about text analysis in chapter 6, including how to use the Analysis form.
- Determine how fields in your documents are analyzed from Schema Browser.
- Get information about the top terms for a field using Load Term Info on the Schema Browser.
- View the status and configuration for plugins from PlugIns / Stats; you'll learn all about plugins in chapter 4.
- View statistics about core Solr cache regions, such as how many documents are in the `documentCache`, from PlugIns / Stats.
- Manage the DIH from Dataimport; this isn't enabled in the example server.

We'll dig into the details for most of these pages throughout the book when it's more appropriate. For instance, you'll learn all about the Analysis page in chapter 6 when we cover text analysis. For now, explore these pages on your own. To give your self-guided tour some direction, see if you can answer the following questions about your Solr server.

1 What's the value of the `lucene-spec` version property for your Solr server?
2 What's the log level of the `org.apache.solr.core.SolrConfig` class?
3 What's the value of the `maxDoc` property for the `collection1` core?
4 What's the value of the `java.vm.vendor` Java system property?
5 What's the `segment count` for the `collection1` core?
6 What's the response time of `pinging` your server?
7 What's the top term for the `manu` field? (Hint: select the `manu` field in the schema browser, and click the Load Term Info button.)
8 What's the current size of your `documentCache`? (Hint: think stats.)
9 What's the analyzed value of the name `Belkin Mobile Power Cord for iPod w/ Dock`? (Hint: select the `name` field on the Analysis page.)

Let's now turn our attention to what needs to be done to start customizing Solr for your specific needs.

2.4   Adapting the example to your needs

Now that you've had a chance to work with the example server, you might be wondering about the best way to proceed with adapting it to your specific needs. You have a couple of choices here. You could use the *example/* directory as is and start making changes to it to meet your needs. But we think it's better to keep a copy of *example/* around and make your application-specific changes in a clone of *example/*. This allows you to refer to *example/* in case you break something when working on your own application.

If you choose the latter approach, you need to select a name for the directory that is more appropriate for your application than *example/*. If we were building the real estate search application described in chapter 1, we might, for example, name the directory *realestate/*. Once you've settled on a name, perform the following steps to create a clone of the *example/* directory in Solr:

1 Create a deep copy of the *example/* directory; for example, `cp -R example realestate`.
2 Clean up the cloned directory to remove unused Solr home directories, such as *example-DIH/* and *multicore/*; they'll be in *example/* if you need to refer back to them.
3 Under the Solr home directory, rename *collection1/* to something more intuitive for your application.
4 Update *core.properties* to point to the name of your new collection by replacing `collection1` with the name of your core from step 3; such as: `name =realestate`.

Note that you don't need to make any changes to the Solr configuration files, such as *solrconfig.xml* or *schema.xml*, at this time. These files are designed to provide a good experience out of the box and to let you adapt them to your needs iteratively without having to swallow such a big pill at once to reconfigure them.

> **Cleaning up your index**
>
> There may come a time when you want to start with a fresh index. After stopping Solr, you can remove all documents by deleting the contents of the *data/* directory for your core, such as *solr/collection1/data/**. When you restart Solr, you'll have a fresh index with 0 documents.

Restart Solr from your new directory using the process from section 2.1.2. For example, to restart our clone for the `realestate` application, we'd execute

```
cd $SOLR_INSTALL/realestate
java -jar start.jar
```

You might be wondering about setting JVM options, configuring backups, monitoring, setting Solr up as a service, and so on. We feel these are important concerns when you're ready to go to production, so we cover these questions in chapter 12 when we discuss taking Solr to production.

2.5 *Summary*

To recap, we started by installing Solr 4.7 from the binary distribution Apache provided. In reality, the installation process was only a matter of choosing an appropriate directory into which to extract the downloaded archive (*.zip* or *.tgz*) and then performing the extraction. Next, we started the example Solr server and added example documents using the *post.jar* command-line application.

After adding documents, we introduced you to Solr's query form and you learned the basic components of a Solr query. Specifically, you learned how to construct queries containing a main query parameter q as well as an optional filter fq. You saw how to control which fields are returned using the fl parameter and how to control the ordering of results using sort. We also touched on ranked retrieval concepts in which results are ordered by relevancy score, which will be covered further in chapter 3. You'll also learn much more about queries in chapter 7.

We introduced you to search components and provided insight into how they work in Solr using the Solritas example UI. Specifically, you saw an example of how the facet component allows users to refine their search criteria using dynamically generated filters called facets. We also touched on how the spellcheck component allows you to prompt users with a "Did you mean *X?*" message when their query contains a misspelled term.

Next, we gave you tips on what other tools are available in the Solr administration console. You'll find many great tools and statistics available about Solr, and we hope you were able to answer the questions we posed as you walked through the administration console in your browser. We also presented the steps to clone the *example/* directory and begin customizing it for your own application. We think this is a good way to start so that you always have a working example to refer to as you customize Solr for your specific needs.

Now that you have a running Solr instance, it's time to learn about key Solr concepts. In chapter 3, you'll gain a better understanding of core search concepts that will help you throughout the rest of your Solr journey.

Key Solr concepts 3

This chapter covers

- What differentiates Solr from traditional database technologies
- The basic structure of Solr's internal index
- How Solr performs complex queries using terms, phrases, and fuzzy matching
- How Solr calculates scores for matching queries to the most relevant documents
- How to balance returning relevant results versus returning all possible results
- How to model your content into denormalized documents
- How Solr scales across servers to handle billions of documents and queries

Now that we have Solr up and running, it's important to gain a basic understanding of how a search engine operates and why you'd choose to use Solr to store and retrieve your content. Our main goal for this chapter is to provide the theoretical underpinnings so you can understand and maximize your use of Solr.

If you have a solid background in search and information retrieval, then you may wish to skip some or all of this chapter, but if not, it will help you understand more advanced topics later in this book and maximize the quality of your users' search experience.

Although the content in this chapter is generally applicable to most search engines, we'll be specifically focusing on Solr's implementation of each of the concepts. By the end of this chapter, you should have a solid understanding of how Solr's internal index works, how to perform complex Boolean and fuzzy queries with Solr, how Solr's default relevancy scoring model works, and how Solr's architecture enables queries to remain fast as it scales to handle billions of documents across many servers.

Let's begin with a discussion of the core concepts behind search in Solr, including how the search index works, how a search engine matches queries and documents, and how Solr enables powerful query capabilities to make finding content a problem of the past.

3.1 Searching, matching, and finding content

Many different kinds of systems exist to help us solve challenging data storage and retrieval problems: relational databases, key-value stores, map-reduce engines operating upon files on disk, and graph databases, among many others. Search engines, and Solr in particular, help to solve a specific class of problem quite well—problems requiring the ability to search across large amounts of unstructured text and pull back the most relevant results.

In this section, we'll describe the core features of a modern search engine, including an explanation of a search "document," an overview of the inverted search index at the core of Solr's fast full-text searching capabilities, and a broad overview of how this inverted search index enables arbitrarily complex term, phrase, and partial-matching queries.

3.1.1 What is a document?

We posted some documents to Solr in chapter 2 and then ran example searches against Solr, so this is not the first time we have mentioned documents. It is important, however, that we have a solid understanding of the kind of information we can put into Solr to be searched upon (a document) and how that information is structured.

Solr is a document storage and retrieval engine. Every piece of data submitted to Solr for processing is a *document*. A document could be a newspaper article, a resume or social profile, or, in an extreme case, an entire book.

Each document contains one or more fields, each of which is modeled as a particular field type: string, tokenized text, Boolean, date/time, lat/long, etc. The number of potential field types is infinite because a field type is composed of zero or more analysis steps that change how the data in the field is processed and mapped into the Solr index. Each field is defined in Solr's schema (discussed in chapter 5) as a particular field type, which allows Solr to know how to handle the content as it's received. Listing 3.1 shows an example document, with the values defined for each field.

Listing 3.1 Example Solr document

```
<doc>
  <field name="id">company123</field>
  <field name="companycity">Atlanta</field>
  <field name="companystate">Georgia</field>
  <field name="companyname">Code Monkeys R Us, LLC</field>
  <field name="companydescription">we write lots of code</field>
  <field name="lastmodified">2013-06-01T15:26:37Z</field>
</doc>
```

When we run a query against Solr, we can search on one or more of these fields (or even fields not contained in this particular document), and Solr will return documents that contain content in those fields matching the query.

It's worth noting that although Solr has a flexible schema for each document, it's not "schema-less." All field types must be defined, and all field names (or dynamic field-naming patterns) should be specified in Solr's *schema.xml*, as we'll discuss further in chapter 5. This does not mean that every document must contain every field, only that all possible fields must be mappable to a particular field type should they appear in a document and need to be processed. Solr *does* contain an ability to automatically guess the field type for previously unseen field names when it first receives a document with a new field name. This is accomplished by inspecting the type of data in the field and automatically adding the field to Solr's schema. Since Solr could potentially guess the wrong field type if the input is confusing, it's a better practice to predefine the field.

A document, then, is a collection of fields that map to particular field types defined in a schema. Each field in a document has its content analyzed according to its field type, and the results of that analysis are saved into a search index in order to later retrieve the document by sending in a related query. The primary search results returned from a Solr query are documents containing one or more fields.

3.1.2 *The fundamental search problem*

Before we dive into an overview of how search works in Solr, it's helpful to understand what fundamental problem search engines are solving.

Let's say you were tasked with creating search functionality that helps users search for books. Your initial prototype might look something like figure 3.1.

Now imagine that a customer wants to find a book on purchasing a new home and searches for *buying a home*. Some potentially relevant book titles you may want to return for this search are listed in table 3.1.

Book Title:

Figure 3.1 Example search interface, as would be seen on a typical website, demonstrating how a user would submit a query to your application

Table 3.1 Books relevant to the query "buying a home"

Potentially relevant books
The Beginner's Guide to Buying a House
How to Buy Your First House
Purchasing a Home
Becoming a New Home Owner
Buying a New Home
Decorating Your Home

All other book titles, as listed in table 3.2, would not be considered relevant for customers interested in purchasing a new home.

Table 3.2 Books not relevant to the query "buying a home"

Irrelevant books
A Fun Guide to Cooking
How to Raise a Child
Buying a New Car

A naïve approach to implementing this search using a traditional SQL database would be to query for the exact text that users enter:

```
SELECT * FROM Books
WHERE Name = 'buying a new home';
```

The problem with this approach is that none of the book titles in your book catalog will match the text that customers type in exactly, which means they will not find any results for this query. In addition, customers will only see results for future queries if the query matches the full book title exactly.

Perhaps a more forgiving approach would be to search for each single word within a customer's query:

```
SELECT * FROM Books
WHERE Name LIKE '%buying%'
  AND Name LIKE '%a%'
  AND Name LIKE '%home%';
```

The previous query, although relatively expensive for a traditional database to handle because it can't use available database indexes, would at least produce one match for the customer that contains all desired words, as shown in table 3.3.

Table 3.3 Results from database `LIKE` **query requiring a fuzzy match for every term**

Matching books	Nonmatching books
Buying *a New* **Home**	*The Beginner's Guide to* **Buying** *a House*
	How to Buy Your First House
	Purchasing **a Home**
	Becoming **a New Home** *Owner*
	A *Fun Guide to Cooking*
	How to Raise **a** *Child*
	Buying *a New Car*
	Decorating Your **Home**

Of course, you may believe that requiring documents to match all of the words your customers include in their queries is overly restrictive. You could easily make the search experience more flexible by only requiring a single word to exist in any matching book titles, by issuing the following SQL query:

```
SELECT * FROM Books
WHERE Name LIKE '%buying%'
    OR Name LIKE '%a%'
    OR Name LIKE '%home%';
```

The results of this query can be seen in table 3.4. You'll see that this query matched many more book titles than the previous query because this query only required a minimum of one of the keywords to match. Additionally, because this query is performing only partial string matching on each keyword, any book title that contains the letter "a" is also returned. The preceding example, which required all of the terms, also matched on the letter "a", but we did not experience this problem of returning too many results because the other keywords were more restrictive.

Table 3.4 Results from database `LIKE` **query only requiring a fuzzy match of at least one term**

Matching books	Nonmatching books
A *Fun Guide to Cooking*	*How to Buy Your First House*
Decorating Your **Home**	
How to Raise **a** *Child*	
Buying *a New Car*	
Buying *a New* **Home**	
The Beginner's Guide to **Buying** *a House*	
Purchasing **a Home**	
Becoming **a** *New* **Home** *owner*	

The first query (requiring all words to match) resulted in many relevant books not being found; the second query (requiring only one of the words to match) resulted in many more relevant books being found but resulted in many irrelevant books being found as well.

These examples demonstrate several difficulties with this implementation:

- It only performs substring matching and is unable to distinguish between words.
- It doesn't understand linguistic variations, such as "buying" versus "buy."
- It doesn't understand synonyms of words such as "buying" and "purchasing" or "home" and "house."
- Unimportant words such as "a" prevent results from matching as expected (either excluding relevant results or including irrelevant results, depending upon whether "all" or "any" of the words must match).
- There's no sense of relevancy ordering in the results; books that match only one of the queried words often show up higher than books matching multiple or all of the words in the customer's query.

These queries will become slow as the size of the book catalog grows or the number of customer queries grows, because the query must scan through every book's title to find partial matches instead of using an index to look up the words.

Search engines like Solr shine in solving such problems. Solr is able to perform text analysis on content and on search queries to determine textually similar words, understand and match on synonyms, remove unimportant words like "a," "the," and "of," and score each result based upon how well it matches the incoming query to ensure that the best results are returned first and that your customers do not have to page through countless less-relevant results to find the content they were expecting. Solr accomplishes all of this by using an index that maps content to documents instead of mapping documents to content as in a traditional database model. This inverted index is at the heart of how search engines work.

3.1.3 *The inverted index*

Solr uses Lucene's inverted index to power its fast searching capabilities, as well as many of the additional bells and whistles it provides at query time. While we'll not get into many of the internal Lucene data structures in this book, it's important to understand the high-level structure of the inverted index. (We recommend *Lucene in Action*, Second Edition, by Michael McCandless, Erik Hatcher, and Otis Gospodnetić [Manning, 2010] if you want a deeper dive.)

Recalling our previous book-searching example, we can get a feel for what an index mapping each term to each document would look like from table 3.5.

While a traditional database representation of multiple documents would contain a document's ID mapped to one or more content fields containing all of the words/terms in that document, an inverted index inverts this model and maps each word/term in the corpus to all of the documents in which it appears. You can tell from looking at

Table 3.5   Mapping of text from multiple documents into an inverted index. The right table contains an inverted search index showing each of the terms, along with its position, within the original documents from the left table.

Original documents		Lucene's inverted index			
Doc #	Content field	Term	Doc #	(Continued)...	
1	A Fun Guide to Cooking	a	1,3,4,5,6,7,8	...	...
2	Decorating Your Home	becoming	8	guide	1,6
3	How to Raise a Child	beginner's	6	home	2,5,7,8
4	Buying a New Car	buy	9	house	6,9
5	Buying a New Home	buying	4,5,6	how	3,9
6	The Beginner's Guide to	car	4	new	4,5,8
	Buying a House	child	3	owner	8
7	Purchasing a Home	cooking	1	purchasing	7
8	Becoming a New Home Owner	decorating	2	raise	3
9	How to Buy Your First House	first	9	the	6
		fun	1	to	1,6,9
		...	...	your	2,9

table 3.5 that the original input text was split on spaces and that each term was transformed into lowercase text before being inserted into the inverted index, but everything else remained the same. It is worth noting that many additional text transformations are possible, not only these simple ones; terms can be modified, added, or removed during the content-analysis process, which will be covered in detail in chapter 6.

Two final important details should be noted about the inverted index:

- All terms in the index map to one or more documents.
- Terms in the inverted index are sorted in ascending lexicographical order.

This view of the inverted index is greatly simplified; we'll see in section 3.1.6 that additional information can also be stored in the index to improve Solr's querying and scoring capabilities.

As you'll see in the next section, the structure of Lucene's inverted index allows for many powerful query capabilities that maximize both the speed and the flexibility of keyword-based searching.

3.1.4   *Terms, phrases, and Boolean logic*

Now that we've seen what content looks like in Lucene's inverted index, let's jump into the mechanics of how a query is able to make use of this index to find matching documents. In this section, we'll go over the basics of looking up terms and phrases in an inverted search index and utilizing Boolean logic and fuzzy queries to enhance these lookup capabilities. Referring back to the book-searching example, let's look at a simple query for *new house*, as portrayed in figure 3.2.

Book Title:

new house		SEARCH

Figure 3.2   Simple search to demonstrate nuances of query interpretation

You saw in the last section that all of the text in the content field was broken up into individual terms when inserted into the Lucene index. Now that there's an incoming query, you need to select from among several options for querying the index:

- Search for two different terms, new and house, requiring both to match
- Search for two different terms, new and house, requiring only one to match
- Search for the exact phrase "new house"

All of these options are perfectly valid approaches depending upon your use case, and thanks to Solr's powerful querying capabilities, built using Lucene, they're easy to accomplish using Boolean logic.

REQUIRED TERMS

Let's examine the first option, breaking the query into multiple terms and requiring them all to match. There are two identical ways to write this query using the default query parser in Solr:

- +new +house
- new AND house

These two are logically identical, and, in fact, the second example gets parsed and ultimately reduced down to the first example. The + symbol is a unary operator that means that the part of the query immediately following it is required to exist in any documents matched; the AND keyword is a binary operator that means that the part of the query immediately preceding and the part of the query immediately following it are both required.

OPTIONAL TERMS

In contrast to the AND operator, Solr also supports the OR binary operator, which means that either the part of the query preceding or the part of the query following it is required to exist in any documents matched. By default, Solr is also configured to treat any part of the query without an explicit operator as an optional parameter, making the following identical:

- new house
- new OR house

NEGATED TERMS

In addition to making parts of a query optional or required, it's also possible to require that they not exist in any matched documents through either of the following equivalent queries:

- new house -rental
- new house NOT rental

In those queries, no document that contains the word rental will be returned, only documents matching new or house.

> **Solr's default operator**
>
> While the default configuration in Solr assumes that a term or phrase by itself is an optional term, this is configurable on a per-query basis using the `q.op` URL parameter with many of Solr's query handlers.
>
> `/select/?q=new house&q.op=OR` versus `/select?q=new house&q.op=AND`
>
> Note that if you change the default operator from `OR` to `AND`, this will switch to requiring all terms specified without an explicit Boolean operator. If the default operator is `OR` for the query `new house`, then only one of the terms is required. If the default operator is `AND` for the same query, then both the terms `new` and `house` are required. You can also explicitly specify the operator between the terms (such as `new AND home` or `new OR home`) to override the default operator.

PHRASES

Solr does not only support searching single terms; it can also search for phrases, ensuring that multiple terms appear together in order:

- `"new home" OR "new house"`
- `"3 bedrooms" AND "walk in closet" AND "granite countertops"`

GROUPED EXPRESSIONS

In addition to the preceding query expressions, one final basic Boolean construct that Solr supports is the grouping of terms, phrases, and other query expressions. The Solr query syntax can represent arbitrarily complex queries through grouping terms using parentheses, as in the following examples:

- `New AND (house OR (home NOT improvement NOT depot NOT grown))`
- `(+(buying purchasing -renting) +(home house residence -(+property -bedroom)))`

The use of required terms, optional terms, negated terms, and grouped expressions provides a powerful and flexible set of query capabilities that allow arbitrarily complex lookup operations against the search index, as we'll see in the following section.

3.1.5   *Finding sets of documents*

With a basic understanding of terms, phrases, and Boolean queries in place, we can now dive into exactly how Solr is able to use the internal Lucene inverted index to find matching documents. Recall the index of books from table 3.5, a part of which is reproduced in table 3.6.

Table 3.6   Inverted index of terms from a collection of book titles

Term	Document	(Continued)...	
a	1,3,4,5,6,7,8	...	...
becoming	8	guide	1,6

Table 3.6   Inverted index of terms from a collection of book titles *(continued)*

Term	Document	(Continued)...	
beginner's	6	home	2,5,7,8
buy	9	house	6,9
buying	4,5,6	how	3,9
car	4	new	4,5,8
child	3	owner	8
cooking	1	purchasing	7
decorating	2	raise	3
first	9	the	6
fun	1	to	1,6,9
...	...	your	2,9

If a customer now passes in a query of new home, how exactly is Solr able to find documents matching that query, given the preceding inverted index?

The answer is that the query new home is a two-term query (there is a default operator between new and home, remember?). As such, both terms must be looked up separately in the Lucene index:

Term	Document
home	2,5,7,8
new	4,5,8

Once the list of matching documents is found for each term, Lucene will perform set operations to arrive at an appropriate final result set that matches the query. Assuming the default operator is an OR, this query would result in a union of the result sets for both terms, as pictured in the Venn diagram in figure 3.3.

Likewise, if the query had been new AND home or if the default operator had been set to AND, then the intersection of the results for both terms would have been calculated to return a result set of only document 5 and document 8, as shown in figure 3.4.

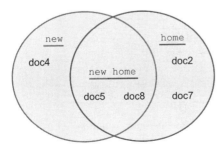

Figure 3.3   Results returned from a union query using the OR operator

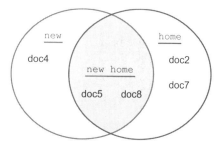

Figure 3.4   Results returned from an intersection query using the AND operator

In addition to union and intersection queries, negating particular terms is also common. Figure 3.5 demonstrates a breakdown of the results expected for many of the result set permutations of this two-term search query (assuming a default OR operator).

As you can see, the ability to search for required terms, optional terms, negated terms, and grouped terms provides a powerful mechanism for looking up single

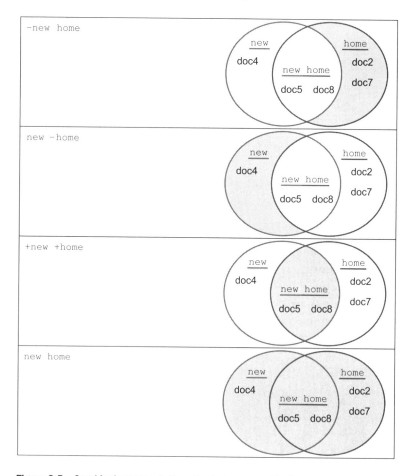

Figure 3.5   Graphical representation of using common Boolean query operators

keywords. As we'll see in the following section, Solr also provides the ability to query for multiterm phrases.

3.1.6 *Phrase queries and term positions*

We saw earlier that, in addition to querying for terms in our Lucene index, it's possible to query Solr for phrases. Recalling that the index contains only individual terms, however, you may be wondering how we can search for full phrases.

The short answer is that each term in a phrase query is still looked up in the Lucene index individually, as if the query new home had been submitted instead of "new home". Once the overlapping document set is found, however, a feature of the index that we conveniently left out of our initial inverted index discussion is used. This feature, called *term positions*, is the optional recording of the relative position of terms within a document. Table 3.7 demonstrates how documents (on the left side of the table) map into an inverted index containing term positions (on the right side of the table).

Table 3.7   Inverted index with term positions

Original documents		Lucene's inverted index with term positions		
Document #	Content field	Term	Document	Term position
1	A Fun Guide to Cooking	a	1	1
2	Decorating Your Home		3	4
3	How to Raise a Child		4	2
4	Buying a New Car		…	…
5	Buying a New Home	cooking	1	5
6	The Beginner's Guide to Buying	decorating	2	1
	a House	your	2	2
7	Purchasing a Home		9	4
8	Becoming a New Home owner	home	2	3
9	How to Buy Your First House		5	4
			7	3
			8	4
		…	…	…
		new	4	3
			5	3
			8	3
		Car	4	4
		The	6	1
		Beginner's	6	2
		House	6	7
			9	6
		Purchasing	7	1
		…	…	…

From the inverted index in table 3.7, you can see that a query for new AND home would yield a result containing documents 5 and 8. The term position goes one step further, telling us where in the document each term appears. Table 3.8 shows a condensed version of the inverted index focused only upon the intersection of the primary terms under discussion: new and home.

Table 3.8   Condensed inverted index with term positions

Term	Document	Term position
home	5	4
	8	4
new	5	3
	8	3

In this example, the term new happens to be in position 3 and the term home happens to be in position 4 in both matched documents. This makes sense, as the book titles were *Buying a New Home* and *Becoming a New Home Owner.* By ensuring that the matched terms appear within one position of each other, Solr can ensure that the terms formed a phrase in the original document. You have now seen the power of term positions; they allow you to reconstruct the original positions of indexed terms within their respective documents, making it possible to search for specific phrases at query time.

Searching for specific phrases is not the only benefit provided by term positions. We'll see in the next section another great example of their use to improve our search results quality.

3.1.7   *Fuzzy matching*

It's not always possible to know up front exactly what will be found in the Solr index for any given search, so Solr provides the ability to perform several types of fuzzy-matching queries. *Fuzzy matching* is defined as the ability to perform inexact matches on terms in the search index. For example, someone may want to search for any words that start with a particular prefix (known as *wildcard searching*), may want to find spelling variations within one or two characters (known as *fuzzy searching* or *edit distance searching*), or may want to match two terms within some maximum distance of each other (known as *proximity searching*). For use cases in which multiple variations of the terms or phrases queried may exist across the documents being searched, these fuzzy-matching capabilities serve as a powerful tool.

In this section, we'll explore multiple fuzzy matching query capabilities in Solr, including wildcard searching, range searching, edit-distance searching, and proximity searching.

WILDCARD SEARCHING
One of the most common forms of fuzzy matching in Solr is the use of wildcards. Suppose you want to find any documents that start with the letters offic. One way to do this is to create a query that enumerates all of the possible variations:

- *Query:* office OR officer OR official OR officiate OR …
  Requiring that this list of words be turned into a query up front can be an unreasonable expectation for customers, or even for you on behalf of your customers.

Because all of the variations you could match already exist in the Solr index, you can use the asterisk (*) wildcard character to perform this same function for you:

- *Query:* `offi*` Matches office, officer, official, and so on

In addition to matching the end of a term, a wildcard character can be used inside of the search term as well, such as if you wanted to match both `officer` and `offer`:

- *Query:* `off*r` Matches offer, officer, officiator, and so on

The asterisk wildcard (*) matches zero or more characters in a term. If you want to match only a single character, you can make use of the question mark (?) for this purpose:

- *Query:* `off?r` Matches offer, but not officer

Leading wildcards

While the wildcard functionality in Solr is fairly robust, it can be expensive to execute certain wildcard queries. Whenever a wildcard search is executed, all of the terms in the inverted index that match the parts of the term prior to the first wildcard must be found. Then, each of those candidate terms must be inspected to see if they match the wildcard pattern in the query. Because of this, the more characters you specify at the beginning of the term before the wildcard, the faster the query should run. For example, the query `engineer*` will not be expensive (because it matches few terms in the inverted index), but the query `e*` will be expensive, as it matches all terms beginning with the letter e.

Executing a leading wildcard query is an expensive operation. If you needed to match all terms ending in *ing* (like caring, liking, and smiling), for example, this could cause major performance issues.

- *Query:* `*ing`

If you need to be able to search using these leading wildcards, a faster solution exists, but it requires additional configuration. The solution is achieved by adding `ReversedWildcardFilterFactory` to your field type's analysis chain (configuring text processing will be discussed in chapter 6).

`ReversedWildcardFilterFactory` works by double-inserting the indexed content in the Solr index (once for the text of each term, and once for the reversed text of each term):

- *Index:*   caring   liking   smiling
                    #gnirac   #gnikil   #gnilims

When a query is submitted with the leading wildcard of `*ing`, Solr knows to search on the reversed version, getting around the performance issues associated with leading wildcard searches by turning them into standard wildcard searches on the reversed content.

Note, however, that turning this feature on requires dual-indexing all terms in the Solr index, increasing the size of the index and slowing down overall searches. Turning this capability on is not recommended unless it's needed within your search application.

One last important point to note about wildcard searching is that wildcards are only meant to work on individual search terms, not on phrase searches, as demonstrated by the following example:

- *Works:*   `softwar* eng?neering`
- *Does not work:* `"softwar* eng?neering"`

If you need the ability to perform wildcard searches within a phrase, you will have to store the entire phrase in the index as a single term, which you should feel comfortable doing by the end of chapter 6.

RANGE SEARCHING

Solr also provides the ability to search for terms that fall between known values. This can be useful when you want to search for a particular subset of documents falling within a range. For example, if you only wanted to match documents created in the six months between February 2, 2012, and August 2, 2012, you could perform the following search:

- *Query:* `created:[2012-02-01T00:00.0Z TO 2012-08-02T00:00.0Z]`

This range `query` format also works on other field types:

- *Query:* `yearsOld:[18 TO 21]`   Matches 18, 19, 20, 21
- *Query:* `title:[boat TO boulder]`   Matches boat, boil, book, boulder, etc.
- *Query:* `price:[12.99 TO 14.99]`   Matches 12.99, 13.000009, 14.99, etc.

Each of these range queries surrounds the range with square brackets, which is the "inclusive" range syntax. Solr also supports exclusive range searching through the use of curly braces:

- *Query:* `yearsOld:{18 TO 21}`   Matches 19 and 20 but not 18 or 21

Though it may look odd syntactically, Solr also provides the ability to mix and match inclusive and exclusive bounds:

- Query: `yearsOld:[18 TO 21}`   Matches 18, 19, 20, but not 21

While range searches perform more slowly than searches on a single term, they provide tremendous flexibility for finding documents matching dynamically defined groups of values that lie within a particular range within the Solr index. It's important to note that the ordering of terms for range queries is exactly that: the order in which they are found in the Solr index, which is a lexicographically sorted order. If you were to create a text field containing integers, those integers would be found in the following order: 1, 11, 111, 12, 120, 13, etc. Numeric types in Solr, at least the ones we'll recommend in the coming chapters, compensate for this by indexing the incoming content in a special way, but it's important to understand that the sort order within the Solr index is dependent upon how the data within the field is processed when it's written to the Solr index. We'll dive much deeper into this kind of content analysis in chapters 5 and 6.

FUZZY/EDIT-DISTANCE SEARCHING

For many search applications, it's important not only to match a customer's text exactly, but also to allow flexibility for handling spelling errors or even slight variations in correct spellings. Solr provides the ability to handle character variations using edit-distance measurements based upon Damerau-Levenshtein distances, which account for more than 80% of all human misspellings.[1]

Solr achieves these fuzzy edit-distance searches through the use of the tilde (~) character as follows:

- *Query:* `administrator~` Matches: adminstrator, administrater, administratior, and so forth

This query matches both the original term (`administrator`) and any other terms within two edit distances of the original term. An *edit distance* is defined as an insertion, a deletion, a substitution, or a transposition of characters. The term `adminstrator` (missing the "i" in the sixth position) is one edit distance away from administrator because it has one character deletion. Likewise the term `sadministrator` would be one edit distance away because it has one insertion (the "s" that was prepended), and the term `administratro` would also be one edit distance away because it has transposed the last two characters ("or" became "ro").

It's also possible to modify the strictness of edit-distance searches to allow matching of terms with any edit distance:

- *Query:* `administrator~1`　Matches within one edit distance.
- *Query:* `administrator~2`　Matches within two edit distances. (This is the default if no edit distance is provided.)
- *Query:* `administrator~N`　Matches within N edit distances.

Please note that any edit distances requested above two will become increasingly slower and will be more likely to match unexpected terms. Term searches with edit distances of one or two are performed using an efficient Levenshtein automaton, but will fall back to a slower edit-distance implementation for edit distances above two.

PROXIMITY SEARCHING

In the previous section, we saw that edit distances could be used to find terms that were close to the original term, but not exactly the same. This edit-distance principle is applicable beyond searching for alternate characters within a term; it can also be applied between terms for variations of phrases.

Let's say that you want to search across a Solr index of employee profiles for executives within your company. One way to do this would be to enumerate each of the possible executive titles within your company:

- *Query:* `"chief executive officer" OR "chief financial officer" OR "chief marketing officer" OR "chief technology officer" OR …`

---

[1] Fred J. Damerau, "A Technique for Computer Detection and Correction of Spelling Errors," *Communications of the ACM*, 7(3):171-176 (1964).

Of course, this assumes you know all of the possible titles, which may be unrealistic if you're searching across other companies with which you're poorly acquainted or if you have a more challenging use case. Another possible strategy is to search for each term independently:

- *Query:* `chief AND officer`

This should match all of the possible use cases, but it will also match any document that contains both of those words anywhere in the document. One problematic example would be a document containing the text: `One chief concern arising from the incident was the safety of the police officer on duty`. This document is clearly a poor match for our use case, but it and similar bad matches would be returned given the preceding query.

Thankfully, Solr provides a basic solution to this problem: proximity searching. In the previous example, a good strategy would be to ask Solr to bring back all documents that contain the term `chief` near the term `officer`. This can be accomplished through the following example queries:

- *Query:*   `"chief officer"~1`
  - *Meaning:*   `chief` and `officer` must be a maximum of one position away.
  - *Examples:* `"chief executive officer"`, `"chief financial officer"`

- *Query:*   `"chief officer"~2`
  - *Meaning:*   `chief` and `officer` must be a maximum of two edit distances away.
  - *Examples:* `"chief business development officer"`,
                 `"officer chief"`

- *Query:*   `"chief officer"~N`
  - *Meaning:*   Finds `chief` within `N` positions of `officer`.

The preceding proximity searches can be seen as "sloppy" versions of traditional phrase searches. In fact, an exact phrase search of `"chief development officer"` could easily be rewritten as `"chief development officer"~0`. These queries will yield the same results, because an edit distance of zero is the definition of an exact phrase search. Both mechanisms make use of the term positions stored in the Solr index (which we discussed in section 3.1.6) to calculate the edit distances. It should also be noted that Solr's proximity searching is not a true use of edit distance because it requires all specified terms to exist, whereas a true edit distance would also allow for substitutions and deletions (as you saw with fuzzy searching on a single term).

The general principle of an edit distance still applies to term proximity queries with regard to term insertions and transpositions, however. Along this line, you may have also noticed that it required a phrase slop of 2 to be specified (`"chief officer"~2`) in order to match the text `officer chief`. This is because the first edit is to move the terms `chief` and `officer` into the same position; the second edit is to move `chief` one more position to come before `officer`. This again underscores the fact that proximity searching does not use a true edit distance (where a transposition may only count as one edit), but is instead asking: "How many positions can be collectively added to a document's text in order to form the exact phrase specified for the proximity search?"

3.1.8 Quick recap

At this point, you should have a basic grasp of how Solr stores information in its inverted index and queries that index to find matching documents. This includes looking up terms, using Boolean logic to create arbitrarily complex queries, and getting results back as a result of the set operations using each of the term lookups. We also discussed how Solr stores term positions and is able to use those to find exact phrases and even fuzzy phrase matches through the use of proximity queries and positional calculations. For fuzzy searching within single terms, we examined the use of wildcards and edit-distance searching to find misspellings or similar words. While Solr's query capabilities will be expanded upon in chapter 7, these key operations serve as the foundation for generating most Solr queries. They also prepare us nicely with the needed background for our discussion of Solr's keyword relevancy scoring model in the next section.

3.2 Relevancy

Finding matching documents is the first critical step in creating a great search experience, but it's only the first step. Most customers aren't willing to wade through page after page of search results to find the documents they're seeking. In our general experience, only 10% of customers are willing to go beyond the first page of any given search on most websites, and only 1% are willing to navigate to the third page.

Solr does a good job out of the box of ensuring that the ordering of search results brings back the best matches at the top of the results list. It does this by calculating a relevancy score for each document and then sorting the search results from the highest score to the lowest. This section will provide an overview of how these relevancy scores are calculated and what factors influence them. We'll dig into both the theory behind Solr's default relevancy calculation and the specific calculations used to compute the relevancy scores, providing intuitive examples along the way to ensure you leave this section with a solid understanding of what, to many, can be the most elusive aspect of working with Solr. We'll start by discussing the Similarity class, which is responsible for most aspects of a query's relevancy score calculation.

3.2.1 Default similarity

Solr's relevancy scores are based upon the Similarity class, which can be defined on a per-field basis in Solr's *schema.xml* (discussed further in chapter 5). Similarity is a Java class that defines how a relevancy score is calculated based upon the results of a query. While you can choose from multiple Similarity classes, or even write your own, it is important to understand Solr's default Similarity implementation and the theory behind why it works so well.

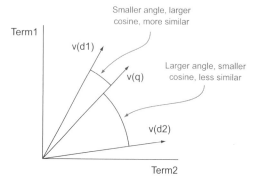

Figure 3.6   **Cosine similarity of term vectors. The query term vector, v(q), is closer to the document 1 term vector v(d1) than the document 2 term vector v(d2), as measured by the cosine of the angle between each document's term vector and the query vector. The smaller the angle between the query term vector and a document's term vector, the more similar the query and the document are considered to be.**

By default, Solr uses Lucene's (appropriately named) DefaultSimilarity class, which uses a two-pass model to calculate similarity. First, it makes use of a Boolean model (described in section 3.1) to filter out any documents that do not match the customer's query. Then it uses a vector space model for scoring and drawing the query as a vector, as well as an additional vector for each document. The similarity score for each document is based upon the cosine between the query vector and that document's vector, as depicted in figure 3.6.

In this vector space scoring model, a term vector is calculated for each document and is compared with the corresponding term vector for the query. The similarity of two vectors can be found by calculating a cosine between them, with a cosine of 1 being a perfect match and a cosine of 0 representing no similarity. More intuitively, the closer the two vectors appear together, as in figure 3.6, the more similar they are. The smaller the angle between vectors or the larger the cosine, the closer the match.

Of course, the most challenging part of this whole process is coming up with reasonable vectors that represent the important features of the query and of each document for comparison. Let's look at the entire, complicated relevancy formula for the DefaultSimilarity class. We'll then go line by line to explain intuitively what each component of the relevancy formula is attempting to accomplish.

Given a query (q) and a document (d), the similarity score for the document to the query can be calculated as shown in figure 3.7.

Wow! That equation can be quite overwhelming, particularly at first glance. Fortunately, it's much more intuitive when each of the pieces is broken down. The math is presented for reference, but you will likely never need to dig into the full equation unless you decide to overwrite the Similarity class for your search application.

The important concepts in the relevancy calculation are demonstrated as pieces of the high-level formula represented in figure 3.7: term frequency (tf), inverse document frequency (idf), term boosts (t.getBoost), field normalization (norm), coordination factor (coord), and query normalization (queryNorm). Let's dive into the purpose of each of these.

Score(q,d) =

$$\sum_{t \text{ in } q} \Big(\textbf{tf}(t \text{ in } d) \cdot \textbf{idf}(t)^2 \cdot \textbf{t.getBoost}() \cdot \textbf{norm}(t,d) \Big) \cdot \textbf{coord}(q,d) \cdot \textbf{queryNorm}(q)$$

Where:

t = term; **d** = document; **q** = query; **f** = field

tf(t in d) = numTermOccurrencesInDocument$^{1/2}$

idf(t) = 1 + log (numDocs / (docFreq +1))

coord(q,d) = numTermsInDocumentFromQuery / numTermsInQuery

queryNorm(q) = 1 / (sumOfSquaredWeights$^{1/2}$)

sumOfSquaredWeights = q.getBoost()^2 $\cdot \sum_{t \text{ in } q}$ (idf(t) $\cdot$ t.getBoost())^2

norm(t,d) = d.getBoost() $\cdot$ lengthNorm(f) $\cdot$ f.getBoost()

Figure 3.7 `DefaultSimilarity` **scoring algorithm. Each component in this formula will be explained in detail in the following sections.**

3.2.2 Term frequency

Term frequency (tf) is a measure of how often a particular term appears in a matching document, and it's an indication of how "well" a document matches the term.

If you were searching through a search index filled with newspaper articles for an article on the President of the United States, would you prefer to find articles that only mention the president once, or articles that discuss the president consistently throughout the article? What if an article happens to contain the phrases `President` and `United States` each one time (perhaps out of context); should it be considered as relevant as an article that contains these phrases multiple times?

In table 3.9, clearly the second article discussed is more relevant than the first, and the identification of the phrases `President` and `United States` multiple times throughout the article provides a strong indication that the content of the second article is more closely related to this query.

Table 3.9 Documents mentioning `President` and `United States`

Article 1 (less relevant)	Article 2 (more relevant)
Dr. Kohrt is the interim `president` of Furman University, one of the top liberal arts universities in the southern `United States`. In 2011, Furman was ranked the 2nd most rigorous college in the country by Newsweek magazine, behind St. John's College (NM). Furman also consistently ranks among the most beautiful campuses to visit and ranks among the top 50 liberal arts colleges nation-wide each year.	Today, international leaders met with the `President` of the `United States` to discuss options for dealing with growing instability in global financial markets. `President` Obama indicated that the `United States` is cautiously optimistic about the potential for significant improvements in several struggling world economies pending the results of upcoming elections. The `President` indicated that the `United States` will take whatever actions necessary to promote continued stability in the global financial markets.

In general, a document is considered to be more relevant for a particular topic (or query term) if the topic appears multiple times.

This is the basic premise behind the `tf` component of the default Solr relevancy formula. The more times the search term appears within a document, the more relevant that document is considered. It's not likely to be the case that 10 appearances of a term make the document 10 times more relevant, however, so tf is calculated using the square root of the number of times the search term appears within the document, in order to diminish the additional contribution to the relevancy score for each subsequent appearance of the search term.

3.2.3   *Inverse document frequency*

Not all search terms are created equal. Imagine if someone were to search a library catalog for *The Cat in the Hat* by Dr. Seuss, and the top results returned were those that included a high term frequency for the words `the` and `in` instead of `cat` and `hat`. Common sense would indicate that words that are more rare across all documents are likely to be better matches for a query than terms that are more common.

Inverse document frequency (idf), a measure of how "rare" a search term is, is calculated by finding the document frequency (how many total documents the search term appears within), and calculating its inverse (see the full formula in figure 3.7 for the calculation).

Because idf appears for the term in both the query and the document, it's squared in the relevancy formula.

Figure 3.8 shows a visual example of the "rareness" of each of the words in the title *The Cat in the Hat* (relative to a generic collection of library books), with a higher idf being represented as a larger term.

Figure 3.8   **Visual depiction of the relative significance of terms as measured by idf. The terms that are rarer are depicted as larger, indicating a larger inverse document frequency.**

Likewise, if someone were searching for a profile for `an experienced Solr development team lead` across a large collection of resumes, we wouldn't expect documents to rank higher that best match the words `an`, `team`, or `experienced`. Instead, we would expect the important terms to resemble the largest terms in figure 3.9.

Clearly the user is looking for someone who knows Solr and can be a team lead, so these terms stand out with considerably more weight when found in any document.

Figure 3.9   **Another demonstration of relative score of terms derived from idf. Once again, a higher idf indicates a rarer and more relevant term, depicted here using larger text.**

Term frequency and inverse document frequency, when multiplied together in the relevancy calculation, provide a nice counterbalance. The term frequency elevates terms that appear multiple times within a document, whereas the inverse document frequency penalizes those terms that appear commonly across many documents. Therefore, common words in the English language such as the, an, and of ultimately yield low scores, even though they may appear many times in any given document.

3.2.4 *Boosting*

It is not necessary to leave all aspects of your relevancy calculations up to Solr. If you have domain knowledge about your content—you know that certain fields or terms are more (or less) important than others—you can supply boosts at either indexing time or query time to ensure that the weights of those fields or terms are adjusted accordingly.

Query-time boosting, the most flexible and easiest to understand form of boosting, uses the following syntax:

- *Query:* `title:(solr in action)^2.5 description:(solr in action)`

This example provides a boost of 2.5 to the search phrase in the title field, while providing the default boost of 1.0 to the description field. Unless otherwise specified, all terms receive a default boost of 1.0 (which means multiplying the calculated score by 1, or leaving it as originally calculated).

Query boosts can also be used to penalize certain terms if a boost of less than 1.0 is used:

- *Query:* `title:(solr in action) description:(solr in action)^0.2`

Note that a boost of less than 1 is still a positive boost. It doesn't penalize the document in absolute terms; it boosts the term less than the normal boost of 1 that it otherwise would have received.

These query-time boosts can be applied to any part of the query:

- *Query:* `title:(solr^2 in^.01 action^1.5)^3 OR "solr in action"^2.5`

Certain query parsers even allow boosts to be applied to an entire field by default, which we'll cover further in chapter 7.

In addition to query-time boosting, it's possible to boost documents or fields within documents at index time. These boosts are factored into the field norm, which is covered in the following section.

3.2.5 *Normalization factors*

The default Solr relevancy formula calculates three kinds of normalization factors (norms): field norms, query norms, and the coord factor.

FIELD NORMS

The *field normalization factor* (field norm) is a combination of factors describing the importance of a particular field on a per-document basis. Field norms are calculated at index time and are represented as an additional byte per field in the Solr index.

norm(t,d) = d.getBoost() · lengthNorm(f) · f.getBoost()

Figure 3.10   Field norms calculation. Field norms combine the matching document's boost, the matching field's boost, and a length-normalization factor that penalizes longer documents. These three fairly separate pieces of data are stored as a single byte in the Solr index, which is the only reason they are combined into this single `field norms` variable.

This byte packs a lot of information: the boost set on the document when indexed, the boost set on the field when indexed, and a length normalization factor that penalizes longer documents and helps shorter documents (under the assumption that finding any given keyword in a longer document is more likely and therefore less relevant). The field norms are calculated using the formula in figure 3.10.

The `d.getBoost()` component represents the boost applied to the document when it's sent to Solr, and the `f.getBoost()` component represents the boost applied to the field for which the norm is being calculated. It's worth mentioning that Solr allows the same field to be added to a document multiple times (performing some magic under the covers to map each separate entry for the field into the same underlying Lucene field). Because duplicate fields are ultimately mapped to the same underlying field, if multiple copies of the field exist, `f.getBoost()` becomes the product of the field boost for each of the multiple fields with the same name.

If the `title` field were added to a document three times, for example, once with a boost of 3, once with a boost of 1, and once with a boost of 0.5, `f.getBoost()` for each of the three fields (or the one underlying field) would be

- *Boost: (3) · (1) · (0.5) = 1.5*

In addition to the index-time boosts, a parameter called the length norm is factored into the field norm. The length norm is computed by taking the square root of the number of terms in the field for which it is calculated.

It is also worth mentioning that document boosts are internally implemented as a boost on every field of the document. In other words, there is no difference between applying a boost to a document versus applying the same boost individually to every field, as all document boosts are ultimately stored per field for each document inside the field norm.

The purpose of the length norm is to adjust for documents of varying lengths, such that longer documents don't maintain an unfair advantage by having a larger likelihood of containing any particular term a given number of times.

Let's say that you perform a search for the keyword `Beijing`. Would you prefer for a news article to come up that mentions `Beijing` five times, or would you rather have an obscure, 300-page book come back that also happens to mention `Beijing` only five times. Common sense would indicate that a document in which `Beijing` is proportionally more prevalent is probably a better match, everything else being equal. This is what the length norm attempts to take into account.

The overall field norm, calculated from the product of the document boost, the field boost, and the length norm, is encoded into a single byte that's stored in the Solr index. Because the amount of information being encoded from this product is larger than a single byte can store, some precision loss does occur during this encoding. In reality, this loss of fidelity generally has negligible effects on overall relevancy, as it's usually only big differences that matter given the variance in all other relevancy criteria.

QUERY NORMS

The *query norm* is one of the least interesting factors in the default Solr relevancy calculation. It does not affect the overall relevancy ordering, as the same `queryNorm` is applied to all documents. It merely serves as a normalization factor to attempt to make scores between queries comparable. It uses the sum of the squared weights for each of the query terms to generate this factor, which is multiplied with the rest of the relevancy score to normalize it. The query norm should not affect the relative weighting of each document that matches a given query.

THE COORD FACTOR

One final normalization factor taken into account in the default Solr relevancy calculation is the *coord factor*. Its role is to measure how much of the query each document matches. Let's say you perform the following search:

- *Query:* Accountant AND ("San Francisco" OR "New York" OR "Paris")

You may prefer to find an accountant with offices in each of the cities you mentioned as opposed to an accountant who has happened to mention "New York" over and over again.

If all four of these terms match, the coord factor is 4/4. If three match, the coord factor is 3/4, and if only one matches, it's 1/4.

The idea behind the coord factor is that, all things being equal, documents that contain more of the terms in the query should score higher than documents that only match a few.

We have now discussed all of the major components of the default relevancy algorithm in Solr. We discussed tf and idf, the two most key components of the relevancy score calculation. We then went through boosting and normalization factors, which refine the scores calculated by tf and idf alone. With a solid conceptual understanding and a detailed overview of the specific components of the relevancy scoring formula, we're now set to discuss Precision and Recall, two important aspects for measuring the overall quality of the result sets returned from any search system.

3.3 *Precision and Recall*

The information retrieval concepts of *Precision* (a measure of accuracy) and *Recall* (a measure of thoroughness) are simple to explain, but are also important to understand when building any search application or understanding why the results being returned are not meeting your business requirements. We'll provide a brief summary here of each of these key concepts.

3.3.1   *Precision*

The Precision of a search results set (the documents that match a query) is a measurement attempting to answer the question, "Were the documents that came back the ones I was looking for?"

More technically, Precision is defined as (between 0.0 and 1.0)

```
# Correct Matches / # Total Results Returned
```

Let's return to our example from section 3.1 about searching for a book on the topic of buying a new home. We've determined by our internal company measurements that the books in table 3.10 would be considered good matches for such a query.

Table 3.10   List of relevant books

Relevant books
1   The Beginner's Guide to Buying a House
2   How to Buy Your First House
3   Purchasing a Home

All other book titles, for the purposes of this example, would not be considered relevant for someone interested in purchasing a new home. A few examples are listed in table 3.11.

Table 3.11   List of irrelevant books

Irrelevant books
4   A Fun Guide to Cooking
5   How to Raise a Child
6   Buying a New Car

For this example, if all of the documents that were supposed to be returned (documents 1, 2, and 3) were returned, and no more, the Precision of this query would be 1.0 (3 Correct Matches / 3 Total Matches), which would be perfect.

If, however, all six results came back, the Precision would only be 0.5, because half of the results that were returned were not correct; that is, they were not precise.

Likewise, if only one result came back from the relevant list (number 2, for example), the Precision would still be 1.0, because all of the results that came back were correct. As you can see, Precision is a measure of how "good" each of the results of a query is, but it pays no attention to how thorough it is; a query that returns one single correct document out of a million other correct documents is still considered perfectly precise.

Because Precision only considers the overall accuracy of the results that come back and not the comprehensiveness of the result set, we need to counterbalance the Precision measurement with one that takes thoroughness into account: Recall.

3.3.2 *Recall*

Whereas Precision measures how correct each of the results being returned is, Recall is a measure of how thorough the search results are. Recall is answering the question: "How many of the correct documents were returned?"

More technically, Recall is defined as

```
# Correct Matches / (# Correct Matches + # Missed Matches)
```

To demonstrate an example of the Recall calculation, the example showing relevant books and irrelevant books from the last section has been recreated in table 3.12 for reference.

Table 3.12 List of relevant and irrelevant books

	Relevant books		Irrelevant books
1	The Beginner's Guide to Buying a House	4	A Fun Guide to Cooking
2	How to Buy Your First House	5	How to Raise a Child
3	Purchasing a Home	6	Buying a New Car

If all six documents were returned for a search query, the Recall would be 1 because all correct matches were found and there were no missed matches (whereas we saw earlier that the Precision would be 0.5).

Likewise, if only document 1 were returned, the Recall would only be 1/3, because two of the documents that should have been returned/recalled were missing.

This highlights the critical difference between Precision and Recall: Precision is high when the results returned are correct; Recall is high when the correct results are present. Recall does not care that *all* of the results are correct. Precision does not care that *all* of the results are present.

In the next section, we'll talk about strategies for striking an appropriate balance between Precision and Recall.

3.3.3 *Striking the right balance*

Though there is clearly tension between the two, Precision and Recall are not mutually exclusive. In the previous example in which the query only returns documents 1, 2, and 3, the Precision and Recall are both 1.0, because all of the results were correct and all of the correct results were found.

Maximizing for full Precision and full Recall is the ultimate goal of most every search-relevancy-tuning endeavor. With a contrived example (or a hand-tuned set of results), this seems easy, but in reality, this is a challenging problem.

Many techniques can be undertaken within Solr to improve either Precision or Recall, though most are geared more toward increasing Recall in terms of the full document set being returned. Aggressive textual analysis (to find multiple variations of words) is a great example of trying to find more matches, though these additional matches may hurt overall Precision if the textual analysis is so aggressive that it matches incorrect word variations.

One common way to approach the Precision versus Recall problem in Solr is to attempt to solve for both: measuring for Recall across the entire result set and measuring for Precision only within the first page (or few pages) of search results. Following this model, better matches will be boosted to the top of the search results based upon how well you tune your use of Solr's relevancy scoring calculations, but you will also find that many poorer matches appear at the bottom of your search results list if you go to the last page of the search results.

This is only one way to approach the problem, however. Because many search websites, for example, want to appear to have as much content as possible, and because those sites know that visitors will never go beyond the first few pages, they can show precise results on the first few pages while still including many less precise matches on subsequent pages. This results in a high Recall score across the entire result set by being lenient about which keywords are able to match the initial query. Simultaneously, the Precision of the first page or two of results is still high due to the elevation of the best matches to the top of the long list of search results.

The decision on how to best balance Precision and Recall is ultimately dependent upon your use case. In scenarios like legal discovery, there's a heavy emphasis placed on Recall, as there are legal ramifications if any documents are missed. For other use cases, the requirement may only be to find a few great matches and find nothing that does not exactly match every term within the query.

Most search applications fall somewhere between these two extremes, and striking the right balance between Precision and Recall is a never-ending challenge: mostly because there is often no one right answer. Regardless, understanding the concepts of Precision and Recall and why changes you make swing you more toward one of these two conceptual goals (and likely away from the other) is critical to effectively improving the quality of your search results. Chapter 16 is dedicated to mastering relevancy, so you can be sure you will see this tension between Precision and Recall surface again.

3.4   *Searching at scale*

One of the most appealing aspects of Solr, beyond its speed, relevancy, and powerful text-searching features, is how well it scales. Solr is able to scale to handle billions of documents and an infinite number of queries by adding servers. Chapters 12 and 13 will provide an in-depth overview of scaling Solr in production, but this section will lay the groundwork for how to think about the necessary characteristics for operating a scalable search engine. Specifically, we'll discuss the nature of Solr documents as denormalized documents and why this enables linear scaling across servers, how distributed searching works, the conceptual shift from thinking about servers to thinking about clusters of servers, and some of the limits of scaling Solr.

3.4.1 The denormalized document

Central to Solr is the concept of all documents being denormalized. A *denormalized document* is one in which all fields are self-contained within the document, even if the values in those fields are duplicated across many documents. This concept of denormalized data is common to many NoSQL technologies. A good example of denormalization is a user-profile document having `city`, `state`, and `postalCode` fields, even though in most cases the `city` and `state` fields will be the same across all documents for each unique `postalCode` value. This is in contrast to a *normalized document* in which relationships between parts of the document may be broken up into multiple smaller documents, the pieces of which can be joined back together at query time. A normalized document would only have a `postalCode` field, and a separate location document would exist for each unique `postalCode` so that the `city` and `state` would not need to be duplicated on each user-profile document. If you have any training whatsoever in building normalized tables for relational databases, please leave that training at the door when thinking about modeling content into Solr. Figure 3.11 demonstrates a traditional normalized database table model, with a big "X" over it to make it obvious that this is not the kind of data-modeling strategy you will use with Solr.

Notice that the information in figure 3.11 represents two users working at a company called "Code Monkeys R Us, LLC." While this figure shows the data nicely normalized into separate tables for the employees' personal information, location, and company, this is not how we would represent these users in a Solr document. Listing 3.2 shows the denormalized representation for each of these employees as mapped to a Solr document.

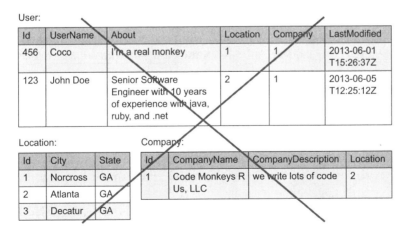

User:

Id	UserName	About	Location	Company	LastModified
456	Coco	I'm a real monkey	1	1	2013-06-01 T15:26:37Z
123	John Doe	Senior Software Engineer with 10 years of experience with java, ruby, and .net	2	1	2013-06-05 T12:25:12Z

Location:

Id	City	State
1	Norcross	GA
2	Atlanta	GA
3	Decatur	GA

Company:

Id	CompanyName	CompanyDescription	Location
1	Code Monkeys R Us, LLC	we write lots of code	2

Figure 3.11 Solr documents don't follow the traditional normalized model of a relational database. This figure demonstrates how *not* to think of Solr documents. Instead of thinking in terms of multiple entities with relationship to each other, a Solr document is modeled as a flat, denormalized data structure, as shown in listing 3.2.

Listing 3.2   Two denormalized user documents

```
<doc>
  <field name="id">123</field>
  <field name="username">John Doe</field>
  <field name="about">Senior Software Engineer with 10 years of
                      experience with java, ruby, and .net
  </field>
  <field name="usercity">Atlanta</field>
  <field name="userstate">Georgia</field>
  <field name="companyname">Code Monkeys R Us, LLC</field>
  <field name="companydescription">we write lots of code</field>
  <field name="companycity">Decatur</field>
  <field name="companystate">Georgia</field>
  <field name="lastmodified">2013-06-05T12:25:12Z</field>
</doc>

<doc>
  <field name="id">456</field>
  <field name="username">Coco</field>
  <field name="about">I'm a real monkey</field>
  <field name="usercity">Norcross</field>
  <field name="userstate">Georgia</field>
  <field name="companyname">Code Monkeys R Us, LLC</field>
  <field name="companydescription">we write lots of code</field>
  <field name="companycity">Decatur</field>
  <field name="companystate">Georgia</field>
  <field name="lastmodified">2013-06-01T15:26:37Z</field>
</doc>
```

❶ Company information for first user.

❷ The same company information repeated for the second user.

Notice that all of the company information is repeated in both the first ❶ and second ❷ user documents, which seems to go against the principles of normalized database design for reducing data redundancy and minimizing data dependency. In a traditional relational database, a query can be constructed that will join data from multiple tables when resolving a query. Although some basic join functionality does now exist in Solr (which will be discussed in chapter 15), it's only recommended for cases in which it's impractical to denormalize content. Solr knows about terms that map to documents but does not natively know about any relationships between documents. That is, if you wanted to search for all users (in the previous example) who work for companies in Decatur, GA, you would need to ensure that the companycity and companystate fields are populated for all of the users for that lookup to be successful.

While this denormalized document data model may sound limiting, it also provides a sizable advantage: extreme scalability. Because we can make the assumption that each document is self-contained, this means that we can also partition documents across multiple servers without having to keep related documents on the same server (because documents are independent of one another). This fundamental assumption of document independence allows queries to be parallelized across multiple partitions of documents and multiple servers to improve query performance, and this ultimately allows Solr to scale horizontally to handle querying billions of documents. This ability to scale across multiple partitions and servers is called *distributed searching*, and it will be covered next.

3.4.2 *Distributed searching*

The world would be a much simpler place if every important data operation could be run using a single server. In reality, however, sometimes your search servers may become overloaded by either too many queries at a time or by too much data needing to be searched through for a single server to handle.

In the latter case, it's necessary to break your content into two or more separate Solr indexes, each of which contains separate partitions of your data. Then every time a search is run, it'll be sent to both servers, and the separate results will be processed and aggregated before being returned from the search engine.

Solr includes this kind of distributed searching capability out of the box. We'll discuss how to manually segment your data into multiple partitions in chapter 12 when we talk about scaling Solr for production. Conceptually, each Solr index (called a Solr core) is available through it's own unique URL, and each of those Solr cores can be told to perform an aggregated search across other Solr cores using the following syntax:

```
http://box1:8983/solr/core1/select?q=*:*&shards=box1:8983/solr/core1,
    box2:8983/solr/core2,box2:8983/solr/core3
```

Notice four features about the preceding example:

- The `shards` parameter is used to specify the location of one or more Solr cores. A shard is a partition of your index, so the `shards` parameter on the URL tells Solr to aggregate results from multiple partitions of your data that are found in separate Solr cores.
- The Solr core being searched on (`box1`, `core1`) is also included in the list of shards; it won't automatically search itself unless explicitly requested as shown previously.
- This distributed search is searching across multiple servers.
- There's no requirement that separate Solr cores be located on separate machines. They can be on the same machine, as is the case here with `core2` and `core3` both being located on `box2`.

The important takeaway here has to do with the nature of scaling Solr. It should scale theoretically linearly because a distributed search across multiple Solr cores is run in parallel on each of those index partitions. Thus, if you split one Solr index into two Solr indexes with the same combined number of documents, the distributed search across the two indexes should be approximately 50% faster, minus any aggregation overhead.

This should also theoretically scale to any other number of servers (in reality, you will eventually hit a limit). The conceptual formula for determining total query speed after adding an additional index partition (assuming the same total number of documents) is

(Query Speed on N+1 indexes) = Aggregation Overhead + (Query Speed on N indexes)/(N+1)

This formula is useful for estimating the benefit you can expect from increasing the number of partitions into which your data is evenly divided. Because Solr scales nearly linearly, you should be able to reduce your query times proportional to the additional number of Solr cores (partitions) you add, assuming you're not constrained by server resources due to heavy load.

3.4.3   *Clusters vs. servers*

In the previous section we introduced the concept of distributed searching to enable scaling to handle large document sets. It's also possible to add multiple more or less identical servers into your system to balance the load of high query volumes.

Both of these scaling strategies rely on a conceptual shift away from thinking about servers and toward thinking about clusters of servers. A *cluster* of servers is defined as multiple servers, working in concert, to perform a unified function.

Take the following example, which should look similar to the example from section 3.4.2:

```
http://box1:8983/solr/core1/select?q=*:*&shards=box1:8983/solr/core1,
    box2:8983/solr/core2
```

This example performs a distributed search across two Solr cores, `core1` on `box1` and `core2` on `box2`. When running this distributed search, what happens to queries hitting `box1` if `box2` goes down? Listing 3.3 shows Solr's response under this scenario, which includes the error message from the failed connection to `box2`.

Listing 3.3   A failed distributed search (`RemoteServer` down)

```
<response>
    <lst name="responseHeader">
        <int name="status">500</int>
        <int name="QTime">1076</int>
        <lst name="params">
            <str name="shards">
                box1:8983/solr/core1,
                box2:8983/solr/core2
            </str>
        </lst>
    </lst>
    <lst name="error">
        <str name="msg">
            org.apache.solr.client.solrj.SolrServerException: IOException
            occurred when talking to server at: http://box2:8983/solr/core2
        </str>
        <str name="trace">...</str>
        <int name="code">500</int>
    </lst>
</response>
```

Notice that the servers for this use case are mutually dependent. If one becomes unavailable for searching, they all become unavailable for searching and begin failing, as indicated in the exception in the listing. It's therefore important to think in terms of clusters of servers instead of single servers when building out Solr solutions that must scale beyond a single box, as those servers are combining to serve as a single computing resource. Solr provides excellent built-in cluster-management capabilities through the use of Apache ZooKeeper, which will be covered in our discussion of Solr-Cloud in chapter 13.

As we wrap up our discussions of the key concepts behind searching at scale, we should be clear that Solr does have its limitations in this area, several of which will be discussed in the next section.

3.4.4 *The limits of Solr*

Solr is an incredibly powerful document-based NoSQL datastore that supports full text searching and data analytics. We have already discussed the powerful benefits of Solr's inverted index and complex, keyword-based, Boolean query capabilities. We have also seen how important relevancy is, and we've seen that Solr can scale more-or-less linearly across multiple servers to handle additional content or query volumes. What then are the use cases in which Solr is not a good solution? What are the limits of Solr?

One limit, as we've already seen, is that Solr is *not* relational in any way across documents. It's not well suited for joining significant amounts of data across different fields on different documents, and it can't perform join operations at all across multiple servers. While this is a functional limit of Solr, as compared to relational databases, this assumption of independence of documents is a tradeoff common among many NoSQL technologies, as it enables them to scale well beyond the limits of relational databases.

We've also already discussed the denormalized nature of Solr documents: data that is redundant must be repeated across each document to which that data applies. This can be particularly problematic when the data in one field that is shared across many documents changes.

Let's say that you were creating a search engine of social networking user profiles and one of your users, John Doe, becomes friends with another user named Coco. Now, I not only need to update John's and Coco's profiles, but I also need to update the "second-level connections" field for all of John's and Coco's friends, which could represent hundreds of document updates for one basic operation: two users becoming friends. This harkens back to the notion of Solr not being relational in any way.

An additional limitation of Solr is that it currently serves primarily as a document-storage mechanism; that is, you can insert, delete, and update documents, but not single fields (easily). Solr does currently have some minimal capability to update a single field, but only if the field is attributed in such a way that its original value is stored in the index, which can be wasteful. Even then, Solr is still updating the entire document based upon reindexing all of the stored fields internally. What this means is that whenever a new field is added to Solr or the contents of an existing field have changed, every single document in the Solr index must be reprocessed in its entirety before the data will be populated for the new field in all documents. Many other NoSQL systems suffer from this same problem, but it's worth noting that adding or changing a field in all documents across the corpus currently requires a nontrivial amount of document-update coordination to ensure the updates make it to Solr and do so in a timely fashion.

Solr is also optimized for a specific use case, which is taking search queries with small numbers of search terms and rapidly looking up each of those terms to find matching documents, calculating relevancy scores and ordering them all, and then only returning a few results for display. Solr is not optimized for processing quite long queries (thousands of terms) or returning quite large result sets to users.

One final limitation of Solr worth mentioning is its elastic scalability: the ability to automatically add and remove servers and redistribute content to handle load. While Solr scales well across servers, it doesn't yet elastically scale by itself in a fully automatic way. Recent work with SolrCloud (covered in chapter 13) using Apache Zoo-Keeper for cluster management is a great first step in this direction, but there are still many features to be worked out. For example, Solr cannot yet automatically reshard its content and increase the number of index replicas to dynamically handle content growth and query load. Many smart people in the community are working toward these long-term goals, however, and Solr continues to move closer and closer with every release.

3.5   *Summary*

In this chapter, we've discussed the key search concepts that serve as the foundation for most of Solr's search capabilities. We discussed the structure of Solr's inverted index and how it maps terms to documents in a way that allows quick execution of complex Boolean queries. We also discussed how fuzzy queries and phrase queries use position information to match misspellings and variations of terms and phrases in the Solr index.

We took a deep dive into Solr relevancy, laying out the default relevancy formula Solr uses and explaining conceptually how each piece of relevancy scoring works and why it exists.

We then provided a brief overview of the concepts of Precision and Recall, which serve as two opposing forces within the field of information retrieval and provide us with a good conceptual framework from which to judge whether or not our search results are meeting our goals.

Finally, we discussed key concepts for how Solr scales, including discussions of content denormalization within documents and distributed searching to ensure that query execution can be parallelized to maintain or decrease search time, even as content grows beyond what can be reasonably handled by a single machine. We ended with a discussion of thinking in terms of clusters as opposed to servers as you scale your search architecture, and we looked at some of the limitations of Solr and use cases for when Solr may not be a great fit.

At this point, you should have all of the conceptual background necessary to understand the core features of Solr throughout the rest of this book and should have a solid grasp of the most important concepts needed for building a killer search application. In the next chapter, we'll begin digging into Solr's key configuration settings, which will enable more fine-grained control over many of the features discussed in this chapter.

Configuring Solr 4

This chapter covers

- Handling a query request
- Extending query processing with search components
- Managing and warming searchers
- Managing cache behavior

Up to this point, you've taken much of what has been presented on faith, without learning how Solr works. We'll change that in this chapter and the next by learning how Solr is configured and how configuration settings impact Solr's behavior. As you'll see, Solr's configuration can be daunting at first look because the configuration file for the example server contains almost every possible configuration setting in Solr. Our main focus in this chapter is to introduce the most important configuration settings for Solr, particularly those that impact how Solr processes requests from client applications. The knowledge you gain in this chapter will be applied throughout the rest of the book. After reading this chapter, you'll have a firm understanding of how queries are executed in the Solr server.

As we learned in chapter 2, Solr works out of the box without requiring any configuration changes. But at some point, you're going to need to optimize Solr for your specific search-application requirements. Broadly speaking, most of the configuration you'll do with Solr focuses around three main XML files:

- *solr.xml*—Defines properties related to administration, logging, sharding, and SolrCloud
- *solrconfig.xml*—Defines the main settings for a specific Solr core
- *schema.xml*—Defines the structure of your index, including fields and field types

In this chapter, we'll focus on *solrconfig.xml*. In chapter 5, we'll learn all about *schema.xml*, which drives how your index is structured. As for *solr.xml*, you won't need to make any changes to that file manually, so we'll skip discussing its purpose until chapter 12, when we introduce the Core Admin API.

As most of Solr's configuration is specified in XML documents, this chapter contains numerous code listings showing XML snippets from *solrconfig.xml*. But our main focus is on the concepts behind the configuration settings, rather than the specific XML syntax, which is mostly self-explanatory.

To begin, let's see what happens from a configuration perspective when you start the Solr server. Recall from chapter 2 that Solr runs as a Java web application in Jetty. The Solr web application uses a global Java system property (solr.solr.home) to identify the root directory from which to look for configuration files. For the example server, the Solr home directory (solr.solr.home) is *$SOLR_INSTALL/example/solr/*.

Next, Solr scans the home directory for subdirectories containing a *core.properties* file, which defines basic properties for autodiscovered cores. For instance, the example server has a *core.properties* file in the *example/solr/collection1/* directory. The *core.properties* file contains a single line defining the name of the core, name=collection1, which is all that is needed to trigger autodiscovery for the collection1 core. Figure 4.1 depicts how *core.properties* and *solrconfig.xml* are used during the Solr initialization process to create and set up the collection1 core.

In earlier versions of Solr, you had to define cores in *solr.xml*, which had the drawback of needing to set up a core directory, then add the core definition to *solr.xml*. With *core.properties*, you no longer need the extra step of adding a core to *solr.xml*. Moreover, the new approach allows cores to be self-contained by removing the need to define all cores in a central configuration file.

The *core.properties* file for the example collection1 core only includes the required name parameter. But you can also set a number of optional parameters to fine-tune the definition of an autodiscovered core. Table 4.1 shows the parameters you can specify in *core.properties* to define an autodiscovered core.

Table 4.1 Configuration properties for autodiscovered cores using *core.properties*

Parameter	Description
name	Names the core; required.
config	Specifies the name of the configuration file; defaults to solrconfig.xml.

Table 4.1   Configuration properties for autodiscovered cores using *core.properties (continued)*

Parameter	Description
dataDir	Specifies the path to a directory containing the index files and update log (tlog); defaults to data under the instance directory.
ulogDir	Specifies the path to a directory containing the update log (tlog).
schema	Sets the name of the schema document; defaults to *schema.xml*.
shard	Sets the shard ID for this core; see chapters 12 and 13 for more information about sharding.
collection	Name of the SolrCloud collection this core belongs to; collections are covered in chapter 13.
loadOnStartup	If true, this core is loaded during the Solr initialization process and a new searcher is opened for the core.
transient	Indicates that this core can be unloaded automatically if Solr's transient-CacheSize threshold is reached (advanced option).

For now, you do not need to worry about any of the properties listed in table 4.1, as our primary focus in this chapter is the *solrconfig.xml* file for the collection1 example core.

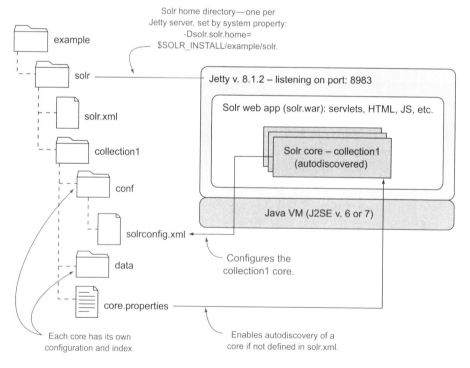

Figure 4.1   Solr discovers the collection1 core using *core.properties* and configures it using *solrconfig.xml* during server initialization.

What's important is to understand that Solr can autodiscover cores during startup using *core.properties*. Once a core is discovered, Solr locates the *solrconfig.xml* file under *$SOLR_HOME/$instanceDir/conf/solrconfig.xml*, where *$instanceDir/* is the directory containing the *core.properties* file. Solr uses the *solrconfig.xml* file to initialize the core.

Now that we've seen how Solr identifies configuration files during startup, let's turn our attention to understanding the main sections of *solrconfig.xml*, as that will give you an idea of what's to come in the rest of this chapter.

4.1 Overview of solrconfig.xml

To illustrate the concepts in *solrconfig.xml*, we'll build upon the work done in chapter 2 by using the preconfigured example server and the Solritas example-search UI. To begin, we recommend that you start the example server we used in chapter 2 using the commands shown in the following listing.

Listing 4.1 Commands to start the example server from the command line

```
cd $SOLR_INSTALL/example
java -jar start.jar
```

Once you've started the server, go to the Solr admin console at http://localhost:8983/solr, click the collection1 link on the left, then the Files link. This will show all the configuration files for the collection1 core as a directory structure. Click on solrconfig.xml to display the active configuration settings for the collection1 core running on your computer. This listing shows a condensed version of *solrconfig.xml*, to give you an idea of the main elements.

Listing 4.2 Condensed version of *solrconfig.xml*

```
<config>
  <luceneMatchVersion>4.7</luceneMatchVersion>
  <lib dir="../../../contrib/extraction/lib" regex=".*\.jar" />
  <dataDir>${solr.data.dir:}</dataDir>
  <directoryFactory name="DirectoryFactory" class="..."/>
  <indexConfig> ... </indexConfig>
  <jmx />
  <updateHandler class="solr.DirectUpdateHandler2">
    <updateLog> ... </updateLog>
    <autoCommit> ... </autoCommit>
  </updateHandler>
  <query>
    <filterCache ... />
    <queryResultCache ... />
    <documentCache ... />
    <listener event="newSearcher" class="solr.QuerySenderListener">
      <arr name="queries"> ... </arr>
    </listener>
    <listener event="firstSearcher" class="solr.QuerySenderListener">
      <arr name="queries"> ... </arr>
    </listener>
  </query>
```

Activates version-dependent features in Lucene (see section 4.1.3).

Lib directives indicate where Solr can find JAR files for extensions (see section 4.1.3).

Index management settings (covered in chapter 5).

Update handler for indexing documents (see chapter 5).

Enables JMX instrumentation of Solr MBeans (see section 4.1.3).

Register event handlers for searcher events; for example, queries to execute to warm new searchers (see section 4.3).

Cache-management settings (see section 4.4).

```
<requestDispatcher handleSelect="false" >
  <requestParsers ... />
  <httpCaching never304="true" />
</requestDispatcher>
<requestHandler name="/select" class="solr.SearchHandler">
  <lst name="defaults"> ... </lst>
  <lst name="appends"> ... </lst>
  <lst name="invariants"> ... </lst>
  <arr name="components"> ... </arr>
  <arr name="last-components"> ... </arr>
</requestHandler>
<searchComponent name="spellcheck"
    class="solr.SpellCheckComponent"> ... </searchComponent>
<updateRequestProcessorChain name="langid"> ...
      </updateRequestProcessorChain>
<queryResponseWriter name="json"
    class="solr.JSONResponseWriter"> ... </queryResponseWriter>
<valueSourceParser name="myfunc" ... />
<transformer name="db"
    class="com.mycompany.LoadFromDatabaseTransformer">
    ...
</transformer>
</config>
```

Unified request dispatcher (see section 4.2.1).

Request handler to process queries using a chain of search components (see section 4.2.4).

Extends indexing behavior using update-request processors, such as language detection.

Example search component for doing spell correction on queries.

Formats the response as JSON.

Declares a custom function for boosting, ranking, or sorting documents.

Transforms result documents.

As you can see, *solrconfig.xml* has a number of complex sections. The good news is that you don't have to worry about these until you encounter a specific need. On the other hand, it's a good idea to make a mental note of what's in *solrconfig.xml*, as it shows how flexible Solr is and what types of behavior you can control and extend.

When organizing this chapter, we chose to present the configuration settings in an order that builds on previous sections rather than follow the order of elements in the XML document. We present Solr's request-handling framework before we discuss caching, even though cache-related settings come before request-handler settings in *solrconfig.xml*. We took this approach because you should understand how requests are handled before you worry about optimizing a specific type of request with caching. But this does mean that you will have to jump around the XML document as you work through this chapter.

Index settings deferred to chapter 5

The *solrconfig.xml* file contains index-management settings. But we'll save our discussion of index-related settings for the next chapter; that way, you can learn about them after gaining a basic understanding of the indexing process. Specifically, you can ignore the following elements until chapter 5:

```
<dataDir> ... </dataDir>
<directoryFactory name="DirectoryFactory" class="..."/>
<indexConfig> ... </indexConfig>
<updateHandler class="solr.DirectUpdateHandler2"> ...
<updateRequestProcessorChain name="langid"> ...
```

4.1.1   *Common XML data-structure and type elements*

As you work through *solrconfig.xml*, you will encounter common XML elements that Solr uses to represent various data structures and types. Table 4.2 provides brief descriptions and examples of the types of elements that Solr uses throughout the *solrconfig.xml* document. You'll also encounter these elements in XML search results, so please spend time getting familiar with this Solr-specific syntax.

Table 4.2   Solr's XML elements for data structures and typed values

Element	Description	Example

`<arr>`	Named, ordered array of objects	`<arr name="last-components">`
		  `<str>spellcheck</str>`
		`</arr>`

`<lst>`	Named, ordered list of name/value pairs	`<lst name="defaults">`
		  `<str name="omitHeader">true</str>`
		  `<str name="wt">json</str>`
		`</lst>`

`<bool>`	Boolean value—true or false	`<bool>true</bool>`

`<str>`	String value	`<str>spellcheck</str>`
		  or
		`<str name="wt">json</str>`

`<int>`	Integer value	`<int>512</int>`
`<long>`	Long value	`<long>1359936000000</long>`
`<float>`	Float value	`<float>3.14</float>`
`<double>`	Double value	`<double>3.14159265359</double>`

The primary difference between `<arr>` and `<lst>` is that every child element of a `<lst>` has a name attribute, but child elements of `<arr>` are unnamed.

4.1.2   *Applying configuration changes*

Learning about configuration is not the most exciting of tasks, so to help keep you interested, we recommend that you experiment with configuration changes as you work through this chapter. Your changes won't be applied until you reload the Solr core, however. Solr doesn't watch for changes to *solrconfig.xml* and apply them automatically; you have to take an explicit action to apply configuration changes. For now, the easiest way to apply configuration changes is to use the Reload button from the Core Admin page of the administration console, as shown in figure 4.2.

If you're running Solr locally, click the Reload button for the `collection1` core to verify that the functionality works. At the end of this chapter, we'll see another way to reload cores programmatically, using the Core Admin API.

Use the Reload button to
apply configuration changes.

Core-specific properties
and index statistics such as
number of documents.

Figure 4.2   Reload a core to apply configuration changes from the Core Admin page.

4.1.3   *Miscellaneous settings*

Now that we've covered some of the configuration background, let's start our tour of
solrconfig.xml by looking at miscellaneous settings for the Solr server. The next listing
shows the configuration settings we'll discuss in this section.

Listing 4.3   Global settings near the top of *solrconfig.xml*

```
<config>
  <luceneMatchVersion>4.7</luceneMatchVersion>          Lucene
                                                        version.
  <lib dir="../../../contrib/langid/lib/" regex=".*\.jar" />
  <lib dir="../../../dist/" regex="solr-langid-\d.*\.jar" />     Loads dependency
  ...                                                            JAR files.
  <jmx />            Enables
  ...                JMX.
</config>
```

LUCENE VERSION

Lucene and Solr take backward compatibility seriously. The `<luceneMatchVersion>`
element controls the version of Lucene your index is based on. If you're starting out,
then use the version that is specified in the example server, such as:

```
<luceneMatchVersion>4.7</luceneMatchVersion>
```

Now imagine that after running Solr for several months and indexing millions of documents, you decide that you need to upgrade to a later version of Solr. When you start

the updated Solr server, it uses the `<luceneMatchVersion>` to understand which version your index is based on and whether to disable any Lucene features that depend on a later version than what is specified.

You'll be able to run the upgraded version of Solr against your older index, but at some point you may need to raise the `<luceneMatchVersion>` to take advantage of new features and bug fixes in Lucene. In this case, you can either reindex all your documents, or use Lucene's built-in index-upgrade tool.[1] Because that's a problem for the future, we'll refer you to the JavaDoc for instructions on how to run the upgrade tool.

LOADING DEPENDENCY JAR FILES

The `<lib>` element allows you to add JAR files to Solr's runtime classpath so that it can locate plugin classes. Let's look at a few of the `<lib>` elements in the example *solrconfig.xml* to see how `<lib>` elements work.

```
<lib dir="../../../contrib/langid/lib/" regex=".*\.jar" />
<lib dir="../../../dist/" regex="solr-langid-\d.*\.jar" />
```

Each `<lib>` element identifies a directory and a regular expression to match files in the directory. Notice that the `dir` attribute uses relative paths, which are evaluated from the core directory root, commonly referred to as the core `instanceDir`. For the `collection1` core in the example server, the `instanceDir` is *$SOLR_INSTALL/example/solr/collection1/*; remember that *$SOLR_INSTALL/* is the variable name for the directory to which you extracted the Solr distribution archive. Consequently, the two example `<lib>` elements shown previously result in the following JAR files being added to Solr's classpath:

- *jsonic-1.2.7.jar* (from *contrib/langid/lib/*)
- *langdetect-1.1-20120112.jar* (from *contrib/langid/lib/*)
- *apache-solr-langid-4.7.0.jar* (from *dist/*)

Note that the version number for the *apache-solr-langid.jar* file may be different, depending on which version of Solr 4 you are using. Alternatively, you can use the `path` attribute to identify a single JAR file, such as

```
<lib path="../../../dist/solr-langid-4.7.0.jar" />
```

You can also put JAR files for plugins in the *$SOLR_HOME/lib/* directory, such as *$SOLR_INSTALL/example/solr/lib/*.

ENABLE JMX

The `<jmx>` element activates Solr's MBeans to allow system administrators to monitor and manage core Solr components from popular system-monitoring tools, such as Nagios. In a nutshell, an *MBean* is a Java object that exposes configuration properties and statistics using the Java Management Extensions (JMX) API. MBeans can be auto-discovered and introspected by JMX-compliant tools. This allows Solr to be integrated into your existing system-administration infrastructure. We'll cover how to enable external monitoring of Solr through JMX in more detail in chapter 12.

---

[1] Class IndexUpgrader, `org.apache.lucene.index.IndexUpgrader`.

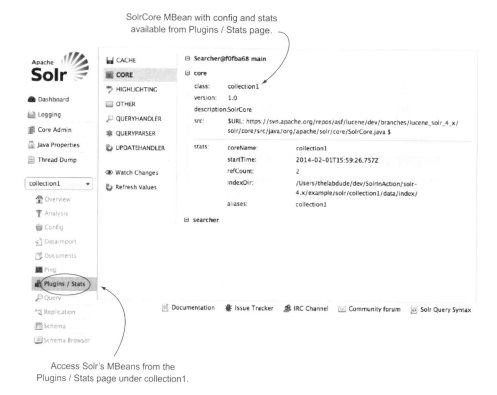

Figure 4.3　Inspecting the SolrCore MBean from the Plugins / Stats page for the `collection1` **core**

You don't need an external JMX-enabled monitoring tool to see Solr's MBeans in action. The Solr administration console provides access to all of Solr's MBeans. Figure 4.3 is a screenshot of the MBean for the `collection1` core.

We'll see more examples of inspecting Solr's MBeans from the administration console throughout this chapter. For now, let's move on to learning how Solr processes requests.

4.2　*Query request handling*

Solr's main purpose is to search, so it follows that handling search requests is one of the most important processes in Solr. In this section, you'll learn how Solr processes search requests and how to customize request handling to better fit your specific search requirements.

4.2.1　*Request-handling overview*

Requests to Solr happen over HTTP. If you want to query Solr, then you send an HTTP GET request. Alternatively, if you want to index a document in Solr, you use an HTTP POST request. The following listing shows an HTTP GET request to query the example Solr server (repeated from listing 2.1).

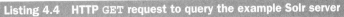

Listing 4.4 HTTP GET request to query the example Solr server

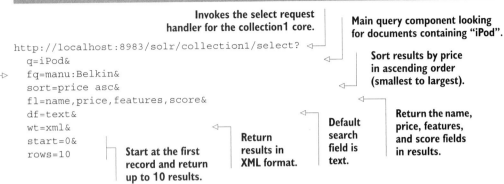

You can input this URL into a web browser, use a command-line tool like curl, or use the example driver application that comes with the book to prevent having to type the query yourself. To execute this request using the example driver, you type

```
cd $SOLR_IN_ACTION
java -jar solr-in-action.jar listing #.#
```

The #.# parameter should be replaced with the number of the listing to execute, such as 4.4. Using the http utility from the book's example code is recommended, because you don't have to do any copying-and-pasting or extra typing to run a code listing, and it works on all Java platforms. The output when running this utility for listing 4.4 is

```
java -jar solr-in-action.jar listing 4.4

INFO [main] (ExampleDriver.java:92) - Found example class sia.Listing for arg
    http
INFO [main] (ExampleDriver.java:125) - Running example Listing with args: -
    listing 4.4
Feb 13, 2013 6:21:32 PM org.apache.solr.client.solrj.impl.HttpClientUtil
    createClient
INFO: Creating new http client,
    config:maxConnections=128&maxConnectionsPerHost=32&followRedirects=false

Sending HTTP GET request (listing 4.4):

    http://localhost:8983/solr/collection1/select?
      q=iPod&
      fq=manu:Belkin&
      sort=price asc&
      fl=name,price,features,score&
      df=text&
      wt=xml&
      start=0&
      rows=10

Solr returned: HTTP/1.1 200 OK

<?xml version="1.0" encoding="UTF-8"?>
<response>
...
</response>
```

The http utility provides other options to allow you to override the address of your Solr server or to change the response type to something other than XML, such as JSON. To see a full list of options, enter java -jar solr-in-action.jar listing -h.

Figure 4.4 shows the sequence of events and the main components involved in handling this Solr request. Starting at the top-left corner of figure 4.4,

1 A client application sends an HTTP GET request to http://localhost:8983/solr/collection1/select?q=.... Query parameters are passed along in the query string of the GET request.

2 Jetty accepts the request and routes it to Solr's unified request dispatcher using the /solr context in the request path. In technical terms, the unified request dispatcher is a Java servlet filter mapped to /* for the Solr web application; see org.apache.solr.servlet.SolrDispatchFilter.

3 Solr's request dispatcher uses the collection1 part of the request path to determine the core name. Next, the dispatcher locates the /select request handler registered in *solrconfig.xml* for the collection1 core.

4 The /select request handler processes the request using a pipeline of search components (covered in section 4.2.4).

5 After the request is processed, results are formatted by a response writer component and returned to the client application; by default, the /select handler returns results as XML. Response writers are covered in section 7.7.

The main purpose of the request dispatcher is to locate the correct core to handle the request, such as collection1, and then route the request to the appropriate request handler registered in the core, in this case /select. In practice, the default configuration for the request dispatcher is sufficient for most applications. On the other hand, it's

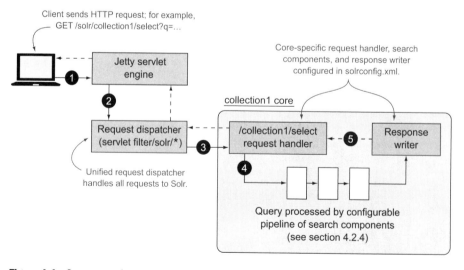

Figure 4.4   Sequence of events to process a request to the /select request handler.

common to define a custom search request handler or to customize one of the existing handlers, such as /select. Let's dig into how the /select handler works, to gain a better understanding of how to customize a request handler.

4.2.2 Search handler

This listing shows the definition of the /select request handler from *solrconfig.xml.*

> **Listing 4.5 Definition of /select request handler from *solrconfig.xml***

```
<requestHandler name="/select"
                class="solr.SearchHandler">
  <lst name="defaults">
    <str name="echoParams">explicit</str>
    <int name="rows">10</int>
    <str name="df">text</str>
  </lst>
</requestHandler>
```

A Java class that implements the request handler.

A specific type of request handler designed to process queries.

A list of default parameters (name/value pairs).

Sets the default page size to 10.

Behind the scenes, all request handlers are implemented by a Java class: in this case, solr.SearchHandler. At runtime, solr.SearchHandler resolves to the built-in Solr class org.apache.solr.handler.component.SearchHandler. In general, anytime you see solr. as a prefix of a class in *solrconfig.xml,* you know this translates to one of Solr's core Java packages: "analysis.", "schema.", "handler.", "search.", "update.", "core.", "request.", "update.processor.", "util.", "spelling.", "handler.component.", or "handler.dataimport." This shorthand notation helps reduce clutter in Solr's configuration documents.

In Solr, there are two main types of request handlers: *search handler* for query processing and *update handler* for indexing. We'll learn more about update handlers in the next chapter, in which we'll cover indexing. For now, let's concentrate on how search request handlers process queries, as depicted in figure 4.5.

The search-handler structure depicted in figure 4.5 is designed to make it easy for you to adapt Solr's query-processing pipeline for your application. For example, you can define your own request handler or, more commonly, add a custom search component to an existing request handler, such as /select. In general, a search handler is comprised of the following phases, and each phase can be customized in *solrconfig.xml*:

1. Request parameter decoration, using
   a. *defaults*—Set default parameters on the request if they are not explicitly provided by the client
   b. *invariants*—Set parameters to fixed values, which override values provided by the client
   c. *appends*—Additional parameters to be combined with the parameters provided by the client
2. *first-components*—An optional chain of search components that are executed first to perform preprocessing tasks

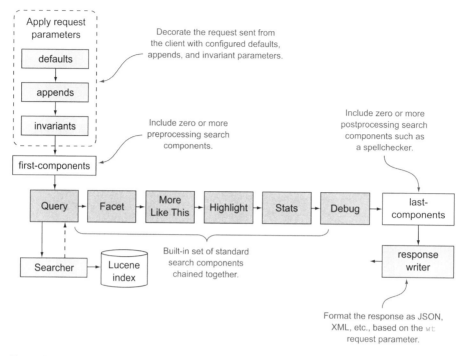

Figure 4.5   Search request handler made up of parameter decoration (defaults, appends, and invariants), first-components, components, and last-components

3   *components*—The primary chain of search components that must at least include the query component

4   *last-components*—An optional chain of search components that are applied last to perform postprocessing tasks

A request handler does not need to define all phases in *solrconfig.xml*. As you can see from listing 4.5, /select defines only the defaults section. This means that all other phases are inherited from the base solr.SearchHandler implementation. If the main components section is not defined, a default list of search components is used. This list of default search components will be covered in section 4.2.4. In practice, customized request handlers are commonly used to simplify client applications. For instance, the Solritas example we introduced in chapter 2 uses a custom request handler, /browse, to power a feature-rich search experience while keeping the client-side code for Solritas simple.

4.2.3   *Browse request handler for Solritas: an example*

Hiding complexity from client code is at the heart of web services and object-oriented design. Solr adopts this proven design pattern by allowing you to define a custom search request handler for your application, which allows you to hide complexity from your Solr client. Rather than requiring every query to send the correct parameters to enable spell correction, for example, you can use a custom request handler that has spell correction enabled by default.

The Solr example server comes preconfigured with a great example of this design pattern at work to support the Solritas example application. This listing shows an abbreviated definition of the `/browse` request handler from *solrconfig.xml*.

Listing 4.6 Browse request handler for Solritas

```
<requestHandler name="/browse" class="solr.SearchHandler">
    <lst name="defaults">
        <str name="echoParams">explicit</str>
        <str name="wt">velocity</str>
        <str name="v.template">browse</str>
        <str name="v.layout">layout</str>
        <str name="title">Solritas</str>
        <str name="defType">edismax</str>
        <str name="qf">text^0.5 features^1.0 ...</str>
        <str name="mlt.qf">text^0.5 features^1.0 ...</str>
        <str name="facet">on</str>
        ...
        <str name="hl">on</str>
        ...
        <str name="spellcheck">on</str>
        ...
    </lst>
    <arr name="last-components">
        <str>spellcheck</str>
    </arr>
</requestHandler>
```

SearchHandler invokes the query-processing pipeline.

Default list of query parameters.

VelocityResponseWriter settings.

Uses the extended dismax query parser.

Query settings.

The setting for the More Like This component.

Enables the facet component.

Enables the highlight component.

Enables spell-checking.

Invokes the spell-checking component as the last step in the pipeline.

We recommend that you go through all the sections of the `/browse` request handler in the *solrconfig.xml* file. One thing that should be obvious is that a great deal of effort was put into configuring this handler in order to demonstrate many of the great features in Solr. When starting out with Solr, you definitely do not need to configure something similar for your application all at once. You can build up a custom request handler over time as you gain experience with Solr.

Let's see the `/browse` request handler in action using the Solritas example. With the example Solr server running, direct your browser to http://localhost:8983/solr/collection1/browse. Enter iPod into the search box, as shown in figure 4.6.

Scan figure 4.6 and look at all of the search features activated for this simple query. Behind the scenes, the Solritas search form submits a query to the `/browse` request handler. In the log, we see

```
INFO: [collection1] webapp=/solr path=/browse params={q=iPod} hits=3 status=0
    QTime=22
```

Notice that the only parameter sent by the search form is `q=iPod`, but the response includes facets, More Like This, spell correction, paging, and hit highlighting.

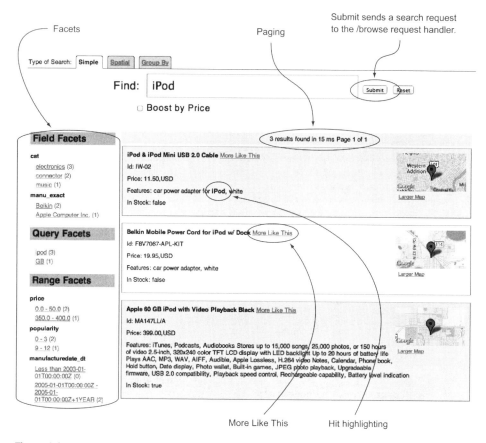

Figure 4.6   A screenshot of the Solritas example powered by the `/browse` request handler

That's an impressive list of features for a simple request like `q=iPod`! As you may have guessed, these features are enabled using default parameters in the `/browse` request handler.

The `defaults` `<lst>` element from listing 4.6 is an ordered list of name/value pairs that provides default values for query parameters if they are not explicitly sent by the client application. For example, the default value for the response-writer type parameter `wt` is `velocity` (`<str name="wt">velocity</str>`). Velocity is an open source templating engine written in Java (http://velocity.apache.org/engine/index.html).

According to the log message shown previously, the only parameter sent by the form was q; all other parameters are set by `defaults`. Let's do a little experiment to see the real query that gets processed. Instead of using response-writer type `velocity`, let's set the `wt` parameter to `xml` so that we can see the response in raw form without the HTML decoration provided by Velocity. Also, in order to see all the query parameters, we need to set the `echoParams` value to `all`. This is a good example of overriding default values by explicitly passing parameters from the client. The next listing shows the query URL and a portion of the `<params>` element returned with the response; remember that you can use the `http` tool provided with the book's source code to execute this request. Notice how the number of parameters sent to the `/browse` request handler is quite large.

Listing 4.7 List of parameters sent to the `/browse` request handler for `q=iPod`

Request

```
http://localhost:8983/solr/collection1/browse?q=iPod&wt=xml&echoParams=all
```

Response

```
...
  <lst name="params">
    <str name="facet">on</str>
    <str name="mlt.fl">text,features,name,sku,id,manu,cat,title,
      description,keywords,author,resourcename</str>
    <str name="f.manufacturedate_dt.facet.range.gap">+1YEAR</str>
    <str name="f.price.facet.range.gap">50</str>
    <str name="q.alt">*:*</str>
    <str name="f.content.hl.fragsize">200</str>
    <str name="v.layout">layout</str>
    <str name="echoParams">all</str>
    <str name="fl">*,score</str>
    <str name="f.price.facet.range.end">600</str>
    <str name="hl.simple.post">&lt;/b&gt;</str>
    <str name="f.name.hl.fragsize">0</str>
    <arr name="facet.field">
      <str>cat</str>
      <str>manu_exact</str>
      <str>content_type</str>
      <str>author_s</str>
    </arr>
    <str name="hl.encoder">html</str>
    <str name="v.template">browse</str>
    <str name="spellcheck.alternativeTermCount">2</str>
    <str name="f.popularity.facet.range.end">10</str>
    <str name="f.manufacturedate_dt.facet.range.start">
      NOW/YEAR-10YEARS</str>
    <str name="spellcheck.extendedResults">false</str>
    <str name="spellcheck.maxCollations">3</str>
    <str name="hl.fl">content features title name</str>
    <str name="f.content.hl.maxAlternateFieldLength">750</str>
    <str name="spellcheck.collate">true</str>
    <str name="wt">xml</str>
    <str name="defType">edismax</str>
    <str name="rows">10</str>
    <str name="facet.range.other">after</str>
    <str name="f.popularity.facet.range.start">0</str>
    <str name="f.title.hl.alternateField">title</str>
    <str name="facet.pivot">cat,inStock</str>
    <str name="f.title.hl.fragsize">0</str>
    <str name="spellcheck">on</str>
    <str name="spellcheck.maxCollationTries">5</str>
    <arr name="facet.range">
```

```
            <str>price</str>
            <str>popularity</str>
            <str>manufacturedate_dt</str>
        </arr>
        <str name="hl.simple.pre">&lt;b&gt;</str>
        <str name="hl">on</str>
        <str name="title">Solritas</str>
        <str name="df">text</str>
        <arr name="facet.query">
            <str>ipod</str>
            <str>GB</str>
        </arr>
        ...
    </lst>
    ...
```

There are many more default parameters in this request not shown here.

From looking at the listing, it should be clear that parameter decoration for a search request handler is a powerful feature in Solr. Specifically, the `defaults` list provides two main benefits to your application:

- It helps simplify client code by establishing sensible defaults for your application in one place. For instance, setting the response-writer type `wt` to `velocity` means that client applications don't need to worry about setting this parameter. Moreover, if you ever swap out Velocity for another templating engine, your client code doesn't need to change!

- By preconfiguring complex components like faceting, you can establish consistent behavior for all queries while keeping your client code simple. As you can see from listing 4.7, the request includes a number of complex parameters needed to configure search components used by Solritas. There are over 20 parameters to configure the faceting component for Solritas.

The `/browse` handler serves as a good example of what is possible with Solr query processing, but it's also unlikely that it can be used by your application, because the default parameters are tightly coupled to the Solritas data model. For instance, range faceting is configured for the `price`, `popularity`, and `manufacturedate_dt` fields, which are specific to the Solritas schema and may not apply to your application. Consequently, you should treat the `/browse` handler as an example, not a 100% reusable solution, when designing your own application-specific request handler.

4.2.4   *Extending query processing with search components*

Beyond a set of defaults, the `/browse` request handler defines an array `<arr>` of search components to be applied to the request after the default set of search components is applied using the `<last-components>` element. From listing 4.6, notice that the `/browse` request handler specifies

```
<arr name="last-components">
    <str>spellcheck</str>
</arr>
```

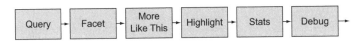

Figure 4.7 Chain of six built-in search components

This configuration means that the default set of search components is applied, and then the spellcheck component is applied. This is a common design pattern for search request handlers. Figure 4.7 shows the chain of six built-in search components that get applied during the `<components>` phase of query processing.

QUERY COMPONENT

The query component is the core of Solr's query-processing pipeline. At a high level, the query component parses and executes queries using the active searcher, which is discussed in section 4.3. The specific query-parsing strategy is controlled by the `defType` parameter. For instance, the `/browse` request handler uses the eDisMax query parser (`<str name="defType">edismax</str>`), which will be discussed in chapter 7.

The query component identifies all documents in the index that match the query. The set of matching documents can then be used by other components in the query-processing chain, such as the facet component. The query component is always enabled, and all other components need to be explicitly enabled using query parameters.

FACET COMPONENT

Given a result set identified by the query component, the facet component, if enabled, calculates field-level facets. We cover faceting in depth in chapter 8. The key takeaway for now is that faceting is built into every search request, and it needs to be enabled with query request parameters. For `/browse`, faceting is enabled using the default parameter: `<str name="facet">true</str>`.

MORE LIKE THIS COMPONENT

Given a result set created by the query component, the More Like This component, if enabled, identifies other documents that are similar to the documents in search results. To see an example of the More Like This component in action, search for hard drive in the Solritas example. Click the More Like This link for the "Samsung SpinPoint P120 SP2514N - hard drive - 250 GB - ATA-133" result to see a list of similar documents, as shown in figure 4.8.

We cover the More Like This component in chapter 16.

HIGHLIGHT COMPONENT

If enabled, the highlight component highlights highly relevant sections of text in matching documents. Hit highlighting is covered in chapter 9.

STATS COMPONENT

The stats component computes simple statistics like min, max, sum, mean, and standard deviation for numeric fields in matching documents. To see an example of what the stats component produces, execute a GET request, as shown in listing 4.8.

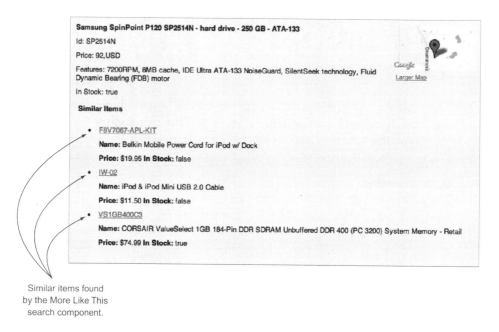

Figure 4.8   Example of similar items found by the More Like This search component

Listing 4.8   Request summary statistics for the `price` field using the stats component

Request
```
http://localhost:8983/solr/collection1/select?
  q=*:*&
  wt=xml&
  stats=true&
  stats.field=price
```
Request statistics for the price field.

Response
```
...
<lst name="price">
  <double name="min">0.0</double>
  <double name="max">2199.0</double>
  <long name="count">16</long>
  <long name="missing">16</long>
  <double name="sum">5251.270030975342</double>
  <double name="sumOfSquares">6038619.175900028</double>
  <double name="mean">328.20437693595886</double>
  <double name="stddev">536.3536996709846</double>
  <lst name="facets"/>
</lst>
...
```
Summary statistics returned for the price field.

DEBUG COMPONENT
The debug component returns the parsed query string that was executed and detailed information about how the score was calculated for each document in the

result set. The parsed query value is returned to help you track down query-formulation issues. The debug component is useful for troubleshooting ranking problems. To see the debug component at work, direct your browser to http://localhost:8983/solr/collection1/browse?q=iPod&wt=xml&debugQuery=true.

Notice that this is the same query that we executed from the Solritas form, except we changed the response-writer type wt to xml (instead of velocity) and enabled the debug component using debug=true in the HTTP GET request. The following listing shows a snippet of the XML output produced by the debug component.

Listing 4.9 Snippet of the XML output produced by the debug component

Request
```
http://localhost:8983/solr/collection1/browse?
  q=iPod&
  wt=xml&                            ◁─┤ Enable the debug
  debug=true                             component.
```

Response
```
...                                           Query produced
<lst name="debug">                            by the eDisMax
    <str name="rawquerystring">iPod</str>     query parser.
    <str name="querystring">iPod</str>
    <str name="parsedquery">(+DisjunctionMaxQuery((id:iPod^10.0 |    ◁─
     author:ipod^2.0 | title:ipod^10.0 | text:ipod^0.5 | cat:iPod^1.4 |
     keywords:ipod^5.0 | manu:ipod^1.1 | description:ipod^5.0 |
     resourcename:ipod | name:ipod^1.2 | features:ipod | sku:ipod^1.5)))/
     no_coord</str>
      ...
    <lst name="explain">              ◁─┤ Explanation of score calculation
      <str name="IW-02">                   for each document in the request.
0.13513829 = (MATCH) max of:
0.045974977 = (MATCH) weight(text:ipod^0.5 in 4) [DefaultSimilarity], result
    of:
    0.045974977 = score(doc=4,freq=3.0 = termFreq=3.0
), ...</str>
    </lst>
...
</lst>
...
```

Notice how the single-term query iPod entered by the user results in a fairly complex query composed of many boosts on numerous fields. The more complex query is created by the eDisMax query parser, which is enabled by the defType parameter under defaults. The eDisMax parser is covered in chapter 7.

ADDING SPELLCHECK AS A LAST-COMPONENT

After the six built-in search components process the request, the /browse search handler invokes the spellcheck component, which is listed in the <last-components> phase. This listing shows the definition of the spellcheck component from *solrconfig.xml*.

Spellcheck
component-
specific
parameters.
See chapter 10.

```
<searchComponent name="spellcheck" class="solr.SpellCheckComponent">
  <str name="queryAnalyzerFieldType">textSpell</str>
  <lst name="spellchecker">
    <str name="name">default</str>
    <str name="field">name</str>
    <str name="classname">solr.DirectSolrSpellChecker</str>
    ...
  </lst>
</searchComponent>
```

Define a search component
named "spellcheck"
of type solr.SpellCheck-
Component.

Notice that the name of the component "spellcheck" matches what is listed in the
<last-components> section of the /browse request handler. You'll need more back-
ground on how Solr's spelling-correction feature works before the settings in listing 4.10
make sense, so we'll return to this configuration element in chapter 10. The key takeaway at this point is seeing how a search component is added to the search request-
handling pipeline using <last-components>.

At this point, you should have a solid understanding of how Solr processes query
requests. Before we move on to another configuration topic, you should be aware that
the Solr administration console provides access to all active search request handlers
under Plugins / Stats > QUERYHANDLER. Figure 4.9 shows properties and statistics for
the /browse search handler, which, as you might have guessed, is another MBean.

Now let's turn our attention to configuration settings that help optimize query
performance.

4.3   *Managing searchers*

The <query> element contains settings that allow you to optimize query performance using techniques like caching, lazy field loading, and new searcher warming.
It goes without saying that designing for optimal query performance from the start
is critical to the success of your search application. In this section, you'll learn about
managing searchers, which is one of the most important techniques for optimizing
query performance.

4.3.1   *New searcher overview*

In Solr, queries are processed by a component called a *searcher*. There is only one
"active" searcher in Solr at any given time. All query components for all search request
handlers execute queries against the active searcher.

The active searcher has a read-only view of a snapshot of the underlying Lucene
index. It follows that if you add a new document to Solr, then it is *not* visible in
search results from the current searcher. This raises the question: How do new documents become visible in search results? The answer is to close the current searcher
and open a new one that has a read-only view of the updated index. This is what it
means to commit documents to Solr. The commit process in Solr is more complicated than what we've described, but we'll save a thorough discussion of the nuances of

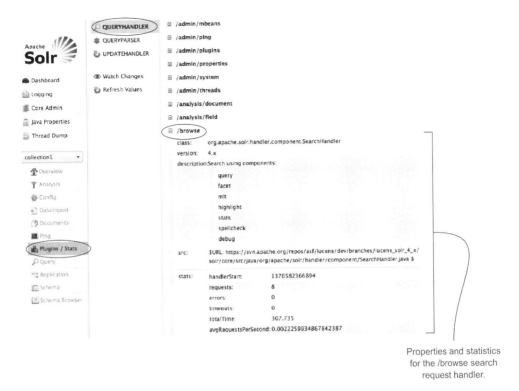

Properties and statistics
for the /browse search
request handler.

Figure 4.9 **A screenshot showing properties and statistics for the** `/browse` **request handler in the Solr administration console under Plugins / Stats > QUERYHANDLER**

commits for the next chapter. For now, think of a commit as a black-box operation that makes new documents and any updates to your existing index visible in search results by opening a new searcher.

Figure 4.10 shows the active searcher MBean for the `collection1` core in the example server, available under the CORE section of the Plugins / Stats page.

On the CORE page, take note of the `searcherName` property (in the diagram, it's Searcher@25082661 main). Let's trigger the creation of a new searcher by resending all the example documents to your server, as we did in section 2.1.4:

```
cd $SOLR_INSTALL/example/exampledocs
java -jar post.jar *.xml
```

Now, refresh the CORE page, and note that the `searcherName` property has changed to be a different instance of the searcher. A new searcher was created because the `post.jar` command sent a `commit` after adding the example documents.

Now that we know that a `commit` creates a new searcher to make new documents and updates visible, let's think about the implications of creating a new searcher. First, the old searcher must be destroyed. But there could be queries currently executing against the old searcher, so Solr must wait for all in-progress queries to complete.

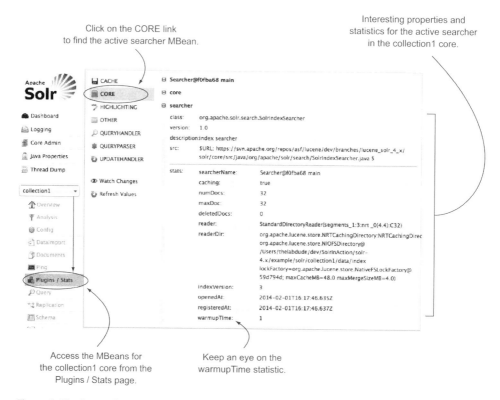

Click on the CORE link
to find the active searcher MBean.

Interesting properties and
statistics for the active searcher
in the collection1 core.

Access the MBeans for
the collection1 core from the
Plugins / Stats page.

Keep an eye on the
warmupTime statistic.

Figure 4.10   Inspecting the active searcher MBean in the `collection1` core from the Solr admin console

Also, any cached objects that are based on the current searcher's view of the index must be invalidated. We'll learn more about Solr cache management in the next section. For now, think about a cached result set from a specific query. As some of the documents in the cached results may have been deleted and new documents may now match the query, it should be clear that the cached result set is not valid for the new searcher.

Because precomputed data, such as a cached query result set, must be invalidated and recomputed, it stands to reason that opening a new searcher on your index is potentially an expensive operation. This can have a direct impact on user experience. Imagine a user paging through search results, and imagine a new searcher is opened after they click on page 2 but before they request page 3. When the user requests the next page, all of the previously computed filters and cached documents are no longer valid. If you don't take care, the user is likely to experience some slowness, particularly if their query is complex.

The good news is that Solr has a number of tools to help alleviate this situation. First and foremost, Solr supports the concept of warming a new searcher in the background and keeping the current searcher active until the new one is fully warmed.

4.3.2　*Warming a new searcher*

Solr takes the approach that it is better to serve stale results for a short period of time than to allow query performance to slow down significantly. This means that Solr does not close the current searcher until a new searcher is warmed up and ready to execute queries with optimal performance.

Warming a new searcher is much like a sprinter warming up in track and field. Before sprinters start a race, they make sure that their muscles are warmed up and ready to perform at full speed when the start gun fires. In the same manner, Solr shouldn't activate "cold" searchers.

In general, there are two types of warming activities: autowarming new caches from the old caches and executing cache-warming queries. We'll learn more about autowarming caches in the next section, in which we dig into Solr's cache-management features.

A *cache-warming query* is a preconfigured query (in *solrconfig.xml*) that gets executed against a new searcher in order to populate the new searcher's caches. The following listing shows the configuration of cache-warming queries for the example server.

> **Listing 4.11　Define a listener for `newSearcher` events to execute warming queries**

Intentionally commented out; configure application-specific queries for your environment.

```
<listener event="newSearcher" class="solr.QuerySenderListener">
  <arr name="queries">
    <!--
    <lst><str name="q">solr</str><str name="sort">price asc</str></lst>
    <lst><str name="q">rocks</str><str name="sort">weight asc</str></lst>
    -->
  </arr>
</listener>
```

Define a listener to handle newSearcher events.

Define a named list of query objects to warm the new searcher.

The configuration settings in the listing register a named list (`<arr name="queries">`) of queries to execute whenever a `newSearcher` event occurs in Solr, such as after a `commit`. Also, note that the queries are commented out! This is intentional, because there is a cost to executing warming queries, and the Solr developers wanted to ensure that you configure warming queries explicitly for your application. The cache-warming queries are application-specific, so the out-of-the-box defaults are strictly for example purposes. You are responsible for configuring your own warming queries.

CHOOSING WARMING QUERIES

Having the facility to warm new searchers by executing queries is only a great feature if you can identify queries that will help improve query performance. As a rule of thumb, warming queries should contain query-request parameters (`q`, `fq`, `sort`, etc.) that are used frequently by your application. Because we haven't yet covered Solr query syntax, we'll table the discussion of warming queries until chapter 7, where you'll learn about Solr's query syntax. After reading chapter 7, you'll know how to construct warming queries. For now, it's sufficient to make a mental note that you need to revisit this topic once you have a more thorough understanding of Solr query construction.

We should also mention that you aren't required to have any warming queries for your application. If query performance begins to suffer after commits, then you'll know it's time to consider using warming queries.

TOO MANY WARMING QUERIES

The old adage of less is more applies to warming queries. Each query takes time to execute, so having many warming queries configured can lead to long delays in opening new searchers. It's best to keep the list of warming queries to the minimal set of the most important queries for your search application.

You might be wondering what the problem is with a new searcher taking a long time to warm up. It turns out that warming too many searchers in your application concurrently can consume too many resources (CPU and memory), leading to a degraded search experience.

FIRST SEARCHER

There is also the concept of warming the first searcher during Solr initialization or after reloading a core. We'll leave it to you to determine if there's value in configuring warming queries for the first searcher. Most Solr users use the same queries for warming new and first searchers. Before we turn our attention to Solr's cache management, we want to mention two additional searcher-related elements in *solrconfig.xml:* `<useColdSearcher>` and `<maxWarmingSearchers>`.

Including XML elements from other sources using XInclude

Solr supports using XInclude to pull XML elements from other files into *solrconfig.xml*. Rather than duplicating your list of warming queries for new and first searchers, for example, you can maintain the list in a separate file and XInclude it in both places, using `<xi:include href="warming-queries.xml" xmlns:xi="http://www.w3.org/2001/XInclude">`.

USECOLDSEARCHER

The `<useColdSearcher>` element covers the case in which a new search request is made and there is no currently registered searcher. If `<useColdSearcher>` is `false`, then Solr will block until the warming searcher has completed executing all warming queries; this is the default configuration for the example Solr server: `<useColdSearcher>false</useColdSearcher>`.

If `<useColdSearcher>` is `true`, then Solr will immediately register the warming searcher regardless of how "warm" it is. Returning to our track-and-field analogy, `false` would mean the starting official waits to start the race until our sprinter is fully warmed up, regardless of how long that takes. A `true` value means that the race will start immediately, regardless of how warmed up our sprinter is.

MAXWARMINGSEARCHERS

It's conceivable that a new commit is issued before the new-searcher warming process completes, which implies that another searcher needs to be warmed up. This is true in particular if your searchers take considerable time to warm up. The `<max-WarmingSearchers>` element allows you to control the maximum number of searchers that can be warming up in the background concurrently. Once this threshold is reached, new commit requests will fail, which is a good thing, because allowing too many warming searchers to run in the background can quickly eat up memory and CPU resources on your server. Solr ships with a default of 2, which is a good value to start with:

```
<maxWarmingSearchers>2</maxWarmingSearchers>
```

If you find your server is reaching the maximum threshold too often, revisit your warming logic to see if new-searcher warming is taking too long.

Hopefully you now have a good sense for what a searcher is and how to configure Solr to manage searchers correctly for your application. Now let's look at more ways to optimize query performance using caching.

4.4 Cache management

Solr provides a number of built-in caches to improve query performance. Before we get into the details of specific Solr caches, it's important to understand cache-management fundamentals in Solr.

4.4.1 Cache fundamentals

There are four main concerns when working with Solr caches:

- Cache sizing and eviction policy
- Hit ratio and evictions
- Cached-object invalidation
- Autowarming new caches

Broadly speaking, proper cache management in Solr is not a set-it-and-forget-it type of process. You'll need to keep an eye on your caches and fine-tune them based on real usage of Solr. Remember that the Solr administration console is your friend when it comes to monitoring important components like caches and searchers.

CACHE SIZING

In terms of cache sizing, you don't want your caches to be so large that they consume all available memory in your JVM. Solr keeps all cached objects in memory and does not overflow to disk, as is possible with some caching frameworks. Consequently, Solr requires you to set an upper limit on the number of objects in each cache. Solr will evict objects when the cache reaches the upper limit, using either a Least Recently Used or Least Frequently Used eviction policy.

Least Recently Used (LRU) evicts objects when a cache reaches its maximum threshold based on the time when an object was last requested from the cache. When a cache is full and a new object is added, the LRU policy will remove the oldest entry; age is determined by the last time each object in the cache was requested. The LRU policy is the default configuration for Solr.

Solr also provides a *Least Frequently Used (LFU)* policy that evicts objects based on how frequently they are requested from the cache. This is beneficial for applications that want to give priority to more popular items in the cache, rather than only those that have been used recently. Solr's filter cache is a good candidate for using the LFU eviction policy, because filters are typically expensive to create and store, so you want to keep the filter cache small and give priority to the most popular filters in your application. We'll learn more about the filter cache in the next section.

A common misconception with cache sizing is that you should make your cache sizes quite large if you have the memory available. The problem with this approach is that once a cache becomes invalidated after a commit, there can be many objects that need to be garbage collected by the JVM. Remember, closing a searcher invalidates all cached values. Without proper tuning of garbage collection, this can lead to long pauses in your server, caused by full garbage collection. We'll learn more about tuning garbage collection parameters for Solr in chapter 12. For now, the important lessons are to avoid defining overly large caches and to let some objects in the cache be evicted periodically.

HIT RATIO AND EVICTIONS

Hit ratio is the proportion of cache read requests that result in finding a cached value. The hit ratio indicates how much benefit your application is getting from its cache. Ideally, you want your hit ratio to be as close to 1 (100%) as possible. A low hit ratio is an indication that Solr is not benefiting from caching.

The eviction count shows how many objects have been evicted from the cache based on the eviction policy described previously. It follows that having a large number of evictions is an indication that the maximum size of your cache may be too small for your application. Eviction count and hit ratio are interrelated, as a high eviction count will lead to a suboptimal hit ratio. Optimizing your hit ratio will be covered in more detail in chapter 12.

CACHED-OBJECT INVALIDATION

In most cache-management scenarios, you need to worry about how to invalidate a cached object, so that your application does not return stale data. But in Solr, this is not a concern, because all objects in a cache are linked to a specific searcher instance and are immediately invalidated when a searcher is closed. Recall that a searcher is a read-only view of a snapshot of your index; consequently, all cached objects remain valid until the searcher is closed.

AUTOWARMING NEW CACHES

As we discussed in section 4.3, Solr creates a new searcher after a commit, but it doesn't close the old searcher until the new searcher is fully warmed. Some of the keys in the soon-to-be-closed searcher's cache can be used to populate the new searcher's cache, a process known as *autowarming* in Solr. Note that autowarming a cache is different than using a warming query to populate a cache, as we discussed in section 4.3.2.

Every Solr cache supports an `autowarmCount` attribute that indicates either the maximum number of objects or a percentage of the old cache size to autowarm. How the objects are autowarmed depends on the specific cache. We'll learn more about cache-specific autowarming strategies soon. The key point for now is that you can configure Solr's caches to refresh a subset of cached objects when opening a new searcher, but as with any optimization technique, you need to be careful to not overdo it.

At this point you should have a basic understanding of cache-management concepts in Solr. Now let's learn about the specific types of caches Solr uses to optimize query performance, starting with one of the most important caches: the *filter cache*.

4.4.2   Filter cache

In Solr, a filter restricts search results to documents that meet the filter criteria, but it does not affect scoring. We saw an example of this in section 2.2.1 in which our first example query filtered documents having the manufacturer field (`manu`) set to `Belkin` using `fq=manu:Belkin`, as seen in this listing.

> **Listing 4.12   Example query using a filter query `fq` on the `manu` field**

```
http://localhost:8983/solr/collection1/select?
  q=iPod&
  fq=manu:Belkin&                                  Filter query
  sort=price asc&                                  fq on the
  fl=name,price,features,score&                    manu field.
  df=text&
  wt=xml&
  start=0&rows=10
```

When Solr executes this query, it computes and caches an efficient data structure that indicates which documents in your index match the filter. For the example server, there are two documents that match this filter.

Now consider what happens if another query is sent to Solr with the same filter query (`fq=manu:Belkin`) but a different query, such as `q=USB`. Wouldn't it be nice if the second query could use the results of the filter query from the first query? This is the purpose of Solr's filter cache! To see this cache in action, navigate to the Query page for the `collection1` core, and submit the query as shown in figure 4.11.

Next, navigate to the Plugins / Stats page for `collection1`, and click on the CACHE link. Figure 4.12 shows the properties and statistics for the `filterCache` MBean. Re-execute the query several times, and you will see the `filterCache` statistics change.

It's difficult to fully appreciate the value of caching filters for a small index, but if you imagine an index with millions of documents, you can see how caching filters can help to optimize query performance. In fact, using filters to optimize queries is one of the most powerful features in Solr, mainly because filters are reusable across queries. For now, we'll save a deeper discussion of filters for chapter 7 and turn our focus to how the filter cache is configured in *solrconfig.xml*. Listing 4.13 shows the default configuration for the filter cache.

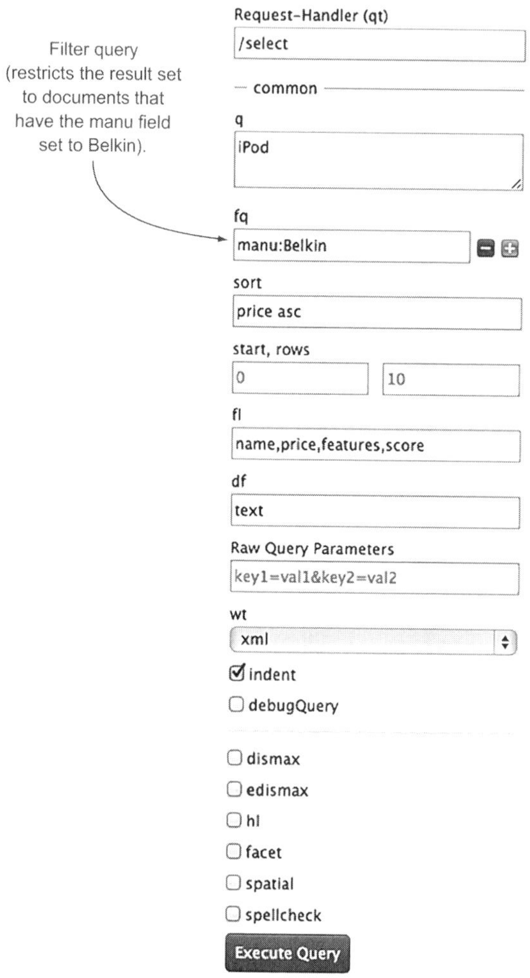

Filter query
(restricts the result set
to documents that
have the manu field
set to Belkin).

Request-Handler (qt)

/select

— common —————————

q

iPod

fq

manu:Belkin

sort

price asc

start, rows

0   10

fl

name,price,features,score

df

text

Raw Query Parameters

key1=val1&key2=val2

wt

xml

☑ indent

○ debugQuery

○ dismax

○ edismax

○ hl

○ facet

○ spatial

○ spellcheck

Execute Query

**Figure 4.11   Execute a query with a
filter query** `fq` **clause to see the filter
cache in action.**

Listing 4.13   Initial settings for the filter cache in the example server

```
<filterCache class="solr.FastLRUCache"                        Uses the LRU
    size="512"                                                eviction policy.
    initialSize="512"              No objects are      Maximum size
    autowarmCount="0"/>            warmed for this cache.   is 512 objects.
```

AUTOWARMING THE FILTER CACHE

A filter can be a powerful tool for optimizing queries, but you can also get into trouble
if you don't manage cached filters correctly. Filters can be expensive to create and
store in memory if you have a large number of documents in your index, or if the filter criteria are complex. If a filter is generic enough to apply to multiple queries in
your application, it makes sense to cache the resulting filter. In addition, you probably
want to autowarm some of the cached filters when opening a new searcher.

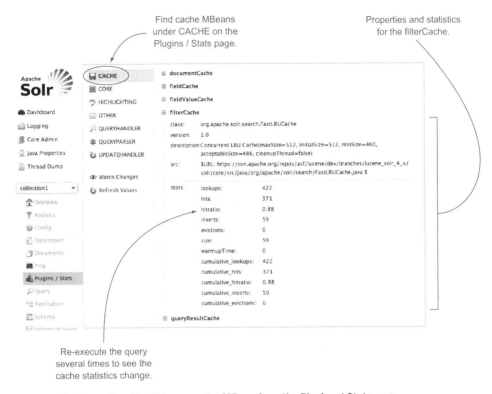

Find cache MBeans
under CACHE on the
Plugins / Stats page.

Properties and statistics
for the filterCache.

Re-execute the query
several times to see the
cache statistics change.

Figure 4.12 Inspecting the `filterCache` MBean from the Plugins / Stats page

Let's look under the hood of the filter cache to understand what happens during autowarming of objects in the filter cache. By now, you should know that objects cannot easily be moved from the old to the new cache because the underlying index has changed, which invalidates cached objects like filters. Each object in the cache has a key. For the filter cache, the key is the filter query, such as `manu:Belkin`. To warm the new cache, a subset of keys is pulled from the old cache and executed against the new searcher, which recomputes the filter. Autowarming the filter cache requires Solr to re-execute the filter query with the new searcher. Consequently, autowarming the filter cache can be a source of performance and resource utilization problems in Solr.

Imagine the scenario in which you have hundreds of filters cached and your `autowarmCount` is set to 100. When warming the new searcher, Solr must execute 100 filter queries. Imagine that it takes 65 seconds to execute the 100 filter queries and your application commits change every minute. Under this scenario, you'll quickly run into problems in which you are warming too many searchers in the background.

We recommend that you enable autowarming for the filter cache, but set the `autowarmCount` attribute to a small number to start. In addition, we think the LFU eviction policy is more appropriate for the filter cache because it allows you to keep the filter cache small and give priority to the most popular filters in your application. Here are the recommended configuration settings for the filter cache:

```
<filterCache class="solr.LFUCache"
    size="100"
    initialSize="20"
    autowarmCount="10"/>
```

Change to use LFU eviction policy.

Keep the size of this cache to a reasonable maximum.

Only autowarm the 10 most popular filters.

You need to experiment with these parameters, depending on how many filters your application uses and how frequently you commit against your index.

In terms of memory usage per cached filter, Solr has different filter representations based on the size of the matching document set. As an upper limit, you can figure that any filter that matches many documents in your index will require MaxDoc (the number of documents in the index) bits of memory. For example, if your index has 10 million documents, then a filter can take up to 10 million bits of memory, or roughly 1.2 MB.

4.4.3   *Query result cache*

The query result cache holds result sets for a query. If you execute the query from listing 4.12 more than once, subsequent results are served from the query result cache, rather than re-executing the same query against the index. This can be a powerful solution for reducing the cost of computationally expensive queries. The query result cache is defined as

```
<queryResultCache class="solr.LRUCache"
    size="512"
    initialSize="512"
    autowarmCount="0"/>
```

Behind the scenes, the query result cache holds a query as the key and a list of internal Lucene document IDs as the value. Internal Lucene document IDs can change from one searcher to the next, so the cached values must be recomputed when warming the query result cache.

To warm the query result cache, Solr needs to re-execute queries, which can be expensive. The same advice we gave about keeping the autowarmCount attribute small for the filter cache applies to the query result cache. That said, we do recommend setting the autowarmCount attribute for this cache to something other than the default zero, so that you get some benefit from autowarming recent queries.

Beyond sizing, Solr provides miscellaneous settings to help you fine-tune your usage of the query result cache.

QUERY RESULT WINDOW SIZE

In section 2.2.4 we stressed the importance of paging your search results in Solr to ensure optimal query performance. The <queryResultWindowSize> element allows you to prepare additional pages when you execute a query.

Imagine your application shows 10 documents per page and in most cases your users only look at the first and second pages. You can set `<queryResultWindowSize>` to 20 to avoid having to re-execute the query to retrieve the second page of results. In general, you want to set this element to two or three times the page size used by your most important queries. But if you set it too large, then every query is paying the price of loading more documents than you are showing to the user. If your users rarely go beyond page 1, then it is better to set this element to the page size. You can determine the percentage of queries for additional pages of results by searching the Solr log files, looking for a `start` parameter greater than zero.

QUERY RESULT MAX DOCS CACHED

As we discussed in section 4.4.1, you have to set a maximum size for Solr caches; but this doesn't affect the size of each individual entry in the cache. As you can imagine, a result set holding millions of documents in the cache would greatly impact available memory in Solr. The `<queryResultMaxDocsCached>` element allows you to limit the number of documents cached for each entry in the query result cache. Users only look at the first couple of pages in most search applications, so you should generally set this to no more than two or three times the page size.

ENABLE LAZY FIELD LOADING

A common design pattern in Solr is to have a query return a subset of fields for each document. For instance, in our example query (listing 4.12), we requested the `name`, `price`, `features`, and `score` fields. But the documents in the index have many more fields, such as `category`, `popularity`, `manufacturedate`, and so forth. If your application adopts this common design pattern, you may want to set `<enableLazyFieldLoading>` to `true` to avoid loading unwanted fields. Our example documents do not have many fields, so it's easy to overlook the benefit of this setting. In practice, most documents have many fields, so it's a good idea to load fields lazily.

4.4.4 *Document cache*

The query result cache holds a list of internal document IDs that match a query, so even if the query results are cached, Solr still needs to load the documents from disk to produce search results. The document cache is used to store documents loaded from disk in memory keyed by their internal document IDs. It follows that the query result cache uses the document cache to find cached versions of documents in the cached result set.

This raises the question of whether it makes sense to warm the document cache. There's a good argument to be made against autowarming this cache, because there's no way to ensure the documents you are warming have any relation to queries and filters being autowarmed from the query result and filter caches. If you are constantly indexing, and the documents a query returns are constantly changing, you could be spending time recreating documents that may not benefit your warmed filter and query result caches. On the other hand, if most of your index is relatively static, the document cache may provide value.

4.4.5   *Field value cache*

The last cache we'll mention is field value, which is strictly used by Lucene and is not managed by Solr. The field value cache provides fast access to stored field values by internal document ID. It is used during sorting and when building documents for the response. As this is an advanced topic, we'll refer you to the Lucene JavaDoc (`org.apache.lucene.search.FieldCache`) for more information.

At this point, you know how Solr processes queries using a request-handling pipeline, and you know how to optimize query performance using new-searcher warming and caching.

4.5   *Remaining configuration options*

We have covered many of the most commonly used settings in the *solrconfig.xml* file in this chapter, but there are many additional features that we have not yet covered. Solr contains many expert-level settings that are unfortunately beyond the scope of what we can cover in this book. One tremendously helpful characteristic of Solr is that the example *solrconfig.xml* shipped with Solr contains extensive comments explaining what most of these additional settings control and how to configure them. We encourage you to spend time exploring *solrconfig.xml* on your own to learn more about all of the knobs you can use to tune Solr's performance and enable new features.

Because *solrconfig.xml* is so central to how you enable new features in Solr, this is not the last time we will see this file. As we cover new features throughout *Solr in Action*, you will see how those features are enabled in *solrconfig.xml*. You will see how to configure response formats, how to define new search handlers and search components specifically for your search application, and how to properly tune your Solr servers for a production environment and for optimal relevancy. In short, there is a lot more to learn about configuring Solr, but you should now have an excellent grasp of what kind of configuration options are available and important as you initially get up and running with Solr.

4.6   *Summary*

Definitely give yourself a pat on the back after working through this relatively long chapter! We know learning about configuration is not the most interesting of topics. At this point you should have a solid understanding of how to configure Solr, particularly for optimizing query-processing performance. Specifically, you learned that Solr's request-processing pipeline is composed of a unified request dispatcher and a highly configurable request handler. We saw how a search-request handler has four phases and that you can customize each phase. The `/browse` handler for the Solritas application served as a good example of using default parameters and custom components (such as `spellcheck`) to enable a feature-rich search experience while simplifying client-application code.

We also learned how Solr processes query requests using a read-only view of the index with a component called a searcher. There is only one active searcher in Solr at any time, and a new searcher needs to be created before updates to the index are visible. Closing the currently active searcher and opening a new one can be an expensive operation that affects query performance. To minimize the impact on query performance, Solr allows you to configure static queries to warm up a new searcher. Properly managing the new searcher warm-up process is one of the most important configuration tasks you'll need to handle for your search application. As such, we'll cover this further in chapter 12.

Solr also provides a number of important caches that need to be fine-tuned for your application. We looked at the filter, query result, document, and field value caches. For each cache, you need to set a maximum size and eviction policy based on the real usage of your application. The Solr administration console provides key statistics, such as the hit ratio, to help you determine if your caches are sized correctly.

Caches can be warmed when creating a new searcher, which also helps optimize query performance. For example, you can use cache autowarming to prepopulate Solr's filter cache with the most popular filters used by queries in your application. Cache autowarming, although powerful, can also lead to large wait times while a new searcher warms up. We advise you to start with small `autowarmCount` values and monitor searcher warm-up time closely. Cache tuning will also be covered further in chapter 12.

Although the configuration options presented in this chapter represent the most important settings you will generally want to adjust, this chapter falls far short of covering every available configuration option (and that is not our goal with this chapter or even this book). Our goal was to get you comfortable with how Solr configuration works, while deferring coverage of many additional configuration options until we introduce the corresponding features throughout the rest of this book and learn about their performance implications.

As we mentioned at the beginning of the chapter, we also chose to skip over the index-related settings in *solrconfig.xml* until we covered the basics of indexing. In the next chapter, you will learn about the Solr indexing process and index-related configuration settings.

Indexing 5

This chapter covers

- Designing your schema for indexing documents
- Defining fields and field types in *schema.xml*
- Using field types for structured data
- Handling update requests, commits, and atomic updates
- Managing index settings in *solrconfig.xml*

In chapter 3, we learned how Solr finds documents using an inverted index, which in its simplest form is a dictionary of terms and a list of documents in which each term occurs. Solr uses this index to match terms in a user's query with the documents in which they occur. In this chapter, we'll learn how Solr processes documents to build the index. A key factor in indexing documents is text analysis. In this chapter, we'll focus on the indexing process and nontext fields, saving a detailed discussion of text analysis until chapter 6.

At the end of this chapter, you'll know how to index documents in Solr and you'll understand key concepts such as fields, field types, and schema design. As a prerequisite, this chapter will be easier to work through if you have the Solr example server running locally, which we covered in chapter 2. You'll still be able to follow along with most examples without running Solr, if you prefer to read this chapter and then come back to do the hands-on activities.

5.1　*Example microblog search application*

Throughout this chapter and the next, we'll design and implement an indexing and text-analysis solution for searching microblog content from popular social media sites like Twitter. We use *microblog* as a generic term for the short, informal messages and other media that people share with each other on social networks. Examples of microblogs are tweets on Twitter, Facebook posts, and check-ins on Foursquare. In this chapter, we'll define the fields and field types to represent microblogs in Solr and learn how to add documents to Solr.

In chapter 6, we'll learn how to do text analysis on microblog content using built-in Solr tools. Let's get started by looking at the types of documents we'll be working with in this example and how users might want to search them.

5.1.1　*Representing content for searching*

To begin, table 5.1 shows some fields from a fictitious tweet that we'll use throughout this chapter to learn about indexing documents in Solr. Even if you're not interested in analyzing social media content, the lessons we learn by working through this example have broad applicability for most search applications.

Table 5.1　Fields of a fictitious tweet

Field	Value
id	1
screen_name	@thelabdude
type	post
timestamp	2012-05-22T09:30:22Z
lang	en
user_id	99991234567890
favorites_count	10
text	#Yummm :) Drinking a latte at Caffé Grecco in SF's historic North Beach. Learning text analysis with #SolrInAction by @ManningBooks on my iPad

Each document in a Solr index is made up of fields, and each field has a specific type that determines how it's stored, searched, and analyzed. In table 5.1, there are eight fields in our microblog document.[1] Think about how a user might find microblogs using these fields. We think the screen_name, type, timestamp, lang,

---

[1]　For a thorough discussion of all the available fields in a tweet, we recommend reading Map of a Tweet: www.slaw.ca/wp-content/uploads/2011/11/map-of-a-tweet-copy.pdf.

and `text` fields are good candidates to use from a search perspective because they contain information that a typical user could use to build a query. For example, you can imagine a user who wants to see all English tweets (`lang:en`) from a specific user (`screen_name:thelabdude`) that occurred after a certain date (`timestamp:[2012-05-01T00:00:00Z TO *]`).

You could index all of these fields, but if you're developing a large-scale system to support millions of documents and high query volumes, you only want to include the fields that will be searched by your users. For example, the `user_id` field is an internal identifier for Twitter so it's unlikely users will ever want to search on this field. In general, each field increases the size of your index, so you should only include fields that add value for users.

The `favorites_count` field is the number of favorites the author of the tweet has, not the number of favorites for the tweet. This field is interesting because it has useful information from a UI perspective, but doesn't seem like a good candidate as a parameter for a search query. We'll address how to handle these display-oriented fields in section 5.2 when we discuss stored versus indexed fields.

Now let's think about how users might build a query using these fields, as that will help us decide how to represent these fields in our Solr index. Figure 5.1 depicts a fictitious search form based on the fields for our example microblog search application.

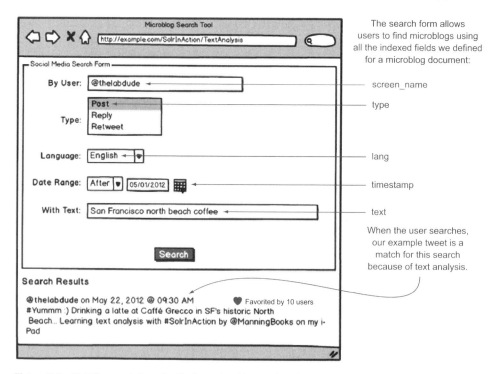

Figure 5.1   Fictitious web form for finding microblogs using the `screen_name`, `type`, `lang`, `timestamp`, and `text` fields.

Each field that we identified as being useful from a search perspective is represented on the form. This is a key point in designing your search application in that you need to think about how users will search a specific field in your index; that will help determine how the field is defined in Solr.

Now we have a conceptual understanding of the fields in our example application and an idea of how users will search for documents using these fields. Next, let's get a high-level understanding of how to add documents to Solr.

5.1.2   Overview of the Solr indexing process

At a high level, the Solr indexing process distills down to three key tasks:

1   Convert a document from its native format into a format supported by Solr, such as XML or JSON.

2   Add the document to Solr using one of several well-defined interfaces, typically HTTP POST.

3   Configure Solr to apply transformations to the text in the document during indexing.

Figure 5.2 provides a high-level overview of these three basic steps to getting your document indexed in Solr.

Solr supports several formats for indexing your document, including XML, JSON, and CSV. In figure 5.2, we chose XML because its self-describing format makes it easy to understand. Here is how our example tweet would look using the Solr XML format.

Listing 5.1   XML document used to index the example tweet in Solr

You can add more than one document at a time, each wrapped in a <doc> tag.

Tell Solr we're adding a new document to the index.

Provide the name and value for each field in the document.

```
<add>
  <doc>
    <field name="id">1</field>
    <field name="screen_name">@thelabdude</field>
    <field name="type">post</field>
    <field name="timestamp">2012-05-22T09:30:22Z</field>
    <field name="lang">en</field>
    <field name="user_id">99991234567890</field>
    <field name="favorites_count">10</field>
    <field name="text">#Yummm :) Drinking a latte at Caffé
        Grecco in SF's historic North Beach... Learning text
        analysis with #SolrInAction by @ManningBooks on my i-Pad</field>
  </doc>
</add>
```

Notice that each field is represented in the XML and that the syntax is rather simple; you only have to define the field name and value for each field. What you don't see is anything about text analysis or field type. This is because you define how fields are analyzed in the *schema.xml* document depicted in figure 5.2.

Recall from our discussion in chapter 2 that Solr provides a basic HTTP-based interface to all of its core services, including a document-update service for adding and updating documents. At the top left of figure 5.2, we depict sending the XML for

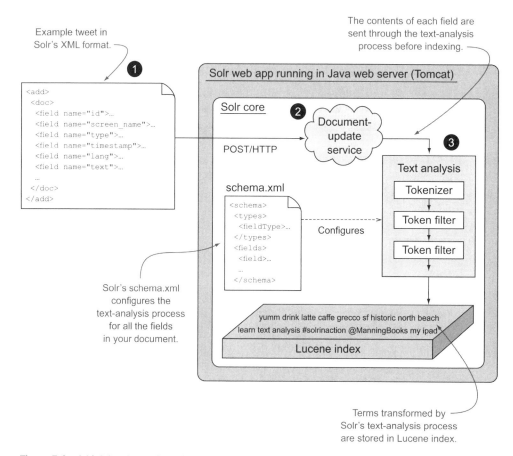

Figure 5.2   A high-level overview of three main steps to indexing a document. In step 1, we represent the tweet in an XML format supported by Solr. In step 2, we send the XML document to Solr's document-update service using HTTP POST. In step 3, each field is analyzed based on the configuration defined in *schema.xml* before being added to the index.

our example tweet using an HTTP POST to a document-update service in Solr. We'll go into more detail about how to add specific document types such as XML, JSON, and CSV later in the chapter. For now, think of the document-update service as an abstract component that validates the contents of each field in a document and then invokes the text-analysis process. After each field is analyzed, the resulting text is added to the index, therefore making the document available for search.

We'll spend more time on how the indexing process works in section 5.5. A high-level overview of the indexing process is sufficient for now, as we need to focus on more foundational concepts first. Specifically, we need to understand how Solr uses the *schema.xml* depicted in figure 5.2 to drive the indexing process.

The *schema.xml* defines the fields and field types for your documents. For simple applications, the fields to search and their types may be obvious. In general, though, it helps to do some up-front planning about your schema.

5.2   Designing your schema

With our example microblog search application, we dove right in and defined what a document is and which fields we want to index. In practice, this process isn't always obvious for a real application, so it helps to do some up-front design and planning work. In this section, we learn about key design considerations for search applications. Specifically, you'll learn to answer the following key questions about your search application:

- What is a document in your index?
- How is each document uniquely identified?
- What fields in your documents can be searched by users?
- Which fields should be displayed to users in the search results?

Let's begin by determining the appropriate granularity of a document in your search application, as that impacts how you answer the other questions.

5.2.1   Document granularity

Determining what a document should represent in your Solr index drives the entire schema-design process. In some cases it's obvious, such as with our tweet example; the text content is typically short, so each tweet will be a document. But if the content you want to index is large, such as a technical computer book, you may want to treat subsections of a large document as the indexed unit. The key is to think about what your users will want to see in the search results. Let's look at a different example to help you think about what a document is for your index.

Imagine searching for `"text analysis"` on a website that sells technical computer books. If the site treated each book as a single document, the user would see *Solr in Action* in the search results, but would need to page through the table of contents or index to find specific places where `"text analysis"` occurs in the book. In figure 5.3, the left-side image depicts how search results might look when an entire book is indexed as a single document.

If the site treated individual chapters in each book as documents in the index, then the search results might show the user the "Text analysis" chapter in *Solr in Action* as the top result, as seen on the right side of figure 5.3. Because text analysis is a central concept in search, however, most of the other chapters in this book and other search books would be included as highly relevant results as well. Being too granular can therefore overwhelm users with too many results to wade through.

You may also need to consider the type of content you're indexing, as splitting a technical computer book by chapter seems to make sense but splitting a fiction novel by chapter doesn't seem like a good approach. In the end, it's your choice what makes a document in your index, but definitely consider how document granularity impacts user experience. In general, you want your documents to be as granular as possible without causing your users to miss the forest for the trees.

Indexing an entire book as a document forces users to go looking in the book contents to find pages relevant to their search.

Indexing each chapter as a document allows you to return results that are more obviously relevant but can overwhelm users with too many results.

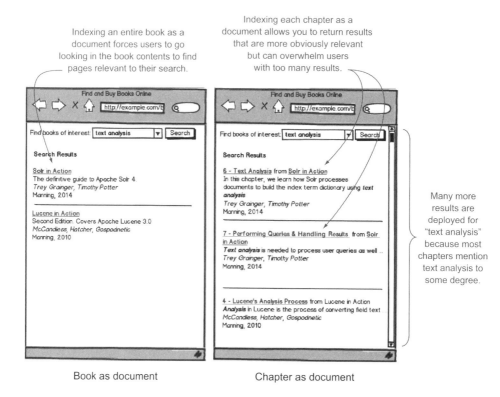

Many more results are deployed for "text analysis" because most chapters mention text analysis to some degree.

Book as document   Chapter as document

Figure 5.3   Comparison of search results when indexing an entire book as a document versus indexing individual chapters as documents

Solr hit highlighting

As a quick aside, we should note that Solr offers a feature called hit highlighting that allows you to highlight relevant sections of longer documents in search results. This is useful when you can't break long documents into smaller units but still want to help your users quickly navigate to highly relevant sections in large documents. For example, we could use hit highlighting to show short snippets of text surrounding the phrase `"text analysis"` in any documents containing that phrase. We discuss hit highlighting in depth in chapter 9.

5.2.2   *Unique key*

Once you've identified what a document is, you should determine how to uniquely identify each document in the index. For a book, this might be the ISBN number. For a chapter, it might be the ISBN number plus the chapter number. Solr doesn't require a unique identifier for each document, but if one is supplied, Solr uses it to avoid duplicating documents in your index. If you have a database background, the unique identifier is similar to a primary key for a row in a table. If a document with the same unique key is added to the index, Solr overwrites the existing record with the latest document. We'll return to the discussion of unique keys in section 5.3.5.

For our example microblog search application from section 5.1, the tweet already includes a unique identifier field: id. But if we index content from a variety of social media sources, we'd probably add something like twitter: as a prefix to differentiate this document from a Facebook post with the same numeric ID value.

5.2.3   *Indexed fields*

Once you've determined what a document represents for your index and how to uniquely identify each document, the next step is to determine the *indexed fields* in the document. The best way to think about indexed fields is to ask whether a typical user could develop a meaningful query using that field. Another way to decide if a field should be indexed is to determine if your users would miss it if you did not provide it as a queryable option in your search form.

For example, every book has a title and an author. When searching for books, people generally expect to find books of interest based on title and author, so these fields should both be indexed. Although every book has an editor, users typically don't search by editor name when trying to find a book to read, so the editor's name would likely not need to be an indexed field. Conversely, if you were building a search index for the book publishing industry, it's likely that your users would want to search by editor name, so you'd include that as an indexed field.

In addition to enabling searching, you will also need to mark your field as indexed if you need to sort, facet, group by, provide query suggestions for, or execute function queries on values within a field. With certain advanced settings enabled (discussed in chapter 9), marking fields as indexed can also be useful for speeding up hit highlighting. Each of these capabilities is covered later in the book, with many getting their own chapter. Essentially, if you need to perform an operation upon the values of a field beyond returning the original field value in the search results, you will most likely need to index the field.

Determining which fields to include in the index is specific to every search application. Take a moment to think about the indexed fields for your documents. Keep these fresh in your mind, as you'll need to refer to them as you work through the rest of this chapter. As we discussed, the screen_name, type, timestamp, lang, and text fields should be indexed for our microblog example. The id and user_id fields are used internally by Twitter and are unlikely to be missed if you don't allow users to search by these fields.

5.2.4   *Stored fields*

Although users probably won't search by editor name to find a book to read, we may still want to display the editor's name in the search results. In general, your documents may contain fields that aren't useful from a search perspective but are still useful for displaying search results. In Solr, these are called *stored fields*. The favorites _count field is a good example of a stored field that isn't indexed but is useful for display purposes. You can imagine users would find it useful to see which authors have more favorites than others in search results, but it's unlikely that users would want to search by this field. Of course, a field may be indexed *and* stored, such as the `screen_name`, `timestamp`, and `text` fields in our microblog search application. Each of these fields can be searched and displayed in results.

As a search-application architect, one of your goals should be to minimize the size of your index. If you're considering Solr, then most likely you have an application that needs to scale to handle large volumes of documents and users. Each stored field in your index consumes disk space and requires CPU and I/O resources to read the stored value to return it in search results. You should choose your stored fields wisely, particularly for large-scale applications.

At this point you should have a good idea about the types of questions you need to answer to design your search application. Once you've settled on a plan, it's time to roll up your sleeves and work with Solr's *schema.xml* to implement your design. As we saw in figure 5.2, *schema.xml* is the main configuration document Solr uses to understand how to index your documents. Let's preview the main sections of *schema.xml* so that we have an idea of what's in store for us over the next couple of sections in this chapter.

5.2.5   *Preview of schema.xml*

In the next few sections, we'll build a valid *schema.xml* document for our example microblog search application. The *schema.xml* file is in the *conf/* directory for your Solr core. The *schema.xml* for the example Solr server is in *$SOLR_INSTALL/example/solr/collection1/conf/*. The following listing contains a condensed version of the example *schema.xml* provided with Solr to give you a feel for the XML syntax and important elements.[2]

Listing 5.2   Major sections of Solr's *schema.xml* document

```
<schema name="example"            ◁─  The schema name is used
    version="1.5">                     only for display purposes.
    <fields>                                       Field elements
        <field name="id" type="string" indexed="true" stored="true" .../>
        <field name="name" type="text_general" indexed="true" stored="true"/>
        <field name="cat" type="string" indexed="true" stored="true" .../>
        ...
        <dynamicField name="*_s" type="string" indexed="true" stored="true"/>
        <dynamicField name="*_t" type="text_general" indexed="true"  .../>
        ...
    </fields>                          Define which field to use to
    <uniqueKey>id</uniqueKey>     ◁─   uniquely identify each document.
    <copyField source="cat" dest="text"/>   ◁─
    ...                                        Copies a value from
    <copyField source="manu" dest="text"/>  ◁─  one field to another.
```

Version is used internally by Solr to enable specific features.

Field elements represent the fields in your documents.

---

[2] To see the full example schema, click the Schema link from the Solr administration page, which loads the *schema.xml* into your browser.

```
<types>
  <fieldType name="string" class="solr.StrField" .../>
  <fieldType name="boolean" class="solr.BoolField" .../>
  ...
  <fieldType name="tint" class="solr.TrieIntField" .../>
  <fieldType name="tfloat" class="solr.TrieFloatField" .../>
  <fieldType name="text_general" class="solr.TextField">
    <analyzer type="index">
      <tokenizer class="solr.StandardTokenizerFactory"/>
      <filter class="solr.StopFilterFactory" .../>
      <filter class="solr.LowerCaseFilterFactory"/>
    </analyzer>
    <analyzer type="query">
      <tokenizer class="solr.StandardTokenizerFactory"/>
      <filter class="solr.StopFilterFactory" .../>
      <filter class="solr.SynonymFilterFactory" .../>
      <filter class="solr.LowerCaseFilterFactory"/>
    </analyzer>
  </fieldType>
  ...
</types>
</schema>
```

> **fieldType elements govern if and how a field is analyzed.**

> **A fieldType configuration useful for analyzing general text.**

At a glance, it's easy to be overwhelmed by all of the details in this document. By the end of this chapter, you'll have a clear understanding of all these details and you'll be well equipped to craft your own *schema.xml*. For now, you'll notice the three main sections of the *schema.xml* document:

1. The `<fields>` element, containing `<field>` and `<dynamicField>` elements used to define the basic structure of your documents
2. Miscellaneous elements, such as `<uniqueKey>` and `<copyField>`, which are listed after the `<fields>` element
3. Field types under the `<types>` element that determine how dates, numbers, and text fields are handled in Solr

We'll work through each of these main sections in the pages to come. Let's begin by looking at the `<fields>` section.

5.3   *Defining fields in schema.xml*

The `<fields>` section in *schema.xml* defines `<field>` elements for all fields in your document. Solr uses the field definitions from *schema.xml* to figure out what kind of analysis needs to be performed for fields in your documents in order to add their content as terms to the inverted search index (covered in chapter 3). In this section, we learn how to define fields, dynamic fields, and copy fields in *schema.xml*. Since we worked through the main concepts behind schema design in section 5.2, we're ready to define the `<field>` elements for our example microblog search application. The next listing defines the indexed and stored fields for our example application.

Listing 5.3   Field elements for our example microblog search application

```
                                                        Define the fields of our example microblog
<schema name="example" version="1.5">                  application under the <fields> element.
    <fields>
      <field name="id" type="string" indexed="true" stored="true"
             required="true"/>
      <field name="screen_name" type="string" indexed="true" stored="true"/>
      <field name="type" type="string" indexed="true" stored="true"/>
      <field name="timestamp" type="tdate" indexed="true" stored="true"/>
      <field name="lang" type="string" indexed="true" stored="true"/>
      <field name="favorites_count" type="int"
             indexed="true" stored="true"/>
      <field name="text" type="text_microblog"
             indexed="true" stored="true"/>
      ...
    </fields>
    ...
</schema>
```

Field used to uniquely identify documents in the index. →

Field is indexed for sorting and is stored for display purposes. →

Fields must define a name and type and whether they're indexed and/or stored.

Text field will be analyzed using a field type called text_microblog.

With these field definitions, Solr knows how to index microblog documents so they can be searched using a form similar to figure 5.1. When defining a field in *schema.xml*, there are a few required attributes you must provide to Solr.

5.3.1   *Required field attributes*

Each field has a unique name that's used when constructing queries. For instance, the query `screen_name:thelabdude` searches the `screen_name` field for value `thelabdude`. In listing 5.3, we defined the `screen_name` field as

```
<field name="screen_name"
    type="string"
    indexed="true"
    stored="true" />
```

In layman's terms, this definition means that the `screen_name` field is indexed and stored and contains `string` values. Each field must define a `type` attribute that identifies the `<fieldType>` to use for that field; we cover field types in detail in the next section. Each field must also define whether it's indexed and/or stored. As we discussed in section 5.2, indexed fields can be searched and sorted upon (among other features we'll discuss throughout the rest of the book), and stored fields can be returned in search results for display purposes. A field can be both indexed and stored, as is the case for most of the fields in our example.

Also notice that there are no nested fields in Solr; all fields are siblings in *schema.xml*, implying a flat document structure. As we discussed in chapter 3, documents in Solr need to be denormalized into a flat structure and must contain all the fields needed to support your search requirements. This means that no relational structure will allow you to join with other documents to pull in additional information to service queries or generate results.

> **Joins in Solr**
>
> You'll undoubtedly encounter content on the web about doing document joins in Solr. We'll address this functionality in detail in chapter 15. For now, it's important to understand that Solr joins are more like subqueries in SQL than joins. A typical use case is to find the parent documents of child documents that match your search criteria. In our example microblog application, for example, we could use Solr joins to bring back the original post instead of retweets.

One thing that can be confusing is that when a field is stored, Solr stores the original value and not the analyzed value. For example, in listing 5.3, we declared the `text` field with `indexed="true"` and `stored="true"`. This means that the `text` field will be searchable and you can return the *original* text in search results. Solr doesn't return the analyzed value in search results when you ask for the field back. Of course, if you don't return a field in search results, it doesn't need to be stored.

Even though it increases the size of your index and therefore slows down queries, there's also a case to be made for storing all fields for a document. If you plan to update fields in documents within Solr after they're indexed (as opposed to resending the full documents from an external source) you'll need to store all fields so that Solr has a copy of the original content for each field. We'll learn more about updating documents in section 5.6.3.

5.3.2 *Multivalued fields*

So far, our microblog search application uses only a small number of simple fields. Let's add a few more fields into the mix to exercise some of Solr's strengths in dealing with more complex document structures. Specifically, let's add support for a `links` field that contains zero or more links associated with each document. As you've probably seen on Twitter, users can embed links to related content, such as a photo or article on the web. Here's an example of another fictitious tweet with two links embedded:

```
Just downloaded the ebook of #SolrInAction from @ManningBooks http://bit.ly/
T3eGYG to learn more about #Solr http://bit.ly/3ynriE
```

The links in this document are shortened URLs provided by http://bitly.com that resolve to the websites shown in table 5.2.

Table 5.2   Real URLs for shortened links in the example tweet

Shortened URL	Real URL
http://bit.ly/T3eGYG	http://manning.com/grainger/
http://bit.ly/3ynriE	http://lucene.apache.org/solr/

From a search perspective, adding resolved links to your index allows users to find social media content that links to a specific website or page. You can imagine users wanting to find all tweets that link to the *Solr In Action* page at http://manning.com/grainger/. Since this example contains two links, we need a way to encode two values for one field. In Solr, fields that can have more than one value per document are called multivalued fields. In *schema.xml*, you declare a multivalued field by setting `multiValued="true"` on the field definition:

```
<field name="link"
    type="string"
    indexed="true"
    stored="true"
    multiValued="true"/>
```

When you add a document that has multiple links, you add multiple `link` fields in the XML document, as depicted in this listing.

Listing 5.4   Representing multivalued fields in XML during indexing

```
<add>
  <doc>
    <field name="id">2</field>
    ...
    <field name="link">http://manning.com/grainger/</field>
    <field name="link">http://lucene.apache.org/solr/</field>
    ...
  </doc>
</add>
```

> Reuse the same field name to populate a multivalued field during indexing.

When you're searching, you can query for `link:"http://manning.com/grainger/"` and Solr will look for matches across all values in a multivalued field.

So far, our microblog documents have had only a small number of fields, which made it easy to declare each field separately in *schema.xml*. In practice, not all documents are so simple or sparse. Let's look at another type of field, called a dynamic field, that helps deal with larger and more complex document structures.

5.3.3   *Dynamic fields*

In Solr, dynamic fields allow you to apply the same definition to any fields in your documents whose names match either a prefix or suffix pattern, such as s_* or *_s. Dynamic fields use a special naming scheme to apply the same field definition to any fields that match this kind of glob-style pattern. Dynamic fields help address common problems that occur when building search applications, including

- Modeling documents with many fields
- Supporting documents from diverse sources
- Adding new document sources

Let's look at each one of these use cases to get a good feel for what you can do with dynamic fields. You should first note that you don't need to use dynamic fields with Solr. It's perfectly acceptable to *not* use dynamic fields if none of these use cases apply to your application.

Also, Solr ignores the dynamic field definitions in your *schema.xml* until you start indexing documents that make use of them. In practice, many Solr users keep the extensive list of dynamic fields provided with the Solr example schema so they're there when needed, but ignored otherwise.

MODELING DOCUMENTS WITH MANY FIELDS

Dynamic fields help you model documents having many fields by allowing you to match a prefix or suffix pattern, applying the same field definition in *schema.xml* to any matching fields. In listing 5.3 we used the `string` field type for the `type`, `screen_name`, and `lang` fields. Moreover, each of these fields is stored and indexed; other than the name, each field definition is exactly the same.

Imagine that in addition to these three fields, we have dozens of `string` fields that are also stored and indexed. You can also type in an explicit definition for each of these fields or you can alternatively define a single `<dynamicField>` element to account for all of these string fields using a suffix pattern on the field name:

```
<dynamicField name="*_s" type="string" indexed="true" stored="true" />
```

With this glob pattern, any field with a name ending in _s will inherit this field definition, such as `subject_s`. Alternatively, you could use a prefix pattern, s_*. Dynamic fields therefore help save typing and simplify your *schema.xml* when you have many fields.

You can also use dynamic fields for multivalued fields, such as our links field in the previous section. The following dynamic field definition has `multiValued="true"`:

```
<dynamicField name="*_ss" type="string" indexed="true" stored="true"
    multiValued="true"/>
```

For multivalued links, your XML document would need to use `link_ss` as the field name for multiple links, as seen in this listing.

Listing 5.5 Using dynamic fields to represent multivalued fields during indexing

```
<add>
  <doc>
    <field name="id">9999012345679</field>
    ...
    <field name="link_ss">http://manning.com/grainger/</field>      ⎫ Including
    <field name="link_ss">http://lucene.apache.org/solr/</field>    ⎬ multiple
    ...                                                              ⎪ links using
  </doc>                                                             ⎪ dynamic
</add>                                                               ⎪ field
                                                                     ⎭ naming.
```

SUPPORTING DOCUMENTS FROM DIVERSE SOURCES

Another benefit of dynamic fields is that they help you support a mixture of documents that share a common base schema, but also have some unique fields. Of course, if your documents don't have a common base schema, they should probably not be in the same index! In our social media example, if we index documents from Twitter, Facebook, YouTube, and Google+, then documents from each of these sources will have some fields that are unique to each social network. We think it's more intuitive and maintainable to handle these source-specific fields as dynamic fields. For example, instead of defining many fields for each source as in the next example

Many Facebook-specific string fields that are stored and indexed.

```
<field name="facebook_f1" type="string" indexed="true" stored="true" />
<field name="facebook_f2" type="string" indexed="true" stored="true" />
<field name="facebook_fn" type="string" indexed="true" stored="true" />
...
<field name="twitter_f1" type="string" indexed="true" stored="true" />
<field name="twitter_f2" type="string" indexed="true" stored="true" />
<field name="twitter_fn" type="string" indexed="true" stored="true" />
```

Many Twitter-specific string fields that are stored and indexed.

you can accomplish the same using a single `string` dynamic field with the `*_s` suffix pattern as the name:

```
<dynamicField name="*_s" type="string" indexed="true" stored="true" />
```

When indexing, you need to send fields with the _s suffix, such as in the next listing.

Listing 5.6   Include source-specific fields during indexing using dynamic fields

```
<add>
  <doc>
    <field name="id">9999012345678</field>
    <field name="screen_name">@thelabdude</field>
    <field name="type">post</field>
    ...
    <field name="facebook_f1_s">hello</field>
    <field name="facebook_f2_s">world</field>
    <field name="twitter_f1_s">foo</field>
    <field name="twitter_f2_s">bar</field>
  </doc>
</add>
```

Matches the `*_s` `<dynamicField>` definition, which is a string field.

ADDING NEW DOCUMENT SOURCES

If you add a new data source for your application that has fields you haven't encountered before, then you can include them during indexing and they will be picked up automatically when using dynamic fields. New social networks seem to come online every day, so we wouldn't want to constantly rework our *schema.xml* to handle documents from these new sources. With dynamic fields, you can include new fields introduced by your new document source without making any changes to the *schema.xml*.

Suppose you want to add support for a new social network that includes a field that captures the phase of the moon when the content was posted to the network (perhaps it's a dating site). With dynamic fields, you can include this field as a string in your documents:

```
<field name="moon_phase_s">waxing crescent</field>
```

Although dynamic fields can be a handy feature on the indexing side, there's no real magic on the query side. When querying for documents that were indexed with dynamic fields, you must use the full field name in the query. You can't formulate queries to find a match in all `string` fields by querying with a prefix or suffix pattern: `*_s:coffee`. Rather, you need to explicitly identify which `string` fields to query, such as `subject_s:coffee keyword_s:coffee`, and so on. But if you want to find matches in more than one field, dynamic or static, Solr provides a clever way to do that with copy fields.

5.3.4 Copy fields

In Solr, copy fields allow you to populate one field from one or more other fields. Specifically, copy fields support two use cases that are common in most search applications:

- Populate a single catch-all field with the contents of multiple fields.
- Apply different text analysis to the same field content to create a new searchable field.

CREATE A CATCH-ALL FIELD FROM MANY FIELDS

In most search applications, users are presented with a single search box in which to enter a query. The intent of this approach is to help your users quickly find documents without having to fill out a complicated form; think about how successful a simple search box has been for Google. In our tweet example, you might think it's an easy decision: search the tweet text and you're done. But with this approach, users wouldn't find our example tweet if they searched for `@thelabdude` because that information is contained in the `screen_name` field and not the `text`. In addition, if a tweet contains shortened bit.ly-style URLs, searches in the text field for the "resolved" URL won't match, as those are stored in the `links` field. What we want here is a catch-all search field that contains the text from the `screen_name`, `text`, and resolved `link` fields. Thankfully, Solr makes it easy to create a single catch-all search field from many other fields in your document using the `<copyField>` directive.

First, you need to define a destination field that other fields will be copied into; let's name this field `catch_all`:

```
<field name="catch_all"
    type="text_en"
    indexed="true"
    stored="false"
    multiValued="true"/>
```

The catch-all field shouldn't be stored as it's populated from another field.

Destination field must be multivalued if any of the source fields are multivalued.

This looks like any other field except there are two important aspects to the definition.

First, notice that this field isn't stored (`stored="false"`), which makes sense because we probably don't want to display a blob of many fields concatenated together to our users. In fact, even if you wanted to do this, you can't because there's no original value for Solr to return for copy fields. Remember that Solr returns the original value for a stored field.

Second, if any of the source fields are multivalued, the destination field must be a multivalued field (`multiValued="true"`). In our case, the `link` field is multivalued, so we must define our copy field as multivalued as well. Also, you must set `multiValued="true"` if you copy more than one source field into the destination field, even if all the source fields are single valued.

Now that we've defined the destination field, we need to tell Solr which fields to copy from, using the `<copyField>` directive. The next listing shows how we'd copy the values from the `screen_name`, `text`, and `link` fields into our `catch_all` field using Solr's `<copyField>` directive:

Listing 5.7   Using the `<copyField>` directive to populate the `catch_all` field

```
<schema>
  <fields>
    ...
  </fields>
  <copyField source="screen_name" dest="catch_all" />      Raw contents of
  <copyField source="text" dest="catch_all" />             screen_name, text, and link
  <copyField source="link" dest="catch_all" />             fields copied into catch_all.
  <types>
    ...
  </types>
</schema>
```

Note that the `<copyField>` element is a sibling of the `<fields>` and `<types>` elements in *schema.xml*. Take a moment to think about why this is the case. The best way to make sense of this is that you must define the source and destination (`dest`) fields first, then connect them with the `copyField` directive after all fields have been defined.

APPLY DIFFERENT ANALYZERS TO A FIELD

You also may want to analyze the contents of a single field differently. As we'll see in chapter 6, stemming is a technique that transforms terms into a common base form, known as a *stem*, in order to improve Recall (covered in chapter 3). With stemming, the terms `fishing`, `fished`, and `fishes` can all be reduced to a common stem of `fish`. Thus, stemming can help your users find documents without having to think about all the possible linguistic forms of a word, which is a good approach for general text search fields.

Consider how stemming would affect a type-ahead suggestion box (autosuggest). In this case, stemming would work against your users in that you could only suggest the stemmed values and not the full terms. With stemming enabled, for example, your search application wouldn't be able to suggest `humane` or `humanities` when the user started typing `human` in the autosuggest box. Solr copy fields give you the flexibility to enable or disable certain text-analysis features like stemming without having to duplicate storage in your index. Consider the following listing from *schema.xml*.

Listing 5.8   Using `copyField` to apply different text analysis to the same text

```
<field name="text"
    type="stemmed_text"
    indexed="true"
    stored="true"/>
<field name="auto_suggest"
    type="unstemmed_text"
```

```
        indexed="true"
        stored="false"
        multiValued="true"/>
...
<copyField source="text" dest="auto_suggest" />   ◁──┐
```

> **Raw text content from the text field copied into the auto_suggest field to be analyzed using the unstemmed_text field type.**

In this case, the text field has field type stemmed_text, which presumably means the text is stemmed. The auto_suggest field isn't stemmed. We use the <copyField> directive to populate the auto_suggest field with unstemmed text from the text field. Under the covers, Solr sends the raw, unanalyzed contents of the text field to the auto_suggest field, which allows a different text-analysis strategy. The original text value is stored only once. To reiterate, you wouldn't return the original value of the auto_suggest field in search results, so it has stored="false". You can learn more about how to implement your own autosuggest capabilities in chapter 10.

5.3.5   *Unique key field*

In section 5.2.2, we discussed that it's a good idea to make your documents uniquely identifiable in the index using a unique ID value. To recap, if you provide a unique identifier field for each of your documents, Solr will avoid creating duplicates during indexing. In addition, if you plan to distribute your Solr index across multiple servers, you must provide a unique identifier for your documents. For these reasons, we recommend defining a unique identifier for your documents from the start. In our microblog example, the id field is unique, so we configure Solr to use that field as the unique key for documents using the <uniqueKey> element in *schema.xml*.

> **Listing 5.9   The <uniqueKey> element identifies the unique ID field for documents**

```
<uniqueKey>id</uniqueKey>
```

One thing to note is that it's best to use a primitive field type, such as string or long, for the field you indicate as being the <uniqueKey/> as that ensures Solr doesn't make any changes to the value during indexing. We've seen instances in which Solr doesn't return results correctly if you don't use string as the type for text-based keys. Save yourself some trouble and use string or one of the other primitive field types for your unique key field.

At this point, we've covered all the basic aspects of defining fields in *schema.xml*. You should also have a good understanding of when to use multivalued, dynamic, and copy fields. It's now time to dig into the next major section of Solr's *schema.xml* to learn how to define field types.

5.4   *Field types for structured nontext fields*

In this section, we learn to define field types for handling structured data like dates, language codes, and usernames. In chapter 6, we learn how to define field types for text fields like the body text of our example tweet. In general, Solr provides a number of built-in field types for structured data, such as numbers, dates, and geo location

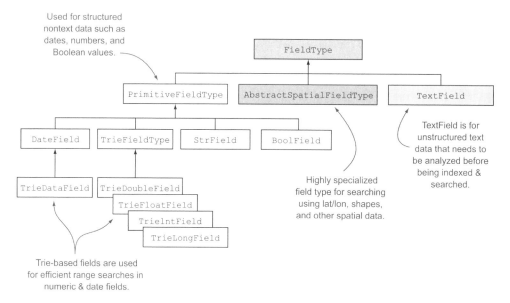

Figure 5.4   Class diagram of commonly used field types from the `org.apache.solr.schema` **Java package**

fields. Figure 5.4 shows a class diagram of some of the more commonly used field types in Solr.

Let's begin our discussion of field types for nontext data by looking at one of the most common field types: `string`.

5.4.1   String fields

For our example tweet, in addition to the `text` field, we decided that `screen_name`, `type`, `timestamp`, and `lang` should be indexed fields. Now we need to decide the appropriate type for each field. It turns out that each of these fields contains structured data that doesn't need to be analyzed. For example, the `lang` field contains a standard ISO-639-1 language code used to identify the language of the tweet, such as en. Users can query the `lang` field to find English tweets, as shown in figure 5.5.

Because the language code is already standardized, we don't want Solr to make any changes to it during indexing and query processing. Solr provides the `string` field type for fields that contain structured values that shouldn't be altered in any way. The next listing shows how the `string` field type is defined in *schema.xml*.

Listing 5.10   Field type definition for `string` **fields in *schema.xml***

```
<fieldType name="string" class="solr.StrField"
    sortMissingLast="true" omitNorms="true"/>
```

Behind the scenes, all field types are implemented by a Java class: in this case, `solr` `.StrField`. At runtime, `solr.StrField` resolves to the built-in Solr class `org.apache`

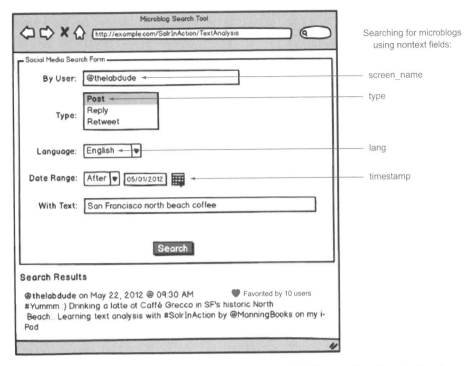

Figure 5.5 Mircoblog search application web form used to find documents using structured nontext fields

.solr.schema.StrField. Any time you see solr. as a prefix of a class in *schema.xml*, you know this translates to the fully qualified Java package org.apache.solr.schema. This shorthand notation helps reduce clutter in your *schema.xml*. The sortMissing-Last and omitNorms attributes are advanced options that we'll discuss in more detail in section 5.4.4.

If we use the string field type for our lang field, Solr will take the value en from our document and store it in the index unaltered as en during indexing. At query time, you also need to pass the exact value en to match English documents. In figure 5.5, the user selected English, which needs to be translated into en when processing the form. The string <fieldType> also seems like a good type for the screen_name and type fields, but what about timestamp?

5.4.2   Date fields

A common approach to searching on date fields is to allow users to specify a date range. In figure 5.5, the user searched for microblogs that occurred after a specified date (05/01/2012). On the query side, this would be a range query on the time-stamp field:

```
timestamp:[2012-05-01T00:00:00Z TO *]
```

Because searching within a date range is such a common use case, Solr provides an optimized built-in `<fieldType>` called `tdate`, shown next.

```
<fieldType name="tdate" class="solr.TrieDateField" omitNorms="true"
    precisionStep="6" positionIncrementGap="0"/>
```

Admittedly, this looks a little scarier than the `string` type! The additional attributes like `precisionStep` and `positionIncrementGap` are advanced options that we'll address in section 5.4.4. Again, the `solr.TrieDateField` is Solr's shorthand notation for specifying the Java class name that implements this field type, which in this case is `org.apache.solr.schema.TrieDateField`. A `trie` is an advanced tree-based data structure that allows for efficient searching for numeric and date values by varying degrees of precision.

During indexing, Solr needs to know how to parse a date. Recall from section 5.1 that the example XML document we sent to Solr for indexing included the `timestamp` field as follows:

```
<add>
   <doc>
      . . .
      <field name="timestamp">2012-05-22T09:30:22Z</field>
      . . .
   </doc>
</add>
```

In *schema.xml*, the `timestamp` field is configured to use the `tdate` type:

```
<field name="timestamp" type="tdate" indexed="true" stored="true" />
```

In general, Solr expects your dates to be in the ISO-8601 Date/Time format (yyyy-MM-ddTHH:mm:ssZ); the date in our tweet (`2012-05-22T09:30:22Z`) breaks down to

```
yyyy = 2012
  MM = 05
  dd = 22
  HH = 09 (24-hr clock)
  mm = 30
  ss = 22
   Z = UTC Timezone (Z is for Zulu)
```

If you send Solr a date in another format, you'll get a validation error during indexing and the document will be rejected.

DATE GRANULARITY

Next you need to decide the granularity of dates in your index. This goes back to understanding how your users need to query using dates. If your users only expect to query for documents by day, then you don't need to index a date with second or millisecond precision. If you need to sort documents by date, then hour-level granularity may be too coarse, in which case you may want to do minute-level granularity.

During indexing, Solr supports date math operations to help you achieve the correct precision for a date field with little effort. Let's say you decide that you only need to index your dates at the hour level of granularity. This saves space in your index, but also means that users can't get more specific than hour ranges when searching. When indexing, you can send your date with /HOUR on the end; the / tells Solr to "round down" to a specific granularity. Let's see how we can index our example tweet with hour granularity:

```
<field name="timestamp">2012-05-22T09:30:22Z/HOUR</field>
```

In the index, the value of the timestamp field for the example document will be equivalent to 2012-05-22T09:00:00Z. In addition to specifying the date/time exactly, Solr also supports the NOW keyword to represent the current system time on your Solr server. You can combine specific dates or the NOW keyword with Solr's date math operations to accomplish powerful date calculations. For example, NOW/DAY evaluates to midnight of the current day, and NOW/DAY+1DAY evaluates to midnight tomorrow. To query for all documents from today, you could do timestamp:[NOW/DAY TO NOW/DAY+1DAY}. We'll dig more into range queries like this in chapter 7.

We'd like to note that the tdate field is a good choice for fields on which you need to do date range queries, but it comes at the cost of requiring more space in your index because more tokens are stored per date value. According to the Solr JavaDocs, a precisionStep="6" is a good value for long fields, which is how Solr stores dates in the index. We cover how to choose the right precisionStep in section 5.4.4.

5.4.3 Numeric fields

For the most part, numeric fields in Solr behave as you'd expect. For example, in section 5.1 we discussed how the favorites_count field indicates the number of times the author of a tweet has been "favorited" by other users. This isn't an intuitive field to search by, but it's useful from a display-and-sorting perspective. In other words, you can imagine having users who want to sort matching tweets by this field to see content from more popular authors. In *schema.xml* we declared the field as

```
<field name="favorites_count" type="int" indexed="true" stored="true" />
```

The int field type is defined as

```
<fieldType name="int" class="solr.TrieIntField"
    precisionStep="0" positionIncrementGap="0"/>
```

Because we don't need to support range queries on this field, we chose precision-Step="0", which works best for sorting without incurring the additional storage costs associated with a higher precision step used for faster range queries. Also, note that you shouldn't index a numeric field that you need to sort as a string field because Solr will do a lexical sort instead of a numeric sort if the underlying type is string-based. In other words, if you index numeric fields using a string-based field type, sorting will return results like 1, 10, 2, 3, ... instead of 1, 2, 3, ... 10.

Up to this point, we've discussed the main concepts for indexing fields that contain structured information. We'll return to specific cases for these types of nontext fields in later chapters. We'll discuss a `<fieldType>` used to represent latitude and longitude when we discuss Solr's geospatial search in chapter 15, for example. For now, let's wrap up this section with a short discussion of some of the advanced configuration options for field types.

5.4.4 *Advanced field type attributes*

Solr supports optional attributes for field types to enable advanced behavior. Table 5.3 covers advanced attributes for `<fieldType>` elements.

Table 5.3   Overview of advanced attributes for `fieldType` elements in *schema.xml*

Attribute	Behavior when enabled (`="true"`)
sortMissingFirst	When sorting results, Solr will list documents that don't have a value for the field at the top of the results.
sortMissingLast	When sorting results, Solr will list documents that don't have a value for the field at the bottom of the results.
precisionStep	Determines the number of terms created to represent a numeric value in the index for doing fast range queries on trie-based fields like `TrieDate` and `TrieLong`; see the JavaDoc for the `NumericRangeQuery` class for more details about the `precisionStep` attribute.
positionIncrementGap	Used to prevent phrase queries from matching the end of one value and the beginning of the next value in multivalued fields.

Let's take a closer look at `precisionStep`, as it's a common source of confusion for new Solr users. You can safely skip the following discussion for now, and come back to this after you've implemented your search application and you're looking for ways to improve the performance of sorting and range queries.

CHOOSING THE BEST PRECISIONSTEP FOR NUMERIC FIELDS

Two common use cases you'll undoubtedly encounter are finding documents that match a range of values for a numeric or date field, called a range query, and sorting results by numeric and date fields. As we discussed earlier, Solr uses a *trie* data structure to support efficient range queries and sorting of numeric and date values. Let's learn how to choose the best value for `precisionStep` to support range queries and sorting in your Solr instance.

First, decide if you even need to worry about `precisionStep` by asking whether you have any numeric or date fields in your index that users would like to find in documents when searching across a range of values in those fields. For each of these fields, think about the range of possible values that will be indexed; are there potentially millions of unique values or only a handful? In Solr terminology, the number of unique values in a field is called the *cardinality* of the field.

Consider a Solr index for finding houses for sale across the United States. Home buyers typically search for houses in a specific area and price range. A typical query in this application might look like: `city:Denver AND price:[250000 TO 300000]`. Home price seems like a good example of a field that needs to support efficient range searches. As this application will have listings from across the United States, the `price` field will have a broad range of values from the low $10,000s to over $10,000,000, so its cardinality will be large.

Next we need to decide on the best field type for listing price. You can imagine that most house prices will be rounded to the nearest dollar, as it's rare to see a home price with cents, so an `int` or `long` field should suffice. Also, the maximum value for an integer in Solr is 2,147,483,647 (2.1 billion), and it's unlikely to see a listing that exceeds this maximum. Keep in mind that you want to be as frugal with your field types as possible; that is, avoid using an eight-byte `long` when a four-byte `int` will suffice. This reduces the size of your index on disk and reduces memory usage during searching and sorting. We can define a field for home listing price as

```
<field name="listing_price" type="tint" indexed="true" stored="true" />
```

To support range queries, the field must be indexed, and because we want to display the home price in search results, the field must also be stored. In the Solr example *schema.xml*, the `tint` field type is defined as

```
<fieldType name="tint" class="solr.TrieIntField"
    precisionStep="8"
    positionIncrementGap="0"/>
```

Let's take a look at what gets indexed for a home price of $327,500 using a `TrieInt` field with `precisionStep="8"`. The intuition behind a trie-based field is that Lucene generates multiple terms for each value in the field, and each term has less precision. In other words, two different home prices will have overlapping terms at lower precisions. Lucene does this to reduce the number of terms that have to be matched to satisfy a range query. Table 5.4 shows the terms that were indexed for a listing price of $327,500 using `precisionStep="8"`.

Table 5.4 Terms indexed for listing price $327,500 using `TrieInt` field with `precisionStep` 8

Precision step (8)	Operation	Indexed term
0: no bits removed	327500 & 0xFFFFFFFF	327500
1: 8 least significant bits removed	327500 & 0xFFFFFF00	327424
2: 16 least significant bits removed	327500 & 0xFFFF0000	262144
3: 24 least significant bits removed	327500 & 0xFF000000	0

The table shows that at each precision step, Lucene removes (8 * step count) least significant bits from the original value, which reduces the precision of the indexed term.

For example, at step 2, home prices $327,500 and $326,800 both would have term 262144 in the index, which means that a range query only needs to match 262144 instead of both prices. In fact, the single term 262144 would be the same for potentially thousands of homes priced between $262,144 and $327,679. In other words, using a precisionStep of 8 allows Solr to match potentially thousands of homes priced between $262,144 and $327,679 using a single term: 262144.

Let's compare this to using precisionStep="4" for listing price to see the impact of using a smaller step size. Table 5.5 shows the terms that would be indexed for price $327,500 if we use precisionStep="4".

Table 5.5   Terms indexed for listing price $327,500 using TrieInt field with precisionStep 4

Precision step (4)	Java bitwise operation	Indexed term
0: no bits removed	327500 & 0xFFFFFFFF	327500
1–4 least significant bits removed	327500 & 0xFFFFFFF0	327488
2–8 least significant bits removed	327500 & 0xFFFFFF00	327424
3–12 least significant bits removed	327500 & 0xFFFFF000	323584
4–16 least significant bits removed	327500 & 0xFFFF0000	262144
5–20 least significant bits removed	327500 & 0xFFF00000	0

The previous table shows that using a smaller precision step equates to more terms being indexed: 6 versus only 4 when using a precision step of 8. In general, a smaller precision step leads to more terms being indexed per value, which increases the size of your index. But having more terms also equates to faster range queries because Lucene can narrow the search space quicker with more terms. The intuition here is that Lucene can search the center of a range using the lowest possible precision in the trie. But the upper and lower boundaries of the range must be searched more precisely, so having more terms indexed allows the range boundaries to be matched more efficiently.

To verify this, we conducted an informal benchmark by indexing 500,000 randomly generated listing prices between $110,000 and $5,000,000. After indexing, we generated 10,000 random range queries to get a feel for average query performance; table 5.6 summarizes the results.

Table 5.6   Results from our informal benchmark to compare index size, term count, and query performance using precisionStep 4 and 8 for our trie-based home listing price field

Precision step	Number of terms indexed	Index size (KB)	RangeQuery performance
8	68,074	28,612	7.0 ms
4	118,170	32,496	6.3 ms

Notice that the index sizes differ by about 8 bytes per document, which agrees with table 5.5 in which we saw two extra 4-byte integer terms created per document when using a smaller step size. To summarize, when selecting a precision step, you have to balance space considerations with range query performance. For our `TrieInt` listing price field, a precision step of 4 leads to more terms being indexed per unique price but slightly faster range searches, particularly when the cardinality of a field is large (many unique values).

5.5 Sending documents to Solr for indexing

We now have enough background on the indexing process to begin adding documents to Solr. In this section, we learn how to send documents to Solr for indexing and get a glimpse of what happens behind the scenes. At the end of this section, you'll be able to start indexing documents to Solr from your application. Let's begin by learning how to index the example tweets we've been working with in this chapter.

5.5.1 Indexing documents using XML or JSON

As we touched on in section 5.1, Solr allows you to add documents using a simple XML document structure. Listing 5.12 shows this structure for the two example tweets we used previously in this chapter. But in this case, we changed the names of the fields to use dynamic fields. For instance, `screen_name_s` will be a `string` because of the `_s` suffix on the name. We do this for convenience, as you can add these documents to the example Solr server without making any changes to *schema.xml*. If you are building a real application, then you may want to declare the fields from listing 5.3 explicitly in your *schema.xml*, but using dynamic fields works fine for this example.

Listing 5.12   XML document used to index example tweets in Solr with dynamic fields

Tell Solr we're adding new documents to the index. → `<add>`

You can add more than one document at a time, each wrapped in a `<doc>` tag.

Use dynamic fields to determine the field type for each field based on the suffix in the name.

```
<add>
  <doc>
    <field name="id">1</field>
    <field name="screen_name_s">@thelabdude</field>
    <field name="type_s">post</field>
    <field name="lang_s">en</field>
    <field name="timestamp_tdt">2012-05-22T09:30:22Z/HOUR</field>
    <field name="favorites_count_ti">10</field>
    <field name="text_t">#Yummm :) Drinking a latte at Caffe Grecco in SF's
        historic North Beach... Learning text analysis with #SolrInAction
        by @ManningBooks on my i-Pad</field>
  </doc>
  <doc>
    <field name="id">2</field>
    <field name="screen_name_s">@thelabdude</field>
    <field name="type_s">post</field>
    <field name="lang_s">en</field>
    <field name="timestamp_tdt">2012-05-23T09:30:22Z/HOUR</field>
    <field name="favorites_count_ti">10</field>
```

```
    <field name="text_t">Just downloaded the ebook of #SolrInAction from
        @ManningBooks http://bit.ly/T3eGYG to learn more about #Solr
        http://bit.ly/3ynriE</field>
    <field name="link_ss">http://manning.com/grainger/</field>
    <field name="link_ss">http://lucene.apache.org/solr/</field>
  </doc>
</add>
```

Let's send this XML document to Solr to index these two tweets. The Solr example includes a simple command-line application that allows you to post XML documents into the example server. Open a command line on your workstation and execute the commands shown in the next listing.

Listing 5.13 Commands to index the example tweets in Solr

Post ch5/tweets.xml to Solr for indexing.

```
cd $SOLR_IN_ACTION/example-docs/        Replace SOLR_IN_ACTION with      Output
java -jar post.jar ch5/tweets.xml       the path on your computer.       from the
                                                                         post.jar
SimplePostTool: version 1.5                                              application.
SimplePostTool: POSTing files to http://localhost:8983/solr/update..
SimplePostTool: POSTing file ch5/tweets.xml
SimplePostTool: COMMITting Solr index changes..    Commit the documents to make
                                                   them visible in search results.
```

The two example tweets should now be indexed in your example Solr server. To verify, navigate with your favorite web browser to the Solr admin panel at http://localhost:8983/solr/#/, click Query under collection1 in the menu on the left, and execute query type_s:post, as shown in figure 5.6.

Behind the scenes, the *post.jar* application sent the XML document over HTTP to Solr's update handler at http://localhost:8983/solr/collection1/update. The update handler supports adding, updating, and deleting documents; we cover the update request handler in more detail in section 5.6.

Beyond XML, Solr's update request handler also supports the popular JSON and CSV data formats. Instead of indexing our example tweets using XML, we could have used JSON as shown in this listing.

Listing 5.14 Using JSON to index documents instead of XML

```
[
  {                                          Wrap all documents to
    "id" : "1",                              index in a JSON array.
    "screen_name_s" : "@thelabdude",
    "type_s" : "post",                       Each document to
    "lang_s" : "en",                         index is a JSON object.
    "timestamp_tdt" : "2012-05-22T09:30:22Z/HOUR",
    "favorites_count_ti" : "10",
    "text_t" : "#Yummm :) Drinking a latte at Caffe Grecco in SF's historic
        North Beach... Learning text analysis with #SolrInAction by
        @ManningBooks on my i-Pad"
  },
```

```
{
  "id" : "2",
  "screen_name_s" : "@thelabdude",
  "type_s" : "post",
  "lang_s" : "en",
  "timestamp_tdt" : "2012-05-23T09:30:22Z/HOUR",
  "favorites_count_ti" : "10",
  "text_t" : "Just downloaded the ebook of #SolrInAction from
      @ManningBooks http://bit.ly/T3eGYG to learn more about
      #Solr http://bit.ly/3ynriE",
  "link_ss" : [ "http://manning.com/grainger/",
                "http://lucene.apache.org/solr/"]          ◁─┐  Multivalued fields
  }                                                            encoded as a JSON array.
]
```

We'll use the *post.jar* utility to send the JSON to Solr, but because XML is the default type, we have to explicitly tell the application that we're sending JSON by setting the type system property to `application/json`:

```
java -Dtype=application/json -jar post.jar ch5/tweets.json
```

Figure 5.6 A screenshot that shows using query `type_s:post` to see the example tweets we added using the *post.jar* command-line utility provided with the Solr example.

The placement of the `-Dtype=application/json` parameter in this command is important; it must be before the `-jar` argument. For a full list of options supported by *post.jar*, you can run `java -jar post.jar --help`.

If you walked through both exercises of adding the XML and JSON documents, then you might think you have four documents in your index. But because we're using the `id` field in our documents, you'll have only two documents in the index. Verify this yourself by reissuing the `type_s:post` query as before. This demonstrates how Solr will update an existing document using the unique key field, which in the example *schema.xml* is `id`.

If you look closely at the output from the *post.jar* application, you'll notice that it also sends a commit to Solr after POSTing the documents. Regardless of how you send documents to Solr, they're not searchable until they're committed. The commit process is quite involved and is covered in detail in section 5.6. Let's continue our discussion of how to index documents by learning about a popular Java-based client for Solr called SolrJ.

5.5.2 *Using the SolrJ client library to add documents from Java*

SolrJ is a Java-based client library provided with the Solr project to communicate with your Solr server from a Java application. In this section, we'll implement a simple SolrJ client to send documents using Java. If you're not a Java developer or your application isn't written in Java, then you'll be happy to know there are many other Solr client libraries available for other languages such as .NET, Ruby, Python, and PHP. See chapter 12 (section 12.8.2) for more information about Solr client libraries available for various languages.

The following listing provides a simple example using SolrJ to add our two example tweet documents to the index and perform a hard commit. After committing, the example code sends a match all docs query (`*:*`) to Solr to get the documents we indexed back in the search results.

Listing 5.15 Example SolrJ client application

```
package sia.ch5;
...
import org.apache.solr.client.solrj.SolrQuery;
import org.apache.solr.client.solrj.SolrServer;
import org.apache.solr.client.solrj.SolrServerException;
import org.apache.solr.client.solrj.impl.HttpSolrServer;
import org.apache.solr.client.solrj.response.QueryResponse;
import org.apache.solr.common.SolrDocument;
import org.apache.solr.common.SolrDocumentList;
import org.apache.solr.common.SolrInputDocument;

public class ExampleSolrJClient {

    public static void main(String[] args) throws Exception {
        String serverUrl = (args != null && args.length > 0) ? args[0] :
                          "http://localhost:8983/solr/collection1";
```

```
                SolrServer solr = new HttpSolrServer(serverUrl);

                SolrInputDocument doc1 = new SolrInputDocument();
                doc1.setField("id", "1");
                doc1.setField("screen_name_s", "@thelabdude");
                doc1.setField("type_s", "post");
                doc1.setField("lang_s", "en");
                doc1.setField("timestamp_tdt", "2012-05-22T09:30:22Z/HOUR");
                doc1.setField("favorites_count_ti", "10");
                doc1.setField("text_t", "#Yummm :) Drinking a latte at Caffe Grecco"
                    in SF's historic North Beach... Learning text analysis with
                    #SolrInAction by @ManningBooks on my i-Pad");

                solr.add(doc1);

                SolrInputDocument doc2 = new SolrInputDocument();
                doc2.setField("id", "2");
                doc2.setField("screen_name_s", "@thelabdude");
                doc2.setField("type_s", "post");
                doc2.setField("lang_s", "en");
                doc2.setField("timestamp_tdt", "2012-05-22T09:30:22Z/HOUR");
                doc2.setField("favorites_count_ti", "10");
                doc2.setField("text_t", "Just downloaded the ebook of #SolrInAction
                    from @ManningBooks http://bit.ly/T3eGYG to learn more about #Solr
                    http://bit.ly/3ynriE");
                doc2.addField("link_ss", "http://manning.com/grainger/");
                doc2.addField("link_ss", "http://lucene.apache.org/solr/");

                solr.add(doc2);

                solr.commit(true, true);

                for (SolrDocument next : simpleSolrQuery(solr, "*:*", 10)) {
                    prettyPrint(System.out, next);
                }
            }

            static SolrDocumentList simpleSolrQuery(SolrServer solr,
                    String query, int rows) throws SolrServerException {
                SolrQuery solrQuery = new SolrQuery(query);
                solrQuery.setRows(rows);
                QueryResponse resp = solr.query(solrQuery);
                SolrDocumentList hits = resp.getResults();
                return hits;
            }

            static void prettyPrint(PrintStream out, SolrDocument doc) {
                List<String> sortedFieldNames =
                        new ArrayList<String>(doc.getFieldNames());
                Collections.sort(sortedFieldNames);
                out.println();
                for (String field : sortedFieldNames) {
                    out.println(String.format("\t%s: %s",
                            field, doc.getFieldValue(field)));
                }
                out.println();
            }
        }
```

Use a SolrInputDocument object to build a document to be indexed.

Connect to the Solr server at the specified URL, such as http://localhost:8983/solr/collection1.

Send the SolrInputDocument to the Solr update request handler over HTTP.

Use the addField method to add multivalues for multivalued fields.

Do a normal or "hard" commit to make these new docs searchable.

Use a SolrQuery object to construct the match all docs query.

prettyPrint each SolrDocument in the results to stdout.

As you can see from this basic example, the SolrJ API makes it easy to connect to Solr, add documents, send queries, and process results. To begin, all you need is the URL of the Solr server, which in our example was http://localhost:8983/solr/collection1. Behind the scenes, SolrJ uses the Apache `HttpComponents` client library to communicate with the Solr server using HTTP. In section 5.5.1, we saw how Solr supports XML and JSON, so you may be wondering if SolrJ is using one of those formats to connect to Solr. It turns out that SolrJ uses an internal binary protocol called javabin by default. When doing Java-to-Java communication, the javabin protocol is more efficient than using XML or JSON.

In addition to sending requests to a single Solr server, SolrJ contains built-in support for batching documents for large-scale indexing, load-balancing between Solr instances, automatically discovering the locations of Solr servers in a SolrCloud configuration, and embedding Solr in a nonserver mode inside your Java application. We will cover each of these options when we take a deeper look at SolrJ in chapter 12.

5.5.3   *Other tools for importing documents into Solr*

We've seen how we can send documents to Solr using basic HTTP POST with the *post.jar* application and with the popular SolrJ client from Java. These aren't the only ways to get your documents into Solr. Being a mature, widely adopted open source technology, Solr offers a number of powerful utilities for adding documents from other systems. In this section, we introduce you to three popular tools available for populating your Solr index:

- Data Import Handler (DIH)
- `ExtractingRequestHandler`, aka Solr Cell
- Nutch

Each tool is powerful and we could easily justify taking an entire chapter to describe each one. For now, we want to give a brief mention of these tools so that you're aware of these options for populating your index.

DATA IMPORT HANDLER

The *Data Import Handler (DIH)* is an extension that pulls data into Solr from one or more external sources, such as websites or relational databases. The DIH works with any database that provides a modern JDBC driver, such as Oracle, Postgres, MySQL, or MS SQL Server. At a high level, you provide the database connection parameters and an SQL query to Solr, and the DIH component queries the database and transforms the results into documents. You can also easily have Solr pull in data from XML files or external websites as documents to be indexed. We cover the DIH in a bit more detail in chapter 12 and provide example data import mappings in appendix C, so for now let's look at another tool for indexing rich binary documents like PDF and MS Word documents.

EXTRACTINGREQUESTHANDLER

`ExtractingRequestHandler`, commonly called Solr Cell, allows you to index text content extracted from binary files like PDF, MS Office, and OpenOffice documents. Behind the scenes, Solr Cell uses the Apache Tika project to do the extraction. Specifically, Tika provides components that know how to detect the type of document and parse the binary documents to extract text and metadata. For example, you can send a PDF document to the `ExtractingRequestHandler`, and it will automatically populate fields like `title`, `subject`, `keywords`, and `body_text` in your Solr index. While we won't cover the many configuration options for the `ExtractingRequestHandler` in this book, we'll discuss it again briefly in chapter 12, where we will also link to a thorough tutorial that can help you index your binary files as documents into Solr.

NUTCH

Apache Nutch is a Java-based open source web crawler. Nutch integrates with Solr out of the box to make the web pages it crawls searchable using Solr. Thus, if your application needs to crawl hyperlinked pages on a massive scale, Nutch is probably a good place for you to start. You can find more information about Nutch at the project's home page, http://nutch.apache.org.

Now that you've seen how to send documents to Solr for indexing, let's learn how those requests are processed in Solr using a component called the update handler.

5.6 *Update handler*

In the previous section, we sent new documents to Solr using HTTP `POST` requests. The request to add these new documents was handled by Solr's update handler. In general, the update handler processes all updates to your index as well as commit and optimize requests. Table 5.7 provides an overview of common request types supported by the update handler.

Table 5.7 Overview of common requests processed by the update handler

Request type	Description	XML example

Add	Adds one or more documents to the index; see listing 5.12 for a full example.	`<add>`
		  `<doc>`
		    `<field name="id">1</field>`
		    `...`
		  `</doc>`
		`</add>`

Delete	Deletes a document by ID, such as deleting a document with ID=1.	`<delete>`
		  `<id>1</id>`
		`</delete>`

Delete by query	Deletes documents that match a Lucene query, such as deleting all microblog documents from a user with `screen_name=@thelabdude`.	`<delete>`
		  `<query>`
		    `screen_name:@thelabdude`
		  `</query>`
		`</delete>`

Table 5.7 Overview of common requests processed by the update handler *(continued)*

Request type	Description	XML example
Atomic update	Updates one or more fields of an existing document using optimistic locking; see section 5.6.3.	```<add> <doc> <field name="id">1</field> <field update="set" name= "favorites_count"> 12 </field> </doc> </add>```
Commit	Commits documents to the index with options to do a soft or hard commit and whether to block on the client until the new searcher is open and warmed.	```<commit waitSearcher="true" softCommit="false" />```
Optimize	Optimizes the index by merging segments and removing deletes.	```<optimize waitSearcher="false"/>```

Although table 5.7 shows examples of update requests using XML, the update request handler supports other formats, such as JSON, CSV, and javabin. Behind the scenes, the update request handler looks at the `Content-Type` HTTP header to determine the format of the request, such as `Content-Type: text/xml`.

The next listing shows the configuration of the update handler in *solrconfig.xml*.

Listing 5.16. Configuration elements for the update handler in *solrconfig.xml*

```
<updateHandler class="solr.DirectUpdateHandler2">
  <updateLog>
    <str name="dir">${solr.ulog.dir:}</str>          Enable the transaction
  </updateLog>                                        log, covered in section
                                                      5.6.2.
  <autoCommit>
    <maxTime>15000</maxTime>
    <openSearcher>false</openSearcher>
  </autoCommit>
  <autoSoftCommit>
    <maxTime>1000</maxTime>                           Configure the soft
  </autoSoftCommit>                                   autocommit policy;
  <listener event="postCommit" ...>                  see section 5.6.1.
    ...
  </listener>                                         Register an update
</updateHandler>                                      event listener.
```

Configure autocommit policy, covered in section 5.6.1.

One of the most important tasks performed by the update handler is to process requests to commit documents to the index to make them visible in search results.

5.6.1 *Committing documents to the index*

In this section, we dig into the details of how Solr makes documents available for searching by committing them to the index. When a document is added to Solr, it won't be returned in search results until it's committed to the index. In other words, from a query perspective, a document isn't visible until it's committed. In Solr 4, there are two types of commits: "soft" commits and normal (sometimes called "hard") commits. Let's first look at how normal commits work, as that will help you better understand the purpose of soft commits.

NORMAL COMMIT

A normal or hard commit is one in which Solr flushes all uncommitted documents to disk and refreshes an internal component called a searcher so that the newly committed documents can be searched. For our purposes, you can think of a searcher as a read-only view of all committed documents in the index. Refer to section 4.3 for a detailed discussion of how a searcher works. For now, let it suffice to say that a hard commit can be an expensive operation that can impact query performance because it requires opening a new searcher.

After a normal commit succeeds, the newly committed documents are safely persisted to durable storage and will survive server restarts due to normal maintenance operations or a server crash. For high availability, you still need to have a solution to failover to another server if the disk fails. We discuss Solr's high-availability features in chapter 13.

SOFT COMMIT

A soft commit is a new feature in Solr 4 to support near real-time (NRT) searching. We discuss NRT searching in more depth in chapter 13. For now, you can think of a soft commit as a mechanism to make documents searchable in near real-time by skipping the costly aspects of hard commits, such as flushing to durable storage. As soft commits are less expensive, you can issue a soft commit every second to make newly indexed documents searchable within about a second of adding them to Solr. But keep in mind that you still need to do a hard commit at some point to ensure that documents are eventually flushed to durable storage.

To summarize

- A hard commit makes documents searchable but is expensive because it has to flush documents to durable storage.
- A soft commit also makes documents searchable but they are not flushed to durable storage.

We'll return to this topic in chapter 13 when we discuss NRT search in the context of SolrCloud.

AUTOCOMMIT

For either normal or soft commits, you can configure Solr to automatically commit documents using one of three strategies:

- Commit each document within a specified time.
- Commit all documents once a user-specified threshold of uncommitted documents is reached.
- Commit all documents on a regular time interval, such as every ten minutes.

Solr's autocommit behavior for hard and soft commits is configured in *solrconfig.xml*. The following XML snippet shows an example configuration in which Solr will commit every 50,000 documents and every 10 minutes:

```
<autoCommit>
   <maxTime>600000</maxTime>
   <maxDocs>50000</maxDocs>
   <openSearcher>true</openSearcher>
</autoCommit>
```

Commit every 10 minutes (value in milliseconds).

Commit every 50,000 documents.

Open a new searcher after committing.

When performing an autocommit, the normal behavior is to open a new searcher. But Solr lets you disable this behavior by specifying `<openSearcher>false</open-Searcher>`. In this case, the documents will be flushed to disk, but won't be visible in search results. Solr provides this option to help minimize the size of its transaction log of uncommitted updates (see the next section) and to avoid opening too many searchers during a large indexing process.

Imagine you have 5 million documents to index and have configured Solr to auto-commit every 50,000 documents. This means that Solr will perform 100 autocommits during the process of indexing 5 million documents. In this scenario, it may make sense to only pay the penalty of warming up a new searcher once all documents are indexed rather than warming up a new searcher 100 times. Of course, your client application can also send an intermittent hard commit request every 1 million documents so that some documents are visible in search results sooner. The main point is that you want to think about whether you need to open a new searcher after every autocommit. If the number of documents you're indexing is larger than your autocommit threshold, you might consider setting `<openSearcher>false</openSearcher>` and have your client issue a final hard commit once all documents are indexed.

Also, don't confuse the `openSearcher` attribute for the `<autoCommit>` element with the `waitSearcher` attribute for the `<commit>` request described in table 5.7. A new searcher is always opened and warmed when you send a `<commit>` request; the `wait-Searcher` attribute indicates whether your client code should block until the new searcher is fully warmed up. As you learned in chapter 4, warming a new searcher can take a long time, so use `waitSearcher="true"` with caution.

You can also configure Solr to do soft commits automatically using the `<autoSoft-Commit>` element in *solrconfig.xml*. But you'll want to use much smaller values for soft commits, such as every second (1000 ms), as shown in this XML snippet:

```
<autoSoftCommit>
   <maxTime>1000</maxTime>
</autoSoftCommit>
```

Do a soft commit every second (1000 ms).

Now let's turn our attention to another powerful feature of the update handler that helps ensure that you don't lose uncommitted updates.

5.6.2 Transaction log

Solr uses a transaction log to ensure that updates accepted by Solr are saved on durable storage until they're committed to the index. Imagine the scenario in which your client application sends a commit every 10,000 documents. If Solr crashes after the client sends documents to be indexed but before your client sends the commit, then without a transaction log, these uncommitted documents will be lost. Specifically, the transaction log serves three key purposes:

- It is used to support real-time gets and atomic updates.
- It decouples write durability from the commit process.
- It supports synchronizing replicas with shard leaders in SolrCloud (covered in chapter 13).

The transaction log is configured for a core in *solrconfig.xml*:

```
<updateLog>
    <str name="dir">${solr.ulog.dir:}</str>       ⟵—  Default location is tlog
</updateLog>                                              subdirectory of data.
```

Every update request is logged to the transaction log. The transaction log continues to grow until you issue a commit. During a commit, the active transaction log is processed and then a new transaction log file is opened. Figure 5.7 illustrates the steps involved in processing an update request.

A few of the components in figure 5.7, such as the request dispatcher and response writer, should be familiar to you already. These are the same components we discussed in chapter 4 when learning about query request processing. Let's walk through the sequence of events in figure 5.7 to highlight some of the important concepts:

1. Client application sends an update request using HTTP POST. The client can send the request as JSON, XML, or Solr's internal binary javabin format. We saw an example client built using SolrJ in listing 5.15.
2. Jetty routes the request to the Solr web application.
3. Solr's request dispatcher uses the "collection1" part of the request path to determine the core name. Next, the dispatcher locates the /update request handler registered in *solrconfig.xml* for the collection1 core.
4. The update request handler processes the request. When adding or updating documents, the update handler uses *schema.xml* to process each field in each document in the request. In addition, the request handler invokes a configurable chain of update request processors to perform additional work on each document during indexing. We'll see an example of this in chapter 6, in which we use an update request processor to do language detection during indexing.
5. The ADD request is written to the transaction log.
6. Once the update request is securely saved to durable storage, a response is sent to the client application using a response writer. At this point, the client application knows the update request is successful and can continue processing.

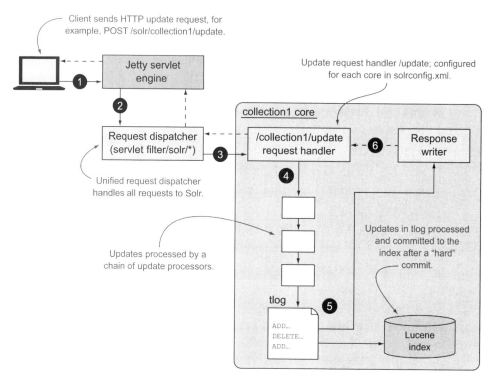

Figure 5.7   Sequence of events and main components used to process update requests, such as adding a new document

With the transaction log, your main concern is balancing the trade-off between the length of your transaction log—that is, how many uncommitted updates—and how frequently you want to issue a hard commit. If your transaction log grows large, a restart may take a long time to process the updates, delaying your recovery process.

For instance, if the average size of your documents is 5 KB and you commit every 100,000 documents, your transaction log can grow to over 3.7 GB. Of course, 5 KB per document is a large document. In contrast, committing microblog documents like we used in this chapter every 100,000 documents wouldn't be a problem. The key takeaway is that you need to consider the size of your transaction log when configuring your auto-commit settings. As you learned in the previous section, you can issue a hard commit without affecting the query side by setting `<openSearcher>false</openSearcher>` for your autocommit settings. But this implies that at some point, your client application must issue a full hard commit to make all updates visible in search results.

5.6.3   *Atomic updates*

You can update existing documents in Solr by sending a new version of the document. But unlike a database in which you can update a specific column in a row, with Solr you must update the entire document. Behind the scenes, Solr deletes the existing document and creates a new one; this occurs whether you change one field or all fields.

From a client perspective, your application must send a new version of the document in its entirety. For some applications in which documents can be created from other sources, this isn't such a big deal. For others that use Solr as a primary data store, recreating a document in its entirety in order to update a single field can be problematic. In practice, this requires users to query for the entire document, apply the updates, and send the fully specified document back to Solr.

This pattern of requesting all fields for an existing document, updating a subset of fields, and sending the new version to Solr is common in practice. Consequently, atomic updates are a new feature in Solr that allows you to send updates to only the fields you want to change. This brings Solr more in line with how database updates work. Solr will still delete and create a new document, but this is transparent to your client application code.

FIELD-LEVEL UPDATES

Returning to our microblog search example, let's imagine that we want to index a new field on existing documents that holds the number of times the tweet has been retweeted. We'll use this new field as an indication of the popularity of a tweet. To keep things simple, we'll update this field once a day. You can imagine a daily volume statistic would also be useful, but we'll stick with an aggregated value to keep things easy. Our focus here is to learn about atomic updates.

Let's name our new field `retweet_count_ti`, which indicates that we're using a dynamic field so that we don't have to update the *schema.xml* to add this new field. The `_ti` suffix applies the following dynamic field (from *schema.xml*):

```
<dynamicField name="*_ti" type="tint" indexed="true" stored="true"/>
```

Here's an example request to update the `retweet_count_ti` field using XML:

```
<add>                                          Slightly unintuitive, but updates must        Identify the
  <doc>                                        be wrapped in an <add> element.              existing document
    <field name="id">1</field>                                                             with id=1.
    <field update="set" name="retweet_count_ti">100</field>
  </doc>                                        Sets the retweet_count_ti field to 100.
</add>
```

Behind the scenes, Solr locates the existing document with id=1, retrieves all stored fields from the index, deletes the existing document, and creates a new document from all existing fields plus the new `retweet_count_ti` field. It follows that all fields must be stored for this to work because the client application is only sending the id field and the new field. All other fields must be pulled from the existing document.

We used the `update="set"` directive to set the `retweet_count_ti` field. Alternatively, because our update process runs daily, we can count them for the previous day and *increment* the existing value using `update="inc"`. In addition to `set` and `inc`, you can use `add` to append a new value to a multivalued field.

OPTMISTIC CONCURRENCY CONTROL

Now consider a slightly more involved example in which we want to use crowd sourcing as a way to classify the sentiment of microblogs. In a nutshell, we'll pay users to classify each document as positive, neutral, or negative. The sentiment field could be useful for allowing users to find negative information about a product or restaurant.

Once classified, each microblog document needs to be updated in Solr with the sentiment label. In our retweet count example, we updated the `retweet_count_ti` field once a day using an automated process. But with sentiment classification, updates to the `sentiment_s` field can happen at any time. Thus, it's conceivable that two users will attempt to update the sentiment label on the same document at the same time. Of course, we could implement some cumbersome process that requires users to explicitly lock a document before labeling, but that would slow them down unnecessarily. Also, we probably don't want to pay for a document to be classified twice. Hence, we need some way to guard against concurrent updates to the same document: enter optimistic concurrency control.

To avoid conflicts, Solr supports optimistic concurrency control using a special version-tracking field, named `_version_`. The special version field should be defined in your *schema.xml* as

```
<field name="_version_" type="long" indexed="true" stored="true"/>
```

> With Solr 4, you shouldn't change or remove this field from your schema.xml.

When a new document is added, Solr assigns a unique version number automatically. When you need to guard against concurrent updates, you include the exact version the update is based on in the update request. Consider the following update request that includes a specific `_version_`:

```
<add>
  <doc>
    <field name="id">1</field>
    <field update="set" name="sentiment_s">positive</field>
    <field update="set" name="classified_by_s">SomeUserID</field>
    <field name="_version_">1234567890</field>
  </doc>
</add>
```

Identify the document to update using its unique ID.

Set the sentiment_s field to "positive".

Track which user classified this tweet so they get paid.

Return the _version_ of the document this update is based on.

When Solr processes this update, it will compare the `_version_` value in the request with the latest version of the document, pulled from either the index or the transaction log. If they match, Solr applies the update. If they don't match, the update request fails and an error is returned to the user. A client application can handle the error response to let the user know the document was already classified by another user. This approach is called "optimistic" because it assumes that most updates will work on the initial attempt and that conflicts are rare.

Using the `_version_` field to enforce concurrency control raises the question: How does the client application get the current `_version_` from Solr? The best technique is to use a real-time `get` request. For instance, to get the `_version_` field for our example document with an id of 1, you'd send this HTTP GET request: http://localhost:8983/solr/collection1/get?id=1&fl=id,_version_.

Real-time get returns the latest version of a document whether or not it's committed to the index. Consequently, real-time get and atomic updates rely on the transaction log being enabled for your index.

Solr has other options for handling concurrent updates with the _version_ field. Table 5.8 gives an overview of how Solr behaves depending on the value of the _version_ in an update request.

Table 5.8 Using the _version_ field to enforce update semantics in Solr

If _version_ field is set to	Solr's behavior is
>1	Versions must match or the update fails.
1	The document must exist.
<0	The document must not exist.
0	No concurrency control desired, existing value is overwritten.

As illustrated by this simple example, atomic updates are a powerful new addition to Solr's arsenal of data-management features. With Solr 4, you can now update existing documents by sending the fields that need to be updated, along with the unique identifier of the document to update.

5.7 Index management

In chapter 4, we delayed a discussion of index-management settings in *solrconfig.xml* until you had more background with Solr indexing. You're now ready to tackle Solr's index-management settings. In this section, we focus on the index-related settings that you're most likely to need to change, beginning with how indexed documents are stored. It should be said that most of the index-related settings in Solr are for expert use only. What this means is that you should take caution when you make changes and that the default settings are appropriate for most Solr installations.

5.7.1 Index storage

When documents are committed to the index, they're written to durable storage using a component called a *directory*. The directory component provides the following key benefits to Solr:

- Hides details of reading from and writing to durable storage, such as writing to a file on disk or using JDBC to store documents in a database.
- Implements a storage-specific locking mechanism to prevent index corruption, such as OS-level locking for filesystem-based storage.
- Insulates Solr from JVM and OS peculiarities.
- Enables extending the behavior of a base directory implementation to support specific use cases like NRT search.

Solr provides several different directory implementations, and no one *best* directory implementation fits all Solr installations. You'll need to do research to decide on the best implementation for your specific application of Solr. In practice, this depends on your OS, JVM type, and use cases. But as you learned in chapter 4, Solr tries to be well configured out of the box. Let's dig into how Solr's index storage is configured by default, which will help you decide if you need to change the default configuration.

DEFAULT STORAGE CONFIGURATION

By default, Solr uses a directory implementation that stores data to the local filesystem in the data directory for a core. For instance, the example server stores its index in *$SOLR_INSTALL/example/solr/collection1/data/*. The location of the data directory is controlled by the <dataDir> element in *solrconfig.xml*:

```
<dataDir>${solr.data.dir:}</dataDir>
```
Default setting from solrconfig.xml; resolves to collection1/data for the example server.

The solr.data.dir property defaults to data but can be overridden in *solr.xml* for each core, such as

```
<core loadOnStartup="true" instanceDir="collection1/"
    transient="false" name="collection1"
    dataDir="/usr/local/solr-data/collection1"/>
```
Directory to store data for the collection1 core.

The first thing you need to consider is whether the data directory for your index has enough storage capacity for your index. Also, it's important that your data directory supports fast reads and writes, with a little more priority usually given to read performance. Strategies for optimizing disk I/O are beyond the scope of this book, but here are some basic pointers to keep in mind:

- Each core shouldn't have to compete for the disk with other processes.
- If you have multiple cores on the same server, it's a good idea to use separate physical disks for each index.
- Use high-quality, fast disks or, even better, consider using solid state drives (SSDs) if your budget allows.
- Spend quality time with your system administrators to discuss RAID options for your servers.
- The amount of memory (RAM) you leave available to your OS for filesystem caching can also have a sizable impact on your disk I/O needs.

These considerations and their impact on Solr's performance will be discussed in detail in chapter 12.

CHOOSING A DIRECTORY IMPLEMENTATION

Once you've tackled storage concerns, you also need to consider the best directory implementation for your storage solution. The default directory implementation used by Solr is solr.NRTCachingDirectoryFactory, which is configured with the <directoryFactory> element in *solrconfig.xml*:

```
<directoryFactory name="DirectoryFactory"
    class="${solr.directoryFactory:solr.NRTCachingDirectoryFactory}"/>
```

The NRTCachingDirectoryFactory is a wrapper class around solr.StandardDirectory-Factory to add support for NRT search. At runtime, the StandardDirectoryFactory selects a specific directory implementation based on your operating system and JVM type, as depicted in figure 5.8.

Based on figure 5.8, there are three possible filesystem-based directory options for Solr:

- MMapDirectory: Uses memory-mapped I/O when reading the index; best option for installations on 64-bit Windows, Solaris, or Linux OSes with the Oracle JVM.
- SimpleFSDirectory: Uses a Java RandomAccessFile; should be avoided unless you're running on 32-bit Windows.
- NIOFSDirectory: Uses java.nio optimizations to avoid synchronizing reads from the same file; should be avoided on Windows due to a long-standing JVM bug.

You can determine which directory implementation is enabled for your Solr server using the Core Admin page in the Solr administration console. Figure 5.9 shows where to find the directory information for the example collection1 core.

You can override the default selection by explicitly setting the directory factory in *solrconfig.xml*. In figure 5.9, for example, Solr is using the NRTCachingDirectory

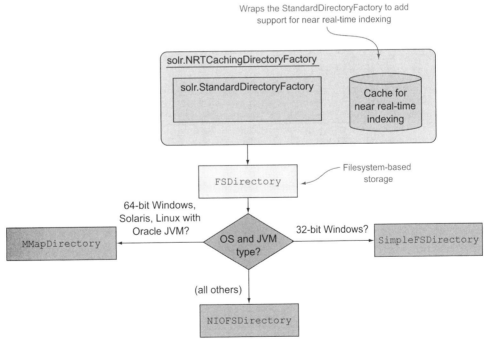

Figure 5.8 **The Solr directory implementation is selected at runtime depending on your specific OS version and JVM type.**

This Solr instance is using
NRTCachingDirectory on top
of the NIOFSDirectory

Figure 5.9   A screenshot of the Core Admin page showing the active directory implementation for the `collection1` core

implementation. If we want to change that to use `MMapDirectory`, then *solrconfig.xml* should be changed to

```
<directoryFactory name="DirectoryFactory"
    class="${solr.directoryFactory:solr.MMapDirectoryFactory}"/>
```

Explicitly use the MMapDirectory implementation.

The `MMapDirectory` implementation is your best option when running on 64-bit Windows, Solaris, and Linux because it optimizes read performance by using the virtual memory management features of these modern operating systems more intelligently.[3]

5.7.2   *Segment merging*

A segment is a self-contained, read-only subset of a full Lucene index; once a segment is flushed to durable storage, it's never altered. When new documents are added to your index, they're written to a new segment. Consequently, there can be many active segments in your index. Each query must read data from all segments to get a complete result set. At some point, having too many small segments can negatively impact query performance. Combining many smaller segments into fewer larger segments is commonly known as *segment merging*.

---

[3] For a deeper understanding of `MMapDirectory`, see Uwe Schindler's blog entry, "Use Lucene's MMapDirectory on 64bit platforms, please!" at http://blog.thetaphi.de/2012/07/use-lucenes-mmapdirectory-on-64bit.html.

SHOULD I OPTIMIZE MY INDEX?

Optimize is an operation that forces Lucene to merge existing segments into a specified number of larger segments, with the default value being 1. For instance, an index with 32 segments will have only one large segment after optimizing. Suffice it to say that optimizing can be an expensive operation in terms of memory, CPU, and disk I/O in Solr, particularly for large indexes; it's not uncommon for a full optimization to take hours for a large index.

One of the most common questions on the Solr user mailing list is whether to optimize your index. This is understandable; who doesn't want an optimized index? But the suggested and current wisdom in the Solr community is that rather than optimizing your index, it's better to fine-tune Solr's segment-merge policy. Moreover, having an optimized index doesn't mean that a slow query will suddenly become fast. Conversely, you may find that query performance is acceptable with an unoptimized index. There are some valid use cases for optimizing your index, however, which we will wait to cover until chapter 12.

EXPERT-LEVEL MERGE SETTINGS

By default, all the segment-merging settings are commented out in *solrconfig.xml*. This is by design, because the default settings should work for most installations, particularly when you're getting started. You should also notice that each element is labeled as an expert-level setting. Table 5.9 provides an overview of segment-merge-related elements from *solrconfig.xml*.

Table 5.9   Overview of segment merge elements from *solrconfig.xml*

Element	Purpose
ramBufferSizeMB	Maximum amount of RAM used to buffer documents during indexing before they're flushed to the directory; default is 100 MB. This shouldn't be confused with commits, which force all buffered documents to be written to durable storage. Increase this value to buffer more documents in memory and reduce disk I/O during indexing.
maxBufferedDocs	Maximum number of documents to buffer during indexing before flushing to the directory (durable storage); default is 1,000 documents. This shouldn't be confused with commits, which force all buffered documents to be written to durable storage and made available for searching.
mergePolicy	Controls how Lucene performs segment merging, such as deciding how many segments to merge at once. Default is the TieredMergePolicy, which will be covered in chapter 12.
mergeFactor	Controls how many segments are merged at once; default is 10. Determining the best value for your index depends on average document size, available RAM, and desired indexing throughput.
mergeScheduler	Controls when segment merging runs; default setting is to run concurrently in the background using the ConcurrentMergeScheduler.

To be clear, even though these expert-level settings are commented out, segment merging is still enabled in your index, running in the background.[4] For now, we recommend that you avoid optimizing and use the default configuration for segment merging until you have a good reason to change these settings. It's likely that doing nothing when it comes to segment merging is the right approach for your server.[5] If indexing throughput becomes an issue for your application, you can revisit these settings, which will be covered further in chapter 12.

HANDLING DELETES

By now, you should know that segments aren't changed after they're flushed to durable storage. This implies that deletes don't delete documents from existing segments. Deleted documents aren't removed from your index until segments containing deletes are merged. In a nutshell, Lucene keeps track of deletes in a separate data structure and then applies the deletes when merging. For the most part, you don't have to worry about this merging process, but we'll dive deeper into how segment merging works and its performance implications in chapter 12.

5.8   *Summary*

At this point you should have a good understanding of the Solr indexing process. To recap, we began this chapter by learning about the schema design process. Specifically, we discussed considerations about document granularity, document uniqueness, and how to determine if a field should be indexed, stored, or both.

Next, we learned how to define fields in *schema.xml*, including multivalued and dynamic fields. We saw how dynamic fields are useful for supporting documents with many fields and documents coming from diverse sources. You also learned how to use Solr's `<copyField>` directive in order to populate a catch-all text search field or to apply different text analysis to the same text during indexing.

Next, we saw how to work with structured data using Solr's support for strings, dates, and numeric field types. We used Solr's round-down operator (`/`) to index date values at different precisions, such as hour-level precision using `/HOUR`. We also learned that Solr provides trie-based fields to support efficient range queries and sorting on numeric and date fields. We saw how to use the `precisionStep` attribute for numeric and date fields to balance the trade-off between having a larger index size or slower range query performance.

Armed with an understanding of *schema.xml*, we learned how to send XML and JSON documents to Solr using HTTP and SolrJ. We introduced additional tools provided by Solr for importing documents from a relational database (DIH) and indexing rich binary documents such as PDFs and Microsoft Word documents using the extracting request handler (Solr Cell).

---

[4] Check out Mike McCandless's blog entry "Visualizing Lucene's segment merges" to see a visualization of segment merging; http://blog.mikemccandless.com/2011/02/visualizing-lucenes-segment-merges.html.

[5] Refer to section 2.13.6 in *Lucene in Action*, Second Edition, for more information about merging.

After documents are processed, they need to be committed using either normal commits or soft commits for NRT search. We showed how Solr uses a transaction log to avoid losing uncommitted updates. Beyond adding new documents, you learned how to update existing documents using Solr's atomic update support. You also saw how you can guard against concurrent updates using optimistic concurrency control with the special _version_ field.

We closed out this chapter by returning to a discussion of index-related settings from *solrconfig.xml*. Specifically, we showed you where and how Solr stores the index using a directory component. You also learned about segment merging and that it's a good idea to avoid optimizing your index or changing segment-merge settings until you have a better understanding of your indexing throughput requirements. We will dive deeper into these expert-level indexing-performance factors in chapter 12.

In the next chapter, you'll continue to learn about the indexing process by diving deep into text analysis. After finishing chapter 6, you'll have a solid foundation for designing and implementing a powerful indexing solution for your application.

Text analysis 6

This chapter covers
- Testing with Solr's Analysis form
- Defining custom field types for advanced text analysis
- Extending text analysis with Solr's Plug-In framework

In chapter 5, we learned how the Solr indexing process works and learned to define nontext fields in *schema.xml*. In this chapter, we get deeper into the indexing process by learning about text analysis.

Text analysis removes the linguistic variations between terms in the index and terms provided by users when searching, so that a user's query for buying a new house can match a document titled purchasing a new home. In this chapter you'll learn how to configure Solr to establish a match between queries containing house and documents containing home.

When done correctly, text analysis allows your users to query using natural language without having to think about all the possible forms of their search terms. You don't want your users to have to construct queries like: buying house OR purchase home OR buying a home OR purchasing a house …

Allowing users to find information they seek using natural language is fundamental to providing a good user experience. Given the broad adoption and sophistication of Google and similar search engines, users are conditioned to expect search engines to be very intelligent, and intelligence in search starts with great text analysis!

The state of the art of text analysis goes well beyond removing superficial differences between terms to address more complex issues like language-specific parsing, part-of-speech tagging, and lemmatization. Don't worry if you're not familiar with some of these terms; we'll cover them in more detail ahead. What's important is that Solr has an extensive framework for doing basic text analysis tasks, such as removing very common words known as *stop words* and doing more complex analysis tasks. To accommodate such power and flexibility, Solr's text analysis framework can seem overly complex and daunting to new users. As we like to say, Solr makes solving very difficult text analysis problems possible, but in doing so it makes simple tasks a little too cumbersome. That is why Solr comes with so many preconfigured field types in its example *schema.xml*: to ensure new users have a good place to start with text analysis when using Solr out of the box. After working through this chapter, we're confident you'll be able to harness this powerful framework to analyze most any content you'll encounter.

The main goal of this chapter is to demonstrate how Solr approaches text analysis and to help you think about how to construct analysis solutions for your documents. To this end, we'll tackle a somewhat complex text analysis problem to demonstrate the mechanics and strategies you need to be successful. Specifically, we'll cover these fundamental components of text analysis with Solr:

- Basic elements of text analysis in Solr, including the analyzer, tokenizer, and chain of token filters.
- How to define a custom field type in *schema.xml* to analyze text during indexing and query processing.
- Common text analysis strategies such as removing stop words, lowercasing, removing accents, synonym expansion, and stemming.

Once we have a solid understanding of the basic building blocks, we'll tackle a harder analysis problem to exercise some of the more advanced features Solr provides for text analysis. Specifically, we'll see how to analyze microblog content from sites like Twitter. Tweets present unique challenges that require us to think hard about how users will use our search solution. Specifically, we show you how to

- Collapse repeated characters down to a maximum of two in terms such as yummm
- Preserve #hashtags and @mentions
- Use a custom token filter to resolve shortened bit.ly-style URLs

6.1 Analyzing microblog text

Let's continue with the example microblog search application we introduced in chapter 5. To recap, we're designing and implementing a solution to search microblogs

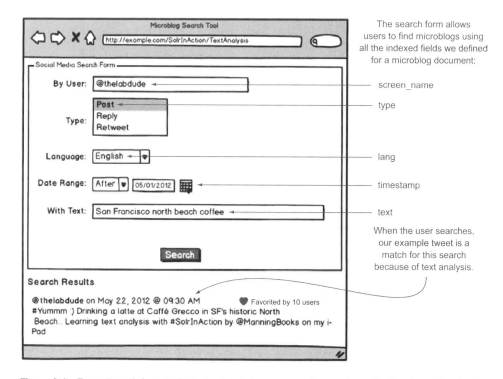

Figure 6.1   Example web form to find microblogs in our example search application from chapter 5

from popular social media sites like Twitter. Because the main focus of this chapter is on text analysis, let's look closer at the text field in our example microblog document. Here is the text we want to analyze:

```
#Yummm :) Drinking a latte at Caffé Grecco in SF's historic North Beach...
Learning text analysis with #SolrInAction by @ManningBooks on my i-Pad
```

As we discussed in the introduction, a primary goal of text analysis is to allow your users to search using natural language without having to worry about all possible forms of their search terms. In figure 6.1, the user searched via the text field for San Francisco north beach coffee, which is a natural query to expect given all the great coffeehouses in North Beach; maybe our user is trying to find a great place to drink coffee in North Beach by searching social media content.

We assert that our example tweet should be a strong match for this query even though exact text matches for San Francisco, north beach, and coffee do not occur in our sample tweet. Yes, North Beach is in our document, but case matters in search unless you take specific action to make your search index case-insensitive. We assert that our example document should be a strong match for this query because of the relationships between terms used in the user's search query and terms in the document shown in table 6.1.

Table 6.1   Query text that matches text in our example tweet

User search text	Text in document
San Francisco	SF's
north beach	North Beach
Coffee	latte, Caffé

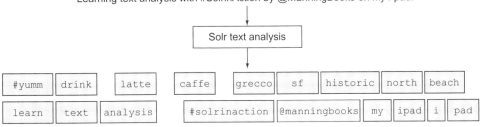

#Yummm :) Drinking a latte at Caffé Grecco in SF's historic North Beach...
Learning text analysis with #SolrinAction by @ManningBooks on my i-pad.

Solr text analysis

| #yumm | drink | latte | caffe | grecco | sf | historic | north | beach |

| learn | text | analysis | #solrinaction | @manningbooks | my | ipad | i | pad |

Figure 6.2   Tweet text transformed into a more optimal form for searching. Each box indicates a unique term in the Solr index after the text analysis process is applied to the text. The extra space between some terms indicates that stop words were excluded from the index.

So the task ahead of us is to use Solr's text analysis framework to transform the tweet text into a form that makes it easier to find. Figure 6.2 shows the transformations we'll make to the text using Solr's text analysis framework, which for now you can think of as a black box. In the remaining sections of this chapter, we'll open up the black box to see how it works.

Can you spot all the transformations that were applied? Table 6.2 provides a summary of the key transformations that were applied using various Solr text analysis tools that we'll go through in detail ahead. Notice that each transformation taken individually is usually quite simple, but collectively they make a big difference in improved user experience with your search application.

Table 6.2   Overview of the transformations made to the microblog text using Solr's text analysis tools. Notice how all transformations are performed using built-in Solr text analysis tools: no custom code required!

Raw text	Transformation	How we did it with Solr
All terms	Lowercased (SF's → sf's)	`LowerCaseFilterFactory`
a, at, in, with, by, on	Removed from text	Very common terms called "stop words" removed from the text using `StopFilterFactory`
Drinking, learning	drink, learn	Stemming with `KStemFilterFactory`

Table 6.2 Overview of the transformations made to the microblog text using Solr's text analysis tools. Notice how all transformations are performed using built-in Solr text analysis tools: no custom code required! *(continued)*

Raw text	Transformation	How we did it with Solr
`SF's`	`sf, san francisco`	Apostrophe s (`'s`) removed by `WordDelimiterFilterFactory`
`Caffé`	`caffe`	Diacritic é transformed to e using `ASCIIFoldingFilterFactory`
`i-Pad`	`ipad, i pad`	Hyphenated word correctly handled using `WordDelimiterFilterFactory`
`#Yummm`	`#yumm`	Collapse repeated letters down to a maximum of two using `PatternReplaceCharFilterFactory`
`#SolrInAction,` `@ManningBooks`	`#solrinaction,` `@manningbooks`	Hashtags and mentions correctly preserved using the `WhitespaceTokenizer` and `WordDelimiterFilterFactory`

Don't worry if some Solr class names look a bit daunting, as we'll cover each of the tools as we progress through the chapter. For now, let's consider a few of the interesting transformations occurring in this text, all of which are provided by built-in Solr tools.

We use Solr's `ASCIIFoldingFilterFactory` to transform caffé into caffe, which means users won't have to enter the diacritical é when searching. Without this transformation, users searching for caffe would not find documents indexed with caffé. The hyphenated term i-Pad is handled by adding two terms to the index using `Word-DelimiterFilterFactory`: ipad and i pad. This means that queries containing ipad, i pad, or i-pad will be a match. It's true that iPad is the correct form, but with search, you want to be as accommodating of simple variations of terms as possible.

Solr also allows you to replace characters and terms using regular expressions with `PatternReplaceCharFilterFactory`. For instance, repeating letters in a word is common in social media content like tweets in order to express emotion (for example, yummm). But from a search perspective, yummm and yumm are more or less equivalent, so we can reduce the number of unique terms in our index by collapsing these repeated letters down to a maximum of two. Later in the chapter, we'll see how to use regular expressions with Solr to make this transformation.

It's worth highlighting that all of the transformations shown previously were provided by built-in Solr tools, meaning that we only had to configure them in Solr's *schema.xml*, not write any Java code. Although Solr's built-in arsenal is powerful, sometimes you need to extend its capabilities. We'll see how to do this by using Solr's Plug-In framework to deal with bit.ly-style shortened URLs in social media content in section 6.4.3.

At this point, you should have a good feel for where we are headed with text analysis in Solr and might be wondering how to get started. Now that we know Solr provides all these great tools to transform text, how do we apply these tools to our documents during indexing? In the next section, we'll start to work with field types for doing text analysis.

6.2 Basic text analysis

As we learned in chapter 5, the `<types>` section in *schema.xml* defines `<fieldType>` elements for all possible fields in your documents, in which each `<fieldType>` defines the format and how the field is analyzed for indexing and queries. The example schema provided with Solr defines an extensive list of field types applicable for most search applications. If none of the predefined Solr field types meets your needs, you can build your own field type using the Solr Plug-In framework. We'll see an example of the Solr Plug-In framework in the last section of this chapter.

If all your fields contained structured data like language codes and timestamps, you wouldn't need to use Solr, because a relational database is efficient at indexing and searching structured data. Dealing with unstructured text is where Solr truly shines. Consequently, the example Solr schema predefines a number of powerful field types for analyzing text. Listing 6.1 provides the XML definition for `text_general`, one of the simpler field types, as a starting point for analyzing our tweet text.

The examples in this chapter depend on a few minor customizations to the *schema.xml* that ships with the Solr example. We recommend that you replace the *schema.xml* file that ships with the Solr example with the customized version in *$SOLR_IN_ACTION/example-docs/ch6/schema.xml*. Specifically, you need to overwrite *$SOLR_INSTALL/example/solr/collection1/conf/schema.xml* by doing

```
cp $SOLR_IN_ACTION/example-docs/ch6/schema.xml
➥ $SOLR_INSTALL/example/solr/collection1/conf/
```

In addition, you need to copy the *wdfftypes.txt* file to the `conf` directory:

```
cp $SOLR_IN_ACTION/example-docs/ch6/wdfftypes.txt
➥ $SOLR_INSTALL/example/solr/collection1/conf/
```

Finally, to start with a clean slate (since we already indexed some test documents in an earlier chapter), you should delete everything in your data directory to start with an empty search index:

```
rm -rf $SOLR_INSTALL/example/solr/collection1/data/*
```

After copying the custom *schema.xml* and *wdfftypes.txt*, you'll need to reload the `collection1` core from the Core administration page in the Solr administration console or restart Solr.

Listing 6.1   Example field type for analyzing general text

```
<fieldType name="text_general"
           class="solr.TextField"
           positionIncrementGap="100">
```

◁— **Use a short, descriptive name based on the type of data.**

Tokenizer splits a field's text into tokens.

```
<analyzer type="index">
  <tokenizer class="solr.StandardTokenizerFactory"/>

  <filter class="solr.StopFilterFactory" ignoreCase="true"
          words="lang/stopwords_en.txt"/>
  <filter class="solr.LowerCaseFilterFactory"/>
</analyzer>

<analyzer type="query">
  <tokenizer class="solr.StandardTokenizerFactory"/>

  <filter class="solr.StopFilterFactory"
          ignoreCase="true" words="lang/stopwords_en.txt"/>
  <filter class="solr.SynonymFilterFactory"
          synonyms="synonyms.txt"
          ignoreCase="true" expand="true"/>
  <filter class="solr.LowerCaseFilterFactory"/>
</analyzer>

</fieldType>
```

Define the analyzer to use for indexing documents.

Define the analyzer to use for analyzing queries.

Let's break this XML definition down into manageable parts. At the top, you define a `<fieldType>`. For fields that handle text data, you should specify the value of the class attribute to be `solr.TextField`. This tells Solr that you want the text to be analyzed. Also, you should use a name that gives a clue about the type of text that will be analyzed using this field type; for example, `text_general` is a good all-purpose type for when you don't know the language of the text you are analyzing.

6.2.1   *Analyzer*

Inside the `<fieldType>` element, you should define at least one `<analyzer>` that determines how the text will be analyzed. In practice, it's common to define two separate `<analyzer>` elements: one for indexing and another for analyzing the text entered by users when searching. The `text_general` field type uses this approach. Think, for a moment, about why you might use different analyzers for indexing and querying. You often need additional analysis for processing queries beyond what's necessary for indexing a document. For example, adding synonyms is typically done during query text analysis only to avoid inflating the size of your index and to make it easier to manage synonyms. We'll see an example of this approach shortly.

Although you can define two separate analyzers, the analysis applied to query terms must be compatible with how the text was analyzed during indexing. Consider the case in which an analyzer is configured to lowercase terms during indexing, but does not lowercase query terms; users searching for North Beach would not find our example tweet because the index contains the lowercased forms north and beach.

6.2.2   *Tokenizer*

In Solr, each `<analyzer>` breaks the text analysis process into two phases: tokenization (parsing) and token filtering. Technically, there is also a third phase that enables preprocessing before tokenization, in which you can apply character filters. We'll discuss character filtering in more detail in section 6.3.1, so for now let's concentrate on tokenization and token filters.

In the tokenization phase, text is split into a stream of tokens using some form of parsing. The most basic tokenizer is a `WhitespaceTokenizer` that splits text on whitespace only. More common is `StandardTokenizer`, which performs intelligent parsing to split terms on whitespace and punctuation and correctly handles URLs, email addresses, and acronyms. To define a tokenizer, you need to specify the Java implementation class of the factory for your tokenizer. To use the common `Standard-Tokenizer`, you specify `solr.StandardTokenizerFactory`.

```
<tokenizer class="solr.StandardTokenizerFactory"/>
```

In Solr, you must specify the factory class instead of the underlying `Tokenizer` implementation class because most tokenizers do not provide a default no-arg constructor. By using the factory approach, Solr gives you a standard way to define any tokenizer in XML. Behind the scenes, each factory class knows how to translate the XML configuration properties to construct an instance of the specific `Tokenizer` implementation class. All tokenizers produce a stream of tokens that can be processed by zero or more filters to perform some sort of transformation of the token.

6.2.3 *Token filter*

A token filter performs one of three actions on a token:

- *Transformation*—Changing the token to a different form such as lowercasing all letters or stemming
- *Token injection*—Adding a token to the stream, as is done with the synonym filter
- *Token removal*—Removing tokens, as is done by the stop word filter

Filters can be chained together to apply a series of transformations on each token. The order of the filters is important as you wouldn't want to have a filter that depended on the case of your tokens listed after a filter that lowercases all tokens.

Let's see this process in action as Solr analyzes our example tweet text, starting with `StandardTokenizer`.

6.2.4 *StandardTokenizer*

At this point, you should have a good understanding of the schema design process and the mechanics of defining fields and field types in *schema.xml*. Let's put this knowledge to work to do basic text analysis of our example tweet text from chapter 5. The first step in basic text analysis is to determine how to parse the text into a stream of tokens using a tokenizer. Let's start by using `StandardTokenizer`, which has been the classic go-to solution for many Solr and Lucene projects because it does a great job of splitting text on whitespace and punctuation, but also handles acronyms and contractions with ease. To see this tokenizer in action, let's use it to parse our example tweet:

```
#Yummm :) Drinking a latte at Caffé Grecco in SF's historic North Beach...
Learning text analysis with #SolrInAction by @ManningBooks on my i-Pad
```

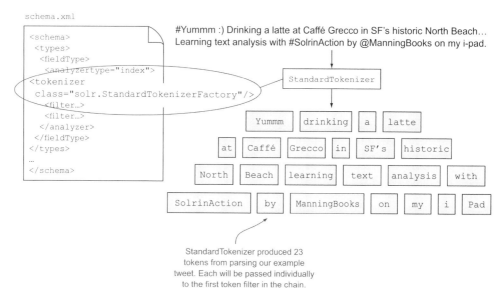

Figure 6.3   Stream of 23 tokens produced by the `StandardTokenizer` for our example tweet

If you are familiar with user-generated content on social networks like Twitter, you'll notice that this tweet is quite well formed compared to most, but it still poses some interesting challenges from a parsing perspective. Figure 6.3 depicts the tokens produced by `StandardTokenizer`.

As you can see, `StandardTokenizer` split the tweet successfully into a stream of 23 separate tokens. Specifically, `StandardTokenizer` provides the following features:

- Splits on whitespace and standard punctuation characters such as period, comma, semicolon, etc. (Notice how the ellipsis … and emoticon `:)` are removed from the stream.)
- Preserves internet domain names and email addresses as a single token.
- Splits hyphenated terms into two tokens; for example, `i-Pad` becomes `i` and `Pad`.
- Supports a configurable maximum token length attribute. Default is 255.
- Strips leading # and @ characters from hashtags and mentions.

Next, let's look at several common token filters provided by Solr to do basic text analysis. Returning to our example tweet, there are a number of issues with the token stream that should be addressed before this text is added to the index. First, there are a few extremely common terms such as `a` or `in` that only serve a grammatical purpose and add little value for differentiating one document from another. Common words that occur in most of the documents in your index are known as *stop words*, and they can be removed from the token stream easily using `StopFilterFactory`.

6.2.5 *Removing stop words with StopFilterFactory*

Solr's `StopFilterFactory` removes stop words from the token stream during analysis, as they add little value to helping your users find relevant documents. Removing stop words during indexing helps reduce the size of your index and can improve search performance as it reduces the number of documents Solr will process and the number of terms that will be scored in the relevancy calculation for queries that contain stop words. To analyze our example tweet, we defined `StopFilterFactory` in listing 6.1 as

```
<filter class="solr.StopFilterFactory" ignoreCase="true"
    words="lang/stopwords_en.txt" />
```

Notice that we specify an English-specific stop word list (`words="lang/stopwords_en.txt"`). Out of the box, Solr provides a basic stop word list that you can customize to meet your needs; see *stopwords_en.txt* in the *lang/* subdirectory under *conf/* (*$SOLR_INSTALL/example/solr/collection1/conf/lang/*). Here are the English stop words included in the example Solr server:

```
a   an   and   are   as   at   be   but   by   for   if   in   into   is   it   no   not   of
on   or   such   that   the   their   then   there   these   they   this   to   was   will
with
```

In general, stop word removal is language-specific. If you are analyzing German text, then you will need a stop word list containing terms like `die` and `ein`. Solr provides custom stop word lists for many languages in the *lang/* subdirectory in the out-of-the-box Solr file path.

> **Advanced approach to removing stop words**
>
> Google owns a patent on its approach to handling stop words, in which it includes all stop words during indexing and selectively removes stop words from queries based on comparing sets of documents retrieved with and without using the stop words; see www.google.com/patents/US7945579. Google's patented approach to stop words is a great example of how search providers use advanced text analysis to achieve competitive advantage. Even with something as simple as removing stop words, there is no one-size-fits-all solution.

6.2.6 *LowerCaseFilterFactory—lowercase letters in terms*

The `LowerCaseFilterFactory` lowercases the letters in all tokens. When indexing our tweet in section 6.2.4, `ManningBooks` became `manningbooks`. As such, the tweet will be found for user queries containing `MANNINGBOOKS`, `ManningBooks`, and `manningbooks`, or any other uppercase/lowercase variation. Defining this filter is trivial:

```
<filter class="solr.LowerCaseFilterFactory"/>
```

As with stop words, it's not always clear whether to apply the lowercase filter to all terms. For example, terms starting with a capital letter in the middle of a sentence

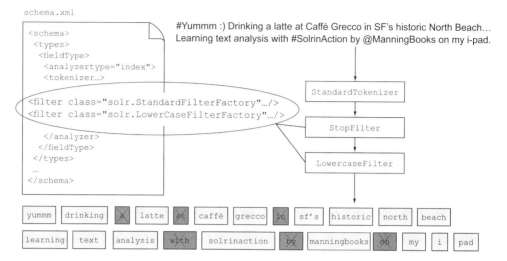

Figure 6.4   Resulting text to be indexed after splitting, using `StandardTokenizer` and applying the stop word and lowercase filters. The terms with an X are the stop words, which would not be included in your index.

typically indicate a proper noun that can greatly improve the precision of your results if users seek the proper noun form of common terms such as North Beach; both north and beach are common terms that appear in other contexts, so the capital letters can help improve precision.

For example, a user searching for North Beach is probably mostly interested in documents about the popular San Francisco neighborhood and would be less interested in a document containing "the waves are stronger on the *north beach* of the island." But using a more nuanced approach to lowercasing terms assumes that your users use the right case when searching. In most cases, you'll want to apply the lowercase filter, but you'll still need to determine where in the filter chain to apply it. If you have a synonym list in all lowercase, then you'll want to apply the lowercase filter before your synonym filter.

Figure 6.4 shows the resulting text after applying the stop word and lowercase filters to the example tweet.

Now we have a basic text analysis solution for our sample tweet. Let's apply what we learned so far to see text analysis in action.

6.2.7   *Testing your analysis with Solr's analysis form*

Solr provides a simple form that allows you to test your text analysis configuration on sample text without having to add a document to the index. The form also allows you to see if a query would match a sample document without having to index the document. With the server running, navigate to the admin console at http://localhost:8983/solr/, and click collection1 as shown in figure 6.5.

Once the form loads in your browser, enter the sample tweet text in the Field Value (Index) text box and text_general in the Field Type box as seen in figure 6.6.

On the Solr Admin panel, click
collection1 to reveal the link
to the Analysis panel

Figure 6.5   How to find the link to the Analysis form from the Solr Admin panel

Once you enter the field type and text to analyze, click the Analyse Values button to see the result. Below the form, Solr reports the steps it takes to analyze the text for indexing using the `text_general` field type. Notice how the text is first parsed with the `StandardTokenizer`, abbreviated as ST, then each token passes through `Stop-Filter` (SF) and `LowercaseFilter` (LCF).

Next, let's try a query against our example tweet to see if it is a match; enter `drinking a latte` in the text box labeled Field Value (Query) as shown in figure 6.7. When you click the Analyse Values button, Solr will highlight any terms in the document that match the query, in this case `drinking` and `latte`.

Next, enter `San Francisco drink cafe ipad`, and click the Analyse Values button again. Although this is a nonsensical query, we would expect our sample document to be a match. We're using this nonsensical query to demonstrate that seemingly small differences in terms can lead to highly relevant documents being missed by your users. Case in point, none of the query terms match the example document! It's easy for a human to see the similarity between the terms in the query and the example document, but to Solr, the terms have no relation to each other! We will use better text analysis to overcome this mismatch.

In our first pass, we resolved a number of text parsing and basic analysis issues with very little overall effort. Still, there are a number of outstanding issues that will make finding this tweet difficult for our users. How many potential issues do you see in the text? Compare your thoughts to figure 6.8.

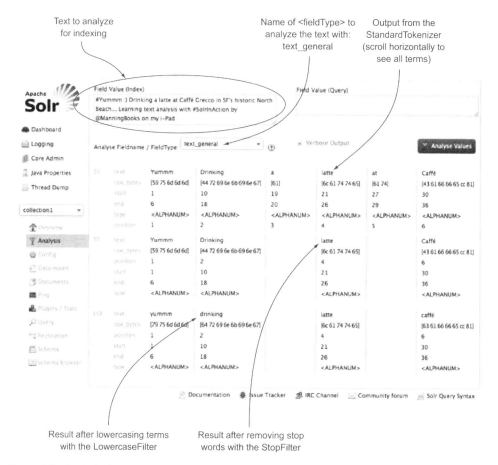

Text to analyze for indexing

Name of <fieldType> to analyze the text with: text_general

Output from the StandardTokenizer (scroll horizontally to see all terms)

Result after lowercasing terms with the LowercaseFilter

Result after removing stop words with the StopFilter

Figure 6.6   Analysis form showing the step-by-step process Solr applies to analyzing a document using the selected `FieldType: text_general`

Unless you are indexing tweets or content from other social media sources, you may not encounter any of the analysis issues shown in figure 6.8. In general, the main point is that you need to study a representative sample of the documents in your index to determine the type of analysis needed, as we've done here.

At this point, it should be clear that the basic text analysis provided by the `text_general` field type is not sufficient to meet our needs. Consequently, we need to implement a new custom field type, building on the tools we've already discussed while learning a few new ones.

6.3   *Defining a custom field type for microblog text*

We made good progress in analyzing social media text, but there are a few outstanding issues we still need to address. In this section, we tackle these remaining issues by introducing a few more of Solr's built-in text analysis tools. To begin, because none of the predefined field types meet all of our needs, we will define a new custom field type

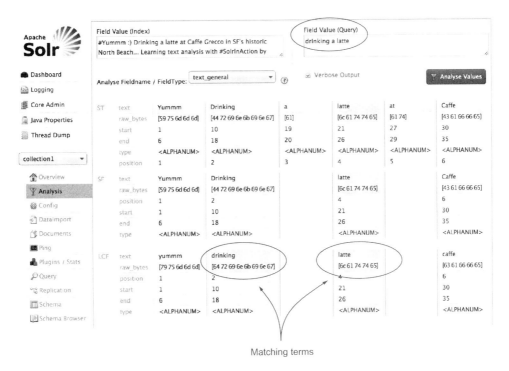

Figure 6.7 **Search for** `drinking a latte` **on the analysis panel, and Solr will highlight matching terms** `drinking` **and** `latte` **in the example document.**

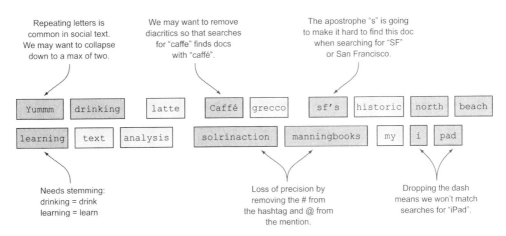

Figure 6.8 **Remaining text analysis issues with our sample tweet after applying the lowercase and stop filters**

in *schema.xml*. Under the `<types>` element in *schema.xml* in the following listing, add
text_microblog.

Listing 6.2   Custom field type for analyzing microblog text

```
<types>
...
  <fieldType name="text_microblog" class="solr.TextField"              ◁──   New field type is added
           positionIncrementGap="100">                                        below the existing field
    <analyzer type="index">                                            ◁──   types inside of <types>.
      <charFilter class="solr.PatternReplaceCharFilterFactory"
                  pattern="([a-zA-Z])\1+"                              Analyzer for
                  replacement="$1$1"/>                                 indexing
      <tokenizer class="solr.WhitespaceTokenizerFactory"/>            documents.
      <filter class="solr.WordDelimiterFilterFactory"
              generateWordParts="1"
              splitOnCaseChange="0"
              splitOnNumerics="0"
              stemEnglishPossessive="1"
              preserveOriginal="0"
              catenateWords="1"
              generateNumberParts="1"
              catenateNumbers="0"
              catenateAll="0"
              types="wdfftypes.txt"/>
      <filter class="solr.StopFilterFactory"
              ignoreCase="true"
              words="lang/stopwords_en.txt"/>
      <filter class="solr.LowerCaseFilterFactory"/>
      <filter class="solr.ASCIIFoldingFilterFactory"/>                 Analyzer for
      <filter class="solr.KStemFilterFactory"/>                        processing
    </analyzer>                                                        user queries.
    <analyzer type="query">                                          ◁──
      <charFilter class="solr.PatternReplaceCharFilterFactory"
                  pattern="([a-zA-Z])\1+"
                  replacement="$1$1"/>
      <tokenizer class="solr.WhitespaceTokenizerFactory"/>
      <filter class="solr.WordDelimiterFilterFactory"
              splitOnCaseChange="0"
              splitOnNumerics="0"
              stemEnglishPossessive="1"
              preserveOriginal="0"
              generateWordParts="1"
              catenateWords="1"
              generateNumberParts="0"
              catenateNumbers="0"
              catenateAll="0"
              types="wdfftypes.txt"/>
      <filter class="solr.LowerCaseFilterFactory"/>
      <filter class="solr.ASCIIFoldingFilterFactory"/>
      <filter class="solr.StopFilterFactory"
              ignoreCase="true"
              words="lang/stopwords_en.txt"/>
      <filter class="solr.KStemFilterFactory"/>
```

```
        <filter class="solr.SynonymFilterFactory"
                synonyms="synonyms.txt"
                ignoreCase="true"
                expand="true"/>
    </analyzer>
  </fieldType>
</types>
```

> **Synonym processing is performed on the query side, not during indexing.**

You should recognize the structure and some of the elements in this field type definition, but there are also a few new ones that we haven't yet discussed. Table 6.3 provides an overview of the new tools we'll cover in this section.

Table 6.3   List of additional Solr text analysis tools needed to analyze microblog text

Solr tool	Description
PatternReplaceCharFilterFactory	Use regular expression to replace characters before tokenizing.
WhitespaceTokenizerFactory	Split text on whitespace only.
WordDelimiterFilterFactory	Intelligently split tokens on punctuation and case change and handle special characters like # and @ on hashtags and mentions.
ASCIIFoldingFilterFactory	Transform diacritics into their ASCII equivalents if possible.
KStemFilterFactory	Stemming on English text; less aggressive than the Porter stemmer.
SynonymFilterFactory	Inject synonyms for common terms into queries.

We'll work through each of these tools in the sections ahead. Let's start with a solution for removing repeated letters from words like "yummm" using a regular expression.

6.3.1   Collapsing repeated letters with PatternReplaceCharFilterFactory

In Solr, a CharFilter (or character filter) is a preprocessor on an incoming stream of characters before they are passed on to the tokenizer for parsing. Much like token filters, CharFilters can be chained together to add, change, or remove characters from text. In Solr 4, there are three built-in CharFilters:

- *solr.MappingCharFilterFactory*—Applies replacements of characters defined in an external configuration file.
- *solr.PatternReplaceCharFilterFactory*—Uses a regular expression to replace characters with an alternative value.
- *solr.HTMLStripCharFilterFactory*—Strips HTML markup from text.

As with most Solr features, you can implement your own using the Plug-In framework. Of the three filters, PatternReplaceCharFilterFactory seems most appropriate for our current text analysis needs as tweets typically do not have embedded HTML, and we do not need to map any characters. Consequently, we won't show how to use the `MappingCharFilterFactory` or `HTMLStripCharFilterFactory` filters in these chapters, so please see the Solr wiki for more details (http://wiki.apache.org/solr/). Let's see how to apply `PatternReplaceCharFilterFactory` to address a few of the issues with our example tweet.

`solr.PatternReplaceCharFilterFactory` is used to filter characters using regular expressions. To configure this factory, you need to define two attributes: `pattern` and `replacement`. The pattern is a regular expression that identifies the characters we want to replace in our text. The replacement attribute specifies the value you want to replace the matched characters with.[1]

Don't worry if you're not a regular expression expert; in most cases you can find the expression you need online using Google or a similar search engine.

Let's use this `<charFilter>` to solve those pesky terms with repeated letters, such as `yummm`. To collapse repeated letters to a maximum of two, we need a regular expression that identifies sequences of repeated letters, so `([a-zA-Z])\1+` will work nicely. In regex speak, `[a-zA-Z]` is a character class that identifies a single letter in lower or uppercase. The parentheses around the character class identify the matching letter as a captured group. The `\1` part is called a numbered backreference that matches a repeat of the first group, and the + part says the repeated letter can occur one or more times.

That covers the pattern to match; what about the replacement? Our goal is to collapse repeated letters to a maximum of two, so what we need is a way to address the part of a term that matches `([a-zA-Z])`. With regular expressions, the `([a-zA-Z])` part of our expression is called a captured group and is addressable as `$1`. Thus, our replacement value is `$1$1`. For example, in `yummm`, `([a-zA-Z])` evaluates to the first "m," and the entire expression evaluates to "mmm," so "mmm" gets replaced with "mm." To make this work in `text_microblog` fieldType, you add the XML shown in this listing.

> **Listing 6.3   Define a `charFilter` to collapse repeated letters using regular expression**

```
<charFilter class="solr.PatternReplaceCharFilterFactory"
    pattern="([a-zA-Z])\1+"
    replacement="$1$1"/>
```

6.3.2   *Preserving hashtags, mentions, and hyphenated terms*

It turns out that a few of the issues we are having with the example tweet are caused by `StandardTokenizer`. Specifically, `StandardTokenizer` is stripping the # and @ characters from hashtags and mentions respectively. In addition, it's splitting hyphenated terms into two tokens, such as `i-Pad` becoming `i` and `Pad`. Consequently, queries for `iPad` won't match our example document, as we saw in the previous section. We'll see

---

[1] If you need a little refresher on regular expressions, we recommend www.regexplanet.com as a resource for learning about and testing regular expressions.

how to handle the iPad issue in a moment. For now, let's dig into why we care about preserving the # and @ characters for hashtags and mentions.

In the previous section, we saw that the @ was removed from @ManningBooks by the StandardTokenizer, which means that we've lost some information about this term. Specifically, @ManningBooks used in a social context has a special meaning in that it identifies a specific social account, in this case the one used by Manning Publications. This mention happens to be pretty specific, but in general, removing the @ during text analysis may lead to unexpected search results, especially when combined with stemming.

The same goes for hashtags. #fail is a hashtag commonly used to denote a person's dissatisfaction with another person, place, or thing such as a brand. If you wanted to find all tweets with #fail, you probably wouldn't want to match tweets with only fail, as in I partied too late last night, I hope I don't fail today's mid-term exam. Thus, during text analysis, you want to preserve the fact that #fail is different than fail by preserving the leading # character. In general, we want to preserve hashtags and mentions so that we have the flexibility to differentiate between, for example, documents with #fail and documents with only fail. The general lesson here is that sometimes you need to preserve context about special terms during text analysis.

We hope you're convinced that we need to preserve the leading # and @ characters in our text. Now we need to figure out how to do it. First, let's make sure we understand how the characters are being removed. StandardTokenizer uses word delimiters to split text into tokens and is treating the # and @ characters as word delimiters. If you are a Java developer, your first inclination might be to extend StandardTokenizer and override the behavior that strips off these two special characters. Unfortunately, StandardTokenizer is not easy to extend, and more importantly, we can do this without writing any custom code! Now we get a chance to learn about two more Solr text analysis tools, namely WhitespaceTokenizerFactory and WordDelimiterFilterFactory.

WHITESPACETOKENIZERFACTORY

WhitespaceTokenizerFactory is a very simple tokenizer that splits text on whitespace only. If you recall, StandardTokenizer split our example tweet into 23 separate tokens. In contrast, WhitespaceTokenizer produces a different set of tokens, as depicted in figure 6.9.

Progress? Maybe. We solved our hashtag, mention, and hyphenated term issues, but we introduced a few more problems in the process. Specifically, the emoticon [:)] is now a token, and the ellipsis (...) is included as part of Beach.... Luckily, with Solr, these issues are easily resolved using WordDelimiterFilterFactory.

WORDDELIMITERFILTERFACTORY

To complement WhitespaceTokenizer's simplistic approach to splitting on whitespace, WordDelimiterFilterFactory offers a powerful solution to resolving most issues caused by splitting on whitespace. At a high level, this filter splits a token into subwords using various parsing rules. Before we cover these rules in detail, let's see how this filter helps us preserve the special characters on our hashtags and mentions. For

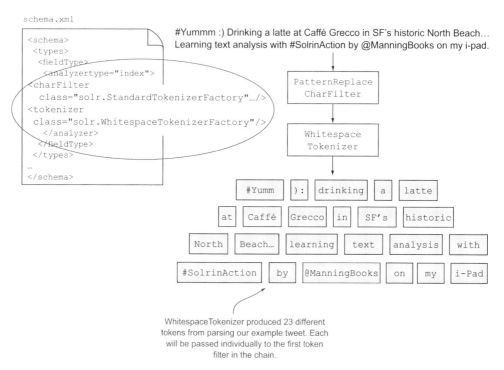

schema.xml

```
<schema>
 <types>
  <fieldType>
   <analyzertype="index">
   <charFilter
    class="solr.StandardTokenizerFactory"…/>
   <tokenizer
    class="solr.WhitespaceTokenizerFactory"/>
    </analyzer>
   </fieldType>
 </types>
…
</schema>
```

#Yummm :) Drinking a latte at Caffé Grecco in SF's historic North Beach…
Learning text analysis with #SolrinAction by @ManningBooks on my i-pad.

PatternReplace
CharFilter

Whitespace
Tokenizer

| #Yumm |): | drinking | a | latte |

| at | Caffé | Grecco | in | SF's | historic |

| North | Beach… | learning | text | analysis | with |

| #SolrinAction | by | @ManningBooks | on | my | i-Pad |

WhitespaceTokenizer produced 23 different
tokens from parsing our example tweet. Each
will be passed individually to the first token
filter in the chain.

Figure 6.9 Tokens produced by `WhitespaceTokenizer`; still 23, but some are different than those produced by `StandardTokenizer`.

our example, we configured `WordDelimiterFilterFactory` using the options in the following listing.

Listing 6.4 Define `WordDelimiterFilterFactory` with options set to preserve #, @

```
<filter class="solr.WordDelimiterFilterFactory"
        generateWordParts="1"
        splitOnCaseChange="0"
        splitOnNumerics="0"
        stemEnglishPossessive="1"
        preserveOriginal="0"
        catenateWords="1"
        generateNumberParts="0"        Define custom character
        catenateNumbers="0"            types for splitting words in
        catenateAll="0"                a file called wdfftypes.txt.
        types="wdfftypes.txt"/>
```

By default this filter will also strip off the # and @ characters from hashtags and mentions. But unlike `StandardTokenizer`, `WordDelimiterFilter` provides an easy way to customize which characters it treats as word delimiters by using a simple "types" mapping file, which in our example is *wdfftypes.txt*. Our *wdfftypes.txt* file contains two mappings:

```
\# => ALPHA
@ => ALPHA
```

These settings map the # and @ characters to the ALPHA class, which means our instance of WordDelimiterFilter won't treat them as word delimiters. The leading backslash on the hash sign is so that Solr won't interpret that line as a comment when reading the *wdfftypes.txt* file. With this simple mapping, hashtags and mentions are preserved in our text.

WordDelimiterFilter also handles hyphenated terms in a robust manner. In our example tweet, the author incorrectly used i-Pad instead of iPad; it would be ideal if our tweet could be matched for all possible forms used in queries, such as i Pad, i-Pad, and iPad. Think about what needs to happen during indexing and query analysis to ensure all three forms produce matches. Hopefully you figured out that Word-DelimiterFilter needs to split i-Pad on the hyphen into two tokens, i and Pad, but also must inject a new token, iPad, into the stream. This is the exact behavior you get from WordDelimiterFilter when you set generateWordParts=1 and catenateWords=1.

In general, WordDelimiterFilter provides a number of options used to fine-tune the transformations it makes to your tokens. Table 6.4 gives an overview of how each option works.

Table 6.4 Configuration options for `WordDelimiterFilterFactory`

Attribute	Behavior if enabled (="1")	Default
generateWordParts	Splits words using built-in parsing rules and other options to create subword parts.	enabled (1)
splitOnCaseChange	Splits camel-case terms when a change in letter case is encountered during parsing; for example, SolrInAction is split into three tokens, Solr, In, and Action.	enabled (1)
splitOnNumerics	Splits terms having a mixture of letters and numbers when a number is encountered; for example, R2D2 is split into four tokens: R, 2, D, and 2.	enabled (1)
stemEnglishPossessive	Removes 's from a term; for example, SF's becomes SF.	enabled (1)
preserveOriginal	Includes the original token in the text in addition to any other tokens produced by this filter; for example, SF's would be included as well as SF.	disabled (0)
catenateWords	Concatenates subword parts into a single token; for example, i-Pad would be split at the hyphen into two tokens, i and Pad, and then concatenated into iPad to produce a third token.	disabled (0)
generateNumberParts	Splits tokens with numeric data separated by punctuation like dashes into multiple tokens; for example, a phone number of 867-5309 would be split into two terms, 867 and 5309.	enabled (1)

Table 6.4   Configuration options for `WordDelimiterFilterFactory` *(continued)*

Attribute	Behavior if enabled (="1")	Default
`catenateNumbers`	If a number token was split, then concatenate the parts into a single term; keeping with our phone number reference, `867-5309` would be split into three tokens: `867`, `5309`, and `8675309`.	disabled (0)
`catenateAll`	When using `generateWordParts="1"` and `generateNumberParts="1"`, concatenate all parts into a single token.	disabled (0)

It may take a bit of experimentation to get a feel for how `WordDelimiterFactory` works with your content. We recommend using Solr's Analysis form to experiment with these settings as we did in section 6.2.7. For now, we've solved the problems with hashtags, mentions, and hyphenated terms, so let's turn our attention to how to handle terms with accent marks, such as `caffé`.

6.3.3   *Removing diacritical marks using ASCIIFoldingFilterFactory*

In search, it's often the case that doing simple things can make a big difference. This is certainly the case when handling characters that have diacritical marks, such as `caffé` (as in our example) or `jalapeño`. In most cases, you can't be sure users will type characters with the diacritical mark when searching, so Solr provides `ASCIIFolding-FilterFactory` to transform characters into their ASCII equivalents, if available. In *schema.xml*, you can include this filter in your analyzer by adding

```
<filter class="solr.ASCIIFoldingFilterFactory"/>
```

It's best to list this filter after the lowercase filter so you only have to work with lower-case characters. `ASCIIFoldingFilter` only works with Latin-based characters; for other languages, look at `solr.analysis.ICUFoldingFilterFactory`, available since Solr 3.1.

6.3.4   *Stemming with KStemFilterFactory*

Stemming transforms words into a base form using language-specific rules. Solr provides a number of stemming filters, each with its own strengths and weaknesses. For now, we'll use a filter based on the Krovetz stemmer: `solr.KStemFilterFactory`. This stemmer is less aggressive in its transformations than other popular stemmers like `PorterStemmer`. For now, we apply `KStemFilterFactory` to remove `ing` from terms like `drinking` and `learning`.[2]

```
<filter class="solr.KStemFilterFactory"/>
```

---

[2] See R. Krovetz, 1993: "Viewing morphology as an inference process," in R. Korfhage et al., Proc. 16th ACM SIGIR Conference, Pittsburgh, June 27–July 1, 1993; pp. 191–202.

Table 6.5 shows some examples of stemming applied to terms using KStemFilter-Factory and PorterStemFilterFactory.

Table 6.5   Comparing stems produced by the KStemmer and Porter algorithms

Original term	Stem (KStemmer)	Stem (Porter)
drinking	drink	drink
requirements	requirement	requir
operating	operate	oper
operative	operative	oper
wedding	wedding	wed
learning	learning	learn

It should be clear from these few examples that the Porter stemming algorithm is much more aggressive than KStemmer. The problem with being too aggressive is that your search application may end up matching documents that have little to do with a user's query (hurting Precision). If a user searches for wedding in July, the term wedding is stemmed to wed using the Porter stemmer, which is also a common abbreviation for Wednesday. Also notice that operating and operative both stem to oper using Porter, so documents containing covert operative and operating system will both be a match for a query for operating capital.

One thing to note is that when KStemmer is applied to our example tweet, it transforms drinking to drink but it does not transform learning to learn as we might expect. This odd behavior occurs because KStemmer uses a list of protected terms that it does not stem, and learning is a protected term.

In general, stemmers expand the set of documents that match a query (improving Recall), but they can negatively impact the Precision of the results. We'll cover stemming in much more detail in our discussion of multilingual search in chapter 14.

6.3.5   *Injecting synonyms at query time with SynonymFilterFactory*

SynonymFilterFactory injects synonyms for important terms into the token stream. For example, you may want to inject home into the token stream when you encounter house. In most cases, synonyms are injected only during query-time analysis. This helps reduce the size of your index and makes it easier to maintain changes to the synonym list. If you inject synonyms during indexing, and you discover a new synonym for one of your terms, then you will have to reindex all of your documents to apply the change. If you only inject synonyms during query processing, new synonyms can be introduced without reindexing. Here's how to define SynonymFilter in your *schema.xml*:

```
<filter class="solr.SynonymFilterFactory"
    synonyms="synonyms.txt"
    ignoreCase="true" expand="true" />
```

This filter is best applied to the query analyzer only, particularly if you have single-term synonyms. You also need to consider where to put it in the chain of filters. To determine this, you need to think about what transformations need to take place before you match synonyms for terms. It often makes the most sense to list this filter last for your query analyzer, so that your synonym list can assume all other transformations have already taken place on a token. Consider what happens if we apply ASCII-FoldingFilter after our synonym filter; this means that our synonym list will need to include the diacritics, such as caffé.

In our example, there are a few tokens that could benefit from synonyms, including SF, latte, and caffe. To map synonyms for these terms in Solr, add the following to the synonyms.txt file identified in your filter definition:

```
sf,san fran,sanfran,san francisco
latte,coffee
caffe,cafe
```

Looking at this, although it's great that Solr provides a way to do this mapping, you might wonder who would want to manually configure thousands of synonyms? That's a fair point, and currently this is a problem in Solr. There are some solutions available as community extensions to Solr, such as a utility to convert the WordNet database of English synonyms into Solr's format (see https://issues.apache.org/jira/browse/LUCENE-2347).

6.3.6 *Putting it all together*

After applying these additional filters to our example tweet, we are left with the text shown in figure 6.10.

Now let's return to the Solr Analysis form to see if the previous query we tried is a match. Recall that the query San Francisco drink cafe ipad was not a match when we used the simple text_general field type in section 6.2.7. But using the text_microblog field type, our example document is a strong match for this query, as shown in figure 6.11.

The query terms shown in table 6.6 are now matches to terms in our example tweet based on text analysis.

Table 6.6   Query terms matching our example tweet based on text analysis

Query term	Matching term in document	Explanation
San Francisco	SF's	WordDelimiterFilter removes the 's from SF's and SynonymFilter injects sf as a synonym for San Francisco during query text analysis.
drink	Drinking	LowercaseFilter changes D to d and KStemFilter removes the ing.

Table 6.6 Query terms matching our example tweet based on text analysis *(continued)*

Query term	Matching term in document	Explanation
cafe	Caffé	LowercaseFilter changes C to c, ASCIIFoldingFilter changes é to e, and SynonymFilter injects caffe as a synonym for cafe during query processing.
iPad	i-Pad	WordDelimiterFilter splits i-Pad on the hyphen, and creates iPad as a new token by concatenating the split terms into one.

This query is a bit contrived for example purposes. The key takeaway is that Solr provides a wealth of built-in text analysis tools that allow you to implement flexible solutions to handle complex text. The ultimate goal is to produce a search application that makes it easier for your users to find relevant documents using natural language, without having to think about linguistic differences in text.

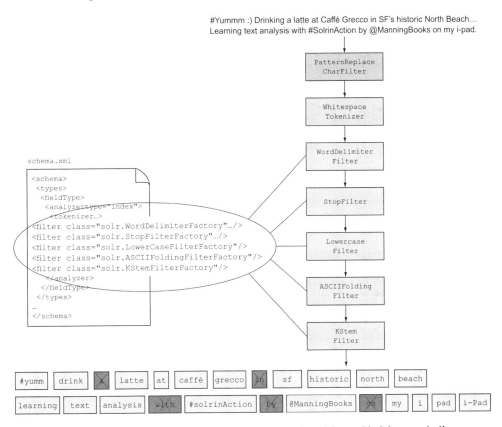

Figure 6.10 Results after applying the new custom `text_microblog <fieldType>` **to the tweet text**

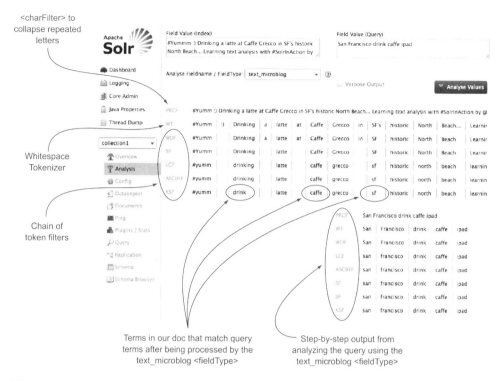

Figure 6.11   Solr Analysis form showing the results of analyzing our example tweet and a query with `text_microblog <fieldType>`

If you are interested in analyzing microblog text or want to see the `text_microblog` field type in action, you can apply the *ch6/schema.xml* from the source code provided with the book to your local Solr server. After applying the *schema.xml*, restart your Solr server and then use the *post.jar* application to add the *tweets.xml* document to your server.

```
cd $SOLR_IN_ACTION/example-docs
java -jar post.jar ch6/tweets.xml
```

You should see output similar to the following:

```
Posting file tweets.xml to http://localhost:8983/solr/collection1/update
<?xml version="1.0" encoding="UTF-8"?>
<response>
  <lst name="responseHeader">
    <int name="status">0</int>
    <int name="QTime">140</int>
  </lst>
</response>

<?xml version="1.0" encoding="UTF-8"?>
<response>
  <lst name="responseHeader">
    <int name="status">0</int>
    <int name="QTime">67</int>
```

```
    </lst>
</response>
```

After indexing the documents, you can search for `catch_all:@thelabdude` to make sure these tweet examples are available when searched. Feel free to experiment with various queries to see Solr text analysis in action. Let's now turn our attention to more advanced topics in text analysis.

6.4   *Advanced text analysis*

Throughout this chapter we built a solution to parse and analyze complex social media text without writing a single line of code. We covered the main tools Solr provides, but in reality we've only touched on the most common tools available. Before we wrap up this chapter, we want to provide an overview of some of the advanced techniques you can use to fine-tune your analysis. Specifically, we'll cover

- Advanced options for text fields in *schema.xml*
- Per-language text analysis
- Extending text analysis using Solr's Plug-In framework

Let's begin by looking at some of the more advanced attributes you can apply to text fields in *schema.xml*.

6.4.1   *Advanced field attributes*

Table 6.7 lists advanced attributes you can set for `<field>` elements, along with a short description of what to expect when the attribute is enabled. We think it is important to be aware of these options, as you will undoubtedly encounter them when looking at the Solr example *schema.xml*. You should be aware also that each of these advanced attributes applies only to text fields and does not impact nontext fields like dates and strings.

Table 6.7   Overview of advanced attributes for field elements in *schema.xml*

Attribute	Behavior when enabled (=`"true"`)	Default value
omitNorms	Disables length normalization and index-time boosting for the field, which helps save storage in your index. Norms help give shorter documents a little boost during relevance scoring. Thus, if most of your documents are of similar size, you could consider omitting norms to help reduce the size of your index. You must not omit norms (`omitNorms="false"`) if you need index-time boosts on a field, as Solr encodes the boost into the norm value. Norms are omitted by default for primitive types such as dates, strings, and numeric fields.	false
termVectors	Solr provides a More Like This feature to find documents that are similar to a specific document. The More Like This feature requires term vectors to be enabled so Solr can compute a similarity measure between two documents. Storing term vectors can be expensive for large indexes, so only enable these if you're sure you need them.	false

Table 6.7   Overview of advanced attributes for field elements in *schema.xml (continued)*

Attribute	Behavior when enabled (=`"true"`)	Default value
`termPositions`	Commonly used to improve the performance of the hit highlighting feature in Solr; covered in depth in chapter 9. Enabling term positions increases the size of your index.	false
`termOffset`	Commonly used to improve the performance of the hit highlighting feature in Solr; covered in depth in chapter 9. Enabling term offsets increases the size of your index.	false

OMITTING FIELD NORMS

Let's take a closer look at the optional `omitNorms` attribute, as that is a common source of confusion for new Solr users. As we discussed in chapter 3, a norm is a floating-point value (Java float) based on a document length norm, document boost, and field boost. Under the covers, Lucene encodes this floating point value into a single byte, which, if you think about it, is pretty cool. The document length norm is used to boost smaller documents. Without going into too much detail, Lucene gives smaller documents a slight boost over longer documents to improve relevance scoring. Conceptually, if a query term matches a short document and a long document, both containing the term "once", Lucene considers the short document to be slightly more relevant to the query because the matching term has more weight in the short document than it does in the long document. In this case, term weight is the term frequency (1) divided by the total number of terms in the document (N). For a short document with 10 terms, the weight would be 0.10, and for a long document with 1000 terms, the weight would be 0.001. Thus, Lucene gives the shorter document a slight boost, which is encoded in the norm.

It stands to reason that if your documents are of similar length, and you are not using field and document boosts at index time, you can set `omitNorms="true"` to save memory during searching. When starting out, we recommend that you use the default value (`omitNorms="false"`) so that results ranking benefits from the document length normalization. Let's look at another advanced attribute for fields, which is used to improve the performance of document similarity calculations.

TERM VECTORS

In chapter 3, we discussed how Solr uses term vectors to compute the similarity between documents and queries. Solr also provides a feature to compute a similarity between documents, commonly known as *More Like This*. This feature in Solr finds documents in the index that are very similar to a specific document. Under the covers, More Like This uses document term vectors to compute the similarity. The term vector for any document can be computed at query time using information stored in the index. For better performance, term vectors can be precomputed and stored during indexing.

The optional `termVectors` attribute allows you to enable term vectors to be stored for each document during indexing. Thus, if you plan to make heavy use of the More Like This feature in your search application, you should set `termVectors="true"` for text fields. Term vectors, in some cases, can also increase the speed of hit highlighting, a feature which will be covered in chapter 9. If you decide to enable term vectors after indexing documents, you will need to reindex all documents.

We will revisit these attributes throughout the rest of the book, when applicable. For example, we'll look closely at the `termPositions` and `termOffsets` attributes in chapter 9 when we discuss hit highlighting. For now, let's turn our attention to another advanced text analysis topic: multilingual analysis and language detection.

6.4.2 Per-language text analysis

Throughout this chapter, we focused on analyzing English text. The key takeaway here is that the text analysis solution you choose is language-specific. The solution we built for analyzing English microblog content won't work very well for German or French tweets. Each language will have its own parsing rules for tokenizing, stop words list, and stemming rules. In general, you will need to develop a specific `<field-Type>` for each language you want to analyze for your index. That said, many of the techniques you learned in this chapter are still applicable for analyzing languages other than English.

How do you select the right text analyzer during indexing? Assuming you want to index all your documents regardless of language in the same index, a simple solution would be to use a unique field for each language. Suppose we want to index French tweets in our microblog search application. We could define the following field:

```
<field name="text_fr" type="text_microblog_fr"
    indexed="true" stored="true" />
```

By now, you know this `<field>` definition means there is a corresponding `<fieldType>` named `text_microblog_fr` that is capable of analyzing French tweets; we'll leave it as an exercise for our French-speaking readers to define the `text_microblog_fr` field type. Out of the box, the Solr example does define the `text_fr` field type, shown in the following listing. This can be used for basic analysis of French text, so we'll use it for this example.

Listing 6.5 Field type definition provided with Solr in an example analyzing French text

```
<fieldType name="text_fr" class="solr.TextField"
            positionIncrementGap="100">
  <analyzer>
    <tokenizer class="solr.StandardTokenizerFactory"/>          ◁─┐  StandardTokenizer
    <filter class="solr.ElisionFilterFactory" ignoreCase="true"      works with most
            articles="lang/contractions_fr.txt"/>                    Latin-based
    <filter class="solr.LowerCaseFilterFactory"/>                    languages.
    <filter class="solr.StopFilterFactory" ignoreCase="true"
            words="lang/stopwords_fr.txt" format="snowball"/>   ◁─┤  French-specific
    <filter class="solr.FrenchLightStemFilterFactory"/>        ◁──    stop words file.
  </analyzer>
</fieldType>
```

French-specific stemming.

There are a few things to note about the `text_fr` field type:

- `StandardTokenizer` is used for tokenizing because it works well with most Latin-based languages, but if you wanted to preserve hashtags and mentions you would need to switch to using `WhitespaceTokenizer`.
- Custom stop words are loaded for French from the *lang/stopwords_fr.txt* file.
- A French-specific stemmer, `FrenchLightStemFilterFactory`, is applied to the text because stemming rules differ for every language.

Now that we have a separate field and field type for French text, we need to populate it during indexing. If you know a document is in French ahead of time, you can manually populate the `text_fr` field when constructing your document to be indexed. For example, assume we have the following tweet, which is a famous quote from Voltaire:

> *Le vrai philosophe n'attend rien des hommes, et il leur fait tout le bien dont il est capable.*
>
> Voltaire

The Solr XML document to index this French tweet is shown in this listing.

Listing 6.6   Example of a French tweet

```
<add>
  <doc>
    <field name="id">3</field>
    <field name="screen_name">@thelabdude</field>
    <field name="type">post</field>
    <field name="lang">fr</field>                        Specifying the language
    <field name="timestamp">2012-05-23T09:35:22Z</field>  of the text explicitly
    <field name="favourites_count">10</field>            during indexing.
    <field name="text_fr">Le vrai philosophe n'attend rien des hommes, et il
      leur fait tout le bien dont il est capable. Voltaire</field>
  </doc>
</add>
```

Specifying the language of the text explicitly during indexing.

Populate the text_fr field so the text is analyzed with the correct field type for French.

Notice how we specify `lang` as `fr` and use the `text_fr` field explicitly. This approach is fine if you already know the text is French, but what do you do when you don't know the language ahead of time? Additionally, what if your content contains multiple languages, and you wish to support searching across all of them? Chapter 14 will cover multilingual search and will provide a deep dive into the many language analysis capabilities in Solr, including language detection, language-specific tokenization, stemming, character handling, and strategies for scaling search to handle any mixture of multilingual content.

6.4.3   *Extending text analysis using a Solr plugin*

We'll wrap up this chapter with an answer to the question, what do you do when Solr doesn't provide a built-in solution for your text analysis problem? As you saw in this chapter, we accomplished some powerful transformations on our microblog content without writing any code, using only built-in Solr tools. Consequently, although it will be rare to encounter text analysis requirements that cannot be addressed with one of the built-in tools, the Solr Plug-In framework can be used to build application-specific text analysis components.

To begin, we need a requirement that Solr can't solve with built-in tools. Recall our discussion of multivalued fields in chapter 5, in which we indexed zero or more URLs into the `links` field. For tweets, any links in the text are going to be shortened links provided by an online service such as bitly.com. For instance, the shortened bit.ly URL for the Solr home page (http://lucene.apache.org/solr/) is http://bit.ly/3ynriE. From a search perspective, the shortened URL isn't very useful, as it's hard to imagine someone entering `bit.ly/3ynriE` in a search box! What we want is a document with a shortened link to be found when someone searches for the resolved URL; that is, searching for `lucene.apache.org/solr` would find a tweet with link http://bit.ly/3ynriE. Thus, during indexing, we need to extract the shortened URL and replace it with the resolved URL. To get the resolved URL, we can use an HTTP `HEAD` request, and follow redirects until we reach the resolved URL or, in the case of bit.ly, we can use its web service API.

Now that we know the problem to solve and have a basic understanding of how we want to solve it, we need to determine where in the Solr text analysis process to plug in our solution. We need to determine the type of plugin we need to build. As we learned in section 6.2, Solr text analysis involves the following components: `Analyzer`, `CharFilter`, `Tokenizer`, and `TokenFilter`. Recall that an analyzer brings together a tokenizer and chain of token filters into a single component. We probably don't want to replace our entire analyzer to resolve a URL, because we want to utilize our existing tokenizer and chain of filters. A tokenizer parses text into a stream of tokens. A token filter transforms, replaces, or removes tokens; again, we probably don't want to redefine our tokenizer unless necessary.

Our solution involves replacing one token, a shortened URL, with a different token, a fully resolved URL. Thus, for this requirement, it makes sense to build a custom `TokenFilter`, which is the most common and easiest way in Solr to customize text analysis. That said, you can also build your own analyzer, tokenizer, or char filter using a process similar to what we illustrate ahead.

To create a custom `TokenFilter`, you need to develop two concrete Java classes: a class that extends Lucene's `org.apache.lucene.analysis.TokenFilter` class to perform the filtering and a factory for your custom filter that extends Lucene's `org.apache.lucene.analysis.util.TokenFilterFactory`. The factory class is needed so that Solr can instantiate configured instances of your `TokenFilter` using configuration supplied in the *schema.xml* file.

CUSTOM TOKENFILTER CLASS

Let's begin by building a custom `TokenFilter`. As our main focus here is to learn how to implement a custom solution for text analysis, we'll leave the implementation details of resolving a URL to the motivated reader. The next listing shows a skeleton of the custom `TokenFilter` class for resolving shortened URLs.

Listing 6.7   A custom Lucene `TokenFilter` class to resolve shortened URLs

```java
package sia.ch6;

import java.io.IOException;
import java.util.regex.Pattern;

import org.apache.lucene.analysis.TokenFilter;
import org.apache.lucene.analysis.TokenStream;
import org.apache.lucene.analysis.tokenattributes.CharTermAttribute;

public class ResolveUrlTokenFilter extends TokenFilter {

    private final CharTermAttribute termAttribute =
                addAttribute(CharTermAttribute.class);
    private final Pattern patternToMatchShortenedUrls;

    public ResolveUrlTokenFilter(TokenStream in,
      Pattern patternToMatchShortenedUrls) {
        super(in);
        this.patternToMatchShortenedUrls = patternToMatchShortenedUrls;
    }

    @Override
    public boolean incrementToken() throws IOException {
        if (!input.incrementToken())
            return false;

        char[] term = termAttribute.buffer();
        int len = termAttribute.length();

        String token = new String(term, 0, len);
        if (patternToMatchShortenedUrls.matcher(token).matches()) {
            termAttribute.setEmpty().
                append(resolveShortenedUrl(token));
        }

        return true;
    }

    private String resolveShortenedUrl(String toResolve) {
        // TODO: implement a way to resolve shortened URLs
        return toResolve;
    }
}
```

- ◁ **Custom filter should extend TokenFilter.**
- ◁ **Custom TokenFilterFactory knows how to construct your TokenFilter.**
- ◁ **Method is called to process each token in the stream.**
- **Token is a shortened URL, resolve it and replace.**
- **Implementation left for the motivated reader.**

If you choose to implement this filter, we encourage you to consider the impact your solution will have on indexing performance. If you have a large volume of documents you need to index, as would typically be the case for social content, then your implementation will need to account for the high latency required to resolve links. A rough outline of a solution would use a distributed caching solution, such as memcached, to avoid resolving links more than once and would take full advantage of web service APIs provided by URL shortening services like bitly.com. Typically, the API-based approach will allow for batching many shortened URLs into a single request, which will be more efficient than using HTTP HEAD requests to resolve the links by following redirects.

CUSTOM TOKENFILTERFACTORY CLASS

When developing a custom `TokenFilter` for Solr, you also need to implement a factory class that knows how to instantiate an instance of your `TokenFilter`. The factory is responsible for taking attributes specified in *schema.xml* and converting them into parameters needed to create `TokenFilter`. Here's how we'll define our token filter in *schema.xml*:

```
<filter class="sia.ch6.ResolveUrlTokenFilterFactory"
    shortenedUrlPattern="http:\/\/bit.ly\/[\w\-]+" />
```

The factory uses the `shortenedUrlPattern` attribute to compile a Java `Pattern` object for matching shortened URLs you want to resolve during text analysis. The example shown here only supports `bit.ly` URLs, so in a real application you would want to extend this regular expression to support all possible shortened URL sources.

Next, think about where in the chain of filters in the `text_microblog` field type you should put this filter. We think it should go immediately after `WhitespaceTokenizer` (before `WordDelimiterFilter`), as you don't want to perform any transformations on the shortened URL before trying to resolve it. The Java implementation for our factory is shown in this listing.

Listing 6.8 Custom Lucene `TokenFilterFactory` to create our custom `TokenFilter`

```java
package sia.ch6;

import java.util.Map;
import java.util.regex.Pattern;

import org.apache.lucene.analysis.TokenFilter;
import org.apache.lucene.analysis.TokenStream;
import org.apache.lucene.analysis.util.TokenFilterFactory;

public class ResolveUrlTokenFilterFactory extends TokenFilterFactory {

    protected Pattern patternToMatchShortenedUrls;

    @Override
    public ResolveUrlTokenFilterFactory(Map<String,String> args) {
        super(args);
        assureMatchVersion();
        String shortenedUrlPattern = require(args, "shortenedUrlPattern");
        patternToMatchShortenedUrls =
                Pattern.compile(shortenedUrlPattern);
    }

    @Override
    public TokenFilter create(TokenStream input) {
        return new ResolveUrlTokenFilter(input,
                    patternToMatchShortenedUrls);
    }
}
```

Custom class must extend TokenFilterFactory so that Solr knows how to instantiate your factory.

Override the init method to access attributes supplied to your factory in schema.xml.

Override the create method to return a fully configured instance of your TokenFilter.

Only a few lines of code are needed to plug in a custom `TokenFilter`! The key takeaway here is that Solr uses your factory class as the intermediary between the filter definition in *schema.xml* and a configured instance of your custom `TokenFilter` used during text analysis.

The last thing you need to do is to place a JAR file containing your plugin classes in a location where Solr can locate them during initialization. To keep things simple, we recommend adding a new directory called *plugins/*, and adding that location to *solrconfig.xml* as we discussed in chapter 4.

```
<lib dir="plugins/" regex=".*\.jar" />
```

When the server starts up, it makes all JAR files in the plugins directory available to the Solr `ClassLoader`. If Solr complains about not being able to find your custom classes during initialization, try entering the full path to your plugins directory.

6.5   *Summary*

Congratulations! You've conquered some pretty complex concepts! At this point you should have a solid understanding of Solr text analysis and the indexing process in general. To recap, we began the chapter by learning how to define field types to do basic text analysis. This is where we learned that field types for unstructured text-based fields are composed of either one analyzer for both indexing and query processing or two separate but compatible analyzers for indexing and query processing. Each analyzer is made up of a tokenizer and chain of token filters. To test our simple analysis solution, we used Solr's Analysis form to see an example document pass through `StandardTokenizer` and a chain of simple filters to remove stop words and lowercase terms.

Our testing demonstrated that the basic text analysis solution was not sufficient to deal with all the nuances of our microblog content. Consequently, we used more built-in Solr tools to tackle these complex requirements. Specifically, we used `PatternReplaceCharFilterFactory` with a simple regular expression to collapse repeated characters down to a maximum of two to deal with terms like `yummm` and `soooo`. We used `WhitespaceTokenizer` and `WordDelimiterFilter` to preserve the leading # and @ characters on hashtags and mentions in tweets. `WordDelimiter` also proved useful for handling hyphenated terms in a more robust manner, such that a search for `iPad` will match documents containing `i-Pad`. We also saw how to use stemming and synonym expansion to improve our search application's matching capabilities. Overall, we developed a powerful solution for analyzing microblog content using only built-in tools and not a single line of custom code.

We finished our tour of text analysis by looking at some advanced concepts. Specifically, we covered advanced attributes for fields, such as setting `omitNorms="true"` to reduce memory and storage in your index if you don't need index-time boosts or field length normalization. Next, we saw how to use Solr's built-in solution for language detection to handle documents in other languages (more to come in chapter 14). Lastly, we developed a custom `TokenFilter` to resolve shortened URLs. The key takeaway was that Solr makes it easy to implement a custom analyzer, tokenizer, token filter, or char filter to implement exotic requirements.

In the next chapter, we'll learn how to query Solr and process results.

Part 2

Core Solr capabilities

In the next six chapters, we'll cover Solr's core capabilities that will help you deliver a powerful search and discovery experience for your users.

The single most critical feature of search is providing relevant search results for queries. In chapter 7, you'll learn how to formulate sophisticated queries, sort and navigate through results, and return responses in various formats.

Although keyword search is Solr's main feature, most search applications require additional functionality to improve the overall user experience. In chapters 8 through 11, we'll cover some of Solr's most common additional features.

Specifically, we'll cover faceting, which helps refine search results; hit highlighting, which provides snippets of text from each document to supply context around matching keywords; spell-checking and autosuggest, a tremendous help for users typing too quickly or those who are poor spellers; and field collapsing/result grouping, which allows excluding multiple similar results to provide a greater diversity of documents.

If the concepts in chapters 8 through 11 do not apply to your current needs, feel free to skip any of those chapters. Result grouping is a common feature in many search engines, for example, but if your data doesn't require it, then feel free to skip past chapter 11 for now.

Finally, chapter 12 will provide in-depth coverage of the considerations important when launching and scaling Solr in a production environment, offering a summary of best practices based upon years of hands-on experience with Solr. Because scalable searching is an inseparable part of Solr's DNA, this chapter nicely rounds out our discussion of Solr's core capabilities.

Performing queries
and handling results

This chapter covers

- Uncovering Solr's capabilities through its numerous request handlers
- Enhancing search results with Solr's pluggable search components
- Combining query parsers for powerful query capabilities
- Returning query results including both static and dynamic values
- Sorting results by values, functions, and relevancy
- Debugging search results

In the previous two chapters, we covered many of the indexing and text analysis capabilities in Solr. As you saw, text analysis is something that takes place both when indexing and when running queries, though our primary focus in the last two chapters was on processing text content into the inverted index for subsequent searching. In this chapter, we will switch tracks somewhat and dive more into the query-side capabilities Solr provides.

This chapter will reintroduce the concepts of request handlers (first discussed in chapter 4), setting the context for discussing `SearchHandler`, Solr's most important request handler. `SearchHandler` runs one or more `SearchComponents`, including `QueryComponent`, which is responsible for executing the main query on a search request. In the process of discussing `QueryComponent`, we'll also introduce the many query parsers available in Solr, demonstrating the powerful query syntax and capabilities Solr provides.

Once you've seen the full query syntax, we'll cover how to manipulate the search results that are returned. We will cover how to sort the results, how to page through them, how to return specific fields and dynamically generated values, and how to manipulate the format of the search results and debug the search request. This chapter covers the core search functionality in Solr, and therefore provides some of the most fundamental information you'll need to build a sophisticated Solr-based search application. In order to dive into Solr's core search capabilities, let us begin by revisiting how Solr processes incoming requests.

7.1 The anatomy of a Solr request

Although the most common type of request sent to Solr is generally a query to find documents within a Solr index, Solr can handle many different kinds of requests. As you learned in chapter 4, essentially all requests (such as document updates and queries) are submitted to Solr through a request handler. The *search handler*, which is the default request handler used to process queries, allows multiple stages of a query to be executed by specifying one or more search components to be invoked, each of which handles a separate part of the search request. For example, the main query is executed through one search component, whereas faceting (covered in chapter 8), highlighting (covered in chapter 9), and spell-checking (covered in chapter 10) are executed through their own separate search components. For requests hitting the main search component, the text of a query also needs to be parsed by one or more query parsers, objects whose job is to understand the syntax of the text query and map that syntax into an appropriate set of query objects to find a relevant set of documents within the Solr index. This section expands upon chapter 4's introduction of request handlers and search components and goes deeper into the anatomy of a Solr request and the interaction between request handlers, search components, and query parsers. Let's begin with a discussion of request handlers.

7.1.1 Request handlers

Request handlers are the entry points for essentially all requests to Solr. Their job is to receive a request, perform some function, and return a response to the client. Solr contains numerous request handlers to cover everything from running a search (`Search-Handler`) to copying Solr indexes from one server to another (`ReplicationHandler`) to sending new documents to update the Solr index (`UpdateRequestHandler`). You can also gain rich insights into the Solr index (`LukeRequestHandler`) and server information such as memory usage and Solr settings (SystemInfoRequestHandler). For simplicity, most request handlers inherit from a Java class called RequestHandlerBase, though this is not required (any class that implements the SolrRequestHandler interface may function as a request handler). Although you can write your own request handlers as plugins for Solr by implementing the SolrRequestHandler interface, most Solr users get by with the built-in request handlers that come with Solr. Figure 7.1 shows an inheritance hierarchy that includes most of Solr's built-in request handlers.

As you can see from figure 7.1, Solr can process many different kinds of requests. SearchHandler is generally the most-used request handler in Solr, as it's the default request handler used to process search requests. Although many of these built-in request handlers will be covered in detail in later chapters, others will be left for you to explore on your own. Table 7.1 includes a brief description of each request handler's intended use.

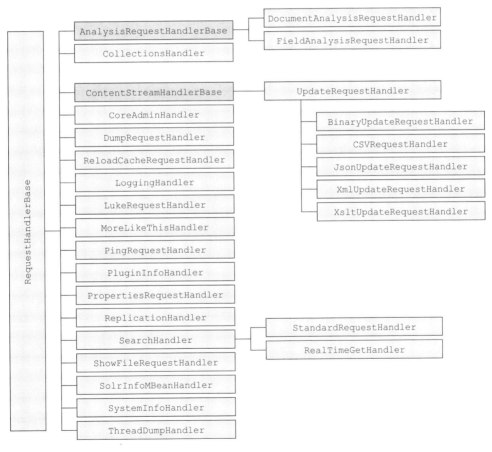

Figure 7.1   A class hierarchy of many of the built-in Solr request handlers that come with the default Solr deployment. AnalysisRequestHandlerBase and ContentStreamHandlerBase are abstract classes, so can't be referenced directly. A few built-in request handlers that do not inherit from RequestHandlerBase are not listed here.

Table 7.1 A brief description of many of Solr's request handlers. All handlers are located in the `org.apache.solr.handler` package unless otherwise specified.

Request handler class name	Description
DocumentAnalysisRequestHandler	Accepts a stream of documents like `Update-RequestHandler`, but returns the postprocessed content instead of adding it to the Solr index. Useful for debugging the content analysis of an entire document. Analyzing documents was covered in chapter 6.
FieldAnalysisRequestHandler	Like `DocumentAnalysisRequestHandler`, but it processes one or more fields instead of an entire document. Useful for debugging the content analysis for specific fields. Text analysis was covered in chapter 6.
UpdateRequestHandler	Accepts a stream of documents to be processed and added to the Solr index. Several request handlers inherit from `UpdateRequestHandler` to handle different content types, such as XML, JSON, CSV, binary input, and XSLT-transformed content. If used directly instead of one of its children classes, `Update-RequestHandler` will attempt to choose the correct child class per request based upon its content type. Sending updates to Solr was covered in chapter 5.
CollectionsHandler	Used to manage SolrCloud collections (covered in chapter 13).
CoreAdminHandler	Used to get details and manage multiple Solr indexes or "cores" inside of a running instance of Solr (covered in chapter 12).
DumpRequestHandler	Useful for verifying/debugging content that is being sent to Solr. When bulk data, such as documents being posted, is sent to Solr, `DumpRequestHandler` can be used to echo the content streams containing that data for debugging.
ReloadCacheRequestHandler	This request handler is located inside the `FlatFileSource` class and is used to reload the cache whenever the file associated with `External-FileField` has changed. `ExternalFileField` allows field information to be stored and updated in an external file outside of the Solr index, but this requires notification to Solr whenever the external file changes. Hitting `ReloadCacheRequestHandler` informs Solr when the external file is updated (covered in chapter 15).
LoggingHandler	Reports and allows control over which loggers and logging levels should be used by Solr when writing out log information.

Table 7.1 A brief description of many of Solr's request handlers. All handlers are located in the `org.apache.solr.handler` package unless otherwise specified. *(continued)*

Request handler class name	Description
`LukeRequestHandler`	Reports meta-information about a Solr index, including information about the number of terms, which fields are used, top terms in the index, and distributions of terms across the index. You may also request information on a per-document basis.
`MoreLikeThisHandler`	Allows textually similar documents to be found based upon an input document. This can be useful for recommending content based upon a document for which a user has already expressed an interest (covered in chapter 16).
`PingRequestHandler`	Returns a status OK message based upon the ability of a Solr core to execute a query and (optionally) the existence of a specified health-check file on the Solr server. This is commonly used as an endpoint for load-balancers to probe to pull Solr servers out of service. If the health-check file exists and Solr can successfully execute queries, the server appears healthy, but if the health-check file is deleted, the server reports as being down but still allows queries to complete successfully for a nonuser, affecting failover. The Solr Admin UI contains an Enable/Disable link to make putting the server in/out of service easy (covered in chapter 12).
`PluginInfoHandler`	Provides information about plugins that have been loaded and are available for use in the running Solr instance.
`PropertiesRequestHandler`	Returns the values for all system properties. If a name parameter is specified, the value associated with the property matching the name parameter is returned.
`ReplicationHandler`	Used by one Solr core (a "slave") to pull index information from another Solr core (a "master"). This allows multiple Solr servers to maintain copies of the same Solr index and keep them in sync, which allows load to be balanced across more than one server (covered in chapter 12).
`ShowFileRequestHandler`	Used to return files stored within the Solr filesystem. It's commonly used to return *schema.xml*, *solrconfig.xml*, or any other config files.
`SolrInfoMBeanHandler`	Used to return stats about all available `SolrMBean` objects in the Solr instance. This includes most of the core Solr objects and is useful for creating Solr monitoring without needing to use JMX.

Table 7.1 A brief description of many of Solr's request handlers. All handlers are located in the `org.apache.solr.handler` package unless otherwise specified. *(continued)*

Request handler class name	Description
SearchHandler	The default request handler for processing searches in Solr. This handler includes pluggable search components (see section 7.1.2) that can enable many search capabilities during a single search request. `SearchHandler` has two subclasses, `StandardRequestHandler` (deprecated) and `RealTimeGetHandler`. Because it can take some time between when Solr receives new content and when it makes it available in the Solr index, the `RealTimeGetHandler` allows new content to be retrieved in search requests in real time from its update logs before the content has been committed to the Solr index. `SearchHandler` will be covered in detail throughout this chapter.
SystemInfoHandler	Provides a point-in-time overview of the operating environment of the Solr instance. This includes Solr/Lucene version data, Java VM information such as memory utilization and JVM version, JMX accessibility, and OS information.
ThreadDumpHandler	Provides the equivalent of a Java thread dump listing the threads running in the current JVM.

Although many of the request handlers in table 7.1 may go unused by most Solr users, it's useful to be aware of their existence to save time should you ever need the information they provide. Each request handler should be defined and configured in *solrconfig.xml* (as covered in chapter 4) in order to be used. The following listing shows an example configuration enabling UpdateRequestHandler (for updating documents), ReplicationHandler (for copying files from one Solr server to another), and several instances of SearchHandler (for searching).

Listing 7.1 Enabling a request handler in *solrconfig.xml*

```
<config>
  ...
  <requestHandler name="/select" class="solr.SearchHandler" />
  <requestHandler name="/update" class="solr.UpdateRequestHandler">
  <requestHandler name="/replication"
                  class="solr.ReplicationHandler"
                  startup="lazy" />

  <!-- The below entries are for demonstrative purposes -->
  <requestHandler name="/private/search " class="solr.SearchHandler" />
  ...
</config>
```

When defining a request handler entry, two attributes are required: the `name` and the `class`. Solr maintains a lookup list of request handlers and routes requests based upon which is specified for each request. The `class` attribute corresponds to the Java class (implementing the `SolrRequestHandler` interface) that should be used to handle requests to the named request handler.

If a request handler's name begins with a / (which is standard practice), the `name` will be used as a relative URL by which the request handler can be reached. For example, starting up Solr's example program (see chapter 2 if you need a refresher on how to do this) using the configuration from listing 7.1, you would be able to hit the following URLs:

- http://localhost:8983/solr/collection1/select/
- http://localhost:8983/solr/collection1/update/
- http://localhost:8983/solr/collection1/replication/
- http://localhost:8983/solr/collection1/private/search/

You will undoubtedly receive errors from some of these request handlers because they require default parameters to be specified for the request to be valid, but you will nonetheless be able to see that you're invoking the expected request handler directly by adding its `name` to the Solr URL.

Two additional points need to be made about listing 7.1. First, notice that the request handlers `/select` and `/private/search` have the same class defined. This is perfectly fine; it will create two separate request handlers that use the same class. Second, notice the use of the `startup="lazy"` attribute on the request handler named `/replication`. It's likely that not all request handlers will be used on every Solr server. By setting this lazy startup option, you're telling Solr to wait until the request handler is invoked the first time to load it, which saves resources at the expense of a slower initial query to that request handler.

If you think back through previous chapters, you have already seen multiple request handlers being used. You have seen `UpdateHandler` and `SearchHandler` in action as early as chapter 4, for example, when adding documents to Solr and searching through those documents. Although discussion of additional request handlers will be saved for later chapters, you should now have a good understanding of what request handlers are and how they're defined. That understanding will be useful as you learn about search components, which are sometimes confused with request handlers due to occasionally overlapping functionality.

7.1.2 Search components

Although the last section introduced many different kinds of Solr request handlers, `SearchHandler` is the one responsible by default for running incoming searches. What exactly should a default search return? Should it include search results only? How about lists of top categories matched, or the highlighted text from the portion of the documents matched? If few or no results were found, should alternative spelling suggestions be returned in the default request?

Based upon the last section, you know that many of these search features can be invoked by sending separate requests to multiple available request handlers. In an ideal world, you would be able to send a single request to Solr and get all of this expected information back with the one request. This is exactly the reason search components exist.

Search components are configurable processing steps that occur within the lifetime of a search handler. Search components allow a search handler to chain together reusable pieces of functionality that can be executed with a single search request.

Search components are configured in *solrconfig.xml*, as discussed in chapter 4. To refresh your memory, the next listing demonstrates the creation of a search handler with the list of default search components included.

> **Listing 7.2   The default list of search components for a search handler**

Any number of search components can be defined.

```
<searchComponent name="query"     class="solr.QueryComponent" />
<searchComponent name="facet"     class="solr.FacetComponent" />
<searchComponent name="mlt"       class="solr.MoreLikeThisComponent" />
<searchComponent name="highlight" class="solr.HighlightComponent" />
<searchComponent name="stats"     class="solr.StatsComponent" />
<searchComponent name="debug"     class="solr.DebugComponent" />

<requestHandler name="/select" class="solr.SearchHandler">
    <arr name="components">
      <str>query</str>
      <str>facet</str>
      <str>mlt</str>
      <str>highlight</str>
      <str>stats</str>
      <str>debug</str>
    </arr>
</requestHandler>
```

Each search handler can chain together any of the defined search components.

Although everything from the listing is default behavior—which means it will occur anyway, even if left out of *solrconfig.xml*—it's useful to examine the listing both to understand how to configure and enable new search components and to understand how searches through the search handler work by default.

If you take a look at the first `<searchComponent />` tag, you will see two attributes defined, a name and a class, with the name being `query` and the class being `solr.Query-Component`. This search component needs to be defined only one time, after which it can be used by any number of request handlers. If you look at the `/select` request handler, you will see an `arr` (array) element with a name of `components`. This element is where the list of search components to include for a search handler is defined. Each entry in the `components` section must correspond with the name of a search component either enabled by default (as are all of the components in listing 7.2) or defined elsewhere in *solrconfig.xml*.

Setting defaults for request handlers and search components

Request handlers and search components generally receive their settings for requests from one of two sources: defaults in code or query string variables passed in on the Solr URL. When configuring a request handler or a search component in *solrconfig.xml*, it's also possible to set up variables that will be automatically added to every request as if they had been passed in on the Solr URL.

In listing 7.3, you will see two sections added to a search component: an `invariants` section and a `defaults` section. `defaults` are values that will be set if no overriding value is passed in on the Solr request URL. This can be useful when you want to enforce safe default settings (such as a `q=*:*` on the query search component so that you do not encounter an exception or receive no results on blank searches).

The `invariants` section works like the `defaults` section, except that invariant parameters can't be overridden by the Solr request URL. This can be useful for enforcing some kind of security filter or, in the case of listing 7.3, ensuring that all requests are always for 25 results (`rows=25`) and that a default field for keyword searches is defined (`df=content_field`). You will see many request handlers and search components defining their configurations using defaults and invariants like this in *solrconfig.xml*.

Most search components allow configuration properties to be set within their XML configuration. If you wish to do this for any of the default components, set the name of the search component to one of the default names (`"query"`, `"facet"`, `"mlt"`, `"highlight"`, `"stats"`, or `"debug"`), and you can override the default configuration for that search component.

Listing 7.3 Setting a default configuration for the `"query"` component

```
<searchComponent name="query" class="solr.QueryComponent">
  <lst name="invariants">
    <str name="rows">25</str>
    <str name="df">content_field</str>
  </lst>
  <lst name="defaults">
    <str name="q">*:*</str>
    <str name="indent">true</str>
    <str name="echoParams">explicit</str>
  </lst>
</searchComponent>
```

Because each default search component exists by default even if it's not defined explicitly in the *solrconfig.xml* file, defining them explicitly as in the previous listing will replace the default configuration. It's also possible to insert components by adding a `first-components` section or a `last-components` section, which can append additional components to the beginning or end of the list of components to be run by the search handler. See chapter 4 (section 4.2) for a refresher on how to add search components to your search handler.

Out of all the search components in the search handler, the query component is the most important, as it's responsible for initially running the query and making the results available in the response (and for other search components to make use of afterward). The query component makes use of a query parser to interpret the incoming query from the request to the search handler. Several query parsers exist in Solr, and they will be covered in the following section.

7.1.3 Query parsers

Query parsers are used to interpret a search syntax into a Lucene query for finding a desired set of documents. Solr supports several query parsers and even enables you to write your own. Just as search components are specific to a single request handler (SearchHandler), query parsers are also specifically used in a single search component (QueryComponent). Figure 7.2 demonstrates this relationship: SearchHandler executes a QueryComponent, which uses QueryParsers.

You can see from figure 7.2 that many query parsers ship with Solr, each implemented as a QParserPlugin class. You can write your own QParserPlugin if you need

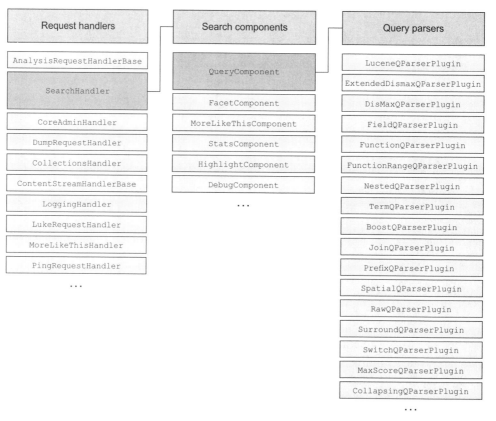

Figure 7.2   Query parsers are used by QueryComponent, the search component specifically responsible for executing the query specified in SearchHandler. Query parser classes are implemented as QParserPlugin classes.

custom query parsing capabilities not supported by any of the available query parsers. The most commonly used query parsers in Solr are Lucene query parser (`Lucene-QParserPlugin`) and eDisMax query parser (`ExtendedDismaxQParserPlugin`), which will be covered in detail in sections 7.4 and 7.5. The additional query parsers listed in figure 7.2 will be covered in section 7.6. Before we dive into the mechanics of each of these query parsers, however, it will be useful to understand the mechanics of working with query parsers.

7.2 *Working with query parsers*

When executing a search, `QueryComponent` handles the primary user query (the `q` parameter) by passing its value along to a query parser. As mentioned in the last section, `LuceneQParserPlugin` is the default query parser in Solr. This default is easy to override and it's possible to combine multiple query parsers in the same query. Each query parser is able to perform its own kind of queries and may accept its own query syntax, so certain query parsers can be more suitable for different scenarios (which will be covered in sections 7.4–7.6). This section will cover the mechanics of working with query parsers, including how to change the default query parser, how to combine query parsers, and how to specify the settings for query parsers.

7.2.1 *Specifying a query parser*

The default query parser type to be used for the `QueryComponent` can be modified using the `defType` parameter on the search request:

```
/select?defType=edismax&q=…
/select?defType=term&q=…
```

When you modify the default query parser type, it changes which query parser will handle the q parameter and therefore will likely change the results of the query. In addition to modifying the default query parser type, you can make use of a special syntax in Solr to modify the query parser to be used inside of your query:

```
/select?q={!edismax}hello world
/select?q={!term}hello
/select?q={!edismax}hello world OR {!lucene}title:"my title"
```

In the third example, you will notice that two different query parsers—eDisMax and Lucene—were invoked within the same query. This is an advantage of specifying the query parser within the query, as opposed to using the `defType` parameter. Solr contains a handful of useful query parsers that will be covered throughout this chapter.

The `{!...}` syntax used to define query parsers inline invokes a feature in Solr known as local params, which will be discussed in more detail in the following section.

7.2.2 *Local params*

Local params provide the ability to localize request parameters to a specific context. Typically you will pass request parameters to Solr on the URL, but sometimes you may only want some parameters to be applied to certain parts of the query. Within the context of a query, local params allow you to pass request parameters only to the specific query parser that you want to consider them, as opposed to making all request parameters global. In the previous section you saw that it's possible to modify your query parser inline inside of your query. Not only can you modify your query parser, you can also modify any request parameter utilizing local params.

LOCAL PARAMS SYNTAX

Local params are a set of key/value pairs representing request parameters that should only be evaluated within the current context. The syntax is as follows:

```
{!param1=value1 param2=value2 … paramN=valueN}
```

A set of local params begins with `{!` and ends with `}` and contains a space-separated list of key/value pairs, where the keys and values are separated by an equals sign. For example,

```
/select?q=hello world&defType=edismax&qf=title^10 text&q.op=AND
```

is functionally equivalent to the following query utilizing local params:

```
/select?q={!defType=edismax qf="title^10 text" q.op=AND}hello world
```

The real difference between these two queries is that, in the first example, all of the request parameters are global, so they will be applied anywhere in the request where they're checked. In the local params example, the `defType`, `qf`, and `q.op` parameters are only defined within the context of the specific q parameter for which they're in scope. If you ever have the need to reuse a query parser more than once in a query with different settings, local params will be the mechanism for that job.

We specified the `defType` parameter inside the local parameters, but it's also possible to override the `defType` with the `type` parameter. As you might imagine, `defType` stands for default type, which means it specifies the default query parser type for all queries. You can override the default type within a specific context using the `type` parameter inside a set of local params:

```
/select?q={!type=edismax qf="title^10 text" q.op=AND}hello world
```

The `type` parameter can only be used within the context of local params; if you want to define a type at the top level to serve as the default, you must use the `defType` parameter. In contrast, the `defType` parameter can be used both at the request level and within a set of local params.

Because some of the local param values may contain special characters (spaces, quotes, and so on), you may need to wrap the local param value in quotes (single or double) or escape the special characters. You can see that the `qf` parameter in the last query is wrapped in double quotes because its value contains a space. To learn more about escaping special characters in Solr, see the end of section 7.4.1.

You may notice a slight inconsistency between section 7.2.1 and this section in terms of how a query parser is specified using the local params syntax. In this section, we specified `{!type=edismax …}`; earlier we used a simpler `{!edismax …}` representation.

Both of these work because `type` is considered the default local param key if only a value is specified. Just as it's possible to run a keyword search without specifying a field and have it search against the default field, so too is it possible to pass in a value for a local param and have it applied against the default local param key of `type`. Because the syntax is shorter, you will generally see query parsers defined using the `{!query-ParserName}` syntax; all other local params must use the full `{!key1=value1 key2=value2 …}` syntax.

PARAMETER VALUE

The value after the local params declaration is the value that is passed into the query parser. Given the following local params declaration, the value passed into the query parser would be `hello world`:

```
/select?q={!edismax qf="title^10 text"}hello world
```

Instead of specifying the value after the local params declaration, however, it can sometimes be easier to define the value inside the local params block. A special local param key of `v` is reserved for this purpose. As such, the previous query can be alternatively defined as

```
/select?q={!edismax qf="title^10 text" v="hello world"}
```

It's worth pointing out that by moving the query value into the `v` parameter in the local params block, you will have to be mindful of escaping special characters; you do not have to worry about this otherwise. For example, if you wanted to search for the quoted phrase `"hello world"`, the following two queries would be equivalent:

```
/select?q={!edismax qf="title^10 text"}"hello world"
/select?q={!edismax qf="title^10 text" v="\"hello world\""}
```

Because of the complexity associated with explicitly defining your query value inside the local params block, and in order to promote reuse of parameters throughout your request syntax, it can often be helpful to make use of parameter dereferencing.

PARAMETER DEREFERENCING

Parameter dereferencing provides the ability to substitute arbitrary variables into your query. This feature is similar to parameterized queries in SQL, as it allows you to define your query input separately from your query syntax. Dereferenced parameter syntax looks like the following:

```
/select?q={!edismax v=$userQuery}&userQuery="hello world"
```

In this example, the `userQuery` parameter is passed in as a user-defined query string variable that Solr does not natively understand. By specifying that the value passed in to the eDisMax query parser should be the dereferenced parameter `$userQuery`, that value can be pulled in from elsewhere on the request. This may seem only moderately useful at first, but because default parameters can be defined in your *solrconfig.xml* for each request handler or query component using defaults, appends, and invariants (covered in chapter 4), you could effectively come up with your own set of request parameters for your application that are substituted into a predefined configuration.

> ### Reducing duplication with parameter dereferencing
>
> Parameter dereferencing can also be useful if you have a need to reuse parts of your query in different ways and do not want to duplicate them on your request. It's also possible to chain dereferenced parameters together such that one dereferenced parameter can be composed of other dereferenced parameters. A good example of this is covered in chapter 15 (section 15.1.4) where the local sales tax is being passed in as a parameter to be used to calculate a total cost for a product document, which is then reused in multiple operations such as sorting and returning the value as a field.

Now you know how to change query parsers and manipulate the values passed to them on both a global and local level. Next, we'll look at how user queries and filters work before we move on to learn how each of the query parsers in Solr works.

7.3   *Queries and filters*

Before moving on to discuss how each of Solr's available query parsers works, it will be useful to have a good understanding of how user queries and filters work: what the difference is, how they interact, and how they ultimately affect the performance and quality of your search requests.

A search in Solr is composed of two main operations—finding the documents that match the request parameters and ordering those documents so that only the top matches need to be returned. By default, the documents are ordered based upon relevancy, which means that after the final set of matching documents has been found, an additional operation is necessary to calculate a relevancy score for each of the matching documents. Both the process of looking up matching documents in Solr's inverted index and the default algorithm for calculating the relevancy score for each document were covered in chapter 3.

7.3.1   *The fq and q parameters*

To efficiently handle the operations of finding matching documents and scoring documents, Solr makes use of two parameters: fq and q. The fq parameter stands for filter query, and the q parameter stands for query. At first glance these parameters may seem indistinguishable, as the same query syntax passed into either of these parameters will return the exact same number of documents. Because of this, many use a single q parameter for their entire search request. Understanding the difference between these parameters allows you to run much more efficient searches.

RELEVANCY IMPACT

So what is the difference between the q and fq parameters? fq serves a single purpose: to limit your results to a set of matching documents.

The q parameter, in contrast, serves two purposes:

- To limit your results to a set of matching documents
- To supply the relevancy algorithm with a list of terms to be used for relevancy scoring

As such, it can be useful to think of the q parameter as a special filter that tells Solr what terms should be considered in the relevancy calculation. Because of this distinction, Solr users tend to put user-entered keywords (such as `keywords:"apache solr"`) in the q parameter and machine-generated filters (such as `category:"technology"`) in the fq parameter.

CACHING AND EXECUTION SPEED

Separating filter queries from the main query serves two purposes. First, because filter queries are often reusable between searches (they typically do not contain arbitrary keywords), it's possible to cache their results in the filter cache (discussed in chapter 4, section 4.4.2). Second, because the relevancy scoring operation must perform calculations on every term in the query (q) for every matching document, by separating some parts of your query into a filter query (fq), those parts in the fq parameter will not result in unnecessary additional relevancy calculations being performed. This can save a substantial amount of work during relevancy scoring for parts of the query that are intended only as filters.

SPECIFYING MULTIPLE QUERIES AND FILTERS

One last important characteristic to note about queries and filter queries is that you can add as many fq parameters as you want to your Solr request, but only a single q parameter. As such, a Solr query for `q=keywords:solr&fq=category:technology &fq=year:2013` will return the same documents in the same order as `q=keywords :solr&fq=category:technology AND year:2013`. With the exception of some caching implications of the fq parameter (each fq parameter will be cached independently), using multiple fq parameters is functionally equivalent to the version combining the parameters into a single fq parameter. Although the many query parsers in the following sections work with both the q and fq parameters, you should be mindful of both the relevancy and caching impacts when choosing which parameter is right for your given use case.

ORDER OF EXECUTION

Because queries and filters both look up document sets and set operations on them, a common question that arises is, "In what order do queries and filters execute?" Some published resources indicate that filters are executed first, some indicate that the query is executed first, and yet others indicate that the query and filters are executed in parallel. So which is true? It's a complicated question, and the answer depends on the use case.

Technically, the order of operations is as follows:

1   Every `fq` parameter is looked up in the filter cache. If it exists, a cached `DocSet` is returned (wrapping an `OpenBitSet`) with one bit (0 or 1) for each document in the index, indicating whether the document is contained in the filter.

2   If a `fq` parameter is not found in the filter cache and caching is enabled, the filter is executed against the index to obtain a new `DocSet`, which can then be cached.

3   All filter `DocSet`s are intersected (`AND`ed together) to yield a single `DocSet`.

4   The `q` parameter is passed in (along with the filter `DocSet`) to be executed as a Lucene query. When executing the query, Lucene plays leapfrog between the query and combined filters, advancing both the query and filter results objects to their next present internal ID (an integer). When both the query result and filter result objects contain the same ID, that ID is collected, a process that includes generating the relevancy score for the document.

5   If the query contains any post filters (discussed in the next section), they will be run as part of the collection process (after both the query and filter have been intersected) and therefore only on the documents that already matched both the combined query and combined filters.

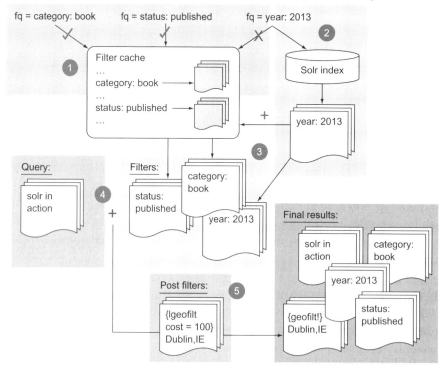

Figure 7.3   **The process of combining queries and filters**

Based on this explanation, it's technically true that filters are executed before the main query when caching is enabled. The query and filters are later evaluated concurrently during the collection process (the leapfrog step), and then special kinds of filters known as post filters can be interjected into that collection process after both the query and filters have found a document that they both match. Figure 7.3 demonstrates the five steps for processing queries and filters for an example search request.

Each of the numbered stages in figure 7.3 corresponds with the steps outlined: ❶ looking up filters in the filter cache; ❷ querying the index for missing filters; ❸ combining each of the filters; ❹ combining the query and (combined) filters using a leapfrog process; and ❺ applying costly post filters. Of course, the last step is to return the final DocSet, calculating relevancy based upon only the query (not the filters) if it's needed for sorting or retrieval, and returning the top documents in the Solr response.

This may sound quite complicated, and indeed it is. Solr does a good job of hiding this complexity from you, but it can be useful to understand this process in order to optimize the performance of expensive filters. Solr provides granular control that enables you to specify which filters will be cached and in which order your filters will be evaluated, including having them evaluated before, after, or concurrently with the main query. The next section will demonstrate how to control the order of execution of your filters by turning caching on/off, specify the order of your filters, and determine whether the filters should be run after the query and other filters are executed.

7.3.2 Handling expensive filters

Filters enable you to save considerable processing time by being cacheable and by bypassing relevancy processing for parts of the query only specified as a filter. Not all filters are created equal, however. If you're trying to filter results to a geographical radius around a particular latitude and longitude (covered in chapter 15 [section 15.2]), this filter will most likely be computationally expensive to calculate due to all the math involved. Additionally, if you're generating different filters for millions of locations, this sheer number of radius filters may be difficult to cache. Alternatively, you may have situations where your application would generate so many unique filters (for example, filtering on a unique ID) that the filter cache would become overloaded and either commonly used filters would be evicted or your searcher's warming time may become excessive. For cases like this, Solr enables you to control both whether any filter should be cached and the order in which filters are evaluated.

TURNING OFF CACHING OF FILTERS

In some cases, you may have a large number of unique filters that are not worth caching. Since you have a fixed upper limit on the number of filters you can cache, the performance of your Solr instance will be best if the most-used filters remain cached at all times. To prevent the cache from being overloaded by less important filters, you can explicitly turn caching off for any filter using the following syntax:

```
fq={!cache=false}id:123&
fq={!frange l=90 u=100 cache=false}
    scale(query({!v="content:(solr OR lucene)"}),0,100)
```

In the preceding filters, the first is so specific that a different filter could be generated for every unique document, so caching the filter would unreasonably fill up the filter cache. In the second example, the filter is also specific: trying to find the most relevant top 10% of documents matching the query content:(solr OR lucene). It does this by getting the relevancy score of the query, scaling the scores of all documents between 1 and 100, and filtering out documents that do not fall between 90 and 100. Because this filter contains a variable input (the input to the query function), it's probably a good candidate for which to turn filtering off. You can add as many filters as you want to your request, with each fq parameter supporting the ability to turn caching on or off independently by either specifying cache=true or (more practically) leaving the cache local parameter off, because cache defaults to true.

CHANGING THE ORDER OF FILTER EXECUTION

If your search request contains multiple filters, the order in which they execute can have a significant impact upon your query speed. It makes logical sense that if filters that reduce the results set the most can be executed first, any additional filters will then have fewer documents to act upon and will therefore execute faster. Likewise, some filters must perform complex calculations—such as geospatial filters trying to filter upon a radius around a point—and the later those filters can be applied, the fewer documents they should have to perform their expensive calculations upon. In cases where you know up front which of your filters is going to be the most expensive to execute, Solr allows you to force them to execute later by supplying an associated cost to the filter. The syntax for supplying a filter cost is as follows:

```
fq={!cost=1}category:technology&
fq={!cost=2}date:[NOW/DAY-1YEAR TO *]&
fq={!geofilt pt=37.773,-122.419 sfield=location d=50 cost=3}&
fq={!frange l=90 u=100 cache=false cost=100}
    scale(query({!v="content:(solr OR lucene)"}),0,100)
```

The higher the cost for a filter, the later it will execute. In the example, the category: technology filter is executed first because it has the lowest cost. It probably makes sense for this filter to have the lowest cost because it can be executed quickly and is likely to greatly reduce the number of documents to a single category of documents. The next filter (with a cost of 2) limits all results to those with a date in the last year. The next most expensive filter is the geofilt operation, which must calculate a radius and limit results to those found within 50 miles of that radius (an expensive operation). The final filter, with a cost of 100, is both expensive (due to the math) and highly variable (because it accepts keywords), so it has both `cost=100` and `cache=false` specified. It may seem odd that we would jump from a `cost` of 3 to a `cost` of `100`. Although the costs do not have to be sequential (they're applied in relative order to each other), a cost greater than or equal to 100 invokes a special feature in Solr called post filtering.

POST FILTERING

In some cases, a filter may be so expensive to execute that you do not want it evaluated until after all other queries and filters. Solr has implemented a special kind of filter called a *post filter* that enables a filter to be applied only during the collection process of documents, when the queries and filters are intersected.

As you recall from section 7.3.1, when the query and combined filter are evaluated in parallel (the leapfrog process), every document that is found in both the query and filter is collected. A post filter is a special filter that is evaluated on a per-document basis only after `"collect"` has been called for that document. This allows all other lower-cost filters to be applied first to limit the total number of results, and for more expensive post filters to be applied only at the end on the smaller document set. The cost parameter defined for a filter, as it turns out, is also the mechanism used to turn a filter into a post filter. Any filter with a cost greater than or equal to 100 will be applied after the fact as a post filter, as long as the filter type implements the post filtering interface.

Post filtering will not necessarily work for all kinds of queries/filters in Solr; it will only work for those implementing the `PostFilter` interface. FRange queries (see section 7.6.3) are one example of a `PostFilter`-capable query type. It's also possible to write your own plugin that implements the `PostFilter` interface, should you need this ability to apply a filter after the main query and filters have executed.

With the difference between queries and filters clearly outlined and the relevancy and performance considerations well understood, we can now dive into the mechanics of the most commonly used query parsers in Solr.

7.4 The default query parser (Lucene query parser)

Most of the queries in the book so far have made use of the standard Solr syntax. This syntax is not the only supported syntax in Solr, but it's the most common and is handled by the default query parser. The default query parser in Solr is confusingly called the Lucene query parser (implemented in the class `LuceneQParserPlugin`), even though it's a Solr-specific class and the default query parser in Solr. The Lucene query parser supports the full range of Lucene syntax (plus some Solr-specific extensions).

7.4.1 Lucene query parser syntax

Most of the Lucene query parser syntax was indirectly covered in chapter 3, but this section will provide a comprehensive overview (and refresher) of the supported query operations in the Lucene query parser. One important characteristic is that the syntax is strictly enforced. If a query does not match the syntax exactly, then a parse exception will be thrown and the request will fail. There is a specific syntax to support many operations you learned about in chapter 3, including fielded and nonfielded term searches, required terms, optional terms, phrase searches, grouped expressions, term proximity, excluded terms, range searches, wildcard searches, and Boolean expressions. This section will cover the correct way to make use of each of these features using the Lucene query parser.

FIELDED TERM SEARCHES

When a value is searched for in the Solr index, it's always looked up in a specific field. The syntax for a fielded search is the name of the field, followed by a colon, followed by the expression to search for within the field:

```
title:solr
title:"apache solr" content:(search engine)
```

Although it's common to run a keyword search without explicitly specifying a field, it's worth noting that this causes the keywords to be searched for against whatever field is defined as the default field. For example, if the default field is defined as the content field (df=content), then the following two queries are equivalent:

```
solr
content:solr
```

It's also worth noting that the scope of the expression after the field and colon must be explicit. The following two queries are equivalent (assuming df=content), even though the user probably meant something different when specifying the first query:

```
title:apache solr
title:apache content:solr
```

If you need to search multiple terms within the same field, you can make use of a grouped expression to specify the scope of the terms within the fielded search:

```
title:(apache solr)
```

If you were trying to search on a phrase, then the scope could be defined with quotation marks instead of parentheses, though this changes the query by requiring both terms to appear together:

```
title:"apache solr"
```

REQUIRED TERMS

In order to specify that one or more terms are required—that a document can't match unless it contains the term(s) specified—the unary + operator can be used on each term. If multiple terms must be included for a document to match, then the binary operators AND or && can also alternatively be used (or you could apply the unary + operator to both terms).

```
+solr
apache AND solr
apache && solr
```

```
+apache +solr
apache solr (assuming default operator is AND)
```

If the default operator is AND (q.op=AND), every term will be required by default if another operator is not explicitly specified. Because every additional required term serves to further limit the total number of results in the document set, you will generally speed up your query by applying more required terms, which further refine the number of results.

OPTIONAL TERMS

Sometimes it's useful to expand the number of matching documents instead of restricting to required terms. If the default operator is OR (q.op=OR), every expression is considered optional unless otherwise specified. Likewise, if the binary operators of OR or || are specified between multiple expressions, this means that a document will match as long as at least one of the expressions is found in the document. The syntax is as follows:

```
apache OR solr
apache || solr
apache solr (assuming default operator is OR)
```

It's worth noting that, because every additional optional term serves to further expand the document set, the OR operation is more expensive than other Boolean operations. For a keyword search, you would generally only want to use OR as your default operator if you have a limited amount of content and want to ensure you're returning something (higher Recall) at the expense of returning noise (hurting Precision). Since documents matching multiple optional criteria will typically yield a higher relevancy score, it's often possible to still yield good results at the top of your search results by using OR as your default operator if you're sorting by relevancy score, though the odds of seeing strange results are much greater when expanding the query as opposed to requiring all of your keywords to match.

PHRASE SEARCHES

If you want to match one or more terms next to each other, you can surround the terms with quotes to form a phrase, such as

```
"apache solr"
"apache software foundation"
```

Such a search does not guarantee that the exact text will match, because the field may contain analyzers that modify the terms in the phrase. For example, a search for "Raining Cats and Dogs" may also match rain cat with dog if the field aggressively stems and removes the terms and and with as stop words. That being said, quoting terms does guarantee that the terms must be found in consecutive term positions, and most reasonably specific phrase searches are unlikely to match other undesired phrases by accident. Phrase searches are a good way to target specific wording and target multiword names in your content.

GROUPED EXPRESSIONS

In order to handle arbitrarily complex Boolean clauses, Solr supports grouping expressions together by wrapping them in parentheses, such as

```
(apache AND (solr OR lucene)) AND title:(apache solr)
```

Grouping expressions also allows you to set the context of expressions (for example, indicating that multiple words should be searched within the same field). Grouped expressions can be nested arbitrarily deep.

TERM PROXIMITY

You saw earlier how to define a phrase search by wrapping multiple terms in quotes. In reality, this is a simplified version of term-proximity searching. It's also possible to search for terms close together, but not necessarily right beside each other, by adding a tilde and the number of positions the terms can be away from each other:

```
"apache solr"~3
"open source software"~5
```

You could think of a plain phrase search as a proximity search with an implied distance of zero. As such, the following queries are equivalent:

```
"apache software foundation"
"apache software foundation"~0
```

The second query can be interpreted as "find all documents where the exact phrase "apache software foundation" can be formed by moving terms not more than 0 spaces combined." Likewise, if the number specified had been 2, then the query would also match any of "apache foundation software", "software apache foundation", "apache [otherWord] [otherWord2] software foundation", or any other variation that can form the original phrase "apache software foundation" by moving terms no more than 2 positions. As discussed in chapter 3, swapping two terms requires two position moves.

With a sufficiently high proximity value specified, it's possible to still match the terms anywhere in the document, similar to an AND query. Thus the following queries should return the same number of documents (assuming the document has less than 1,000,000 terms in it).

```
apache AND solr
"apache solr"~1000000
```

One interesting side effect of using a term-proximity query is that the closer the terms are in a document, the higher their relevancy score will be for the proximity query. Because the first query does not care about the positions of the terms, and the second query cares but has a tolerance beyond the range of terms in the documents, the only difference between these two queries will ultimately be the relevancy score and the cost of calculation. (It's much more expensive to calculate the distances than to do the Boolean lookup.) Both queries will return the same number of documents. Using a proximity boost like this to boost the relevancy of documents that have terms closer together will be discussed further in chapter 16.

CHARACTER PROXIMITY

Not only can you perform proximity searching between terms, you can also perform edit distances on the characters within a term you're querying to find similarly spelled terms. The syntax is the same as with a term-proximity search minus the quotes, because you're only dealing with one term:

```
solr~1
supercalifragilisticexpialidocious~5
```

The first query will find any term within 1 edit distance of `solr` (`sol`, `sor`, `slr`, `salr`, `olr`, etc.), and the second query will find any term off by up to 5 edit distances from the much longer and more difficult word supercalifragilisticexpialidocious. In some applications, where it's better to return some results than no results, it may make sense to replace a zero results search with the same terms having an edit distance applied to see if any similarly spelled words match the query. This can assist your users with spelling corrections (though there are perhaps better ways to handle spelling corrections, which will be covered in chapter 10).

EXCLUDING TERMS

Sometimes it's useful to explicitly exclude certain terms from a query. This can be accomplished through the use of the – (minus sign) unary operator on an expression or the NOT Boolean operator between expressions:

```
solr -panel
solr NOT panel
solr AND NOT (panel OR electricity)
-badterm
```

In the first three examples, an attempt was made to separate documents with a misspelled version of `solar` (meaning from the sun and generally in reference to solar power) from the correctly spelled `solr` search engine. These examples demonstrate how to apply the - and NOT operators, as well as how to distribute a NOT across multiple terms in the third query. The final example shows that it's possible in Solr to perform a pure exclusion query, which is the equivalent of specifying `*:* -badterm`; it finds all matching documents and removes any containing the excluded expression.

RANGE SEARCHES

Sometimes you do not want to match only a single value with a query expression, but rather a whole range of values. This can be a numerical range (say a price between $20 and $25), a date range (any document modified in the last year), or a string range (any word whose spelling lies between `ape` and `apple`, such as `appetite`). The syntax to perform an inclusive (including the values specified) range search is the field name and a colon, followed by square brackets:

```
number:[12.5 TO 100]
date:[2013-11-04T10:05:00Z TO NOW-1DAY]
string:[ape TO apple]
```

It's worth noting that the date format must be specified in either Zulu time or using date math; otherwise it will throw an exception. If you do not have a specific minimum or maximum value upon which you want to limit a range, you can use a wildcard (*) to leave either the lower or upper end of the range open:

```
number:[* TO 0]
number:[100 TO *]
date:[NOW-1Year TO *]
```

Technically, you can even leave both the lower and upper ends of the range open:

```
field:[* TO *]
```

Although it may seem silly to do a range search without limiting the upper or lower end of the range, this serves the purpose of finding all documents that have any value in the field. (A value exists between something and something else.) It's also possible in recent versions of Solr to perform this search by specifying `field:*`, so the range search in this case is probably overkill.

Using square brackets performs an inclusive range search, but it's also possible to exclude the lower and upper range values through the use of curly braces:

```
number:{0 TO 100}
```

In this example, if the field is an integer field, the lowest matched value will be 1 and the highest will be 99. It's also possible to mix and match inclusive and exclusive brackets. The following queries achieve the same results on an integer field as the previous example:

```
number:[1 TO 100}
number:{0 TO 99]
```

Range searches can be useful for many kinds of operations in Solr, from drawing a bounding box around a location (`latitude:[min TO max] AND longitude:[min TO max]`) to generating queries for arbitrarily slicing and dicing documents by date ranges.

WILDCARD SEARCHES

Sometimes it can be useful for your users to match variations of words or phrases in your Solr index. Although techniques like stemming hopefully make this unnecessary for most keywords your users would type in, it's nevertheless possible to find all documents beginning with a particular set of characters or to allow a single character to be replaced. The syntax for *wildcard* queries is the text you're looking for, with an asterisk (*) to stand in place for "one or more characters" and a question mark (?) to stand in place for a single character substitution. You may include as many wildcard characters as you wish in a phrase:

```
hel* w?rld, t??s is awe*m?
```

This phrase would match the text `hello world, this is awesome`. It's worth keeping in mind that Solr is able to do incredibly fast keyword searching because it generally does direct lookups in an inverted index for exact tokens. In the case of wildcard searching, Solr must scan the index to find the many terms that match the wildcard query, which means the more characters that you include before a wildcard, the fewer terms Solr has to scan through and use in the search. To understand more about the performance implications of wildcards and how to optimize for wildcards early in a search term, you may want to revisit chapter 3 (section 3.1.7).

BOOSTING EXPRESSIONS

Boosting expressions will be covered more fully in chapter 16, but it should suffice for now to demonstrate the syntax:

```
(apache^10 solr^100 is^0 awesome^1.234) AND (apache lucene^2.5)^10
```

Any expression, whether a term, a phrase, or another grouped expression, can have its relevancy boosted if a caret (^) and number are specified after the expression. This can be useful if you know that certain expressions are more important than others or if you're trying to allocate a certain amount of relevancy for different aspects of the query.

SPECIAL CHARACTER ESCAPING

Certain characters are reserved characters in Solr, meaning that they will be interpreted as query syntax instead of as terms to be searched against. In Solr, these characters include:

```
+ - && || ! ( ) { } [ ] ^ " ~ * ? : /
```

In some use cases, you may need to include reserved characters as part of the terms to be searched upon in your query. For example, if you tried to run the query q=content:(I'm so happy!!! :)), you would get the following response from Solr:

```
org.apache.solr.search.SyntaxError: Cannot parse 'content:( I'm so
happy!!! : ) )': Encountered " ")" ") "" at line 1, column 30. Was expecting
one of: <BAREOPER> ... "(" ... "*" ... <QUOTED> ... <TERM> ... <PREFIXTERM>
... <WILDTERM> ... <REGEXPTERM> ... "[" ... "{" ... <LPARAMS> ... <NUMBER>
...
```

If you do need to search upon reserved characters, you must either wrap the characters in a quoted phrase or escape them with a backslash:

```
q=content:"I'm so happy!!! : )"
q=content:(I\'m so happy\!\!\! \: \))
```

In the first example, wrapping the entire phrase in quotes changes the meaning of the query to search for the entire phrase as opposed to the terms individually, so it may not be appropriate for many use cases. You could alternatively wrap each individual term in quotes to accomplish the same effect as using the backslash:

```
q=content:("I'm" "so" "happy!!!" ": )")
```

This works fine if you want to preparse all of your terms, but doing this is a lot of work and is generally not practical. It also does not handle the use case in which a double quote is one of the characters you need to escape. As such, the recommended approach for handling reserved characters in keywords is either to strip them before passing them to Solr (if they do not add value or will be stripped by your fields' analyzers anyway) or to escape each with a backslash.

As you can see, the syntax for the Lucene query parser allows for arbitrarily complex queries across your data. Unfortunately for many users, the syntax is strictly enforced, and any special characters or poorly formed queries will result in an exception being returned instead of search results. Although the Lucene query parser is good for queries that are built up programmatically, it's not well suited for user-entered keyword queries that you have limited control over (unless you want to preprocess those queries to clean them up yourself). Thankfully, Solr provides an excellent query parser to handle user-entered queries: the eDisMax query parser.

7.5   Handling user queries (eDisMax query parser)

The Lucene query parser, as you saw in the previous section, includes an expressive syntax for creating arbitrarily complex Boolean queries, but it has a few major drawbacks that make it less than ideal for handling user queries. The most problematic of these is that the Lucene query parser expects a strict syntax that, if broken, will throw an exception. Because it's often unreasonable to expect your users to understand and always enter perfect Lucene query syntax when typing in their keywords, this relegates the Lucene query parser to not being user-friendly enough for many applications.

An additional drawback of the Lucene query parser is its inability to search across multiple fields by default. The `df` parameter allows you to define which single field the Lucene query parser should search across, but what if you want to search across multiple fields with different weights (such as a title field and a content field, with the title field assigned a higher relevancy boost)? To do this with the Lucene query parser, you would have to prepare the user's query from `q=some keywords` to `q=title:(some keywords) OR content:(some keywords)` if you required all keywords to match within a single field, or to `q=(title:some OR content:some) AND (title:keywords OR content:keywords)` if you wanted to allow the keywords to match in either of the fields as long as both keywords appeared in the document. Doing this kind of preparsing of the query, for most Solr developers, is an unreasonable amount of work. To work around these limitations of the Lucene query parser and to enable user queries to be passed directly to Solr and handled gracefully, the Extended Disjunction Maximum (eDisMax) query parser was created.

7.5.1   eDisMax query parser overview

The eDisMax query parser is essentially a combination of two other query parsers, the Lucene query parser and Disjunction Max (DisMax) query parser. The DisMax query parser is an older version of the eDisMax query parser that only accepts keywords and a few basic Boolean operations, but which allows those keywords to be searched across multiple fields. Because the DisMax query parser is a subset of the eDisMax query parser, the original DisMax query parser should be considered deprecated in favor of the newer extended version. As such, we will not be covering the DisMax query parser independently, even though many of its features will be included by reference in our discussion of the eDisMax query parser.

The eDisMax query parser, although not the default query parser in Solr, is probably the best choice for applications that accept keywords directly from users, as it's tolerant of errors in query syntax, unlike the Lucene query parser. The next section will demonstrate the common query parameters for the eDisMax query parser.

7.5.2 *eDisMax query parameters*

The eDisMax query parser supports the full range of query syntax from the Lucene query parser. The only major difference is that, instead of throwing an exception on invalid input syntax, the eDisMax query parser will treat the invalid input as a literal string to search upon. It's also a bit more tolerant in interpreting the syntax, allowing special keywords such as AND and OR to be understood when lowercased. This flexibility and tolerance makes it much better for handling user input than the Lucene query parser.

7.5.3 *Searching across multiple fields*

In addition to safely handling user-inputted text and liberally interpreting query syntax, one of the most useful features of the eDisMax query parser is its ability to search across multiple fields. Instead of being forced into copying all searchable content into a default content field and searching it, the eDisMax query parser lets you put each piece of your content in its own field (such as a title field, a description field, and an author field). With the Lucene query parser, you would have to construct a query for Solr in Action to look something like this:

```
(((title:solr) OR (description:solr) OR (author:solr)) AND ((title:in) OR
(description:in) OR (author:in)) AND ((title:action) OR (description:action)
OR (author:action)))
```

In comparison, the eDisMax query parser can do this for you with ease, allowing you to specify your query and the query fields (qf) you want to search across:

```
q=solr in action&qf=title description author
```

This example query is much simpler to construct and it enables you to keep your content separated into multiple fields. Other than keeping your data better organized (by not cramming it all into one field), this also may help your relevancy scoring by keeping your idf statistics separated out per field. An additional benefit of keeping your fields separate is that you can assign different boosts to each field if you want:

```
q=solr in action&qf=title^1.5 description author^3
```

You can choose to modify these boosts on a per-query basis if you prefer. Figure 7.4 demonstrates how this kind of boosted field search works.

In figure 7.4, you can see that each keyword is searched across every field specified in the qf parameter. The size of the field names corresponds to the relative relevancy weights of each of the fields as defined by the specified boost. In addition to boosting particular fields, you can also boost content based upon how closely terms are found

q=solr in action
&qf=title^1.5 description author^3

Keywords being searched for

solr   in   action

title   description   **author**

Fields being searched across, sized by boost

Figure 7.4   A demonstration of how the eDisMax query parser distributes terms across multiple fields with different boosts. The size of the fields represents the relative boosts of the fields used for relevancy scoring.

together (similar to term-proximity boosting discussed in the Lucene query parser section), which will be covered in the next section.

7.5.4   *Boosting queries and phrases*

One of the great features of the eDisMax query parser is its ability to natively boost the relevance of terms that appear closer together. A typical query using the Lucene query parser treats the relevancy of all terms the same, regardless of whether they appear closer to each other or in a phrase together. Another feature of the eDisMax query parser is its ability to apply arbitrary relevancy boosts to functions independent of the main user query. These relevancy-affecting capabilities will be covered further in chapter 16, but it's worth mentioning each of these relevancy-affecting parameters to give general insight into what they do.

THE PF (PHRASE FIELDS), PF2, AND PF3 PARAMETERS

The pf parameter can be used to boost the score of documents in which all of the terms in the q parameter appear in close proximity. The pf parameter uses the same format as the qf parameter, taking a list of fields and optional corresponding boosts. The eDisMax query parser will attempt to make phrase queries out of all the terms in the q parameter, and if it's able to find the exact phrase in any of the phrase fields, it will apply the specified boost to the match for that document.

In addition to the pf parameter, the eDisMax query parser supports the pf2 and pf3 parameters. These parameters function similarly to the pf parameter, but instead of requiring all of the terms in the q parameter, they break the terms up into bigrams (for pf2) or trigrams (for pf3) and boost documents containing only a few of the terms together. In the case of the query Solr finds relevant documents, the pf3 parameter would boost documents containing the phrases "solr finds relevant" or "finds relevant documents", whereas the pf2 parameter would boost documents containing the phrases "solr finds", "finds relevant", and "relevant documents".

THE PS (PHRASE SLOP), PS2, AND PS3 PARAMETERS

When using the pf parameter, you may not want to require all terms in the query to appear as an exact phrase. You can make use of the ps (phrase slop) parameter to specify how many term positions the terms in the query can be off by to be considered a match on the phrase fields.

The eDisMax query parser also supports the ps2 and ps3 parameters, which allow the phrase slop to be overridden for the pf2 and pf3 parameters. If ps2 and ps3 are not specified, their values default to that of the ps parameter.

THE QS (QUERY PHRASE SLOP) PARAMETER

Just as the ps parameter allows you to define the amount of slop (edit distances) on phrases matching in the phrase fields (pf parameter), the qs parameter allows you to do the same for phrases the user explicitly specifies in the main q parameter. Think of the qs parameter as redefining what an exact match is, allowing you to change the slop from the default of 0 (terms must appear beside each other) to a higher number.

THE TIE (TIE BREAKER) PARAMETER

The tie parameter is used to determine what happens when a query term is matched in more than one field in a document. A score is calculated for each term for each field in which it matches, and by default, only the top-scoring field in each document is used in the relevancy calculation for the term. This is the maximum score for the disjunction (after which the query parser gets its name, "disjunction maximum"). This stands in stark contrast to the Lucene query parser, which always adds up the relevancy score for each term in each field to compute the composite relevancy score per document.

The tie parameter determines how much each term's relevancy score in the other fields besides the top-matching field should contribute to the overall relevancy score. A tie of 0.0 is the default and means that other fields will contribute no weight. A tie of 1.0 means that all fields will contribute their full weight to the overall relevancy score, as in the Lucene query parser. In this case, the scoring performs as a disjunction sum instead of a disjunction maximum.

THE BQ (BOOST QUERY) PARAMETER

The bq parameter accepts a query string that will be included with the main query (q parameter) to influence the score. It does not modify the number of documents matched, only the order in which they will be returned. If you wanted to add a relevancy boost for recent documents, you could add the following to your request:

```
bq=date:[NOW/DAY-1YEAR TO NOW/DAY]
```

This will effectively boost all documents with a date within the last year. You can specify multiple bq parameters, which allow the query to be parsed with separate boosts for separate clauses.

THE BF (BOOST FUNCTIONS) PARAMETER

Just as the bq parameter is able to boost the relevancy of the main query with another query, the bf parameter is able to boost the score of the main query with a function query. Function queries will be covered fully in chapter 15, but here's an example of how you would use a function to provide a relevancy boost for more recent documents:

```
recip(rord(date),1,1000,1000)
```

The bf parameter accepts any function supported by Solr, along with a boost value.

7.5.5 Field aliasing

Sometimes, you may need to use an internal field name in Solr that is not suitable for displaying to your users. This can be particularly true for dynamic fields, where your field name may be something like `title_t_en`, but you would prefer to enable a more user-friendly syntax for searching, such as `title:"some title"`. The eDisMax query parser provides such a mechanism for aliasing fields to alternate names.

Field aliasing can be enabled for an eDisMax query by adding a parameter, `f.{alias}.qf={realfield}`, to your request. In the previous example, your Solr query would look like

```
/select?defType=edismax&q=title:"some title"&f.title.qf=title_t_en
```

In this example, the query run will be against the `title_t_en` field, because it will be substituted in anywhere the `title` field appears in the query. The field aliasing parameter is modeled after the default `qf` parameter, which means it's possible to map a single alias to multiple internal fields with respective boosts. It's also possible to add as many aliases as you want to your request. For example, if you have the following fields,

```
personFirstName, personLastName, itemName, companyName, cityName, stateName,
postalCodeName
```

you could simplify the query for your users with the following Solr request:

```
/select?defType=edismax&
  f.who.qf=personLastName^30 personFirstName^10&
  f.what.qf=itemName company^5&
  f.where.qf=city^10 state^20 country^35 postalCode^30&
  q=...
```

In a request like this, users can query using the following syntax:

```
who:(trey grainger) what:(solr) where:(decatur, ga)
```

Figure 7.5 demonstrates how the keywords in this query across the field aliases of `who`, `what`, and `where` will be distributed across the fields in your Solr index.

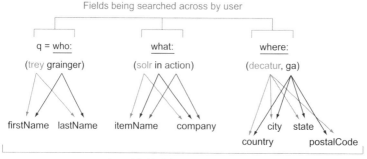

Figure 7.5 **How searches on field aliases expand queries to their true underlying fields. This mechanism effectively allows you to create your own** `qf` **parameter for any virtual field you define, instead of being constrained to only defining a virtual default field.**

As you would probably expect, a search across multiple aliased fields operates like a search across the default field, in which each query term is divided across the query fields defined for the alias. The only difference is that instead of one qf parameter defined for the default field, you can now define a separate qf field per alias. As such, the parts of the query associated with each alias will search across separate lists of fields.

Figure 7.5 demonstrated how terms would be divided across fields, but it did not represent the field boosts associated with each of the underlying queries. The query specified internally would automatically be expanded by the eDisMax query parser to run the following full query against the Solr index:

```
((
    (personFirstName:trey^10.0 | personLastName:trey^30.0)
    (personFirstName:grainger^10.0 | personLastName:grainger^30.0)
)(
    (itemName:solr | company:solr^5.0)
)(
    (state:decatur^20.0 | postalCode:decatur^30.0
        | country:decatur^35.0 | city:decatur^10.0)
)(
    (state:ga^20.0 | postalCode:ga^30.0
        | country:ga^35.0 | city:ga^10.0)
))
```

This ability to map any number of field aliases to a list of query fields enables you to provide a much simpler query syntax to your users. This should allow you to implement any number of field weighting rules without having to resort to pre-parsing your user queries or relying solely on the default qf parameter. Of course, it's possible that you may not want to expose all of your fields or aliases to each of your users. The next section will demonstrate how you can handle per-field (or per-alias) access restrictions.

7.5.6 *User-accessible fields*

In many cases, you will only want your users to be able to execute keyword queries against the default field and (possibly) a small list of additional fields. Since you may have some internal fields with somewhat sensitive information (such as user IDs or other internal identifiers), you likely will not want your users to be able to guess additional fields from your Solr index to begin querying upon.

Although the eDisMax query parser allows the main query (q parameter) to query across any field, it's possible to restrict this with the uf (user fields) parameter. The default value is uf=*, which allows all fields to be queried with the syntax field:expression. If you would like to restrict the available fields to a single title field, you can specify uf=title. You can also allow access to multiple fields by separating them with a space: uf=title city date. If you want to disable all fields to users, you can also use the negation syntax: uf=-*. If you want to enable access to all fields except a specific list of fields, you can specify this with the syntax: uf=* -hiddenField1 -hiddenField2.

To maintain full control over your user queries, you can combine the uf parameter with the field aliasing parameter discussed in the last section. The uf parameter will accept either a real field or an alias, so you could construct a query such as the following:

```
/select?defType=edismax&
  &df=text&
  f.who.qf=lastName^30 firstName^10&
  f.what.qf=itemName companyName^5&
  uf=who what&
  q=+who:(timothy potter) +what:(solr in action) +"big data"
```

In this example, the query would be expanded to search for timothy and potter in the firstName and lastName fields, and for solr and in and action in the itemName and companyName fields. It would also search for the phrase "big data" in the default (text) field. Had the query attempted to search across any other fields except for the who and what aliased fields, however, the query would not have worked. For example, consider the following query:

```
q=+who:(timothy potter) +what:(solr in action) +firstName:timothy
```

In this example, the query would not interpret firstName as a field, but would instead search for the full phrase in the default (text) field as a keyword. Thus, unless you have a document which matches the search text:"firstName:timothy", this query will return zero results, protecting your search engine from unauthorized field access. If you have this need to restrict the accessible fields in your search application, the eDisMax query parser should have you covered.

7.5.7 *Minimum match*

In our discussion of Boolean logic to this point, two binary operators have been discussed: AND and OR. These are internally represented in Lucene with the concepts of must match and should match. The expression hello AND world can be rewritten +hello +world, meaning hello must match and world must match. The query big OR brown OR cow means that at least one of the terms big, brown, or cow must match. But how would you model a query for which you want to require more than a single expression to match, but do not care which ones?

The eDisMax query parser provides the ability to blur the lines of traditional Boolean logic through the use of the mm (minimum match) parameter. The mm parameter allows you to define either a specific number of terms or a percentage of terms in a query that must match in order for a document to be considered a match. This can be a great tool for manipulating the Precision and Recall characteristics of your search application, because it does not take an absolute approach requiring all terms to match (default operator of AND) or only requiring a single term out of many to match (default operator of OR).

The syntax for the mm parameter is expressive, and can be tricky to get right at first. Table 7.2 walks you through various mm values, describing how they're interpreted.

Table 7.2　Minimum match syntax examples

Description	mm value	Interpretation
Positive integer	`2`	Two optional clauses must match (or all clauses if less than two are present).
Negative integer	`-3`	All but three optional clauses must match.
Positive percentage	`75%`	75% of all optional clauses must match (rounded down to the nearest integer, so less than 75% is possible).
Negative percentage	`-30%`	Up to 30% of all optional clauses can be missing (rounded down to the nearest integer, so no more than 30% will be missing).
Conditional percentage	`3<80%`	All clauses must match if three or fewer exist. If more than three clauses exist, 80% are required (using the positive percentage rules in this case).
Multiple conditional percentages	`3<-1 5<4 7<-30%`	If three or fewer clauses exist, they all must match. If four to five clauses exist, one can be missing. If six to seven clauses exist, four must match. If more than seven clauses exist, up to 30% do not have to match.

From table 7.2, you can see that the minimum match specification syntax is expressive. It can be defined in terms of how many expressions must match (a positive integer), how many can be missing (a negative integer), the percentage of expressions that must match (a positive percentage), or the percentage which can be missing (a negative percentage). For more control, you can also define different minimum match rules based upon how many expressions are present in the query.

As an example, consider the following query structure:

```
/select?q={!edismax mm="2<50% 4<-45%" v=$example}&example=…
```

Given that query, the following rules would be in effect for different example parameter values:

`example=solr`	all terms must match
`example=solr is`	all terms must match
`example=solr is a`	1 term must match (33% present, rounded up to 50%)
`example=solr is a search`	2 terms must match (50% present exactly)
`example=solr is a search engine`	2 terms must match (40% missing, rounded up to 45%)

The minimum match capability in the eDisMax query parser enables you to have fine-grained control over the quality and quantity of matches for queries with many

q={!edismax mm="40%"}solr is a search engine

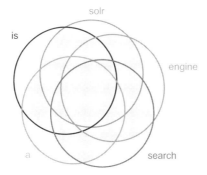

Figure 7.6   Minimum match of 40% of five terms. In this case, two out of five terms must match, allowing for a different set intersection than the traditional Boolean AND (all terms) and OR (only one term) operators discussed in chapter 3.

keywords. Figure 7.6 demonstrates how a minimum match threshold works from a set intersection standpoint.

In this figure, the shaded portion represents the documents that would match this query given the presence of the terms contained in the associated circles. You will notice that because only 40% of the terms must match (two out of five), the Venn diagram looks different than that of the traditional AND and OR Boolean operations discussed in chapter 3. Whereas a default operator of AND would require all terms to match, and a default operator of OR would only require a single term to match, by using the mm parameter you're able to achieve a much more nuanced approach. Effectively, by increasing the mm parameter you will usually increase Precision, and by reducing the mm parameter you will usually increase Recall. (Precision and Recall were covered in chapter 3.)

There are a couple of important points to note when using the mm parameter, however. First, if the calculations ever determine that no clauses are required (such as when specifying that more expressions can be missing than are present in the query), the default Boolean logic of requiring at least one clause will still be applied. The same applies for the upper limit. Essentially, a derived minimum match value less than 1 will never be used (at least one will be required), and a value greater than the number of clauses will never be used (the max will be the number of clauses in the query). Second, it's useful to note that, when dealing with percentages, positive percentages and negative percentages can be used to obtain different behaviors around edge cases. When dealing with five clauses, 80% and -20% yield the same behavior, but when dealing with four clauses, 80% means that three clauses are required (80% rounds down to 3 out of 4 present, not up to 4 out of 4 present), whereas -20% means that all four are required (-20% rounds down to zero out of 4 missing, not up to 1 out of 4 missing). These kinds of nuances and the overall expressiveness of the minimum match capability in the eDisMax query parser make it a powerful tool in your query toolkit.

7.5.8   *eDisMax benefits and drawbacks*

The eDisMax query parser supports the full range of query syntax provided by the Lucene query parser and enables many additional features, such as searching across multiple fields, sanitizing user input, aliasing and restricting fields, and applying multiple query modifications to improve the relevancy of phrases and other boost factors. Because the eDisMax query parser acts as a superset of the available capabilities in the Lucene query parser, you may wonder why anyone would ever consider using the Lucene query parser directly.

For typical user-facing applications, the eDisMax query parser is generally used. It doesn't make sense to reimplement the user-friendly query functionality provided by the eDisMax query parser in your application layer unless you have some fairly specific needs in your application. For applications that generate all of the Solr queries, however, you may prefer to use the Lucene query parser directly if you do not need the additional functionality (or overhead) provided by the eDisMax query parser.

There are drawbacks to using the eDisMax query parser. The first has to do with how the eDisMax query parser handles searching across multiple fields. If you put all of your terms into a single field and search across that field, your query is generally going to execute more quickly than when you use the eDisMax query parser to run the same query expression across multiple fields. This is not a benefit of the Lucene query parser over the eDisMax query parser, per se, because you can still use the eDisMax query parser to only search upon a single field like the Lucene query parser. Instead, it's a comment on the extra expense added to many Solr-based applications by choosing to search across many fields because it's made so easy to do by the eDisMax query parser.

There is one particular characteristic of the eDisMax query parser related to relevancy scoring which should be taken into consideration. Unlike the Lucene query parser, which will consider the relevancy of each term in the q parameter regardless of the field it's searched against, the eDisMax query parser only counts the relevancy of the top scoring field in which a term matches (by default). For example, consider the following two queries:

```
/select?q={!edismax qf=title content}solr
/select?q=title:solr OR content:solr
```

In theory, you would expect these queries to return the same relevancy score for the documents they match, because in the eDisMax query you're asking Solr to search across both fields for you. Internally, however, an eDisMax query only uses the relevancy of the top field the term appeared within by default. Thus, if the relevancy of `solr` is higher in the `title` field, then only the relevancy of the `title` field will be used in the score, and vice versa for the `content` field. This is different than the Lucene query parser, which will add the relevancy of the scores from each field and therefore allow a more composite (and nuanced) relevancy score to be returned. The full name of the eDisMax query parser—Extended Disjunction Maximum—implies this behavior; it only uses the maximum of the disjunction scores by default. Because of the fact that some fields count more than other fields, this means that the eDisMax query parser is scoring how well each document matched a term in its best field, not how well the document as a whole scored.

In fairness, you may get a better relevancy score through this approach for many use cases, but you should at least be aware that the magic provided by the eDisMax query parser includes this relevancy behavior. The eDisMax query parser also allows you to change this behavior through the use of the `tie` request parameter. If you specify `tie=0` (the default), you get the disjunction maximum behavior described. If you set the value to 1.0, however, you get the same kind of behavior as you would with the Lucene query parser (in this case, the disjunction sum).

You can also put the value anywhere between 0.0 and 1.0, with the top field provided receiving most of the relevancy weight the closer the `tie` parameter is to 0.0. Most Solr applications are not so sensitive to relevancy that this difference between scoring would even be noticed, so using the eDisMax query parser with its default settings is generally recommended for most newly built search applications. If your relevancy needs are so critical that you're concerned about such details, you will likely find even bigger ways to improve the relevancy of your search application in chapter 16.

With the two most commonly used query parsers (Lucene query parser and eDisMax query parser) covered in detail, it's worthwhile to at least mention others available in Solr. The next section will provide an overview of some of these other interesting query parsers.

7.6   Other useful query parsers

Solr contains several other query parsers out of the box. This section will provide a quick overview of some of the more interesting ones.

7.6.1   Field query parser

The Field query parser can be used to search for a term or phrase within a specific field, making use of any defined text analysis for the field. The `f` parameter represents the field upon which the term or phrase should be searched. The syntax is as follows:

```
{!field f=myfield}hello world
```

This syntax is equivalent to searching for the phrase `myfield:"hello world"` using the Lucene query parser.

7.6.2   Term and Raw query parsers

Term query parser can be used to look up values directly in the Solr index. This is in contrast to the Field query parser, which can take in text values and apply the defined text analysis for the field. The Term query parser can be useful for filtering on values returned from faceting (covered in the next chapter) or the terms component, which are pulled directly from the Solr index. The syntax for the Term query parser is as follows:

```
{!term f=mystemmedtextfield}engin
{!term f=mystringfield}Single Term with Spaces
{!term f=myintfield}1.5
```

In each of the preceding examples, the value being searched for is the readable version of the token in the Solr index for the field in question. As with the Field query parser, the f parameter references the field to search against.

Solr also contains a similar implementation in the form of the Raw query parser. The only difference between the Term and the Raw query parsers is that the Raw query parser searches for the *exact* token in the Solr index, but the Term query parser searches for the *readable* version of the term.

In certain kinds of fields, such as numeric fields that internally store values in a trie structure for greater search efficiency, the Term query parser will accept the readable version of the number (1.5), whereas the Raw query parser will accept the machine-readable version (the internal representation of the field in the index). The number 1 in an integer field may be represented by a `trie` structure in the Solr index with a token such as `` `#8;#0;#0;#0;#1; ``. The following queries would both return a document containing the integer value 1.

```
{!term f=myintfield}1
{!raw f=myintfield}`#8;#0;#0;#0;#1;
```

The Raw query parser, as you can probably tell, is an advanced feature that is rarely used in typical search applications. Part of the beauty of Solr is that it allows users to run efficient queries without having to fully understand the internal data structures necessary to make searching so efficient. As such, you should almost always opt to use the Term query parser over the Raw query parser.

7.6.3 Function and Function Range query parsers

One of the more powerful capabilities in Solr is its ability to use function queries to generate dynamic values during a search. Such dynamically computed values can include determining geospatial distances, doing math calculations, doing string transformations, or running arbitrary code you include in your own function plugin. Functions can be fairly complex and represent such a large topic, so we will devote most of a chapter to covering their use in detail. We will defer coverage of the Function query parser and Function Range query parser until chapter 15, at which point we will even show you how to write your own function plugin.

7.6.4 Nested queries and the Nested query parser

Each query parser discussed so far has been discussed in isolation. You have seen how to change the query parser for any given query, but what if you have a need to combine multiple query parsers in unique ways?

The query syntax for the Lucene query parser (or eDisMax query parser) supports a special _query_ operator that enables you to easily substitute other query parsers in the middle of the default Lucene query parser. This enables you to combine different query parsers inside of any arbitrarily complex Boolean expression.

The syntax for executing nested queries is: _query_:"[QUERY]", where [QUERY] represents any query you could otherwise use independently in the q or fq parameter. Consider the following query:

```
/select?q=category:("technology" OR "business") AND
  _query_:"{!edismax qf=title^10 category^4 text}solr lucene hadoop mahout"
```

In this example, an eDisMax query is nested inside of a request to the Lucene query parser. The full nested query must be wrapped in quotes, which means that any quotes inside the query must be escaped with a backslash. It should be noted that, in many cases, the use of the explicit _query_ syntax is not necessary, as the Lucene query parser and eDisMax query parser can often infer the need for a nested query when it discovers a local params syntax embedded within the query. The more complicated the query, the greater the likelihood that you will need to wrap your nested query in the _query_ syntax to ensure it's parsed as expected.

In addition to the special _query_ operator, Solr contains a built-in Nested query parser that is also able to handle nested queries. The type local param for the Nested query parser is query, which means you could invoke it as follows:

```
/select?q={!query v=$nestedQuery}
```

When defining your query this way, you can then substitute in any query, including a new local params section. This can be particularly useful if you want to predefine parts of your query in your *solrconfig.xml* and substitute in both the query parser type and the value for the query dynamically:

```
<lst name="defaults">
  <str name="nestedQuery">{!func}product(popularity, 0.25)
</str>
```

In this example, a function query was substituted into the query from the *solrconfig.xml* without the process creating the query having to know what kind of query would be substituted. Of course, you can combine the use of the Nested query parser with the special _query_ nested query syntax to create much more complex expressions, even nesting and substituting queries multiple levels deep. In practice, however, most search applications never get this sophisticated.

This nested query capability enables you to substitute any number of subqueries to different query parsers within your main query, allowing for the full scope of Boolean expressions to determine how to combine the queries. This can be particularly useful for boosting the relevance of a query by function, including geospatial distance or other function calculations in the relevancy score.

7.6.5   *Boost query parser*

The Boost query parser enables you to apply an arbitrarily defined relevancy boost based upon whether a document matches a particular query, without also filtering out documents that do not match the boosting query. You will recall that the q parameter is typically used to both filter your search results and to inform the similarity implementation about expressions to consider in relevancy scoring. The Boost query parser allows you to submit terms that should only be considered for relevancy scoring and not applied as a filter. The syntax for the Boost query parser is as follows:

```
{!boost b=1000}shouldboost:true
{!boost b=log(popularity}category:trending
{!boost b=recip(ms(NOW,articledate),3.16e-11,1,1)}category:news
```

Each of these examples boosts the relevancy of any documents that match the query value specified, but doesn't restrict documents to only those matching the query value. You can also combine the Boost query parser with another query parser through the use of a nested query:

```
/select?q=_query_:"{!edismax qf=title content}data science" AND
        _query_:"{!boost b=log(popularity)}*:*" AND
        _query_:"{!boost b=recip(
                ms(NOW,articledate),3.16e-11,1,1)}category:news"
```

This query will run a search for the keywords data science, boosting all documents by their popularity and by how recently they were posted if they fall within the "news" category. The number of results will be the same as the search for data science; the boost clauses only serve to affect document relevancy.

7.6.6 *Prefix query parser*

The Prefix query parser can be used in place of a wildcard query. The syntax is

```
{!prefix f=myfield}engin
```

This query is equivalent to searching for myfield:engin* with the Lucene query parser, which will match terms in myfield such as engine, engineer, and engineering. It should be noted that the prefix is searched directly against the Solr index, so no text analysis will be performed on the input before it's compared against the index. As such, you will need to know the indexed representation of the terms you're searching for in order to avoid a mismatch between your prefix input and the index representation of terms for which you're searching. In most cases, you will probably do better to use a wildcard search using the Lucene query parser or eDisMax query parser.

7.6.7 *Spatial query parsers*

Solr contains rich geospatial capabilities, allowing you to define a geographical point or a shape at both index and query time. With such a point, you can run a search that filters documents to those falling within a certain distance of a given point. Given the latitude and longitude of San Francisco, you can filter to all documents within a 50-kilometer radius. Solr contains two query parsers meant to handle spatial queries, the Spatial Box query parser (bbox) and the Spatial Filter query parser (geofilt). Because geospatial searching is such an important topic in Solr, we have devoted a large portion of chapter 15 to covering the details of how to maximize your use of

Solr's available geographical and spatial capabilities. An overview of the available spatial query parsers will be deferred until then.

7.6.8   Join query parser

The Join query parser in Solr allows you to run subqueries that perform a pseudo-join across document sets. For example, you can limit a query by running a subquery against a different set of documents and restricting your original query's result set to documents that contain field values present in the subquery's documents. Such join functionality can even work across documents existing in different Solr cores. This join functionality is an advanced feature that, like the function query functionality and the spatial functionality, will be covered fully in chapter 15. We will defer discussion of the Join query parser until then.

7.6.9   Switch query parser

The Switch query parser allows you to choose between multiple query/filter elements based upon some logical condition. It operates like the `switch` statement present in many programming languages. The syntax for the Switch query parser can be demonstrated through the following example:

```
fq={!switch
      case.day='date:[NOW/DAY-1DAY TO *]'
      case.week='price:[NOW/DAY-7DAYS TO *]'
      case.month='date:[NOW/DAY-1MONTH TO *]'
      case.year='date:[NOW/DAY-1YEAR TO *]'
      case.else='*:*'
      v=$withinLast}
```

Given this filter, you could pass any of the following parameters in on the Solr request to have one of the cases applied: `withinLast=day`, `withinLast=month`, `withinLast=month`, `withinLast=year`. Because of the `case.else`, any other values will default to searching all documents.

You could probably think of many other ways to use the Switch query parser beyond this simple date example. Any value can be checked, and any query can be executed as a result of matching the `case` statement, so you can use the Switch query parser to map your own business rules to queries in Solr that can be easily invoked with a simple request parameter.

7.6.10   Surround query parser

To round out the list of query parsers which ship with Solr, we will cover a fairly niche one, the Surround query parser. This query parser is designed to make thorough use of *span queries*, which are queries that understand the positional relationships of terms with each other. The Surround query parser makes use of the special operators `n` (ordered) or `w` (unordered) preceded by an integer value between 1 and 99. Consider the following examples:

```
{!surround}3w(solr, action)
{!surround}5n(solr, action)
{!surround}solr 3w action
{!surround}solr 3n in 2w action
```

The first example will find the term `solr` within three positions (unordered, forward or backward) of the term `action`. The second example will find the term `solr` followed by the word `action` within five positions (`action` must occur after `solr`). Both of these examples use a prefix notation, in which the terms are enclosed in parentheses and the operators (`3w` and `5u`) serve as a function being operated upon the input values.

The third example is logically the same as the first, using infix notation instead of prefix notation. The final example demonstrates the combination of multiple terms together, in which the term `solr` must be followed by the term `in` within three positions, and the term `action` must exist within two positions before or after the term `in` appears.

The Surround query parser additionally supports the `AND` and `OR` operators in prefix notation, along with the `AND`, `OR`, `NOT`, and `()` operations in infix notation. Although the added proximity operators seem to be powerful additions to Solr's available query syntax, the Surround query parser suffers from one major limitation: its lack of support for text analysis. Unfortunately, like the Term query parser, the Surround query parser looks terms up directly against the Solr index without first running them through the defined analyzers for their field type. Although the Surround query parser does contain support for common query operations such as boosts (`field^10`) and wildcards (`hel* w?rld`), the lack of support for text analysis makes it much less useful for typical keyword searching situations, unless you have deep insights into the text analysis required for a field and can reproduce it when constructing your query.

7.6.11 *Max Score query parser*

When a query is scored using the Lucene query parser, each term/clause is scored and all of those scores are summed together to yield the total relevancy score for each document. Sometimes, it may be more useful to use the maximum score of multiple clauses as opposed the sum of the clauses. You can do this with the `MaxScoreQParser-Plugin` as follows:

```
{!maxscore}term1 term2 term3
```

In this query, each of the three terms will be scored for each document, and the score of the top-scoring term will be used as the entire relevancy score (as opposed to the sum of the three terms' scores). You can also combine both query parsers in the same query if you have the need:

```
/select?q=one OR two OR _query_:"{!maxscore v=$maxQ}"&
  maxQ=three OR four OR five
```

The total score for all documents matching this query will be the score for `one` plus `two` plus the maximum score across `three`, `four`, and `five`. The `MaxScoreQParser-Plugin` extends the `LuceneQParserPlugin`, so it is easy to use the two query parsers interchangeably based upon when you want to sum the scores of all clauses versus just using the maximum score across all the clauses.

7.6.12 Collapsing query parser

The Collapsing query parser provides the ability to remove duplicate documents (documents containing identical values in some field you specify) from a set of search results. This capability, called *field collapsing*, can be very useful for ensuring diversity among your search results. There are two ways to achieve field collapsing in Solr. The first is by using a larger suite of capabilities called *result grouping*, which enables you to group all documents with identical values in a field and only return a specifiable number of documents per group. The other way to collapse documents to a unique field value is by utilizing the Collapsing query parser. The topic of result grouping/field collapsing has a dedicated chapter (chapter 11) later in the book, so you can find all of the specifics on how to use the Collapsing query parser in section 11.7.

You have now seen a multitude of query parsers available in Solr. In addition to the ones that come standard in Solr, it's also possible to write your own query parser as a Solr plugin, though most users find everything they need in the built-in query parsers. With a solid understanding of how to construct queries using one or more query parsers, it's now time to dive into how to handle the retrieval of results from your query.

7.7   *Returning results*

This chapter has covered how to construct a query to find a desired set of matching documents, but the end result of running a query is to return some kind of response. In many cases you will want to return a small number of documents to display on a page, to bring back one or more fields in each of those documents, and to sort those documents based upon relevancy. In other cases, it may be useful to return dynamically calculated values with each document, to page through results by specifying a maximum number of documents to return and an offset into the full document list, or to sort documents based upon some criteria other than relevancy. This section will walk you through the mechanics of sorting your results and returning the desired fields and number of documents in the desired response format for your search application.

7.7.1 Choosing a response format

Most of the responses shown throughout the rest of *Solr in Action* are shown in JSON format for readability. You have previously seen several examples returning responses in XML (the default format). From Solr's standpoint, the response format is fairly inconsequential. As you learned in chapter 4, Solr can return a response in XML, JSON, Ruby, Python, PHP, Binary Java, or even a format that you create yourself.

You can modify the response format through use of the wt (writer type) parameter. Available response wts included with Solr are listed in table 7.3.

Table 7.3 Available Solr response writers

wt **value**	**Associated Solr class**
csv	CSVResponseWriter
json	JSONResponseWriter
php	PHPResponseWriter
phps	PHPSerializedResponseWriter
python	PythonResponseWriter
ruby	RubyResponseWriter
xml	XMLResponseWriter
xslt	XSLTResponseWriter
javabin	BinaryResponseWriter

In order to change the Solr response format, you need to set the wt parameter on your request to one of the values in table 7.3. This listing demonstrates a response in several of the available formats.

Listing 7.4 Sample Solr responses in different formats

Query 1
```
/select?wt=json&indent=true&q=*:*&fl=id,title&rows=2
```

Response 1
```
{
   "responseHeader":{
     "status":0,
     "QTime":1,
     "params":{...},
     "response":{"numFound":1000,"start":0,"docs":[
       {
         "id":"1",
             "title":"solr in action",
       },
       {
         "id":"2",
         "title":"lucene in action",
       }]
   }}
```

Query 2
```
/select?wt=xml&indent=true&q=*:*&fl=id,title&rows=2
```

Response 2
```
<?xml version="1.0" encoding="UTF-8"?>
<response>

<lst name="responseHeader">
  <int name="status">0</int>
```

```
<int name="QTime">1</int>
<lst name="params">
  ...
</lst>
</lst>
<result name="response" numFound="1000" start="0">
  <doc>
    <str name="id">1</str>
    <str name="title">solr in action</str>
  </doc>
  <doc>
    <str name="id">2</str>
    <str name="title">lucene in action</str>
</doc>
</result>
</response>
```

Query 3
```
/select?wt=csv&indent=true&q=*:*&fl,title=id&rows=2
```

Response 3
```
id,title
1,solr in action
2,lucene in action
```

As you can see, Solr's response format is easily configurable using the `wt` request parameter. If you have the need, you can also write your own response writer to output a format specifically designed for your application. In order to do this, you would create a class inheriting from the `QueryResponseWriter` class in Solr. Then, you must register your response writer in your *solrconfig.xml* file as follows:

```
<queryResponseWriter name="myapp" class="….MyAppResponseWriter" />
```

Because most modern programming languages have easy-to-use libraries for dealing with XML and JSON formats, it may not be the best use of your time to implement your own response writer, but it's certainly possible. If you have strong security requirements, for example, you may want to implement a response writer (and require its use), which encrypts your response before returning it to a requestor. Alternatively, you may have a need to restrict the fields returned from Solr, which will be discussed in the next section.

7.7.2   *Choosing fields to return*

When you specify fields in the Solr schema, one of the options you can specify is whether the field should be stored. Storing fields, as you may recall from chapter 5 on indexing, makes the original text available to be returned with search results. Not all stored fields have to be returned with every document in your search results, however. Indeed, if you only need a subset of the available fields, you can greatly speed up the search response by limiting the number of fields returned in (and therefore the size of) the results.

RETURNING STORED FIELDS

As you probably remember from chapter 2, the field list (fl) parameter controls which fields will be returned from Solr. The field list is a comma-separated list of fields that you want returned with each document in your search results in the following format:

```
/select?...&fl=id,name
/select?...&fl=*
```

The first example returns the stored value of the id field and the name field for each document. If you want to return all stored fields, Solr provides a wildcard (the asterisk in the second example) option that prevents you from having to explicitly specify fields. In addition to returning stored fields, Solr also allows you to return dynamically generated values as pseudo-fields in your documents.

RETURNING DYNAMIC VALUES

In addition to the stored fields in your documents, one of the most useful pieces of information to know about each document is the relevancy score. You can return the relevancy score by requesting the special score field to be returned:

```
/select?...&fl=*,score
```

This example returns all stored fields plus an additional (dynamically generated) field containing the relevancy score of the document. Since the relevancy score is not one of the stored fields, the score is not automatically returned using the wildcard and therefore must be explicitly requested. Of course, it isn't necessary to return all fields to obtain the score (you need to request the score field).

The score is far from the only dynamically generated field you can return within your documents. Solr also contains a feature called function queries that enables you to compute all kinds of interesting values for your documents. As an example, you could return the computed value of a mathematical function as a pseudo-field:

```
/select?...&fl=id,sum(integerField,10)
```

This example will add 10 to the value of the integer field and return it as an additional field along with the id field for each document. The power of function queries to do these kinds of dynamic calculations will be covered in detail in chapter 15. In addition to dynamically calculating values for fields, it's also possible to invoke special document transformation steps that can further supplement the information that can be returned for a document.

DOCUMENT TRANSFORMERS

Sometimes it can be useful to pull back extra information about documents before the final documents are written to the Solr response. This may include a readable explanation of how the relevancy score was calculated for each document, the shard in which a document was found for a distributed search (see chapter 12 for an overview of sharding and distributed search), or even the internal Lucene doc

ID. Solr enables this kind of information to be returned through the use of document transformers (doc transformers for short). Doc transformers can be invoked as follows:

```
/select?...&fl=*,[explain],[shard]
```

This example request invokes two special fields: [explain] and [shard]. These fields, [square brackets], invoke doc transformers to pull back additional meta-information about each document. Table 7.4 contains a list of the most common doc transformers built into Solr.

Table 7.4   Common doc transformers in Solr

Example	Meaning
[docid]	The Lucene internal document ID (an integer)
[shard]	The ID of the shard that produced the result
[explain]	The relevancy calculation explanation
[explain style=nl|text|html]	The relevancy calculation explanation in a particular format (style)
[value v=? t=int|double|float|date]	A specific value, the same for each document

The [docid] field will generally only be used if you need to interact at a low level with the Lucene index (not a common use case for most Solr users), the [shard] field will be mostly useful for finding the server and Solr core containing each document in a distributed search, the [explain] field (covered in chapter 16) can be useful for understanding the math behind why your documents received their relevancy score, and the [value] field is used to return a static value on every document.

In addition to these built-in doc transformers, it's also possible to write your own doc transformer as a plugin by inheriting from the org.apache.solr.response.transform .DocTransformer class and implementing the transform method that passes in the entire document for you to manipulate. To make your transformer available to Solr, you also need to create a factory which wraps your doc transformer (inheriting from org.apache.solr.response.transform.TransformerFactory), and you need to register your transformer factory in your *solrconfig.xml* file:

```
<transformer name="magic" class="magicTransformer" >
   <string name="yourSetting">abracadabra</string>
</transformer>
```

Although certainly not one of the most commonly used features in Solr, doc transformers nevertheless provide a useful extension point for document manipulation (the ability to add, remove, or edit fields) prior to documents being returned in the search results.

RETURN FIELD ALIASES

In addition to the ability to return pseudo-fields with dynamically generated values, Solr provides a way to rename fields before they're returned in the search results. By supplying an alias followed by a colon before the field name, the search results will return the value from the actual field name (or dynamically generated value) in a new field, using the alias as its key:

```
/select?...&fl=id,betterFieldName:actualFieldName
```

This feature can be particularly useful if you make use of dynamic fields such as `fieldname_t_is` (a text field that is indexed and stored) but want to return documents with a more user-friendly field name called `fieldname` instead of `fieldname_t_is`. You would accomplish this by specifying `fieldname:fieldname_t_is` in your field list. You can rename any field to any other name. If one of your requested fields is a function query, this makes it easy to provide a more meaningful field name than the function syntax (the default field name).

Chapter 15 will cover further how to use functions as fields in your documents. When you do return documents, particularly when you request many fields back, it's important to make sure that you're not retrieving too many documents at a time in order to keep the response size reasonable. This often requires bringing back smaller numbers of documents at a time and paging through them in multiple requests as necessary, which will be covered in the following section.

7.7.3 *Paging through results*

A query may match many documents (hundreds or even billions), but only enough results are generally brought back to display a page of results to a user. Solr is designed to be incredibly efficient at finding millions or billions of documents that match a query in milliseconds, but it's not optimized for returning large numbers of documents. Solr is good at returning tens or sometimes hundreds of documents, but when you start returning thousands of documents, the request time and throughput slow down considerably. The best practice with Solr is to return only a page representing the top results, and then to allow users to proceed through multiple pages of results. This way, each request to Solr pulls back a limited number of documents, thus preventing a single search request from hogging resources and slowing down other queries by trying to pull back too much data at once.

Paging through results in Solr requires the use of two request parameters that were introduced in chapter 2: `start` and `rows`. The `start` parameter indicates an offset into the result set, beginning at zero. The `rows` parameter indicates how many documents to return for the request. Assuming you have 100,000 documents with IDs 1–100000, the next listing demonstrates a few combinations for the rows and start parameters.

Listing 7.5   Paging through search results

Query 1
```
/select?q=*:*&sort=id&fl=id&
  rows=5&
  start=0
```

Results 1
```
{...
    "response":{"numFound":100000,"start":0,"docs":[
        {
         "id":"1"},
        {
         "id":"2"},
        {
         "id":"3"},
        {
         "id":"4"},
        {
         "id":"5"}]
}}
```

Query 2
```
/select?q=*:*&sort=id&fl=id&
  rows=5&
  start=5
```

Results 2
```
{...
    "response":{"numFound":100000,"start":5,"docs":[
        {
         "id":"6"},
        {
         "id":"7"},
        {
         "id":"8"},
        {
         "id":"9"},
        {
         "id":"10"}]
}}
```

Query 3
```
/select?q=*:*&sort=id&fl=id&
  rows=2&
  start=50000
```

Results 3
```
{...
    "response":{"numFound":100000,"start":50000,"docs":[
        {
         "id":"50001"},
        {
         "id":"50002"}
}}
```

Query 4

```
/select?q=*:*&sort=id&fl=id&
  rows=10&
  start=99997
```

Results 4

```
{...
    "response":{"numFound":100000,"start":99997,"docs":[
        {
          "id":"99998"},
        {
          "id":"99999"},
        {
          "id":"100000"}]
}}
```

As you can see, pulling back results a page at a time is straightforward. Queries 1 and 2 demonstrate that in order to see the next page of results (to see page 2 after page 1, for example), all that is necessary is to add the number of results in your rows parameter to the current start parameter and re-execute the query. Query 3 demonstrates that you can start your document offset at any number within the range of your search results, and query 4 demonstrates that on the last page of results, you will see fewer results than on the other pages. Consequently, if you set the start parameter's offset higher than the number of matching documents, you will get no returned results. Paging through results works pretty much as you would expect any search engine to work.

In this simple example, all of the results were in sorted order. In fact, you may have even noticed the sort parameter being used in listing 7.5. It's possible to sort on many things, including combinations of fields and dynamically calculated values. The next section will demonstrate these sorting capabilities.

7.8 Sorting results

After a search is executed, the results are returned in a sorted order. The default is by keyword relevancy (score), but any content can be sorted upon: dates, words, numbers, functions, and so forth. This section will demonstrate the mechanics of sorting search results.

7.8.1 Sorting by fields

When you run a keyword search, the search results are sorted (by default) by the relevancy score of each document in descending order (top scores higher, bottom scores lower). For any documents with the same score, the tie is broken based upon the order of the internal Lucene document IDs in the search index (by doc ID in ascending order). If there is no relevancy score, this means that the documents will be ordered only by the internal ID. This default sorting can easily be overridden using the sort parameter on the search request:

```
sort=someField desc, someOtherField asc
sort=score desc, date desc
sort=date desc, popularity desc, score desc
```

As you can see, the syntax for sorting on any field is a comma-separated list of field and direction pairs (with field and direction separated by a space). Any field you wish to sort on must be marked as `indexed=true` in the *schema.xml*, and the valid directions to sort are `asc` (ascending) or `desc` (descending).

Sorting by fields is fairly straightforward, though a few edge cases are worth mentioning. First, you should be aware that sorting is based upon the order of terms in the index. For example, if you use a string field to index the values 1, 2, 3, 10, 20, 30, they will be sorted lexicographically in the order 1, 10, 2, 20, 3, 30.

Additionally, because some languages sort in different orders than others, Solr includes built-in token filters for language-specific character collation (see http://wiki.apache.org/solr/UnicodeCollation for more information). If your field makes use of one of these token filters, your results are likely to sort correctly for the language at hand, but differently than they would in a standard string field.

It's important to also keep in mind that, because sorting takes place using indexed tokens, if you modify the tokens to something other than the original value of a field, the sorting may not make sense to the end user. If you're doing some kind of term substitution inside of Solr, for example, then the final indexed value will be the sort key instead of the original value that was sent to Solr.

SORTING MISSING VALUES

One edge case that may be important to you is the sort order of documents that are missing a value in the `sort` field. Since Solr does not require most fields to exist by default, it's easy to have a field that only exists in a subset of your document. In this case, if you were to sort on this field, would you expect the documents that match your query but do not have the `sort` field to show up at the top of your results or the bottom of your results? Because use cases may vary, Solr allows you to choose the behavior which best suits your field through the `sortMissingLast` and `sortMissingFirst` attributes on the field type definition in your *schema.xml*:

```
<fieldType name="string" class="solr.StrField"
    sortMissingLast="true"
    sortMissingFirst="false" />
```

If the `sortMissingLast` attribute is set to `true`, all documents without a value for the field will appear at the bottom of any sorted list of documents (regardless of sort direction). If the `sortMissingFirst` attribute is set to `true`, all documents without a value for the field will appear at the top of any sorted list of documents (regardless of sort direction). By default, both `sortMissingLast` and `sortMissingFirst` are set to `false`. Under this default setting, missing documents appear at the top of any sort in ascending order (`asc`), and at the bottom of any sort in descending order (`desc`).

SORTING'S MEMORY FOOTPRINT

One final point regarding sorting: it's a memory-intensive process. In order for documents to be sorted, Solr makes use of Lucene's field cache, which loads every unique value inside the field into memory the first time a sort is requested (unless it's already in the cache for other reasons). This means that for indexes with many millions of unique terms, sorting can consume a lot of memory per field sorted upon. It also means that the first time a sort is requested on a field, an in-memory structure will need to be built, which may cause the initial sorting query to be slow. This is not to say that you should not sort your documents, but you should be aware that you will need sufficient memory to perform sorting. Additionally, you may want to prewarm your Solr instance with sample searches (warming queries) to warm the cache, as discussed in chapter 4. You may also want to avoid sorting on fields with millions of unique terms if you have a choice to model the data differently.

7.8.2 Sorting by functions

In addition to sorting on fields, it's possible to sort on the calculated values from function queries. For example, you may want to sort based upon geographical distance from a point (using the `geodist` function) or based upon a combination of the popularity and age of a document (using a math function on a `popularity` field and a `date` field). You can even combine field sorts with function sorts in interesting ways. Function queries will be covered in detail in chapter 15, and you can find details on how to sort on functions in section 15.1.4.

7.8.3 Fuzzy sorting

Sorting is often thought of as an all-or-nothing operation. In reality, it's possible to create somewhat of a fuzzy sort by relying on Solr's relevancy calculation. If you think of the relevancy calculation as a composite of multiple factors (usually keywords, but you could also search on anything else), you have the ability to distinguish between the weights of each factor in the query by applying boosts to them.

If you apply a large boost on one query element that is thousands of times larger than another query element, you have effectively hard-banded your relevancy scores such that all documents will be sorted based upon matching the first element and then matching the second element. If you reduce the magnitude of your scores to something closer together, you alternatively have the ability to have a fuzzy sort: two components of a score in which one is generally higher than the other, but where there is some overlap such that documents from the lower group can beat out some documents from the higher group if they're relevant otherwise.

This fuzzy sorting concept is more of a relevancy concern in most cases, and it can be handled in any number of ways. Chapter 11 covers how to return a fixed number of documents from separate selection criteria, and chapters 15 and 16 cover how to use function queries to influence the ordering of documents to maximize the relevancy of your search application. In many cases, it makes the most sense to sort based upon relevancy and manipulate the query to ensure your documents come back in the expected order as opposed to utilizing the hard-sorting techniques on fields discussed in the previous sections. There is a time and place for both, based upon the needs of your search application.

7.9   *Debugging query results*

Even though you're well on your way to becoming an experienced Solr user, there will likely still be times when you're baffled by the results you're seeing. Sometimes, the query will result in a different number of results than you're expecting due to query parsing weirdness, sometimes the relevancy scores will seem off, and sometimes the timing of your queries will seem excessive. Thankfully, the search handler ships with a special search component—DebugComponent—that may be of assistance in these scenarios.

7.9.1   *Returning debug information*

The easiest way to gain insight into what is going on internally during your Solr request is to turn debugging on by passing in the debug=true parameter on your request. This activates DebugComponent on the request, which brings back information about the same, such as that shown in the next listing.

> **Listing 7.6   Query debug Information**

Query
```
/select?q=*:*&rows=3&debug=true
```

Result
```
{
    "responseHeader":{...},
    "response":{... docs":[
        {
          "id":"1"},
        {
          "id":"2"},
        {
          "id":"3"}]
        },
    "debug":{
      "rawquerystring":"*:*",
      "querystring":"*:*",
      "parsedquery":"MatchAllDocsQuery(*:*)",
      "parsedquery_toString":"*:*",
      "explain":{ ... },
      "QParser":"LuceneQParser",
      "timing":{ ... }
}
```

1 Query passed in to Solr.
2 Internal representation of query after parsed.
3 Readable version of the parsed query.
4 Explanation of relevancy score.
5 Default query parser.
6 Timing information for each SearchComponent.

From the listing you can see that the DebugComponent brings back several useful pieces of information: **1** the original query (rawquerystring), **2** the parsed query as it would be represented in Lucene objects (parsedquery), **3** a more readable version of the parsed query (parsedquery_toString), **4** a section providing the math calculations involved in the relevancy score calculation for each document (explain), **5** the default query parser used in the query (QParser), and **6** the amount of time each SearchComponent took to process (timing).

In addition, it's possible to bring back only particular sections by being more specific in the debug parameter. Instead of specifying debug=true, if you specify debug=query you will only see the section's debug information associated with query parsing. If you specify debug=results, you see the explain section, which provides the relevancy score calculations. Debugging this relevancy explanation will be demonstrated further in chapter 16. If you specify debug=timing, you will see a breakdown of the time taken for each SearchComponent, which can be useful for debugging slow requests. By invoking these aspects of DebugComponent, you can gain greater insight into how your queries are being parsed internally and where the most time is being spent in your Solr requests, which can help you more effectively construct your Solr requests.

7.10 Summary

In this chapter, we reviewed the request flow introduced in chapter 4 for performing queries. For a search, this includes hitting SearchHandler with your request, which invokes one or more SearchComponents. The most important SearchComponent, QueryComponent, is responsible for running the main query. We discussed how Solr handles queries and filters, including diving into many of the query parsers available in Solr and their syntax. We specifically covered the benefits of the eDisMax query parser versus the default Lucene query parser for handling user queries and searching across fields. We covered how to submit queries, return fields, sort and page through results, use local params and dereferenced parameters, and debug query issues using the DebugComponent. We also demonstrated how to combine multiple query parsers in the same query to enable use of the full spectrum of query capabilities within a single request.

At this point, you should feel well equipped to perform queries and handle and debug the main result set of those queries. Once you arrive at your main result set, however, it's often useful to pull in aggregate information about your result set to help you better understand your results at a high level and refine them. This is generally accomplished through the faceting capability in Solr, which will be the topic of the next chapter.

Faceted search

This chapter covers

- Using facets for discovery, analytics, and filtering of search results
- Showing top values in any field for matching documents via field facets
- Using range facets to get bucketized counts for numeric and date ranges
- Using query facets to get document counts for arbitrarily complex queries
- Faceting upon values not included in search results

Faceting is one of Solr's most powerful features, particularly when you compare it to traditional databases and other NoSQL data stores. Faceted search, also called faceted navigation or faceted browsing, allows users who are running searches to see a high-level breakdown of their search results based upon one or more aspects (facets) of their documents. This allows users to select filters to drill into those search results.

When you run a search on a news site, you expect to see options to filter your results by time frame (last hour, last 24 hours, last week) or by category (politics, technology, local, business). When searching a job search site, you likewise expect to see options to filter results by city, job category, industry, or even company name. Generally, these filtering options display not only the available values for each of these facets, but also a count of the total search results matching each of those values. Because you can display only a limited number of values on the screen for each facet, search engines often sort the values for each facet based upon the most prevalent values (those matching the most documents). This allows users to quickly see a bird's-eye view of their results set without having to look through every single search result.

Faceting in Solr enables this kind of dynamic metadata to be brought back with each set of search results. Although the most basic form of faceting shows only a breakdown of unique values within a field shared across many documents (a list of categories, for example), Solr also provides many advanced faceting capabilities. These include faceting based upon the resulting values of a function, the ranges of values, or even arbitrary queries. Solr also allows for hierarchical and multidimensional faceting and multiselect faceting, which allows returning facet counts for documents that may have already been filtered out of a search result. We'll investigate each of these capabilities in this chapter, which will give you the knowledge to implement your own powerful faceted search experience.

To get the most out of this chapter, you should be familiar with how to perform queries and how query parsers work (chapter 7) and how fields are defined in Solr's *schema.xml* to analyze text (chapters 5 and 6). A basic understanding of how the Lucene index stores terms (chapter 3) is useful, but not required.

Let's begin with examples demonstrating how faceting in Solr enables you to navigate through content and visualize search results at a glance.

8.1 *Navigating your content at a glance*

In this section, you'll see a high-level overview of faceting, including several examples demonstrating powerful ways to visualize facets for maximum usability. Faceted search is generally composed of two separate steps: calculating and displaying facets to users (which we'll refer to going forward as "bringing back facets" or sometimes just as "faceting") and allowing users to select one or more facet values by which their results should be filtered (which we'll refer to as "selecting" or "filtering" on a facet).

At this point, you may be wondering exactly what a facet looks like when it's brought back from the search engine. If you were searching through a set of restaurant documents, you might expect several facets to be represented as a navigational element in the user interface, such as in figure 8.1, depicting the facets to be returned for the query hamburger.

This navigational element provides a clear visual demonstration of what faceting is, and it provides an initial glimpse into the power faceting provides. Each of the categories (Restaurant Type, State, Price Range, and City) is individually considered one facet. You can think of each facet as a slice of information that describes the results of a search. In this case, you have at least 14,000 search results matching

► Restaurant Type	► State	► Price Range	► City
Fast Food (10073)	New York (4020)	< $5 (5674)	New York, NY (2021)
Sit-down Chain (2530)	California (3459)	$5 - $10 (7000)	San Francisco, CA (1499)
Coffee Shop (1530)	Illinois (2450)	$10 - $20 (1007)	Chicago, IL (850)
Local Sit-down (998)	Georgia (1620)	$20 - $50 (1300)	Atlanta, GA (620)
Upscale (400)	Texas (1501)	$50+ (550)	Austin, TX (501)
	. . .		. . .

Figure 8.1   Navigational elements in a search results UI depicting a breakdown of various facets of the content returned for a search query of `hamburger`.

the query for `hamburger`, but you're able to easily see that most of them are for fast food restaurants, most are in large cities, and most restaurants' menus fall within the $5 to $10 range.

Although the information in figure 8.1 is useful, there are many potentially better ways to visualize these facets. One downside of including each of the previously mentioned values is that you can only display a few at a time for each facet. Figure 8.2 demonstrates an alternate way to view the state facet.

As you can see, when you use modern visualization techniques, it's possible to use facets to represent important metadata about a user's search results to provide an enhanced searching experience. Figure 8.3 illustrates a similarly appropriate visualization for the restaurant type facet.

Although geographic maps and pie charts may be useful for demonstrating discrete values, representing continuous values such as numbers and dates can often be best represented through line graphs, as demonstrated in figure 8.4.

The line graph demonstrating the price range facet is particularly interesting because this visualization can be used to represent any range of values that can be plotted in a continuous series: numbers, dates and times, prices, distances, or even function values calculated inside of Solr. This isn't a chapter on data visualization, so we won't belabor the point here, but it's important to take away from this section that faceting provides an incredibly powerful ability to generate real-time analytics on user searches, which can greatly enhance your users' search experiences.

Before we dive into the mechanics of implementing facets in Solr, it's also important to note that facets are calculated in real time for each set of search results (or

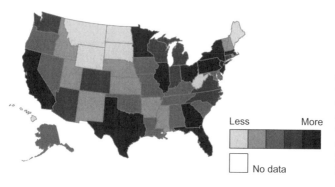

Less   More

No data

Figure 8.2   Representation of a facet on state in a visually appealing way. This visualization allows for display of all 50 states within the United States in the UI at one time, preventing the user from being overwhelmed by information.

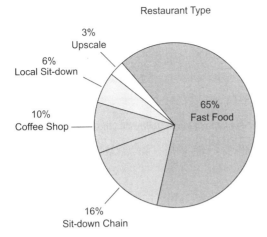

Figure 8.3 Visualization representing the restaurant type facet as a pie chart

possibly pulled from a cache for a repeated search). Each facet brings back a list of values (such as Fast Food, Sit-down Chain, Local Diner, and Upscale for the restaurant type facet) along with a count for each of those values indicating how many documents contain that value. The count is *not* how many times the value exists across all documents (as a value may exist multiple times within a single document); it's only a count of the number of documents matched. The fact that all facet values are calculated based upon a search result set means that every time a new search is fired, different values and counts will be returned for each facet. This allows users to run a search, see the facets that are returned from the search result, and perform another search that filters on any values for which they want to limit the next set of search results.

Given our example in figure 8.1, what would have happened if a user had clicked the value of California in the state facet and your application executed another search filtering on that value? Figure 8.5 demonstrates the facet values that would have resulted from this second search.

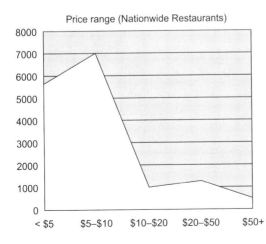

Figure 8.4 The price range facet is visually represented as a continuous line graph, allowing users to interpret all of the values in the facet with one glance.

▶ Restaurant Type	▶ State	▶ Price Range	▶ City
Fast Food (1704)	California (3459)	< $5 (800)	San Francisco, CA (1499)
Sit-down Chain (799)		$5 - $10 (1600)	Los Angeles, CA (701)
Coffee shop (456)		$10 - $20 (580)	San Diego, CA (535)
Local Sit-down (301)		$20 - $50 (298)	San Jose, CA (356)
Upscale (199)		$50+ (181)	Sacramento, CA (178)
			...

Figure 8.5   Demonstration of how facet values change when California (the state facet) is filtered upon after the search request in figure 8.1. Notice that all cities in the city facet are now located in California, because all documents within our search results must now be in California.

Although figure 8.5 only filters on a single value (California), you can apply as many filters as you want on any given search, and each facet will calculate its values based upon all of the filters being applied. If you explore the price range facet for the first search (nationwide) and compare it to the results of the second search (California), you'd be able to spot a noticeable price difference between California and the rest of the United States, as figure 8.6 demonstrates.

You'll see in section 8.5 how to apply these filters to facet values, but the key takeaway from this section is that facets can provide rich insights into the results of any given search, allowing your users to easily measure the quality of their searches and drill down into the aspects of the results they find most interesting.

8.2   Setting up test data

Before we dive into the mechanics of faceting, we need to load sample data into Solr that we'll use for the examples in the rest of this chapter. Our sample data will be a small subset of documents similar to our restaurants example from section 8.1. This

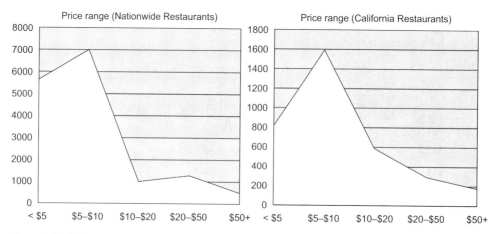

Figure 8.6   Price range facet (nationwide) versus price range facet (state of California). A noticeable trend is evident when the facet values are compared side by side: restaurants in California, on the whole, are more expensive than restaurants in the rest of the country.

section will get you up and running with a handful of restaurant documents upon which you'll be able to facet throughout the rest of this chapter. In order to feed these example documents to Solr, we first need to include the fields defined in the next listing in Solr's *schema.xml* file (covered in chapter 5).

Listing 8.1 *Schema.xml* defining fields for example restaurant documents

```
<?xml version="1.0" encoding="UTF-8" ?>
<schema name="example" version="1.5">
 <fields>                                                        Six fields.
    <field name="id" type="string" indexed="true" stored="true" />
    <field name="name" type="string" indexed="true" stored="true" />
    <field name="city" type="string" indexed="true" stored="true" />
    <field name="type" type="string" indexed="true" stored="true" />
    <field name="state" type="string" indexed="true" stored="true"/>
    <field name="tags" type="string" indexed="true" stored="true"
     multiValued="true" />
    <field name="price" type="double" indexed="true" stored="true" />
 </fields>                                                        Three
<uniqueKey>id</uniqueKey>          Should have a unique ID.        field
  <types>                                                         types.
    <fieldType name="string" class="solr.StrField" sortMissingLast="true" />
    <fieldType name="boolean" class="solr.BoolField" sortMissingLast="true"/>
    <fieldType name="double" class="solr.TrieDoubleField" precisionStep="0"
     positionIncrementGap="0"/>
  </types>
</schema>
```

The schema defines each of the fields upon which we'll attempt to facet in this chapter. Each is defined as both indexed and stored, but they are stored only for demonstration purposes. Faceting only makes use of the indexed values for a field, so you can mark your documents as only indexed if you do not need to otherwise retrieve them. The following listing contains each of the documents upon which we'll facet.

Listing 8.2 Documents upon which faceting will be demonstrated

```
[
  {
    "id":"1", "name":"Red Lobster", "city":"San Francisco, CA", "type":"Sit-
    down Chain", "state":"California", "tags":["sea food", "sit down"],
    "price":33.00                                    Each document has
  },                                                 all seven fields.
  {
    "id":"2", "name":"Red Lobster", "city":"Atlanta, GA", "type":"Sit-down
    Chain", "state":"Georgia", "tags":["sea food", "sit-down"],
    "price":22.00                                    The id field is unique
  },                                                 per restaurant.
  {
    "id":"3", "name":"Red Lobster", "city":"New York, NY", "type":"Sit-down
    Chain", "state":"New York", "tags":["sea food", "sit-down"],
    "price":29.00                                    The name field has
  },                                                 one nonunique value.
```

```
{
    "id":"4", "name":"McDonalds", "city":"San Francisco, CA", "type":"Fast
    Food", "state":"California", "tags":["fast food", "hamburgers",
    "coffee", "wi-fi", "breakfast"], "price":9.00
},
```

The city field has one nonunique value.

```
{
    "id":"5", "name":"McDonalds", "city":"Atlanta, GA", "type":"Fast Food",
    "state":"Georgia", "tags":["fast food", "hamburgers", "coffee", "wi-fi",
    "breakfast"], "price":4.00
},
{
    "id":"6", "name":"McDonalds", "city":"New York, NY", "type":"Fast Food",
    "state":"New York", "tags":["fast food", "hamburgers", "coffee", "wi-
    fi", "breakfast"], "price":4.00
},
```

The state field has one nonunique value.

```
{
    "id":"7", "name":"McDonalds", "city":"Chicago, IL", "type":"Fast Food",
    "state":"Illinois", "tags":["fast food", "hamburgers", "coffee", "wi-
    fi", "breakfast"], "price":4.00
},
```

The tags field contains multiple nonunique values.

```
{
    "id":"8", "name":"McDonalds", "city":"Austin, TX", "type":"Fast Food",
    "state":"Texas", "tags":["fast food", "hamburgers", "coffee", "wi-fi",
    "breakfast"], "price":4.00
},
```

The price field is a positive number.

```
{
    "id":"9", "name":"Pizza Hut", "city":"Atlanta, GA", "type":"Sit-down
    Chain", "state":"Georgia", "tags":["pizza", "sit-down", "delivery"],
    "price":15.00
},
{
    "id":"10", "name":"Pizza Hut", "city":"New York, NY", "type":"Sit-down
    Chain", "state":"New York", "tags":["pizza", "sit-down", "delivery"],
    "price":24.00
},
{
    "id":"11", "name":"Pizza Hut", "city":"Austin, TX", "type":"Sit-down
    Chain", "state":"Texas", "tags":["pizza", "sit-down", "delivery"],
    "price":18.00
},
{
    "id":"12", "name":"Freddy's Pizza Shop", "city":"Los Angeles, CA",
    "type":"Local Sit-down", "state":"California", "tags":["pizza", "pasta",
    "sit-down"], "price":25.00},
{
    "id":"13", "name":"The Iberian Pig", "city":"Atlanta, GA",
    "type":"Upscale", "state":"Georgia", "tags":["spanish", "tapas", "sit-
    down", "upscale"], "price":45.00
},
{
    "id":"14", "name":"Sprig", "city":"Atlanta, GA", "type":"Local Sit-
    down", "state":"Georgia", "tags":["sit-down", "gluten-free", "southern
    cuisine"], "price":15.00
},
```

```
{
    "id":"15", "name":"Starbucks", "city":"San Francisco, CA",
    "type":"Coffee Shop", "state":"California", "tags":["coffee",
    "breakfast"], "price":7.50
},
{
    "id":"16", "name":"Starbucks", "city":"Atlanta, GA", "type":"Coffee
    Shop", "state":"Georgia", "tags":["coffee", "breakfast"], "price":4.00
},
{
    "id":"17", "name":"Starbucks", "city":"New York, NY", "type":"Coffee
    Shop", "state":"New York", "tags":["coffee", "breakfast"], "price":6.50
},
{
    "id":"18", "name":"Starbucks", "city":"Chicago, IL", "type":"Coffee
    Shop", "state":"Illinois", "tags":["coffee", "breakfast"], "price":6.00
}
{
    "id":"19", "name":"Starbucks", "city":"Austin, TX", "type":"Coffee
    Shop", "state":"Texas", "tags":["coffee", "breakfast"], "price":5.00
},
{
    "id":"20", "name":"Starbucks", "city":"Greenville, SC", "type":"Coffee
    Shop", "state":"South Carolina", "tags":["coffee", "breakfast"],
    "price":3.00
}
]
```

You can also find the example *schema.xml* and the example documents (called *restaurants.json*) from listings 8.1 and 8.2 in the downloadable source code available from the *Solr in Action* page on Manning's website (http://manning.com/grainger). After downloading the source code and extracting the files to a folder we'll refer to as $SOLR_IN_ACTION, you can execute the following commands to configure and start Solr with the schema for restaurant documents from listing 8.1:

```
cd $SOLR_INSTALL/example/
cp -r $SOLR_IN_ACTION/example-docs/ch8/cores/restaurants/ solr/restaurants/
java -jar start.jar
```

Once Solr is successfully up and running, you can then send the documents from listing 8.2 to Solr with the following commands:

```
cd $SOLR_IN_ACTION/example-docs/
java -Durl=http://localhost:8983/solr/restaurants/update
    -Dtype=application/json
    -jar post.jar ch8/documents/restaurants.json
```

The last line in the previous example indexes the restaurants from a text file using the *post.jar* utility that comes with Solr (specifying that the file is in JSON format as opposed to the default XML format). If everything is successful, you should see output like the following:

```
SimplePostTool version 1.5
Posting files to base url
```

```
http://localhost:8983/solr/restaurants/update using content-type
➥ application/json..
POSTing file restaurants.json
1 files indexed.
COMMITting Solr index changes to
➥ http://localhost:8983/solr/restaurants/update..
Time spent: 0:00:00.102
```

Once you've successfully indexed the restaurant documents, you should be able to hit the standard Solr search handler and verify that your documents are in the engine (along with all of the fields from listing 8.2) using the following URL: http://localhost:8983/solr/restaurants/select?q=*:*

Changing Solr's response format

Note that most documents and Solr responses in this chapter and the chapters to come are in JSON format, not XML. Even though XML is Solr's default response type, JSON is a more human-readable format that's more compact and is therefore easier to use for demonstration purposes. A parameter of `wt=json` was added to the Solr request to change the response type from XML to JSON format. If you haven't changed your default response type from XML to JSON in your *solrconfig.xml*, you'll need to add this `wt=json` parameter to all of the Solr requests in this chapter to return them in the same format.

You'll also notice that all Solr responses in this chapter appear nicely indented. You can do this by adding an `indent=on` parameter to your Solr URL. Requesting this indented response format isn't recommended for a production application (it works, but adds unnecessary extra processing whitespace for your application to process), but it does make Solr responses more human readable, which is why we've used it for all of the examples in this chapter.

To eliminate redundancy in the listings, this chapter assumes that you've set `&wt=json&indent=on` as default parameters (see chapter 4 for how to do this) on all of your queries.

The response you receive from Solr should include all 20 of the example restaurant documents, with each containing the seven fields defined in the schema and the example restaurants dataset:

```
{
  "responseHeader":{
    "status":0,
    "QTime":0,
    ...},
  "response":{"numFound":20,"start":0,"docs":[
      {
        "id":"1",
        "name":"Red Lobster",
        "city":"San Francisco, CA",
        ""type":"Sit-down Chain",
        "state":"California",
```

```
            "tags":["sea food", "sit down"],
            "price":33.0,
            ...},
        },
        ...
    ]}
}
```

With the 20 example documents now searchable, we're ready to begin running faceted searches. We'll begin with the most common form of faceting, which is faceting upon each of the unique values within a field.

8.3 *Field faceting*

Field faceting is the most common form of faceting: when you perform a search, you request back the unique values found in a particular field, along with the number of documents in which they're found. In section 8.1, we demonstrated visually how to use several field facets from the restaurants example: a facet on the restaurant `type` field, a facet on the `state` field, and a facet on the `city` field. In this section, you'll learn how to construct a Solr query to request a field facet, and you'll learn the faceting parameters that allow you to tweak how the facet values are calculated and returned from Solr.

For demonstration purposes for the rest of the chapter, we're going to be faceting upon the documents we indexed in section 8.2. Let's start by running our first facet:

```
http://localhost:8983/solr/restaurants/select?q=*:*&rows=0&
    facet=true&facet.field=name
```

The results of this query appear in this listing.

Listing 8.3   Facet results for a field facet on a single-valued field

```
{
    "responseHeader":{
        "status":0,
        "QTime":43},
    "response":{"numFound":20,"start":0,"docs":[]
    },                                              ◁──── The root node
    "facet_counts":{                                       for all facets.
        "facet_queries":{},                         ◁──── Lists all field facets.
        "facet_fields":{
            "name":[                                 ◁──── We requested a facet
                "Starbucks",6,                              on the name field.
                "McDonalds",5,
                "Pizza Hut",3,                       Starbucks was found
                "Red Lobster",3,                     in six documents.
                "Freddy's Pizza Shop",1,
                "Sprig",1,                           ◁──── Sprig was found in
                "The Iberian Pig",1]},                       one document.
        "facet_dates":{},
        "facet_ranges":{}}
}
```

This example demonstrates the most basic form of faceting in Solr: field faceting on a single-valued field. In this kind of faceting, each unique value is examined, along with a count of documents in which that value is found. Because you only have one value per document, the sum of all of the counted values (company names in this case) will also equal the total number of documents.

Not all fields in Solr contain a single value, however. The `tags` field is an example of a multivalued field. Let's see what happens when we try to facet upon the `tags` field in this listing.

Listing 8.4   Faceting upon a multivalued field

Query

```
http://localhost:8983/solr/restaurants/select?q=*:*&facet=true&facet.field=tags
```

Results

```
...
"facet_fields":{
       "tags":[
           "breakfast",11,
           "coffee",11,
           "sit-down",8,
           "fast food",5,
           "hamburgers",5,
           "wi-fi",5,
           "pizza",4,
           "delivery",3,
           "sea food",3,
           "gluten-free",1,
           "pasta",1,
           "sit down",1,
           "southern cuisine",1,
           "spanish",1,
           "tapas",1,
           "upscale",1]
}
...
```

> **The name of the field we faceted upon.**

> **Adds up to > 20 due to documents matching multiple tags.**

It's interesting to note that the tags `breakfast` and `coffee` were the two most prevalent across the entire corpus of restaurant documents. This is because two restaurants, `Starbucks` and `McDonalds`, fell into both categories. If you were to search for `breakfast` or `coffee`, this fact would become readily apparent from the results returned from Solr.

It's also important to note that the sum of the counts for each of the `tags` facet values is much greater than 20, which is the total number of documents in the search engine. This is because each document contains more than one term, which means that many of the individual terms can map to the same document (and therefore most of the documents are counted toward more than one facet value).

In section 8.1 we discussed several methods for visualizing facets. This tag faceting example lends itself to what's probably a distinctly obvious kind of visualization: a tag

Figure 8.7 **A tag cloud representation of a field facet on a multivalued `tags` field. The size of the text is relative to the number of documents in which the phrase was found. This demonstrates again the many ways you can visualize facets.**

cloud. Figure 8.7 demonstrates mapping the facet values from the multivalued field facet result on the `tags` field.

Tag clouds are common ways for users to see a high-level overview of the results of their search from a categorical standpoint. In addition to using tags such as those in this example, it's also common to facet upon a raw content field containing everyday language to glean these kinds of insights (such as the full text of a restaurant's description in this case). The problem with using a raw content field is that much more noise exists in such a field, because everyday language contains junk words (such as the *and*, *of*, and *like* stop words), making it less reliable in describing the document than explicit tags would be.

An additional important point to keep in mind when you're faceting is that the values returned for a field facet are based upon the indexed values for a field. This means that if you pass in the term San Francisco, CA, but you tokenize the field as a text field that splits on spaces and commas and also lowercases the text, then the values in the Solr index for that field would be ca, francisco, and san. Therefore, unless you want to bring back facet counts for each of those terms individually and lowercased, you have to consider how you want to facet on a field when you create the field definition in Solr's *schema.xml*. It's fairly standard for Solr developers to create a separate field into which they'll put a duplicate copy of certain content for the sole purpose of faceting (so that the original text can be preserved in a facetable form).

At this point you should have a solid grasp of what a facet is, and you should also have a good feel for requesting a facet on either a single-valued field or a multivalued field. To this point, you've been exposed only to the default settings for bringing back a facet. Faceting seems easy when you're only dealing with 20 documents, but what happens when you have thousands or millions of unique terms that would come back from Solr on a faceting request? Fortunately, Solr has many faceting options that allow fine-tuning of how facets are returned on a per-query basis. This list of field facet options is given in table 8.1.

Table 8.1 Field faceting parameters that can be specified on the Solr URL to modify faceting behavior

Solr parameter	Possible values	Description
facet	true, false	Enables or disables all faceting for the current search.
facet.field	the name of any indexed field	Determines which field a facet should be calculated upon. This parameter may be specified multiple times to return multiple facets.
facet.sort	index, count	Sorts the facet values by highest number of occurrences (count) or by lexicographical order in the index (index). This parameter can be specified on a per-field basis.
facet.limit	An integer >= -1	Determines how many unique facet values will be returned for each facet. This parameter can be specified on a per-field basis.
facet.mincount	An integer >= 0	Sets a minimum number of documents in which a facet value must appear before it will be returned. By default, terms with zero matches in the current search will be included in facet results, so it's common to set facet.mincount to at least 1. This parameter can be specified on a per-field basis.
facet.method	enum, fc, fcs	The enum method loops over all terms in the index, calculating a set intersection with those terms and the query. The fc (field cache) method loops over the documents that match the query and finds the terms within those documents. The fc method is faster for fields that contain many unique values, whereas the enum method is faster for fields that contain few values. The fc method is the default for all fields except Boolean fields. The fcs method invokes per-segment field caching for single-valued string fields, which can perform better if your index is constantly changing. It also accepts a threads local param, which can speed up faceting by specifying the number of available threads for handling different index segments. This parameter can be specified on a per-field basis.
facet.enum .cache.minDf	An integer >= 0	Advanced: Specifies the minimum number of documents required to match a term before filterCache should be used for that term. The default is 0, meaning that filterCache should always be used. Setting this value > 0 can reduce memory consumption at the expense of slower queries. This parameter can be specified on a per-field basis.
facet.prefix	Any string	Limits facet values to terms beginning with the string specified. Useful for finding similar terms and is often used to build autocomplete capabilities.
facet.missing	true, false	Specifies whether to return a count of all matching documents that do not contain a value (the value is "missing") in the facet's field.

Table 8.1 Field faceting parameters that can be specified on the Solr URL to modify faceting behavior *(continued)*

Solr parameter	Possible values	Description
`facet.offset`	An integer >= 0	Allows paging through facet values. `offset` defines how many of the top values to skip in lieu of returning later facet values.
`facet.threads`	An integer	Specifies the number of processing threads to be used when executing multiple field facets. A value of 0 is the default, which will cause all field facets to execute serially. A negative number ("unlimited") will create a thread for each field facet, and a positive number will create up to the number of `threads` specified. If many field facets are executed per search, this can greatly speed up faceting time.

One important takeaway from table 8.1 is that multiple facets can be requested by specifying the `facet.field` parameter multiple times. Additionally, several of the facet parameters are listed as being specifiable on a per-field basis. This can be accomplished using the following syntax:

```
f.<fieldName>.<FacetParameter>=<value>
```

If you want to bring back a facet for all 50 U.S. states (in alphabetical order) with at least one restaurant, all restaurant names even if they don't match the query, and the top five matching tags, you could perform the query in this listing.

Listing 8.5 Mixing field faceting parameters on a field-by-field basis

Query
```
http://localhost:8983/solr/restaurants/select?q=*:*&       Default for all facets
  facet=true&                                               unless overridden.
  facet.mincount=1&
  facet.field=state&
  f.state.facet.limit=50&       Only modifies
  f.state.facet.sort=index&     the state facet.
  facet.field=name&
  f.name.facet.mincount=1&          Only modifies
  facet.field=tags&                 the name facet.
  f.tags.facet.limit=5
```
Results
```
...
"facet_fields":{
  "state":[
    "California",4,
    "Georgia",6,
    "Illinois",2,
    "New York",4,
    "South Carolina",1,
    "Texas",3],
```
Only modifies
the tags facet.

```
"name":[
    "Starbucks",6,
    "McDonalds",5,
    "Pizza Hut",3,
    "Red Lobster",3,
    "Freddy's Pizza Shop",1,
    "Sprig",1,
    "The Iberian Pig",1],
"tags":[
    "breakfast",11,
    "coffee",11,
    "sit-down",8,
    "fast food",5,
    "hamburgers",5]
}
...
```

As you can see, this listing combines multiple facet options on multiple fields in a custom way to return exactly what was desired in the search results. Although the query required many parameters, the flexibility these faceting options provide can be well worth the additional complexity.

At this point you've learned how to request field facets back in Solr so that you can see how many documents match each unique value in any of your indexed fields. Although field faceting is a powerful feature, there are still even more flexible faceting options available. The next realm of faceting we'll explore is query faceting, the ability to bring back facet counts for literally any query—no matter how complex.

8.4   *Query faceting*

Although it's great to be able to return the top values within any indexed field as a facet, as discussed in the previous section, it can also be extremely useful to bring back counts for arbitrary subqueries so you know how many results might match a future search and provide analytics based upon that number. Solr provides this capability through its implementation of *query faceting*.

The best way to demonstrate this feature is through an example. Referring to our restaurant-searching dataset from section 8.2, let's say you want to run a query for restaurants falling within the price range of $5–$25, but you also want to know how many of them were on the East Coast, on the West Coast, or in the Central United States. You could certainly accomplish this by running three different queries, as indicated in this next listing.

> **Listing 8.6   Running multiple queries to obtain document counts for subqueries**

```
http://localhost:8983/solr/restaurants/select?q=*:*&fq=price:[5 TO 25]
...
"response":{"numFound":11 ...

http://localhost:8983/solr/restaurants/select?q=*:*&fq=price:[5 TO 25]&
    fq=state:("New York" OR "Georgia" OR "South Carolina")
```

```
...
"response":{"numFound":5 ...

http://localhost:8983/solr/restaurants/select?q=*:*&fq=price:[5 TO 25]&
  fq=state:("Illinois" OR "Texas")

...
"response":{"numFound":3 ...

http://localhost:8983/solr/restaurants/select?q=*:*&fq=price:[5 TO 25]&
  fq=state:("California")

...
"response":{"numFound":3 ...
```

The example demonstrates the most brute-force method for finding search result counts for subqueries in Solr—running each subquery as a separate search and seeing how many results are found. Although the pain may not seem enormous in this small, contrived example, it's nevertheless unnecessary. The following listing demonstrates how such a query can be easily combined into a single query using query facets.

Listing 8.7 Running a single query facet to obtain document counts for subqueries

Query
```
http://localhost:8983/solr/restaurants/select?q=*:*&fq=price:[5 TO
    25]&facet=true&
  facet.query=state:("New York" OR "Georgia" OR "South Carolina")&
  facet.query=state:("Illinois" OR "Texas")&
  facet.query=state:("California")
```

Results
```
...
  "response":{"numFound":11,"start":0,"docs":[]},
    "facet_counts":{
      "facet_queries":{
        "state:(\"New York\" OR \"Georgia\" OR \"South Carolina\")":5,
        "state:(\"Illinois\" OR \"Texas\")":3,
        "state:(\"California\")":3},
      ...
}
```

As you can see, multiple subqueries can be combined into a single request to Solr through the use of query facets. The previous example is specific to our dataset (because it requires knowing all possible values at query time), but you've already seen an example in section 8.1 that's a great use case for query facets: faceting upon price, in a case in which the price ranges needed aren't evenly spaced out. We can recreate this example using our test data, as indicated in this listing.

Listing 8.8 Query facets based upon multiple price ranges

Query
```
http://localhost:8983/solr/restaurants/select?q=*:*&rows=0&facet=true&
  facet.query=price:[* TO 5}&
  facet.query=price:[5 TO 10}&
  facet.query=price:[10 TO 20}&
```

```
facet.query=price:[20 TO 50}&
facet.query=price:[50 TO *]
```

Results

```
...
  "response":{"numFound":20,"start":0,"docs":[]    },
    "facet_counts":{
      "facet_queries":{
        "price:[* TO 5}":6,
        "price:[5 TO 10}":5,
        "price:[10 TO 20}":3,
        "price:[20 TO 50}":6,
        "price:[50 TO *]":0}, ...
```

This example demonstrates how query facets can effectively be used to create new buckets of information at query time in any Solr query. In reality, you could have easily created a new field in Solr, called price_range, that contained each of these bucketized values. Had you done so, you could have performed a field facet upon the new price_range field to pull back each of the five bucketized values. This would also require you to apply these bucketizing rules at index time when you're feeding your content to Solr. Any future changes to these buckets would therefore require a complete reindex of your documents, a process that can be painful, particularly as your amount of content in Solr begins to grow. Query facets provide a nice alternative that allows you complete flexibility at query time to specify and redefine which facet values should be calculated and returned.

Although the examples in this section have been simple, they demonstrate the complete flexibility that faceting upon any arbitrary query provides. Because Solr provides many powerful query capabilities, including nested queries (chapter 7) and function queries (chapter 15), the possibilities for advanced query-based faceting are only limited by one's imagination. Imagine taking a radius query in Solr and creating concentric circles (<5 kilometers, 5–10 kilometers, 10–20 kilometers, 20+ kilometers) around a particular location to create a facet based upon distance away from a location. Alternatively, imagine generating a query facet on the calculated values of a custom relevancy function you've generated as a function query. The ability to extend faceting in this way is tremendously powerful; anything you can search upon, you can facet upon.

Although query facets are incredibly flexible, they can become burdensome at times to request from Solr, as every single value upon which you want to generate facet counts must be explicitly specified. As we'll see in the next section, Solr also provides a convenient range faceting capability that makes faceting upon numeric and date values much easier in this regard.

8.5   *Range faceting*

Range faceting, as its name implies, provides the ability to bucketize numeric and date field values into ranges such that the ranges (and their counts) get returned from Solr as a facet. This can be particularly useful as a replacement for creating many different query facets to represent multiple ranges of values.

In the previous section, a query facet was demonstrated based upon the `price` field in our example data from section 8.2. Had the values needed from the search engine been evenly spread out, similar facet counts could have been returned from Solr using a range facet, as indicated in the next listing.

Listing 8.9 Example range facet on the `price` field

Query

```
http://localhost:8983/solr/restaurants/select?q=*:*&facet=true&
  facet.range=price&
  facet.range.start=0&
  facet.range.end=50&
  facet.range.gap=5
```

Results

```
. . .
  "response":{"numFound":20,"start":0,"docs":[]    },
    "facet_counts":{
      . . .
      "facet_ranges":{
        "price":{
          "counts":[
            "0.0",6,
            "5.0",5,
            "10.0",0,
            "15.0",3,
            "20.0",2,
            "25.0",2,
            "30.0",1,
            "35.0",0,
            "40.0",0,
            "45.0",1],
          "gap":5.0,
          "start":0.0,
          "end":50.0}
        }}}
```

The output of this example is similar to the result of listing 8.8, with two notable exceptions. First, range faceting returns counts for every range (bucket of values) falling between the `facet.range.start` and `facet.range.end` parameters on the query, even those ranges containing no documents. Second, unlike the query facet example in listing 8.7, the buckets in range faceting are equally spaced out based upon the `facet.range.gap` parameter. You can adjust the gap to create larger or more granular buckets based on the needs of your application. This is a great time saver if you want to bring back all of the range buckets within your range, as it prevents you from writing countless `facet.query` parameters manually to accomplish a similar effect.

Additional range faceting parameters are available, including `facet.range.hardend`, `facet.range.other`, and `facet.range.include`. Table 8.2 lists each available range faceting parameter and its available options.

Table 8.2   A list of the range faceting parameters that can be specified on the Solr URL to modify faceting behavior

Solr parameter	Possible values	Description
`facet.range`	The name of any indexed numerical or date field.	Determines which field a range facet should be calculated upon. This parameter may be specified multiple times to return multiple facets.
`facet.range .start`	The numerical or date value at which the first range should begin.	This parameter specifies the lower bound of your ranges. No value lower than this will be included in the counts for this facet. This parameter can be specified on a per-field basis.
`facet.range .end`	The numerical or date value at which the first range should end.	This parameter specifies the upper bound of your ranges. No value higher than this will be included in the counts for this facet. This parameter can be specified on a per-field basis.
`facet.range .gap`	For dates, a `DateMath` expression (`+1DAY`, `+2MONTHS`, `+1HOUR`, and so on). For other numeric fields, a number is expected.	The size of each range. To create the ranges, this gap will be added to the lower bound (`facet.range.start`) successively until the upper bound (`facet.range.end`) is reached. This parameter can be specified on a per-field basis.
`facet.range .hardend`	`true`, `false`	If the gap (`facet.range.gap`) doesn't divide evenly between the lower bound and the upper bound, the size of the last bucket is different than previous buckets. If `hardend` is set to `true`, the final range will stop at the upper bound, leaving a potentially smaller final bucket. If `hardend` is `false`, final bucket size will be increased above the upper bound such that it's the same size as the other buckets (the size of the `gap`). This parameter can be specified on a per-field basis.
`facet.range .other`	`before`, `after`, `between`, `all`, `none`	Indicates additional ranges that should be included in the ranges. The `before` option creates a bucket for all values prior to the lower bound. The `after` option creates a bucket for all values after the upper bound. The `between` option creates a bucket for all values between the lower and upper bounds. This parameter may be specified multiple times to include multiple values. The `all` option is a shortcut for saying `before`, `after`, and `between`. If the `none` option is present, it will override any other parameters that are specified. This parameter can be specified on a per-field basis.
`facet.range .include`	`lower`, `upper`, `edge`, `outer`, `all`	`lower` means all ranges include their lower bound. `upper` means all ranges include their upper bound. `edge` means the first range includes its lower bound and the last range includes its upper bound. `outer` means that the `before` and `after` buckets (from `facet.range .other`) include their lower and upper bounds, respectively. This parameter may be specified multiple times to include multiple values. `all` is a shortcut for specifying each of the parameters separately. This parameter can be specified on a per-field basis.

The parameters in table 8.2 show the rich options available when performing range faceting in Solr. As with field faceting, several range faceting parameters can be specified on a per-field basis using `f.<fieldName>.<FacetParameter>=<value>`.

Range faceting often provides a more convenient and succinct query syntax than query faceting when faceting upon ranges of number or date values. Query faceting can alternatively be used when the range queries become overly complicated, allowing for some powerful queries as we discussed in section 8.4 (and will see further in chapter 15). Of the three types of faceting we discussed, field faceting is the most widely used and the most simple. For each faceting type, we've explored how you can request facet values back from Solr. What we've yet to discuss is how you'd go about refining your subsequent search once a facet is selected by a user, which will be the topic of the next section.

8.6 Filtering upon faceted values

Returning facets from Solr is the first step toward allowing your users to refine their search results. Once you've shown the breakdown of faceted values to your users, your next step is to allow them to click on one or more facet values to apply that value as a filter. In this section, we'll discuss the best approaches for applying these filters.

8.6.1 Applying filters to your facets

At the most basic level, applying filters upon a facet is no more difficult than adding an extra filter (the `fq` parameter) to your query. Assume you wanted to return three facets with your searches—a field facet on the `state` field, a field facet on the `city` field, and a query facet on the `price` field. The initial query and results would look similar to the next listing.

> **Listing 8.10 Faceting upon the `tags` field in the example restaurant data**

Query
```
http://localhost:8983/solr/restaurants/select?q=*:*&facet=true&
  facet.field=state&
  facet.field=city&
  facet.query=price:[* TO 10}&
  facet.query=price:[10 TO 25}&
  facet.query=price:[25 TO 50}&
  facet.query=price:[50 TO *]
```

Results
```
...
  "facet_counts":{
    "facet_queries":{
      "price:[* TO 10}":11,
      "price:[10 TO 25}":5,
      "price:[25 TO 50}":4,
      "price:[50 TO *]":0},
```

```
        "facet_fields":{
          "state":[
            "Georgia",6,
            "California",4,
            "New York",4,
            "Texas",3,
            "Illinois",2,
            "South Carolina",1],
          "city":[
            "Atlanta, GA",6,
            "New York, NY",4,
            "San Francisco, CA",3,
            "Austin, TX",3,
            "Chicago, IL",2,
            "Greenville, SC",1,
            "Los Angeles, CA",1]},
        "facet_dates":{},
        "facet_ranges":{}}
        ...
```

All states contained in all documents (no filter).

All cities contained in all documents (no filter).

Search results will also be returned (not shown in listing 8.10), and your UI is likely to display these facet values for your users to select from this wide-open query. In this example, how would you go about filtering upon a facet value? You already know how to do this; you add a filter to your query for each selected facet value. The following listing demonstrates a second search, for which the user has clicked the state of California.

Listing 8.11   Filtering upon a field facet

Query

```
http://localhost:8983/solr/restaurants/select?q=*:*&facet=true&facet.mincount=1&
  facet.field=state&
  facet.field=city&
  facet.query=price:[* TO 10}&
  facet.query=price:[10 TO 25}&
  facet.query=price:[25 TO 50}&
  facet.query=price:[50 TO *]&
  fq=state:California
```

A filter limiting the results.

Results

```
...
  "facet_counts":{
    "facet_queries":{
      "price:[* TO 10}":2,
      "price:[10 TO 25}":0,
      "price:[25 TO 50}":2,
      "price:[50 TO *]":0},
    "facet_fields":{
      "state":[
        "California",4,],
      "city":[
        "San Francisco, CA",3,
        "Los Angeles, CA",1]},
```

Resulting facet counts reflect the reduced result set.

```
  "facet_dates":{},
  "facet_ranges":{}}
...
```

The point to take away from listings 8.10 and 8.11 is that users typically use facets in succession. They run a base search bringing back facets, then they select a facet to run a subsequent search and narrow down their search results with a filter. This could continue with the user running a third search, such as in this listing.

Listing 8.12 Filtering upon both a field facet and a query facet

Query

```
http://localhost:8983/solr/restaurants/select?q=*:*&facet=true&facet.mincount=1&
  facet.field=state&
  facet.field=city&
  facet.query=price:[* TO 10}&
  facet.query=price:[10 TO 25}&
  facet.query=price:[25 TO 50}&
  facet.query=price:[50 TO *]&
  fq=state:California&                      Two filters have been applied
  fq=price:[* TO 10}                        from previous facets.
```

Results

```
...
  "facet_counts":{
    "facet_queries":{
      "price:[* TO 10}":2,
      "price:[10 TO 25}":0,
      "price:[25 TO 50}":0,
      "price:[50 TO *]":0},            All facet counts
    "facet_fields":{                   are limited by all
      "state":[                        applied filters.
        "California",2,],
      "city":[
        "San Francisco, CA",2,]},
    "facet_dates":{},
    "facet_ranges":{}}
...
```

As the user applies both a filter of `state:California` and a filter of `price:[* TO 10}`, you can see that the results narrow down even further, leaving only two restaurants in `California` that match this narrowed query—both of which happen to be in `San Francisco, CA`.

It's worth noting that each of the examples you've seen to this point operates on a field containing only one value. As such, as soon as you filter upon that value, no documents matching any other values for that facet will be returned. This makes sense in our single-valued fields; if a document can only have one `price` or only appear in one `state`, it can't appear in a facet in which another `price` or `state` was selected. But not all fields contain only a single value. Any field that's marked as multivalued in Solr's *schema.xml* file or that's of a field type that's analyzed into multiple tokens may contribute multiple terms to a facet. We can see this in action by using the multivalued tags field in our restaurants index. This listing shows several searches that successively apply filters on the `tags` field.

Listing 8.13   Applying several filters on a faceted field containing multiple values

NO FILTERS APPLIED
Query
```
http://localhost:8983/solr/restaurants/select?q=*:*&facet=true&facet.mincount=1&
    facet.field=name&
    facet.field=tags
```

Results
```
...
"facet_fields":{
  "name":[
    "Starbucks",6,
    "McDonalds",5,
    "Pizza Hut",3,
    "Red Lobster",3,
    "Freddy's Pizza Shop",1,
    "Sprig",1,
    "The Iberian Pig",1],
  "tags":[
    "breakfast",11,
    "coffee",11,
    "sit-down",8,
    "fast food",5,
    "hamburgers",5,
    "wi-fi",5,
    "pizza",4,
    "delivery",3,
    "sea food",3,
    "gluten-free",1,
    "pasta",1,
    "sit down",1,
    "southern cuisine",1,
    "spanish",1,
    "tapas",1,
    "upscale",1]},
  ...
```

11 restaurants have coffee, 5 have hamburgers, and 5 have wi-fi.

ONE FILTER APPLIED
Query
```
http://localhost:8983/solr/restaurants/select?q=*:*&facet=true&facet.mincount=1&
    facet.field=name&facet.field=tags&fq=tags:coffee
```

Results
```
...
"facet_fields":{
  "name":[
    "Starbucks",6,
    "McDonalds",5],
  "tags":[
    "breakfast",11,
```

```
        "coffee",11,                    With the coffee filter applied,
        "fast food",5,                  all 5 hamburger and wi-fi
        "hamburgers",5,                 restaurants remain.
        "wi-fi",5]},
    ...
```

TWO FILTERS APPLIED
Query
```
http://localhost:8983/solr/restaurants/select?q=*:*&facet=true&facet.mincount=1&
    facet.field=name&facet.field=tags&fq=tags:coffee&fq=tags:hamburgers
```

Results
```
    ...
    "facet_fields":{
        "name":[
            "McDonalds",5],
        "tags":[
            "breakfast",5,
            "coffee",5,                   All restaurants with
            "fast food",5,               hamburgers also have
            "hamburgers",5,              coffee and wi-fi.
            "wi-fi",5]},
        ...
```

You can see that fields containing multiple values will allow the other values to continue being returned as long as they still exist in the documents matching all applied filters. It's worth noting that, even though these examples specify each selected filter value as its own `fq` parameter on the Solr URL, there is no requirement that this be done. In fact, the filters applied in the last search of the previous listing could easily be converted from `fq=tags:coffee&fq=tags:hamburgers` to `fq=tags:(coffee AND hamburgers)` (or any logically equivalent Boolean expression). This will require fewer lookups in the Solr filter cache (discussed in chapter 4), and will also provide more control over how your filter values interact.

Nothing requires you to `AND` together each of the facet filters. It could be a perfectly valid use case for you to `OR` values together, such as when allowing users to select multiple cities in their facet while filtering to only the cities selected. The discussion of multiselect faceting in section 8.7 will highlight how you might accomplish the display of such a facet with multiple filters selected at once, even on a single-valued field.

8.6.2 Safely filtering on faceted values

All of our examples of applying facet filters to this point have applied filters based upon a single-valued term, such as `coffee` or `hamburgers`. In reality, the terms brought back in facets may be more challenging to handle (such as dealing with multiword terms). What happens, for example, if you want to facet upon the multiword term `Los Angeles`? As you already know, the filter `fq=city:Los Angeles` is invalid as it syntactically says to find documents containing a city of `Los` and the term `Angeles` in the default field(s). In order to allow for phrases separated by a space, most Solr developers decide to quote all terms they facet upon. Therefore, the query syntax would look like `fq=city:"Los Angeles"`.

Unfortunately, you'll even run into a problem with blindly quoting the terms you're filtering upon; if the term has quotes within it, the syntax will break unless you escape it. Therefore, if you were searching on a search index containing songs and faceting upon the song the `"in"` crowd, you'd need to escape the quotes to pass this term safely to Solr: `fq=name:"the \"in\" crowd"`. If quoting and escaping quotes weren't already enough trouble, you also have to be mindful of all text processing taking place on the field upon which you're faceting. As you saw in chapter 6, text analysis upon a field can be defined differently for content indexing versus querying. Therefore, if any kind of configuration mismatch exists (which is generally a bad practice), it's possible that a value you're trying to filter upon doesn't match the same number of documents as reported by the facet.

Thankfully, we have a fairly simple solution to ensure the values returned by a facet and matched by a subsequent filter find the exact same documents: using Solr's Term query parser (`TermQParserPlugin`), discussed in chapter 7. One of the benefits of this query parser is that it bypasses the defined text-analysis chain for your field and instead matches the term passed in directly against the Solr index. This saves text-processing time, and it prevents the other quoting and escaping logic discussed previously from being necessary. The syntax using the Term query parser for our `Los Angeles` example would be `fq={!term}Los Angeles`, and the syntax for our the `"in"` crowd example would be `fq={!term}the "in" crowd`.

The one downside of using the Term query parser for all of your facet filters is that it doesn't support Boolean syntax, so if you want to combine multiple facet values together in a filter, you may need to utilize the nested query syntax (chapter 7). The following listing demonstrates the use of both approaches: using a separate filter for each facet term and combining multiple facet terms into a single filter utilizing the Term query parser.

Listing 8.14   Using the Term query parser to filter on facet values

APPROACH 1: SEPARATE FILTERS PER TERM
Query
```
http://localhost:8983/solr/restaurants/select?q=*:*&facet=true&facet.mincount=1&
  facet.field=name&facet.field=tags&
  fq={!term f=tags}coffee&fq={!term f=tags}hamburgers
```

APPROACH 2: ONE FILTER FOR ALL TERMS
Query
```
http://localhost:8983/solr/restaurants/select?q=*:*&
  facet=true&facet.mincount=1&facet.field=name&facet.field=tags&
  fq=_query_:"{!term f=tags}coffee" AND _query_:"{!term f=tags}hamburgers"
```

Regardless of which approach you use for implementing your facet filters, using the Term query parser should make your queries faster. If you end up using the nested query syntax in approach 2, you'll still need to escape quotes within your terms (because the whole nested query is in quotes), but this is a minor inconvenience if you want the capability to still use Boolean logic in your facet filters.

In this section, you've seen that applying filters to your facets is no different than applying any other filter in Solr. You've also seen that it's possible to apply a separate filter per facet value or one filter for multiple facet terms. In addition, you saw that it's possible to use the Term query parser to bypass text processing and avoid difficult-to-handle character escaping when applying a faceting filter. At this point, you should be able to request and filter upon all of the basic facet types, but there's still more to explore. In the next section, you'll uncover useful ways to rename facets for display purposes and even to bring back facet counts for documents that have already been filtered out.

8.7 Multiselect faceting, keys, and tags

When requesting a facet back from Solr, the name of the facet isn't always the most useful for purposes of displaying results back to the user or even handling them within your application stack. Solr provides a convenient ability to rename facets when they're returned, making facets much more user-friendly for many use cases. Solr also provides the ability to bring back facet counts for documents that have been filtered out. This can be incredibly useful for implementing multiselect faceting: an ability to filter search results but still see the number of documents that would have matched had the filter not been applied. In this section, you'll be introduced to the concepts of the `key`, `tag`, and `exclude` local params (local params were introduced in chapter 7), which enable these useful facet renaming and multiselect capabilities.

8.7.1 Keys

All facets have a name that allows developers to distinguish them from each other. By default the name of a facet is the field name (for field facets and range facets) or the query (for query facets) upon which the facet values and counts are calculated. By using the `key` local param, however, it's easy to rename any facet, as demonstrated in this listing.

Listing 8.15   Renaming the key of a facet

DEFAULT SOLR FACETING NAMES
Query
```
http://localhost:8983/solr/restaurants/select?q=*:*&facet=true&facet.mincount=1&
   facet.field=city&                          ◁─────┐  A field facet is
   facet.query=price:[* TO 10}&                      │  named after its
   facet.query=price:[10 TO 25}&                     │  field by default.
   facet.query=price:[25 TO 50}&
   facet.query=price:[50 TO *]
```

Results
```
...
   "facet_counts":{                     A query facet is
      "facet_queries":{                 named after its
         "price:[* TO 10}":11,          query by default.
         "price:[10 TO 25}":5,
         "price:[25 TO 50}":4,
         "price:[50 TO *]":0},
```

```
    "facet_fields":{
      "city":[
        "Atlanta, GA",6,
        "New York, NY",4,
        "Austin, TX",3,
        "San Francisco, CA",3,
        "Chicago, IL",2,
        "Greenville, SC",1,
        "Los Angeles, CA",1]},
    "facet_dates":{},
    "facet_ranges":{}}}
  ...
```

A field facet is named after its field by default.

RENAMING FACETS BY SPECIFYING AN EXPLICIT KEY

Query

```
http://localhost:8983/solr/restaurants/select?q=*:*&facet=true&facet.mincount=1&
  facet.field={!key="Location"}city&
  facet.query={!key="<$10"}price:[* TO 10}&
  facet.query={!key="$10 - $25"}price:[10 TO 25}&
  facet.query={!key="$25 - $50"}price:[25 TO 50}&
  facet.query={!key=">$50"}price:[50 TO *]
```

Results

```
  ...
  "facet_counts":{
    "facet_queries":{
      "<$10":11,
      "$10 - $25":5,
      "$25 - $50":4,
      ">$50":0},
    "facet_fields":{
      "Location":[
        "Atlanta, GA",6,
        "New York, NY",4,
        "Austin, TX",3,
        "San Francisco, CA",3,
        "Chicago, IL",2,
        "Greenville, SC",1,
        "Los Angeles, CA",1]},
    "facet_dates":{},
    "facet_ranges":{}}}
  ...
```

Query facets being given more readable names.

A field facet being renamed from city to Location.

The ability to rename a facet can be useful in many scenarios. It allows your search application to request query facets, for example, without requiring the application to interpret the queries from the result set during a postprocessing stage. It also allows for user-friendly names to be assigned to facets regardless of the underlying field or query associated with the facet, which can make displaying the results in a UI more straightforward. Additionally, by enabling each facet to be assigned a unique name, this capability to specify keys allows for more than one facet to be defined on the same field (which can be useful for field facets or range facets), with each facet coming back under a unique name. One last advantage of this approach is that it allows multiple fields to be mapped into the same name depending upon query-time rules.

Say you have a search index with a field called `SecretInformationOnlyAvailable-ToSomeUsers` and another called `InformationAvailableToAllUsers`. With such a setup, you could create a facet at query time that either specified `facet.field={!key="Information "}InformationAvailableToAllUsers` or `facet.field={!key="Information "}SecretInformationOnlyAvailableToSomeUsers`. This layer of indirection can be handy in many scenarios, including any time you want to redefine a facet to point to a different field with minimal changes to your application stack. In addition to renaming facets, Solr provides the ability to tag certain filters so you can control their interaction with other Solr features.

8.7.2 Tags, excludes, and multiselect faceting

When filters are applied to a Solr query request, the results must include every single filter. By default, the same holds true for facets. But one of the problems this presents is that it's often useful to see facet counts for values that have been excluded from the query already. Figure 8.8 demonstrates this problem by requesting some facets on the restaurant test data from section 8.2 and applying a filter for the state of California.

Even though you'd expect your search results to only display documents in California given the previous UI, you'd also expect the facets to continue displaying the other states so that you could expand your query. The same principle applies for price ranges and cities; it's silly to only allow your users to search for one value per facet at a time.

Fortunately, Solr has a solution to this problem through a feature called facet exclusions. *Facet exclusions* allow you to add documents removed by any groups of filters applied on your search request. By adding the removed documents to the facet counts, you can make the counts on each facet effectively ignore any filters applied based upon that facet. The parameters necessary to implement this are the `tag` local param and the `ex` local param. Listing 8.16 demonstrates using these parameters to implement multiselect faceting on the example from figure 8.8.

FACETS BEFORE ANY FILTERS ARE APPLIED

▶ State	▶ Price Range	▶ City
☐ Georgia (6)	☐ < $5 (6)	☐ Atlanta, GA (6)
☐ California (4)	☐ $5 - $10 (5)	☐ New York, NY (4)
☐ New York (4)	☐ $10 - $20 (3)	☐ Austin, TX (3)
☐ Texas (3)	☐ $20 - $50 (6)	☐ San Francisco, CA (3)
☐ Illinois (2)	☐ $50+ (0)	☐ Chicago, IL (2)
…		…

FACETS AFTER A FILTER IS APPLIED ON STATE:CALIFORNIA

▶ State	▶ Price Range	▶ City
☑ California (4)	☐ < $5 (0)	☐ San Francisco, CA (3)
	☐ $5 - $10 (2)	☐ Los Angeles, CA (1)
	☐ $10 - $20 (0)	
	☐ $20 - $50 (2)	
	☐ $50+ (0)	

Figure 8.8 By default, after filtering upon a facet, the facet values that are returned no longer include the documents that were filtered out. This is problematic if you want to allow your user to select multiple values to include in the search, as they'll never be able to OR any additional facet filters for the values because they're no longer visible as options.

Listing 8.16   Using tags and excludes to implement multiselect faceting

Query

```
http://localhost:8983/solr/restaurants/select?q=*:*&facet=true&facet.mincount=1&
    facet.field={!ex=tagForState}state&
    facet.field={!ex=tagForCity}city&
    facet.query={!ex=tagForPrice}price:[* TO 5}&
    facet.query={!ex=tagForPrice}price:[5 TO 10}&
    facet.query={!ex=tagForPrice}price:[10 TO 20}&
    facet.query={!ex=tagForPrice}price:[20 TO 50}&
    facet.query={!ex=tagForPrice}price:[50 TO *]&
    fq={!tag="tagForState"}state:California
```

> The state facet should
> ignore filters tagged
> tagForState.

> The query results will
> be limited to the state
> of California.

Results

```
...
"facet_counts":{
    "facet_queries":{
        "{!ex=tagForPrice}price:[* TO 5}":0,
        "{!ex=tagForPrice}price:[5 TO 10}":2,
        "{!ex=tagForPrice}price:[10 TO 20}":0,
        "{!ex=tagForPrice}price:[20 TO 50}":2,
        "{!ex=tagForPrice}price:[50 TO *]":0},
    "facet_fields":{
        "state":[
            "Georgia",6,
            "California",4,
            "New York",4,
            "Texas",3,
            "Illinois",2,
            "South Carolina",1],
        "city":[
            "San Francisco, CA",3,
            "Los Angeles, CA",1]},
    "facet_dates":{},
    "facet_ranges":{}}}
...
```

> The state facet
> ignores the filter
> on state:California.

> Other facets respect the
> filter on state:California.

As you can see, a filter was applied on the query that limited the search to the state of California, but the total count of all documents matching the rest of the query was still returned for each state—not only for California. Figure 8.9 demonstrates how these multiselect faceting results compare with the original nonfiltered facets.

In terms of the mechanics of the query, `tagForState` was applied on the filter for the state of California. This was accomplished using the syntax `fq={!tag="tag-ForState"}state:California`. When the `state` facet was requested, it was told to exclude all filters tagged with `tagForState` using the syntax `facet.field={!ex=tag-ForState}state`.

Even though you can't see the search results in listing 8.16, it's important to keep in mind that the documents returned from Solr are still constrained to the state of California (because the filter was applied to the query), even though the `state` facet isn't limited by that filter. It's also important to understand that all of the other facets not tagged with `tagForState` are still constrained to the state of California for the same reason.

FACETS BEFORE ANY FILTERS ARE APPLIED

▶ State	▶ Price Range	▶ City
☐ Georgia (6)	☐ < $5 (6)	☐ Atlanta, GA (6)
☐ California (4)	☐ $5 - $10 (5)	☐ New York, NY (4)
☐ New York (4)	☐ $10 - $20 (3)	☐ Austin, TX (3)
☐ Texas (3)	☐ $20 - $50 (6)	☐ San Francisco, CA (3)
☐ Illinois (2)	☐ $50+ (0)	☐ Chicago, IL (2)
. . .		. . .

FACETS AFTER A FILTER IS APPLIED ON STATE:CALIFORNIA

▶ State	▶ Price Range	▶ City
☐ Georgia (6)	☐ < $5 (0)	☐ San Francisco, CA (3)
☑ California (4)	☐ $5 - $10 (2)	☐ Los Angeles, CA (1)
☐ New York (4)	☐ $10 - $20 (0)	
☐ Texas (3)	☐ $20 - $50 (2)	
☐ Illinois (2)	☐ $50+ (0)	
. . .		

Figure 8.9 **All fields are filtered by the state:California filter except the state facet, because it was marked to exclude the `tagForState` tag that was applied to the state facet. This allows users to continue selecting additional states for a multiselect faceting experience.**

Also note that each of the other requested facets (on `city` and `price`) also contained exclusion tags, but they didn't correspond with any tagged filters. Although these exclusion tags were unnecessary, they didn't cause any problems and were ignored. If someone were to rerun the query and add a filter (using one of those excluded tags) on one of the additional facet values, the currently unused exclusion tag would kick into effect. Whether you choose to apply exclusion tags on facets prior to the existence of any filters containing the excluded tags is up to you, but the point here is that doing so, although possibly wasteful syntax-wise, won't negatively impact the returned results.

It's possible to build some interesting UIs and data analytics capabilities by mixing and matching tags and facets, but those use cases go well beyond what this chapter can cover. Feel free to experiment with these capabilities in Solr if you want to learn more.

At this point you've seen Solr's most common faceting capabilities, including field, query, and range faceting. In the next section, we'll briefly touch on some of the more advanced topics related to faceting, topics which we'll dive into in more detail in chapter 15 when discussing complex query operations.

8.8 *Beyond the basics*

This chapter provides a solid overview of the most used faceting capabilities in Solr, but this isn't the last time you'll see faceting discussed. Faceting makes heavy use of Solr's caches, so you'll need to optimize your use of Solr's built-in caches in order to maximize the performance of your faceting requests. Working with caches will be discussed further in chapter 12.

In addition to performance tuning, you'll see more advanced forms of faceting in chapter 15. One of these advanced faceting capabilities is called pivot faceting, and it provides the ability to facet in many dimensions. Say it wasn't sufficient for your application to only know the top values from the `tags` field but that you really needed to know the top `tags` per `city`. How would you go about accomplishing this? You could run a first search to get a facet for all the values in the `city` field and then run subsequent searches for each `city` to get its `tags` facet. Unfortunately, this approach doesn't scale well and can easily result in your having to run dozens or hundreds of searches as your document set grows larger. Solr has a solution for this problem, *pivot facets*, which allow you to facet across multiple dimensions to pull back these kinds of calculations in a single search. To learn more, check out the advanced faceting section of chapter 15 (section 15.3).

8.9   *Summary*

Congratulations on wrapping up an in-depth chapter on one of Solr's most powerful features. As you've seen, faceting provides a fast way to let users see a high-level overview of the kinds of documents their queries match. You'd be hard put to find a major search-powered website today that doesn't provide some form of faceting to allow users to drill down and explore their search results. With Solr, you have the ability to bring back the top values within each field using field facets, to bring back bucketed ranges of numbers or date values using range facets, or to bring back the counts of any number of arbitrarily complex queries by using query faceting.

You also saw that it's possible to use `keys` to rename facets as they're being returned, you learned how to use `tags` and facet excludes to implement multiselect faceting (which returns counts even for documents that are filtered out by a query), and you explored multiple ways of applying filters to a query once your users click on your facets.

Finally, you were made aware of Solr's multidimensional pivot faceting capabilities, which we'll discuss in detail in chapter 15, which focuses on complex query operations. At this point, you should be able to implement some fairly sophisticated search applications using all but the most complex forms of faceting available in Solr.

In the next chapter, you'll learn how to use another common Solr feature, hit highlighting, which allows the snippets of text matched in each document during a search to be returned for display in your list of search results, providing a potentially important insight to your users as to whether a document in your search results is worth exploring.

Hit highlighting

This chapter covers

- Highlighting query terms in search results
- Selecting the best snippets to display for each search result
- Refining highlighting behavior using optional parameters
- Improving highlighting performance using `FastVectorHighlighter`
- Using Solr's newest highlighter implementation, `PostingsHighlighter`

In this chapter, we introduce a core Solr feature, hit highlighting, in which query terms are highlighted in search results. Hit highlighting helps users quickly scan results to determine which results are worth investigating further, or whether they should navigate to the next page, or even issue a different query.

To have a little fun while learning about hit highlighting, we use a dataset containing thousands of unidentified flying object (UFO) sightings from across the United States, collected into a free dataset provided by Infochimps (www.infochimps .com/datasets/60000-documented-ufo-sightings-with-text-descriptions-and-metada).

Our UFO search application allows users to type in a few keywords about a sighting and see if there have been similar sightings.

We chose this example because it provides two important learning devices that you have not been exposed to in this book so far. First, unlike the canned examples we've encountered in previous chapters, the UFO dataset can't be added to Solr without doing some upfront data modeling and preprocessing. Having to adapt a raw dataset into a form that can be indexed is a common requirement when building search applications. Second, this example application gives us a chance to build upon all the concepts we've covered in the book. Specifically, we will need to index UFO sightings (chapter 5), perform text analysis (chapter 6), configure a search component in *solrconfig.xml* (chapter 4), explore sighting-related facets (chapter 8), and execute queries to find similar sightings (chapter 7). Our main focus is on hit highlighting, but we also implement the foundation of a search application by using tools you learned about in previous chapters.

Although conceptually very simple, hit highlighting in Solr can be confusing to new users because there are many optional configuration parameters, and it's not always clear when to use each parameter. Moreover, Solr provides three different highlighter implementations out of the box, which makes it hard to decide which implementation you need. We cover all three highlighters in this chapter and give you pointers to help you decide when to use which. To begin, let's set the stage for how hit highlighting is used in our UFO sighting search application.

9.1   *Overview of hit highlighting*

Let's imagine we saw a blue fireball in the sky on a rainy day. We'll use our UFO search application to find similar sightings. Highlighting will help the sighting jump out as relevant or not. Consider the example in figure 9.1, where a user queries for `blue fireball in the rain` to find similar UFO sightings.

In figure 9.1, the UFO search application uses highlighting to put query terms in context in search results. The user searched for `blue fireball in the rain` and the search results show matching query terms `blue`, `fireball`, and `rain` in bold and highlighted. Based on this contrived example, you might be thinking, what's the big deal about highlighting the terms `blue`, `fireball`, and `rain` in these documents? Highlighting query terms in these results can easily be accomplished with simple pattern matching and HTML markup. But what might not be immediately apparent is that Solr also selected a small section of each document, called a snippet, which best represents the user's query. The text being displayed for each result in figure 9.1 is dynamically selected based on the user's query and is not the full description of the sighting. For instance, the full text description of the first sighting in figure 9.1 is

```
Bright blue fireball in the distance during a rain storm. Not a lightning
storm, no thunder. No relevant towers or objects in the area.
```

To be clear, highlighting query terms for display is only a small part of Solr's highlighting feature. What makes this feature powerful is deciding which text in each search result should be highlighted.

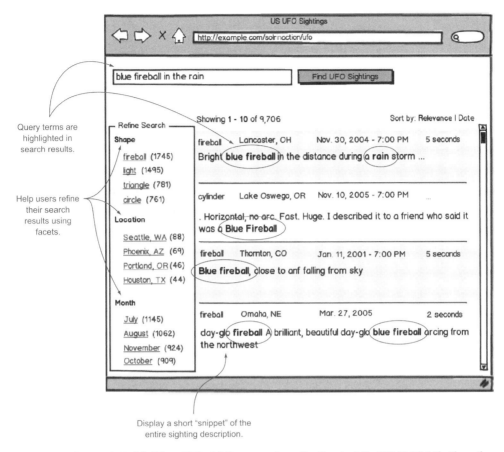

Figure 9.1 Screenshot of fictitious UFO sightings search application depicting hit highlighting in action

In most search applications, you have limited screen real estate to dedicate to a single result, as is the case in figure 9.1. If a document is short and can be displayed in its entirety in the results list, then limited screen space is not much of an issue. But in most cases, you're only able to display a small portion of each document. This raises the question, how do you select a subsection of a document to be displayed? Ideally, you want to display a snippet of each result based on how closely it matches the user's query. Selecting the best snippet to display for a given query is the core functionality provided by Solr's hit highlighting framework.

9.2 *How highlighting works*

Let's see how to implement the hit highlighting solution for the example UFO search application we saw in figure 9.1. The first step is to get the UFO sightings loaded into Solr. Download the UFO sightings from www.infochimps.com/datasets/ 60000-documented-ufo-sightings-with-text-descriptions-and-metada. Once downloaded, extract the compressed archive (ZIP or TGZ) to a temp folder on your computer, and take note of the full path to the *ufo_awesome.json* file, such as */tmp/chimps_16154-2010-10-20_14-33-35/ufo_awesome.json*.

Next, start Solr if it's not already running. We'll be adding around 54,000 documents to your server for this example, so we recommend starting your Solr server with a large maximum heap size (`-Xmx512m`) to avoid running out of memory while indexing.

```
cd $SOLR_INSTALL/example/
java -Xmx512m -jar start.jar
```

9.2.1 Set up a new Solr core for UFO sightings

Now, let's use some of the knowledge we gained in chapter 4 to create a new core instead of using the `collection1` core; let's call the new core for this chapter `ufo`. To do this, you need to copy the *collection1/* directory under *$SOLR_INSTALL/example/* to a new directory named *ufo/*. For now, you do not need to make any other configuration changes, but we do recommend deleting the data directory under *ufo/* so that your new core starts with an empty index.

```
cd $SOLR_INSTALL/example/solr
cp -r collection1 ufo
rm -rf ufo/data
rm ufo/core.properties
```

Navigate to the Core Admin page in the Solr administration console, and click the Add Core button. Fill out the form as shown in figure 9.2.

9.2.2 Preprocess UFO sightings before indexing

Let's take a peek at the raw data from *ufo_awesome.json* that we'll use to build our Solr index. The first two lines in the file are

```
{"sighted_at": "19951009", "reported_at": "19951009", "location": " Iowa
City, IA", "shape": "", "duration": "", "description": "Man repts. witnessing
&quot;flash, followed by a classic UFO, w/ a tailfin at back.&quot; Red color
on top half of tailfin. Became triangular."}

{"sighted_at": "19951010", "reported_at": "19951011", "location": "
Milwaukee, WI", "shape": "", "duration": "2 min.", "description": "Man  on
Hwy 43 SW of Milwaukee sees large, bright blue light streak by his car,
descend, turn, cross road ahead, strobe. Bizarre!"}
```

Each line is a JSON object containing fields about a specific UFO sighting. As we've mentioned numerous times, Solr supports JSON natively. Consequently, you might be thinking that we can send this JSON file directly to Solr and it will index it automatically. Unfortunately, this won't work because the data does not conform to the *schema.xml* of the `ufo` core, which was cloned from the `collection1` example core. Think about where the UFO sighting data does not conform to the *schema.xml* for the `ufo` core. Remember that you can view the *schema.xml* file from the Solr administration console.

To adapt the raw sighting data to our schema, we need to develop a custom client application. To save some typing, we provided an example application to preprocess the UFO data and send it to Solr; see the `sia.ch9.IndexUfoSightings` Java class.

Click the Add Core button on the Core Admin page to create the ufo core.

Add the new ufo core from the ufo directory you copied from collection1.

Figure 9.2   Add a new core named `ufo` from the Core Admin page in the Solr administration console.

At a high level, the `IndexUfoSightings` application performs simple preprocessing on the raw data to prepare it for indexing, then uses the `ConcurrentUpdateSolrServer` class from the SolrJ library to send UFO sightings to Solr. We won't review the source code in detail here, but we recommend you take a look at it as it serves as another good example of using SolrJ to index documents. Instead of walking through the code, let's review some of the important preprocessing steps the application performs on the raw data:

1 Ensures each sighting has required fields: `sighted_at`, `location`, and `description`.

2 Creates a unique identifier for each sighting to populate the required `id` field.

3 Validates and converts the `sighted_at` and `reported_at` values into Java `Date` objects.

4 Extracts the month from the `sighted_at` date and indexes it into a separate field called `month_s`, which is useful for faceting.

5 Replaces XML character entity references with the represented character; for example, `&quot;` becomes a double quote (`"`) character.

6 Collapses all whitespace in the sighting description to a single space character.

7 Splits the location field into city and state fields.

8 Adapts field names in the JSON sighting information to Solr dynamic fields; for example, `shape` becomes `shape_s` and `description` becomes `sighting_en`.

9 Fixes missing spaces between words and the end of sentences; for example, `"fog.We"` becomes `"fog. We"`; this improves the display of sighting descriptions.

The key takeaway is that when working with datasets derived from user-generated content, sometimes you need to do preprocessing in your indexing client code to improve the user experience with your search application.

Now that we have a basic understanding of what the client application does, let's run it to populate the Solr index. Change directories into the *$SOLR_IN_ACTION/* directory, and execute the following:

```
java -jar solr-in-action.jar ufo -jsonInput
   ➥ $FULL_PATH_TO_UFO_SIGHTINGS_DIR/ufo_awesome.json
```

The indexing application should run very quickly and complete in less than one minute. You should see the following output at the end of the application, indicating that 54,190 sightings were sent to Solr for indexing:

```
INFO [main] (IndexUfoSightings.java:106) - Sent 54190 sightings (skipped
   6877) took #.# seconds
```

Notice that 6,877 documents were skipped due to validation errors. Now execute the match all documents query against the `ufo` core to see how many sightings are indexed. Figure 9.3 shows the results of the match all documents (`*:*`) query from the query form at http://localhost:8983/solr/#/ufo/query.

9.2.3 *Exploring the UFO sightings dataset*

Table 9.1 provides an overview of the UFO sightings document structure created by the `IndexUfoSightings` application.

Table 9.1 UFO sightings document

Name	Type	Description	Example
id	string	Synthetic unique identifier created from other fields	20041130/20041204/ ...
sighted_at_dt	date	Date/time of UFO sighting	2004-11-30T07:00:00Z
reported_at_dt	date	Date/time sighting was reported to authorities	2004-12-04T07:00:00Z
month_s	string	Month when sighting occurred	November
city_s	string	U.S. city where sighting occurred	Lancaster
state_s	string	U.S. state where sighting occurred	OH
location_s	string	U.S. city and state where sighting occurred	Lancaster, OH

Table 9.1 UFO sightings document *(continued)*

Name	Type	Description	Example
shape_s	string	Shape of UFO	fireball
duration_s	string	How long the UFO was visible	5 seconds
sighting_en	text_en	Free-form text description of sighting	Bright blue fireball in the distance during a rainstorm. Not a lightning storm, no thunder. No relevant towers or objects in the area.

Two things should stand out from table 9.1. First, we are using dynamic fields by applying built-in suffixes on the Solr field names, such as _s for string fields and _dt for date fields. Dynamic fields were covered in chapter 5. Second, we derived new fields from the raw data to facilitate faceting. We extracted the month when each sighting occurred from the sighted_at_dt field into month_s to allow us to focus on the month of the year. Although this is not required, it gives our users another facet to explore the dataset with, in this case to answer questions like "is a particular shape more frequent in certain months?" In general, this is a good example of designing your data model to help provide a better user experience.

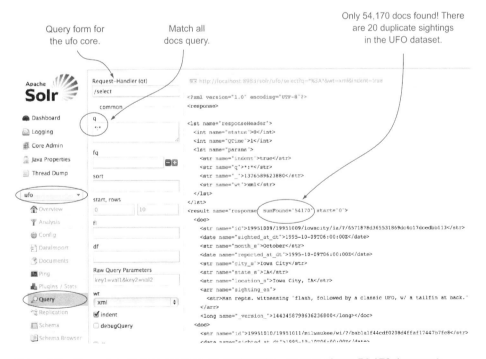

Figure 9.3 The match all docs query (*:*) against the ufo core shows 54,170 documents indexed; the client application sent 54,190 documents with 20 duplicates.

Our UFO dataset has a mixture of short one or two sentence descriptions of a sighting as well as some documents with longer descriptions. The average description length is about 1,100 characters and 216 terms. But there are thousands of sightings that have over 3,000-character descriptions, making Solr's hit highlighting a necessary feature for this dataset. We are now ready to do some hit highlighting!

9.2.4   *Hit highlighting out of the box*

At this point in the book, it should not surprise you that Solr comes preconfigured to do hit highlighting with little effort on your part. Highlighting is a core feature of Solr and an important capability for any search application in general. In this section, you'll learn how to enable hit highlighting and how to control the number of highlighted snippets created for each document in search results.

BASIC HIT HIGHLIGHTING

This listing shows the Solr query that produced the results shown in figure 9.1.[1]

Listing 9.1   Simple query with highlighting enabled

Query

```
http://localhost:8983/solr/ufo/select?q=blue fireball in the rain&
    df=sighting_en&
    wt=xml&
    rows=10&
    hl=true
```

◁──┐ Set the default search field for
     this query to be sighting_en.

◁──┐ Enable the built-in hit highlighting
     search component named "highlight".

Results

```
<response>
    <lst name="responseHeader"> ... </lst>
    <result name="response" numFound="9687" start="0">
        <doc>
            <str name="id">20041130/.../2bbc6dc90efcbb8fb8f54ba23e07bd0a</str>
            ...
            <arr name="sighting_en">
                <str>Bright blue fireball in the distance during a rain storm.
                    Not a lightning storm, no thunder. No relevant towers or
                    objects in the area.</str>
            </arr>
            <long name="_version_">1431225103138422786</long>
        </doc>
    </result>
    <lst name="highlighting">
        <lst name="20041130/.../2bbc6dc90efcbb8fb8f54ba23e07bd0a">
            <arr name="sighting_en">
                <str>Bright &lt;em&gt;blue&lt;/em&gt; &lt;em&gt;fireball&lt;/em&gt;
                    in the distance during a &lt;em&gt;rain&lt;/em&gt; storm. Not a
                    lightning storm, no thunder</str>
            </arr>
        </lst>
```

◁──┐ All fields for the first document
     in the search results.

◁──┐ Highlighting results
     returned in a separate
     section of the response
     XML document.

Highlights
for the first
document
in the
search
results. ⟶

◁──┐ Snippet from the first document
     with highlights using <em> tag.

```
    </lst>
```

---

[1]   Remember that you can use the query listing tool described in chapter 4 to execute this request to your local Solr server: `java -jar solr-in-action.jar listing 9.1`.

```
    </lst>
</response>
```

Notice that Solr returns highlighted snippets in a separate element: `<lst name="highlighting">`. Therefore, your client application must process this information to create the display. The highlighted snippet for the first document in the results is shown here without the XML escape sequences:[2]

```
Bright blue fireball in the distance during a rain storm. Not a lightning
storm, no thunder
```

The highlighted snippet looks pretty close to what is displayed in figure 9.1, except that it includes the additional terms `Not a lightning storm, no thunder`. We'll see how to get the exact results shown in figure 9.1 later in the chapter, when we use the `PostingsHighlighter`.

For now what's important is that with very little effort (passing one additional query parameter, `hl=true`), we have hit highlighting support. As with most search components in Solr, the highlighter supports a number of optional configuration parameters to fine-tune the behavior. Let's work with a few of the optional parameters to get a feel for the process.

GENERATING MULTIPLE SNIPPETS PER RESULT

In some cases, a single snippet per result may not give the user enough context to decide if a result is worth investigating further. For example, the highlighted text for the second document returned from our query is

```
. Horizontal, no arc. Fast. Huge. I described it to a friend who said it was
a "Blue Fireball
```

At a glance, this result looks promising because it mentions a blue fireball, but it seems as if there is more to this story, particularly because it's listed as the second-most-relevant document in the index for this query. Let's use the `hl.snippets` parameter to try to tease out more context from this and other documents in the results. The following listing shows the results when setting `hl.snippets=2` to allow a maximum of two snippets per document to be highlighted.

> **Listing 9.2   Generating more snippets per document using the `hl.snippets` parameter**

Query
```
http://localhost:8983/solr/ufo/select?q=blue fireball in the rain&
    df=sighting_en&
    wt=xml&                                  Ask Solr to generate
    hl=true&                                 up to two snippets
    hl.snippets=2                            per document.          Highlighting section
                                                                    of the XML response
                                                                    document.
```
Results
```
<lst name="highlighting">
    <lst name="20041130/20041204/lancaster/oh/fireball/
```

---

[2]   Solr returns highlighted terms encoded with XML escape sequences, such as < escaped as <. We display highlighted terms in **bold** and highlighted to improve readability as you work through this chapter.

```
            2bbc6dc90efcbb8fb8f54ba23e07bd0a">
          <arr name="sighting_en">
            <str>Bright &lt;em&gt;blue&lt;/em&gt; &lt;em&gt;fireball&lt;/em&gt;
                in the distance during a &lt;em&gt;rain&lt;/em&gt; storm. Not a
                lightning storm, no thunder</str>
          </arr>
        </lst>
        <lst name="20051110/20051116/lakeoswego/or/cylinder/
            4bae25d796ba82677ea0d77b36d08faf">
          <arr name="sighting_en">
            <str>. Horizontal, no arc. Fast. Huge. I described it to a friend
                who said it was a
                "&lt;em&gt;Blue&lt;/em&gt; &lt;em&gt;Fireball&lt;/em&gt;</str>
            <str>Brilliant &lt;em&gt;blue&lt;/em&gt; oblong object zooms
                horizontally across southern sky at 2 in the morning. I
                awoke
            </str>
          </arr>
        </lst>
        ...
      </lst>
```

Only one snippet returned for the first document in the results. *(annotation pointing to `<arr name="sighting_en">`)*

First snippet for second document in the results. *(annotation pointing to first `<str>` of second lst)*

Second snippet for second document in the results. *(annotation pointing to second `<str>` of second lst)*

Here are the two snippets generated for the second result without all the XML escape sequences:

1 Horizontal, no arc. Fast. Huge. I described it to a friend who said it was a "**Blue Fireball**

2 Brilliant **blue** oblong object zooms horizontally across southern sky at 2 in the morning. I awoke

Unfortunately, there is still no mention of rain in the second snippet for this document. One interesting aspect of these results is that the snippets are sorted by relevance score, with the snippets with the closest similarly to the query listed first. In fact, the first snippet comes after the second one in the sighting text. We leave it as an exercise for the reader to verify that this is the case by inspecting the results returned from executing listing 9.2.

Setting `hl.snippets=2` does not guarantee two snippets will always be generated for each document, as seen by the highlighting result for the first document in our results. Only the first sentence of that result is applicable to the query, so Solr only returns one snippet. The value of the `hl.snippets` parameter should be considered an upper limit on the number of snippets returned per result.

9.2.5 *Nuts and bolts*

Now that you've seen highlighting in action, let's dig into the details to see what happens behind the scenes. Recall from chapter 4 that the highlight component is included in the default components list of the search request handler. Figure 9.4 depicts where the highlight search component is in the search handler query processing chain.

There is a corresponding search component entry named `highlight` defined in *solrconfig.xml*. Listing 9.3 shows an abbreviated definition of the highlight search component.

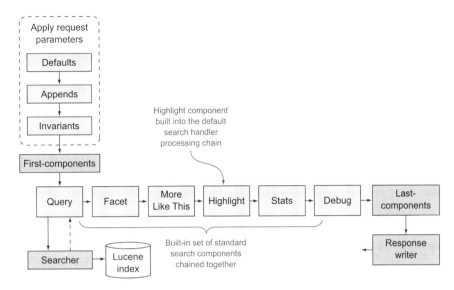

Figure 9.4 Query processing pipeline showing the highlight component in the chain of components for a search handler

Listing 9.3 XML definition of default `highlight` search component in *solrconfig.xml*

```
<searchComponent class="solr.HighlightComponent" name="highlight">    ◁── Define the
  <highlighting>                                                              highlight
    <fragmenter name="gap" default="true"          ◁── Use the               search
        class="solr.highlight.GapFragmenter">          GapFragmenter as the  component.
      ...                                                 default fragmenter.
    </fragmenter>
    <fragmenter name="regex" class="solr.highlight.RegexFragmenter">  ◁── Alternative
      ...                                                                   fragmenter
    </fragmenter>                                        Highlight terms      using
    <formatter name="html" default="true"       ◁──     using HTML           regular
        class="solr.highlight.HtmlFormatter">           markup.              expressions.
      ...
    </formatter>
    <encoder name="html" class="solr.highlight.HtmlEncoder" />
    <fragListBuilder name="simple"
        class="solr.highlight.SimpleFragListBuilder"/>
      ...
    <fragmentsBuilder name="default" default="true"
        class="solr.highlight.ScoreOrderFragmentsBuilder">
      ...
    </fragmentsBuilder>
    ...
  </highlighting>
</searchComponent>
```

Used by the FastVector-Highlighter to create fragments from term vectors.

An important thing to notice in figure 9.4 is that the highlight component is downstream from the query component. Consequently, the highlighter only works with a page of search results at a time. Our example query from listing 9.1 requests 10 documents (rows=10) so the highlight component will only work on 10 documents per request. It follows that if you use large page sizes, such as 1,000, you're asking the highlighter to do more work per request, which will negatively impact query response time.

The highlight component needs to know which fields in your documents you want it to perform highlighting on, which is specified using the hl.fl parameter. If your query does not specify the hl.fl parameter, as is the case with our example, then Solr falls back to the default query field specified using the df parameter, which in our example is sighting_en. For our sample application, the only field that makes sense to highlight is sighting_en. A good example of using multiple fields is where you have a title and body field, and you want to highlight query terms in both fields. In this case you would need to specify hl.fl=title,body to perform highlighting on the title and body fields.

For each field in the hl.fl list, the highlighter determines how many snippets to generate based on the hl.snippets parameter, which defaults to 1. This sets the maximum number of snippets to generate per field. If hl.snippets=2, then Solr may create zero, one, or two snippets per field. We saw an example of this parameter in the previous section.

At this point, the highlighter has a small set of documents to work on (rows=10), knows which fields to generate highlighted snippets for (df=sighting_en), and knows how many snippets to create per field (hl.snippets=2). The next step is to reanalyze the text to be highlighted. Figure 9.5 illustrates how the highlighter works to produce highlighted snippets.

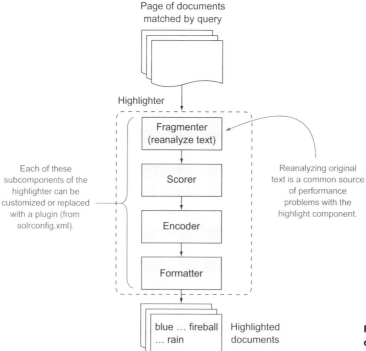

Figure 9.5 Main components of the Solr highlighter

TEXT ANALYSIS

Before Solr can highlight, it needs access to the original text. As you learned in chapter 5, to access the original text for a field, it needs to be stored. In our example, we are highlighting the `sighting_en` field, which is a dynamic field declared in *schema.xml* as

```
<dynamicField name="*_en" type="text_en"
    indexed="true" stored="true" multiValued="true" />
```

Once Solr has the original text for the field, it needs to reanalyze it using the configured index-time analyzer. For `sighting_en`, the analyzer is configured by the `text_en` field type (refer to *schema.xml* for the full definition):

```
<fieldType name="text_en" class="solr.TextField" positionIncrementGap="100">
  <analyzer type="index">
    <tokenizer class="solr.StandardTokenizerFactory"/>
    <filter class="solr.StopFilterFactory" .../>
    <filter class="solr.LowerCaseFilterFactory"/>
    <filter class="solr.EnglishPossessiveFilterFactory"/>
    <filter class="solr.KeywordMarkerFilterFactory" .../>
    <filter class="solr.PorterStemFilterFactory"/>
  </analyzer>
  ...
</fieldType>
```

We covered text analysis in chapter 6, but we'll do a quick review here so you have a good feel for the text transformations performed by the `text_en` analyzer. Consider the following sighting description: `It was raining when I saw a blue fireball`. Figure 9.6 shows the transformations applied to this fictitious sighting text using the `text_en` analyzer.

As you can see in figure 9.6, Solr removes `it`, `was`, and `a` as stop words, lowercases all terms, and stems `raining` to `rain` and `fireball` to `firebal`. The transformations are straightforward, but what might not be clear is why Solr needs to reanalyze the stored text for highlighting.

Reanalyzing the original text for each document is required for two main reasons. First, the terms in fragments must be comparable to terms in the query. We expect Solr to make the following highlights for our example query `blue fireball in the rain`: It was **raining** when I saw a **blue fireball**. By analyzing the original text before highlighting, the term `raining` becomes `rain` using stemming, as shown in figure 9.6.

Second, Solr needs to know the position offsets of the terms in the original text so it can highlight the terms in the snippet. We wouldn't want Solr to produce a snippet where it misses the `ing` part of `raining`, for example: It was **rain**ing when I saw a **blue fireball**. Solr needs to know the start and end offsets of `raining` in the original text. Position offsets are also important so that Solr knows when to highlight a phrase and not the parts of a phrase.

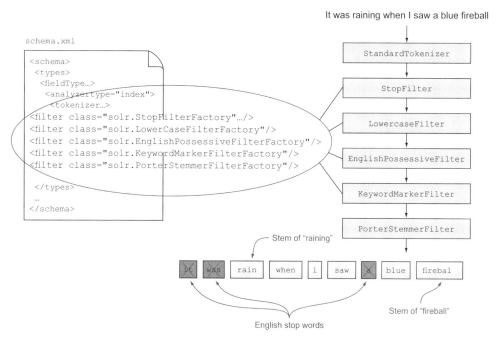

Figure 9.6   Text analysis applied to a fictitious sighting by the text_en analyzer

FRAGMENTING

Fragmenting is the process of selecting zero or more subsections of a text field to high-light. To this point we've been using the term *snippet*, which you can think of as a ranked and formatted fragment that scored high enough to be returned in the results. Solr breaks text into fragments and generates a score for each fragment; the highest N scoring fragments are returned as snippets, where N is determined by the `hl.snippets` parameter.

There are two basic approaches to fragmenting in Solr, `GapFragmenter` and `Regex-Fragmenter`. `GapFragmenter`, the default, selects fragments based on a target length. By default, the target fragment length is 100, but that can be changed using the `hl.fragsize` parameter. But `hl.fragsize` does not translate into a firm fixed-length fragment, as `GapFragmenter` creates fragments at token boundaries. It doesn't split tokens to enforce a fixed-length fragment. `GapFragmenter` gets its name because it also avoids creating fragments that span a large position gap, such as the gap between distinct values in a multivalued field set by the `positionIncrementGap` attribute in the field definition in *schema.xml*. We'll see an example of `GapFragmenter` respecting the gap between values in a multivalued field in the next section.

Table 9.2 shows the eight fragments generated by `GapFragmenter` for the second document in our search results; the sighting description is 742 characters long, so generating eight fragments makes sense (seven fragments of roughly 100 characters and one short fragment with the remaining characters).

Table 9.2 Breakdown of eight fragments with scores generated for an example UFO sighting

Fragment	Score
Brilliant **blue** oblong object zooms horizontally across southern sky at 2 in the morning. I awoke	1.0
suddenly because of the silence. **Rain** had been thundering on the glass ceiling, but suddenly I woke up	1.0
realizing the **rain** had stopped and there was complete silence (I sleep with windows open.) I looked	1.0
at the clock ... 2 AM ... and I looked at the sky through the glass ceiling. (I live on a lake so have a clear	0.0
view of the southern sky with no interference from trees, lights or houses.) Every star in the universe	0.0
was shining and suddenly, across the horizon, zoomed a brilliant **blue** something ... from west to east	1.0
. Horizontal, no arc. Fast. Huge. I described it to a friend who said it was a "**Blue Fireball**	2.0
." It was a beautiful experience.	0.0

Solr also provides RegexFragmenter, which selects fragments from text using a regular expression. For example, if you wanted to produce sentences as fragments in English text, you could use a pattern like [-\w ,/\n\"']{20,200}, which incidentally is the preconfigured pattern in *solrconfig.xml*.

SCORING

The fragmenter uses a subcomponent called a scorer to score fragments. The default scorer implementation (QueryScorer) counts how many query terms occur in each fragment. The following fragment from the first document matching our example query would get a score of 3.0.

```
Bright blue fireball in the distance during a rain storm. Not a lightning
storm, no thunder
```

We'll see another type of scorer later in the chapter when we learn about the Postings-Highlighter, which uses a more advanced scoring algorithm.

ENCODING AND FORMATTING

The hl.formatter parameter specifies a formatter that performs the highlighting on each term. The default formatter (hl.formatter=simple) wraps arbitrary text around each term. This approach works well for using HTML tags to highlight query terms. By default, the simple formatter wraps terms in <em> tags. But you can override the default using the hl.simple.pre and hl.simple.post parameters. For example, if you wanted to use cascading style sheets (CSS) to format the highlighted terms, you could add the following parameters to your query:

```
hl.simple.pre=<span class="foo">&
hl.simple.post=</span>
```

Using these parameters would result in highlighted terms of form `<span class="foo">term</span>`. You can then define the style for the `foo` class in a CSS file.

The encoder component encodes special characters before each fragment is passed to a formatter. When generating HTML highlighted fragments, the HTML encoder will escape special characters with HTML character entity references; for example, double-quote (") is encoded as `&quot;`.

9.2.6   *Refining highlighter results*

Now that we've covered the basic process of how Solr determines which snippets to highlight for each document, let's work through additional examples to learn more about how to refine highlighting results.

WORKING WITH FACETS

Recall from chapter 8 that facets allow users to refine their search criteria and explore a dataset. With the UFO dataset, there are three fields that make sense to produce facets for: shape, location, and month. Month was derived from the sighting date specifically to support faceting. Listing 9.4 shows the query to generate facets and highlighting information.

Listing 9.4   Example query with facets and highlighting enabled

```
http://localhost:8983/solr/ufo/select?q=blue fireball in the rain&
    df=sighting_en&
    wt=xml&
    hl=true&                          Enable highlighting.
    hl.snippets=2&                    Generate up to two snippets per document.
    hl.fl=sighting_en&                Highlight the sighting_en field.
    facet=true&                       Enable faceting.
    facet.limit=4&                    Generate up to four categories per facet field.
    facet.field=shape_s&
    facet.field=location_s&           Produce facets for the shape_s, location_s, and month_s fields.
    facet.field=month_s
```

Figure 9.7 shows the top four values for each of these facets, generated using the query in listing 9.4.

From these results, it should be clear that Seattle, WA, is the location with the most frequent sightings, and light is the most frequently reported shape. Consider what happens if the user selects the light option for the shape facet. The results will be filtered to only include sightings that specified light as the shape. The query will include filter query `fq=shape_s:light`; applying facets using filter queries was covered in section 8.6. Our concern here is how this applies to highlighting.

Since the user has provided more information about what they're looking for, it stands to reason that we should incorporate the facet information into the highlighter.

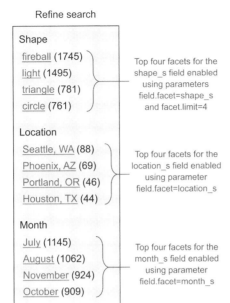

Refine search

Shape

fireball (1745)

light (1495)

triangle (781)

circle (761)

Top four facets for the
shape_s field enabled
using parameters
field.facet=shape_s
and facet.limit=4

Location

Seattle, WA (88)

Phoenix, AZ (69)

Portland, OR (46)

Houston, TX (44)

Top four facets for the
location_s field enabled
using parameter
field.facet=location_s

Month

July (1145)

August (1062)

November (924)

October (909)

Top four facets for the
month_s field enabled
using parameter
field.facet=month_s

**Figure 9.7   Top four shape, location,
and month facet values generated from
the results of our example query,** `blue
fireball in the rain`

Specifically, the highlighter should also consider `light` when selecting the best fragments to display. But when we apply the filter, the highlighter does not incorporate the additional `light` term into the fragment selection or highlighting because the `light` is in a filter query (`fq`) and is not in the `q` part of the query. What we need is a way to control the query terms the highlighter is using without having to change the query we use to match documents.

It is a common use case in Solr for you to want to use a slightly modified query to drive the highlighting, versus what is being used to match documents. Solr supports this using a custom `hl.q` parameter. The following listing shows how to use the `hl.q` parameter to add the term `light` to the query used by the highlighter.

Listing 9.5   Using a parameter to incorporate facet terms into highlighting results

```
http://localhost:8983/solr/ufo/select?q=blue fireball in the rain&
  df=sighting_en&
  wt=xml&
  hl=true&
  hl.snippets=2&
  hl.fl=sighting_en&
  hl.q=blue fireball in the rain light&
  fq=shape_s:light
```

**Also include the facet
term "light" in the
highlighting query.**

**Filter by the light
shape facet.**

Solr returns the following two snippets for the top hit after applying the light facet filter and including `light` in the `hl.q` parameter, which we think is more user-friendly than not including `light` in the highlighted results:

1   and orange as well as **blue light** and what appeared to be a **fireball**. After
that no more **lights** and no more

2 Neon **Blue** Flashes of **light** around Perry Ohio Nuclear Power PLant **light** up night sky and cause power

HIGHLIGHTING PHRASES

The example query we've been working with so far (blue fireball in the rain) is very broad in that it matches all documents that contain blue, fireball, or rain regardless of position. If you enable query debugging (debug=true), you will see that the Lucene query that gets executed (after query text analysis) is

```
sighting_en:blue OR sighting_en:firebal OR sighting_en:rain
```

This query matches 9,706 documents. Now consider a more rigid query for which we only care about sightings in documents in which the exact phrase "blue fireball" occurs. The underlying Lucene query for this is slightly different: sighting_en:"blue firebal" **AND** sighting_en:rain. This query matches two documents because it's very restrictive.

What's important is that Solr correctly highlights occurrences of the phrase "blue fireball", but does not highlight blue or fireball when they're separate terms. For example, the second instance of fireball will not be highlighted in this fictitious snippet:

```
I saw a blue fireball in the sky, it was an awesome fireball.
```

Behind the scenes, the hl.usePhraseHighlighter parameter controls this behavior; it's enabled (true) by default. If you set hl.usePhraseHighlighter=false, Solr may return snippets that have only blue or fireball highlighted. The key takeaway is that Solr behaves correctly when highlighting queries with phrases because the hl.use-PhraseHighlighter parameter is enabled by default in Solr 4.

HIGHLIGHTING MULTIVALUED FIELDS

Solr also handles highlighting in multivalued fields. Imagine that we also had a multi-valued field to capture short descriptions of other objects near the UFO at the time of the sighting. This is completely fictitious and is not part of the UFO sighting data-set, but our example indexing application created one document with the nearby _objects_en field populated with

```
<arr name="nearby_objects_en">
   <str>arc of red fire</str>
   <str>cluster of dark clouds</str>
   <str>thunder and lightning</str>
</arr>
```

The next listing shows a query that matches and highlights the nearby_objects_en field.

Listing 9.6 Query to highlight a multivalued field

```
http://localhost:8983/solr/ufo/select?q=fire cluster clouds thunder&
   df=nearby_objects_en&
   wt=xml&                              ◁─┐  Match and highlight
   hl=true&                               │  on our fictitious
   hl.snippets=2                          │  multivalued field.
```

Based on the query (`fire cluster clouds thunder`), you might expect to see fragments like `fire cluster of dark clouds thunder`, but Solr takes care to not generate snippets that span across distinct values in a multivalued field. Solr correctly produces two highlighted snippets for this query:

- **cluster** of dark **clouds**
- arc of red **fire**

This works because `GapFragmenter` respects the gap Solr places between values based on the `positionIncrementGap` attribute, which is 100 for the `text_en` field type. Also, if you want Solr to highlight all values of the multivalued field, then you can use `hl.preserveMulti=true`, in which case Solr will return all three values for our sample document.

SUMMARY OF HIGHLIGHTING PARAMETERS

Let's summarize what we know about the default Solr highlighter before moving on to learn about Solr's other highlighter implementations. Table 9.3 provides an overview of the parameters supported by the default highlighter, including a few parameters we haven't covered yet; but they're mostly self-explanatory.

Table 9.3 Most common parameters that apply to the default highlighter implementation

Parameter	Description	Default value
`hl`	Set to `true` to enable hit highlighting for your query.	`false`
`hl.snippets`	Maximum number of snippets to generate per field.	`1`
`hl.fl`	List of one or more fields, separated by commas, to generate highlighted snippets for.	<no default> falls back to using `df` field
`hl.fragmenter`	Specify the fragmenter component to use; the fragmenter should be defined in *solrconfig.xml*.	`gap`
`hl.fragsize`	Sets the target length of each fragment; not a strict upper limit.	`100`
`hl.q`	Alternative query to use for highlighting, which gives you the flexibility to highlight different terms than you're using to query (q).	<no default>
`hl.alternateField`	Specify a stored field to display when no snippets can be highlighted for a field.	<no default>
`hl.formatter`	Specify the formatter component to use; the formatter should be defined in *solrconfig.xml*.	`simple`
`hl.simple.pre`	Arbitrary text to be prepended to each highlighted term.	`<em>`

Table 9.3   Most common parameters that apply to the default highlighter implementation *(continued)*

Parameter	Description	Default value
`hl.simple.post`	Arbitrary text to be appended to each highlighted term.	`</em>`
`hl.requireFieldMatch`	When highlighting multiple fields, require a field to match the query in order to be highlighted.	`false`
`hl.maxAnalyzedChars`	Used to restrict the analysis to a maximum number of characters when fragmenting very large fields.	`51200`
`hl.usePhraseHighlighter`	If enabled, Solr will only highlight phrase matches; the individual terms of a phrase will not be highlighted when they occur elsewhere in the text.	`true`
`hl.mergeContiguous`	Set to `true` to have Solr merge adjacent fragments into a single fragment.	`false` (for backwards compatibility)
`hl.highlightMultiTerm`	Set to `true` to enable highlighting for range/wildcard/fuzzy/prefix queries.	`false`
`hl.preserveMulti`	Set to `true` to perform highlighting on all values of a multivalued field and preserve the order of the values.	`false`

FIELD-LEVEL OVERRIDES

You can also use per-field-level overrides for many of the highlighter parameters. For example, imagine a search application that has a `title` and `body` field. Titles are usually short, so only one snippet is required, but you may want to generate up to three snippets for the longer `body` field. To override the default value of `1` for the `body` field only, you can do this: `f.body.hl.snippets=3`. In general, you can apply a field-level override for any parameter by prepending `f.<fieldname>.` to the parameter, such as `f.body.hl.snippets`.

At this point you should have a solid understanding of the default Solr highlighter component and how to refine its behavior using optional parameters. Let's now turn our attention to other Solr highlighter options that were invented to overcome some of the shortcomings of the default highlighter.

9.3   *Improving performance using FastVectorHighlighter*

The most common problem faced with the default highlighter is that it can be too slow to do highlighting on large text fields. The main cause for slowness is the need to reanalyze the original text at query time. This is true for large text fields or when your text analysis is complex. To work around this issue, Solr provides `FastVector-Highlighter`, which can be faster than the default because it skips the analysis step when generating fragments.

> ### Default highlighter performance
>
> It should be mentioned that we were not able to find a case with the UFO sightings dataset where the default highlighter was too slow. Using an informal benchmark of sending thousands of randomly generated queries, the default highlighter was always extremely fast, even when using an unusually large page size of 50. If you have much larger documents or are highlighting many fields, you *could* run into a slowdown. Although we say `FastVectorHighlighter` can help if the default is too slow, this does not imply that the default will be too slow for your data.

The `FastVectorHighlighter` still needs access to term position and offset information to do highlighting, so it relies on using information computed during indexing time. Therefore, to use `FastVectorHighlighter`, any field that needs to be highlighted must be indexed with `termVectors`, `termPositions`, and `termOffsets` enabled. To enable `FastVectorHighlighter` for our `sighting_en` field, we would need to define it as

```
<field name="sighting_en" type="text_en" indexed="true" stored="true"
    termVectors="true" termPositions="true" termOffsets="true" />
```

That seems easy enough; what's the catch? For starters, you need to reindex all documents to apply these settings. But the bigger concern is that these attributes can greatly increase the size of your index. For our small UFO sightings dataset, the index grew from 69 MB to 109 MB. The increase in index size doesn't matter for small datasets, but at large scale, this growth may be a concern. Storing term vectors, positions, and offsets also slows down indexing (slightly), which may be a concern in high-throughput environments needing near real-time search.

To use `FastVectorHighlighter`, you need to reindex all documents. For this example, all you need do is add the new field definition (see previous section) for `sighting_en` to *schema.xml*, restart your Solr server, and rerun the `IndexUfoSightings` application using

```
java -jar solr-in-action.jar ufo -jsonInput
    ➥ FULL_PATH_TO_UFO_SIGHTINGS_DIR/ufo_awesome.json
```

To activate `FastVectorHighlighter`, you need to pass `hl.useFastVectorHighlighter` `=true` in your request as shown in the next listing.

Listing 9.7   Enable `FastVectorHighlighter`

```
http://localhost:8983/solr/ufo/select?q=blue fireball in the rain&
  df=sighting_en&
  wt=xml&
  hl=true&                                          Must explicitly enable
  hl.snippets=2&                                    FastVectorHighlighter.
  hl.useFastVectorHighlighter=true    ◁─────
```

The highlighting results between `FastVectorHighlighter` and the default highlighter are comparable. In terms of performance, you will only notice an improvement if your text analysis is complex or you're highlighting large text fields. Unfortunately, the UFO dataset does not provide enough complexity to see the performance benefits of `FastVectorHighlighter`. We introduced it here so you're aware of alternatives if the default highlighter causes performance issues for your application.

9.4   *PostingsHighlighter*

Before we wrap up this chapter, we want to introduce Solr's newest highlighter implementation, `PostingsHighlighter`, which promises to be faster than the default without needing the term vector overhead of `FastVectorHighlighter`. `Postings-Highlighter` gets its name because it relies on term offsets stored with the postings information in the inverted index. In contrast to `FastVectorHighlighter`, which requires a separate data structure in the index to retrieve term positions and offsets, `PostingsHighlighter` accesses the same information directly from the postings list, which is a new capability in Lucene 4. Recall from our introduction of Lucene's inverted index that a postings list contains a list of documents where a term occurs along with the term frequency in each document. As of Lucene 4.0, you also have the option to store term positions and offsets in the postings list.

To use `PostingsHighlighter`, fields must be indexed with `storeOffsetsWith-Positions="true"`. For our example, we need to add the `sighting_en` field definition in *schema.xml*:

```
<field name="sighting_en" type="text_en" indexed="true" stored="true"
    storeOffsetsWithPositions="true" />
```

Previously, we relied on the _en suffix on the name to apply a dynamic field. But because we need to add the `storeOffsetsWithPositions` parameter, we need to explicitly define the `sighting_en` field in *schema.xml*. After adding the field definition, you will need to restart Solr and reindex all documents. Recall from section 9.3 that enabling term vectors, positions, and offsets for the `FastVectorHighlighter` expanded the index from 69 MB to 109 MB. In contrast, enabling offsets and positions in the postings list only expands the index from 69 MB to 85 MB, which can be a significant difference for large indexes.

Unlike `FastVectorHighlighter`, you also need to configure the `Postings-Highlighter` component in *solrconfig.xml* using the XML definition shown in listing 9.8.

Listing 9.8   Configure `PostingsHighlighter` in *solrconfig.xml*

Override the default "highlight" component.

```
<searchComponent class="solr.HighlightComponent" name="highlight">
    <highlighting class="org.apache.solr.highlight.PostingsSolrHighlighter"
        preTag="&lt;b&gt;"
        postTag="&lt;/b&gt;"
        ellipsis="... "
        maxLength="10000"/>
</searchComponent>
```

Use Postings-Highlighter.

Separate highlighted snippets with an ellipsis.

Append </b> to highlighted terms.

Prepend <b> to highlighted terms.

Note that you must add the XML definition in listing 9.8 after the existing highlighter or remove the default highlighter from *solrconfig.xml*. After applying the configuration changes, re-execute listing 9.2 using the `http` utility to see `Postings-Highlighter` in action:

```
java -jar solr-in-action.jar listing 9.2
```

The highlighted snippets returned from `PostingsHighlighter` are similar to the default highlighter, with the first document having this snippet:

```
Bright blue fireball in the distance during a rain storm.
```

Notice that the additional terms returned by the default highlighter (`Not a lightning storm, no thunder`) are not returned by `PostingsHighlighter`. Behind the scenes, `PostingsHighlighter` uses a sentence-aware approach to fragmenting based on Java's `BreakIterator` class (see `java.text.BreakIterator`). For the second document in the results set for listing 9.2, `PostingsHighlighter` returns

```
Brilliant blue oblong object zooms horizontally across southern sky at 2 in
the morning. ... Rain had been thundering on the glass ceiling, but suddenly
I woke up realizing the rain had stopped and there was complete silence (I
sleep with windows open.)
```

Unlike the other highlighters, `PostingsHighlighter` returns all snippets in one continuous string separated by an ellipsis (…).

In addition to the benefits of speed and reduced indexing overhead, `Postings-Highlighter` uses a more advanced similarity calculation, called BM25, for scoring fragments. In contrast to the default scorer, which counts the frequency of query terms in each fragment, BM25 is a state-of-the-art tf-idf scoring function for calculating the similarity between a document or fragment and a query.[3] The BM25 scorer gives a natural boost to fragments containing terms that occur less frequently in the index. We see evidence of this in the results for the second document where `rain` stands out because it's a less frequent term in the index than `blue` or `fireball`, so it's given more weight by BM25 scoring.

The primary drawback of `PostingsHighlighter` is that it requires accurate term offsets to be set on terms during indexing. Let's use the Solr Analysis form we worked with in chapter 6 to see how term offsets are calculated during text analysis. Figure 9.8 shows term offsets calculated during analysis of the example sighting we've been working with throughout this chapter.

From figure 9.8, you can see that the `StandardTokenizer` used by the `text_en` field calculates the start and end offset positions for terms. For instance, `fireball` starts at position 12 and ends at position 20, using zero-based positional counting. Unfortunately, there are some tokenizers and token filters that do not accurately

---

[3] The mathematics behind BM25 are beyond the scope of this book, so we'll refer you to the Wikipedia page for BM25; see http://en.wikipedia.org/wiki/Okapi_BM25.

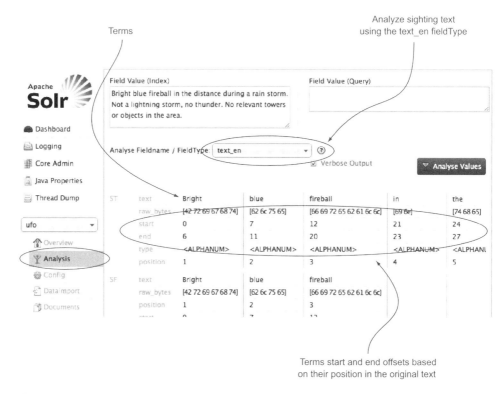

Figure 9.8   Screenshot of the Analysis form showing term start and end offsets calculated during text analysis

report term offsets.[4] Consequently, depending on your text analysis requirements, you may not be able to use PostingsHighlighter.

9.5   *Summary*

In this chapter, we implemented the foundation for a search application for finding UFO sightings. Specifically, we designed a client application to preprocess and index UFO sightings from the public dataset provided by Infochimps. Once indexed, we learned how to display short snippets with query terms highlighted. The snippets were generated dynamically based on their similarity to the query using a built-in search component called a highlighter. Selecting the best snippet to display for each search result makes up the core functionality of a highlighter.

Part of what makes Solr's hit highlighting confusing to new users is that there are many optional parameters. In this chapter, we focused on the most common uses of highlighting and saw how to apply some of the optional parameters to refine highlighting

---

[4] For an up-to-date list of problematic token filters, refer to https://issues.apache.org/jira/browse/LUCENE-4641.

results. We also covered the three highlighter implementations provided by Solr: the default, `FastVectorHighlighter`, and `PostingsHighlighter`.

The default highlighter is easy to use and provides fast results for our UFO dataset. For large text fields, the default highlighter may be too slow, in which case you can use `FastVectorHighlighter`. The performance gains afforded by `FastVector-Highlighter` come at the cost of increasing the size of your index. The newest highlighter is `PostingsHighlighter`, which is more efficient than the default and does not increase the size of your index as much as `FastVectorHighlighter`. Consequently, we recommend that you experiment with `PostingsHighlighter`, in particular, if you need to highlight large text fields. The main drawback to using `PostingsHighlighter` is that it's not compatible with all text analyzers, including `WordDelimiterFilter`, which we used in chapter 6.

In the next chapter, you'll learn about another core function provided by Solr: making suggestions as users type queries into a search box.

Query suggestions

In this chapter, we introduce two simple features to help improve the usability of your search solution. Specifically, we cover spell-checking and autosuggest. *Spell-checking* addresses the problem of misspelled query terms, leading to poor search results. You've probably seen an incarnation of spell-checking when using your favorite web search engine and it asks, *Did you mean …?* Spell-checking is a crucial feature for helping users who don't take the time to craft perfect queries, especially in mobile environments.

Autosuggest helps users as they type by providing instant suggestions from terms in your index; it allows users to quickly hone in on query terms as they formulate their query. Autosuggest gives immediate feedback to users by showing valid query terms available in the index as they type. Let's begin by learning how Solr's spell-check search component works, as that provides the foundation for autosuggest.

10.1 Spell-check

In this section, you'll learn how to use Solr's spell-check search component. Automated spell-checking is a core search feature that most users expect to just work without having to think. When it comes to spell-checking, there are four general scenarios you need to consider:

1 Query contains one or more misspelled terms leading to no relevant hits; if a suggestion is available, your search client should autoexecute the suggested term and show the user an informational message such as: *Searched for atmosphere instead of atmosphear.*

2 Query contains a rare term resulting in a few hits; suggestions are available and have more hits, so you may want to prompt the user with *Did you mean ... ?*

3 Query contains a correctly spelled term; suggestions are available, but they have fewer or about the same hits as the query term. In this case, your search solution should not prompt the user with any alternate decision.

4 Query contains a term that does not exist in your index; suggestions are not available.

From these four scenarios, we can derive two key requirements of a spell-checking solution. First, we need a way to identify suggested terms for each term in our query; that is, some sort of dictionary to look up terms that are similar to terms entered by users. Second, we need to know how many documents each suggested term matches, as that will help us decide if and how to prompt the user. We'll see how Solr addresses each of these requirements ahead.

To illustrate the concepts in this chapter, we'll build a search index to support an online encyclopedia similar to Wikipedia. In fact, we'll use a small sample of English-language articles from Wikipedia to populate our index. The Wikipedia data provides a variety of topics from which to make suggestions, and it's high-quality, curated content, so we can be confident about the quality of our suggestions. Specifically, we selected 13,000 articles at random from a recent XML dump provided by Wikipedia.[1] We provide a small sample because the full dump is over 40 GB and takes several hours to download, extract, and index.

10.1.1 Indexing Wikipedia articles

Our first task is to import articles from Wikipedia into Solr. To simplify the process, we preconfigured a Solr core named `solrpedia`, which is defined in `$SOLR_IN_ACTION/example-docs/ch10/cores/solrpedia/`. To get this core (as well as this chapter's other example cores) set up, you can execute the following commands:

```
cd $SOLR_IN_ACTION/example-docs/
cp -r ch10/cores/ $SOLR_INSTALL/example/solr/
```

---

[1] Index of /enwiki/latest/, http://dumps.wikimedia.org/enwiki/latest/.

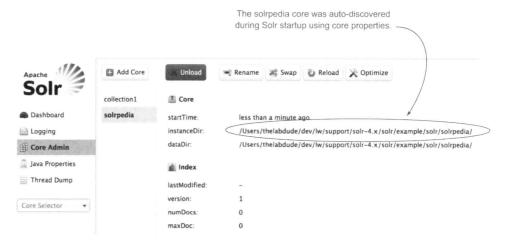

Figure 10.1   **Verify the preconfigured `solrpedia` core is available in the Solr administration console.**

Be sure to start the example Solr server on your local workstation (or stop and restart it if it is already running):

```
cd $SOLR_INSTALL/example/
java -jar start.jar
```

Next, verify the `solrpedia` core is available in the Solr administration console as shown in figure 10.1.

We preconfigured the `solrpedia` core to import articles from a Wikipedia XML data dump file using Solr's Data Import Handler (DIH) framework. As our focus in this chapter is on spell-checking and autosuggest, we'll cover how to kick off an import from our predefined DIH configuration for use in this chapter. If you want to understand how to configure the DIH for importing Wikipedia documents, see appendix C.

Before you can run the data importer, you need to copy the *SOLR_IN_ACTION/ example-docs/ch10/documents/solrpedia.xml* file to *$SOLR_INSTALL/example/* so that the DIH can locate the XML document to import. You can open the *solrpedia.xml* file in any text editor if you're curious what the data looks like before it's imported.

After copying the *solrpedia.xml* file, you're ready to run the data import process to build the `solrpedia` index. Reload the administration console and select the Dataimport page under the `solrpedia` core. Fill out the form and click the Execute button as shown in figure 10.2.

You should have 13,000 documents in the `solrpedia` index. To verify, you can execute the match all documents query (`*:*`) using the Query form as we've done throughout this book. Now that we have data, let's see Solr spell-checking in action.

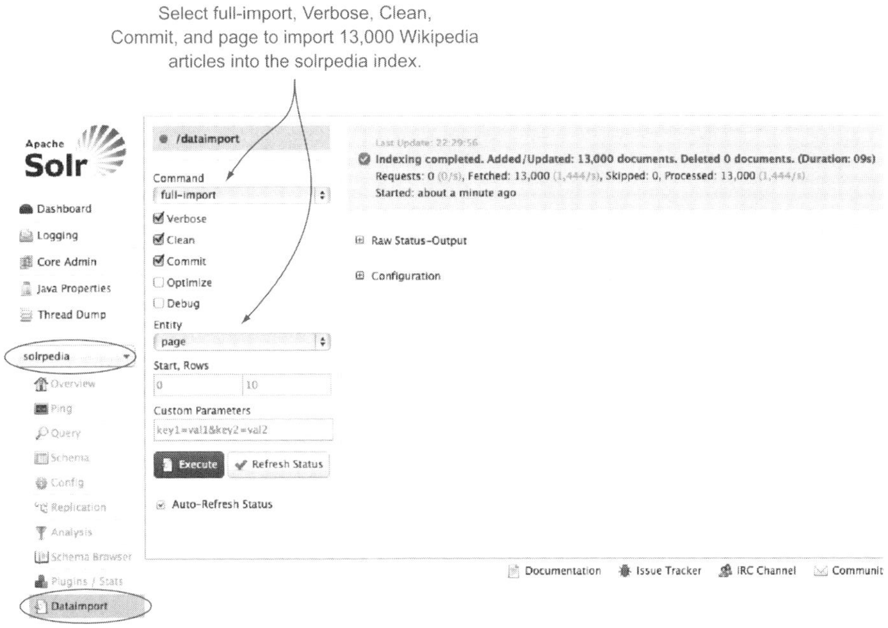

Select full-import, Verbose, Clean,
Commit, and page to import 13,000 Wikipedia
articles into the solrpedia index.

Figure 10.2 Import articles from *solrpedia.xml* into the `solrpedia` core using the Dataimport page.

10.1.2 *Spell-check example*

You can use the `http` command-line utility for executing code listings to query Solr with the misspelled term `atmosphear`, as seen in this listing.

Listing 10.1 Query Solr with a misspelled query term "`atmosphear`"

Query

```
http://localhost:8983/solr/solrpedia/select?q=atmosphear    ⟵┤ Query with
                                                               misspelled term.
```

Response

```
<response>
  <lst name="responseHeader">...</lst>
  <result name="response" numFound="0" start="0"></result>    ⟵┐ Response found
  <lst name="spellcheck">                                       │ 0 documents.
    <lst name="suggestions">
      <lst name="atmosphear">
        <int name="numFound">1</int>
        ...
        <arr name="suggestion">
          <str>atmosphere</str>                      ⟵┐ Spell-check component
        </arr>                                         │ suggests "atmosphere."
      </lst>
      <lst name="collation">
        <str name="collationQuery">atmosphere</str>     ⟵┐ Suggested term has
        <int name="hits">86</int>                        │ 86 hits in the corpus.
```

```
        <lst name="misspellingsAndCorrections">
          <str name="atmosphear">atmosphere</str>
        </lst>
      </lst>
    </lst>
  </lst>
</response>
```

Recall that you can execute the query using `java -jar solr-in-action.jar`
listing 10.1. Notice that the response suggests `"atmosphere"` as a replacement
term for the misspelled query term `atmosphear`. The response also includes a collation section that indicates how many documents the suggested term occurs in,
which in this case is 86. Your search client can process the suggestion information
to determine that this result matches the first case we discussed. Consequently, you
can automatically execute `collationQuery` behind the scenes and present the user
with an informational message stating *Searched for atmosphere instead of atmosphear*.
You could prompt the user with *Did you mean atmosphere?*; but since there are no
hits for the user's original query and many hits for `collationQuery`, you're safe to
assume the user did mean *atmosphere*, and execute `collationQuery` automatically
behind the scenes.

Now try searching article titles for `anaconda` and notice that Solr was not able to
find any documents or come up with a suggestion, as shown next.

Listing 10.2   Searching the title field for a term that doesn't exist

Query
```
http://localhost:8983/solr/solrpedia/select?q=title:anaconda
```

Response
```
<response>
  <lst name="responseHeader">...</lst>
  <result name="response" numFound="0" start="0"></result>
  <lst name="spellcheck">
    <lst name="suggestions"/>                          ⊣    No suggestions
  </lst>                                                     found for anaconda.
</response>
```

The response illustrates the expected behavior when a user searches for a term that
does not exist in the index. In this case, no documents are found, and Solr is not able
to make an intelligent suggestion. The `spellcheck` component uses the terms in your
index to make suggestions; you'll learn more about this in the next section. The best
thing you can do in this case is to analyze your log files for frequent examples that
result in no hits or suggestions, and add them to an external dictionary.

Let's see an example in which suggestions shouldn't be applied. The next listing
shows the results from searching for `Julius`, which is a correct spelling, but Solr still
returns some suggestions.

Listing 10.3   Query illustrating the case of when to ignore Solr's suggestions

Query

```
http://localhost:8983/solr/solrpedia/select?q=Julius&
  df=suggest&
  fl=title
```

> Use the suggest field as the default search field.

> Only return the title to keep results short for this example.

Response

```
<response>
<lst name="responseHeader">...</lst>
<result name="response" numFound="4" start="0">
  <doc><str name="title">Julius Wegscheider</str></doc>
  ...
</result>
<lst name="spellcheck">
  <lst name="suggestions">
    <lst name="julius">
      <int name="numFound">2</int> ...
      <arr name="suggestion">
        <str>justus</str>
        <str>julian</str>
      </arr>
    </lst>
    <lst name="collation">
      <str name="collationQuery">justus</str>
      <int name="hits">2</int>
      ...
    </lst>
    ...
  </lst>
</lst>
</response>
```

> Found four documents matching Julius.

> Found two suggestions, justus and julian.

> Suggested term justus only found in two documents.

Solr found results for our query term and also suggestions. Notice that the number of results for the query term `Julius` exceeds the number of results for the suggestions. Specifically, `Julius` matched four documents, and `justus` matched two. In this case, it's probably not a good idea to display *Did you mean justus?* because it's less frequent than `Julius`. The key takeaway is that your client application needs to decide when it makes sense to present the *Did you mean ...?* prompt to your users. In most cases, if the query term provides more or about the same number of results as the suggested term(s), you probably do not need to show the prompt. Now that you've had a chance to see Solr's spell-checking in action, let's dig into the details of how it works.

10.1.3 *Spell-check search component*

One important thing to notice about the query requests in listings 10.1–10.3 is that they are processed by the normal `/select` request handler we discussed in chapter 4. Also notice that there are no parameters in the query that have anything to do with spell-checking, yet we are clearly getting spell-checking support in the response. The `spellcheck` component is already integrated into the default `/select` request handler defined in *solrconfig.xml*, as shown in the next listing; refer to section 7.1 if you need a refresher on search request handlers and components.

Listing 10.4   Integrate spell-check support into the `/select` request handler

```
<requestHandler name="/select" class="solr.SearchHandler">
  <lst name="defaults">
    <str name="echoParams">explicit</str>
    <int name="rows">10</int>
    <str name="df">text</str>

    <str name="spellcheck">on</str>
    <str name="spellcheck.extendedResults">false</str>
    <str name="spellcheck.count">5</str>
    <str name="spellcheck.alternativeTermCount">2</str>
    <str name="spellcheck.maxResultsForSuggest">5</str>
    <str name="spellcheck.collate">true</str>
    <str name="spellcheck.collateExtendedResults">true</str>
    <str name="spellcheck.maxCollationTries">5</str>
    <str name="spellcheck.maxCollations">3</str>
  </lst>
  <arr name="last-components">
    <str>spellcheck</str>
  </arr>
</requestHandler>
```

Configuration of the /select request handler in solrconfig.xml.

Enable spell-checking by default.

Fine-tune spell-check behavior; see table 10.1.

Run the spellcheck component last.

In a nutshell, this approach builds spell-checking support into the /select request handler because it's a core feature we want enabled for all queries by default. In addition, it alleviates the need for your client application to pass all the spell-check parameters in every query. If a specific query does not want spell-checking enabled, it can be disabled by passing spellcheck=false. Also, it makes sense to apply the spellcheck component as a last step because we still want the default search components, such as query, facet, and debug, to execute during query processing. If you enable collation using spellcheck.collate=true, as we've done here, spellcheck must be listed as a last component because generating the collation query requires the query component to have already executed. In general, we recommend configuring spell-check as a last component in your request handler.

Table 10.1 provides a summary of the available spell-check parameters you can specify when integrating spell-checking into a request handler.

Table 10.1   Overview of spell-check parameters

Spell-check parameter	Description
spellcheck	Used to enable (true) or disable (false) spell-checking for a query request.
spellcheck.q	Specifies the query to spell-check; Solr applies spell-checking to the q parameter if this parameter is not provided.
spellcheck.build	If true, instructs Solr to build the spell-check dictionary if it does not exist; this option is not needed for the DirectSolrSpellChecker because the dictionary is based on the main index.

Table 10.1 Overview of spell-check parameters *(continued)*

Spell-check parameter	Description
spellcheck.reload	If true, causes Solr to reload the spell-checker implementation; this has no effect on the DirectSolrSpellChecker, as it is always up to date.
spellcheck.count	Specifies the maximum number (integer) of suggestions to provide.
spellcheck.dictionary	Sets the name of the dictionary to use to create suggestions, such as default; you can activate multiple spell-checkers in one request by including this parameter for each dictionary (see listing 10.8 for an example).
spellcheck.onlyMorePopular	If true, restricts suggested queries to only those that match more documents than the original query.
spellcheck.maxResultsForSuggest	Sets a threshold (integer) on the number of results matched for a query before Solr attempts to create suggestions; this allows you to avoid paying the cost of suggestions for queries that match a sufficient number of documents. If you set this to 10 and a query matches 12 documents, suggestions will be disabled.
spellcheck.accuracy	Float value between 0 and 1 to determine if a suggestion is valid; larger values indicate more accuracy but can result in fewer suggestions.
spellcheck.extendedResults	Requests additional information about the suggested terms, such as term document frequency.
spellcheck.collate	If true, requests Solr to generate an alternative query based on the suggested spelling corrections; your client application can execute the collate query if the user clicks the *Did you mean …?* link. Collation queries are guaranteed to return some results, which implies that Solr must execute the collation query in the background before returning results.
spellcheck.maxCollations	Limits the number (integer) of collation queries Solr will generate.
spellcheck.maxCollationTries	Maximum number (integer) of collation attempts; lower values provide better performance at the cost of not providing suggestions in all cases.

As seen in the previous listing, the spellcheck search component is integrated into the /select request handler as a last component. To reiterate what we covered in section 4.2.4, a last component runs after the built-in core components: query, facet, and so forth (see figure 4.5). Listing 10.5 shows the configuration of the spellcheck search component from *solrconfig.xml*.

Listing 10.5 Configure the `spellcheck` search component in *solrconfig.xml*

Build a
dictionary of
terms from
the suggest
field.

Use the
main index
to generate
suggestions.

Field type defined
in schema.xml to
analyze query terms.

Use Levenshtein
string distance
to find similar
terms.

Accuracy of
suggestions; value
between 0 and 1.

Additional
spell-checker
implementation
named
"wordbreak."

```
<searchComponent name="spellcheck" class="solr.SpellCheckComponent">
  <str name="queryAnalyzerFieldType">text_suggest</str>

  <lst name="spellchecker">
    <str name="name">default</str>
    <str name="field">suggest</str>
    <str name="classname">solr.DirectSolrSpellChecker</str>
    <str name="distanceMeasure">internal</str>
    <float name="accuracy">0.5</float>
    ...
  </lst>

  <lst name="spellchecker">
    <str name="name">wordbreak</str>
    <str name="classname">solr.WordBreakSolrSpellChecker</str>
    <str name="field">suggest</str>
    <str name="combineWords">true</str>
    <str name="breakWords">true</str>
    <int name="maxChanges">10</int>
    <int name="minBreakLength">5</int>
  </lst>
  ...
</searchComponent>
```

At a high level, the configuration settings you see in the listing configure the `spellcheck` component to base its suggestions off of terms in the `suggest` field of our main index. Let's break this configuration down into manageable parts, starting with `DirectSolrSpellChecker`.

DIRECTSOLRSPELLCHECKER

The default spell-checker implementation in Solr 4 is `DirectSolrSpellChecker`. This component gets its name because it provides suggestions directly from the main index. In previous versions of Solr, you needed to build a separate spell-check index based on the main index. Basing suggestions off the main index is preferred over maintaining a secondary index because you do not need to rebuild any secondary index after your main index changes, as was the case in previous versions.

 `DirectSolrSpellChecker` supports a number of parameters to let you fine-tune its behavior. The three most important parameters are `field`, `distanceMeasure`, and `accuracy`. The `field` parameter identifies the field in your index to use for suggestions. In our example, we use the `suggest` field, which is defined in *schema.xml* as

```
<field name="suggest" type="text_suggest" indexed="true" stored="false"/>
```

The `suggest` field is populated from the `title` field using the `<copyField>` directive:

```
<copyField source="title" dest="suggest"/>
```

Using a copy field allows us to apply different text analysis strategies to the `title` field in our Wikipedia articles. You could additionally pull terms from other fields, such as the `article` text field, to add more terms to your spell-checking dictionary. We'll leave it as an exercise for the reader to add terms from the text field to the suggest field.

The `distanceMeasure` parameter tells Solr how to determine suggestions for query terms. While an in-depth discussion of how spell-checking identifies terms in a dictionary is beyond the scope of this text, the intuition behind the process is quite simple. A spell-checker uses some function to compute the string distance (edit distance) between a query term and each term in a dictionary, as we discussed in chapters 3 and 7 when we covered fuzzy searching. One way to think about *distance* between two terms is by considering how many changes you have to make to one of the terms to change it to the other term. For example, the distance between `atmosphear` and `atmosphere` is 2: one change to remove the `a` and another to add an `e` on the end. A well-known algorithm for calculating the string distance between two terms is the *Levenshtein distance*;[2] setting `distanceMeasure` to `internal` uses the Levenshtein distance algorithm.

The `accuracy` parameter is a floating value between `0` and `1` that determines how accurate the suggestions need to be. The higher the number, the more accurate the suggestions will be, but you will also have more misses, cases for which no suggestions are available. If you set `accuracy` too low, Solr will generate more suggestions but they may not always make sense to your users.

Next, let's look at the `queryAnalyzerFieldType` setting, which identifies the field type used to analyze query terms and create suggestions.

TEXT ANALYSIS FOR SPELL-CHECKING

Think about the type of text analysis you should perform on terms you want in the spell-checker dictionary. For the most part, you want the text analysis to be fairly minimal, specifically avoiding filters that make drastic changes to terms, such as stemming or phonetic analysis. As you can see from the following listing, we are using the `text_suggest` field type defined in *schema.xml*. The listing shows the relevant portions of the `text_suggest` field type.

> **Listing 10.6** `text_suggest` **field type for analyzing terms for spell-checking**

```
<fieldType name="text_suggest" class="solr.TextField"
           positionIncrementGap="100">
  <analyzer>
    <tokenizer class="solr.UAX29URLEmailTokenizerFactory"/>
    <filter class="solr.StopFilterFactory" ignoreCase="true"
            words="stopwords.txt"/>
    <filter class="solr.LowerCaseFilterFactory"/>
    <filter class="solr.ASCIIFoldingFilterFactory"/>
    <filter class="solr.EnglishPossessiveFilterFactory"/>
  </analyzer>
</fieldType>
```

---

[2] "Levenshtein distance," http://en.wikipedia.org/wiki/Levenshtein_distance.

If you worked through chapter 6, then this definition should be self-explanatory. Effectively, this field type splits text on whitespace and punctuation, while preserving URLs and email addresses (UAX29URLEmailTokenizer), removing stop words (Stop-Filter), lowercasing terms (LowerCaseFilter), folding Latin characters into their ASCII equivalents (ASCIIFoldingFilter), and removing English possessives (English-PossessiveFilter). All of these are considered safe transformations from a spell-checking perspective. Also, we apply the same analysis during indexing and queries. For our example query in listing 10.1, the query Julius becomes julius. The ASCII-FoldingFilter is useful for providing suggestions to users who enter query terms that should contain accented characters, such as jalapeño, as it's rare for users to type the accented form when constructing a query.

Recall that DirectSolrSpellChecker is configured to use the suggest field to build its dictionary (listing 10.5), and as you might have guessed, suggest also uses the text_suggest field type. In general, you need to analyze query terms for spell-checking using the same analysis strategy that was used to build the spell-checker dictionary. This ensures that the spell-checker is working with compatible analysis schemes between the dictionary and the query terms.

ADDITIONAL SPELL-CHECK IMPLEMENTATIONS

One of the powerful features of Solr spell-checking is that you can chain together multiple spell-check implementations to create a composite spell-checker. For instance, in listing 10.5, we see that WordBreakSolrSpellchecker is configured as an additional spell-checker implementation. The WordBreakSolrSpellchecker finds suggestions by breaking query terms into multiple parts or by combining query terms. Consider a misspelled query such as northatlantic curent, for which the user is intending to find topics related to the North Atlantic Current. The default spell-checker we've been working with so far will have no trouble producing a valid suggestion for curent, but it comes up short on northatlantic, as seen in this listing.

Listing 10.7   Default spell-checker has trouble with terms that should be broken apart

Query
```
http://localhost:8983/solr/solrpedia/select?
  q=northatlantic curent&df=suggest&wt=xml
```

Response
```
<response>
  <lst name="responseHeader">...</lst>
  <result name="response" numFound="0" start="0"></result>
  <lst name="spellcheck">
    <lst name="suggestions">
      <lst name="current">
        ...
        <arr name="suggestion">
          <str>current</str>
          <str>cent</str>
        </arr>
      </lst>
```

Spellchecker found suggestions for "curent", but nothing for "northatlantic".

```
    <lst name="collation">
      <str name="collationQuery">northatlantic current</str>
      <int name="hits">1</int>
      <lst name="misspellingsAndCorrections">
        <str name="curent">current</str>
      </lst>
    </lst>
    ...
  </lst>
  </lst>
</response>
```

What we need is for Solr to recognize that `northatlantic` is actually two terms, and our user didn't put a space between them. In general, misplacing a space between query terms is a common user error, so you should plan to correct for it in your spell-checking solution. `WordBreakSolrSpellchecker` is able to come up with the correct suggestion by splitting the query term into multiple terms, then looking up the split terms in the index. The following listing shows an example of `WordBreakSolrSpellchecker` in action.

Listing 10.8 Query request that invokes `wordbreak` and default `spellcheckers`

Query
```
http://localhost:8983/solr/solrpedia/select?
  q=northatlantic curent&
  wt=xml&df=suggest&q.op=AND&
  spellcheck.dictionary=wordbreak&
  spellcheck.dictionary=default
```
> Activate the wordbreak spellchecker.
> Activate the default spellchecker.

Response
```
<response>
...
<result name="response" numFound="0" start="0"></result>
<lst name="spellcheck">
  ...
  <lst name="collation">
    <str name="collationQuery">(north atlantic)
      current</str>
    ...
  </lst>
</lst>
</response>
```
> Both spell-checkers working together found the best suggestion.

The listing illustrates how using the `default` and `wordbreak` spell-checkers together in the same request results in an accurate suggestion being created for a poorly formed query. In this case, your search client can execute the `collationQuery` behind the scenes without prompting the user and then show the user *Searched for north atlantic current instead.* The key takeaway here is that Solr provides great flexibility in how you generate suggestions by allowing you to combine multiple spell-checker implementations into a unified solution.

Now that you are familiar with Solr's spell-checker, let's move on to autosuggest, which uses many of the same techniques as spell-checking.

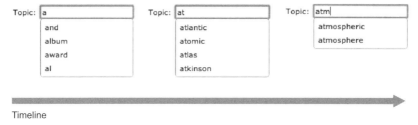

Timeline

Figure 10.3   Timeline of type-ahead suggestions from the solrpedia index

10.2   Autosuggesting query terms

Spell-checking is a nice feature to have, but you can also go a long way to preventing spelling errors in the first place by suggesting query terms as users type. Autosuggest is especially helpful in mobile environments where "fat-finger" style errors are common. In this section, we focus on the Suggester that is built into Solr 4.

Before we get into details of how Solr's Suggester works, it helps to think about how autosuggest should work in the abstract. The UI is quite simple—a list of suggestions is presented to the user as they type. Each additional character changes the suggestion list as depicted in figure 10.3.

In general, we need the autosuggest feature to satisfy two main requirements:

- It must be fast; there are few things that are more annoying than a clunky type-ahead solution that cannot keep up with users as they type. The Suggester must be able to update the suggestions as the user types each character, so milliseconds matter.

- It should return ranked suggestions ordered by term frequency, as there is little benefit to suggesting rare terms that occur in only a few documents in your index, especially when the user has typed only a few characters.

With this basic conceptual understanding of autosuggest, let's see how it works in Solr, starting with a custom request handler specifically designed to support autosuggest.

10.2.1   Autosuggest request handler

In this section, we'll work through the process of building an autosuggest solution for `solrpedia` using the built-in Solr Suggester. To begin, we need to define a specific request handler for generating suggestions. In the previous section, we integrated spell-checking into the default `/select` request handler. It turns out that design approach is not the best way to handle autosuggest. For one thing, we don't need the spell-checking support we added to the `/select` handler. In addition, we don't need any of the built-in components, such as `query`, `facets`, and `highlighting`. Solr is specifically designed for you to define custom request handlers to encapsulate complex behavior behind a simple interface, as is done in object-oriented programming. The next listing shows the definition of our custom request handler to support autosuggest.

Listing 10.9   Define the /suggest request handler in *solrconfig.xml*

```
<requestHandler name="/suggest"                                    ⊲── Custom
    class="org.apache.solr.handler.component.SearchHandler">          request
  <lst name="defaults">                                                handler for
    <str name="echoParams">none</str>                                  autosuggest
    <str name="wt">json</str>                                          only.
    <str name="indent">false</str>
    <str name="spellcheck">true</str>
    <str name="spellcheck.dictionary">suggestDictionary</str>    ⊲── Identify the
    <str name="spellcheck.onlyMorePopular">true</str>                dictionary to
    <str name="spellcheck.count">5</str>                             use for
    <str name="spellcheck.collate">false</str>                       suggestions.
  </lst>                                       Override the built-in
  <arr name="components">                      component pipeline.
    <str>suggest</str>                ⊲──
  </arr>                                    Execute the suggest
</requestHandler>                            component.
```

One thing that should stand out about the definition in the listing is that it overrides the search component definition to only include the suggest search component. It replaces the default component stack (query, facet, debug, etc.) with a single search component named suggest. Remember that the main requirement of autosuggest is fast performance, so we don't want to pay the expense of executing any other search component in our /suggest handler.

To receive suggestions, a client application must send requests to /suggest; the following listing shows an example of the /suggest request handler in action.

Listing 10.10   Example of /suggest request handler in action

Query
```
http://localhost:8983/solr/solrpedia/suggest?q=atm       ⊲── Send atm prefix to
                                                             /suggest request
```
Response   handler.
```
{
  "responseHeader":{...},
  "spellcheck":{
    "suggestions":[
      "atm",{ "numFound":2,
        ...
        "suggestion":["atmosphere", "atmospheric"]    ⊲── Suggestions from
      }                                                   the suggest field in
    ]                                                      the solrpedia index.
  }
}
```

Now let's see how the suggest search component used by the /suggest request handler works.

10.2.2 *Autosuggest search component*

When the /suggest handler receives a request, it invokes the suggest search component to make the suggestions. The following listing shows the configuration of the suggest search component from *solrconfig.xml*.

Listing 10.11   Suggest search component definition from *solrconfig.xml*

Name the Suggester dictionary.

Lookup implementation class.

Built on top of the spell-checking framework.

Based on the suggest field.

Rebuild the lookup data structure after every commit.

```
<searchComponent class="solr.SpellCheckComponent" name="suggest">
  <lst name="spellchecker">
    <str name="name">suggestDictionary</str>
    <str name="classname">org.apache.solr.spelling.suggest.Suggester</str>
    <str name="lookupImpl">org.apache.solr.spelling.suggest.fst
      .FSTLookupFactory</str>
    <str name="field">suggest</str>
    <float name="threshold">0.</float>
    <str name="buildOnCommit">true</str>
  </lst>
</searchComponent>
```

There's a key difference between spell-checking and autosuggest. Spell-checking has a complete query term from which to generate suggestions; autosuggest only has a prefix. As you learned in the previous section, spell-checking uses a string distance function, such as Levenshtein, to find terms similar to a query term. Autosuggest doesn't have a complete term to work from, so string distance provides little value.

The naïve approach to autosuggest would be to apply a wildcard search as the user types. Unfortunately, wildcard searches can be too slow for autosuggest, so a different approach is needed. The built-in Suggester uses a prefix tree data structure, which supports extremely fast lookups using a prefix, which is exactly what is needed for type-ahead suggestions.

The main intuition behind the lookup structure in Solr is that it is efficient for finding terms by prefix, so when the user types at, for example, Solr can quickly home in on terms that start with at. In a large index, there can be many terms matching a prefix, so we also need a way to sort the suggestions by popularity, as we don't want low-frequency, rare terms polluting our suggestion lists. Think of it in terms of doing the most good for the most users; if a term only occurs in a few documents out of millions, it's probably not a good suggestion.

In listing 10.11, we're using the org.apache.solr.spelling.suggest.fst.FST-Lookup class, which uses a data structure based on finite state automaton (FST) to provide fast, constant-time lookups regardless of prefix length. The FSTLookupFactory implementation is slower to build but requires a smaller memory footprint, which makes it a good choice for large-term dictionaries.

The suggestion dictionary must be rebuilt to incorporate new terms as new documents are indexed. In our configuration, we chose to rebuild the dictionary after every commit (buildOnCommit=true). The dictionary is held in memory and builds quickly, so it's not usually a source of performance issues.

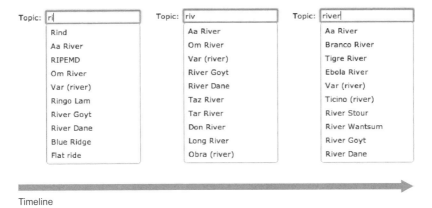

Timeline

Figure 10.4   Suggesting topics vs. terms as the user types

10.3   *Suggesting document field values*

Suggester provides a good solution for suggesting specific query terms as the user types, but it doesn't work as well for suggesting phrases or short fields such as titles. In this section, we'll investigate an alternative approach that's good for suggesting field values from your documents.

Using our `solrpedia` example, we could suggest topic titles as the user types. If the user types `river`, the Solr Suggester we covered in the previous section will suggest `rivers`, `riverdale`, and `riverside`. Alternatively, we can display a list of topics that includes the term `river` as suggestions, as shown in figure 10.4.

It should be said that either approach can be valid for your search application; for `solrpedia`, we think suggesting topics is more appropriate, because of the specific search application. You'll need to think about which approach makes sense for your users. Let's see how we implemented the solution shown in figure 10.4.

10.3.1   *Using n-grams for suggestions*

As you can see in figure 10.4, our topic Suggester matches topics that do not start with the letters `riv`. We're getting suggestions if the prefix `riv` occurs anywhere in the title. One way to achieve this type of behavior is to use a wildcard query against the `suggest` field, such as `riv*`. There are two problems with this approach, however. Wildcard queries can be slow to execute (as previously discussed), especially in fields with a large number of terms. You have little control over the ranking of documents returned when using wildcards.

A better approach is to create edge *n-grams* for terms during text analysis; an n-gram is a sequence of contiguous characters generated for a word or string of words, where the *n* signifies the length of the sequence. For instance, a 1-gram, also known as a unigram, is an n-gram of size one. Similarly, a bigram (2-gram) is a sequence of two contiguous characters. The bigrams for `river` are: `ri`, `iv`, `ve`, and `er`. *Edge n-grams* are a special type of n-gram generated for one side or edge of a term, typically the left edge for English terms. The edge n-grams for the term `river` are: r, ri, riv, rive, and `river`. Solr provides `EdgeNGramFilter` to generate edge n-grams for terms during text analysis.

For making suggestions, n-grams work like a precomputed wildcard search, and so they avoid the aforementioned performance problems. At query time, a search in the `suggest` field for the prefix `riv` results in an exact match of the `riv` 3-gram for any topics that contain the term `river`. If you use the `EdgeNGramFilter` to analyze topic names, all the possible prefixes for every term get indexed. It follows that using n-grams can greatly increase the size of your index, because you are creating many n-grams for every term indexed. Since we are only generating n-grams for the topic field, which are typically two to three terms, the impact on our index size will be manageable.

To create n-grams during text analysis, we defined a new field type in *schema.xml* named `text_suggest_ngram`, as shown in the next listing.

Listing 10.12   Field type to create general n-grams during text analysis

```
<fieldType name="text_suggest_ngram"
    class="solr.TextField" positionIncrementGap="100">
  <analyzer type="index">
    <tokenizer class="solr.UAX29URLEmailTokenizerFactory"/>
    <filter class="solr.StopFilterFactory" ignoreCase="true"
        words="stopwords.txt"/>
    <filter class="solr.LowerCaseFilterFactory"/>
    <filter class="solr.ASCIIFoldingFilterFactory"/>
    <filter class="solr.EnglishPossessiveFilterFactory"/>
    <filter class="solr.EdgeNGramFilterFactory"
        maxGramSize="10" minGramSize="2"/>
  </analyzer>
  <analyzer type="query">
    <tokenizer class="solr.UAX29URLEmailTokenizerFactory"/>
    <filter class="solr.StopFilterFactory" ignoreCase="true"
        words="stopwords.txt"/>
    <filter class="solr.LowerCaseFilterFactory"/>
    <filter class="solr.ASCIIFoldingFilterFactory"/>
    <filter class="solr.EnglishPossessiveFilterFactory"/>
  </analyzer>
</fieldType>
```

Token filter to generate n-grams during analysis for indexing only.

One important aspect of the `text_suggest_ngram` field type is that it uses a different, yet compatible, analysis strategy for indexing and queries. Since we're using this field type to produce suggestions from prefixes entered by the user, we do not need to generate n-grams during query processing, only during indexing. Also, to avoid infusing n-grams into the `suggest` field used by the Solr Suggester, we'll define a new field to use the `text_suggest_ngram` field type and populate it using the `<copyField>` directive as we did previously.

```
<field name="suggest_ngram" type="text_suggest_ngram"
    indexed="true" stored="false"/>

<copyField source="title" dest="suggest_ngram"/>
```

It should be obvious that you would not want to use the `suggest_ngram` field as a source for term-level suggestions, as you will be suggesting incomplete terms like `rive`. Now let's see how to use the `suggest_ngram` field to produce the results shown in figure 10.4.

10.3.2 N-gram-driven request handler

Let's create a search request handler to generate suggested titles using n-grams. When thinking about how to configure our request handler to use n-grams, one thing you want to consider is that some n-grams will be complete terms. In most cases you want to rank exact matches higher than partial (n-gram) matches. If a user types `long`, the results should show exact matches `Long Valley` and `Long River` above partial matches `Longo` and `Longitude`, as depicted in figure 10.5.

The search request handler definition in the following listing achieves the desired result using Solr's eDisMax query parser, which is discussed in section 7.5.

Listing 10.13   Using the eDisMax query parser to boost exact matches

```
<requestHandler name="/suggest_topic"
    class="org.apache.solr.handler.component.SearchHandler">
  <lst name="defaults">
    <str name="wt">json</str>
    <str name="defType">edismax</str>          ◁──┘  Use the eDisMax
    <str name="rows">10</str>                         query parser.
    <str name="fl">title</str>                 ◁──   Return the title
    <str name="qf">suggest^10 suggest_ngram</str>  ◁── field for displaying
  </lst>                                             suggestions.
</requestHandler>
```

Use the eDisMax query parser.

Return the title field for displaying suggestions.

Boost exact matches above partial n-gram matches.

In the listing, we boost exact matches in the `suggest` field by 10 times any matches in the `ngram` field. The key takeaway is that we're using Solr's built-in document scoring framework to find the best suggestions as a user types a query. It should also be clear that since we can match against multiple fields, you can apply any number of text-analysis strategies using additional fields and weight matches against those fields differently. For example, you could produce suggestions based on phonetic matching to suggest `hybrid` if a user types `highbred`. Contrast this approach with the built-in Suggester that ranks suggestions based on term frequency in the index. Either approach is valid depending on your specific requirements.

Topic: long

Long Valley
Long River
Long County
Richard Long
MTV Video Music Award for Best Long Form Video
Luigino Longo
Board of Longitude
Longsword (disambiguation)

Figure 10.5   Ranked suggestions, with a boost given to exact matches over partial matches

Before we wrap up this chapter, we want to introduce another possible approach to making suggestions, based on past user activity.

10.4   Suggesting queries based on user activity

One of the limitations of the solutions we developed in this chapter is that they do not take into account previous queries entered by users. The built-in Suggester from section 10.2 was good at suggesting query terms, and the n-gram-based Suggester from section 10.3 was good at suggesting fields from documents using partial term matches. In both cases, however, the suggestions do not take into account the popularity of terms based upon user behavior with your search engine.

Basing suggestions off of past user query behavior is a form of collective intelligence; you may have seen this type of suggestion when using Google Instant.[3] The basic idea is to execute the most likely query as the user types, where the query is selected from a secondary database of recently popular queries. If a user types `justin b`, then a collective-intelligence-based suggestion engine might return the results for `Justin Bieber`, a popular celebrity on the web. The benefit to your users is an experience that saves them keystrokes and seems intelligent, especially when they are searching for popular topics.

A rough sketch of a solution using Solr would use a similar configuration to the n-gram solution we developed in section 10.3. But, instead of matching on a field in the main index, you would need to query a secondary Solr index containing user queries mined from your query logs. You will need to develop a tool to analyze your query logs to compute popularity scores for each query. Your analysis must be ongoing in order to update popularity scores and incorporate new queries. When querying the secondary index for suggestions, you will need to incorporate the popularity of a query into the score, or sort by popularity in descending order.

SCHEMA DESIGN

We'll leave the query-log mining as an exercise for the reader. To keep things simple, let's imagine we have the data shown in table 10.2, mined from the `solrpedia` query logs.

Table 10.2   Sample query popularity data mined from query logs

Query	Last executed on date	Frequency (past 30 days)
Prince William	August 10, 2013	20,000
Fort William	July 15, 2013	20,005
William and Mary	July 22, 2013	19,995

---

[3] "About Google Instant," www.google.com/insidesearch/features/instant/about.html.

We'll store our queries and their popularities in a secondary Solr core named solrpedia_instant. The main fields in the *schema.xml* for our secondary index are shown in this listing.

Listing 10.14 Fields for suggesting popular queries from the `solrpedia_instant` core

```
                   <field name="id" .../>
Raw        ⮑       <field name="query" type="string" indexed="false" stored="true"/>
query              <field name="query_ngram" type="text_suggest_ngram"    ⮜
text                     indexed="true" stored="false"/>
mined              <field name="popularity" type="tfloat"                 ⮜
from the                 indexed="true" stored="true"/>
query              <field name="last_executed_on" type="tdate"            ⮜
logs.                    indexed="true" stored="true"/>
                   <field name="_version_" .../>
```

Field to hold n-grams of query text (see section 10.3).

Popularity score computed from analyzing query logs.

Last date this query was found in the logs.

Notice that the query_ngram field uses the text_suggest_ngram field type we developed in section 10.3. Using the schema from the previous listing, we can index the data from table 10.2 using JSON.

```
[
  {
    "id" : "1",
    "query" : "Prince William",
    "last_executed_on" : "2013-08-10T00:00:00Z/DAY",
    "popularity" : 20000
  },
  {
    "id" : "2",
    "query" : "Fort William",
    "last_executed_on" : "2013-07-15T00:00:00Z/DAY",
    "popularity" : 20005
  },
  {
    "id" : "3",
    "query" : "William and Mary",
    "last_executed_on" : "2013-07-22T00:00:00Z/DAY",
    "popularity" : 19995
  }
]
```

To send these documents to Solr, just execute the following commands:

```
cd $SOLR_IN_ACTION/example-docs/
java -Durl=http://localhost:8983/solr/solrpedia_instant/update
  ⮑ -Dtype=application/json -jar post.jar ch10/documents/
  ⮑ solrpedia_instant.json
```

Now that we have a basic design for our secondary index, let's move on to learning how to find the most popular query to execute against our main index.

FIND MOST POPULAR QUERY

How many characters do the users need to type before you activate the instant behavior? Unlike type-ahead suggestions of query terms, you're trying to predict what the user wants to see based on past user activity, so you'll likely need more characters from the user before you try to predict their intentions. For instance, in solrpedia, we might activate the instant behavior after the user types six characters. Before six characters, we rely on type-ahead suggestions, using the techniques covered in the previous sections.

Based on the data in table 10.2, if the user types willia, our suggestion engine will match the popular query for Fort William and then display the results instantly. The following listing shows the query we could use against the solrpedia_instant core to find suggested queries as the user types.

Listing 10.15   Query to find suggested queries based on popularity

```
http://localhost:8983/solr/solrpedia_instant/select?
  q=query_ngram:willia&                                          Query the
  sort=popularity desc&                         Descending       field containing
  rows=1&                           Return      sort by          n-grams.
  fl=query&            Return the   only one    popularity.
  wt=json              query text   suggestion.
                       from the logs.
{
  "response": {
    "numFound":3,
    "start":0,
    "docs":[                              Suggested query is
      {"query":"Fort William"}            "Fort William" based
    ]                                     on table 10.2.
  }, ...
}
```

Querying our secondary index for willia returns Fort William, which matches our expectation based on the popularity score of 20,005 from table 10.2. What if in addition to popularity, we wanted to sort the results based on the age of each query's popularity score? How do we take the recency of a query's popularity into account?

BOOSTING MORE RECENT POPULARITY

When thinking of the popularity of queries, it's also important to consider the age of the popularity score so that we can boost more recent queries as well as penalize previously popular queries that have fallen out of interest. In table 10.2, we see that a query for Fort William is slightly more popular than for Prince William, but it's also older. It stands to reason that if we took the age of the query popularity into account, Prince William would be a better suggestion when a user types willia, because it's more recent.

Why not incorporate the *age* of the popularity calculation into the popularity score? The problem with that approach is that age changes every day, so you would need to reindex every document in your secondary index every day, which can be significant for busy search engines. We think a better approach is to index the last executed date with each document, and compute a boost for the age dynamically using a Solr function query.

Let's imagine that we keep up to 30 days of queries in our secondary index. When we process query logs on a daily basis, not every query in our secondary index will show up in the logs every day. To take into account the age of a query's popularity score without having to reindex every query, we can keep a last executed on date field with each document in the index; the value of this field is the last date we saw a given query in our logs. Then, during indexing, we only need to update the queries that have activity on a given day. Let's say the `Prince William` query had 19,980 queries as of August 9, 2013, and when processing the logs from August 10, 2013, you find 20 more queries. You would then want to update the secondary index with the following data:

```
{
    "id" : "1",
    "query" : "prince william",
    "last_executed_on" : "2013-08-10T00:00:00Z/DAY",
    "popularity" : 20000
}
```

The `last_executed_on` field gets updated to reflect the last day you found the query in your logs, and popularity is the aggregated number of queries over 30 days (20,000 = 19,980 previous + 20 new). Now we can use Solr's `boost` function query to boost documents by popularity and age, as shown in the next listing.

Listing 10.16   Using Solr's `boost` function to boost by popularity and age

```
http://localhost:8983/solr/solrpedia_instant/select?      ◁──┐  Boost function
    q={!boost b=$recency v=$qq}&                                with local params.
    sort=score desc&              ⟵── Sort by score, descending.
    rows=1&
    wt=json&                                  Local qq param to search
    qq=query_ngram:willia&        ◁──         the query_ngram field.
    recency=product(recip(ms(NOW/HOUR,last_executed_on),
        1.27E-10,0.08,0.05),popularity)    ⟵── Local recency param to boost by popularity and age.
```

The result of this query is that `Prince William` is returned as the top hit, even though `Fort William` has a larger popularity score. This is because the boost function penalizes older popularity scores, using a time-based decay function. Table 10.3 breaks down the request in the previous listing into its basic components to get a better understanding of how it works.

Table 10.3   Boosting by age and popularity

Query parameter	Explanation
`q={!boost b=$recency v=$qq}`	Uses the Boost query parser to boost results matching the query indicated by v, using a function query identified by the b parameter. We use Solr's local parameter support to simplify the syntax of this query; see section 7.2.2.
`sort=score desc`	Explicitly sorts by the score in descending order; this is the default sort criteria, but we are showing it here so that it's clear we are sorting by the boosted score.

Table 10.3   Boosting by age and popularity *(continued)*

Query parameter	Explanation
`qq=query_ngram:willia`	Searches the `query_ngram` field as the user types `willia`; uses the local `params` syntax.

`recency=product(`
`    recip(ms(NOW/HOUR,`
`        last_executed_on),`
`    1.27E-10,0.08,0.05),`
`    popularity)`
	Computes the product of the popularity and the age boost. The age boost is computed using Solr's `recip` function: `recip(x,m,a,b) = a / (m*x + b)`, where x is the document age and m, a, and b are parameters used to compute the age penalty. Document age is based on the number of milliseconds between the current time and the `last_executed_on` field.

Figure 10.6 shows how the age boost function penalizes popularity scores as they age; you can change the values of the m, a, and b parameters to affect the shape of the boost function. We chose m=1.27E-10, a=0.08, and b=0.05 to rapidly penalize older popularity scores.

After querying the secondary index, your search application can send the suggested query to the main index behind the scenes. This will give the user the impression that your search engine is predicting what they are searching for as they type. But we should caution you that this feature can increase the query volume of your main index dramatically, as your search application is executing queries in the background before users have formulated a full query. As with any user-experience-related feature, you need to monitor actual user behavior to determine if this feature benefits or hinders user productivity with your search application.

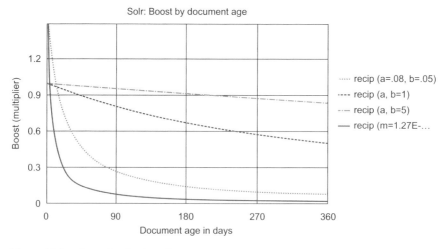

Figure 10.6   Chart showing how Solr's `recip` **function works to boost or penalize the popularity of a query based on age; any value below 1.0 works as an age penalty.**

10.5 *Summary*

In this chapter, we implemented query suggestions to help improve the usability of your search application. Specifically, we saw how to implement *Did you mean …?* style query suggestions to handle misspelled terms. In addition, we used Solr's built-in Suggester component to return suggested query terms as the user types. The approaches are complementary and are typically used together to form a robust query-suggestion solution.

Next we tackled a different approach to generate suggested topics instead of raw query terms. We used Solr's `EdgeNGramFilter` to generate n-grams during indexing so that we could query for suggested documents using a prefix efficiently. We finished up this chapter with a brief discussion of how to use Solr to implement an instant search suggestion feature.

In the next chapter, you'll learn about result grouping.

Result grouping/
field collapsing

This chapter covers

- Excluding duplicate documents from search results

- Returning multiple groups of query results in a single search request

- Ensuring variety in search results by showing multiple document categories

- Grouping query results by field values, queries, or functions

- Data-partitioning strategies necessary for scaling Solr's grouping functionality

Result grouping is a useful capability in Solr for ensuring that an optimal mix of search results is returned for a user's query. *Result grouping*, commonly referred to as field collapsing, is the ability to ensure only one document (or some limited number) is returned for each unique value (actual or dynamically computed) within a field. This can be useful if you have multiple similar documents—products from the same company, locations for the same restaurant chain, or companies with multiple offices—but do not want an entire page of search results to only represent a single product, restaurant, or company.

You've probably seen implementations of this capability when using your favorite web search engine. If you've ever seen messages telling you that many results matched your query, but only one (or the top few) were being displayed, you've encountered field collapsing. Often, such a message will provide a link users can click to see the fully expanded list of search results, along with a count of how many additional documents would have been returned had the search results not been collapsed.

In addition to collapsing search results to remove duplicate documents, the result grouping functionality in Solr provides other useful features. In many ways, you can view result grouping in Solr as a more verbose form of faceting. Instead of only returning separate facet sections along with the counts for each value, result grouping returns the unique values and their counts (like faceting) plus some number of documents that contain each of the specified values. One way in which grouping is different than faceting is that it returns the requested groups within the search results section, which means the groups and values within the groups are sorted based on the sorts specified for the documents in the query. Grouping can be performed based upon field values, functions, or queries, making its applications numerous. Although this may sound complex initially, we will cover several use cases to demonstrate this incredibly useful and (mostly) straightforward feature. Before jumping in, it will be useful to clarify the sometimes confusing distinction between the terms *result grouping* and *field collapsing*.

11.1 Result grouping vs. field collapsing

One question commonly asked is why is the result grouping functionality in Solr referred to by two different names: *result grouping* and *field collapsing*? Field collapsing is the more commonly used term for this functionality in other search engines, referring to the act of returning a normal set of results with duplicate values removed. An early version of this functionality was being developed for Solr and was unofficially called the field collapsing patch. The decision was later made to make this capability more generic, and the result grouping name was chosen to signify the more generic capabilities now available.

Although returning a single results set collapsed on the duplicate values within a field (field collapsing) is certainly a supported option using Solr's result grouping functionality, it's also possible to return multiple result sets, or groups, from a single query. The result grouping name thus signifies a more generic capability than the traditional field collapsing use case. As of Solr 4.6, an alternate implementation (covered in section 11.7) also exists in Solr and is capable of more efficient field collapsing in cases where duplicate document removal is the only required feature. This approach has some limitations, such as limited support for sorting documents prior to collapsing, but it may prove useful in some cases.

This chapter will primarily focus on the many uses for Solr's result grouping functionality, starting with the most common one—field collapsing—to remove duplicate documents from a set of search results.

11.2 Skipping duplicate documents

Let's say you are running an online e-commerce website that sells user-posted items. Although it may be nice to run a search for an item and see thousands of copies of identical products, you may provide a much better user experience if instead you only show one document per unique item (possibly along with a count of how many of each item exist). This will allow some diversity in the search results, in case the duplicate items that show up at the top are not exactly what the user was trying to find. Say a user searched for the term `spider-man`. If the top match was `The Amazing Spider-man–2012`, and you had 100 copies of this same item, the top 100 results would be for this one product, assuming they all had the same relevancy score based upon their content. If, instead, you were to group on the name of the product and ask for only one item per group, `The Amazing Spider-man–2012` would show up only once amid other possibilities like `Spider-man–2002`, `Spider-man 2–2004`, and `Amazing Spider-man Comic #2`. Figure 11.1 demonstrates this phenomenon.

In most scenarios, using result grouping to collapse search results will provide a better user experience. This definitely seems to be the case for figure 11.1, where the default option of listing `The Amazing Spider-man–2012` at least 100 times before showing the next unique result would likely frustrate any users searching for a different Spider-man product.

To demonstrate this capability in action, some example e-commerce product documents have been added in the source code that accompanies this book. After downloading a clean version of Solr, you can start up Solr and add these example documents using the commands in listing 11.1.

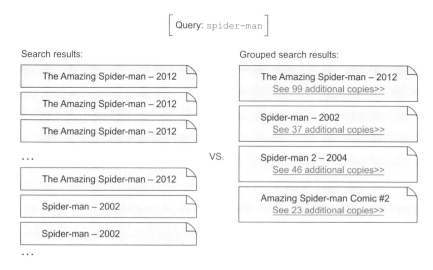

Figure 11.1   Standard search results on the left show duplicate documents; grouped search results on the right show unique results and collapsed counts of duplicates.

Listing 11.1 Indexing example documents for e-commerce site

```
cd $SOLR_INSTALL/example/
cp -r $SOLR_IN_ACTION/example-docs/ch11/cores/ecommerce/ solr/ecommerce/
java -jar start.jar
cd $SOLR_IN_ACTION/example-docs/
java -Durl=http://localhost:8983/solr/ecommerce/update
    ➥ -jar post.jar ch11/documents/ecommerce.xml
```

With our e-commerce search engine up and running, we can now demonstrate Solr's result grouping capabilities in action. The following listing demonstrates a standard search request for the query spider-man without grouping turned on.

Listing 11.2 Standard search containing duplicate documents

Request
```
http://localhost:8983/solr/ecommerce/select?
    fl=id,product,format&
    sort=popularity asc&                          Basic keyword query,
    q=spider-man                                  no grouping turned on.
```

Response
```
{
  "responseHeader":{
    "status":0,
    "QTime":2},
  "response":{"numFound":18,"start":0,"docs":[
    {
      "id":"4",
      "format":"dvd",
      "product":"The Amazing Spider Man - 2012"},      Multiple products
    {                                                   with the same name
      "id":"5",                                         are shown in a
      "format":"blu-ray",                               standard search.
      "product":"The Amazing Spider Man - 2012"},
    {
      "id":"6",
      "format":"dvd",
      "product":"Spider Man - 2002"},
    {
      "id":"7",
      "format":"blu-ray",
      "product":"Spider Man - 2002"},
    {
      "id":"8",
      "format":"dvd",
      "product":"Spider Man 2 - 2004"},
    {
      "id":"9",
      "format":"blu-ray",
      "product":"Spider Man 2 - 2004"},
    {
      "id":"11",
```

```
    "format":"xbox 360",
    "product":"The Amazing Spider-Man"},
  {
    "id":"12",
    "format":"ps3",
    "product":"The Amazing Spider-Man"},
  {
    "id":"13",
    "format":"xbox 360",
    "product":"Spider-Man: Edge of Time"},
  {
    "id":"14",
    "format":"ps3",
    "product":"Spider-Man: Edge of Time"}]
}}
```

The results almost certainly represent a bad user experience, as they seem to present every format (such as Blu-ray and DVD) of the same product as separate results, listing it multiple times. By turning grouping on, however, the results appear much more diverse and provide a cleaner user experience, as demonstrated in this listing.

Listing 11.3   Grouped search results collapsing on the product field

Request
```
http://localhost:8983/solr/ecommerce/select?
  fl=id,product,format&
  sort=popularity asc&
  q=spider-man&
  group=true&                          ❶ Turns grouping
  group.field=product&                   on by product.
  group.limit=1  ◁───────┐
                         │     Returns only the top one
**Response**             │   ❷ document per group.
{
  "responseHeader":{
    "status":0,
    "QTime":3},
  "grouped":{
    "product":{
      "matches":18,
      "groups":[{                                    ❸ Grouped
        "groupValue":"The Amazing Spider Man - 2012",    results have
        "doclist":{"numFound":2,"start":0,"docs":[       a detailed
          {                                              response
            "id":"4",                                    format.
            "format":"dvd",
            "product":"The Amazing Spider Man - 2012"}]
        }},
      {
        "groupValue":"Spider Man - 2002",
        "doclist":{"numFound":3,"start":0,"docs":[
          {
            "id":"6",
            "format":"dvd",
```

```
            "product":"Spider Man - 2002"}]
      }},
  {
    "groupValue":"Spider Man 2 - 2004",
    "doclist":{"numFound":3,"start":0,"docs":[
      {
        "id":"8",
        "format":"dvd",
        "product":"Spider Man 2 - 2004"}]
    }},
  {
    "groupValue":"The Amazing Spider-Man",
    "doclist":{"numFound":2,"start":0,"docs":[
      {
        "id":"11",
        "format":"xbox 360",
        "product":"The Amazing Spider-Man"}]
    }},
  {
    "groupValue":"Spider-Man: Edge of Time",
    "doclist":{"numFound":2,"start":0,"docs":[
      {
        "id":"13",
        "format":"xbox 360",
        "product":"Spider-Man: Edge of Time"}]
    }},
  {
    "groupValue":"Spider-Man Halloween Costume",
    "doclist":{"numFound":1,"start":0,"docs":[
      {
        "id":"15",
        "format":"costume",
        "product":"Spider-Man Halloween Costume"}]
    }},
  {
    "groupValue":"Boys Spider-Man T-shirt",
    "doclist":{"numFound":1,"start":0,"docs":[
      {
        "id":"21",
        "format":"shirt",
        "product":"Boys Spider-Man T-shirt"}]
    }},
  {
    "groupValue":"Amazing Spider-Man Comic #1",
    "doclist":{"numFound":1,"start":0,"docs":[
      {
        "id":"22",
        "format":"paperback",
        "product":"Amazing Spider-Man Comic #1"}]
    }},
  {
    "groupValue":"Amazing Spider-Man Comic #2",
    "doclist":{"numFound":1,"start":0,"docs":[
      {
        "id":"23",
```

4 Each group has a groupValue, numFound, and list of docs.

```
      "format":"paperback",
      "product":"Amazing Spider-Man Comic #2"}]
    }},
  {
    "groupValue":"Amazing Spider-Man Comic #3",
    "doclist":{"numFound":1,"start":0,"docs":[
      {
        "id":"24",
        "format":"paperback",
        "product":"Amazing Spider-Man Comic #3"}]
    }}]}}}
```

The listing demonstrates several noteworthy properties of grouping. First, notice that grouping must be turned on by specifying the group=true parameter ❶, in addition to specifying what to group on (the product field). The group.limit parameter ❷ was set to 1, indicating that only one document should be returned for each unique value within a group. It can be useful to set the group.limit to an integer higher than 1, as you will see in section 11.4, but for removing all duplicate documents you would generally only want one document returned per unique value upon which you are collapsing.

You will also notice that the results format ❸ is substantially different than the default Solr results format. This more verbose format is necessary to communicate all of the information associated with grouped search results: the name of the field that is grouped upon ❹, the unique terms within that field (groupValue) that define each group, and the total number of results (numFound) before collapsing occurred in each group.

Unfortunately, it can often be inconvenient to support parsing out two separate Solr results formats to handle grouping. Thankfully, if you are looking to remove duplicates and do not need all of this additional grouping information, Solr provides a group.main parameter which, if set to true, will merge the results from each group back into a flat list and return it in the main results format. The following listing demonstrates the same query as listing 11.3, but with group.main set to true.

> **Listing 11.4   Flattening grouped results into the main search results format**

Request

```
http://localhost:8983/solr/ecommerce/select?
  fl=id,product,format&
  sort=popularity asc&
  q=spider-man&
  group=true&
  group.field=product&
  group.main=true
```

Collapses docs from all groups into the main search response.

Response

```
{
  "responseHeader":{
    "status":0,
    "QTime":8},
```

```
"response":{"numFound":18,"start":0,"docs":[
  {
    "id":"4",
    "format":"dvd",
    "product":"The Amazing Spider Man - 2012"},
  {
    "id":"6",
    "format":"dvd",
    "product":"Spider Man - 2002"},
  {
    "id":"8",
    "format":"dvd",
    "product":"Spider Man 2 - 2004"},
  {
    "id":"11",
    "format":"xbox 360",
    "product":"The Amazing Spider-Man"},
  {
    "id":"13",
    "format":"xbox 360",
    "product":"Spider-Man: Edge of Time"},
  {
    "id":"15",
    "format":"costume",
    "product":"Spider-Man Halloween Costume"},
  {
    "id":"21",
    "format":"shirt",
    "product":"Boys Spider-Man T-shirt"},
  {
    "id":"22",
    "format":"paperback",
    "product":"Amazing Spider-Man Comic #1"},
  {
    "id":"23",
    "format":"paperback",
    "product":"Amazing Spider-Man Comic #2"},
  {
    "id":"24",
    "format":"paperback",
    "product":"Amazing Spider-Man Comic #3"}]
}}
```

Collapsed documents are now unique.

The main disadvantage of using the group.main option is that you lose access to the total number of uncollapsed results within each group, but if this is not important in your search application, then this may be a fair trade-off in return for not having to handle two different search results formats. You also lose the name of the group in this simple format, but this can often be derived from the results by returning the field in each document that you grouped upon (assuming it's a single-valued field). Another disadvantage of using the group.main format is that it only supports a single group being requested.

One other major disadvantage of using result grouping to perform field collapsing is that it can be significantly slower than executing a standard search request. Fortunately, as of Solr 4.6 there is a much more efficient implementation of field collapsing that relies upon a special query parser (`CollapseQParserPlugin`) to collapse documents. This capability, covered in section 11.7, will yield results in the standard Solr search results format (just like using `group.main=true` with result grouping), but should provide a significant performance boost for indexes containing a large number of documents with distinct values upon which to be collapsed. If you are using a version of Solr 4 prior to Solr 4.6, however, you will have to get by utilizing the slower result grouping capability as described earlier in this section.

Thus far, we've only specified a single `group.field=product` parameter, but Solr supports returning multiple groups. For example, you could ask for both a `group.field=type` and a `group.field=format`, and Solr would return both groups in the grouped results format. If you specify `group.main=true`, however, Solr will only return the last group that you specify in the Solr request URL.

There is also another option between the advanced grouping format (the default) and the `group.main` format: the simple grouping format. By specifying `group.format=simple`, you can return multiple groups (like the default advanced grouping format) while still returning the results for each group request in a flat list like the `group.main=true` option. In fact, from an implementation standpoint, setting `group.main=true` uses the `group.method=simple` capability and returns the last specified group in the main results list. The following listing demonstrates the same query as in listings 11.3 and 11.4, but using the simple grouping format.

Listing 11.5   The simple grouping format

Request
```
http://localhost:8983/solr/ecommerce/select?
  fl=id,product,format&
  sort=popularity asc&
  q=spider-man&
  group=true&
  group.field=product&          Turns the simple
  group.format=simple           grouping format on.
```

Response
```
{
  "responseHeader":{
    "status":0,                     Overall group count
    "QTime":2},                     information is still
  "grouped":{                       returned.
    "product":{
      "matches":18,
      "doclist":{"numFound":18,"start":0,"docs":[         The per-group
        {                                                 groupValue and
          "id":"4",                                       numFound no
          "format":"dvd",                                 longer returned.
          "product":"The Amazing Spider Man - 2012"},
        {
          "id":"6",
          "format":"dvd",
          "product":"Spider Man - 2002"},
```

```
    {
      "id":"8",
      "format":"dvd",
      "product":"Spider Man 2 - 2004"},
    {
      "id":"11",
      "format":"xbox 360",
      "product":"The Amazing Spider-Man"},
    {
      "id":"13",
      "format":"xbox 360",
      "product":"Spider-Man: Edge of Time"},
    {
      "id":"15",
      "format":"costume",
      "product":"Spider-Man Halloween Costume"},
    {
      "id":"21",
      "format":"shirt",
      "product":"Boys Spider-Man T-shirt"},
    {
      "id":"22",
      "format":"paperback",
      "product":"Amazing Spider-Man Comic #1"},
    {
      "id":"23",
      "format":"paperback",
      "product":"Amazing Spider-Man Comic #2"},
    {
      "id":"24",
      "format":"paperback",
      "product":"Amazing Spider-Man Comic #3"}]
}}}}
```

You've seen throughout this section how to collapse the results of a query into groups so as to remove duplicate documents. You've also seen three formats in which grouped search results can be returned: the default advanced grouping format, the simple grouping format, and the returning of a single collapsed group in the main search results. Each of these formats strikes a balance between backward compatibility with the standard search results format and the richness of information available to describe the identified groups. The collapsing of results down to a single document per unique field value represents the essence of what is meant by the use of the traditional term *field collapsing*.

Throughout the remainder of this chapter, you will see more advanced use cases for the more generic grouping capabilities available in Solr. The next section will begin by demonstrating how to request multiple documents per group in a single query.

11.3 *Returning multiple documents per group*

Collapsing to a single document per unique field value is not the only practical use case for Solr's grouping function. Returning to our e-commerce search engine example from the previous section, imagine that if instead of only collapsing duplicate

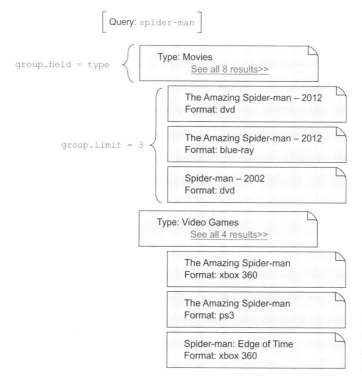

Figure 11.2   Returning multiple documents per group by setting `group.limit > 1`.

documents, we could guarantee that we would return no more than a fixed number of results from each product category. In our search for `spider-man` in section 11.2, imagine that instead of returning a flat list of collapsed (deduplicated) documents, we instead returned up to three documents per unique category. Figure 11.2 demonstrates such a query.

The example documents that were indexed in listing 11.1 contain a `type` field that we can group upon, requesting a limit of three documents per group. Additionally, let's request that a maximum of five total groups be returned. This listing demonstrates such a query.

Listing 11.6   Returning multiple values per group

Request

```
http://localhost:8983/solr/ecommerce/select?
  q=spider-man&
  fl=id,product,format&
  sort=popularity asc&
  group=true&
  group.field=type&
  group.limit=3&
  rows=5&
  start=0&
  group.offset=0
```

❶ Up to three results per group will be returned.

❷ Up to five groups will be returned.

Response

```
{
  "responseHeader":{
    "status":0,
    "QTime":2},
  "grouped":{
    "type":{
      "matches":18,
      "groups":[{
        "groupValue":"Movies",
        "doclist":{"numFound":8,"start":0,"docs":[
          {
            "id":"4",
            "format":"dvd",
            "product":"The Amazing Spider Man - 2012"},
          {
            "id":"5",
            "format":"blu-ray",
            "product":"The Amazing Spider Man - 2012"},
          {
            "id":"6",
            "format":"dvd",
            "product":"Spider Man - 2002"}]
        }},
      {
        "groupValue":"Video Games",
        "doclist":{"numFound":4,"start":0,"docs":[
          {
            "id":"11",
            "format":"xbox 360",
            "product":"The Amazing Spider-Man"},
          {
            "id":"12",
            "format":"ps3",
            "product":"The Amazing Spider-Man"},
          {
            "id":"13",
            "format":"xbox 360",
            "product":"Spider-Man: Edge of Time"}]
        }},
      {
        "groupValue":"Clothing",
        "doclist":{"numFound":2,"start":0,"docs":[
          {
            "id":"15",
            "format":"costume",
            "product":"Spider-Man Halloween Costume"},
          {
            "id":"21",
            "format":"shirt",
            "product":"Boys Spider-Man T-shirt"}]
        }},
      {
        "groupValue":"Comic Books",
        "doclist":{"numFound":3,"start":0,"docs":[
```

```
      {
        "id":"22",
        "format":"paperback",
        "product":"Amazing Spider-Man Comic #1"},
      {
        "id":"23",
        "format":"paperback",
        "product":"Amazing Spider-Man Comic #2"},
      {
        "id":"24",
        "format":"paperback",
        "product":"Amazing Spider-Man Comic #3"}]
    }},
  {
    "groupValue":"Action Figures",
    "doclist":{"numFound":1,"start":0,"docs":[
      {
        "id":"25",
        "format":"n/a",
        "product":"Marvel Legends Icon: Spider Man 12\" Action Figure"}]
    }}]}}}
```

Several important points can be gleaned here. First, notice that no group contains more than three results, but not all groups contain three results. Even though the group.limit is set to 3 ❶, this only sets the upper limit, as any group without three documents cannot return a full three documents. Second, notice that the rows=5 parameter ❷ is controlling not how many documents are returned, but how many groups are returned. In the default advanced grouping format, both the rows and start parameters apply to the groups instead of to the documents within each group. That is, rows controls how many groups are returned, whereas group.limit controls how many documents are returned within each group. Likewise, the start parameter controls the group offset for paging through groups; the group.offset parameter controls the document offset for paging through the documents within each group.

One final important aspect of grouping can be gleaned from listing 11.6: the way sorting interacts with grouping. Conceptually, all groups are sorted based upon the order in which their top document is sorted. What this means is that, assuming groupings were not enabled, all of the documents would appear in their sorted order (by relevancy score by default). If the highest sorted document were to have a type field value of Movies, the second highest a value of Comic Books, the third highest again a value of Movies, and the fourth highest a value of Clothing, then the sorted order of the groups would be Movies, Comic Books, Clothing.

Inside each group, the documents are also sorted, by default, in the order of their first appearance. This means that because Movies is the top category group, and because three movies are requested to appear within the Movies category group, the second and third movies are likely to be less relevant (sorted lower) in an absolute sense even though they show up higher in the results because they get promoted up to the top group of Movies. For this reason, it's generally uncommon for someone to request a `group.limit` of greater than 1 when using the `group.main` or the `group.format=simple` formats, as the sorted order of results may appear quite strange without the structure provided by the advanced grouping format to distinguish when one group ends and another begins.

Although grouping on the values within a field provides useful search capabilities, as shown in the preceding examples, much more is possible with Solr's result grouping capabilities. The next section will begin by demonstrating the ability to group on more than field values; you will see how to group by arbitrary queries and functions, as well.

11.4 Grouping by functions and queries

In addition to supporting grouping by unique field values, Solr supports two more grouping use cases. The first is similar to grouping on a field, but it instead allows grouping by dynamically computed values by using function queries. The second is Solr's query grouping capability, which allows multiple queries to be run concurrently and returned as separate result sets.

11.4.1 Grouping by function

Grouping based upon functions is accomplished using the `group.func` parameter. We will not cover all of the possible functions here (see chapter 15 for full coverage of functions in Solr), but the following listing demonstrates a search result grouped by a function. In this case, the function is trying to group the search results into three groups by popularity (most popular = 1, somewhat popular = 2, least popular = 3).

Listing 11.7 Search result grouped by a function

Request
```
http://localhost:8983/solr/ecommerce/select?
  fl=id,product,format&
  sort=popularity asc&
  q=spider-man&
  group=true&
  group.limit=3&                                    Requests
  rows=5&                                           grouping by
  group.func=map(map(map(popularity,1,5,1),6,10,2),11,100,3)   ◁─── a function.
```

Response
```
{
  "responseHeader":{
    "status":0,
    "QTime":3},                                     Response format is
  "grouped":{                                       similar to grouping
    "map(map(map(popularity,1,5,1),6,10,2),11,100,3)":{  ◁─── by field.
      "matches":18,
      "groups":[{
```

```
    "groupValue":1.0,
    "doclist":{"numFound":2,"start":0,"docs":[
      {
        "id":"4",
        "format":"dvd",
        "product":"The Amazing Spider Man - 2012"},
      {
        "id":"5",
        "format":"blu-ray",
        "product":"The Amazing Spider Man - 2012"}]
    }},
  {
    "groupValue":2.0,
    "doclist":{"numFound":4,"start":0,"docs":[
      {
        "id":"6",
        "format":"dvd",
        "product":"Spider Man - 2002"},
      {
        "id":"7",
        "format":"blu-ray",
        "product":"Spider Man - 2002"},
      {
        "id":"8",
        "format":"dvd",
        "product":"Spider Man 2 - 2004"}]
    }},
  {
    "groupValue":3.0,
    "doclist":{"numFound":12,"start":0,"docs":[
      {
        "id":"11",
        "format":"xbox 360",
        "product":"The Amazing Spider-Man"},
      {
        "id":"12",
        "format":"ps3",
        "product":"The Amazing Spider-Man"},
      {
        "id":"13",
        "format":"xbox 360",
        "product":"Spider-Man: Edge of Time"}]
}}]}}}
```

The computed value from the function becomes the groupValue.

As you can see, grouping by a function is conceptually the same as grouping by a field value, except that the value you group upon is computed dynamically. In this case, all popularity values were mapped into three groups (popularity 1–5 was mapped into group 1, popularity 6–10 was mapped into group 2, and popularity 11–100 was mapped to group 3). Functions can be nested, as you see in this example that nests three map functions, which means you have full control over the values that are computed if you want to manipulate them by combining multiple functions. If function grouping is too limiting for your use case, it's also possible to group by a query so that you can specify your own arbitrary values upon which to group.

11.4.2 Grouping by query

In section 11.3, you saw that it's possible to collapse search results so that no more than a few documents are returned matching a particular value within a field (using the group.field parameter). In addition to grouping on predefined field values, it can be useful to dynamically group on arbitrary queries. A customer-centric user experience, for example, could be highly customized to return three sets of search results: those within 50 kilometers of the user, those within the customer's price range, and those within the customer's favorite category. Because Solr allows multiple group.query parameters to be sent in the same request, it's possible to bring back each of these sets of search results as a separate group.

To demonstrate this capability using our dataset for this chapter, let's see what it would look like to request three somewhat arbitrary query groups: one query that matches all movies, one query that matches anything matching the keyword games, and one query which is for the specific product named The Hunger Games. This listing demonstrates how to accomplish this.

Listing 11.8 Search results grouped by multiple queries

Request
```
http://localhost:8983/solr/ecommerce/select?
  sort=popularity asc&
  fl=id,type,format,product&
  group.limit=2&
  q=*:*&
  group=true&
  group.query=type:Movies&        ❶ Requests three
  group.query=games&                 separate query
  group.query="The Hunger Games"     groups.
```

Results
```
{
  "responseHeader":{
    "status":0,
    "QTime":1},
  "grouped":{
    "type:Movies":{
      "matches":26,
      "doclist":{"numFound":11,"start":0,"docs":[
        {
          "id":"1",
          "type":"Movies",
          "format":"dvd",
          "product":"The Hunger Games"},
        {                                          ❷ The same docs
          "id":"4",                                  can appear in
          "type":"Movies",                           multiple query
          "format":"dvd",                            groups.
          "product":"The Amazing Spider Man - 2012"}]
      }},
```

```
"games":{
  "matches":26,
  "doclist":{"numFound":7,"start":0,"docs":[
    {
      "id":"1",
      "type":"Movies",
      "format":"dvd",
      "product":"The Hunger Games"},
    {
      "id":"2",
      "type":"Video Games",
      "format":"xbox 360",
      "product":"Dance Dance Revolution"}]
  }},
"The Hunger Games":{
  "matches":26,
  "doclist":{"numFound":2,"start":0,"docs":[
    {
      "id":"1",
      "type":"Movies",
      "format":"dvd",
      "product":"The Hunger Games"},
    {
      "id":"3",
      "type":"Books",
      "format":"paperback",
      "product":"The Hunger Games"}]
}}}}
```

The example demonstrates three important takeaways:

- It's possible ❶ to request multiple groups back from Solr. This is true for any kind of grouping query (group.field, group.func, or group.query); any number of groups can be returned from Solr within a single request.

- A query group is a way to perform multiple subsearches of the original search. In this case, the initial query was a wide-open search (q=*:*), which allows you to run as many queries as you want within a single request, each returning separate sets of results.

- Although it's true that a document will only appear once within a grouped result set, it's important to note that when multiple group parameters are used in a Solr request, each set of grouped results ❷ can contain that document again. It's as if you are literally running multiple searches within the same request, because each of the separately requested query groups can contain the same documents if the query in their corresponding group.query parameter matches those documents.

With this ability to run multiple subsearches in a single Solr request, interesting interactions take place between Solr's grouping functionality and the results paging and document sorting that also occur during the request. The next section will dive into these interactions.

11.5 *Paging and sorting grouped results*

Grouping, because of its richer search results structure, introduces additional complexity when paging through and sorting search results. You will recall from chapter 7 that Solr uses the rows parameter to determine how many documents to return from Solr for a standard search query. When grouping results, however, there is an extra layer of complexity: what is it you are trying to put a limit upon? Do you wish to return a certain number of documents per group, a certain number across all groups, or a certain number of groups? Similar questions exist when using Solr's start parameter to page through grouped search results and the sort parameter to sort the grouped search results. What does it mean to page through and sort search results in the context of multiple groups of search results?

In order to handle this additional complexity, Solr's grouping functionality applies these global parameters—rows, start, and sort—to the groups themselves. The rows parameter determines how many groups to return, the start parameter controls paging through available groups, and the sort parameter controls how groups are sorted (based upon their top document) as opposed to how documents are sorted within groups.

Should you additionally need to increase the number of documents per group, page through the results within a group, or sort the results within the groups differently, Solr's result grouping functionality has separate parameters to control this. As indicated in section 11.3, the group.limit parameter specifies the maximum number of results to return per group, performing the behavior that the rows parameter performs on a nongrouped search. The group.offset parameter allows you to page through the results within a group, performing the behavior that the start parameter provides on a nongrouped search. Figure 11.3 demonstrates the interaction between the start, rows, group.limit, and group.offset parameters for paging through grouped search results.

In figure 11.3, you can see that the first result that would have been returned in each group is faded out to indicate that document is not returned. The document is skipped because the group.offset value, which enables paging through the results in each group, is set to 1. Two documents are still returned per group because group.limit is set to 2, and two groups are returned because rows is set to 2. Because start is set to 0, the top group is returned first, though you could skip straight to the second group (as we did with the first document in each group) by setting the start parameter to 1.

A final parameter, group.sort, allows you to re-sort the documents within your groups, even though they have already been sorted initially by the sort parameter to determine the order in which the groups will appear. Some interesting uses for this two-pass sorting could be implemented, with one phase finding the relevant groups of documents and the other phase sorting the documents within that group based upon some other business need. Figure 11.4 demonstrates how the group.sort parameter for documents within groups interacts with the default sorting of the overall groups, which relies upon the sort parameter.

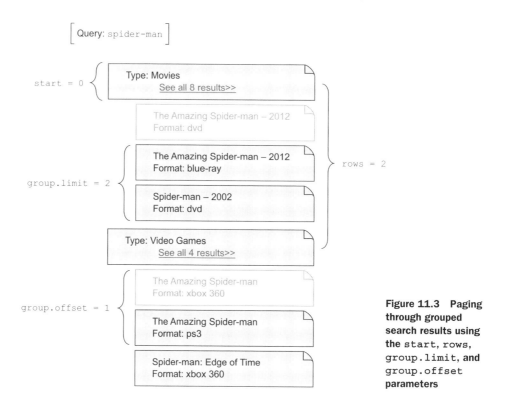

Figure 11.3 Paging through grouped search results using the `start`, `rows`, `group.limit`, and `group.offset` parameters

As you can see, grouping can lead to interesting interactions when you return multiple documents per group. In figure 11.4, you will notice that Document 5 moved from the fifth overall spot to the third spot because it was the lowest-sorted document in the top group when grouping was turned on. Document 5 moved up even higher once the documents within each group were re-sorted using the `group.sort` parameter, but the groups remained sorted in the same way (based upon the top document within each group) as per the `sort` parameter.

At the end of the day, perhaps the easiest way to think of paging, sorting, and limiting the results in a grouped request is to think of the groups as the documents Solr is returning. You can page, sort, and limit those document groups as you would page, sort, and limit single documents in a standard search request. Solr then provides the additional group parameters (`group.limit`, `group.offset`, and `group.sort`) to help you refine the documents within the groups for display.

11.6 *Grouping gotchas*

Although Solr's grouping capabilities prove useful for many cases, there are a few aspects of this functionality that can be a bit tricky to navigate. Understanding these details is important for determining how to partition your data, what facet counts represent, and how your query performance will be impacted.

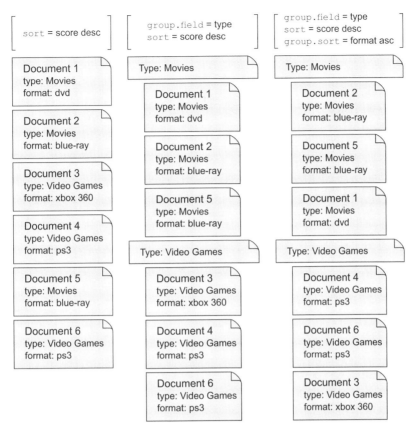

Figure 11.4   Example of sorting with grouping turned on. The left column shows default search sorting of documents by score, the middle column shows default sorting of groups by score with documents within those groups using that same sort, and the right column shows default sorting of groups by score, with the documents within each group re-sorted using the `group.sort` parameter.

11.6.1 Faceting upon result groups

By default, facet counts are based upon the original query results, not the grouped results. This means that whether or not you turn grouping on for a query, the facet counts will be the same. It's possible to only return facet counts for collapsed results by setting the parameter `group.facet=true`.

If you were to turn faceting on and facet on the `type` field using the e-commerce data for this chapter, you would get the results in the following listing.

Listing 11.9   Standard faceting on grouped search results

Request

```
http://localhost:8983/solr/ecommerce/select?
  fl=product&
  group=true&
```

```
sort=popularity asc&
q=*:*&
facet=true&
facet.mincount=1&
group.format=simple&
fq=type:Movies&
facet.field=type&
group.field=product
```

| **Turning grouping and faceting on independently.**

Response

```
{
  ...
  "grouped":{
    "product":{
      "matches":11,
      "doclist":{"numFound":11,"start":0,"docs":[
        {
          "product":"The Hunger Games"},
        {
          "product":"The Amazing Spider Man - 2012"},
        {
          "product":"Spider Man - 2002"},
        {
          "product":"Spider Man 2 - 2004"},
        {
          "product":"Top Gun"},
        {
          "product":"A Beautiful Mind"}]
      }}},
  "facet_counts":{
    ...
    "facet_fields":{
      "type":[
        "Movies",11]},
  ...
}}
```

❶ Only six groups/unique docs remain after collapsing by product.

❷ Facet counts represent the 11 total results, not the six grouped results.

The first characteristic of the listing that you should notice is that although 11 documents matched the filter for type:Movies, only six documents were returned in the grouped search results ❶ when the results were collapsed by the product field. This is because several of the movies contained duplicate documents corresponding to different movie formats (DVD, Blu-ray, and even VHS), so the duplicate documents with the same product name were collapsed out. The second characteristic you may notice is that the facet counts ❷ are still based upon the total number of documents and not the collapsed number of documents.

From a customer's perspective, however, there are not 11 unique movies upon which they should be able to facet. The customer most likely does not care about all the format variations and simply wants to see that there are six unique movies. Thankfully, by setting the parameter group.facet=true, as shown in the next listing, you can achieve this desired result.

Listing 11.10 Limiting facet counts to grouped search results

Request

```
http://localhost:8983/solr/ecommerce/select?
  fl=product&
  group=true&
  sort=popularity asc&
  q=*:*&
  facet=true&
  facet.mincount=1&
  group.format=simple&
  fq=type:Movies&
  facet.field=type&            ⊳ Requests facets on
  group.field=product&           count of groups vs.
  group.facet=true               count of docs.
```

Response

```
{
  ...
  "grouped":{
    "product":{                              ⊳ Total number of
      "matches":11,                            docs matching
      "doclist":{"numFound":11,"start":0,"docs":[  ⊲ query was 11.
        {
          "product":"The Hunger Games"},         ⊲
        {
          "product":"The Amazing Spider Man - 2012"},  ⊲
        {
          "product":"Spider Man - 2002"},        ⊲   Total
        {                                             groups/unique
          "product":"Spider Man 2 - 2004"},     ⊲   docs was six.
        {
          "product":"Top Gun"},                 ⊲
        {
          "product":"A Beautiful Mind"}]         ⊲
      }}},
  "facet_counts":{
    ...
    "facet_fields":{
      "type":[
        "Movies",6]},        ⊳ Facet value is six, the number
  ...                          of groups/unique docs.
}}
```

This ability to group on a field and then facet on the collapsed group can come in handy for situations like those previously covered. If you don't want to apply the `group.facet=true` setting to all facets, you can also turn it on selectively by specifying `f.<field>.group.facet=true`, where `<field>` represents the field associated with the field facet upon which you want the `group.facet` behavior applied. It's worth noting that grouped faceting cannot be applied to multiple requested groups (when multiple `group` parameters are requested on the Solr URL). As such, if you do turn on grouped faceting, you should be aware that it only applies to the first requested result grouping.

11.6.2 *Distributed result grouping*

One important consideration when using Solr's result grouping functionality is how it interacts with distributed search. Unlike standard searches, result grouping cannot be said to fully work in distributed mode; instead, it's more accurate to say that it works in a pseudo-distributed mode. Grouping does return aggregated results in distributed mode, but the results are only the aggregates of the groups calculated locally on each Solr core.

Why does this matter? It matters because if the values you are grouping on are randomly distributed across Solr cores, the counts of grouped documents are going to be inaccurate. If you were grouping a query for products by a field containing the product manufacturer's name (to see all the unique products for that manufacturer), your total count of groups would be roughly the sum of the group counts for each Solr core you searched against in a distributed search. If, and only if, your documents are partitioned into separate shards by manufacturer name would you get the correct group count, because each group would be guaranteed to only exist on one shard. This is an important consideration to keep in mind if you plan on using Solr's grouping functionality in a distributed mode and require that the count of groups (returned by `group.ngroups=true`) is accurate. If your data is not sharded by the field you are grouping on and you are performing a distributed search, the count of groups that is returned will merely be an upper limit. We cover how to partition your documents by a field, such as manufacturer name, using a feature called custom hashing in section 13.7.1.

In addition to these data partitioning limitations, a few of the grouping parameters simply do not currently work in a distributed mode (`group.truncate` and `group.func`), so be careful using these if you think your data will grow beyond what one Solr core can handle.

11.6.3 *Returning a flat list*

You saw in section 11.2 how to return grouped results in the simple (flat) grouped format instead of the default advanced grouping format by setting the parameter `group.format =simple`. You also saw that you could return the first group in the main default results format (such as a nongrouped query) by setting the `group.main=true` parameter. Although both of these options are useful, you should think long and hard whether you can live without the extra information provided by the advanced grouping format. Without the advanced format, Solr cannot return the number of groups. If you are using grouping to collapse documents, this means that you will not know how many unique values were found without using the advanced format. Because it can often be challenging to change the response format in your application down the line, you should carefully consider which format(s) to use during your initial application development.

11.6.4 *Grouping on multivalued and tokenized fields*

Grouping doesn't work at all on multivalued fields (defined as `multivalued="true"` in the *schema.xml*); it'll throw an exception if you try it. In contrast, grouping on tokenized fields (fields in which text is split into multiple tokens) will return results, but the results are unreliable and largely undefined. Specifically, if you group on a tokenized field, the `groupValue` will only represent one of the tokens within the field for each document, and you do not get to choose which token is used. As such, you won't see a separate `groupValue` for each token; you'll be grouping on a seemingly random token from within the field you are grouping. Because Solr is trying to treat the tokenized field as a single token field, this makes grouping mostly unsuitable for use on any field containing more than one token. Grouping on a field, in almost all use cases, should only be performed on a single-token, non-multivalued field.

11.6.5 *Grouping performance*

Although grouping is a powerful feature, it's considerably slower than a standard Solr query. With a large number of documents with unique values to be grouped on, a grouped query can take many times longer than a nongrouped search request.

In order to help speed up grouping, a cache can be turned on for your grouping queries using the `group.cache.percent` query parameter. This parameter defaults to `0`, so setting it to any value between `1` and `100` will turn it on. Grouping in Solr internally requires two searches to be executed, and the `group.cache.percent` parameter represents a percentage of documents (out of all documents in the index) that can be cached along with their scores from the first search in order to speed up the second search. The higher this percentage is set, the more memory your grouping queries will consume, so you should experiment with different values in order to get the maximum speed with the lowest number possible. It's an advanced feature, but it has been demonstrated to improve the performance of queries, whether Boolean, wildcard, or fuzzy. Be careful, as it has also been shown to decrease performance on simple queries such as term queries and match all (`*:*`) queries.

You will need to measure the performance impact for your own search application, including whether or not to turn group caching on, but a query using result grouping is most likely going to demonstrate a performance slowdown relative to a nongrouped query. You should certainly take this performance impact into consideration when determining whether Solr's grouping capabilities make sense for your use case.

If your use case only requires collapsing results down to a single unique document per field value and doesn't need to support sorting by multiple values prior to collapsing, there is a much more efficient implementation of field collapsing available as of Solr 4.6, which will be described in the next section.

11.7 *Efficient field collapsing with the Collapsing query parser*

Solr 4.6 introduced the Collapsing query parser (`CollapsingQParserPlugin`), which enables you to collapse search results to a single result per unique field value without the complexity of invoking the full result grouping stack. This capability can be invoked just as any other query parser:

```
/select?q=*:*&fq={!collapse field=fieldToCollapseOn}
```

This query will return only one document per unique value within the field called `fieldtoCollapseOn`, where that document is the one containing the highest relevancy score among all documents containing that unique field value. In addition to returning the document with the highest score, it is also possible to return the document with the minimum or maximum value within a numeric field or function query.

```
/select?q=*:*&fq={!collapse field=fieldToCollapseOn min=numericFieldName}
/select?q=*:*&fq={!collapse field=fieldToCollapseOn max=numericFieldName}
/select?q=*:*&fq={!collapse field=fieldToCollapseOn max=sum(field1, field2)}
```

One final feature of the Collapsing query parser is the ability to handle missing values in multiple ways through a `nullPolicy`. The `nullPolicy` determines what happens to documents that do not contain a value in the field upon which you are collapsing. Three choices exist for the `nullPolicy`: ignore, expand, and collapse. You can remove all documents with `null` values by specifying a `nullPolicy` of ignore (which is also the default if no `nullPolicy` is specified):

```
/select?q=*:*&fq={!collapse field=fieldToCollapseOn nullPolicy=ignore}
/select?q=*:*&fq={!collapse field=fieldToCollapseOn}
```

Alternatively, if you want to treat a missing value as its own group, you can specify a `nullPolicy` of collapse, which will collapse to a single value for all documents containing a `null` value:

```
/select?q=*:*&fq={!collapse field=fieldToCollapseOn nullPolicy=collapse}
```

Finally, if you only want to collapse documents with duplicate values in the `fieldToCollapseOn` field but want to return all documents with a `null` value, you should specify a `nullPolicy` of expand.

```
/select?q=*:*&fq={!collapse field=fieldToCollapseOn nullPolicy=expand}
```

Conceptually, the Collapsing query parser will return results similar to what you would see when using grouping (`group=true`) and specifying the `group.main=true`, `group.limit=1`, and `sort=score desc` (or sorting by a numeric field's value if you specify a `min` or `max` instead of a `field` parameter to the Collapsing query parser).

If you are interested in using the Collapsing query parser, there is one major limitation of which you should be aware: it does not respect the `sort` parameter passed in on the search prior to collapsing. Grouping first sorts all of the documents prior to collapsing them, but the Collapsing query parser only looks at a single factor (the relevancy score or the `min`/`max` value). As such, if you need to sort on anything other than the score or `min`/`max` value, the Collapsing query parser does not currently support this. As of Solr 4.7, however, the Collapsing query parser does support sorting documents based upon the calculated value of a function, which means you can technically implement your own combination of sorting criteria using a function:

```
/select?q=*:*&fq={!collapse field=fieldToCollapseOn max=sum(product(field1,
    1000000), cscore())}
```

In this example, we are effectively sorting by `field1 desc` and then the `cscore desc` (a special "collapse score" function for getting the score of a document before collapsing), since `field1`'s value should always be higher than the `cscore` function. If you need to sort your documents prior to collapsing based upon something you cannot model through a function query, however, you'll need to stick with the full grouping implementation for now.

11.8 Summary

This chapter has demonstrated Solr's result grouping/field collapsing capabilities. This functionality enables many query options, including removing duplicate or near duplicate documents dynamically at query time, ensuring results come from diverse categories, or even executing multiple queries with a single request. Result grouping can also be used to modify the results used for faceting, preventing duplicate documents from being considered each time for facet counts. You also saw how to return multiple documents per group and how to group on fields, functions, and queries. Finally, you got to see some of the trickier gotchas associated with using Solr's result grouping functionality, and you saw both the performance impacts of result grouping and the formats in which grouped results can be returned.

The last five chapters have covered many of Solr's key search features, and by now you should feel prepared to build a world-class search application based upon Solr. Taking that search application to production will require additional work, and that effort is the subject of our next chapter.

Taking Solr to production

This chapter covers

- Building and deploying your Solr distribution
- Monitoring for and debugging issues with Solr
- Scaling Solr across servers to handle large content and query volumes
- Choosing the right configuration (hardware, OS, JVM, and Solr caches)

Most of the examples in previous chapters have used small datasets intended to demonstrate how Solr's core functionality works. At some point, however, you will want to move beyond a prototype and into a production system capable of handling a large number of queries and/or documents. This means that you will have additional concerns beyond Solr's functional capabilities: You will care about server configuration (CPU, RAM, and OS), how many servers you need, how the servers communicate, which Solr settings need to be "tuned" to handle load, how to monitor performance issues and debug Solr's code, and how to fix problems when they arise. You will also have to worry about writing code to communicate with Solr (or using libraries) to run queries, and how to most efficiently get your data indexed into Solr. This chapter will cover some of these practical nuts and bolts of taking Solr to production.

12.1 Developing a Solr distribution

A new version of Solr (along with Lucene) is officially released several times per year, but since it is completely open source, the most recent trunk version of Solr is available to be pulled and built at any time. The trunk version of Solr contains all committed changes, though any functionality in trunk could still be subject to change since it has not yet made it into an official release.

In addition to newly committed changes, there is a large collection of patches available on Solr's JIRA page (https://issues.apache.org/jira/browse/SOLR) that have been contributed by developers all around the world. Many of these patches will be committed to the trunk version of Lucene/Solr once a Solr committer agrees to review and approve the changes contributed in the patch. Since all of this code is publicly available and free to use, you can create your own custom Solr distribution if you need features or bug fixes not available in an official release.

Because most readers will stick with officially released versions of Solr (as opposed to building their own), we have chosen not to slow this chapter down with a discussion of how to pull the source code for the many branches of Solr. Instead, we have covered this material in appendix A, along with information on how to

- Apply Solr patches
- Set up Solr in the IntelliJ IDEA and Eclipse integrated-development environments (IDEs)
- Build your own Solr distribution
- Debug the Solr codebase (both locally and on remote servers)
- Contribute patches back to the open source community containing your own Solr modifications

Whether you want to debug through the Solr codebase in your favorite IDE or pursue your own branch of Solr development, appendix A should provide you with all the steps you need to quickly get off the ground developing code to integrate with Solr. Once you've finished your Solr development (or downloaded the most recent official release to use out of the box), you'll be ready to build Solr and deploy it to a production environment, which is covered in the following section.

12.2 Deploying Solr

Solr builds into a standard Java web application archive (WAR file), which means it can be deployed in any modern servlet container. If you are unfamiliar with how WAR files integrate into Java servlet containers to power web applications, you can check out http://en.wikipedia.org/wiki/WAR_file_format_(Sun) for a quick introduction. When you launch the example Solr application (using *start.jar* as we have throughout the book), an embedded version of Jetty, a Java servlet container, is launched to run the *solr.war* file, though many users choose to deploy Solr into Apache Tomcat or other servlet containers. If you're writing another Java application, it's also possible to add direct code references to the Solr libraries and embed Solr within your application.

This section will cover the process of building a Solr distribution and basic production deployment.

12.2.1 Building your Solr distribution

When you download an official distribution of Solr, it ships with a *$SOLR_INSTALL/dist/* folder that contains a *solr-*.war* file (where * corresponds to the Solr version number). It's recommended that you rename the *solr-*.war* file to *solr.war* for simplicity. This WAR file and the Solr home directory (*$SOLR_INSTALL/example/solr/*) are all that are necessary to deploy Solr into your servlet container.

BUILDING THE *SOLR.WAR* FILE

If you have pulled the Lucene/Solr codebase yourself, the *solr.war* file will not be present until you build Solr. You can build the *solr.war* file by running the `ant dist` target from your *lucene-solr/solr/* directory, where *lucene-solr/* is the home directory of the Lucene/Solr codebase you pulled in appendix A:

```
cd lucene-solr/
cd solr/
ant dist
```

Once the command successfully finishes, all you need do is copy the *lucene-solr/solr/dist/solr-*.war* file and the *lucene-solr/solr/example/solr/* directory (or your own Solr home directory if you have customized your Solr configuration) to your servlet container. If you are unfamiliar with this process, specific instructions for setting up most popular servlet containers, such as Jetty, Tomcat, GlassFish, JBoss, Resin, WebLogic, and WebSphere, can be found at http://wiki.apache.org/solr/SolrInstall.

DEPLOYING SOLR WITH JETTY

Solr ships with an embedded version of Jetty that starts up whenever you start the Solr example by executing the `java -jar start.jar` command from your *lucene-solr/solr/example/* directory. If you were to try starting up Solr this way after only running the `ant dist` command, you would get an exception stating that the *solr.war* file could not be found.

This is because Jetty looks for a *solr.war* file in your *lucene-solr/solr/example/webapps/* directory, and `ant dist` builds the *solr.war* file elsewhere. To use the `java -jar start.jar` command, you need to either manually copy the *solr.war* file into *lucene-solr/solr/example/webapps/* (as you would for any other servlet container) or use the familiar `ant example` command as a shortcut to both run `ant dist` and copy the WAR file to *lucene-solr/solr/example/webapps/* for you:

```
ant example
```

If you deploy the *lucene-solr/solr/example/start.jar* file along with the *lucene-solr/solr/example/solr/* home directory to your production server, this is all you need (other than Java) to successfully start up Solr in your production environment.

12.2.2 *Embedded Solr*

In addition to deploying the *solr.war* file to a servlet container, it is also possible to run Solr embedded within another Java application. This can be particularly useful if you need to add search functionality to your application but want to keep Solr self-contained within the scope of your application and not exposed as a service that could be hit by other applications or across your network. The process of starting Solr embedded within your Java application makes use of the SolrJ Java client for Solr and will be covered, along with SolrJ, in section 12.8.3. Regardless of whether you are embedding Solr within an application or running it as a standalone server, making sure that you have the right kind of hardware for your use case and having your system properly configured are important for performance. The next section will dive into some of these considerations.

12.3 *Hardware and server configuration*

Solr is able to scale to handle as many queries as you need across billions of documents in tens to hundreds of milliseconds. Handling thousands of queries per second and hundreds of millions of documents or more, however, is generally beyond the scope of what a single server can handle. For large documents, Solr may only be able to store a few million documents per server, whereas for small documents Solr may be able to store hundreds of millions and still maintain reasonable query speed. Although there is no magic formula for determining the right server configuration for any particular use case, there are some general guidelines that can lead you in the right direction.

12.3.1 *RAM and SSDs*

If you're running your own servers (as opposed to using a cloud-based service like Amazon EC2 or Rackspace Cloud Servers), one of the best investments you can make for Solr's performance is to add more RAM to your servers. RAM is incredibly cheap relative to other parts of your server, and Solr can be quite a memory hog. Even if you are using a cloud provider, you should consider experimenting with larger instances containing more RAM to see if the extra performance boost justifies the cost.

For its core operations, Solr caches consume memory for things like faceting, sorting, indexing documents, and query results caching, and you need to ensure you have allocated enough memory to hold these data structures safely. You can see how much memory is both available and allocated from the main Solr admin page.

Equally important to the speed of your queries, however, can be whether your Solr index can fit completely into the available memory not allocated to your JVM. If the Solr index is larger than the amount of extra RAM available on your server, this means hard disk seeks will be necessary throughout the course of your search requests in order to load files into memory, which can significantly affect both query speed and query throughput.

Some Solr users counteract the expense of disk seeks by purchasing SSDs (solid-state hard drives). This can definitely speed up disk seeks, but wouldn't it be better if you didn't have to perform them in the first place? Indeed, you're likely to see the best possible query performance out of Solr if you guarantee that you have more than enough memory to ensure that the entire index is always in memory and never swaps back out to disk. If you need more indexing throughput, SSDs may provide a larger benefit since indexing is a more disk I/O constrained operation.

In most modern OSes (including Linux, which is most common for production in Solr deployments), once a file is loaded one time, it is kept in memory until the system requires the memory for some other need. Keeping files recently loaded from disk in this OS filesystem cache in memory until nearly all available memory has been used (and RAM allocated to files accessed less recently must be freed up for new data) allows applications that reuse files to pull them from memory on subsequent access attempts.

Because Solr's job is to access the same large chunks of data (the data in the Solr index) over and over, this makes the OS filesystem cache extremely important to the overall performance of your Solr server. Although many Solr indexes can be hundreds of gigabytes and beyond the realm of how much RAM it's practical to put in a server today, it's nevertheless true that if you can manage to ensure your Solr index size is always less than the total amount of RAM in your system, you will essentially never have to seek to disk in order to execute a Solr query once all files have been initially loaded into memory. In this scenario, you effectively have an in-memory search engine, which enables considerably faster indexing throughput and faster query times. The takeaway from this section should be that, although SSDs are good, RAM is usually better, and you should consider adding enough RAM to your server to fit your entire index (plus whatever memory you allocate the JVM to run Solr) if you require the fastest speeds.

12.3.2 *JVM settings*

This is not a book about garbage collection or the JVM, but there are settings which you should be aware of that affect Solr's performance. First, instead of relying on the JVM to grab more from the OS when needed, you will do best to allocate a predetermined amount of memory to the JVM running Solr:

```
java -Xms2g -Xmx2g -jar start.jar
```

or

```
java -Xms2048m -Xmx2048m -jar start.jar
```

In the example, 2 GB was set as both the minimum and maximum amount of memory that will be allocated to Solr's JVM. Your Solr instance may need 1 GB of memory, or it may need 20 GB of memory, but if you predefine the minimum (Xms) and maximum (Xmx) amount of memory, you will ensure that Solr isn't slowed down by the process of growing or shrinking the available memory on demand. As discussed in the previous section, it's ill-advised to allocate more memory to Solr's JVM than is necessary for Solr to keep its key data structures (caches, Solr cores, and other in-memory structures) in memory and perform its query operations. As such, it's important for your OS to be able to cache files from your Solr index in any available spare memory. If you allocate too much memory, then your garbage-collection times will increase, since more will be garbage collected at once, and you will starve your OS's filesystem cache (discussed in the previous section) of available memory to keep your Solr index files in memory without going back to your hard drive. The general rule of thumb is to give Solr only what it needs plus a little buffer, and leave the rest to the OS. Solr provides a memory gauge on the main admin page (shown later in figure 12.1) that can help you measure how much memory is being consumed by your running Solr instance.

GARBAGE COLLECTION IN SOLR

Garbage collection in Java is a painful science. People often ask which garbage collector is best for Solr, but results vary from deployment to deployment. If you need the best possible performance most of the time and are willing to accept long pauses (that is, Solr becoming unresponsive) some of the time, then you may be fine with the throughput garbage collector, which is turned on by default in a 64-bit server configuration.

If you need more consistent performance, in which queries can be slower on average but pauses (Solr becoming unresponsive) are rare and last for much shorter durations, then the concurrent marksweep garbage collector may be best for you:

```
java -server
    -XX:+UseConcMarkSweepGC
    -XX:+UseParNewGC
    -XX:CMSInitiatingOccupancyFraction=80
    -Xmx$JAVA_HEAP_SIZE
    -Xms$JAVA_HEAP_SIZE
    -jar start.jar
```

These settings are an example that works well for many Solr users, but you should consult your JVM vendor's documentation on garbage collection options, and experiment based upon the performance characteristics of your Solr server in your environment. Many garbage collectors and combinations of optional settings are available to optimize your JVM's garbage collection process, but good garbage collection tuning is a complicated topic that is well beyond the scope of this book. If you determine that garbage collection is having a material impact on your Solr server's performance, there are many external resources available online independent of Solr that you can find to help in this area.

12.3.3 *The index shuffle*

In the previous two sections, we discussed the importance of RAM and the OS filesystem cache's ability to keep recently accessed Solr index files in memory. What happens when new documents are added to Solr and the index changes? This process of index restructuring can have a significant impact on performance that's worth understanding.

INCREMENTAL INDEXING

Solr internally uses Lucene to create an inverted index of the documents it receives. This index follows an *incremental indexing* process by which changes are always written to new files and never applied to previously written files.

Conceptually, this means that once an index file is written, it will never change. It also means that in order to copy an updated index from one server to another, only the new files containing the incremental changes need to be copied. Since indexes can often be tens or hundreds of gigabytes large, the incremental nature of the index is beneficial in several ways:

- Disk space needs are reduced since previous index files are shared across multiple newer index versions.
- Replication of changes from one server to another requires moving small incremental files.
- The OS's filesystem cache already contains most of an index (the old files) whenever a new index version is committed.

This incremental indexing process does come with a few costs, however. Chief among these is the fact that since old files can never be updated, any document updates or deletes actually take up extra space, because they are written to entirely new files. As such, if you send the same document over and over to Solr, you will see your index size continue to grow, since both the old and new versions of the documents remain in the index. In the case of a document delete, a blacklist is kept telling Solr to ignore the old version of the document, but the old version still remains in a preexisting index segment. If you are reindexing all of your content (into a Solr instance already containing the old content), you can expect the size of your index to grow considerably during this process, even though not much of the incoming content may have actually changed.

When we say that old files are never changed, this needs some clarification. At some point after many commits, so many index segments will exist that it is necessary to merge segments to form new combined segments within your index. This merging process does not technically modify previous segments; it instead writes new segments that make the old segments no longer necessary. At some point after the old index segment files are no longer being referenced by Solr, they will be deleted in order to free up disk space.

As discussed in chapter 5, in order for the documents in a new index segment to become live and available for searching, a commit must occur. A hard commit (which must occur) kicks off a process by which the searcher for the old index is swapped out for a searcher across the new index (old index segments plus new incremental segments).

INDEX FLIPPING AND CACHE WARMING

When a hard commit occurs, a new searcher is created, which has a reference to the previous index segments still in the index plus any new index segments that have been added. Since Solr may be continually receiving search requests, it's important that the query experience isn't impacted whenever the new index becomes available for searching.

Solr accomplishes a seamless transition from the old index version to the new index version by having two searchers running in parallel. The old searcher (pointing only to the old index segments) continues receiving request traffic while the new searcher (pointing to the old index segments plus any new segments) is loaded.

Because Solr makes use of caches to keep previous queries, filters, field values, and other data in memory and speed up search time, it is important that these caches continue to work when the new searcher begins accepting queries. Unfortunately, since the caches are tied to a specific version of the index, this means that time must be spent warming new caches for the new searcher based upon values in the caches for the previous searcher. To clarify, every time a hard commit occurs, a new searcher is created, along with new caches that need to be warmed for the new searcher. The configurations for total cache size and the number of cached items to populate in the new searcher from the old searcher's caches are specified in the *solrconfig.xml* when each of the caches is defined:

```
<fieldValueCache class="solr.FastLRUCache" size="500" initialSize="50"
    autowarmCount="500" />
<filterCache class="solr.FastLRUCache" size="500" initialSize="500"
    autowarmCount="250" />
<queryResultCache class="solr.LRUCache" size="100" initialSize="100"
    autowarmCount="0" />
<documentCache class="solr.LRUCache" size="500" initialSize="500"
    autowarmCount="0" />
```

In each of these examples, the maximum size of each cache is between 100 and 500 items. In some instances you may want much larger cache sizes, especially if you have plenty of memory allocated to your JVM and your hit rate continues to increase linearly as you increase the cache size (see section 12.9.2 for more information about cache hit rates). The larger you increase the cache size, however, the more items there are to be autowarmed anytime a new searcher starts up.

Although it's okay to set a large cache size for your caches (if you have enough memory to support it), you may have to be more pragmatic when setting your `autowarmCount`. The larger your autowarm count, the longer it will take to autowarm any new searchers, and therefore the longer it will take for your commits to finish and for your documents to become active.

For the `filterCache`, in particular, if you have many expensive filters, it can take minutes or even hours (in a fringe case) to autowarm a searcher, which is not realistic for many search applications. Nevertheless, if you set your `autowarmCount` too low, you are likely to negatively impact the initial performance of the new searcher once it begins receiving traffic. This could result in slower user query times and potentially introduce unexpected pauses in responses from Solr while common expensive queries (such as those generating facets for the first time) are executed. You will need to tune your cache sizes (through trial and error) to arrive at a reasonable `autowarmCount` setting that optimizes for both cache effectiveness on a new searcher and time required to autowarm.

SEGMENT MERGING AND OPTIMIZING

As discussed in chapter 5, when index segments get too big, they are automatically merged to compress the index (removing deleted documents and duplicate versions of documents). The decision to merge index segments is based upon the merge policy defined in your *solrconfig.xml* file. The *merge scheduler* and the *merge policy* determine when and how segments are merged:

```
<mergeScheduler class="org.apache.lucene.index.ConcurrentMergeScheduler">
  <int name="maxMergeCount">4</int>
  <int name="maxThreadCount">4</int>
</mergeScheduler>

<mergePolicy class="org.apache.lucene.index.TieredMergePolicy">
  <int name="maxMergeAtOnce">10</int>
  <int name="segmentsPerTier">10</int>
</mergePolicy>

<mergeFactor>10</mergeFactor>
```

TieredMergePolicy is the default merge policy in Solr, and is generally the most effective. Two parameters, maxMergeAtOnce and segmentsPerTier, determine when segments will be merged. The segmentsPerTier setting determines how many segments can be created before Solr begins merging them. The maxMergeAtOnce setting determines how many segments can be merged into a new segment at once. By default, both values are set to 10, and if either isn't defined for the TieredMergePolicy, its value is set to the value of the separately defined mergeFactor parameter (which also defaults to 10).

In general, the higher you set your mergeFactor (or the individual maxMergeAtOnce and segmentsPerTier options), the faster Solr will be able to index documents since the cost of merging is experienced less often. A larger number of segments slows down searching, as more files must be searched through in the index, and each of those files is likely to have old copies of documents and deleted documents that have not yet been merged out. The default mergeFactor of 10 works well for most use cases, but you may want to increase or decrease the value based upon whether you are more concerned with indexing quickly or searching quickly.

In some cases, you may need to merge all documents down to a single segment by initiating an optimize. If you only need to perform a one-time index of your data, for example, you may want to optimize your index down to one clean segment after you finish indexing in order to make searches on the index as fast as possible. Additionally, if you perform a lot of updates on your index (such as updating most of your documents every day), it might make sense to optimize periodically in a low-volume search time in order to recover some of the space consumed by keeping multiple copies of old documents in your index. To optimize your entire index, you can post an <optimize/> tag to your /update handler from your web client. If you are issuing the command manually, you can alternatively pass in the posted content stream using the convenience parameter of stream.body on a get request: http://localhost:8983/solr/collection1/update?stream.body=<optimize/>.

Keep in mind that an `optimize` is an expensive operation—it is rewriting your entire index line by line—and may take a long time and consume an excessive amount of system resources. Your merge policy, if set aggressively enough, may eliminate the need to optimize your index, since your segments are being merged frequently enough to reasonably clean up the accumulated waste. Because your entire index is being rewritten during an `optimize`, you may also have issues fitting both the old and the new index segments into your OS's buffer cache at the same time, which means your query speed may suffer if you do not have enough RAM to accommodate both indexes. You can mitigate this if your index is broken into multiple Solr cores on the same server by optimizing only one Solr core at a time, but be aware of the potential impact that optimizing your index can have when making the decision as to whether the benefit after the `optimize` is finished warrants the expense that will be incurred during the process of optimizing.

In addition to these indexing optimizations and the hardware and JVM setting optimizations in the last section, the next section will cover OS-level settings that can have an effect on the speed and stability of your Solr servers.

12.3.4 *Useful system tricks*

Solr's code is written in Java, which means it should be able to run on about any OS. That being said, most production Solr clusters (and production servers in general) are run on a Linux OS. This section will outline useful tricks that can enhance the performance of a production system running Linux.

AUTOWARMING THE OS FILESYSTEM CACHE

As discussed in section 12.3.1, having enough RAM on your server to fit your entire Solr index (plus the memory you allocate to your JVM) can tremendously help Solr's performance, as it allows the OS's filesystem cache to keep loaded files from the hard drive in memory after the first time the files are loaded. Unfortunately, it still requires all of the files to be loaded initially, which means the first time you start up Solr after a system restart (or after a long delay in which other files are loaded and kick the Solr index out of memory), Solr will run much more slowly than usual—every time it hits a file it hasn't used before—until it has eventually been able to pull all files back into memory.

There is a clever trick to bypass the slowness associated with files in the Solr index lazy loading on the first access: preload all of the files into memory before Solr even starts using the following command.

```
find $SOLR_INSTALL/example/solr/*/data/ -type f -exec cat {} \; > /dev/null
```

Assuming that you use the default directory structure for storing your Solr indexes for each Solr core (*$SOLR_INSTALL/example/solr/$CORE_NAME/data/*), this command will load all of the files one by one into memory from disk for each of your Solr cores without trying to display them anywhere. If you store your data directories elsewhere, you need to modify the path in the command accordingly. For large indexes (tens to hundreds of gigabytes), the process of preloading all files into the OS filesystem cache can take several minutes to finish executing, but searches will run much faster if you run the command before starting Solr, especially if you have just restarted your server.

To test that this is working, run the command twice: once right after a system restart, and once right after the first run. You will notice that the second time you run the command it's considerably faster (nearly instantaneous), demonstrating that the files were loaded directly from memory on the second attempt, and showing why this trick can be so helpful when first starting up Solr.

Do keep in mind that if your Solr index is larger than your free memory, not every file will still be in memory after executing this trick. In fact, if you already have a running Solr instance and then push your entire index through memory like this, you're likely to actually push out some more important files Solr has been using in the process. If you have plenty of memory, use this trick liberally, but otherwise, proceed with caution.

INCREASING AVAILABLE FILE DESCRIPTORS

Due to the nature of Lucene's incremental indexing process, an index can be composed of hundreds of files, all of which may need to be opened at once. If you have many indexes in Solr, this means that Solr can have thousands of files that it must keep open at any given time to enable searching. Unfortunately, having this many files open at once can exceed the upper limit for available file handles set as the default on some Unix-based OSes. Hitting this upper limit can result in Solr crashing due to being unable to open additional index files during the normal course of index fragmentation. The number of file descriptors Solr is using relative to the limit (the maximum number of files that can be opened at once) is tracked on the main dashboard on the Solr Admin page, as shown in figure 12.1.

In figure 12.1, you can see that the number of files Solr has open (mostly from indexes belonging to multiple Solr cores) has reached the system file descriptor limit, which means Solr is likely about to crash. This is fortunately an easy problem to fix through the use of the `ulimit -n` command. Issuing the `ulimit -n` command will tell you the user limit for file descriptors available. In order to increase this limit, which is important for safely running Solr, you need to specify a new limit.

```
ulimit -n 100000
```

Many systems have a default file descriptor limit of 1024, but since each Solr index can consist of hundreds of files (or even thousands depending upon your `MergePolicy` settings), it may be necessary to increase this limit to 100,000 (from our example) or something even higher, especially if you expect to have many Solr cores on your server. You will probably want to set this limit permanently (running the command only applies to the current bash session) by setting it in a system-wide configuration such as */etc/security/limits.conf*. You should ensure that your new file descriptor limit is sufficiently large that you will never run the chance of hitting it.

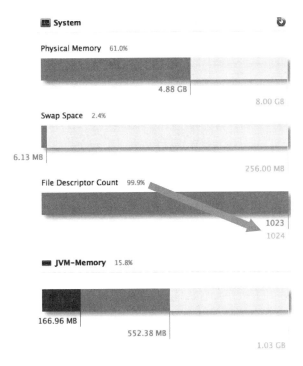

Figure 12.1   The file descriptor usage and limit displayed with other system resource information on the Solr Admin page.

12.4   Data acquisition strategies

So far, you have seen one way to post documents to Solr: through sending a document over HTTP to the Solr /update handler. We have utilized an included *post.jar* file as a convenience library for posting files containing Solr documents primarily in XML format, but under the covers it posts the contents of a file to Solr's /update handler for you. It's also possible to have Solr ingest documents in other ways, either through pushing documents to Solr in other formats or through having Solr import documents itself from any number of external data sources.

UPDATE FORMATS, INDEXING TIME, AND BATCHING

As you saw in chapter 5 (section 5.5), Solr supports the posting of content to the /update handler in many different formats out of the box, such as XML, JSON, and CSV. You also saw how to make use of SolrJ to send documents to Solr in a Java binary format to help reduce extra serialization and deserialization costs. One important point to keep in mind when posting documents to Solr is that the total time it takes to index documents is composed of many factors. Some of the internal Solr configuration settings affecting indexing were covered in the "Segment merging and optimizing" part of section 12.3.3, but the input format of documents, the number of network calls and network latency, and the speed of pulling content from the original data source and threading requests to Solr all factor into the total time required to get your content into Solr.

Although you may or may not be able to do much about your networking latency between your content sending server and your Solr server, you can definitely do your part to reduce the total number of round-trip requests to Solr by batching up your documents into one request. If you remember from section 5.5, it's possible to send multiple documents to the /update handler at a time:

```
<add>
  <doc>
  ...
  </doc>
  <doc>
  ...
  </doc>
    ...
</add>
```

Batching your documents instead of creating a separate request for each update request to Solr can yield a huge increase in indexing throughput, as you remove the latency of extra network calls and allow Solr to do more work at once. In general, sending hundreds of medium to large documents at a time is often reasonable, and sending many thousands can be realistic for small documents. You will have to experiment with the size of your update batches based upon the size of your documents and the time it takes per request for Solr to accept all of the content in order to determine the best threshold for your application.

In addition to batching documents, you can have a material impact on your indexing throughput by choosing your input format carefully. Parsing XML requires a lot of processing, meaning that choosing another document-input format such as Java binary (javabin) or CSV should provide a large improvement in indexing time.

Finally, for any process you write that sends content to Solr, it's important that the process is able to overcome any basic bottlenecks: not using enough threads to send documents to Solr while other threads are busy preparing requests or otherwise making Solr wait around for content instead of staying busy actually indexing it. One of the biggest bottlenecks in an indexing process is loading content from an external database and converting it into Solr documents; in many cases, Solr is hardly working because the indexing process allows itself to become bottlenecked when doing this kind of work prior to even talking to Solr. In short, most applications will run into bottlenecks long before Solr's indexing throughput becomes saturated. You should monitor the CPU and other system resources on your Solr server to determine whether it is being stressed by the amount of content it's receiving before assuming that Solr's indexing process is running too slowly. If you determine this to be the case, your best option is to divide your content into multiple Solr cores across several servers and partition your update requests across the servers (or use SolrCloud to manage this process for you, as shown in chapter 13).

DATA IMPORT HANDLER

In addition to writing a process to send content to Solr, you can make use of the Data Import Handler to have Solr pull your content from an external data source. You saw the DIH in action in chapter 10 when we imported 13,000 Wikipedia entries to test out different forms of query suggestions.

The Data Import Handler can reach out to databases, web addresses, or flat files containing data in various formats, and it can use rules you specify to execute queries or look for patterns in the content from those resources to construct Solr documents.

It is able to do full dataset imports (indexing an entire document set) or incremental imports (pulling in changes since the last import), which makes it a useful tool for getting your data into Solr without having to write an external process to send it.

To use the DIH, three important configuration steps are required.

First, in *solrconfig.xml*, we need to use the `<lib>` directive to load the JAR files for the Data Import Handler and its dependencies:

```
<lib dir="../../../contrib/dataimporthandler/lib" regex=".*\.jar" />
<lib dir="../../../dist/" regex="solr-dataimporthandler-.*\.jar" />
```

Second, in *solrconfig.xml*, we need to define the `/dataimport` request handler:

```
<requestHandler name="/dataimport"
    class="org.apache.solr.handler.dataimport.DataImportHandler">
  <lst name="defaults">
    <str name="config">data-config.xml</str>
  </lst>
</requestHandler>
```

The third step for setting up the DIH is to provide a data import configuration file. When defining the DIH in the *solrconfig.xml* file, we had to specify the location of a data import configuration file, which we called *data-config.xml*, in the example request handler configuration. The path to the file you specify is relative to the *conf/* directory for your Solr core. This file includes references to all the external data sources from which data should be pulled, as well as steps for how to transform the records into Solr documents. DIH supports many kinds of external data sources and complex content transformation logic (including support for executing arbitrary scripting code to manipulate data as it is imported), the scope of which is well beyond what can be covered in this chapter. A thorough guide to using the Data Import Handler is located at http://wiki.apache.org/solr/DataImportHandler, which should demonstrate how to import your data automatically.

For some chapters in this book, it has been and will be useful to have large, interesting document sets upon which to experiment. We have decided to reference two large and freely available document sets: the Wikipedia and Stack Exchange data dumps. To demonstrate the power of the Data Import Handler, we have included instructions and example data import configurations in appendix C, which will allow you to quickly get up and running with a full working copy of the Wikipedia or Stack Exchange data in Solr.

Once you have your *data-config.xml* file defined to correctly pull in data and transform it into documents, you can go to the Dataimport tab from the Solr Admin page

Figure 12.2   A data import currently in progress

to kick off a data import or see the status of a current import run. Figure 12.2 demonstrates a data import in progress.

In figure 12.2, you can see the status of a current data import, including an indication of the number of records processed so far. On the left, you have the option to execute a new data import (full or incremental, selected from a dropdown), and on the right you can see the current *data-config.xml* configuration, the status of the current or last import, and the option to abort any current import in progress. If you would like to experiment more with the process of importing datasets directly into Solr, you can get started by using the examples in appendix C to import either the Wikipedia or the Stack Exchange dataset.

EXTRACTING TEXT FROM FILES WITH SOLR CELL

In addition to importing text from databases, websites, and files, Solr is able to extract text out of nontext document types such as PDFs, images, Word documents, Excel spreadsheets, PowerPoint presentations, and other common file formats. This capability is available through the /extraction request handler that is enabled in the example configuration files that ship with Solr. The name of this functionality is Solr Cell, which is derived from the original name of the *Solr Content Extraction Library*. This capability makes use of Apache Tika (http://tika.apache.org/) to do the heavy lifting of extracting text information from numerous file types. You can find configuration options on the Solr Cell wiki page at http://wiki.apache.org/solr/ExtractingRequestHandler.

At this point, it should be clear that Solr provides many options for ingesting content—from accepting content posted to Solr's REST API in many different formats, to automatically importing data from databases, URLs, and files, to extracting information from nontext documents through Solr Cell. Once you begin indexing all of this content, at some point you may have too much content to fit within a single Solr core or a single server. You may also reach the point where your query volumes are too high for a single server to handle. The next section will cover how to scale Solr to handle such increased content and query volumes through sharding and replication.

12.5   *Sharding and replication*

In chapter 3 (section 3.4.2), we introduced the concept of sharding and distributed searching with Solr. Solr allows you to create multiple search indexes, each of which is represented by a Solr core. It is possible to partition your content across multiple Solr indexes (called sharding), as well as to create multiple copies of any partition of the data (called replication). Although you already know how to perform a distributed search across multiple Solr cores from chapter 3, this section will discuss how to determine the number of shards and replicas you need for your Solr cluster. These same factors will be important considerations in chapter 13 when we discuss SolrCloud, which is able to automatically handle management of shards for you.

12.5.1   *Choosing to shard*

Sharding can be useful if you have too many documents to comfortably handle on a single server. Figure 12.3 demonstrates how a simple sharded Solr cluster would look if you chose to partition documents between two shards based upon a simple modulus operation on the hash code of each document's `id` field.

Because each document appears only within one of the two shards in figure 12.3, it's necessary to execute a distributed search across both shards in order to search all documents. See chapter 3 (section 3.4.3) for a refresher on how to execute a distributed search across multiple shards using the `shards` parameter on your query request.

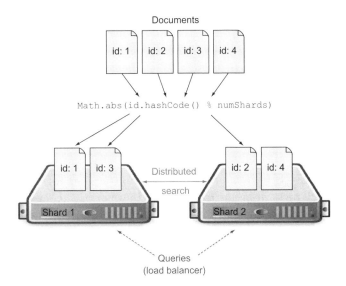

Figure 12.3   Partitioning documents between two shards based upon their document id. Each document will only appear on one shard, and a query to either server will need to execute a distributed search across both shards in order to search all documents.

One decision you need to make when setting up a Solr cluster is the number of shards to split a collection into. You can have one shard or hundreds, depending on the size of your index. If you have only one shard for a collection, your index is not considered sharded. This section provides guidance on how to decide how many shards you need, but since there are too many variables to consider, you'll need to test with your own data to determine the optimal value.

The number of shards has nothing to do with fault tolerance. It is strictly to help scale as the size of your collection of documents grows. Before we get into the details of how to decide on the number of shards, you should realize that, as of Solr 4.3.1, you can easily split an existing shard into two smaller ones within Solr. Consequently, you're not stuck with your initial value. But you don't want to pick the initial value arbitrarily, as shard splitting is intended to deal with the natural growth of your index over time. In general, there are five primary factors you need to consider when deciding on how many shards you need:

1 Total number of documents
2 Document size
3 Required indexing throughput
4 Query complexity
5 Expected growth

TOTAL NUMBER OF DOCUMENTS

One of the upper limits in Solr is that an index cannot contain more than 2^{31} documents, due to an underlying limitation in Lucene. In practice, most installations run into other problems long before they hit this upper limit. As your index becomes large, you'll start to have performance and memory issues when sorting, constructing facets, and caching filter queries.

Let's consider a scenario to help illustrate why sharding a large index is beneficial. Imagine a query that matches 10 million documents and has a custom sort criterion to return documents sorted by timestamp in descending order (`sort=timestamp_tdt desc`). When generating the results for this query, Solr has to sort all 10 million matching hits to produce a page size of 10; the sort alone will require roughly 80 MB of memory to order the results. However, if your 100 million docs are split across 10 shards, each shard is sorting roughly 1 million docs in parallel. There is a little overhead in that Solr needs to re-sort the top 10 hits per shard (100 hits total), but it should be obvious that sorting 1 million documents on 10 nodes in parallel will always be faster than sorting 10 million documents serially on a single node. This is an extreme example; most queries do not match 10 million documents, but the same logic applies for smaller result sets as well. The bottom line is that as the number of documents in your index grows, the more benefits you'll see from sharding.

Sharding also helps you manage memory more effectively. In chapter 5, we introduced `MMapDirectory` as the recommended directory implementation on 64-bit Linux and Windows OSes because it reads the primary data structures of your index from the OS filesystem cache. The basic premise is that you optimize query performance by loading your index into memory-mapped I/O. It stands to reason that the smaller your index, the more of it will fit in the OS filesystem cache. This is one example where we see the benefit of horizontal scaling over vertical scaling.

For example, 3 m1.xlarge servers in Amazon EC2 will provide 12 CPUs, 45 GB of RAM, high network performance, and will cost roughly $1.44/hour. Alternatively, a system with only 8 CPUs, fast network performance, and 68 GB of RAM (m2.4xlarge) would cost $1.64 per hour. So by distributing an index across three nodes, each having roughly 15 GB of memory and 4 CPUs, you increase performance and save money compared to running a single index on one machine with more RAM. As you can see, scaling up the amount of memory within a cloud environment can currently be more expensive than scaling out by using more modest hardware. The figures are obviously subject to change over time, but the principle remains the same.

If you are scaling physical servers instead of cloud servers, however, you may see a different cost/benefit curve for adding additional RAM due to the relatively inexpensive cost of physical memory relative to purchasing and installing new servers. As you add more and more documents, you may eventually have to scale out anyway; it's still best to optimize each server even in a horizontally scaled Solr cluster in order to optimize for the overall performance relative to the cost.

DOCUMENT SIZE

You also need to factor in the size of your documents in terms of the number of fields and amount of content in each field. In general, you'll want more shards for indexes containing documents with a large number of fields because the data structures needed to support search use more memory.

Consider a search application that supports many unique filters. Each cached filter requires maxDoc/8 bytes, so in an index containing 160 million documents, each filter will require roughly 20 MB of RAM in cache. That's not much of a concern unless you have hundreds of filters that need to be cached. If you split the index into 4 shards, each shard contains only about 40 million documents, and each filter only requires 5 MB of RAM, not to mention that you spread the computation of building a filter across 4 nodes running concurrently. The bigger your documents, the fewer documents you will be able to store on a single shard and still maintain reasonable resource utilization and performance.

REQUIRED INDEXING THROUGHPUT

If you are constantly adding and updating documents, then having more shards will help distribute the indexing load. Consider the scenario in which you need to index 5,000 documents per second. If you split the index into ten shards, you'll have roughly ten servers performing indexing concurrently instead of one server. Thus, a sharded collection can typically index more documents per second than a nonsharded collection, especially when doing batch updates. There is some overhead involved in distributed indexing, however, so your indexing throughput will probably not scale in a perfect linear fashion.

QUERY COMPLEXITY

If your index is split among 10 shards, you can use a distributed search to parallelize query processing across those 10 shards for most Solr capabilities (such as searching, faceting, and highlighting). As the complexity of your query increases and your query time grows, splitting your collection of documents into more shards will allow you to further parallelize your queries and speed up final response times. On the flip side, some features, such as grouping and joins, require special index partitioning strategies to work in a distributed mode in order to ensure that related documents are colocated on the same shard and/or server.

EXPECTED GROWTH

You also need to consider how much your index will grow over the next few months. You want to build in room for growth initially. If you know your index will double in size in the next three months, for example, you should choose the number of shards based on the ideal number for three months down the road.

Unfortunately, there's no simple equation to compute the proper number of shards for your application. It's up to you to weigh the factors we discussed. In practice, most Solr installations tend to overshard slightly to allow for growth. If you decide your search application needs four shards, you might consider starting with six to allow for future growth.

TESTING THIS IN DEVELOPMENT

It should be obvious that determining how many shards you need will take experimentation with your own data. Obviously, you probably do not want to experiment with hitting the breaking point in production when testing different shard sizes. One approach we've had success with is to build up a small Solr cluster, such as with two shards, in a development environment, and grow the shards to the same size as they would be in production with a larger number of shards. For example, if you have 200 million documents spread across 10 shards in production, you can build a similar cluster in development having only 40 million documents in 2 shards (both environments having roughly 20 million documents per shard). In addition, you should match your production hardware as closely as possible.

With this setup, you can grow the development shards until you start to see issues, such as out-of-memory errors, slow indexing, or poor query performance. This will give you an idea of the breaking point for the size of shards containing your data without having to build a 200 million document index in development. The bottom line is that a 20 million document shard in development will behave similarly to a 20 million document shard in production, even though your production environment has many more documents spread across more shards.

12.5.2 *Choosing to replicate*

Once you have determined the number of shards to divide your content into, it's possible to run a distributed search across all of your shards, as demonstrated in chapter 3 (section 3.4.2). At this point, you have a fully functioning search experience with a single copy (replica) of each partition of the index. Based upon the performance characteristics of your Solr cluster (such as system configuration, number of documents and fields, size of documents, and complexity of queries and text analysis), however, it's possible that your Solr cluster will not be able to keep up with the query volumes necessary to support your application.

SIMPLE REPLICATION SCENARIO

If your Solr cluster can handle 100 queries per second but your application needs to support 150 queries per second, you have a problem. Rather than breaking your index into additional partitions (adding shards), you would want to create multiple identical copies of your index and load balance traffic across each of the copies. In the simple example in which you have a Solr server with a Solr core that can handle 100 queries per second, if you need to handle 150 queries, you would create a replica of the original shard and balance incoming traffic across the original shard and the replicated shard. Figure 12.4 demonstrates how this server configuration would look.

In figure 12.4, you can see that all documents are still being sent to a single server for indexing (the top server, labeled Master). This server in our example is the original server that could handle 100 queries per second. Figure 12.4 shows that the indexes being generated from the original master server are now being replicated (copied) from the master server to a new server, labeled Slave. Since both servers have an identical copy of the index, you can send half of your queries to the first server and half of your queries to the second server and now collectively handle at least 200 queries per second, providing plenty of capacity to handle your application's search needs.

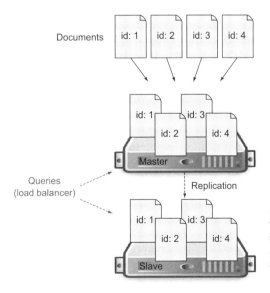

Figure 12.4 Replicating a copy of the index from a primary (master) Solr core on one server to a replica (slave) Solr core on another server. All documents exist on both servers. The replication is for redundancy and/or to increase query capacity.

SEPARATING INDEXING FROM SEARCHING

Since the slave server does not have to deal with the potentially expensive indexing operation, it is possible that the slave server could be able to handle more queries per second than the master server. In many cases, it can even be useful to have a master server dedicated and configured entirely for maximizing indexing through-put, and to have multiple slave servers replicating the index and dedicated entirely to searching. By having this kind of separation in your cluster, you can allow search performance to be relatively unaffected by rapid reindexing of content, even if that reindexing completely overloads the master server. You may want to use replication either when you want to isolate indexing from searching operations to different servers within your cluster or when you need to increase available queries-per-second capacity.

FAULT TOLERANCE

It's great that we can increase our overall query capacity by adding another server and replicating the index to that server, but what happens when one of our servers eventually crashes? When our application had only one server, the application clearly would have stopped. Now that multiple, redundant servers exist, one server dying will simply reduce our capacity back to the capacity of however many servers remain. If you want to build fault tolerance into your system, it's a good idea to have additional resources (extra slave servers) in your cluster so that your system can continue functioning with enough capacity even if a single server fails. Through using replication, you can build this kind of redundancy into your system to greatly reduce the chances of your application going offline in the event of a single server failure.

SETTING UP REPLICATION

Now that you understand why you would want to replicate, we can take a look at how to set up replication in your Solr cluster. Fundamentally, replication requires a server to perform indexing (the master server), and a server to pull a copy of the index from the master (the slave server). The `/replication` handler in Solr must be configured on both the master and slave servers in order for the slave to be able to check with the master periodically and copy any updated index files. The following listing demonstrates how you would set up replication on both servers.

> **Listing 12.1   Setting up replication between a master and slave server**

Master server's *solrconfig.xml*

```
(http://masterserver:8983/solr/core1)
<requestHandler name="/replication" class="solr.ReplicationHandler">
    <lst name="master">
        <str name="enable">true</str>
        <str name="replicateAfter">commit</str>
        <str name="replicateAfter">optimize</str>
        <str name="replicateAfter">startup</str>
    </lst>
</requestHandler>
```

Slave server's *solrconfig.xml*

```
(http://slaveserver:8983/solr/core1)
<requestHandler name="/replication" class="solr.ReplicationHandler">
    <lst name="slave">
        <str name="enable">true</str>
        <str name="masterUrl">
            http://masterserver:8983/solr/core1/replication
        </str>
        <str name="pollInterval">00:00:15</str>
    </lst>
</requestHandler>
```

The interesting parameters you will notice for the master configuration are the various `replicateAfter` directives. The master server has to indicate to the slaves when the index needs to be replicated, so by specifying `commit`, `optimize`, and `startup`, we are ensuring that the slave servers get the newest copy of the index after each of these important events. For the slave server's configuration, the most interesting parameter is `masterUrl`, which tells the slave Solr core from which master server and Solr core to replicate. `pollInterval` in the slave configuration tells the slave how frequently to check with the master Solr core for updates to the index, and you can configure this to a few seconds or even to days or weeks if you only build your index infrequently.

One final interesting parameter is the `enable` option in both the master and slave configurations. By setting this value to `true` or `false`, you can control whether replication is enabled for either master or slave mode for any given Solr core. This will come in handy in section 12.7.2 when we try to generalize the Solr configuration files.

COMBINING SHARDING AND REPLICATION

At this point you know how to scale Solr to handle either more content (by sharding) or more query load (by replicating). If you are lucky enough to have both a large dataset and a large number of users trying to query your data, however, you may need to set up a cluster utilizing both sharding and replication. If you often have a large amount of indexing going, you may also want to separate your indexing operation and your query operation onto separate servers. Figure 12.5 demonstrates the architecture for a complicated Solr cluster like this.

As you can tell from figure 12.5, setting up a Solr cluster to handle both sharding and replication can quickly become a maintenance nightmare. Querying load balancing between multiple manually defined Solr cores and ensuring replication is configured and enabled between each Solr core on the slave servers and the associated Solr core on the master server can become complex quickly. If you ever have a failure in one of your nodes, it can cause multiple nodes in the cluster to fail. If the single master server in figure 12.5 fails, for example, the entire cluster will stop receiving updates. Likewise, if one slave fails, any other slaves trying to run a distributed search dependent upon the failed slave will also fail their queries.

Thankfully, SolrCloud was created to take over management of these kinds of complexities for you. Manual scaling of Solr was introduced in this chapter to explain how scaling fundamentally works in Solr and to provide tools you need to handle use cases

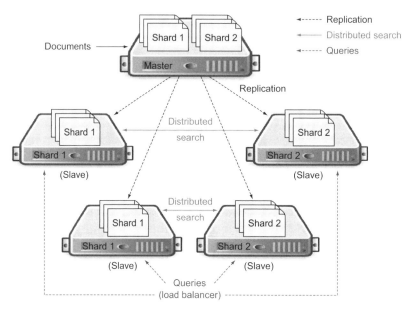

Figure 12.5   A complex Solr cluster containing a dedicated indexing server (master) with all shards and two sets of replicas (slaves).

that SolrCloud cannot currently handle. Chapter 13 will demonstrate how you can delegate most of the fault tolerance and distributed query routing concerns to Solr-Cloud to make scaling Solr a more manageable process. Regardless of which scaling approach you take, it can be useful to understand how to interact with your Solr cores without having to restart Solr to make changes. The next section will dive into Solr's Core Admin API, which provides rich features for managing Solr cores.

12.6   *Solr core management*

In the previous section we discussed how to scale Solr using sharding (for large document sets) and replication (for fault tolerance and query load). Solr contains a suite of capabilities collectively called SolrCloud (covered in depth in the next chapter) that makes managing collections of documents through shards and replicas somewhat seamless. Although most Solr users will want to let SolrCloud manage their Solr clusters for them, SolrCloud can be overly complex for simple use cases (a single shard collection, for instance), and it may not provide enough control for more complicated Solr implementations. These more complicated needs may include controlling exactly which servers do indexing versus searching, dynamically creating new indexes per customer, controlling when replication occurs, or manually copying indexes into place from outside data sources. This section will introduce you to Solr's Core Admin API, which enables manual control over the creation of Solr cores.

DEFINING CORES
Prior to Solr 4.4, all cores for a Solr instance had to be centrally defined in the *solr.xml* file. Although this capability will continue to exist in all versions of Solr up until Solr 5.0,

Solr now defaults to using the core autodiscovery mode described in chapter 4, using *core.properties* files located in each core's directory. The *core.properties* files contain most of the same kinds of configuration options previously present in *solr.xml* (such as name, config, and schema), but they allow for cores to be defined in a more decentralized manner, instead of forcing them to be defined all in one place in the *solr.xml*.

Limitations of core management through core autodiscovery

Although using the new *core.properties* autodiscovery mode is the way of the future, there are several current limitations to the new approach that have not yet been worked out. Chief among those is the inability to use a shared configuration directory (still true as of Solr 4.7). Because of this limitation, the examples in this section assume you are using the older *solr.xml* configuration (available for all Solr 4.x releases), which allows for a single instanceDir to be defined and shared across multiple Solr cores. The core creation action, for example, will not allow you to dynamically create new Solr cores from a shared, preexisting configuration file without using the old, centralized core configuration mechanism. These limitations of core autodiscovery mode should be worked out prior to the release of Solr 5.0.

That being said, there are a few capabilities of the *solr.xml* format that are not yet supported in the new *core.properties* files. Although all of the example Solr core configurations that ship with *Solr in Action* utilize the new core autodiscovery format, the Core Admin Handler (discussed next) still works best along with the old *solr.xml* format, particularly for creating new cores (see the sidebar for more info). As such, please keep in mind that all of the examples in this section assume you are using a *solr.xml* file in the old, centralized format.

CREATING CORES THROUGH THE CORE ADMIN API

In addition to defining Solr cores beforehand in *solr.xml* or using a *core.properties* file, it is possible to ask Solr to create new Solr cores through the Core Admin Handler. As mentioned, the Core Admin Handler still works best as of Solr 4.7 when used in conjunction with the old *solr.xml* format, which allows a shared instanceDir between multiple cores. The path to the Core Admin Handler can be overridden in the *solr.xml* file:

```
<solr persistent="true" sharedLib="lib">
  <cores adminPath="/admin/cores">
    <core name="core1" instanceDir="shared" dataDir="core1/data"  />
    <core name="core2" instanceDir="shared" dataDir="core2/data" />
  </cores>
</solr>
```

Assuming the admin path does not override the default of /admin/cores, you would hit the Core Admin Handler at http://localhost:8983/solr/admin/cores. It's worth pointing out that the Core Admin Handler, unlike most other request handlers, is defined at a global level, not at a per-core level. This is because the Core Admin Handler is responsible for managing cores and is therefore not run from inside of any particular cores.

In order to dynamically add a Solr core, you need to send a CREATE request to the Core Admin Handler:

```
http://localhost:8983/solr/admin/cores?
  action=CREATE&
  name=coreX&
  instanceDir=path_to_instance_directory&
  config=solrconfig_file_name.xml&
  schema=schema_file_name.xml&
  dataDir=data&
  loadOnStartup=true&
  transient=false
```

For the action of CREATE, only the name and instanceDir parameters are required. If you want to reference a *schema.xml* or *solrconfig.xml* file in a different directory or by a different name, you can optionally also specify the schema and dataDir parameters. Finally, Solr supports the idea of lazy loading (and unloading) Solr cores, so you can specify loadOnStartup=true|false to enable lazy loading and transient=true|false to enable unloading of the core if the system needs to free up resources.

You should note that if the persist=false option is set in your *solr.xml* file, any Solr cores you create through the Core Admin Handler will only exist until Solr is restarted. This could come as an unpleasant surprise when you restart Solr and can no longer see your Solr cores defined and loaded, so please be sure to determine whether or not you want your dynamically created cores to have their configurations persisted. It's also worth mentioning that you can create a Solr core only once; if you use the CREATE action more than once with the same name parameter, you will receive an exception.

In addition to creating Solr cores, it's possible to perform actions on existing Solr cores such as reloading, renaming, name swapping, unloading, index splitting, and index merging.

RELOADING CORES

If you make changes to a Solr core's configuration files (such as *solrconfig.xml*, *schema.xml*, and other files in the *conf/* directory), those changes generally do not become immediately available. Issuing a RELOAD action, however, will cause the Solr core to reload its configuration files and reinitialize:

```
http://localhost:8983/solr/admin/cores?
  action=RELOAD&
  core=coreX
```

The current version of the Solr core will stay active and accept requests until the newly loaded version of the Solr core is ready for use so that requests are not interrupted during this process. There are a few settings, such as dataDir for the Solr core and some of the IndexWriter settings from *solrconfig.xml*, which cannot be modified for a Solr core without restarting Solr, but a RELOAD action should take care of updating most other settings. It's also worth noting that any caches and collected request handler statistics will be lost during a Solr core reload.

RENAMING AND SWAPPING CORES

Sometimes, it can be useful to rename a Solr core. You may have an old version of an index, for example, and you want to signify that it is out of date. You can do this with the RENAME action:

```
http://localhost:8983/solr/admin/cores?
  action=RENAME&
  core=coreX&
  other=coreX_old
```

In this example, the Solr core named coreX will be renamed coreX_old. If you were trying to introduce a new Solr core currently called coreX_new to replace the old Solr core, you could perform this as a series of two renames: the first to move the old core out of the way (rename coreX to coreX_old), and the second to rename the new Solr core to the name formerly used by the old Solr core (rename coreX_new to coreX). The obvious problem with this approach is that during the time between renames, there will be no Solr core named coreX, which means that any requests to a core by that name will fail.

To account for this use case, Solr includes a SWAP action that performs an atomic rename of two Solr cores by swapping their names. In our previous example, you would perform a two-step process. First, you would issue a SWAP command to swap the coreX_new with coreX:

```
http://localhost:8983/solr/admin/cores?
  action=SWAP&
  core=coreX&
  other=coreX_new
```

Once you have swapped the two Solr cores, you can monitor to make sure that the new Solr core (now called coreX) is functioning as expected. If you find a problem, you can always swap the two Solr cores back again. In this way, it becomes much less dangerous to make large-scale changes (such as reindexing data), since you can reindex data to an entirely new core and do a live swap, with the option to revert back in a split second if anything goes wrong.

Assuming the new coreX is functioning as expected, you would want to either rename the previous Solr core (inaccurately now called coreX_new due to the swap) to something more meaningful like coreX_old or delete the old Solr core if you no longer need it.

UNLOADING AND DELETING CORES

Once you determine that you no longer need one of your Solr cores loaded, you can send the UNLOAD action to the Core Admin Handler:

```
http://localhost:8983/solr/admin/cores?
  action=UNLOAD&
  core=coreX_old&
  deleteInstanceDir=false&
  deleteDataDir=false&
  deleteIndex=false
```

Only the `core` parameter is required along with the `UNLOAD` action. Unloading a Solr core does not, by default, delete the index, the data directory, or the instance directory from disk. This means that you could easily unload a core and, later, reload it using the `CREATE` action if you use the same `instanceDir` (and `schema` and `config` options if you have overridden them). If you want to completely wipe away the data and configuration associated with the Solr core, you can delete the instance directory by adding the `deleteInstanceDir=true` parameter to the `UNLOAD` request. If you only want to delete the data directory, you can add the `deleteDataDir=true` command, and if you only want to delete the index inside the data directory but not the entire data directory, you can specify `deleteIndex=true`.

SPLITTING AND MERGING INDEXES

Sometimes your current Solr cores will grow so large that you need to split them into multiple shards. Although you would normally set up new shards and then reindex your data from source, Solr provides a mechanism for splitting your Solr cores into multiple shards without reindexing. If you want to split a core into three new cores, for example, you would make use of the `SPLIT` action as follows:

```
http://localhost:8983/solr/admin/cores?
  action=SPLIT&
  core=oldCore&
  targetCore=newCore1&
  targetCore=newCore2&
  targetCore=newCore3
```

Your original Solr core name should be passed into the `core` parameter, and you must specify at least one `targetCore` based upon how many shards you want to divide the old index into. It is important to note that each of the target cores must already be created and live on the Solr server for this command to work (you can use the `CREATE` action to do this first). If there are preexisting documents in one of the target cores you specify, they will be merged with the new documents from the Solr core you are splitting. Because you can split an index into a single `targetCore`, you can also use this command to make a backup of the current core to a target core.

   If you do not already have each of your target core shards running, you can alternatively specify the directories on disk to which you want the new shards saved:

```
http://localhost:8983/solr/admin/cores?
  action=SPLIT&
  core=oldCore&
  path=/path/to/newCore1/data/&
  path=path/to/newCore2/data/&
  path=path/to/newCore3/data/
```

If you follow this latter approach, you can issue a `CREATE` action to the Core Admin Handler to bring the new Solr cores live after the `SPLIT` action finishes. It is important to note that this method (splitting into indexes by specifying paths) assumes the indexes in the paths are unloaded and are not receiving any updates. If any changes are being made to the indexes you are splitting into, you may end up with a corrupt index as the result of this operation. If the cores you want to split into are already loaded, you should use the `targetCore` parameter instead to ensure that all index writes are synchronized and that no index corruption occurs.

   If you need to go in the other direction—merging indexes instead of splitting them—Solr's Core Admin Handler also supports the `MergeIndexes` action:

```
http://localhost:8983/solr/admin/cores?
  action=MERGEINDEXES&
  core=newCore&
  srcCore=oldCore1&
  srcCore=oldCore2&
  srcCore=oldCore3
```

When using the `MERGEINDEXES` action, you must specify the new core you want to merge indexes into (the `core` parameter) as well as one or more source cores (the `srcCore` parameters) from which you want to merge documents.

   As with the `SPLIT` action, it's also possible to merge from static indexes on disk without having to first load them into Solr. To do this, replace the `srcCore` parameters with `indexDir` parameters referencing the index location on disk:

```
http://localhost:8983/solr/admin/cores?
  action=MERGEINDEXES&
  core=newCore&
  indexDir=/path/to/oldCore1/data/&
  indexDir=path/to/oldCore2/data/&
  indexDir=path/to/oldCore3/data/
```

As with splitting indexes, it's important that no updates are being written to the `indexDir` indexes during the split. If the cores you're merging from are already loaded and running in your Solr instance, it's better to use `srcCore` parameters instead of `indexDir` parameters to ensure that no index corruption occurs. It's also interesting to point out that performing a `SPLIT` action with a single `targetCore` or a `MERGEINDEXES` action with a single destination `core` will ultimately result in the same outcome: a single core which is a copy of the original core merged with whatever documents were already in the destination core.

GETTING THE STATUS OF CORES

In addition to all of the ways you can manipulate Solr cores, it's possible to get a list of Solr cores and their statuses through the `STATUS` action:

```
http://localhost:8983/solr/admin/cores?
  action=STATUS
```

This will bring back a list of all Solr cores live on the server, as well as information about their configurations, index sizes, and general performance information. If you only want information about a single Solr core, you can optionally pass in the `core=coreName` parameter to limit the scope of the information returned.

   The ability to pull back statuses of cores can help you better understand the state of each Solr core before making changes to it, and any monitoring tools you may have pointing at your server can use this action to programmatically pull back information about the data on the server. When you are only dealing with a few servers, your management and configuration of Solr cores will likely be manual, but, if not, the next section will cover some tricks for helping you reduce complexity as you scale your Solr clusters to multiple servers.

12.7 Managing clusters of servers

As you move beyond a single Solr instance, managing your Solr cluster becomes much more complicated. If you have a sharded search environment, taking one server down can actually cause searches to fail on other servers that are trying to execute a distributed search using the server you took down. Likewise, if one or more of your replicas starts having an application-affecting problem, you need some way to identify which servers are healthy enough to remain in your production load balancer. Additionally, as you begin adding more and more servers, you may notice that the complexity of managing unique configurations for every server (*solrconfig.xml, schema.xml,* etc.) becomes a maintenance headache. This section will discuss tricks that can help with these problems.

12.7.1 Load balancers and Solr health check

If you have a distributed Solr cluster containing shards and/or replicas, you will want a way to balance traffic between each of the servers in your cluster. If you are fortunate enough to work for a company with a hardware load balancer, you probably already know how to set up a virtual IP address into which you can put each of your Solr servers, or you know someone within your company who does. If you are using Amazon EC2 instances in the cloud, you can use Amazon's Elastic Load Balancer to set up load balancing in a similar way. If you are running a smaller operation, you may consider installing HAProxy for use as a load balancer. Regardless of which solution you use, you will want some kind of "health check" option—something the load balancer can check on the server to determine whether the server is healthy and should be in service or is in a failed state and should be removed.

To facilitate these kinds of health checks, Solr maintains the Ping Request Handler, which can be enabled by adding a special `requestHandler` entry in your *solrconfig.xml*. The Ping Request Handler is responsible for determining if a server is supposed to be enabled to receive traffic and is able to successfully execute queries. To enable it, you need to make sure it is configured in your *solrconfig.xml*:

```
<requestHandler name="/admin/ping" class="solr.PingRequestHandler">
    <lst name="invariants">
      <str name="q">choose_any_query</str>
      <str name="shards">
         localhost:8983/solr/core1,remotehost:8983/solr/core2
    </lst>
    <str name="healthcheckFile">server-enabled</str>
</requestHandler>
```

With the Ping Request Handler enabled, now all you have to do is point your load balancer to http://servername:8983/solr/admin/ping for each of your servers, and if the load balancer gets a `Status 200 OK` response it means your Solr cluster is healthy and should remain in the load balancer; if you get an HTTP error code (any other status besides `200` in this case), it means there is a problem with the server and that the load balancer should stop sending traffic to the server.

An optional feature useful for pulling a server in and out of a load balancer (while Solr is running in a healthy state) can be turned on with the `healthcheckFile` setting. If this setting is included in the request handler configuration, then, prior to attempting the health check query, the Ping Request Handler will first check for the existence of the health check file on disc (in the *conf/* directory for your Solr core) with the name you specify. If that file does not exist, the Ping Request Handler will automatically return an error code, and will not even attempt to execute the query.

This optional health check file feature provides you with the ability to explicitly pull a Solr server out of the load balancer without having to shut down Solr to make queries fail. You can then either manually create and delete the file on your Solr server, or you can ask the Ping Request Handler to do it for you:

- *Enable ping*: http://servername:8983/solr/core1/ping?action=enable
- *Disable ping*: http://servername:8983/solr/core1/ping?action=disable

You can then interrogate the Ping Request Handler to get the status of the health check file or see if the server is healthy:

- *Check health check file*: http://servername:8983/solr/core1/ping?action=status
- *Check health check file (if enabled) plus query execution success*: http://servername:8983/solr/core1/ping

You may have also noticed that we added a `shards` parameter to the Ping Request Handler configuration section. The Ping Request Handler does support distributed searching, which means that the health check will fail if any of the shards defined or passed in using the (optional) `shards` parameter fail to respond successfully. This will cause the entire cluster to be pulled out at nearly the same time if all servers reference the same failed shard(s), since they will all be unable to successfully execute their distributed test query. This is what you want in most scenarios, since you need all shards to successfully complete the request.

If you are running Solr behind a load balancer, the Ping Request Handler can make your interaction with the load balancer much simpler by preventing you from having to interact directly with the load balancer beyond initially setting up the health check. Everything you need to pull Solr in and out can be controlled from Solr through a simple API. As you continue scaling Solr, one other area of maintenance pain may become the deployment and versioning of many different configuration files for your various Solr servers. The next section will provide tips for managing this complexity.

12.7.2 Generic vs. customized configuration

Solr is incredibly customizable. You can have separate *schema.xml* and *solrconfig.xml* settings per Solr core, fields hardcoded into the *schema.xml* file with specific names and attributes defined for each separate use case. This works phenomenally well for small Solr deployments. Once you begin adding tens or hundreds of servers, however, a large level of customization of the Solr configuration files can become difficult to manage. Every time you want to upgrade and/or redeploy your version of Solr across many servers with different configurations, you end up having to manually upgrade each of the Solr-specific configuration files (*core.properties*, *solrconfig.xml*, *schema.xml*, and so on).

One strategy to reduce the operational costs associated with maintaining a large number of Solr servers is to attempt to generalize as much of the configuration as possible. Companies building cloud-based search services based upon Solr, for example, will often define all of their available field types as dynamic fields, allowing customers to create new fields at any time without having to modify the Solr schema on any of their deployed Solr instances. In this way, every Solr server in their infrastructure can have the exact same *schema.xml*, which means redeploying to any one cluster is the same as redeploying to all clusters.

Such a generalized configuration suffers from a few problems, the biggest being that you will have to predefine all available field types in terms of dynamic fields. This requires considerable up-front thinking. Say you have a text field, and you want to create variations which have the field indexed, stored, and including norms (the opposite of omitNorms="true"). If you want to support any combination of those attributes from your client application, you would need to add each of the following to your *schema.xml* for this one field type:

```
<dynamicField name="*_t" type="text"
    indexed="false" stored="false" omitNorms="true" />
<dynamicField name="*_t_i" type="text"
    indexed="true" stored="false" omitNorms="true" />
<dynamicField name="*_t_s" type="text"
    indexed="false" stored="true" omitNorms="true" />
<dynamicField name="*_t_n" type="text"
    indexed="false" stored="false" omitNorms="true" />
<dynamicField name="*_t_is" type="text"
    indexed="true" stored="true" omitNorms="true" />
<dynamicField name="*_t_in" type="text"
    indexed="true" stored="false" omitNorms="false" />
<dynamicField name="*_t_sn" type="text"
    indexed="false" stored="true" omitNorms="true" />
<dynamicField name="*_t_isn" type="text"
    indexed="true" stored="true" omitNorms="false" />
```

Although such a generalized configuration makes your Solr deployment scripts much simpler, it also leads to trade-offs between simplicity and performance. Are you going to support *all* possible configuration options for each field type? For numeric field types, for example, what precision levels are you going to support? In a customized *schema.xml*, you have full control over every detail of your configuration, but in a generalized configuration, you'll need to choose carefully the level of customization you'll provide, and you'll also need to avoid allowing incompatible options like we (somewhat confusingly) did in our example.

In addition to generalizing the schema, it is possible to generalize the *solrconfig.xml*. This may seem more challenging up front, since different servers will have different resource needs and therefore different settings, but it's still possible through careful use of core-specific attributes.

Recall from listing 12.1, which covered how to set up replication between a master and slave server, that we had to tell the /replication handler on the slave specifically which server to replicate from. In a large cluster of servers, you may have different slave servers replicating from different master servers. The next listing demonstrates how you would do this.

Listing 12.2 Generalizing your *solrconfig.xml* through the use of variables

Generic *solrconfig.xml*

```
...
<requestHandler name="/replication" class="solr.ReplicationHandler">
    <lst name="master">
        <str name="enable">${master.replication.enabled:false}</str>
        <str name="replicateAfter">commit</str>
        <str name="replicateAfter">optimize</str>
        <str name="replicateAfter">startup</str>
    </lst>
    <lst name="slave">
        <str name="enable">${slave.replication.enabled:false}</str>
        <str name="masterUrl">
            http://${masterserver:}/solr/${solr.core.name}/replication
        </str>
        <str name="pollInterval">00:00:15</str>
    </lst>
</requestHandler>
...
```

Slave server's *solrcore.properties* file

```
...
slave.replication.enabled="true"
masterserver="masterserver:31000"
...
```

Master server's *solrcore.properties* file

```
...
master.replication.enabled="true"
...
```

You can see that the properties specific to this particular slave Solr core have been abstracted out of the *solrconfig.xml* and turned into variables that are only defined in the *solrcore.properties* file for the Solr core. The *solrcore.properties* file, if it exists in your Solr core's *conf/* directory, will be used to pass in properties specific to the Solr core. This means that the very same *solrconfig.xml* can now be used on any server in your entire Solr infrastructure. In fact, you will also notice that there are both a ${master.replication.enabled:false} parameter and a ${slave.replication.enabled:false} parameter defined in the *solrconfig.xml*. This syntax means that the default value of both of these is false (replication is disabled for that particular master or slave mode), unless the value of `true` is explicitly passed in from elsewhere (in this case, the *solrcore.properties* file). Thus, any server in your Solr infrastructure can share the same *solrconfig.xml* file regardless of whether it is a master or a slave, and regardless of what master server it needs to point to if it is a slave. This greatly reduces the number of configuration files you have to maintain and makes it much easier to generically deploy Solr across your servers and to upgrade your configuration files between Solr versions.

Once you have your server configuration worked out, you're likely ready to begin using Solr from your application. The next section will cover methods for sending requests to Solr that may help expedite this process.

12.8   Querying and interacting with Solr

Although the examples in this book so far have mainly focused on interacting with Solr over its REST API, there are other ways which may work better for your search application. This section will cover various approaches for interacting with Solr from your web application.

12.8.1   REST API

The standard REST API, demonstrated throughout this book, is the most common mechanism for interacting with Solr. Because this API only relies upon the HTTP protocol, it is possible to interact with Solr from any programming language that can connect over your network to your Solr server.

As you saw in chapter 7 (section 7.7.1), it is possible to receive responses from Solr in a format already serialized into the syntax of many common programming languages (Python, Ruby, PHP, JavaScript/JSON, and many more). Despite the useful response formats, if you are getting started with Solr, it can be a pain to have to write custom code in your preferred programming language to send queries to Solr. Thankfully, earlier developers have already written client libraries to handle interaction with Solr's REST API for you, through the use of objects directly from your application code. The next section will cover a few of those available language-specific libraries.

12.8.2   Available Solr client libraries

Although Solr's REST API exposes all available features in Solr, several client libraries have been written to abstract the interaction with the REST API into objects. Not all of the libraries are up to date with the most recent Solr release (and several appear to be unmaintained at this point), but Solr does a great job of maintaining backward compatibility in its public API, which means you will likely be able to use most features even if the client library is a bit out of date.

Some of the most popular client libraries are RSolr (Ruby), Solarium (PHP), Scala-LikeSolr (Scala), SolPython (Python), SolJSON (JavaScript), SolrNet (.NET), and Sol-Perl (Perl). Several languages contain multiple client libraries to choose from, and a published list can be found at http://wiki.apache.org/solr/IntegratingSolr.

In addition to these languages, a Java client library called SolrJ (introduced in chapter 5) ships with Solr. Since Solr is written in Java, SolrJ allows you to communicate with Solr using a binary object representation (by default) instead of requiring usage of the typical XML request/response format. SolrJ will be covered in even more detail in the next section.

12.8.3 Using SolrJ from Java

As you may remember from chapter 5, SolrJ enables you to communicate with Solr from your own application's Java code. SolrJ ships with Solr, which means that when you pull the Solr code or download a Solr release, the correct version of the SolrJ library is pulled as well. SolrJ can also (optionally) utilize a Java binary request/response format, reducing the serialization/deserialization overhead associated with other communication formats. Using SolrJ, you can communicate across an HTTP connection, as with any other client library, but you can also embed Solr within your application and talk to it directly without exposing an HTTP connection on your server.

ADDING SOLRJ TO YOUR PROJECT

SolrJ is compiled into the *apache-solr-solrj-*.jar* file in your *$SOLR_INSTALL/dist/* directory, where *** represents your version of Solr. SolrJ contains dependencies on various other libraries, located in the *$SOLR_INSTALL/dist/solrj-lib/*, *$SOLR_INSTALL/dist/*, and *$SOLR_INSTALL/example/lib/* directories. You will need to include each of these dependencies in your classpath or else use a dependency manager like Maven to pull these in automatically for you. If you are using Maven, you can add the following (specifying your current Solr version) to your project's *pom.xml* file to add SolrJ and its dependencies:

```
<dependency>
  <groupId>org.apache.solr</groupId>
  <artifactId>solr-solrj</artifactId>
  <version>4.7.0</version>
</dependency>
```

Once you have added SolrJ to your project, you need to create a `SolrServer` object to interact with Solr. You can create either `HttpSolrServer` or `EmbeddedSolrServer`, based upon whether you want to connect to a running Solr instance (over HTTP) or to use Solr in an embedded mode on your current system without exposing Solr over HTTP.

CONNECTING TO A SOLR SERVER OVER HTTP WITH SOLRJ

The most common way to use SolrJ is to connect to an already running Solr server over HTTP. In this way, SolrJ is being used as any other client library to interact with Solr, while not preventing additional connections from being made from other sources.

To tell SolrJ about your Solr server, you need to create a `SolrServer` object. Several implementations of `SolrServer` exist for you to choose from, each listed in table 12.1.

Table 12.1 Available SolrServer implementations for SolrJ

SolrServer implementation	Description
HttpSolrServer	The default `SolrServer` used to communicate an end-to-end request to Solr.

Table 12.1   Available SolrServer implementations for SolrJ *(continued)*

SolrServer implementation	Description
ConcurrentUpdateSolrServer	Meant for sending update/delete requests. Handles batching document updates in a queue to increase indexing throughput.
LBHttpSolrServer	Enables load balancing of requests across more than one Solr endpoint.
CloudSolrServer	Allows dynamic discovery (through ZooKeeper) of Solr endpoints to load balance across a SolrCloud cluster.
EmbeddedSolrServer	Enables use of Solr in an embedded mode on the current system, without enabling HTTP access.

As you can probably infer from the table, HttpSolrServer is the most basic Solr-Server implementation. You can send all requests through HttpSolrServer and they will be executed immediately against a single specified Solr endpoint. Since sending a single document at a time to Solr is inefficient when indexing multiple documents, ConcurrentUpdateSolrServer enables the queuing of documents as you add them to be later batched and sent to Solr once a specifiable number of documents or amount of time has been exceeded. ConcurrentUpdateSolrServer is specifically designed to send update requests, so it's recommended that you use one of the other SolrServer implementations for your queries. If you have a multiserver Solr cluster, you can use LBHttpSolrServer instead, which will load balance requests across a list of Solr endpoints that you specify. If you are using SolrCloud (covered in chapter 13), CloudSolrServer will automatically determine which servers to load balance your queries across based upon information pulled from ZooKeeper. If you want to embed Solr in your application instead of running it as a web application in its own Java process, you would want to make use of EmbeddedSolrServer.

INTERACTING WITH SOLR THROUGH SOLRJ

As you can see, you have many SolrServer implementations from which to choose based upon the specific nature of your application and Solr configuration. Because HttpSolrServer serves as the lowest common denominator among your options, we will use it to demonstrate the basic SolrJ operations. You saw how to use SolrJ to send documents to Solr for indexing in chapter 5 (section 5.5.2). In addition to sending document updates, SolrJ can be used to invoke the full range of Solr requests directly from Java. The following listing demonstrates how to perform basic document updates, deletes, and searches.

Listing 12.3   Using SolrJ to interact with Solr

```
SolrServer server = new
  HttpSolrServer("http://localhost:8983/solr/collection1");

server.deleteByQuery( "*:*" );
```

⊲— **Instantiate a SolrServer to talk to a core.**

⊲— **Delete any preexisting documents.**

```
SolrInputDocument doc1 = new SolrInputDocument();
doc1.addField( "id", "1", 1.0f );
doc1.addField( "cat", "health", 1.0f );
doc1.addField( "price", 100 );

SolrInputDocument doc2 = new SolrInputDocument();
doc2.addField( "id", "2", 1.0f );
doc2.addField( "cat", "entertainment", 1.0f );
doc2.addField( "price", 150 );

SolrInputDocument doc3 = new SolrInputDocument();
doc3.addField( "id", "2", 1.0f );
doc3.addField( "cat", "entertainment", 1.0f );
doc3.addField( "price", 99 );

Collection<SolrInputDocument> docs = new ArrayList<SolrInputDocument>();
docs.add( doc1 );
docs.add( doc2 );
docs.add( doc3 );

server.add( docs );
server.commit();

SolrQuery query = new SolrQuery();
query.setQuery( "*:*" );
query.addSortField( "price", SolrQuery.ORDER.desc );

QueryResponse rsp = server.query( query );
SolrDocumentList docs = rsp.getResults();
...

SolrQuery solrQuery = new  SolrQuery()
  .setQuery("*:*")
  .setFacet(true)
  .setFacetMinCount(1)
  .setFacetLimit(10)
  .addFacetField("cat");

QueryResponse rsp = server.query(solrQuery);
...

server.deleteByQuery("*:*");
```

- Create a document and add fields.
- Three field parameters: name, value, and boost.
- Add each document to a collection (for batch updating).
- Send the batch of documents to Solr.
- Commit the documents so they can be searched.
- Query for all documents.
- Add a sort to the query.
- Execute the search and process the results.
- Enable faceting for this query.
- Clean up (delete) all documents once finished.

SolrJ supports most Solr operations, so the previous listing is only scratching the surface of how you can go about interacting with the SolrJ API from within your Java code. You should check out the JavaDoc that ships with SolrJ for information about additional features provided by the SolrJ API.

EMBEDDING SOLR WITHIN YOUR APPLICATION THROUGH SOLRJ

In addition to using SolrJ to interact with a running Solr server over HTTP, we mentioned in section 12.2.2 that it is possible to embed Solr directly within another Java application. Now that you know how to use SolrJ, embedding Solr should come naturally, since all that is required is that you use an `EmbeddedSolrServer` instead of the `HttpSolrServer` when writing your SolrJ code. Since you will be starting up Solr cores directly, you must also pass in your Solr configuration files into your `EmbeddedSolr-Server`, as shown in this listing.

Listing 12.4   Embedding Solr within another Java application

```
File home = new File( "/path/to/solr/home" );
File file = new File( home, "solr.xml" );
CoreContainer container = new CoreContainer();
container.load( "/path/to/solr/home", file );
EmbeddedSolrServer server = new EmbeddedSolrServer(
    container, "core1" );

SolrQuery query = new SolrQuery();
    query.setQuery( "*:*" );
...
QueryResponse rsp = server.query( query );
SolrDocumentList docs = rsp.getResults();
```

As you can see, embedded Solr utilizes the SolrJ library as it does a traditional server instance of Solr. The only code difference is that instead of creating `HttpSolrServer`, you create `EmbeddedSolrServer` and pass in the path to your Solr home directory and location, your *solr.xml* file, and the name of the Solr core to which you want to send requests.

The embedded Solr server does have one giant drawback relative to the other `Solr-Server` types: it does not support distributed search. In fairness, if you are embedding Solr within your application, it's unlikely you would be sharding across multiple servers anyway, but not being able to at least search across multiple Solr cores on the same server is a pretty significant limitation.

SolrJ VERSIONING AND SERIALIZATION

Solr does a decent job of backward compatibility with SolrJ; newer versions of SolrJ are typically able to talk with previous versions of Solr within the same major release. This is largely due to the fact that SolrJ uses Solr's XML request and response format to communicate with Solr, and previously supported capabilities are rarely deprecated.

That being said, it's possible to change the default transport mechanism from XML to a Java binary format, which will greatly decrease the serialization/deserialization costs associated with your Solr requests. To do this you need to set the request parser and request writers for your `HttpSolrServer`:

```
SolrServer server = new
  HttpSolrServer("http://localhost:8983/solr/collection1");
  server.setParser(new BinaryResponseParser());
  server.setRequestWriter(new BinaryRequestWriter());
```

If you do change the request writer or the response parser to use the Java binary format, you may have issues if you try to use a different version of SolrJ than your version of Solr. If you need to use different versions (for upgrade reasons, for example), you will probably want to stick with the default XML request and response format.

12.9   *Monitoring Solr's performance*

When you put Solr into production under real traffic, it is important to understand the performance characteristics of your Solr cluster. If query speed is too slow under a light load, you may need to further shard your content, reduce the complexity of your queries, or increase the resources of your servers. If you are getting hammered by too many queries, you may need to add additional replicas of your content to balance out the query load. Under either of these scenarios, you may have suboptimal cache performance or you may have errors in your queries, which need to be debugged. This section will show you how to dig into Solr's internal performance statistics and log files to find the performance information you need.

12.9.1 Solr's Plugins / Stats page

From the Solr Admin page, after you select a Solr core, a link will appear along the left column to see Solr's Plugins / Stats page. Figure 12.6 demonstrates what this Plugins / Stats page looks like from the Solr Admin page.

From the Plugins / Stats page, you can dig into performance characteristics of most of the core Solr components.

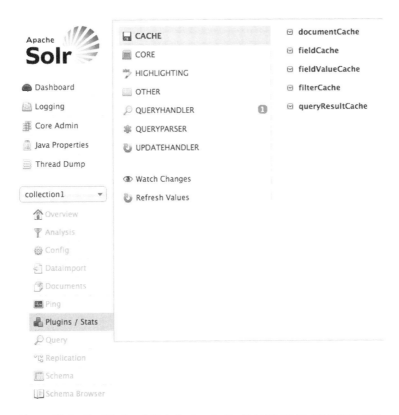

Figure 12.6 The Plugins / Stats feature in the Solr Admin UI. From here, you can drill into statistics about caches, cores, query handlers, or the performance of other Solr components and plugins.

QUERY AND UPDATE REQUEST STATISTICS

If you want to check on the rate of queries coming in to Solr and their historical response time, you can click the QUERYHANDLER link, then select the /select request handler (or any other handler which you have defined), as demonstrated in figure 12.7.

As you can see from figure 12.7, each request handler logs the average time over the last 5 minutes and the last 15 minutes, as well as the overall average and median times since the core was last reloaded. It also keeps track of the total number of requests and errors, as well as several important percentiles for request time so that you can understand the typical range of response times. This can be useful for tracking historical changes to the performance of your Solr cluster, or for comparing servers with each other in the case where one server is having issues. It can also be useful for helping you determine if Solr is performing as expected with your current document and query volumes.

In addition to monitoring query response rates, you can monitor the update-Handler section to gain insight into the processing of documents being sent to Solr for indexing. Figure 12.8 demonstrates the kinds of information you can find about the indexing process.

Figure 12.7   Stats for available query-related request handlers

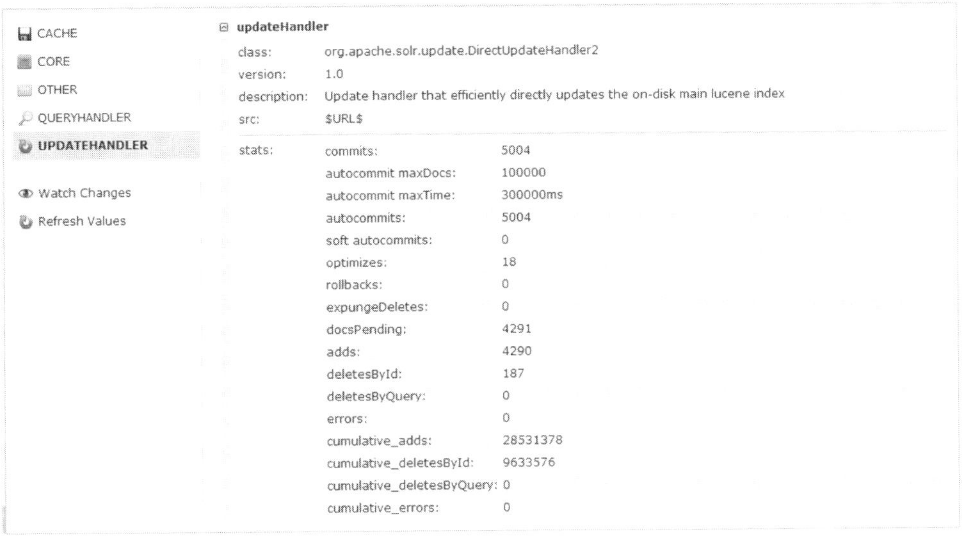

Figure 12.8   Available indexing statistics from the `updateHandler` section on the Solr Admin's UPDATEHANDLER page

As you can see from figure 12.8, the `updateHandler` stats include information about the number of documents added, the number of commits, the number of deletes (by query and ID), the number of errors, and the pending number of documents received but not yet committed. This information can be useful for gauging your throughput and, in the case of missing documents, whether they may be missing due to an error, due to a pending commit, or due to never having been received.

SOLR CORE STATISTICS

Another useful section of the Plugins / Stats page is the CORE section where you can find a list of all currently registered searchers. If you remember from section 12.3, every time a commit occurs, a new searcher is opened (or the previous one is reopened). As part of this process, the caches of the new searcher will be autowarmed, a process that prepopulates values in the new searcher's caches from the old searcher. If your caches are large, this autowarming process can take a long time. Additionally, if the `maxWarmingSearchers` option in your *solrconfig.xml* file is greater than 1, it is possible that multiple commits will result in multiple pending searchers being warmed up and prepared to be swapped in for the current searcher. Figure 12.9 demonstrates the information which is available under the CORE option on the Plugins / Stats page.

When a new searcher is loaded and in the process of warming, you will see multiple searchers listed under the CORE section of the Plugins / Stats page. The `searcher` entry is a variable containing a reference to the currently active searcher (in figure 12.9, the actual underlying searcher object is `Searcher@6cf33940`); whenever the warming searcher is ready to begin receiving searches, the `searcher` parameter's reference is updated to point to the new underlying searcher object. Any requests that went to the

Figure 12.9   Available statistics about searchers from the CORE option on the Solr Admin page

previous searcher will complete, and once all queries and references to the previous searcher complete (since new requests are already being directed to the new searcher), the old searcher will be discarded.

One of the important statistics for the searchers on the admin page is their `warm-upTime`. In figure 12.9, `warmupTime` for the searcher was 32 seconds (32120 milliseconds). This means that from the time a hard commit (or finished replication) occurs, it is taking 32 seconds for the next searcher to warm its caches and become available to receive searches. If the warming time for a new searcher exceeds the time between commits, it's possible for your Solr instance to get into a death spiral where new searchers are being created faster than their caches can warm, resulting in your index flipping being unable to keep up with the rate of new commits. In this scenario, you could run out of memory and overuse your available CPUs for autowarming if you allow many warming searchers. As such, it may be a good idea to keep your `maxWarmingSearchers` parameter in your *solrconfig.xml* to a low number (like 1) if you are doing a lot of cache warming. If you have a Solr instance with caches turned off in which you are indexing documents rapidly (such as an indexing-only server), it probably makes sense to keep `maxWarmingSearchers` set to a higher number to enable frequent commits.

In the example from figure 12.9, as long as hard commits are consistently happening more than 32 seconds (plus some reasonable buffer) apart, new searchers warming should have no trouble keeping up with the commit rate. Whether you are willing to accept a 32 second delay before your documents appear after every commit is a question only you can answer, however. If you do determine that the amount of time it is taking to commit and warm your caches is excessive, you can take a look at the

CACHE section of the Plugins / Stats page to tune your caches. Solr cache performance will be discussed in the following section.

12.9.2 *Solr cache performance*

Your Solr caches can be critical to the overall performance of your Solr server. Section 12.3.3 showed you how to modify the `size` and `autowarmCount` for your caches, but how do you know what values to choose? In the case of figure 12.9, it was taking 32 seconds to autowarm each new searcher. In general, most of the autowarm time comes from cache autowarming. If you click the CACHE option on the Plugins / Stats page, you can see important statistics for each of your defined caches. Figure 12.10 demonstrates what these statistics look like for the `filterCache`.

The three most important statistics from figure 12.10 for tuning your cache are the cache `size` (1067), `hitratio` (0.98), and `warmupTime` (30 seconds). This figure was pulled from the same server as the searcher with a total `warmupTime` of 32 seconds, which means `filterCache` was single-handedly responsible for 30 out of 32 seconds of the total searcher warming time.

In tuning your caches, you have to balance a good hit ratio with the warm-up time (and ultimately amount of memory) necessary to achieve that hit ratio. Hit ratios tell you how many times an entry was found in the cache (`hits`) relative to the number of total cache lookups. A hit ratio of 1 is perfect (all requested values are cached), whereas a hit ratio of 0 means that the cache has never been useful. A hit ratio above

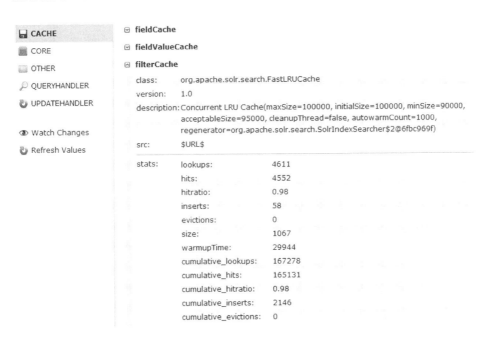

Figure 12.10 Statistics for the `filterCache`, showing a high hit ratio (0.98) but also a high `warmupTime` (30 seconds).

0.5 means that the cache helps the query more than half the time. For caches with low hit ratios, you should consider either disabling the cache entirely (since the cache is not adding much value and is causing extra cache-checking operations) or increasing the size of the cache if that would help increase the hit ratio.

In the case of figure 12.10, the hit ratio of 0.98 is nearly perfect with 1067 items in the cache. The question at hand, then, is whether reducing the size of the cache (and the warm-up time) would still result in a high hit ratio. For example, if the size of the cache were reduced to 500, the warm-up time would probably be reduced to about 15 seconds. What would happen to the hit ratio in this case? It is possible that the hit ratio would not change much if most of the queries only make use of the top 500 filters. Another way of saying this is that in the original case, 98% of queries made use of only 1067 filters. It could be the case that 96% of queries only make use of the top 500 filters, or even that 90% of queries only make use of the top 50 filters. If the latter case were true, you could reduce the total warm-up time from 32 seconds to 1.5 seconds while still achieving a cache hit on 9 out of 10 queries.

This is the process by which you will want to tune each of your caches: figure out the cost of the cache (in warm-up time or memory required) and the hit ratio, and then determine how to maximize the cost versus the value by increasing or decreasing the size of the cache.

Most of the examples discussed so far for monitoring Solr include using information from Solr's Admin page. The following sections will cover other ways to pull useful monitoring information from Solr.

12.9.3 *Pulling stats from request handlers and MBeans*

Although the previous section demonstrated how to pull a lot of useful performance information from the Solr Admin pages, it is worth noting that those pages are actually convenient ways to access information that's exposed through Solr's request handlers.

All of the information on the replication page, for example, can be pulled through Solr's Replication Handler, defined in the *solrconfig.xml* by default with a path of /replication. Likewise, all of the cache, Solr core, and request handler information can be found through the MBeans Handler. The following listing shows example output from the MBeans Handler.

> **Listing 12.5   Solr performance statistics from the MBeans Handler**

Request
```
/solr/core1/admin/mbeans?stats=true&wt=json
```

Response
```
{
  ...
  "solr-mbeans":[
    "CORE",{
      "core":{
```

```
    ...
      "stats":{
        "coreName":"core1",
          ...
          "searcher":{
            ...
            "stats":{
              "searcherName":"Searcher@362c975a main",
              "caching":true,
              "numDocs":1069399,
              "maxDoc":1137777,
              "deletedDocs":68378,
              ...
              "indexVersion":163412,
              "openedAt":"2013-07-30T04:39:04.509Z",
              "registeredAt":"2013-07-30T04:39:26.564Z",
              "warmupTime":22053}},
... }}},
"QUERYHANDLER",{
  ...
  "standard":{
    ...
      "stats":{
        "requests":238083,
        "errors":0,
        "timeouts":0,
        "totalTime":2.0561250266E7,
        "avgRequestsPerSecond":17.51375685220339,
        "5minRateReqsPerSecond":20.355573970348654,
        "15minRateReqsPerSecond":18.66862341791267,
        "avgTimePerRequest":86.36241558965226,
        "medianRequestTime":75.787,
        "75thPcRequestTime":99.09899999999999,
        "95thPcRequestTime":166.72789999999995,
        "99thPcRequestTime":260.87716000000006,
        "999thPcRequestTime":869.9387500000016}}
...}]}
```

Information broken down for each Solr core.

Searcher statistics such as warm-up time.

Searcher statistics such as warm-up time.

Query response times, errors, and related stats.

The data in the listing should look familiar to you; it's the same kind of information that was presented on the Solr Admin pages in figures throughout sections 12.9.1 and 12.9.2. This makes it easy to pull in server performance information programmatically from anywhere—even from outside of Solr.

12.9.4 *External monitoring options*

In addition to being able to pull MBean information from Solr's MBean Handler, you can expose it to external monitoring tools through the use of JMX. If you recall from chapter 4, JMX is a protocol for exposing system information across a network for management and monitoring. To enable JMX, you first need to add a single line to your solrconfig.xml:

```
<JMX/>
```

Once JMX is enabled in Solr, you need to tell your JVM to remotely expose the JMX parameters by starting Solr up with the following extra parameters:

```
java -Dcom.sun.management.jmxremote
    -Dcom.sun.management.jmxremote.port=9001
    -Dcom.sun.management.jmxremote.ssl=false
    -Dcom.sun.management.jmxremote.authenticate=false
    -jar start.jar
```

These settings are all configurable, based upon how your JMX monitoring solution is configured. If you're not using the default Jetty configuration (`java -jar start.jar`), you'll need to separately configure your Java servlet container or bootstrap settings to ensure that these extra JVM parameters are enabled. Most modern application performance monitoring tools are able to read JMX beans and provide long-term collection and graphing of metrics, often along with monitoring and alerting when the numbers deviate significantly beyond performance metrics you can set. In addition, several application performance monitoring tools—including cloud-based ones—now exist with direct support and understanding of Solr's internals. A simple web search for `Solr application performance monitoring` will help you find a long list of companies interested in helping you further monitor the performance of your Solr cluster.

12.9.5 Solr logs

As with most applications, logs provide the richest source of information about the state of your cluster at any time. They demonstrate what queries have been run, the full set of parameters for each request, how long each request took to execute, and any errors or significant operations which took place during or between requests. Solr's logs also show detailed information about when documents were received, when commits and segment merges occur, when replications begin and end, and any number of other operations based upon the level of detail you have requested in your logging configuration. For detailed information about configuring logging in Solr, check out http://wiki.apache.org/solr/SolrLogging.

12.9.6 Load testing

One of the best ways to determine the capacity of your Solr cluster—besides putting production traffic on it—is to perform offline load testing. Replaying historical logs, for example, is a good mechanism for simulating user traffic to help determine your server's query and indexing capacity.

Although no tool is perfect, an open source project called *SolrMeter* provides a great mechanism specifically designed to load test Solr. SolrMeter allows you to specify which queries or documents you want to send to Solr and how fast you want to send them. SolrMeter then measures the performance of various parts of your request, the utilization of your caches, and the details of what's going on with your cluster (such as commits or optimizes) at the time. Figure 12.11 demonstrates a basic histogram of query load versus query response time, which is one of the many measurements that SolrMeter provides.

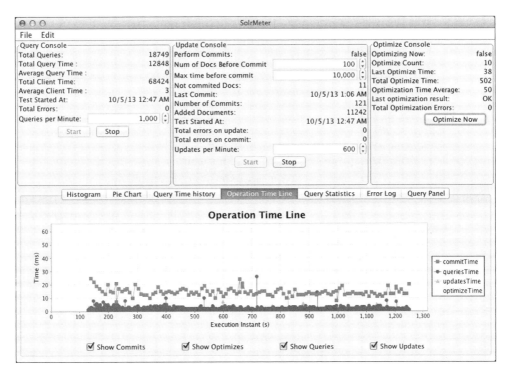

Figure 12.11 Screenshot of SolrMeter, a load-testing tool for Solr

In addition to the histogram in figure 12.11, SolrMeter will provide a pie chart breakdown of time ranges of queries, a list of errors that occur during the test run, and even the hits, lookups, and evictions in each of your caches during the test run. If you are looking for a way to quickly test the capacity of your Solr application, you can find more information about SolrMeter at https://code.google.com/p/solrmeter/.

12.10 *Upgrading between Solr versions*

Solr is constantly under development, which means that from time to time you will need to upgrade from a previous version of Solr to a new version in order to get the latest and greatest features and performance improvements. The absolute best way to perform an upgrade is to install the new version of Solr, make any customizations necessary to your configuration files and plugins, and rebuild your index from scratch under the new version by feeding all of your content in from an external source.

Technically, every officially released version of Solr is supposed to support automatically upgrading the index files from a previous major release. This means that if you have an index build on a Solr 3.x version, and you install Solr 4.x and start it up with the old indexes, it should be able to upgrade the previous index files. If you follow this approach, you will want to issue an `optimize` after starting up the new version to ensure all of the index files are successfully upgraded.

Just because you *can* upgrade index files this way, however, does not mean that you should. Various text analysis components change from version to version of Solr (even between minor versions), which means that the index built under one version may result in different tokens than in a previous Solr version. Unfortunately, an index-format upgrade will not be able to overcome this limitation, which means you could have some mismatch between index and query time analysis resulting in data integrity issues.

If you happen to store all of the fields in your index, you could alternatively use something like the DIH in the new version of Solr to import all of your documents from your old running Solr instance. This is functionally no different than reimporting all of your documents from an external data store. Regardless of the source of your data (be it another version of Solr or some other data source), if you can reindex your data from scratch you stand the lowest chance of having any data-integrity issues associated with your upgrade.

12.11 Summary

This chapter was designed to walk you through the practical considerations associated with taking Solr from development to production. We covered the process of building the Solr source code and deploying Solr to a production environment, as well as sending requests to Solr through one of the available client libraries like SolrJ.

Hardware and OS considerations were discussed, including tips and tricks for maximizing your utilization of RAM and other system resources. We additionally covered the important performance characteristics of Solr and how to monitor, tune, and test many of those settings.

One of the important topics introduced in this chapter was how to scale Solr through sharding (splitting) and replicating (copying) your data to multiple servers. Scaling Solr can actually prove to be a big server and configuration management hassle, so the next chapter will demonstrate how Solr can greatly reduce some of that hassle for you.

Part 3

Taking Solr to the next level

As your knowledge and experience with Solr grows, so too will your desire to tackle more complex problems related to search. In these final chapters, we'll cover advanced topics that have proven challenging for many organizations offering a world-class search application to their users. It's unlikely that you'll be interested in every topic, but it is likely you'll deal with many of them frequently, and these chapters will ease your way.

SolrCloud, a set of distributed features that makes it easy to shard and replicate your indexes across a cluster of machines, is introduced first. Chapter 13 is more theory than hands-on activities, but by chapter's end you should understand how to use SolrCloud to achieve your scalability and high-availability needs.

The world is becoming smaller and smaller and as more organizations extend their reach, handling multiple languages is a common requirement for many search applications. How do you handle multilingual content within Solr? Turn to chapter 14 for a comprehensive overview of both basic and advanced techniques.

Solr is able to perform a robust set of complex data operations at query time, which will be the topic of chapter 15. Specifically, we will cover dynamically generating field values in Solr through function queries (useful for returning, sorting, and ranking), faceting and advanced data analytics across multiple dimensions, geospatial search, joining across documents and indexes, and referencing data external to the Solr index.

It's quite common for organizations to start out with basic keyword search, then need to fine-tune how documents are ranked based on domain-specific knowledge.

How to implement an expert-level relevancy model is the focus of chapter 16. Much of the content in this chapter is based on the authors' real-world experience implementing personalization and recommendation systems in Solr, demonstrating how Solr can be more than just a keyword search engine in your technology stack.

13

SolrCloud

This chapter covers

- Scaling Solr with the SolrCloud architecture
- Managing configuration information with ZooKeeper
- Distributing indexing and queries
- Administering the SolrCloud system
- Shard splitting and custom hashing

In this chapter, you'll learn how to design, configure, and operate a large-scale Solr cluster using a set of features known collectively as SolrCloud. This chapter will be challenging because there are new concepts and terminology with which you may not be familiar. Rest assured that by the end of this chapter, you should have a solid understanding of managing Solr clusters and a good feel for what it takes to set up and run a robust, large-scale distributed search engine.

There's more theory in this chapter than hands-on activities. You'll find that enabling SolrCloud mode is quite simple. Moreover, any existing client code for indexing and queries should not need to change. A SolrCloud cluster looks like any other Solr server to client applications.

To illustrate the core concepts in SolrCloud, we use the example of a search engine to power a log aggregation and analytics service called logmill. This fictitious application aggregates log messages from many systems into a centralized search engine to power monitoring, data visualization, and analytics of application activity.

SolrCloud is well suited for this type of problem because it supports near real-time indexing and can scale to handle an immense number of log messages generated by hundreds of applications; many of the queries, such as facets to analyze log metrics, will be complex.

Our main focus in this chapter is on the main SolrCloud concepts, but in cases in which a simple example helps illustrate a difficult concept, we'll use `logmill` as the example. We chose this example because it's conceptually simple but also presents real scalability challenges to deal with the massive amount of information created by enterprise and web applications in today's large organizations.

13.1   Getting started with SolrCloud

Before we get into the details of the SolrCloud architecture, we think it's helpful to start a SolrCloud cluster on your local computer. This will give you some exposure to the core concepts and allow us to ease into more complex concepts once you've seen them in action.

13.1.1   Starting Solr in cloud mode

In this section, we will launch a Solr cluster for our log aggregator service, `logmill`. Specifically, our first Solr cluster will have a single index split across two instances of Solr running on your local workstation. Each split, known as a shard, will contain roughly half the documents for the `logmill` application.

In SolrCloud, an index split across multiple nodes is called a *collection*. Up to this point, you have only worked with Solr cores (a single index on one node) and have not encountered the concept of a Solr collection. We'll dig deeper into the details of a collection in section 13.2.1. For now, think of a collection as an index split across multiple Solr nodes. For our example application, we'll call the collection `logmill`.

SolrCloud also depends on a distributed coordination service called Apache ZooKeeper, which we will cover in section 13.2.2. For now, it's easiest to think of Zoo-Keeper as an abstract service that manages cluster state and distributes configuration files to nodes joining the cluster. To keep things simple, we'll run ZooKeeper embedded in the same Java process as Solr.

CREATE THE LOGMILL CORE

Now that we have a plan for our first cluster, let's start by copying the example directory to a new directory named *shard1/*; remember that *$SOLR_INSTALL* is the top-level directory to which you extracted the Solr installation archive in chapter 2. This step is necessary because we need to run multiple instances of Solr on the same computer, bound to different ports.

```
cd $SOLR_INSTALL/
cp -r example/ shard1/
```

Next, create a core directory for `logmill` by cloning the *collection1/* directory under *shard1/solr.* Delete the data directory so that you start with an empty index. Next, remove the *core.properties* files for all preexisting core directories so that the cores will not be added to the SolrCloud cluster automatically. Finally, enable core autodiscovery by setting the `name` of the core in *core.properties* to `logmill`.

```
cd shard1
cp -r solr/collection1/ solr/logmill/
rm -rf solr/logmill/data/
find . -name "core.properties" -type f -exec rm {} \;
echo "name=logmill" > solr/logmill/core.properties
```

New feature as of Solr 4.4 to enable autodiscovery of Solr cores.

You are now ready to start Solr in cloud mode.

STARTING SOLR IN CLOUD MODE

When first starting a SolrCloud cluster, you need to start one Solr node that lays the groundwork for all other nodes to come. We'll refer to this first node as our bootstrap node, as it performs special *one-time* initialization work for the rest of the cluster. You'll see that these special one-time operations are quite simple.

Use the command in the following listing to start Solr in cloud mode.

Listing 13.1   Start Solr in cloud mode

Set up the logmill collection on SolrCloud.

```
java -Dcollection.configName=logmill
    -DzkRun
    -DnumShards=2
    -Dbootstrap_confdir=./solr/logmill/conf
    -jar start.jar
```

Run ZooKeeper embedded in the same JVM as Solr.

Upload the logmill configuration files to ZooKeeper.

Split the logmill index into two shards.

This will start the shard1 Solr server in cloud mode. Let's look closer at the command-line parameters specified with `-D` that are needed to bootstrap a SolrCloud cluster. The `collection.configName` parameter specifies the name of a configuration directory in ZooKeeper, in this case `logmill`. Every collection in SolrCloud needs to identify a named configuration directory in ZooKeeper; for our example, the `logmill` collection will use the `logmill` configuration directory. You can host multiple collections in the same cluster, but we'll only be working with one for now. The `zkRun` parameter tells Solr to launch an embedded instance of ZooKeeper in the same JVM as Solr. The embedded ZooKeeper instance listens on port 9983. The `numShards` parameter should be self-explanatory. As stated before, we decided to distribute the `logmill` collection across two shards.

The `bootstrap_confdir` parameter tells the bootstrap node to upload its configuration files to ZooKeeper. One of the primary features provided by ZooKeeper in Solr-Cloud is a centralized configuration store. Centralized configuration allows all nodes in the cluster to download their configurations from a central location instead of a system administrator having to push configuration changes to multiple nodes. Before ZooKeeper can provide centralized configuration, you need to upload the configuration from the bootstrap server.

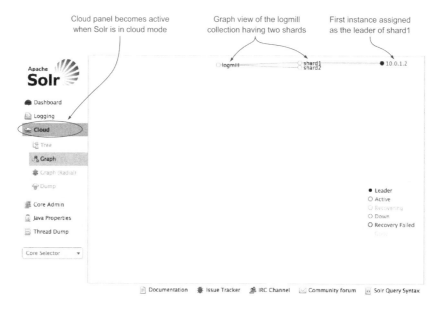

Figure 13.1   Cloud panel, showing the graph view of the `logmill` collection containing two shards. The first Solr instance we started is the leader for shard1.

Direct your web browser to the Solr administration console at http://localhost:8983/solr. Figure 13.1 shows the Cloud panel that becomes active when Solr is running in cloud mode.

Notice from figure 13.1 that there are two shards, shard1 and shard2, but only shard1 has a node assigned. This makes sense because you have only started one Solr server at this point. We'll start another Solr server for shard2 in a moment.

Also notice that the first node is the leader for shard1, as indicated by the black dot on figure 13.1. We won't get into the full details of what a shard leader does until the next section, but in a nutshell, a *shard leader* handles additional responsibilities when processing update requests to the shard, such as assigning a unique version number for each document being created or updated.

Select the `logmill` core and execute the match all docs query (`*:*`), as you've done many times throughout the book. In this case, Solr returns a 503 error with the message *no servers hosting shard*. The query fails because we configured Solr to break the `logmill` index into two shards (`-DnumShards=2`), but only one shard has a running instance. This is an important concept to understand: every shard must have an active server for distributed queries to work. If a shard does not have an active server, you cannot query Solr.

LAUNCH ANOTHER SOLR SERVER FOR SHARD2

Next, let's launch another Solr server to host shard2. Recall that Solr binds to port 8983 by default. To start another server on your computer, you need to bind to another port, such as 8984. Back at the command line, run the following:

```
cd $SOLR_INSTALL/
cp -r shard1/ shard2/
cd shard2/
rm -rf solr/logmill/conf/
java -DzkHost=localhost:9983 -Djetty.port=8984 -jar start.jar
```

The zkHost parameter activates SolrCloud mode by telling Solr to register itself with the specified ZooKeeper server during initialization. ZooKeeper will assign the initializing Solr instance to a specific shard and assign a role for that shard, either leader or replica. In our simple example, the second instance we started on port 8984 is assigned the leader role for shard2. This process works for all nodes that join the cluster after the bootstrap node.

Think what would happen if you start another instance on port 8985. Because both shards have active leaders, the third node will be assigned as a replica for shard1. If you start a fourth instance, it will be a replica for shard2. Put simply, SolrCloud takes the most logical action when new nodes join the cluster so you don't have to worry about manually assigning nodes to shards.

Another important process occurs when the second instance initializes. Recall that you cloned the *shard1/* directory to create the *shard2/* directory. We also had you delete the *shard2/solr/logmill/conf/* directory intentionally, so that it's clear that any new nodes that join the cluster after the bootstrap node receive their configuration from ZooKeeper and not from the local filesystem.

Now that both instances are running, let's look again at the Cloud panel in the administration console. Figure 13.2 shows a SolrCloud cluster with two shards and one host per shard; be sure to refresh the page after starting the second server.

Notice that Solr automatically assigned the second server running on 8984 to shard2. The other option would be to make the new node a replica of shard1. However,

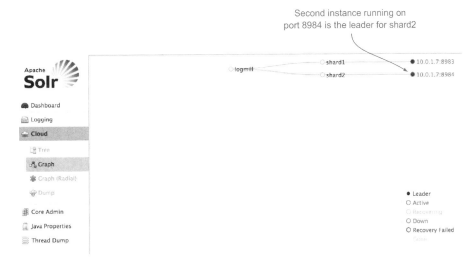

Figure 13.2   Cloud panel, showing leaders for shard1 and shard2: the logmill **collection is now fully operational in cloud mode.**

Solr ensures that all shards have at least one host before assigning replicas as new nodes join the cluster. Both servers should be green, indicating they are active. Also, because each shard only has one host, both servers are leaders, depicted with the black circle. The cluster state depicted in figure 13.2 is stored in ZooKeeper.

DISTRIBUTED QUERIES AGAINST SOLRCLOUD

Re-execute the match all docs query (*:*) against the `logmill` core to see that queries now execute successfully. Of course we have not added any documents to the `logmill` collection, so the result shows zero documents. Let's fix this by adding a few example documents.

Because our fictitious `logmill` search application is for log files, let's index an example log file containing Solr log messages using a simple utility provided in the example code.

```
cd $SOLR_IN_ACTION
java -jar solr-in-action.jar indexlog -log=example-docs/ch13/solr.log
```

The `indexlog` utility parses the specified *solr.log* file and indexes a new document for every log message. Re-execute the match all docs query (*:*) after running the `indexlog` utility to verify that the `logmill` index contains 300 documents. When a document is indexed in SolrCloud, it is routed to one of the shards based on a hash of its unique ID by default. We'll cover the details of how documents get routed in section 13.3. A document can exist in only one shard. Each shard covers an exclusive hash range, and the hash function attempts to distribute documents evenly between shards so that each shard in your cluster remains about the same size. We'll cover distributed indexing in more detail in section 13.3. Table 13.1 shows the distribution of documents after running the `indexlog` utility.

Table 13.1   Distribution of documents created by the `indexlog` utility

Shard	Number of documents
shard1	143
shard2	157
Total:	**300**

Let's try additional query parameters to show you how we determined the document counts in table 13.1. Add the `distrib=false` parameter to the Solr URL and re-execute the query. Notice that only about half the documents (143) are found. The `distrib =false` parameter disables distributed search, so the query only executes against shard1. Next, pass the `shards=shard2` parameter instead of `distrib=false` to query shard2. In this case, the result set will only include documents from shard2, even though you sent the query to the Solr instance running on port 8983.

Let's recap what we've accomplished so far. We created a new core named `logmill` with zero documents. After creating the new core, we restarted Solr in cloud mode by specifying the number of shards (two) and enabling an embedded instance of Zoo-Keeper. The first instance we start with the `numShards` parameter is our bootstrap node. You learned that every shard must have an active server in order to execute queries in SolrCloud. When a distributed query is executed (the default in cloud mode), the query is sent to all shards, and a final result set is compiled from docs from all shards. You also learned that documents are assigned to only one shard using a hash function of the unique document ID field. Now that you have a running SolrCloud cluster, let's take a step back and learn about the motivating factors that drive the architecture behind SolrCloud.

13.1.2 *Motivation behind the SolrCloud architecture*

In section 13.2 we'll look closer at core concepts like collections, ZooKeeper, shard leaders, and cluster-state management. But we think it is important to first review the motivating factors behind the SolrCloud architecture before getting into the implementation details. There are five main properties of a distributed search engine that drive the architecture behind SolrCloud:

- Scalability
- High availability
- Consistency
- Simplicity
- Elasticity

Let's dig into each of these in more detail to see how they apply to large-scale search engines in general and Solr in particular.

SCALABILITY

A *scalable* software system is one that can handle an increased workload by expanding capacity in one or more dimensions. There are two general approaches to achieving scalability: horizontal and vertical scaling. *Vertical scaling* involves increasing the computing resources of a single server, such as increasing RAM, adding more or faster CPUs, and upgrading disk I/O performance, such as by using SSDs. *Horizontal scaling* involves adding more nodes to a system to *distribute* the workload to multiple servers in parallel.

SolrCloud favors horizontal scaling using sharding and replication. Sharding breaks a large index into multiple smaller indexes, which allows you to operate massive indexes that cannot fit on one server and parallelize complex query execution and indexing operations. Replication creates additional copies of a Solr index across multiple servers to add redundancy in case of failures. With multiple copies of each document in your index, Solr remains operable if one of the copies fails.

Replication also helps increase the number of queries an index can execute concurrently. A distributed query gets sent to one replica per shard, so it follows that if you have ten replicas per shard, you can execute roughly ten times more queries concurrently. You'll learn the details of distributed queries in section 13.4.

A common goal when scaling a system like Solr is to make it *linearly scalable*, which means a system's computing capacity increases linearly with more resources. If you double the number of nodes in a cluster, for example, linear scalability implies the system can support double the workload. In practice, we aim for near linear scalability because adding more nodes typically introduces additional overhead to manage those nodes. We'll discuss the overhead of distributing indexing and queries in sections 13.3 and 13.4.

Of the two approaches, horizontal scaling is more popular because it's more cost-effective than vertical scaling, given the availability of low-cost commodity hardware and on-demand cloud-computing services like Amazon EC2. Although SolrCloud is primarily focused on horizontal scaling, it would be wrong to think you can achieve all your scalability needs by just adding more machines to a SolrCloud cluster. Specifically Solr works best with fast, multicore CPUs, large amounts of RAM, and fast disks. In practice, most, if not all, large-scale Solr installations use both approaches. To achieve maximum query performance, for example, you'll need enough RAM to cache the index in OS cache and still accommodate caching, sorting, and faceting in the JVM. If the searchable data structures of your index require 20 GB of memory and you need 8 GB allocated to the JVM, you'll want roughly 28 GB of RAM dedicated to Solr. Solr can also be disk I/O intensive (particularly when indexing documents), so having fast disks such as SSDs is also recommended.

Scaling a search engine is not a one-size-fits-all type of problem, as there are a number of dimensions that require different strategies to address correctly. Table 13.2 provides a summary of scalability concerns in a search engine and strategies available in SolrCloud to address these concerns.

Table 13.2   Scalability concerns in a search engine and ways to address them using SolrCloud

Scalability / limitation	Mitigation strategy
Number of documents indexed: Having a large number of documents in an index impacts the performance of faceting, sorting, and constructing filters. Also, we are currently limited to ~2.1 billion documents per Lucene index due to the document ID being stored as an integer.	Split large indexes into multiple smaller indexes using sharding; see section 12.5 for a deeper discussion of sharding.
Document size and complexity: Having many fields or large text fields requires more memory and faster disk I/O.	Add more RAM and faster disks.
Indexing throughput: You may need to index thousands of documents per second.	Distribute indexing operations across multiple nodes using sharding.
Document volatility: If existing documents change frequently, your indexes will be more volatile, requiring constant segment merging.	Get faster disks to facilitate constant segment merging; see section 12.3.3 for more information about segment merging.
Query volume (typically measured by QPS—queries per second).	Use replication to increase the number of threads available to execute queries.
Query complexity: This includes facets, grouping, custom sorting impact, and query execution performance.	Use sharding and replication to parallelize complex query computations such as faceting and sorting.

HIGH AVAILABILITY

Once you achieve the desired level of scalability, you need to plan for expected and unexpected outages. The ultimate goal is to have zero downtime, but in practice achieving this is expensive and beyond the capabilities of most organizations. A reasonable compromise is to create a system that makes high availability a business decision, as opposed to a technical one. You want high availability of your search engine to be a question of how much you can spend, rather than being restricted by some inherent limitation of the architecture.

To be highly available, a system needs two main properties: the ability to *failover* to healthy services when critical services fail, and *data redundancy* so that large datasets, such as search indexes, do not need to be moved to healthy nodes in the event of a failure. Moving 100 GB of data takes time, even on fast networks. In general, there are four types of outages you need to plan for with a distributed system like Solr:

1 Unexpected outages that affect a subset of the nodes in your cluster due to issues such as hardware faults and loss of network connectivity
2 Planned outages due to upgrades and system maintenance tasks
3 Degraded service due to heavy system load
4 Disasters that take your entire cluster/data center offline

SolrCloud provides a solid solution for failover and redundancy between servers within the same data center, which covers the first three types of outages. There is still work to be done to distribute Solr between multiple, geographically diverse data centers, which serves as a disaster recovery solution. As of Solr 4.7, there is no built-in support for clustering Solr across data centers. Of course you could distribute nodes across different data centers as all internode communication happens over HTTP, but in practice the network latency between data centers is too high to allow for acceptable search performance. What we mean here is that Solr does not have any built-in support for replicating data between two separate SolrCloud clusters operating in different data centers. You would have to set something up manually.

At the most basic level, Solr provides two services: indexing and query execution. Either or both of these services may need to be highly available. You may decide that Solr must always respond to queries, but you can accept downtime for indexing. It's possible that you cannot accept any outage of both core services. One of the key design principles in SolrCloud is that every node in the cluster performs indexing and executes queries. Contrast this with a master-slave architecture in which master nodes perform indexing, and slave nodes execute queries. SolrCloud allows you to achieve high availability of both core services.

To ensure that Solr continues to serve queries, SolrCloud supports redundancy by having multiple replicas per shard. To ensure that Solr continues to serve update requests (indexing), SolrCloud can automatically failover to select a new shard leader if the current leader fails.

Solr can also help minimize downtime during upgrades by using rolling restarts, where each Solr server only contacts other Solr servers using the stable, HTTP-based

API. Consequently, you're able to run different versions of Solr in the same cluster temporarily, such as to do a rolling upgrade.

Another type of outage is one in which Solr is online and responding to queries, but is under heavy load to the point it cannot respond to requests quickly enough to meet its service-level agreements (SLA). The main point here is that a search engine that does not respond to queries quickly enough is unavailable even if the servers are still running. One of the common outages with Solr is from full garbage-collector pauses in the JVM, which prevent any other threads from executing. You can guard against this type of outage by having a solid monitoring system in place and being able to quickly add more nodes to your cluster to respond to increased workload. SolrCloud allows you to quickly add new replicas to your cluster to meet increased demand.

There's also the aspect of building more fault-tolerant hardware systems. A discussion of these techniques is beyond the scope of this book, but it's worthwhile to invest in a conversation with your system administrators to discuss how to make your Solr nodes more fault-tolerant at the hardware level, such as by using RAID configurations for your disks.

CONSISTENCY

The *CAP theorem* provides a conceptual model for understanding trade-offs in a distributed system.[1] The theorem states that there are three desired properties of a distributed system—consistency (C), availability (A), and partition tolerance (P)—but only two of the three can be achieved simultaneously. In practice, distributed system designers assume that failures will occur, so the P is a must; designers are forced to choose between consistency and availability.[2]

Consistency means that an operation either succeeds or fails. When thinking about consistency in a distributed system like Solr, it boils down to the question of what can be expected from a read after a write. SolrCloud makes the assumption that once a write succeeds, all active replicas will return the same version of a document. This implies that update requests must succeed on all replicas, or the request fails. For instance, if shard1 has replicas A, B, and C, then the write is not considered successful until all three replicas accept the update. If A and B work and C fails, the write fails.

You'll learn more about the details of distributed indexing in section 13.3. The key point is that SolrCloud does not allow replicas participating in queries to have different versions of the same documents. The index may not be fully up to date because writes are failing, but it will not return inconsistent results depending on which replicas participate in a query.

Solr emphasizes *consistency over write availability* and is not tunable as is the case with some other NoSQL technologies. (You can specify the desired consistency level on a write to Cassandra [a NoSQL database] to emphasize consistency or write availability.)

---

[1] Read more about the CAP theorem, also known as Brewer's theorem, at http://en.wikipedia.org/wiki/CAP_theorem.

[2] "CAP Confusion: Problems with 'partition tolerance'," Henry Robinson, April 26, 2010, http://blog.cloudera.com/blog/2010/04/cap-confusion-problems-with-partition-tolerance/.

Solr 4 does not have the concept of configurable consistency levels; a write must succeed on all active replicas of a shard. But Solr only considers active and recovering replicas when determining if a write succeeds. It does not consider an offline replica to need the update, as that will be addressed once the failed replica recovers, using a built-in recovery process. Put simply, Solr will continue to accept writes as long as there is one active host per shard.

Contrast this with a system that favors write availability over consistency. In this case, the system would accept update requests on any replica for a shard, and the replica would try to propagate the update to the other replicas in the same shard. If the update fails on some of the replicas, the write may still be considered successful. Some systems allow the client application to specify their tolerance for this weak consistency in favor of having highly available writes; this is commonly known as *eventual consistency* because replicas eventually have a consistent state. SolrCloud currently has zero tolerance for weak consistency; the write must succeed on all replicas for a shard.

Why does Solr emphasize consistency over write availability? For one thing, it simplifies the API when writing client applications. Your Solr indexing client code does not need to worry about partial failures, because an update request either succeeds or fails on all replicas in a shard. Another reason is to ensure that you get consistent search results from every query to the same shard no matter which replicas participate in the query. Imagine the scenario of the real estate portal that we introduced in chapter 1. If replicas are allowed to be inconsistent, then one user might see a new house listing, and another would not. You can imagine it would be hard to establish and maintain trust in your search application if your application served inconsistent results based on which replicas participate in a query. You'll learn more about distributed indexing and consistency in section 13.3.

SIMPLICITY

It might surprise you to learn that Solr provided a solution for scalability, high availability, and consistency before SolrCloud. What was missing was simplicity! One of the main design goals of SolrCloud was to make it easy to achieve these important system properties. It isn't enough to be scalable and fault tolerant if achieving those goals requires manual intervention to recover or requires difficult setup and maintenance on a daily basis. Simplicity is more subjective, but we think SolrCloud achieves this goal in two areas:

- *Day-to-day operations*—Once set up, running a Solr cluster is no more complicated than running a single Solr instance.
- *Recovering from node failures*—Once you've fixed the issue that caused a node to fail, adding it back to the cluster is easy and automated. The recovered node will sync up with its shard leader. We'll cover basic system administration tasks later in the chapter.

SolrCloud does require additional components, most notably ZooKeeper. As you'll learn in the next section, ZooKeeper is mostly a black-box technology that you don't need to worry about too much other than the initial configuration. Of course, Solr-Cloud is still evolving, and there are some rough edges—especially in terms of monitoring a large cluster.

ELASTICITY

The final property of the ideal search system is the ability to expand capacity in an automated fashion. Specifically, with Solr, we need the ability to add more replicas to distribute query processing and split shards into smaller shards as they grow larger. For query capacity, you can add more replicas to the cluster and they will automatically sync with the leader.

Another issue that arises in large-scale clusters is that a shard may outgrow the server it's hosted on and need to be split into multiple smaller shards. Solr supports splitting one shard into two smaller ones. This can be useful if your cluster has reached a level at which you can double the number of nodes. We'll discuss shard splitting in the final section of this chapter.

13.2 Core concepts

At this point, you've started a SolrCloud cluster, indexed some documents, and executed distributed queries. You've also learned about the ideal properties of large-scale search engines and how they drive the SolrCloud architecture. Now let's dig into the details of the core concepts we introduced in the previous section, starting with collections versus cores.

13.2.1 Collections vs. cores

Up to this point in the book, we've only worked with Solr cores. To recap, a Solr core is a uniquely named, managed, and configured index running in a Solr server; a Solr server can host one or more cores. A core is typically used to separate documents that have different schemas. In chapter 1, we used the example of a real estate search application that separated home listings and land listings into different cores because the schema for each type of document is quite different.

SolrCloud introduces the concept of a collection, which extends the concept of a uniquely named, managed, and configured index to one that is split into shards and distributed across multiple servers. The reason SolrCloud needs a new term is because each shard of a distributed index is hosted in a Solr core, as depicted in figure 13.3.

When talking about SolrCloud, it helps to no longer think in terms of cores, but rather to think of shards, which are mutually exclusive slices of an index. The fact that a shard is backed by a Solr core is simply an implementation detail. Consequently, we won't use the term core in this chapter unless it is to draw reference back to non-SolrCloud behavior.

Just as a single Solr server can host multiple cores, a SolrCloud cluster can host multiple collections. If you need to represent documents with different schemas, you will use multiple collections in SolrCloud as you would use multiple cores in a single

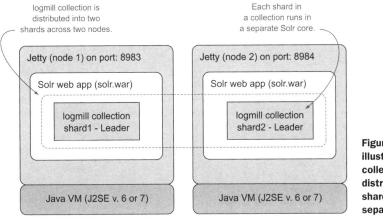

Figure 13.3 **A diagram illustrating the** `logmill` **collection being distributed into two shards on two separate nodes**

server setup. Now that we have a basic understanding of collections, let's learn about ZooKeeper, which is a critical component in the SolrCloud architecture.

13.2.2 *ZooKeeper*

ZooKeeper is a coordination service for distributed systems. Solr uses ZooKeeper for three critical operations:

- Centralized configuration storage and distribution
- Detection and notification when the cluster state changes
- Shard-leader election

The designers of SolrCloud chose to use ZooKeeper because it is mature, stable, and widely used by a number of complex distributed systems. In this section, we cover the most important concepts you need to understand about ZooKeeper as it relates to SolrCloud. One of the main strengths of ZooKeeper is that it provides robust solutions for common problems that arise in distributed systems. The ZooKeeper community calls these *recipes*, which are similar to design patterns in object-oriented design: that is, "We've seen this problem before, and it is best solved using approach X." Let's begin by understanding ZooKeeper's data model, as that will help you understand how Solr uses ZooKeeper for cluster-state management.

ZOOKEEPER DATA MODEL

ZooKeeper organizes data into a hierarchical namespace similar to a filesystem. Each level in the hierarchy is called a *znode*. Each znode encapsulates basic metadata such as creation time and last-modified time and can also store a small amount of data.

It's important to recognize that znodes are not intended to store large data objects; as such, ZooKeeper comes preconfigured with a maximum size of 1 MB of storage available for each znode. This restriction is because ZooKeeper keeps znodes in memory for performance reasons. It's also there as a reminder that ZooKeeper is not a general-purpose data-storage system; it's intended for storing small bits of metadata

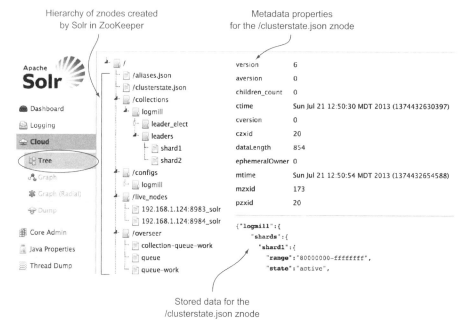

Figure 13.4   Tree view of znodes needed to coordinate a SolrCloud cluster

that need to be accessed by a large number of distributed servers. ZooKeeper's design favors speed and ability to service many requests concurrently over flexibility in the size and type of data you can store. Figure 13.4 shows some of the znodes used by SolrCloud.

A central concept in ZooKeeper is the *ephemeral znode*, which requires an active client connection to keep the znode alive. If the client application that created the ephemeral znode goes away, the ephemeral znode is automatically deleted by Zoo-Keeper. When a Solr node joins the cluster, it creates an ephemeral znode under the /live_nodes node. Solr keeps an active connection to this node using the ZooKeeper API. If Solr crashes, the connection to the ephemeral znode is lost, causing that node to be considered gone. When the state of a znode changes, ZooKeeper notifies the other nodes in the cluster that one of the nodes is down. This is important so that Solr doesn't try to send distributed query requests to the failed node. You can see the ephemeral znodes for the two live Solr servers we started in the previous section in the Cloud panel under the tree view in figure 13.5.

ZNODE WATCHER

Another core concept in ZooKeeper is that of a *znode watcher*. Any client application can register itself as a watcher of a znode. If the state of the znode changes, Zoo-Keeper will notify all registered watchers of the change. For instance, Solr registers as a watcher of the /clusterstate.json znode so that it can receive notifications when the state of the cluster changes, as when there is a new replica or a node is offline.

Figure 13.5   Ephemeral znodes created by each Solr instance when it joins the cluster

PRODUCTION CONFIGURATION

ZooKeeper is also a distributed system that can be deployed to be fault tolerant and highly scalable. When starting out, you can have Solr run an embedded ZooKeeper instance in the same process as one of your Solr nodes, as we did in section 13.1.1. But, you are strongly discouraged from running ZooKeeper on the same nodes as Solr in production.

For production, you need to set up a separate ZooKeeper ensemble made up of at least three nodes,[3] as ZooKeeper relies on a majority of nodes (commonly known as a quorum) agreeing on the state of a znode at all times. If you deploy three nodes, you can lose one without experiencing any downtime. If ZooKeeper goes offline, Solr can still respond to queries but will refuse to accept updates. This is a safeguard mechanism. Solr can respond to queries because each node caches the cluster state received from ZooKeeper.

Once you have a running ensemble, you will need to know the connection string to pass to Solr using the zkHost parameter. Recall that we used zkHost=localhost:9983 when using the embedded ZooKeeper instance. Change this to the ZooKeeper connection string when you're ready to run SolrCloud in production. If you set up a three-node ensemble on zk1.example.com:2181, zk2.example.com:2181, and zk3.example.com:2181, you will need to pass the following parameter when starting Solr in production:

```
-DzkHost=zk1.example.com:2181,zk2.example.com:2181,zk3.example.com:2181
```

---

[3] "ZooKeeper: Because Coordinating Distributed Systems is a Zoo," Hadoop, Nov. 19, 2012, http://zookeeper .apache.org/doc/r3.4.5/.

ZOOKEEPER CLIENT TIMEOUT

The second most important parameter you need to understand is the ZooKeeper client timeout. As discussed earlier, Solr creates ephemeral znodes when it joins a cluster to indicate there is a live node. If a Solr node crashes, ZooKeeper will detect the crash after the timeout period. Consequently, you want the timeout to be as brief as possible to ensure the cluster state managed in ZooKeeper reflects the current state of your cluster. The default timeout in Solr is 15 seconds. To change it, you can set the `zkClientTimeout` parameter to an integer value in milliseconds: `-DzkClientTimeout =30000`, for example, will change the timeout to 30 seconds.

> ### Full garbage collection and the ZooKeeper client timeout
>
> As an aside, be aware of the impact that full garbage collection in the Java VM has on the ZooKeeper session. The JVM pauses all executing threads when running a full garbage collection, including the thread that keeps the ZooKeeper session alive. It follows that if a full garbage collection takes longer than the ZooKeeper client timeout, then the instance will appear as being offline to ZooKeeper. This is a good thing because the instance cannot accept requests while it is performing full garbage collection. Solr will attempt to reestablish the ZooKeeper connection once the full garbage collection pause is over. If you notice that nodes keep dropping their session with ZooKeeper, we recommend enabling verbose garbage collection logging to see if full garbage collection activities are taking too long to finish. Refer to the documentation for your JVM for information on how to enable verbose garbage collection logging.

CENTRALIZED CONFIGURATION STORAGE AND DISTRIBUTION

One of the great features provided by ZooKeeper is centralized configuration management and distribution. When you bootstrap a new collection in a SolrCloud cluster, you need to upload the configuration files such as *solrconfig.xml* and *schema.xml* into ZooKeeper. When Solr launches in cloud mode, it will pull the configuration files from ZooKeeper automatically. We saw this in section 13.1.1 when we started our second instance after deleting the *conf/* directory. If you need to change a setting in *solrconfig.xml*, upload the updated version to ZooKeeper, and reload your collection to trigger all nodes in your cluster to apply the updates from a centralized location.

This is a powerful feature of SolrCloud because it allows you to add nodes at any time, and you know they will have the most up-to-date configuration files. Imagine you manage a Solr cluster composed of 100 servers, and you need to make a change to *solrconfig.xml*. Let's say you need to add a new warming query to the new searcher listener configuration element in *solrconfig.xml* (`<listener event="newSearcher">`). The configuration change needs to be pushed out to all servers, and then the collection needs to be reloaded. Wouldn't it be nice if you could just publish the configuration change to one centralized location and have all servers pull the update automatically? This is one of the important processes that ZooKeeper supports with SolrCloud.

Figure 13.6   Screenshot showing the configuration files for the `logmill` collection stored in ZooKeeper

Figure 13.6 shows where the configuration files are stored in ZooKeeper. One caveat is that ZooKeeper is not meant to store large files. The default size limit is set to 1 MB.

Now that we have a basic understanding of ZooKeeper concepts, let's discuss how to determine the appropriate number of shards and replicas for your collection.

13.2.3 Choosing the number of shards and replicas

In chapter 12 (section 12.5) we discussed how to go about choosing the right number of shards into which your data will be partitioned, and the number of replicas that will contain a copy of your sharded data. You may choose to have one shard or hundreds of shards, based upon the performance and fault-tolerance factors, such as the total number of documents, document sizes, your desired indexing throughput, your query complexity, and the projected index-size growth over time.

When choosing the number of shards and replicas in a SolrCloud configuration, the same performance factors apply as discussed in chapter 12. Fundamentally, all searches run across one or more Solr shards regardless of whether you explicitly execute a distributed search (using the `shards` request parameter on your query) or whether you allow SolrCloud to find copies of every shard in your collection. SolrCloud hides the complexity of tracking where each of your shards is located. Thus, the same guidelines for handling data volumes and query volumes that governed our sharding and replication decisions in chapter 12 still apply when using SolrCloud to manage your cluster instead of doing it manually. SolrCloud does provide a much simpler mechanism for managing your distributed search environment, however, which we will dive into more in the next section.

13.2.4   *Cluster-state management*

Distributed indexing and search depend on every node knowing the state of every other node in the cluster. A shard leader, for instance, needs to know about all the replicas that need to receive updates. At any given time, there are a number of possible node states that determine if a node is eligible to process a query or receive an update request. Table 13.3 provides an overview of the possible states of an instance in SolrCloud.

Table 13.3   **Short description of instance states in SolrCloud**

Status	Description
Active	Active nodes are happily serving queries and accepting update requests. Active replicas are in sync with their shard leader. A healthy cluster is one in which all nodes are active.
Inactive	Used during shard splitting to indicate that a Solr instance is no longer participating in the collection. Shards that get split enter this state once the splits are active.
Construction	Used during shard splitting to indicate that a split is being created. Shards in this state buffer update requests from the parent shard but do not participate in queries.
Recovering	Recovering instances are running but can't serve queries. They do accept update requests while recovering so that they don't continue to fall behind the leader.
Recovery Failed	The instance attempted to recover but encountered an error. In most cases, you will need to consult the logs and manually resolve the issue preventing the instance from recovering.
Down	The instance is running and is connected to ZooKeeper but is not in a state in which it can recover, such as when Solr is initializing. A downed instance does not participate in queries or accept updates. The down state is usually temporary, and the node will transition to one of the other states.
Gone	The instance is not connected to ZooKeeper and has probably crashed. If a node is still running but ZooKeeper thinks it's gone, the most likely cause is an `OutOfMemoryError` in the JVM.

Ideally, you want all nodes in your cluster to be active at all times, but SolrCloud was designed to gracefully handle node failures as well as new nodes joining the cluster. Solr relies heavily on ZooKeeper for cluster-state management.

Behind the scenes, SolrCloud uses an overseer component to store a snapshot of the current cluster state in the `/clusterstate.json` znode in ZooKeeper. There is only one overseer per cluster, but Solr can automatically select a new one if the current one fails. Thus, the overseer is not a single point of failure. The overseer is elected using a leader election process, similar to how shard leaders are elected.

Every Solr instance registers as a watcher of the /clusterstate.json znode to receive state-change notifications. For example, if a new replica joins the cluster, then the overseer will update the /clusterstate.json znode to incorporate the new node. When the znode changes, ZooKeeper notifies all nodes in the cluster, which triggers them to refresh their cached view of the cluster state.

In addition to each node having a discrete state in the cluster, a node can be either a shard leader or a replica. Let's turn our attention to understanding how shard-leader election works, which is the final core concept you need to understand about SolrCloud.

13.2.5 *Shard-leader election*

A shard leader is responsible for accepting update requests and distributing them to replicas in a coordinated fashion. Specifically, the shard leader provides the following additional responsibilities for handling update requests beyond a replica:

- Accepts update requests for the shard
- Increments the value of the _version_ field on the updated document and enforces optimistic locking
- Writes the document to its update log
- Sends the update (in parallel) to all replicas and blocks until a response is received

Shard leaders do not perform any additional responsibilities when handling query requests. Any host per shard can be the leader, and all other hosts per shard are replicas. As with replicas, leaders also participate in distributed queries. Contrast this with a master-slave setup in which master nodes only index, and slave nodes only respond to queries. In SolrCloud, both leaders and replicas perform indexing and execute queries.

Before we cover the details of how a shard leader is selected, it's important to know that you really shouldn't care which node in a shard is the current leader and shouldn't try to control it. SolrCloud was designed so that any host for a shard could be the leader, and a new leader can be elected automatically. For the most part, shard leaders are an implementation detail that has little bearing on how you set up or operate your cluster.

There are two essential aspects to leader election: choosing the initial leader and automatically selecting a new leader if the current leader fails. Leader election needs to be centrally coordinated, as you don't want two hosts from the same shard thinking they are both the leader. As you may have guessed, ZooKeeper plays a critical role in shard leader election. In fact, leader election is a common requirement for many distributed systems, and as such it's codified into a ZooKeeper recipe.

To illustrate how leader election works, consider the scenario in which a shard has four replicas that join the cluster simultaneously. One of the replicas needs to be elected

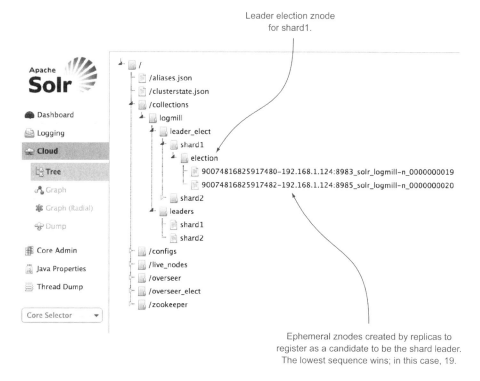

Figure 13.7   Znodes used for shard leader election

as the shard leader, so it stands to reason that the first of the four nodes to register itself should be elected as the leader. Behind the scenes, Solr uses ZooKeeper sequence flags to keep track of the order in which nodes register themselves as candidates to be the leader. Sequence flags are incremented in an atomic fashion, so it doesn't matter how many clients attempt to increment the sequence concurrently. Figure 13.7 shows the znodes used for leader election for shard1 in our example `logmill` collection.

In a nutshell, the node with the lowest sequence number wins as leader of the shard. Now let's consider what happens when the current leader fails. When this occurs, a new leader needs to be elected before indexing can continue. It turns out that the next healthy node in the sequence becomes the leader. If you're interested in the details of how leader failover works, we encourage you to read the ZooKeeper documentation.[4]

13.2.6 *Important SolrCloud configuration settings*

SolrCloud introduces additional configuration settings you need to be aware of as you plan your cluster. The default *solr.xml* provided with the example server includes a

---

[4] "ZooKeeper Recipes and Solutions," Hadoop, Oct. 9, 2013, http://zookeeper.apache.org/doc/trunk/recipes .html - sc_leaderElection.

`<solrcloud>` element where you can control various configuration properties related to SolrCloud. The good news is that you don't need to worry about changing these parameters while learning about SolrCloud. We're including them here so that you know they are available when you're ready to roll SolrCloud out to production. You can safely skip this subsection and come back to it when you're further along in the process. If you are curious about SolrCloud configuration parameters, the following listing shows the `<solrcloud>` elements from the *solr.xml* file provided with the example server.

Listing 13.2 SolrCloud parameters in the *solr.xml* provided with the example server

SolrCloud-
related
parameters
in solr.xml.

```
<solr>
  <solrcloud>
    <str name="host">${host:}</str>
    <int name="hostPort">${jetty.port:8983}</int>
    <str name="hostContext">${hostContext:solr}</str>
    <int name="zkClientTimeout">${zkClientTimeout:15000}</int>
    <bool name="genericCoreNodeNames">${genericCoreNodeNames:true}</bool>
  </solrcloud>
  <shardHandlerFactory name="shardHandlerFactory"
    class="HttpShardHandlerFactory">
    <int name="socketTimeout">${socketTimeout:0}</int>
    <int name="connTimeout">${connTimeout:0}</int>
  </shardHandlerFactory>
</solr>
```

Let's dig into each of the parameters to get a basic understanding of how it is used in SolrCloud. In general, most of these parameters control how a Solr instance registers itself with ZooKeeper when joining a SolrCloud cluster.

HOST

ZooKeeper needs to know the host and port of every Solr instance in the cluster. This information is stored in the `/clusterstate.json` znode so that all nodes have access to all other nodes in the cluster. When a Solr instance joins the cluster, it registers a host and port. By default, the host will be set to the IP address and the port will be the port Jetty is bound to. We showed an example of this in figure 13.1 where the first instance of Solr we started registered itself with ZooKeeper using IP address 10.0.1.7 on port 8983; 10.0.1.7 is an internal IP address issued by our local router. Using the IP address of your local workstation is fine for development and testing, but when you're ready to deploy SolrCloud in production, we recommend setting the `host` parameter to a hostname instead of an internal IP address, as that will make the Cloud panel in the Solr Admin Console easier to read. Moreover, it is typically easier to change a DNS entry to assign a hostname to a different server than to update an IP address in `/clusterstate.json`.

Imagine that we want to set the `host` property of one of our Solr instances to hostname solr1.example.com. Of course we can edit *solr.xml* to set the host using `<str name="host">solr1.example.com</str>`. But that approach requires us to edit the *solr.xml* file for every instance in our cluster, which can be a pain for system administrators. By default, *solr.xml* sets the host parameter to `<str name="host">${host:}</str>`. The value `${host:}` is a special configuration syntax that allows you to set a parameter using a Java system property and specify a default value after the colon. In this case, the default value for the host property is empty. We can pass `-Dhost=solr1.example.com` on the command line when starting Solr, which avoids having to edit *solr.xml* separately for every instance in our cluster.

PORT

The `hostPort` parameter sets the port that Solr is listening on, such as 8983. In most cases, you want to leave the default value set to `${jetty.port:8983}`, which simply uses the value of the `jetty.port` system property. If the `jetty.port` system property is not set, the `hostPort` parameter defaults to 8983. Recall that we set the `jetty.port` system property using `-Djetty.port=8984` when starting the second instance on our local workstation in section 13.1.1. In general, we recommend that you always pass the `jetty.port` system property when starting a Solr instance with Jetty in a production cluster.

SOLR HOST CONTEXT

Solr is a Java web application that runs under the solr context in Jetty. If you change the Solr web application or deploy the *solr.war* file under the root context (/ in Jetty), you must set the `hostContext` parameter. If you deployed the Solr web application under the search context in Jetty, you would need to set `-DhostContext=search` when starting Solr. It should be noted that changing the Solr web application context, and consequently the `hostContext` parameter, is not common for most Solr installations.

ZOOKEEPER CLIENT TIMEOUT

We discussed the concepts behind the ZooKeeper client timeout in section 13.2.2. As with the other parameters in the *solr.xml* file, we recommend that you use the Java system property to change the value of the `zkClientTimeout` parameter. Because this value should be the same for all nodes in your cluster, it would be acceptable to edit *solr.xml* instead of using the command-line approach.

CORE NODE NAMES

The `genericCoreNodeNames` parameter should stand out as being somewhat confusing and probably unnecessary for an example *solr.xml* file. For the most part, you can ignore this parameter and leave it set to `true`. Briefly, this parameter controls the naming strategy Solr uses when creating unique names for cores in a collection. As we described in section 13.2.1, a collection is distributed across multiple cores. Each core in a cluster needs to have a unique name. If the `genericCoreNodeNames` parameter is set to `true`, Solr assigns a generic name, such as `core_node1`. If `false`, then the value of the `host` parameter is included in the core name, such as `10.0.1.7:8983_solr_logmill`.

LEADER VOTE WAIT PERIOD

There is an optional parameter that is not included in the example *solr.xml* that controls how long a node will wait for other nodes to vote to be a shard leader before assuming the shard leader role. The `leaderVoteWait` parameter provides a safety mechanism intended to prevent a node with stale data from automatically assuming the leader role until other nodes hosting the same shard have had a chance to vote to be the leader.

Consider the scenario where there are two instances hosting a shard; specifically node X is the leader and node Y is a replica of shard1. Now imagine that node Y crashes but node X continues to accept update requests as the leader. In this scenario, node Y becomes out of sync with the shard leader while it is offline. If node X crashes before node Y recovers, then node Y should not immediately assume the role as the shard leader when it is restarted because node Y has stale data compared to node X. The `leaderVoteWait` parameter, which defaults to three minutes, protects against situations described in this fictitious scenario. If node X comes back online within the `leaderVoteWait` period, it will resume the leader status and node Y will recover as a replica. This only protects the case where node X and Y are offline for a short period of time, of course.

The implication of this safety mechanism is that node Y will not become active in the cluster within the `leaderVoteWait` period if node X is offline. Specifically, node Y will enter a waiting period to see if other nodes for the same shard join the cluster. This implies that shard1 will remain offline until node X rejoins the cluster or until the `leaderVoteWait` period ends. This situation only occurs when all nodes hosting a shard go offline, which can be mitigated by using more replicas per shard.

Before we move on, let's recap some of the essential points described in this section.

- SolrCloud uses the term *collection* to describe an index split across multiple Solr instances. It's better to think in terms of shards than cores; Solr cores should be treated as an implementation detail.
- ZooKeeper is a critical service in SolrCloud that provides centralized configuration management, cluster-state management, and shard-leader election.
- You must specify the number of shards when defining a collection, based on the number of documents, document size, indexing throughput, query complexity, and projected growth of your index over time.
- The overseer component updates the `/clusterstate.json` znode to notify all nodes when the state of the cluster changes.
- Shard leaders provide additional responsibilities during indexing; leaders are elected automatically using a recipe provided by ZooKeeper.
- If the current shard leader fails, a new one is elected automatically.

Now let's apply the core concepts we learned in this section to understanding how the distributed-indexing process works.

13.3 Distributed indexing

From a client's perspective, indexing documents in SolrCloud remains the same. In fact, you should be able to use any existing indexing client application without having to make any changes, but there are potential optimizations you can add to your indexing client application to improve performance and to support near real-time search. On the Solr server side, indexing has changed considerably. In this section, you'll learn how distributed indexing works with SolrCloud.

The overall goal behind distributed indexing in SolrCloud is to be able to send a document to any node in the cluster and have that document be indexed in the correct shard. Moreover, distributed indexing in SolrCloud is designed to remove all SPoFs, which is essential to achieving high availability. We'll begin our discussion of distributed indexing by learning how documents are assigned to shards.

13.3.1 *Document shard assignment*

When a new document is indexed in Solr, it needs to be assigned to one of the shards. A document is assigned to one and only one shard per collection. Solr uses a component called a *document router* to determine which shard a document should be assigned to. There are two basic document-routing strategies supported by Solr-Cloud: compositeId (default) and implicit. We won't discuss implicit routing in this book, as it places all of the routing logic on your application client code. You can customize shard assignment, but in this section we're going to discuss the out-of-the-box approach; we discuss custom document routing in the last section of this chapter.

As we discussed previously in this chapter, you must set the number of shards to initialize a collection. Once Solr knows the number of shards, it assigns each shard a range of 32-bit hash values. For the two-shard example cluster we set up in section 13.1, shard1 was assigned hash range 80000000-ffffffff, and shard2 was assigned hash range 0-7fffffff (hexadecimal values). The 32-bit hash range is split evenly between each shard.

The default compositeId router computes a numeric hash of the unique ID field in a document and assigns the document to the shard whose range includes the computed hash value. This implies that every document sent to SolrCloud must have a unique document ID. Keeping with our two-shard example, if the hash value for the unique ID field for a document is 80000001 (hexadecimal), then the document would be assigned to shard1.

This raises the question: How is the hash value for a given document ID computed? There are two basic goals for a hash function used for document routing: it must be fast, because determining the shard assignment for a document is a fundamental operation in distributed Solr, and it should distribute documents evenly across all shards. You wouldn't want one of your shards to end up with twice as many documents as the other shards in the collection, for example, because of a biased hashing function. The reason you want a balanced distribution of documents around your cluster is that distributed queries are only as fast as the slowest shard to respond. If one of the shards has twice as many documents as the other shards, it would likely be the bottleneck for all your distributed queries.

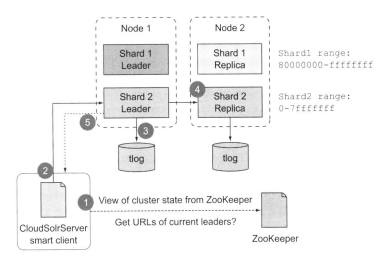

Figure 13.8 The distributed-indexing process using Solr's smart client, `CloudSolrServer`

If you're curious, Solr uses the *MurmurHash* algorithm,[5] because it's fast and creates an even distribution of hash values, which keeps the number of documents in each shard balanced (roughly). Now that we understand how documents are assigned to shards, let's see how distributed indexing works in our two-shard `logmill` collection.

13.3.2 Adding documents

As you learned in chapter 5, there are four types of update requests in Solr: `add`, `update`, `delete`, and `commit`. In this section, we'll learn how documents are added to the index, as that provides the foundation for understanding how the other types of update requests work in SolrCloud. Figure 13.8 depicts the distributed-indexing process in SolrCloud.

Let's walk through the steps depicted in figure 13.8, beginning in the lower left. Previously, we stated that existing indexing client applications do not need to change. You can send update requests to any node in the cluster, and the request will be forwarded to the correct shard leader. However, SolrJ does include a new `SolrServer` implementation, called `CloudSolrServer`, that helps make indexing in SolrCloud a little more robust. The following steps explain figure 13.8.

STEP 1: SEND THE UPDATE REQUEST USING CLOUDSOLRSERVER
As depicted in figure 13.8, `CloudSolrServer` connects to ZooKeeper to get the current state of the cluster. This means that your indexing client knows the state of each node in the cluster and which nodes are leaders. Because `CloudSolrServer` takes current cluster-state information into account when generating requests, it's considered to be a smart client. Having access to the current cluster state provides two advantages.

---

[5] "MurmurHash," http://en.wikipedia.org/wiki/MurmurHash.

First, `CloudSolrServer` knows which nodes are shard leaders. Because `update` requests must be routed to shard leaders before their replicas, `CloudSolrServer` can save time by sending them directly to a shard leader instead of to a replica. Think what must happen on the client side in `CloudSolrServer` for direct updates to work. We hope you guessed that `CloudSolrServer` must implement the document-routing strategies we described in section 13.3.1. We'll describe how this works in a moment.

The second advantage of `CloudSolrServer` is it provides basic load balancing and retry logic on the client side. If a node crashes while your client application is indexing documents, `CloudSolrServer` will get a notification from ZooKeeper that the node is unavailable so it can stop sending requests to that node; that is, it'll take it out of the list of load-balancing candidates. If the node that failed was a leader, then `CloudSolrServer` will also get a notification of the new shard leader. All of this happens automatically behind the scenes because `CloudSolServer` registers a watcher on the `/clusterstate.json` and `/live_nodes` znodes in Zookeeper. (Refer to section 13.2.2 for a review of znode watchers.)

The indexing tool we used in section 13.1 uses `CloudSolrServer`. The primary difference is that you need to specify the ZooKeeper connection address instead of the Solr URL, as shown in the following listing.

Listing 13.3 Create an instance of `CloudSolrServer` using the ZooKeeper address

```
String zkHost = cli.getOptionValue("zkhost", ZK_HOST);
String collectionName = cli.getOptionValue("collection", COLLECTION);
int zkClientTimeout =
    Integer.parseInt(cli.getOptionValue("zkClientTimeout", "15000"));

CloudSolrServer solr = new CloudSolrServer(zkHost);
solr.setDefaultCollection(collectionName);
solr.setZkClientTimeout(zkClientTimeout);
solr.connect();
```

Connect to SolrCloud using the ZooKeeper connection string.

Specify the default collection name, such as logmill.

Set the ZooKeeper client timeout (see section 13.2.2).

Open the connection to ZooKeeper to read cluster state.

As you add documents to `CloudSolrServer`, it will load balance across all shard leaders in your cluster.

STEP 2: ROUTE THE DOCUMENT TO THE CORRECT SHARD

Returning to step 2 in figure 13.8, `CloudSolrServer` needs to decide which shard to send a document to using the document-routing process described in section 13.3.1. For instance, in figure 13.8, the document is sent to shard 2, which covers the hash range of 0-7fffffff. Once the shard leader is selected, `CloudSolrServer` sends the update request to the correct shard leader using the HTTP-based Solr API.

Conceptually, this process is very simple for a single document, but now let's consider what happens if you add a batch of multiple documents to `CloudSolrServer` in your indexing application. When processing multiple documents, `CloudSolrServer` needs to determine the correct shard assignment for each document in the batch individually. Behind the scenes, `CloudSolrServer` divides the batch into *S* sub-batches, where *S* is the number of shards. `CloudSolrServer` then assigns each document in the batch to one of the sub-batches using the document-routing process. Lastly, `Cloud-SolrServer` sends the sub-batches to the correct shard leaders in parallel, which allows for very high throughput indexing in SolrCloud.

STEP 3: LEADER ASSIGNS VERSION ID

The shard leader indexes the document locally before sending it to replicas. This serves to validate the document and ensures that it's safely persisted to durable storage using the update log before forwarding to the replicas. In addition, the leader assigns a version number to the new document. For existing documents, the leader will validate the version number against the current version of the document, to support the optimistic locking process described in chapter 5.

STEP 4: FORWARD REQUEST TO REPLICAS

Once a document has been validated and versioned, the leader determines which replicas are available and sends the update request to each one in parallel using multiple threads. For any update request, there may be some replicas in the gone or down states. The leader does not care about them, as they will recover any missed documents using a recovery process discussed in section 13.3.4. What might not be obvious is that the leader will send the update request to any replicas that are in the recovering state. The recovering node persists the update request to its update transaction log while recovery is running.

STEP 5: ACKNOWLEDGE WRITE SUCCESS

Once the leader receives an acknowledgement from all active and recovering replicas, it returns confirmation to the indexing client application. Update requests will continue to be accepted by Solr so long as there is at least one active replica for a shard. However, this approach favors write-availability at the potential expense of lost consistency.

Recall the scenario we described in section 13.2.6 when we discussed the `leader-VoteWait` configuration setting. As we discussed, a recovering replica will wait for a specified time before assuming the leader role, which can help alleviate the chance of having inconsistencies in a shard. However, if the previous leader does not recover within the specified timeout, then the replica may assume the leader role, which would mean some accepted writes would be lost in our scenario.

A planned future improvement in Solr is to provide an option to enforce a majority quorum approach to accepting updates in SolrCloud.[6] This option would allow you to favor consistency over write-availability in that writes would fail if they cannot be accepted by a majority of total replicas for a shard. In our scenario, writes would no longer be accepted if there were only one active replica for a shard because one node does not constitute a majority in a shard containing two replicas. If a shard

---

[6] SOLR-5468, "Option to enforce a majority quorum approach to accepting updates in SolrCloud," https://issues.apache.org/jira/browse/SOLR-5468.

were replicated on three nodes, then writes would be accepted if one node failed because there would still be two active nodes for the shard.

Of course, causing writes to fail on the server side just moves the problem to the client application, but at least that will remove the chance for inconsistencies between a leader and a replica. This issue illustrates that when building distributed systems there will be trade-offs between write-availability and consistency.

COMMIT

As you know, documents are not visible in search results until they are committed. In distributed indexing, when you send a commit to any node, it gets forwarded to all nodes in the cluster so that every shard is committed. Put simply, your client-application code should send the hard commit request when you need to open a new searcher, and SolrCloud will do the right thing by propagating the commit to all nodes in the cluster.

13.3.3 *Near real-time search*

Discussion of SolrCloud would not be complete without a look into *near real-time* (NRT) search, which was one of the main drivers behind the design of SolrCloud. NRT makes documents visible in search results within seconds of their being indexed, hence the use of the *near* qualifier. To allow documents to be visible in NRT, Solr provides a soft commit mechanism, which skips the costly aspects of hard commits, such as flushing documents stored in memory to disk.

As you learned in the previous section, shard leaders forward update requests to all replicas before responding to the indexing client application. This ensures that all shards produce consistent search results. It turns out that the design decision to send updates to all replicas is largely driven by the need to support NRT search. In contrast, a master-slave setup cannot support NRT search because the intent of the search is to make documents visible in search results within about one second of their being added to the index. Master–slave-based replication relies on moving entire segments from the master to the slave. If Solr had to replicate segments to slaves every second, your engine would build up many small segments, and query performance would suffer greatly.

Let's see how to use NRT search in our `logmill` example application. Log aggregation is a good use case for this type of search, as most organizations want to see errors being generated by critical applications as quickly as possible. It turns out that you can use any existing client application to index in near real-time. Enabling NRT behavior simply requires a configuration change in *solrconfig.xml*. The following listing shows the changes needed to enable automatic soft commits.

> **Listing 13.4 Enable automatic soft commits in *solrconfig.xml***

```
<autoSoftCommit>
  <maxTime>1000</maxTime>
</autoSoftCommit>
```
◁—| **Issue a soft commit every 1000 milliseconds.**

As soft commits are less expensive, you can issue a soft commit every few seconds to make newly indexed documents visible in NRT. However, keep in mind that you still need to do a hard commit at some point to ensure documents are eventually flushed to durable storage.

When you perform a soft commit, Solr must open a new searcher to make the soft committed documents visible in search results. This implies that Solr must also invalidate all caches to remain consistent with the changes applied by the soft commit. When opening a new searcher after a soft commit, Solr warms caches and executes warming queries configured in *solrconfig.xml*. Consequently, this implies that your cache autowarming settings and warming queries must execute faster than your soft commit frequency. For instance, if you perform soft commits every two seconds, your warming queries and autowarmed caches should not take longer than two seconds to complete, otherwise you will end up with too many open searchers, which causes subsequent commits to fail. The key takeaway is that when doing soft commits, you need to ensure your cache and warming query configuration settings are properly tuned for NRT search. Put simply, you should rely on a minimal amount of cache autowarming and warming queries.

Although NRT search is a powerful feature, you do not have to use it with Solr-Cloud. It's perfectly acceptable to not use soft commits, and we recommend not using them unless you really need indexed documents to be visible in near real-time. Do not feel like you must use NRT search when using SolrCloud. One of the drawbacks to using soft commits is that your caches are constantly being invalidated.

Let's move on to learn how Solr keeps leaders and replicas in sync after a failure occurs during distributed indexing.

13.3.4 *Node recovery process*

A good rule to live by when designing and running a large-scale distributed system is to plan on node failures as a common occurrence. This is especially true when scaling out on commodity hardware; instead of investing in expensive fault-tolerant hardware, you simply use replication to protect your system when a node fails. Moreover, you will also need to upgrade Solr to apply bug fixes and new features or change JVM settings. The bottom line is that at any given time, there may be an offline node in your cluster. The good news is that SolrCloud was designed to handle offline nodes gracefully.

SolrCloud supports two basic recovery scenarios: *peer sync* and *snapshot replication*. The recovery process for these two scenarios is differentiated by how many update requests (`add`, `delete`, `update`) the recovering node missed while it was offline.

- *Peer sync*—If the outage was short-lived and the recovering node missed only a few updates, it will recover by pulling updates from the shard leader's update log. The upper limit on missed updates is currently hardcoded to 100. If the number of missed updates exceeds this limit, the recovering node pulls a full index snapshot from the shard leader.
- *Snapshot replication*—If a node is offline for an extended period of time such that it becomes too far out of sync with the shard leader, it uses Solr's HTTP-based replication, based on the snapshot of the index.

For the most part, you don't need to worry about either of these processes, as a node determines the state of its index compared to the leader and initiates the appropriate process automatically. This also means that you can add a new replica to your cluster at any time, and it will pull the full index from the shard leader.

That covers how distributed indexing works in SolrCloud. Let's now look at how distributed queries work.

13.4 Distributed search

Once you shard your index, you have a new problem: you must query all shards to get a complete result set. Querying across all shards in a collection to create a unified result set is known as a *distributed query*. The `distrib` parameter determines if a query is distributed or local; when SolrCloud mode is enabled, `distrib` defaults to `true`. Setting `distrib=false` disables distributed queries and executes the query against the local index only.

13.4.1 Multistage query process

Distributed queries work differently than nondistributed queries because Solr needs to gather results for all shards, then merge the results into a single response to the client. Solr uses a multistage query process to execute distributed queries, as depicted in figure 13.9 and explained in the following steps.

STEP 1: CLIENT SENDS QUERY TO ANY NODE

The distributed query process begins when a client application sends a query to any node in the cluster. It's common to use a load balancer to distribute queries to different nodes in the cluster. If your application is using SolrJ, the `CloudSolrServer` class works as a simple load balancer for distributing queries to your cluster. If you're not using SolrJ, you can use a load balancer or something simple like a round-robin DNS address to access your cluster.

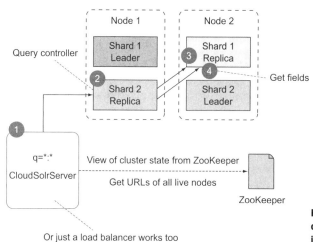

Figure 13.9 Two-stage distributed-query process in SolrCloud

STEP 2: QUERY CONTROLLER RECEIVES REQUEST

A distributed query happens in multiple stages. The node that receives the initial request is the *query controller* (or aggregator) and is responsible for creating a unified result set to return to the client. Any node in the cluster can be the controller for any query.

In SolrCloud, the query controller needs to know the status of all nodes in the cluster, which it gets from ZooKeeper. But the query controller does not request cluster-state information from ZooKeeper on every request, as that would quickly become a major bottleneck. Instead, each node registers as a watcher of cluster-state changes, as discussed in section 13.2.4. When the cluster state changes, ZooKeeper notifies each watcher of the change. It's possible that a request will be sent to a failed node before ZooKeeper sends the notification. Solr has basic fault tolerance to guard against this by retrying the request on other hosts for the same shard.

STEP 3: QUERY STAGE

The query controller sends a nondistributed query (`distrib=false`) to every shard to identify matching documents in the shard. The controller determines which nodes to query using cluster information provided by ZooKeeper. The query controller uses the SolrJ API to execute the query in parallel on all shards. This implies that a distributed query is only as fast as the slowest shard to respond, which is why you want an even distribution of documents across all your shards.

The query that is sent to every shard only requests the `id` and `score` fields. It does this to avoid reading stored fields prematurely. Consider a query with a page size of 10 (`rows=10`) sent to a cluster with 10 shards. Each shard will identify up to 10 documents, so the query controller will have to merge and sort up to 100 documents to create the final page of 10 results. Thus, rather than requesting all the stored fields for 100 documents, the query controller waits until the final 10 documents are identified.

Optionally, if the query specifies a custom sort parameter, any fields mentioned in the sort are also requested so the query controller can apply the sort when merging results. When merging, the query controller also calculates the total number of hits for the query by summing the total hit count per shard.

Before moving on to a discussion of the second stage in a distributed query, it's important to realize the implications of using large page sizes with SolrCloud. Consider a distributed query that requests 1,000 documents (`rows=1000`) against a collection split across 10 shards. Behind the scenes, the query controller must request 1000 documents from every shard, which means it needs to read and sort 10,000 documents to create the final result set.

STEP 4: GET FIELDS STAGE

Once the matching documents have been determined from the first query, the controller sends a second query to a subset of nodes to get the rest of the fields needed to fulfill the request. If the query requests 10 rows, then 10 documents are requested in the get-fields stage. The documents needed from each node are known from the first query (step 3). If you only need the IDs of the documents, this second query to get additional fields is not needed. Only shards containing documents to be returned will receive the second query—if all documents identified come from shard1, for example, then Solr only sends the second query to shard1.

What happens if there are no servers hosting a shard at the time of a query? In the query stage, the controller will attempt to query the offline shard. The request will fail; the merge stage can't complete, because Solr chooses to not return an incomplete result set for your query. You can override this behavior by specifying `shards.tolerant=true` as a query parameter to indicate that you'll accept incomplete results.

Ask yourself whether the warming queries we discussed in chapter 4 should be distributed. Of course the simple answer is that they should not be, as the purpose of a warming query is to warm the local searcher only. SolrCloud automatically appends `distrib=false` to warming-query parameters to ensure they are executed against the local index only.

13.4.2 *Distributed search limitations*

Unfortunately, not all Solr query features work in distributed mode. Specifically, there are three main limitations you should be aware of:

1 Inverse document frequency (idf) is based on the frequency of a term in the local index only. It is used when scoring documents, so there can be some bias introduced when ranking documents in a distributed query. Because documents are randomly distributed across shards (by default), the idf for a term in shard1 is typically close to the idf for a term across all shards.[7]

2 Joins do not work in distributed mode unless you use the custom hashing solution we'll describe in section 13.7.1.

3 In order to use Solr's grouping functionality (chapter 11) in SolrCloud, you need to use custom hashing to collocate documents that will be collapsed into the same group.

These limitations are well known, and the Solr community is actively seeking solutions to resolve these issues, but joins and grouping in particular present difficult challenges in a distributed environment due to the current need to compare large amounts of data across servers.

13.5   *Collections API*

In chapter 12, you learned about the Core Admin API, which allows you to manage Solr cores programmatically (section 12.6). SolrCloud provides a Collections API that works on collections distributed across multiple physical nodes. Under the covers, the Collections API may use the Core Admin API to perform tasks on individual cores in a

---

[7] A better solution for distributed idf is being developed; see https://issues.apache.org/jira/browse/SOLR-1632.

cluster. When you reload a collection, for instance, the Collections API uses the Core Admin API to reload the core on each server.

The Collections API supports creating, deleting, and aliasing collections. It also provides support for splitting shards, an advanced topic that will be covered in section 13.7.2.

13.5.1 *Create a collection*

At the beginning of this chapter, we had you create the `logmill` core manually and then boot Solr in cloud mode to distribute the `logmill` index across multiple nodes. We took that approach because we wanted to cover the process of bootstrapping a new SolrCloud cluster from scratch. Moreover, our goal was to get you up and running with SolrCloud quickly, so we didn't want to spend much time describing the Collections API at that point. But now that you have a SolrCloud cluster running on your local workstation, let's see how to use the Collections API to create collections, as the process we used originally would be a bit cumbersome for creating a new collection in an existing cluster.

To work through this section, let's create a new collection that will contain support requests from customers. The basic idea behind this new collection is to allow support engineers to find issues reported by customers in the `support` collection, and correlate those with log messages in the `logmill` collection.

One of the tricky aspects of creating a collection is that you need to upload the configuration files to ZooKeeper prior to creating the collection using the Collections API. The configuration for a new collection must exist in ZooKeeper before the collection is created. Alternatively, if your new collection uses the same configuration as an existing one, you don't need to duplicate the configuration files. This approach would be useful for a multitenant environment where you need to keep each tenant's documents in a separate collection but they share the same configuration files.

To create our `support` collection, we need to upload the configuration files to ZooKeeper. For this scenario we don't have to change any configuration files, but a real application may have different settings in *solrconfig.xml* and *schema.xml*. We'll simply copy the `logmill` configuration files to keep things simple.

```
cd $SOLR_INSTALL/shard1/
cp -r solr/logmill/conf /tmp/support_conf
```

The previous command recursively copied the `logmill` *conf/* directory to a temporary location on our workstation. Now let's use a simple command-line utility provided by Solr to upload the configuration files to ZooKeeper.

The *cloud-scripts/* directory contains shell scripts to interact with the Solr ZkCLI client application. Open a command line, and execute the *zkcli.sh* script for your platform from the *$SOLR_INSTALL/shard1/cloud-scripts/* directory. On Linux, you would enter

```
cd $SOLR_INSTALL/shard1/scripts/cloud-scripts/
./zkcli.sh
```

This will show the usage information for the utility. To upload the configuration files for the support collection, you use the upconfig command, as shown in the next listing.

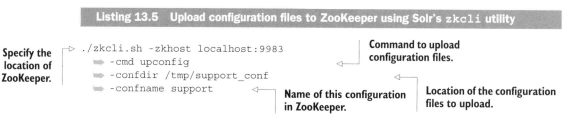

Listing 13.5   Upload configuration files to ZooKeeper using Solr's zkcli utility

Specify the location of ZooKeeper.

```
./zkcli.sh -zkhost localhost:9983
    -cmd upconfig
    -confdir /tmp/support_conf
    -confname support
```

Command to upload configuration files.

Location of the configuration files to upload.

Name of this configuration in ZooKeeper.

upconfig uploads the configuration files from your local workstation to ZooKeeper. After running the command in the previous listing, the configuration files will be stored in ZooKeeper under /configs/support, as shown in figure 13.10.

Now we are ready to use the Collections API to create the collection. Before running the command, let's review the available options when creating a new collection. Table 13.4 provides an overview of the parameters you can set when creating a collection.

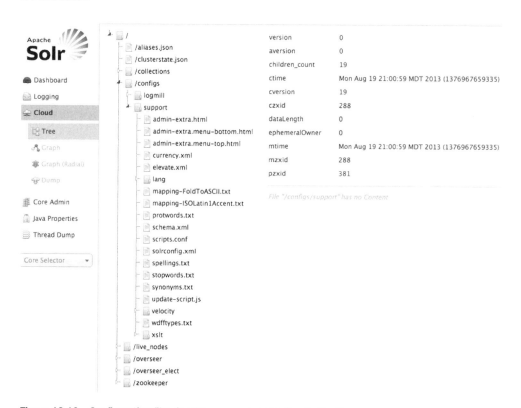

Figure 13.10   Configuration files for the support collection in ZooKeeper

Table 13.4 Summary of parameters for creating a new collection

Parameter	Explanation
`name`	Unique name of the collection to create; for example, `support`.
`numShards`	Number of shards to distribute the collection across.
`replicationFactor`	Number of replicas per shard, which includes the leader. Setting `replicationFactor=2` will result in one leader and one replica for each shard. This value can also be interpreted as the number of copies of a document in a collection.
`maxShardsPerNode`	Enforces a maximum number of shards per physical node. If you set this value to 1 (the default), you must have at least as many nodes as the value of `numShards * replicationFactor`. For instance, if you set `maxShardsPerNode=1`, `numShards=10`, and `replicationFactor=2`, you must have 20 nodes in your cluster to distribute the new collection across. You need at least `(replicationFactor * numShards)/maxShardsPerNode` nodes in your cluster to provision a new collection.
`createNodeSet`	Allows you to specify the set of nodes in your cluster to provision the new collection; this parameter is only useful if your cluster is larger than `(replicationFactor * numShards)/maxShardsPerNode`. You could use this parameter to provision your new collection on specific nodes that have more available resources than other nodes in your cluster.
`collection.configName`	The name of the configuration to use for this collection, such as `support` for our example `support` collection. The configuration must exist in ZooKeeper prior to creating the new collection.

Now that you have a basic understanding of the parameters available when creating a new collection, let's invoke the Collections API to create the `support` collection. Specifically, let's create the `support` collection to only have one shard with a replication factor of two. This makes sense because the number of support requests should be much smaller and occur less frequently than log messages, so we don't need as many shards. The following listing shows the command to create the `support` collection.

Listing 13.6 Use the Collections API to create the `support` collection

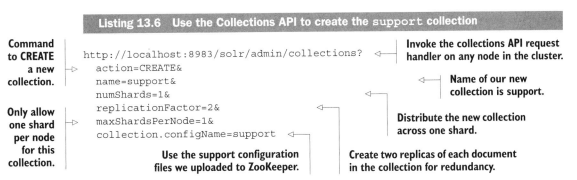

Command to CREATE a new collection.

Only allow one shard per node for this collection.

```
http://localhost:8983/solr/admin/collections?
  action=CREATE&
  name=support&
  numShards=1&
  replicationFactor=2&
  maxShardsPerNode=1&
  collection.configName=support
```

Invoke the collections API request handler on any node in the cluster.

Name of our new collection is support.

Distribute the new collection across one shard.

Use the support configuration files we uploaded to ZooKeeper.

Create two replicas of each document in the collection for redundancy.

The key takeaway is that the Collections API allows you to define a new collection in an existing cluster and gives you control over how to distribute it across the nodes in the cluster. Contrast this with how we initially created the `logmill` collection by bringing new nodes online one by one and allowing Solr to assign shards and roles dynamically as new nodes joined the cluster. In general, when you already have a cluster, you need more control over how to allocate a new collection on the existing nodes. The Collections API gives you this control.

It's also worth pointing out that you do not need to provision a collection on all nodes in your cluster. Put simply, you shard and replicate your collection based on its specific requirements and do not need to split it across more nodes than necessary.

The Collections API also supports deleting an existing collection using the `action=DELETE` parameter. As this is self-explanatory, we'll leave it as an exercise for you to delete the `support` collection we created previously. It should be noted that the `DELETE` action does not actually delete the index data files on disk, so you can recover them manually if needed.

Before we move on to other uses of the Collections API, keep in mind that you can reuse an existing configuration set in ZooKeeper for a new collection. If you wanted to partition log messages into different collections based on date, the configuration would be the same, and you'd just add new collections for new date partitions. If you wanted to keep log messages in separate collections by month, then the `January`, `February`, etc. collections could all share the same configuration.

13.5.2 *Collection aliasing*

Solr supports the concept of a collection alias that is composed of one or more collections under the covers. Collection aliases are useful for a couple of reasons. You can change the underlying index without affecting client applications, which is useful if you need to reindex a collection. You can also use a collection alias to query across multiple collections. Let's start by seeing how to use collection aliases to support flexible reindexing operations.

COLLECTION ALIAS TO SUPPORT FLEXIBLE REINDEXING

In figure 13.11 we have a collection with many client applications that send update requests (indexing) and a number of other client applications that send query requests (search). As you can see in the diagram, we use separate aliases for writing to and reading from the `logmill` collection.

In a moment, we'll see how this allows us to reindex our collection without impacting our client applications. The next listing shows the command to create the `logmill-write` alias.

Listing 13.7   The command to create the `logmill-write` alias

```
http://localhost:8983/solr/admin/collections?
    action=CREATEALIAS&
    name=logmill-write&
    collections=logmill
```

Link this alias to the logmill collection.

Name the new alias.

Execute the CREATEALIAS command.

Invoke the Collections API request handler on any node.

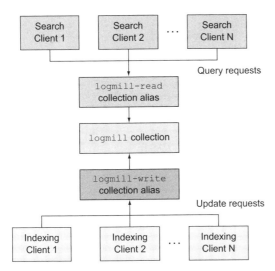

Figure 13.11 Using separate aliases for sending update and query requests to the `logmill` collection

We'll leave creating the `logmill-read` alias as an exercise for you. After creating it, you'll need to update your indexing client applications to use the `logmill-write` context, such as http://localhost:8983/solr/logmill-write/update. This provides insulation for your indexing client applications in case the underlying collection they are writing to needs to change. It's much easier to update a single alias in one place using the Collections API than it is to track down all the possible applications that send update requests to `logmill`, especially because making a configuration change might require redeploying production applications. It's important to realize that there is nothing related to *writing* in the alias. The alias exists to allow you to configure your indexing applications to send writes to this alias.

The indexing client applications in figure 13.11 are not aware of the actual `logmill` collection, as they only work with the `logmill-write` alias. Conversely, search clients only see the `logmill-read` alias. This means that you can reindex to a new collection, say `logmill2`, by changing the `logmill-write` alias. Search clients continue to query `logmill` through the `logmill-read` alias until `logmill2` is ready, as depicted in figure 13.12.

To implement the scenario depicted in figure 13.12, we need to update the `logmill-write` alias to point at the `logmill2` collection. To update an existing alias, you use the CREATEALIAS command and change the value of the `collections` parameter, as shown in the next listing.

Listing 13.8 Update an existing collection by changing the `collections` parameter

```
/admin/collections?
  action=CREATEALIAS&
  name=logmill-write&
  collections=logmill2
```

Update the existing alias to point at a different collection.

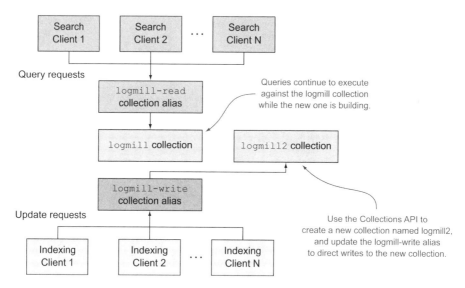

Figure 13.12   Update the `logmill-write` alias to direct writes to the `logmill2` collection.

USE A COLLECTION ALIAS TO QUERY ACROSS MULTIPLE COLLECTIONS

Another common use case for collection aliases is to query across multiple collections, such as to support a date/time-based partitioning scheme for your collection. Imagine that we wanted to organize log documents in separate collections partitioned by month; we would have the `August2013` collection, `September2013` collection, and so on.

We can then use two separate aliases: `logmill-recent` and `logmill-all`. The `logmill-recent` alias contains the current and past month; the `logmill-all` alias covers collections for all months. When we roll over to a new month, we can update the aliases using the Collections API. Specifically, if we need to add a new collection for `October2013` to the `logmill-all` alias, we would use the command shown in the next listing.

Listing 13.9   Add the `October2013` collection to the `logmill-all` alias

```
/admin/collections?
  action=CREATEALIAS&
  name=logmill-all&
  collections=August2013,September2013,October2013
```
**Include all collections
to include in the alias.**

The `collections` parameter should be a comma-delimited list of all collections to include in the alias. To query across all collections, we'd simply send query requests to the `logmill-all` alias, such as http://localhost:8983/solr/logmill-all/select?q=*:*.

The two scenarios we described in this section are the most common use cases of collection aliasing. The key takeaway is that an alias decouples the view of a client application from the underlying implementation details in your SolrCloud cluster. Now let's move on to learning about basic system-administration tasks for SolrCloud.

13.6   *Basic system-administration tasks*

In this section, we cover a few basic system-administration tasks that apply to Solr-Cloud. Let's begin by learning how to propagate configuration changes to all nodes in your cluster.

13.6.1   *Configuration updates*

One of the most common system-administration tasks you'll need to do is to update the Solr configuration, such as *solrconfig.xml*. Updating the configuration in SolrCloud is a two-stage process: upload your changes to ZooKeeper using Solr's `zkcli` command-line utility and reload the collection using the Collections API. Let's work through a simple example to update cache settings for the `logmill` application. To begin, change the filter cache settings in *$SOLR_INSTALL/shard1/solr/logmill/conf/solrconfig.xml* to

```
<filterCache class="solr.FastLRUCache"
    size="60"
    initialSize="20"
    autowarmCount="20" />
```

STAGE 1: UPLOAD CHANGES TO ZOOKEEPER
Upload your changes to ZooKeeper using the `zkcli` utility provided by Solr:

```
cd $SOLR_INSTALL/shard1/cloud-scripts
./zkcli.sh -zkhost localhost:9983
    -cmd upconfig
    -confname logmill
    -confdir ../solr/logmill/conf
```

Notice that you need to specify the ZooKeeper connection string using the `-zkhost` parameter. In our local SolrCloud setup, this will typically be `localhost:9983`, but in a production system, this will be a comma-delimited list of ZooKeeper host and port pairs. The `upconfig` command will upload all configuration files in the directory identified using the `-confdir` parameter (recursively).

STAGE 2: RELOAD THE COLLECTION
Reload the collection using the Collections API: http://localhost:8983/solr/admin/collections?action=RELOAD&name=logmill.

The reload operation will reinitialize the core on each node in the collection and open a new searcher. Consequently, reload can be expensive and should be done during a maintenance window.

13.6.2   *Rolling restart*

Imagine you need to change a JVM system setting in order to fine-tune your garbage collection behavior. This will require a JVM restart on all nodes. The best way to handle this is to do a *rolling restart* so that you don't introduce any unnecessary outages. Specifically, you need to restart nodes one by one to make sure you don't take any shards offline during the restart. The best approach is to restart a node, then wait until that node is active in the cluster again before proceeding to restart the next node. This implies that the restart will take some time to complete, but it will allow you to upgrade your nodes one by one without any downtime. You can use this same process to upgrade Solr. We'll leave the OS-specific details of restarting a node to you, but you can use the mechanism described in section 13.6.4 to test whether a node is healthy and active.

13.6.3 Restarting a failed node

If one of your nodes crashes, then the cluster state will be updated to mark that node as being gone so that the other nodes stop sending requests to it. Before restarting the node, be sure to capture the logs to help you diagnose the cause of the crash. After you resolve the issue, you can restart the node, and it will try to synchronize its index with the current shard leader. The other nodes will be notified when the recovered node is active, and they will begin sending requests to it.

13.6.4 Is node X active?

One of the issues with SolrCloud is determining if a server is healthy and responding to queries using HTTP. At first glance, you might think you can just ping the server. Unfortunately, a ping may return a false positive because it doesn't take into account ZooKeeper's state of the node. A Solr instance may respond to a query with a 200 code (OK) even if ZooKeeper thinks the node is gone.

You can determine if a node is healthy by executing a query against the node using the `distrib=false` parameter to only search against the local index. The current state of the node can be retrieved from ZooKeeper. Ideally, what we want is the ability to send a simple HTTP request to a Solr instance to determine if it's responding to queries and if its state is active in ZooKeeper. Solr already provides a ping request handler to check whether the index is responding to query requests, so we'll use that as our starting point for adding the additional cluster state check.

Specifically, the example code provided with the book includes the `sia.ch13` `.ClusterStateAwarePingRequestHandler` utility that extends Solr's `PingRequest-` `Handler` to verify that the cluster state of the replica is active. We leave it as an exercise for you to review the source code for this utility. You can enable this extension by changing the definition of the `/admin/ping` request handler in *solrconfig.xml* to something like listing 13.10.

Listing 13.10   Extension to the `PingRequestHandler` to verify a replica is active

```
<requestHandler name="/admin/ping"
    class="sia.ch13.ClusterStateAwarePingRequestHandler">      ⟵  Use the full
  <lst name="invariants">                                           class name of
    <str name="q">id:0</str>                                        the extension
    <bool name="distrib">false</bool>   ⟵                           provided in the
  </lst>                                                            source code
  ...                                                              for the book.
</requestHandler>
```

Local only—do not distribute the ping query. | A fast query for your index.

13.6.5 *Adding a replica*

You can add more replicas at any time in a live cluster. As the replicas come online, they will receive their shard assignment from ZooKeeper based on the current cluster state. In most cases, you'll want to add a new replica for every shard in your cluster. When using the default document-routing logic, it doesn't help all that much to have one shard with two replicas and all other shards with one, as the documents should be evenly distributed to all shards. But it may make sense to have unbalanced replicas when doing custom sharding, because one shard may have many more documents than other shards.

To add a replica for a shard, simply start a new Solr instance, and pass the shard ID as a startup parameter. For example, `-Dshard=shard1` will create a new replica for shard1.

13.6.6 *Offsite backup*

Replication guards against the occasional failure of a few nodes, but will not help if your entire data center goes offline due to natural disaster or major malfunction at the facility hosting your cluster. You can definitely run multiple Solr clusters in different data centers, but that can be expensive, and there is little support built into Solr for distributing documents across data centers. Another approach is to perform frequent backups of your index, and move them offsite so that you can rebuild your cluster from backups in another data center. If you decide to do offsite backups, we have a few suggestions on how to implement them.

We've provided a simple utility to drive the backup process in SolrCloud in the sample code for this book; see the `sia.ch13.BackupDriver` class. Here are some key points about how the `BackupDriver` utility works.

- You can't back up the index directory directly, as it could be in a state that will make the backup unusable. The safest approach is to use the built-in backup support provided by Solr's replication handler. The following GET request will back up the index for shard1 of our `logmill` collection: http://localhost:8983/solr/logmill/replication?command=backup.
- You need to create the backup for every shard in the collection, so this command should be sent to every shard leader after issuing a hard commit.
- The actual backup process runs in the background, so the backup request will return immediately. Consequently, you need a mechanism to determine when the actual backup is complete, as it can take several minutes to back up a large index. Our utility polls the replication handler's details action until we receive a completed-on date for the backup.
- Once all the backups are complete, you can move them offsite, such as to Amazon S3. Moving the backup files offsite is not provided by `BackupDriver`.

To run the utility against the `logmill` example on your local workstation, execute the following command:

```
java -jar $SOLR_IN_ACTION/solr-in-action.jar backup
```

At this point, we hope you have a sense for the types of administration tasks you need to plan for when running SolrCloud. Now let's move on to a discussion of some advanced topics related to SolrCloud.

13.7   Advanced topics

In this section, we introduce a few advanced topics related to SolrCloud, namely custom hashing and shard splitting. We consider these advanced topics because they are not necessary for many SolrCloud installations, not because they are difficult to understand or use. Our main goal in this section is to make you aware of these features if you need to go beyond the normal use of SolrCloud. You can use custom hashing to give you control over the shard to which a document gets assigned. Shard splitting may be useful if your collection outgrows your hardware in the future.

13.7.1   Custom hashing

As you learned in section 13.3.1, the default document-routing strategy is to distribute documents evenly across all shards using a hash of the unique ID field. The default strategy works well for situations in which the bulk of your queries need to search the entire corpus of documents. Consider the situation where the bulk of your queries can be scoped to a specific subset of documents based on some common property between the documents. For instance, *multitenant search* applications may host documents for different customers in the same index. Most, if not all, queries in a multitenant index must be targeted to a specific tenant ID. In this scenario, distributing the documents for a specific tenant ID across all shards is not the most efficient solution. *Custom hashing* allows you to route documents to specific shards based on some common field value, such as tenant ID. Another example of this would be routing documents based on category.

Keeping with our `logmill` example, imagine that after analyzing usage patterns, we determined that end users mostly queried using a specific source-application ID, such as `solr`. In this case, it may make sense to route all documents with the same application ID to the same shard. Of course, you could simply distribute documents for the same application ID to all shards and use the application ID in a filter query. Routing documents with the same application ID has two main advantages, though: the bulk of your queries are executed against a much smaller index (a single shard), and you can use query features that do not work easily in distributed mode, such as joins and grouping.

COMPOSITE DOCUMENT ID

Solr has built-in support for routing documents based on one or more common fields, so all you need do is create document ID values using a specific syntax. Specifically, you'll create composite document-ID values with a prefix containing the common field value and an exclamation point (`!`). To send all of the log messages generated by Solr to the same shard, you would create document-ID values such as `solr!doc123`. The general format is `shardKey!docID`, where the value before the exclamation point is known as the *shard key*.

Under the covers, the default `compositeId` router in Solr uses 16 bits from the hash value of the shard key and 16 bits from the hash value of the document ID to create a composite 32-bit hash value, which is then mapped into the correct shard based on the standard shard range we discussed in 13.3.

This should not be confused with *implicit routing* (also called *direct routing*) in which the client application specifies the exact shard to index to. With custom hashing, you are guaranteed that all documents with the same shard key will end up in the same shard, but you can't control which shard.

TARGET A SPECIFIC SHARD AT QUERY TIME

Once you route documents to specific shards based on a common field value, you need to query the correct shard. In this case, your client application needs to pass the shard key in the `_route_` parameter. If we want to query the shard holding log messages for `solr`, we need to include `_route_=solr!` as a query parameter. You can query additional shards by separating shard keys with a comma; for example, `_route_=solr!,squid!` will query the shard for the `solr` and `squid` applications (Squid is a caching HTTP-proxy server). Of course, you can still query across all shards by not using the `_route_` parameter when querying.

LIMITATIONS OF CUSTOM HASHING

The biggest concern when using custom hashing is that it may create unbalanced shards in your cluster. If one of the applications that sends messages to `logmill` creates ten times more log messages than other applications, then the shard hosting those messages will be much larger than other shards. For this reason, you will need to understand your data to determine if you need to further subdivide shard keys or avoid their use altogether.

13.7.2 Shard splitting

If you are constantly adding new documents to SolrCloud and not removing any previously indexed documents, your shards will eventually outgrow the hardware they are deployed on. Of course, the rate of growth determines if this is a short- or long-term problem for you. Keeping with our `logmill` application, let's imagine that our organization has deployed a number of new high-volume applications in the past several months, and our two-node `logmill` cluster is increasingly under too much strain to handle the new load. Specifically, indexing throughput is beginning to slow gradually because our indexes are much larger and are changing more frequently. In addition, the average execution time of our queries is increasing because of the increase in index size.

At this point, we've decided that we want to add two more nodes to the cluster. Because one of our goals is to handle more documents and maintain fast indexing throughput, we cannot just add replicas to the existing shards, as adding more replicas will only help with increasing query volume. What we really need is to split our existing two shards into four shards to distribute the indexing work across four nodes instead of two.

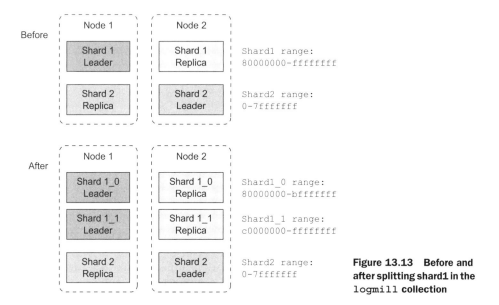

Figure 13.13   Before and after splitting shard1 in the `logmill` **collection**

Solr provides a solution for this scenario; it allows you to split an existing shard into two *subshards*. The shard splitting process involves the following steps applied to each shard individually:

1 Use the `SPLITSHARD` action of the collections API to split an existing shard into two subshards.
2 Issue a hard commit after the split process completes to make the new sub-shards active.
3 Unload the original shard from the cluster.
4 Optionally, migrate one of the splits to a new server.

Let's apply these steps to split shard1 of our `logmill` collection.

```
curl -i -v "http://localhost:8983/solr/admin/
➥collections?action=SPLITSHARD&collection=logmill&shard=shard1"
```

```
curl -i -v "http://localhost:8983/solr/logmill/update" -H 'Content-
➥type:application/xml' --data-binary "<commit waitSearcher=\"true\"/>"
```

Figure 13.13 shows the before and after states of the `logmill` collection when splitting shard1.[8] Notice that the splits were replicated just as the original shard was replicated. This is an important feature, because you wouldn't want to lose your replication strategy when splitting shards.

Alternatively, if we decided that we really needed five shards to address our current and projected growth, Solr does not yet support rebalancing a cluster to add

---

[8] Hopefully you don't suffer from triskaidekaphobia! See http://en.wikipedia.org/wiki/Triskaidekaphobia.

an arbitrary number of new nodes.[9] Keep in mind that Solr embraces an iterative development methodology and likes to release features as they stabilize, even if there is more work to be done, as is the case with shard splitting.

13.8 Summary

We hope this chapter has given you a solid understanding of how to use SolrCloud to achieve your scalability and high-availability needs. To recap, we started out by launching Solr in cloud mode to support a fictitious log aggregation index named `logmill`. Cloud mode is enabled by connecting Solr to a ZooKeeper instance. In our example, we used an embedded instance via the `-DzkRun` parameter. For production, you should set up a ZooKeeper ensemble on separate hardware. The local SolrCloud cluster provided hands-on experience with splitting an index into two shards, routing documents into those distributed shards at index time, and executing distributed queries.

After launching the cluster, we covered the five key drivers behind the SolrCloud architecture: scalability, high availability, consistency, simplicity, and elasticity. SolrCloud provides a solid foundation for achieving these goals, though it's still continuing to improve on simplicity and elasticity.

Next, we covered core concepts such as collections, ZooKeeper, shard count, clusterstate management, and shard-leader election. Using your new knowledge of these core concepts, we covered distributed indexing. You saw how update requests are sent to shard leaders, which then distribute the update requests to all replicas to ensure consistency across the cluster. Solr uses a document router to distribute documents to shards, in which the default `compositeId` router uses the MurmurHash algorithm to evenly distribute documents across all shards. You also saw how distributed queries require a two-stage process driven by a query controller.

Next we introduced the Collections API, which allows you to create, delete, and alias collections in an existing SolrCloud cluster. You learned that new collections can reuse an existing configuration in ZooKeeper; alternately, you must upload a new configuration directory before creating a new collection. You also learned how collection aliases support flexible reindexing schemes and querying across multiple collections as if they were one unified collection.

After covering the nuts and bolts of SolrCloud, we outlined some of the systemadministration processes you need to plan for as you roll out SolrCloud to production. Lastly, you learned about two advanced topics related to SolrCloud: custom hashing and shard splitting. Custom hashing is useful for distributing documents to shards using a shard key to group documents together. Shard splitting is useful for doubling the capacity of your cluster by splitting an existing shard into two subshards. Shard splitting is a good step toward true elasticity, but there is still work to be done to allow you to add an arbitrary number of nodes to a SolrCloud cluster.

In the next chapter, you'll learn about multilingual search with Solr.

---

[9] "Implement true re-sharding for SolrCloud," Apache Software Federation, July 10, 2013, https://issues.apache.org/jira/browse/SOLR-5025.

Multilingual search

14

This chapter covers

- Using Solr's stemming and language identification libraries
- Searching multiple languages using separate fields
- Searching multiple languages in the same field through separate Solr cores
- Searching multiple languages in the same field and Solr core

Solr comes out of the box with a robust suite of linguistic libraries that enable searching across a wide spectrum of languages from around the world. This chapter will provide an overview of these libraries and will demonstrate how to most effectively make use of them in your search applications. An understanding of Solr's *schema.xml* (covered in chapter 5) and the process of text analysis (covered in chapter 6) is assumed in this chapter, so you may need to refer back to those chapters as necessary.

Many languages present challenges to text searching—some contain various forms of the same word that should all return in a search, some (such as French and Spanish) contain special accents, some (German and Dutch, for example) contain compound words made up of subwords, and some (such as Chinese, Japanese, and Korean) may have no whitespace between words to distinguish them from one another. Linguistic analysis can help overcome these complexities within your text by performing analysis using language-specific rules associated with the language(s) represented within your documents. Although Solr provides many preconfigured field types in its example *schema.xml*, these examples are designed to be used with only one language at a time. This chapter will cover the available language libraries in Solr and will also show how you can use them to create a powerful multilingual search experience that can even handle mixed-language content within a single document or field.

14.1 *Why linguistic analysis matters*

Imagine the sentence, "John approached the bank." This probably makes you think of a person named John walking up to a particular kind of place: a financial institution. If the text instead read "After sailing for hours, John approached the bank," you would likely be thinking about a person named John on a boat floating toward the shore. Both sentences state that "John approached the bank," but the context plays a critical role in ensuring the text is properly understood.

Due to advances in the field of Natural Language Processing (NLP), many important contextual clues can be identified in standard text. These can include identification of the language of unknown text, determination of the parts of speech, discovery or approximation of the root form of a word, understanding of synonyms and unimportant words, and discovery of relationships between words through their usage. You will notice that the best web search engines today go to great lengths to infer the meaning of your query. If you type into Google `define Solr`, it might respond that *Solr is an open source enterprise search platform*. If you ask it to `navigate to the Statue of Liberty`, it might draw a map and offer directions from your location to Ellis Island in New York City. Google is able to process the words from your query and infer your meaning, delivering results based upon the most probable interpretation.

Can Solr pull off this same level of query sophistication? Well…no, at least not out of the box. It's your job to add on those intelligent capabilities based upon your particular domain expertise. You can certainly build a layer of intelligence on top of Solr—using mostly open source technologies—that can pull this off. Apache UIMA (Unified Information Management Architecture) is an excellent open source framework that enables complex content analysis pipelines to be built from smaller, reusable components. Apache UIMA includes integration with many tools to extract knowledge from within your content, and Solr provides connectors for Apache UIMA, so these may be worth looking into if you need to build sophisticated content analysis capabilities into your search application.

Other clustering and data classification techniques can also be used to enrich your data, which can lead to a far superior search experience than keyword searching alone. Although implementing most of these capabilities is beyond the scope of this book, Grant Ingersoll, Thomas Morton, and Andrew Farris provide a great overview of how to implement these kind of natural language processing techniques in *Taming Text: How to Find, Organize, and Manipulate It* (Manning, 2013), including a chapter on building a question-and-answer system similar to some of the previous examples.

What Solr *does* provide out of the box, however, are the building blocks for these kinds of systems. This includes dozens of language-specific stemmers, a synonym filter, a stop words filter and language-specific stop word lists, character/accent normalization, query correction (spell-check) capabilities, and a language identifier.

Most of these building blocks have been introduced in earlier chapters, but it's the proper use of these components together that unlocks intelligence within your Solr-based search products. It would be a pity if your customers searched for documents about the keyword `engineer`, and all the documents containing the plural form `engineers` were missing altogether. Without the use of an English stemmer or similar token filter to remove the plural "s" from the end of `engineers`, this would be the outcome.

In tests the authors have run, without stemming or other linguistic analysis turned on, search results have demonstrated up to 49% lower Recall across common English words (this number varies across languages). As you may remember from section 3.3, Recall is a measure of how much of the expected content is found. As a result, if you're searching language-specific text content and are not using some form of linguistic analysis, your number of search results will most likely be artificially low. This chapter will show you how to make the most of Solr's built-in language handling capabilities to improve the Recall of language-specific content. To start, we'll take a look at two different approaches to solving the problem of word variations.

14.2   Stemming vs. lemmatization

Stemming, which you were introduced to in chapter 6, is the process of algorithmically trying to determine the base forms of words. An English-language stemmer, for example, is likely to remove word endings such as *s*, *es*, *ed*, and *ing*. As such, an English stemmer will correctly reduce the word `engineers` to `engineer` (by removing the *s*), but it may also reduce other words like `nurses`, `nursing`, or `nurse` to fake words like `nurs`. In practice, as long as all variants of a word reduce to the same thing (even if it's a fake word), this is fine because the same stemming behavior will be applied both at index time and query time. This means that each search for any variation will still match every other variation.

Stemming becomes problematic in a couple of cases, however. First, if not all variations of a word map to the same stem, your searches will have a mismatch. Using the common English Porter Stemmer, the word `mice` stems to `mice`, and the word `mouse` stems to `mous`. Similarly, the word `dry` stems to `dry`, but the word `dries` stems to `dri`. In these scenarios, the word `mouse` will never successfully match on the word `mice`, and the word `dry` will never successfully match the word `dries`, all because they algorithmically map to different stems.

A second problem caused by stemmers is that they often cause overmatching. Consider the words `generally`, `generation`, `generations`, `generative`, `generous`, `generator`, `general`, and `generals`. The English Porter Stemmer comes up with a stem of `gener` for each of the preceding words, even though many of those words do not represent the same meaning. Likewise, it comes up with a stem of `anim` for both `animal` and `animated`, and it comes up with a stem of `iron` for both the metal `iron` and for the word `ironic`. The consequence of this overly aggressive stemming is that many words can falsely match other (incorrect) words, resulting in a loss of Precision in searches. Instead of not seeing enough results (with stemming turned off), users can start seeing extra, bad results with stemming turned on. One way to overcome this problem is by using a less aggressive stemming algorithm. The other way is to use a more intelligent version of base-word identification: lemmatization.

Lemmatization is the process of determining the root form of a word. In contrast with stemming, which tries to algorithmically find a common base for a word, lemmatization typically makes use of dictionaries to find the root form of a word. Lemmatization would map the word `went` to `go` and would map the words `am`, `is`, `are`, `was`, `were`, `being`, and `been` all to the root form `be`. From our previous examples, lemmatization would also map `engineers` to `engineer`, `mice` to `mouse`, and `nurses` to `nurse`. Figure 14.1 demonstrates the difference between stemming and lemmatization on some example terms.

You can see that the particular stemming algorithm used in figure 14.1 did not map `goose` and `geese` to the same term, and it mapped several unrelated terms like `several` and `severity` to the same stemmed term. The lemmatizer, however, was able to look up the original terms and map them to their dictionary forms. As you can probably guess, lemmatization can be considerably more accurate than stemming, but coming up with good dictionaries is much more difficult to pull off.

Other techniques exist for finding suitable root forms of words. *Morphological analysis* tools, using statistical NLP techniques to learn about a language structure from a large corpus of text from that language, can perform quite well. Unfortunately, most lemmatization and morphological libraries with trained language models are typically only available today from commercial vendors. The Precision vs. Recall trade-off (refer to

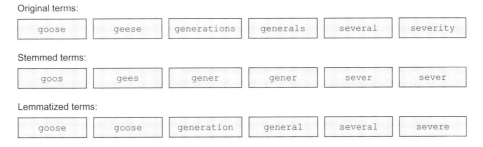

Figure 14.1 Stemming versus lemmatization output for some example terms. As you can see, the lemmatized output generally looks more accurate, because it's using true dictionary forms of words instead of programmatically removing/replacing letters.

the discussion in section 3.3) should be a key consideration in the decision to implement stemming or lemmatization in your search application. The reality is that performing no stemming will get you high Precision searches, as all the results returned contain exact matches for the keywords searched; (many) stemming algorithms yield a fairly high Recall score, but lower Precision due to incorrectly matching bad stems. If you're sensitive to both Precision and Recall, you may want to pursue commercial vendors for lemmatization or morphological libraries, as several companies offer off-the-shelf integration with Solr. It's always worth at least trying the built-in stemmers that come with Solr, as they are often good enough for many use cases out of the box. The next section will demonstrate how to use some of the most common English stemmers in Solr.

14.3 *Stemming in action*

In section 6.3.4, you were introduced to the idea of stemming, with a demonstration of two English language stemmers, invoked by `PorterStemFilterFactory` and `KStem-FilterFactory`. In this section, we'll walk through a few more English-language stemming examples before diving into the other supported languages in Solr.

To set up this example, let's add three new field types to our *schema.xml*, as laid out in the following listing.

> **Listing 14.1   Example English language `fieldType` configurations**

```
<fieldType name="text_en_porter" class="solr.TextField"
    positionIncrementGap="100">
  <analyzer>
    <tokenizer class="solr.StandardTokenizerFactory"/>
    <filter class="solr.StopFilterFactory"
        ignoreCase="true"
        words="lang/stopwords_en.txt"/>
    <filter class="solr.LowerCaseFilterFactory"/>
    <filter class="solr.EnglishPossessiveFilterFactory"/>
    <filter class="solr.KeywordMarkerFilterFactory"
        protected="protwords.txt"/>
    <filter class="solr.PorterStemFilterFactory"/>
  </analyzer>
</fieldType>

<fieldType name="text_en_minimalstem" class="solr.TextField"
    positionIncrementGap="100">
  <analyzer>
    <tokenizer class="solr.StandardTokenizerFactory"/>
    <filter class="solr.StopFilterFactory"
        ignoreCase="true"
        words="lang/stopwords_en.txt"/>
    <filter class="solr.LowerCaseFilterFactory"/>
    <filter class="solr.EnglishPossessiveFilterFactory"/>
    <filter class="solr.KeywordMarkerFilterFactory"
        protected="protwords.txt"/>
    <filter class="solr.EnglishMinimalStemFilterFactory"/>
```

```
    </analyzer>
</fieldType>

<fieldType name="text_en_kstem" class="solr.TextField"
    positionIncrementGap="100">
  <analyzer>
    <tokenizer class="solr.StandardTokenizerFactory"/>
    <filter class="solr.StopFilterFactory"
        ignoreCase="true"
        words="lang/stopwords_en.txt"/>
    <filter class="solr.LowerCaseFilterFactory"/>
    <filter class="solr.EnglishPossessiveFilterFactory"/>
    <filter class="solr.KeywordMarkerFilterFactory"
        protected="protwords.txt"/>
    <filter class="solr.KStemFilterFactory"/>
  </analyzer>
</fieldType>
```

After adding these three field types to your *schema.xml*, it's easy to test them out using the Analysis page in Solr's Admin UI. To make this testing easier, we've included an example *schema.xml* in `/example-docs/ch14/english-examples/schema.xml` in the accompanying source.

> ### Firing up this chapter's preconfigured examples
>
> In this chapter, the configuration files for each example have been preconfigured in separate Solr cores to allow you to start Solr one time and easily navigate through all of the chapter's examples. To get Solr immediately up and running with all of the chapter's examples available, execute the following:
>
> ```
> cd $SOLR_INSTALL/example/
> cp -r $SOLR_IN_ACTION/example-docs/ch14/cores/ solr/
> cp $SOLR_IN_ACTION/solr-in-action.jar solr/lib/
> java -jar start.jar
> ```

With Solr running and using the provided configuration, you should now be able to hit the Analysis page at http://localhost:8983/solr/#/english-examples/analysis. On that page, you will be able to compare the results of the analysis process for any field types: in this case, `text_en_porter`, `text_en_minimalstem`, or `text_en_kstem`. Figure 14.2 demonstrates using the Analysis page to test the output for these field types (with Verbose Output turned off).

As you can see from figure 14.2, the `text_en_porter` field results in the word engineering being stemmed down to engin. Is this good or bad? If you want engineer to match documents containing the words engine, engines, engineer, and engineers, then it would be a good thing, as you will find, that each of these words stems down to the same form (engin). If this is too aggressive for you, you may consider using one of the less aggressive stemmers (using `EnglishMinimalStemFilterFactory` or `KStem-FilterFactory`). If you try out these other stemmers, you will see that they are not as aggressive, as demonstrated in figure 14.3.

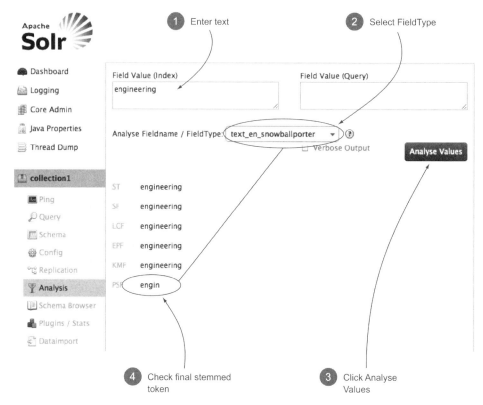

Figure 14.2   The PorterStemFilterFactory stemming *engineering* down to *engin*

Figure 14.2 demonstrates the `PorterStemFilterFactory` stemming `engineering` down to `engin`, and figure 14.3 demonstrates that both `EnglishMinimalStemFilterFactory` and `KStemFilterFactory` result in less aggressive stemming that leaves the

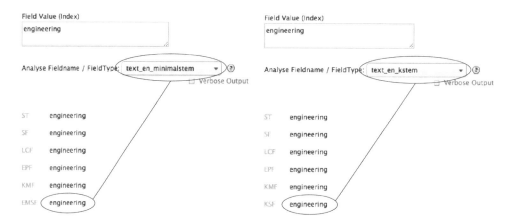

Figure 14.3   Checking the English Minimal Stem and KStem output using the Analysis page in the Solr UI

word `engineering` as is. Although they resulted in the same output for this particular example, in practice the KStem algorithm tends to be somewhere in between the Porter and the English Minimal Stem algorithms in terms of aggressiveness. In order to give you a better sense for the distinctions between each of these stemmers, table 14.1 provides a comparison of a number of common English words and their resulting stems.

Table 14.1 Comparison of English stemmer output for common words

Original	PorterStemFilter	KStemFilter	EnglishMinimalStemFilter
country	countri	country	country
countries	countri	country	country
dogs	dog	dogs	dog
runs	run	runs	run
running	run	running	running
association	associ	association	association
associates	associ	associate	associate
listing	list	list	listing
investing	invest	invest	investing
investments	invest	investment	investment
investors	investor	invest	investor
organizations	organ	organization	organization
organize	organ	organize	organize
organic	organ	organic	organic
generous	gener	generous	generous
generals	gener	general	general
generalizations	gener	generalization	generalization

Each of the stemmers demonstrated in table 14.1 has its strengths and weaknesses. Although the Porter Stem algorithm is virtually always the most aggressive, and the English Minimal Stem algorithm is typically the least aggressive, there are a few clear counterexamples. In the case of the input `investors`, for example, the KStem algorithm reduces down to `invest`, and the Porter algorithm stays with the less aggressive `investor`. In the case of the input `dogs`, the KStem algorithm retains `dogs` as the stem (because a dictionary form apparently exists containing the "s"), where the English Minimal Stem algorithm reduces down to `dog`. These counterexamples may be few and far between, but they do exist.

Wait, which stemmer do I use?

In this section, we demonstrated the output from several different English stemmers: `PorterStemFilter`, `KStemFilter`, and `EnglishMinimalStemFilter`. To add confusion to an already crowded space, Solr also contains a separate stemmer known as `SnowballPorterFilter` containing many different stemming implementations, configurable through the `language` parameter (see section 14.5). For the `Snowball-PorterFilter`, if you specify the `language` as `Lovins`, you'll get the first English stemmer ever published.[1] If you specify the `language` as `Porter`, you'll get the originally published Porter stemmer algorithm.[2] If you specify the `language` as `English`, you'll get a more recently modified version of the Porter algorithm, often called Porter2.[3] The implementation of the Porter stemmer algorithm provided in the `PorterStemFilter` is a slightly modified version of the original Porter stemming algorithm, but it's generally still considered inferior to the Porter2 algorithm. What's the practical takeaway? First, if you're going to use the `SnowballPorterFilter`, you should generally opt for the most recent Porter2 algorithm (`language="English"`), as is recommended by Martin Porter himself (http://tartarus.org/~martin/Porter-Stemmer/). In speed tests, however, `PorterStemFilter` has been shown to be twice as fast as the `SnowballPorterFilter` (due to Lucene implementation details), and it's often recommended as the default for handling English because the stemming quality differences are probably not material to most search applications. If you need an aggressive stemmer, you should choose one of these two, with the `PorterStemFilter` representing a sizable speed advantage at the expense of some small stemming improvements.

At the end of the day, no stemming algorithm is perfect, so you have to pick the one that arrives closest to your desired output for the most examples. As a rule of thumb, if you care more about Recall than Precision, you may want to go with a more aggressive stemmer, whereas a higher Precision focus may call for a less aggressive stemmer. When stemming leads you astray, Solr provides helpful tools to let you straighten things out, as you'll see in the following section.

14.4   Handling edge cases

No stemming algorithm will be perfect for every example you will encounter in your application. Sometimes a stemmer may produce incorrect stems, or you may have domain-specific words that you do not want to be modified by a stemmer. Thankfully, Solr provides several capabilities that can help you overcome the limitations inherent in any of the stemming implementations.

---

[1] The Lovins stemming algorithm, including links to resources, http://snowball.tartarus.org/algorithms/lovins/stemmer.html.

[2] The Porter stemming algorithm, including links to resources, http://snowball.tartarus.org/algorithms/porter/stemmer.html.

[3] The English (Porter2) stemming algorithm, including links to resources, http://snowball.tartarus.org/algorithms/english/stemmer.html.

14.4.1 *KeywordMarkerFilterFactory*

At times, you may have particular words that you want to prevent from being stemmed. These will often be names (such as `Manning Publications`, where the word `Manning` may stem down to merely `man`), but they could be any terms for which you have determined that your chosen stemmer is reducing down to an undesired output. The `KeywordMarkerFilterFactory` allows you to specify a list of protected terms that all stemmers in Solr will ignore. If you insert `KeywordMarkerFilterFactory` above your stemmer in the analysis chain and specify a file containing your protected words, your problematic stemming output will be a thing of the past. We included `Keyword-MarkerFilterFactory` in our previous English stemmer examples, such as the recommended KStem definition:

schema.xml
```xml
<fieldType name="text_en_kstem" class="solr.TextField"
    positionIncrementGap="100">
  <analyzer>
    <tokenizer class="solr.StandardTokenizerFactory"/>
    <filter class="solr.StopFilterFactory"
        ignoreCase="true"
        words="lang/stopwords_en.txt"/>
    <filter class="solr.LowerCaseFilterFactory"/>
    <filter class="solr.EnglishPossessiveFilterFactory"/>
    <filter class="solr.KeywordMarkerFilterFactory"
        protected="protwords.txt"/>
    <filter class="solr.KStemFilterFactory"/>
  </analyzer>
</fieldType>
```

protwords.txt
```
listing
manning
```

In this case, the *protwords.txt* file should contain all of the protected keywords (`listing`, `manning`) that you want ignored by the subsequent `KStemFilterFactory`. This enables you to create your own list of terms that you want stemming to leave untouched based upon your particular domain needs.

14.4.2 *StemmerOverrideFilterFactory*

At times, it may not be sufficient to merely protect words from being incorrectly stemmed through the use of `KeywordMarkerFilterFactory`. If your desire is to *fix* the problematic stems, `StemmerOverrideFilterFactory` is the tool for the job. It uses a custom dictionary of stemmer mappings that takes precedence over any subsequent stemmers that are run:

schema.xml
```xml
<fieldType name="text_en_kstem_with_overrides" class="solr.TextField"
    positionIncrementGap="100">
```

```
  <analyzer>
    <tokenizer class="solr.StandardTokenizerFactory"/>
    <filter class="solr.StopFilterFactory"
        ignoreCase="true"
        words="lang/stopwords_en.txt"/>
    <filter class="solr.LowerCaseFilterFactory"/>
    <filter class="solr.EnglishPossessiveFilterFactory"/>
    <filter class="solr.KeywordMarkerFilterFactory"
        protected="protwords.txt"/>
    <filter class="solr.StemmerOverrideFilterFactory"
        dictionary="stemdict_en.txt" />
    <filter class="solr.KStemFilterFactory"/>
  </analyzer>
</fieldType>
```

stemdict_en.txt
```
dogs       dog
runs       run
investors  investor
```

By combining KeywordMarkerFilterFactory and StemmerOverrideFilterFactory in your analysis chain, you should have all of the major tools you need to both protect words and correct mistakes from whichever stemming algorithm you choose. We've so far demonstrated several English stemmers such as the Porter Stem, English Minimal Stem, and KStem filters. We also covered the additional English stemming algorithms available through the SnowballPorterFilter, such as the Lovins, original Porter, and English (Porter2) stemmers. This currently represents the English language and is only the tip of the iceberg of available language handling capabilities in Solr.

14.5 *Available language libraries in Solr*

Although English was used to demonstrate common stemming implementations, Solr also supports many other languages. Although we'll not demonstrate input/output examples for each language (you can easily do that yourself using the Analysis page on Solr's Admin UI), it's at least worth listing the available stemmers in Solr with which you can experiment.

14.5.1 *Language-specific analyzer chains*

Because of the wide variations between languages, there is not a single, consistent model to follow when defining a field in Solr to properly handle a language. Some languages require their own stemming filters, others require multiple filters to handle different language characteristics (such as normalization of characters, removal of accents, and even custom lowercasing functionality), and some languages require their own tokenizers due to the complexity of parsing the language. Table 14.2 demonstrates the level of variation common across language-specific analyzer chains, with language-specific components listed in bold.

Table 14.2 Variation among language-specific analyzer chains

Language	Example analyzer chain

Arabic	`StandardTokenizerFactory`
	`LowerCaseFilterFactory`
	`StopFilterFactory` `[words="lang/`**`stopwords_ar.txt`**`"]`
	`ArabicNormalizationFilterFactory`
	`ArabicStemFilterFactory`

CJK (Chinese, Japanese, Korean)	`StandardTokenizerFactory`
	`CJKWidthFilterFactory`
	`LowerCaseFilterFactory`
	`CJKBigramFilterFactory`

Greek	`StandardTokenizerFactory`
	`GreekLowerCaseFilterFactory`
	`StopFilterFactory` `[words="lang/`**`stopwords_el.txt`**`"]`
	`GreekStemFilterFactory`

Hindi	`StandardTokenizerFactory`
	`LowerCaseFilterFactory`
	`IndicNormalizationFilterFactory`
	`HindiNormalizationFilterFactory`
	`StopFilterFactory` `[words="lang/`**`stopwords_hi.txt`**`"]`
	`HindiStemFilterFactory`

Japanese	**`JapaneseTokenizerFactory`** `[userDictionary="lang/`**`userdict_ja.txt`**`"]`
	`JapaneseBaseFormFilterFactory`
	`JapanesePartOfSpeechStopFilterFactory` `[tags="lang/`**`stoptags_ja.txt`**`"]`
	`CJKWidthFilterFactory`
	`StopFilterFactory` `[words="lang/`**`stopwords_ja.txt`**`"]`
	`JapaneseKatakanaStemFilterFactory`
	`LowerCaseFilterFactory`

Persian	**`PersianCharFilterFactory`**
	`StandardTokenizerFactory`
	`LowerCaseFilterFactory`
	`ArabicNormalizationFilterFactory`
	`PersianNormalizationFilterFactory`
	`StopFilterFactory` `[words="lang/`**`stopwords_fa.txt`**`"]`

Romanian	`StandardTokenizerFactory`
	`LowerCaseFilterFactory`
	`StopFilterFactory` `[words="lang/`**`stopwords_ro.txt`**`"]`
	`SnowballPorterFilterFactory` `[language="`**`Romanian`**`"]`

As you can see from table 14.2, Solr natively supports a wide range of language-specific analysis, with varying levels of configuration complexity. A longer, more complete list of language configuration examples can be found in appendix B. If you would like to add any of these languages to your schema, most of the per-language token and filter combinations in the table are also represented as their own field types in the example *schema.xml* that comes with Solr.

Although there isn't room to include the XML configurations for every language in this chapter, there are a few particular configurations that are worth pointing out. First, let's take a look at the suggested configuration for Romanian, the simplest of those listed:

```
<analyzer>
  <tokenizer class="solr.StandardTokenizerFactory"/>
  <filter class="solr.LowerCaseFilterFactory"/>
  <filter class="solr.StopFilterFactory" ignoreCase="true"
      words="lang/stopwords_ro.txt"/>
  <filter class="solr.SnowballPorterFilterFactory"
      language="Romanian"/>
</analyzer>
```

This analyzer chain—StandardTokenizerFactory, LowerCaseFilterFactory, Stop-FilterFactory, and SnowballPorterFilterFactory—models the basic structure for many languages. Most languages are able to make use of StandardTokenizer-Factory, followed by some form of lowercasing. Some languages have their own lowercasing filter to handle language-specific lowercasing (such as with Turkish-LowerCaseFilterFactory, IrishLowerCaseFilterFactory, and GreekLowerCase-FilterFactory), but most can make use of the standard LowerCaseFilterFactory. Solr also comes with custom stop words files for many languages that can be used with StopFilterFactory.

Several languages, as you can tell from table 14.2, also require special character normalization filters. This includes languages such as Arabic, Persian, and Hindi. You will notice several other filters interspersed throughout the recommended analyzer chains for various languages, but the previously mentioned filters take care of most language-specific characteristics and generally improve the quality of search results across these languages.

The final characteristic of most of these analyzer chains is the use of stemmers. Most of the languages have one or more available language-specific stemmers. In languages with more than one stemmer, you must make the choice between stemmers based upon how aggressively you want to stem your content. Remember that the more aggressive the stemmer you use, the higher the Recall will generally be for your queries (more of the expected documents will be returned), but the lower the Precision will be (you will return more documents which you're not expecting). It's up to you to make the determination as to which of these is preferred for your search application.

Generally speaking, the name of the stemmer will provide insight into how aggressively it stems. A MinimalStem filter will generally be the least aggressive, followed by a LightStem filter, followed by a StemFilter, followed by the SnowballPorter filter. Table 14.3 provides examples of each of these.

The main takeaway from table 14.3 is that Solr provides out-of-the-box stemming options for many languages with varying levels of Precision and Recall. The Snowball-Porter stemmer includes implementations for many languages and is often used as the default, even though it's generally considered aggressive. It's worth testing multiple

Table 14.3 Comparison of stemmers from least to most aggressive per language

Least aggressive	Less aggressive	More aggressive	Most aggressive
PortugueseMinimalStem*	PortugueseLightStem*	PortugueseStem*	SnowballPorter*
FrenchMinimalStem*	FrenchLightStem*		SnowballPorter*
GermanMinimalStem*	GermanLightStem*		SnowballPorter*
NorwegianMinimalStem*	NorwegianLightStem*		SnowballPorter*
GalicianMinimalStem*			
	SpanishLightStem*	GalicianStem*	SnowballPorter*
	HungarianLightStem*		SnowballPorter*
	ItalianLightStem*		SnowballPorter*
	RussianLightStem*		SnowballPorter*
	SwedishLightStem*		SnowballPorter*
		ArabicStem*	
		BulgarianStem*	
		CzechStem*	
		GreekStem*	
		HindiStem*	
		IndonesianStem*	
		JapaneseKatakanaStem*	
		LatvianStem*	

* The full name of each stemmer ends with `FilterFactory` when referenced in *schema.xml*. For example: `PortugueseMinimalStemFilterFactory`. This factory internally creates the `Token-Filter` for stemming.

stemmers out in the languages you care about if you want to arrive at the best possible search experience for your use case. Although the details of how each of these stemmers handles its respective language are beyond the scope of this chapter, the information presented so far should be sufficient to demonstrate the commonly used stemming libraries in Solr and how you can begin testing and making use of them.

14.5.2 *Dictionary-based stemming (Hunspell)*

Solr also provides support for another stemming filter invoked through the `Hunspell-StemFilterFactory`. As the `SnowballPorterFilter` supports many languages, so too does the Hunspell stemming algorithm. In fact, the Hunspell stemmer currently supports 101 different languages, so if you haven't seen support for your language(s) yet, the Hunspell stemmer may be worth checking out. It is a dictionary-based stemmer, which means it only works for words that are contained within a supplied dictionary. As such, the Hunspell stemmer requires downloading custom files (called dictionary and affix files) per language, configured as follows (in this example, for the Slovak language from Slovakia):

```
<filter class="solr.HunspellStemFilterFactory"
    dictionary="sk_SK.dic"
    affix="sk_SK.aff"
    ignoreCase="true" />
```

Because it's dictionary-based, the quality of the Hunspell stemmer varies considerably from language to language based upon the quality of the publicly available dictionary and affix files. If you choose to use the Hunspell stemmer, you may determine that it's necessary to create your own custom dictionaries in order to better handle your domain-specific terms. Although many Solr users tend to shy away from Hunspell stemmers due to these limitations, if your language is not otherwise supported natively by Solr or if you have a need to build up domain-specific dictionaries for your application, the Hunspell stemmer may be worth a try.

Now that we've seen the many kinds of the language-specific text analysis components available in Solr, it's time to dive into how you can combine these to search multilingual content.

14.6 *Searching content in multiple languages*

Many companies need to search content across multiple languages. Up to this point, we've seen Solr's ability to handle content across a variety of languages, but this discussion has been relegated to configuring searching within a single language at a time. Although it's useful to be able to create an English language field or a German language field, for example, what happens when you need to search content across both languages?

This section will cover techniques for searching multilingual content in which you may have different languages across your documents or even multiple languages within a single document or field. There are three primary ways to implement these kinds of multilingual search capabilities:

- Create a separate field per language (as you have seen so far), and spread your query across each of them.
- Use multiple Solr indexes containing the same field name, with each index having the field configured to handle a different language.
- Implement a field type which is natively able to index and search across multiple languages at the same time.

Each technique represents a different level of complexity and is better for different use cases, which we'll cover in the following subsections.

14.6.1 *Separate field per language*

Searching across multiple language-specific fields is the simplest and most commonly used multilingual setup in Solr. At a high level, it requires knowing up front which language or languages are associated with your content, and making sure that the content is fed into those fields at index time. At search time, you must know which languages you wish to search across and must include each of those fields in your search query. Figure 14.4 provides a diagram for the indexing and querying model for a field-per-language multilingual search setup.

As you can see from figure 14.4, the field-per-language multilingual search model requires both separating your content into individual fields by language and duplicating your query keywords across each of those fields. This approach of maintaining

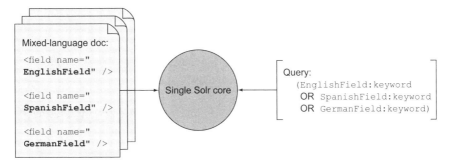

Figure 14.4 Diagram of the indexing and querying configuration for implementing multilingual search using the field-per-language model

a separate field per language is the easiest to set up of the three approaches we'll cover, but it also scales the least well as you add more and more language-specific fields. The scalability problem occurs on two fronts:

- If you're unable to reduce your query to a small number of specific languages at query time, you will likely have to spread your search across all of the defined language-specific fields in your document, and each additional field you search against slows your query down.
- If you need to support multiple languages in a single document, you may end up having to duplicate your content in multiple fields, which will increase the size of your index. This will both slow queries down and reduce the amount of content you can hold within your index without additional sharding of your index.

Field-per-language overview

Pros:

- Simplest method to implement out of the box.
- Built-in support for searching across fields using a DisMax-style query parser.
- Language-detection for mapping to language-specific fields works out of the box.
- Works in a single Solr core or sharded Solr setup.

Cons:

- Multilingual documents may require dual-storing content per language field, increasing index size and subsequently slowing down searches.
- Search speed slows as more languages are searched per query.
- You're forced to use a DisMax-style query parser or to manually craft a multi-field query.
- Does not support mixed-language proximity/phrase searching.

Because of the ease of setup and limited complexity of most multilingual search implementations, this approach is the most commonly used and best-supported way of handling multilingual search in Solr.

The following listing demonstrates how you would set up your schema to search across three languages: English, Spanish, and French.

Listing 14.2   Schema supporting three separate language fields

```xml
<fieldType name="text_english" class="solr.TextField"
    positionIncrementGap="100">
  <analyzer>
    <tokenizer class="solr.StandardTokenizerFactory"/>
    <filter class="solr.StopFilterFactory"
        ignoreCase="true"
        words="lang/stopwords_en.txt"/>
    <filter class="solr.LowerCaseFilterFactory"/>
    <filter class="solr.EnglishPossessiveFilterFactory"/>
    <filter class="solr.KeywordMarkerFilterFactory"
        protected="protwords.txt"/>
    <filter class="solr.KStemFilterFactory"/>
  </analyzer>
</fieldType>

<fieldType name="text_spanish" class="solr.TextField"
    positionIncrementGap="100">
  <analyzer>
    <tokenizer class="solr.StandardTokenizerFactory"/>
    <filter class="solr.LowerCaseFilterFactory"/>
    <filter class="solr.StopFilterFactory" ignoreCase="true" words="lang/
        stopwords_es.txt" format="snowball"/>
    <filter class="solr.SpanishLightStemFilterFactory"/>
  </analyzer>
</fieldType>

<fieldType name="text_french" class="solr.TextField"
    positionIncrementGap="100">
  <analyzer>
    <tokenizer class="solr.StandardTokenizerFactory"/>
    <filter class="solr.ElisionFilterFactory" ignoreCase="true"
        articles="lang/contractions_fr.txt"/>
    <filter class="solr.LowerCaseFilterFactory"/>
    <filter class="solr.StopFilterFactory" ignoreCase="true" words="lang/
        stopwords_fr.txt" format="snowball"/>
    <filter class="solr.FrenchLightStemFilterFactory"/>
  </analyzer>
</fieldType>
...
<field name="id" type="string" indexed="true" stored="true" />
<field name="title" type="string" indexed="true" stored="true" />
<field name="content_english" type="text_english" indexed="true"
    stored="true" />
<field name="content_spanish" type="text_spanish" indexed="true"
    stored="true" />
```

```
<field name="content_french" type="text_french" indexed="true"
    stored="true" />
...
```

With a field set up for each language in your schema, the next step is to index your documents, with each document's content being mapped into the appropriate language-specific fields. The following commands take care of sending your documents to Solr:

```
cd $SOLR_IN_ACTION/example-docs/
java -Durl=http://localhost:8983/solr/field-per-language/update
  ➥ -jar post.jar  ch14/documents/field-per-language.xml
```

Before we begin searching the documents you added to Solr, it's worth taking a look at a few of them to understand their layout first. The following listing provides a good overview of several documents containing quotes from famous books.

> **Listing 14.3   A sampling of documents with separate fields per language**

```
<doc>
  <field name="id">1</field>
  <field name="title">The Adventures of Huckleberry Finn</field>
  <field name="content_english">YOU don't know about me without you have read
  a book by the name of The Adventures of Tom Sawyer; but that ain't no
  matter. That book was made by Mr. Mark Twain, and he told the truth,
  mainly. There was things which he stretched, but mainly he told the truth.
  <field>
</doc>
<doc>
  <field name="id ">2</field>
  <field name="title">Les Misérables</field>
  <field name="content_french">Nul n'aurait pu le dire; tout ce qu'on savait,
  c'est que, lorsqu'il revint d'Italie, il était prêtre.
  </field>
</doc>
<doc>
  <field name="id">3</field>
  <field name="title">Don Quixote</field>
  <field name="content_spanish">Demasiada cordura puede ser la peor de las
  locuras, ver la vida como es y no como debería de ser.
  </field>
</doc>
<doc>
  <field name="id">4</field>
  <field name="title">Proverbs</field>
  <field name="content_spanish"> No la abandones y ella velará sobre
  ti, ámala y ella te protegerá. Lo principal es la sabiduría; adquiere
  sabiduría, y con todo lo que obtengas adquiere inteligencia.
  </field>
  <field name="content_english">Do not forsake wisdom, and she will
  protect you; love her, and she will watch over you. Wisdom is supreme;
  therefore get wisdom. Though it cost all you have, get understanding.
  </field>
```

```
<field name="content_french">N'abandonne pas la sagesse, et elle te
gardera, aime-la, et elle te protégera. Voici le début de la sagesse:
acquiers la sagesse, procure-toi le discernement au prix de tout ce que tu
possèdes.
<field>
</doc>
```

You will notice two important aspects in the listing. A separate content field exists for each language (content_english, content_french, and content_spanish) and although most documents only make use of one of these fields, there is no limitation requiring this. In the document with id 4, for example, you will notice that a translation exists for each language, which will allow a document to be searched upon in any of the three languages. There is also no requirement that the text in the three fields be exact translations; if different parts of a document could be divided across multiple languages, then it would be perfectly reasonable to put independent sections of content in the appropriate language field.

With these documents indexed in Solr, we can now take care of the last step: allowing searching across each of these languages. Recall from chapter 7 that the eDisMax query parser makes it easy to search across multiple fields. The next listing demonstrates how to easily execute a search across each of the defined language fields in this section's example.

Listing 14.4   Performing a search across multiple language-specific fields

Query

```
http://localhost:8983/solr/field-per-language/select?
  fl=title&
  defType=edismax&
  qf=content_english content_french content_spanish&
  q="he told the truth" OR "il était prêtre" OR "ver la vida como es"
```

Response

```
{
   "responseHeader":{
     "status":0,
     "QTime":1},
   "response":{"numFound":3,"start":0,"docs":[
      {
        "title":["The Adventures of Huckleberry Finn"]},
      {
        "title":["Don Quixote"]},
      {
        "title":["Les Misérables"]}]
}}
```

If you perform the query, Solr will return three book documents in the search results: *Don Quixote* (matching the phrase "ver la vida como es" in the content_spanish field), *The Adventures of Huckleberry Finn* (matching the phrase "he told the truth" in the content_english field), and *Les Misérables* (matching the phrase "il était prêtre" in the content_french field). This example demonstrates that it's relatively simple to search across content in different languages, where each document contains a single language in a separate language-specific field.

What happens, however, when a single document needs to contain multiple languages? The next listing demonstrates searching for a multilingual document.

Listing 14.5 Searching for multilingual documents with one language per field

Query 1

```
http://localhost:8983/solr/field-per-language/select?
  fl=title&
  defType=edismax&
  qf=content_english content_french content_spanish&
  q="wisdom"
```

Query 2

```
http://localhost:8983/solr/field-per-language/select?
...
q="sabiduría"
```

Query 3

```
http://localhost:8983/solr/field-per-language/select?
...
q="sagesse"
```

Response (same for queries 1–3)

```
{
    "responseHeader":{
      "status":0,
      "QTime":1},
    "response":{"numFound":1,"start":0,"docs":[
        {
          "title":["Proverbs"]}]
}}
```

The document returned in the listing contains three translations of the content: one in the `content_english` field, one in the `content_spanish` field, and one in the `content_french` field (refer to listing 14.3 for the full text in each of these fields). As such, each of the three queries (a query for the translated word *wisdom* in each of the three languages) finds the same document. This demonstrates how to support documents with multiple translations, though there is no requirement that the content in each of these fields contains exact translations. If you have documents that contain separate sections in various languages, it would make sense to divide those sections into language-specific fields if you're able to determine the language of each section ahead of time.

As you can see from this section, it's easy to support multilingual content by dividing language-specific content into separate language-specific fields and then searching across each of these fields. This separate field per language model works well until you have many languages to support. Since every query must search across the multiple language-specific fields, if the number of languages/fields you need to search across becomes large, obviously your queries may become unreasonably slow. If this ends up being the case, then you may want to consider one of the more advanced multilingual search approaches in the coming sections.

14.6.2 Separate index per language

In addition to creating multiple language-specific fields in your search index and searching across them all at query time, it's possible to search upon a single field and accomplish the same goal. One common way to do this is to create a separate Solr index (Solr core) per language. As opposed to creating a separate Solr field per language in the same index (demonstrated in the previous section), creating a separate Solr core per language allows you to keep the same field name in each index while changing the field type that the field references in each index to handle a different language. This allows your queries to stay simple. Searching a single field will increase the speed of your queries at scale by parallelizing searches in different languages across multiple Solr cores (and CPU cores and/or servers), as opposed to expanding the query across multiple fields in the same Solr index. Figure 14.5 demonstrates the architecture for this kind of multilingual search implementation.

As you can see from figure 14.5, the core-per-language implementation is a bit more complex than the field-per-language approach we discussed in the previous section. It requires managing separate Solr indexes and manually directing content to them based upon the language of the content. Queries are fairly simple, because you

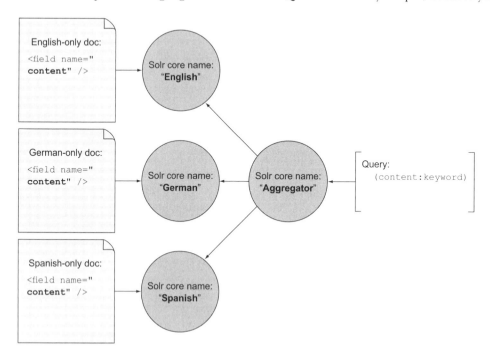

Figure 14.5   Diagram of the indexing and querying configuration for implementing multilingual search using the separate core-per-language model.

can configure Solr to automatically aggregate search results across multiple Solr indexes, but the overall architecture definitely presents more moving parts to manage.

> ## Core-per-language overview
> **Pros:**
> - Fast search across many languages—searches each language's content in parallel.
> - Supports any query parser because it only requires searching on a single field.
>
> **Cons:**
> - Managing multiple Solr cores adds complexity to your environment.
> - You must manually shard documents by language before sending to Solr.
> - Doesn't support multilingual documents unless you duplicate them in multiple cores.
> - Can yield suboptimal relevancy scores, because relevancy statistics are calculated per language, then merged with other disjointed languages.

How does one go about creating a separate Solr index for each language? If you recall from prior chapters (specifically chapters 3 and 12), Solr supports the creation of multiple Solr cores, each of which contains a unique Solr index. Each core can be defined to use different configuration files, including *schema.xml.* When an aggregated search across multiple cores occurs, each of the Solr cores searches its own data using its own configuration before returning results to be combined by another core. Because of this, it's possible to have many language-specific cores with their own definitions for a particular field, which means that all documents and queries in that field will be handled differently on a per-Solr-core basis. The following listing demonstrates how you would configure such an option.

Listing 14.6 Configuring multiple language-specific Solr cores

File: *english/conf/schema.xml*

```
...
  <field name="content" type="text_english" indexed="true" stored="true" />
...
```

The same field name is used for each separately defined language.

File: *spanish/conf/schema.xml*

```
...
  <field name="content" type="text_spanish" indexed="true" stored="true" />
...
```

File: *french/conf/schema.xml*

```
...
  <field name="content" type="text_french" indexed="true" stored="true" />
```

Core definitions: (*core.properties* files)

```
$SOLR_INSTALL/example/solr/english/core.properties
$SOLR_INSTALL/example/solr/spanish/core.properties
$SOLR_INSTALL/example/solr/french/core.properties
$SOLR_INSTALL/example/solr/aggregator/core.properties
```

Each language-specific core uses a language-specific schema.

The aggregator is for searching other cores (contains no data).

In this particular example, separate Solr cores have been defined for each language, each of which uses a custom schema containing a `content` field defined to use a language-specific field type. With your language-specific Solr cores set up like listing 14.6, as should already be done for you if you started the chapter example, you can now send content to each of the Solr cores:

```
cd $SOLR_IN_ACTION/example-docs/
java -jar -Durl=http://localhost:8983/solr/english/update post.jar
  ➥ ch14/documents/english.xml
java -jar -Durl=http://localhost:8983/solr/spanish/update post.jar
  ➥ ch14/documents/spanish.xml
java -jar -Durl=http://localhost:8983/solr/french/update post.jar
  ➥ ch14/documents/french.xml
```

With Solr running with content in each of the language-specific cores, the last step is to send a query:

```
http://localhost:8983/solr/aggregator/select?
  shards=localhost:8983/solr/english,
    localhost:8983/solr/spanish,
    localhost:8983/solr/french&
  df=content&
  q=*:*
```

In this query, a distributed request is sent to each of the language-specific cores using the `shards` parameter, resulting in each language's content being searched independently and in parallel with the other languages. Because the `content` field (listing 14.6) is defined differently in each language-specific core, the work of handling each language is delegated to that core.

Although this core-per-language setup allows querying across all languages or a subset of languages similar to the field-per-language approach in section 14.6.1, it offers the additional advantage that it parallelizes the search across multiple smaller indexes, as opposed to searching across a growing number of fields in a much larger index. This means that, given enough CPU cores, this approach will generally result in faster queries at scale. The cost of this approach, however, comes in the complexity of managing a multitude of Solr cores. One caveat of the core-per-language approach is that it can potentially lead to unusual relevancy scores. If you remember from section 3.2.3, idf is a measure of how rare a term is, and this metric is an important part of Solr's default relevancy algorithm. Because idf is a statistic based upon all documents in a single Solr index (Solr core) it typically works best if the distribution of terms is randomized across each Solr core. In the case of sharding content by language, this will clearly not be the case, so you could inadvertently end up with higher relevancy scores in one language than another based solely upon how the content was sharded.

Additionally, one aspect of the field-per-language approach that's difficult to replicate in the core-per-language approach is the ability to handle multiple languages in the same document. Because each document only contains one `content` field in the core-per-language example seen in this section, each document can only handle one language configuration per Solr core. The only way to get around this limitation would be to send the same document to multiple language cores, but this isn't recommended because it will cause the document to be counted twice in any search metadata (facets, hits, etc.). Handling multiple languages per document is not a requirement in many systems, but this is certainly worth considering before trying to implement this approach.

In addition to the field-per-language approach and the core-per-language approach, it's possible to implement multilingual search by allowing a single field to support multiple languages, which will be covered in the next section.

14.6.3 *Multiple languages in one field*

Managing a separate Solr core for every language can create a management headache, as it requires you to create a custom sharding implementation that directs documents to separate Solr cores for each language. Additionally, if you have a small number of documents, the aggregation overhead of using distributed search may slow down your queries. With the implementation in section 14.6.2 you saw that the core-per-language approach also does not easily support having multiple languages per document. Maintaining a separate field per language causes queries to be more complex, and if you're using any query parser not in the DisMax query parser family (such as the eDisMax query parser) you have to manually spread your queries across every language-specific field.

It would be much simpler in certain use cases if you could have the key benefits of both approaches: a single field across multiple languages, not having to manage language-specific Solr cores, and the ability to support multilingual documents. This can be accomplished by creating a field type that's able to support any combination of language configurations.

Multiple languages per field overview

Pros:

- Supports any combination of languages in a single field.
- Works in a single Solr core or sharded Solr setup.
- Supports any query parser because it only requires searching on a single field.
- Supports true multilingual searching, including mixed-language phrases.
- Does not require dual-storing content per language, reducing index size and subsequently increasing search speed.
- Allows dynamically trying different language combinations at query time.
- Still supports language identification (through example code in this chapter).

Cons:

- Not available out of the box, so requires custom code (included with this chapter).
- Each document field and query term must be prefixed with the languages in which it should be analyzed, adding complexity.
- Potential exists to not find terms if languages chosen at index and query time do not match.

Supporting multiple languages per field is not something Solr (currently) provides out of the box, but with a little work we can create this capability ourselves. There are many strategies to pull this off. The simplest method would be to place multiple stemmers (stemming filters) within the same `TextField`'s analyzer chain defined in *schema.xml*. The disadvantage here is that a previous stemmer may destroy the token's original format before it hits a later stemmer, creating undesired or incorrect resulting tokens in your index.

You could solve this particular problem by creating a custom `TokenFilter` that buffers tokens and creates multiple copies of the original token stream before passing the original input into separate stemmers. With this approach, you would end up with multiple token streams you would then have to either stack or concatenate. This approach would work well if you only need to support a few predefined languages, and those languages only need to swap out a `TokenFilter` in one place in the analysis chain.

If you want to support many different languages with different configurations (`CharFilters`, `Tokenizers`, and ordering of `TokenFilters` are all variables), you will need a much more flexible solution. To provide an example solution for this problem, we've created a special field type in this chapter—the `MultiTextField`—that will effectively allow you to stack multiple field types into a single field. In the next section, we'll demonstrate how this field type works and how you can use it to support highly flexible multilingual search within the same field.

14.6.4 *Creating a field type to handle multiple languages per field*

When you send documents and queries to Solr, the content for each field is analyzed based upon the field type defined for the field. This field type can contain a single analyzer per mode: `index` mode versus `query` mode versus `multiTerm` mode (for wildcard queries). In the case of multilingual content, however, it would be useful if you could specify multiple analyzers (one per language) for your content, because you sometimes want a fully separate analysis chain for each language (with separate `CharFilter`, `Tokenizer`, and `TokenFilter` configurations).

In such a scenario, you would need to specify the languages you wanted to be considered for each field at index time and for each term at query time. Figure 14.6 provides a model of what documents and queries would look like in such a configuration.

The key takeaway from figure 14.6 is that at both index time and query time, the languages of the content must be specified. As many languages can be combined as you desire, and they can be different on every document and query, but something has to tell the special field type which language configurations to use to analyze the content in order for this to be possible. For the implementation in this chapter, the list of languages is prepended to the content itself.

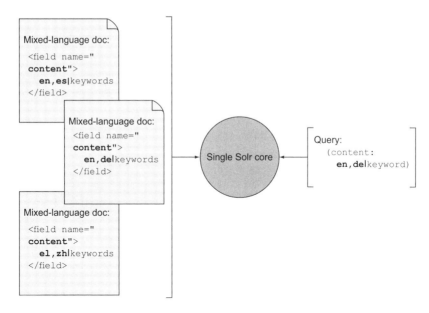

Figure 14.6 Diagram of the indexing and querying configuration for implementing multilingual search combining multiple languages into a single field in the same Solr core

An example document may look like this:

```
<doc>
  <field name="content">
    en,de,fr|this field contains English, dieses feld enthält Deutsch,
    et ce champ contient du français
  </field>
</doc>
```

Likewise, an example query may look like this:

```
/select?q=en|contains OR de|enthält OR en,fr|contient
```

In the indexing example, the leading list of languages indicates that the content should be processed in English (en), German (de), and French (fr). Likewise, in the query, the first term should be processed as an English term, the second as a German term, and the third should be run through both English and French analysis. To pull this off, we would need to create an analyzer that could switch between and combine other analyzers on demand. The next listing demonstrates the first steps for creating such a mechanism by implementing custom TextField and Analyzer classes.

Listing 14.7 Implementing `MultiTextField` and `Analyzer`

```
public class MultiTextField extends TextField {
... //Skipped code which reads in settings, available in full source
```

```
  @Override
  protected void init(IndexSchema schema, Map<String,String> args) {
    super.init(schema, args);

    MultiTextFieldSettings indexSettings = new MultiTextFieldSettings();
    indexSettings.analyzerMode = AnalyzerModes.index;
    MultiTextFieldSettings querySettings = new MultiTextFieldSettings();
    querySettings.analyzerMode = AnalyzerModes.query;
    MultiTextFieldSettings multiTermSettings = new MultiTextFieldSettings();
    multiTermSettings.analyzerMode = AnalyzerModes.multiTerm;

...

    MultiTextFieldAnalyzer indexAnalyzer = new
    MultiTextFieldAnalyzer(schema, indexSettings);
    MultiTextFieldAnalyzer queryAnalyzer = new
    MultiTextFieldAnalyzer(schema, querySettings);
    MultiTextFieldAnalyzer multiTermAnalyzer = new
    MultiTextFieldAnalyzer(schema, multiTermSettings);

    this.setAnalyzer(indexAnalyzer);
    this.setQueryAnalyzer(queryAnalyzer);
    this.setMultiTermAnalyzer(multiTermAnalyzer);
  }
}

public class MultiTextFieldAnalyzer extends Analyzer {

  protected IndexSchema indexSchema;
  protected MultiTextFieldSettings settings;

  public MultiTextFieldAnalyzer(IndexSchema indexSchema,
    MultiTextFieldSettings settings) {
      super(new PerFieldReuseStrategy());
      this.settings = settings;
      this.indexSchema = indexSchema;
  }

  @Override
  public TokenStreamComponents createComponents(String fieldName,
    Reader reader) {

    MultiTextFieldTokenizer multiTokenizer = new MultiTextFieldTokenizer(
      indexSchema, reader, fieldName, Settings);

        Tokenizer source = multiTokenizer;
        TokenStream result = multiTokenizer;
        if (Settings.removeDuplicates){
          result = new RemoveDuplicatesTokenFilter(multiTokenizer);
        }

        return new TokenStreamComponents(source, result);
  }
}
```

As you can see from this listing, `MultiTextField` and `MultiTextFieldAnalyzer` do nothing particularly impressive. Because `TextField` contains three separate `Analyzers`—one
for indexing content, one for querying, and one for wildcard and similar queries—
`MultiTextField` ensures that a separate copy of `MultiTextFieldAnalyzer` is specified

for each of these configurations. Because the `MultiTextFieldAnalyzer` needs to load appropriate `Analyzers` for each subfield requested, assigning a different `MultiText-FieldAnalyzer` that knows which `Analyzer` (index, query, or `multiTerm`) to choose in its subfields is necessary. The other important thing to notice is that `MultiTextField` and `MultiTextFieldAnalyzer` pass in `IndexSchema` to `MultiTextFieldTokenizer`, providing it with access to all other field types and their configurations. Typically, `Tokenizers` do not have access to `IndexSchema` or other field types, but because the `MultiTextField` serves as a sort of meta field, its `Analyzer` and `Tokenizer` need access to the configurations for other available fields whose analysis pipelines may be requested.

The `MultiTextFieldTokenizer`, initialized in the previous listing, is where the hard work will take place. This listing introduces the `MultiTextFieldTokenizer`.

Listing 14.8 Implementing the `MultiTextField`'s `Tokenizer`

```
public class MultiTextFieldTokenizer extends Tokenizer {
  protected String fieldName;
  protected IndexSchema indexSchema;
  protected MultiTextFieldSettings settings;
  protected LinkedHashMap<String, Analyzer> namedAnalyzers;
  protected MultiTextFieldInput multiTextInput;

  private CharTermAttribute charTermAttribute;
  private OffsetAttribute offsetAttribute;
  private TypeAttribute typeAttribute;
  private PositionIncrementAttribute positionAttribute;
  private LinkedList<Token> tokens;
  private Integer startingOffset;

  protected MultiTextFieldTokenizer(IndexSchema indexSchema, Reader input,
      String fieldName, MultiTextFieldSettings settings) {
    super(input);
    this.indexSchema = indexSchema;
    this.fieldName = fieldName;
    this.settings = settings;
    init();
  }

  private void init() {
    charTermAttribute = addAttribute(CharTermAttribute.class);
    offsetAttribute = addAttribute(OffsetAttribute.class);
    typeAttribute = addAttribute(TypeAttribute.class);
    positionAttribute = addAttribute(PositionIncrementAttribute.class);
  }

  @Override
  public void reset() throws IOException {
    super.reset();
    this.tokens = null;
    if (this.multiTextInput == null) {
      this.multiTextInput = new MultiTextFieldInput(
          this.input, this.settings.keyFromTextDelimiter,
          this.settings.multiKeyDelimiter);
```

① Constructor takes input Reader with original text.

② Preprocessing of input is performed during reset method.

③ MultiTextField-Input splits requested FieldTypes from text.

Allows ❹
different
analyzers
to be
specified
per search
term.

```
        } else {
          this.multiTextInput.setReader(this.input);
        }
      this.namedAnalyzers = getNamedAnalyzers();
      this.startingOffset = this.multiTextInput.StrippedIncomingPrefixLength
          >= 0 ? this.multiTextInput.StrippedIncomingPrefixLength : 0;
    }

  private LinkedHashMap<String, Analyzer> getNamedAnalyzers() {

      LinkedHashMap<String, Analyzer> namedAnalyzers =
          new LinkedHashMap<String, Analyzer>();

      FieldType fieldType;
      for (int i = 0; i < this.multiTextInput.Keys.size(); i++) {

        String fieldTypeName = this.multiTextInput.Keys.get(i);
        if (this.settings.fieldMappings != null) {
          fieldTypeName = this.settings.fieldMappings
              .get(this.multiTextInput.Keys.get(i));
        }

        fieldType = this.indexSchema.getFieldTypeByName(fieldTypeName);
        if (fieldType != null) {
          if (this.settings.analyzerMode == AnalyzerModes.query) {
            namedAnalyzers.put(fieldTypeName, fieldType.getQueryAnalyzer());
          } else if (this.settings.analyzerMode == AnalyzerModes.multiTerm) {

            namedAnalyzers.put(fieldTypeName,
                ((TextField) fieldType).getMultiTermAnalyzer());
          } else {
            namedAnalyzers.put(fieldTypeName, fieldType.getAnalyzer());
          }
        } else {
          if (!this.settings.ignoreMissingMappings) {
            throw new SolrException(SolrException.ErrorCode.BAD_REQUEST,
                "Invalid FieldMapping requested: '"
                    + this.multiTextInput.Keys.get(i) + "'");
          }
        }
      }
```

If no named
analyzers are
specified, use
the default
FieldType.

```
    if (namedAnalyzers.size() < 1) {
      if (this.settings.defaultFieldTypeName != null
          && this.settings.defaultFieldTypeName.length() > 0) {
        if (this.settings.analyzerMode == AnalyzerModes.query) {
          namedAnalyzers.put(
              "",
              this.indexSchema.getFieldTypeByName(
                  this.settings.defaultFieldTypeName).getQueryAnalyzer());
        } else if (this.settings.analyzerMode == AnalyzerModes.multiTerm) {
          namedAnalyzers.put("", ((TextField) this.indexSchema
              .getFieldTypeByName(this.settings.defaultFieldTypeName))
              .getMultiTermAnalyzer());
        } else {
          namedAnalyzers.put(
```

```
                    "",
                this.indexSchema.getFieldTypeByName(
                    this.settings.defaultFieldTypeName).getAnalyzer());
        }
      }
    }

    if (namedAnalyzers.size() == 0) {
      throw new SolrException(SolrException.ErrorCode.BAD_REQUEST,
          "No FieldMapping was Requested, and no DefaultField"
              + " is defined for MultiTextField '" + this.fieldName
              + "'. A MultiTextField must have one or more "
              + "FieldTypes requested to execute a query.");
    }

    return namedAnalyzers;
  }

  @Override
  public boolean incrementToken() throws IOException {
    if (this.tokens == null) {
      String data = convertReaderToString(this.multiTextInput.Reader);
      if (data.equals("")) {
        return false;
      }

      this.tokens = mergeToSingleTokenStream(
          createPositionsToTokensMap(this.namedAnalyzers, data));

      if (this.tokens == null) {
        return false;
      }
    }

    if (tokens.isEmpty()) {
      this.tokens = null;
      return false;
    } else {
      clearAttributes();
      Token token = tokens.removeFirst();

      this.charTermAttribute.copyBuffer(token.buffer(), 0, token.length());
      this.offsetAttribute.setOffset(token.startOffset(), token.endOffset()
          + this.startingOffset);
      this.typeAttribute.setType(token.type());
      this.positionAttribute.setPositionIncrement(
          token.getPositionIncrement());

      return true;
    }
  }

  private SortedMap<Integer, LinkedList<Token>>
      createPositionsToTokensMap (LinkedHashMap<String, Analyzer>
      namedAnalyzers, String text) throws IOException {

    SortedMap<Integer, LinkedList<Token>> tokenHash =
        new TreeMap<Integer, LinkedList<Token>>();
```

❺ All tokens are buffered on the first call to increment-Token().

Creates a map of positions to tokens, merging tokens from each TokenStream.

```
       for (Map.Entry<String, Analyzer> namedAnalyzer :
           this.namedAnalyzers.entrySet()) {

         String subFieldName = (this.fieldName + " "
             + namedAnalyzer.getKey()).trim();

         addTokenStreamForFieldType(tokenHash, namedAnalyzer.getValue()
             .tokenStream(subFieldName, new StringReader(text)));
       }

     return tokenHash;
   }

   private void addTokenStreamForFieldType(
     SortedMap<Integer, LinkedList<Token>> tokenHash,
     TokenStream tokenStream) throws IOException {

     tokenStream.reset();
     int position = 0;

     CharTermAttribute charTermAtt = null;
     PositionIncrementAttribute posIncrAtt = null;
     OffsetAttribute offsetAtt = null;
     TypeAttribute typeAtt = null;

     if (tokenStream.hasAttribute(CharTermAttribute.class)) {
       charTermAtt = tokenStream.getAttribute(CharTermAttribute.class);
     }

     if (tokenStream.hasAttribute(PositionIncrementAttribute.class)) {
       posIncrAtt =
      tokenStream.getAttribute(PositionIncrementAttribute.class);
     }

     if (tokenStream.hasAttribute(OffsetAttribute.class)) {
       offsetAtt = tokenStream.getAttribute(OffsetAttribute.class);
     }

     if (tokenStream.hasAttribute(TypeAttribute.class)) {
       typeAtt = tokenStream.getAttribute(TypeAttribute.class);
     }

     for (boolean hasMoreTokens = tokenStream.incrementToken();
         hasMoreTokens; hasMoreTokens = tokenStream.incrementToken()) {

       String multiTermSafeType = null;

       if (charTermAtt == null
           || offsetAtt == null
           || (typeAtt == null &&
               this.settings.analyzerMode != AnalyzerModes.multiTerm)) {
         return;
       }

       if (typeAtt != null) {
         multiTermSafeType = typeAtt.type();
       }

       Token clone = new Token(charTermAtt.toString().trim(),
           offsetAtt.startOffset(), offsetAtt.endOffset(), multiTermSafeType);
```

TokenStreamComponents are cached per field, so must simulate subfields.

6

Gets a separate TokenStream from each requested analyzer for the input.

```
      position += ((posIncrAtt != null) ?
         posIncrAtt.getPositionIncrement() : 1);

      if (!tokenHash.containsKey(position)) {
        tokenHash.put(position, new LinkedList<Token>());
      }

      tokenHash.get(position).add(clone);
    }
    tokenStream.close();
  }

  private static LinkedList<Token> mergeToSingleTokenStream
      (SortedMap<Integer, LinkedList<Token>> tokenHash) {

    LinkedList<Token> result = new LinkedList<Token>();

    int currentPosition = 0;
    for (int newPosition : tokenHash.keySet()) {
      int incrementTokenIndex = result.size();

      LinkedList<Token> brothers = tokenHash.get(newPosition);
      int positionIncrement = newPosition - currentPosition;

      for (Token token : brothers) {
        token.setPositionIncrement(0);
        result.add(token);
      }

      if (result.size() > incrementTokenIndex
          && result.get(incrementTokenIndex) != null) {
        result.get(incrementTokenIndex)
          .setPositionIncrement(positionIncrement);
      }

      currentPosition = newPosition;
    }

    return result;
  }
}
```

7 Merges the tokens in the positions to tokens map into a final TokenStream.

The `MultiTextFieldTokenizer` may seem complicated based upon the amount of code within it, but its implementation can be broken down into fairly straightforward steps.

1. Like all `Tokenizers`, a field name and a `Reader` **1** are passed in through the constructor or through the **setReader()** method in the base class. The `setReader` method allows the object to be reused with a different `Reader` in subsequent searches without having to create a new `Tokenizer` object for each request.

2. Like all `Tokenizers`, the **reset()** method **2** will be called every time the `Reader` changes. The `Reader` contains the text to be analyzed, so it will change every time new text is passed in for analysis. The `MultiTextTokenizer` uses the `reset()` method to parse the text in the `Reader` and uses the **3** `MultiText-FieldInput` class (not shown) to separate the language mappings from the

field content. It then creates a list of `Analyzers` in the **`getNamedAnalyzers()`** method ❹, to be used in subsequent processing, corresponding with the fields requested at the beginning of the content in the reader.

3 When **`incrementToken()`** ❺ is called on the `MultiTextFieldTokenizer`, a separate copy of the incoming `Reader`'s text is passed (wrapped in another `Reader`) to **`addTokenStreamForFieldType()`** ❻ for each field type requested. For each requested field type, this method gets the `Analyzer` and calls **`tokenStream()`** on it, returning a `TokenStream` that makes use of that `Analyzer`'s `TokenStream-Components` (`CharFilters`, `Tokenizer`, and `TokenFilters`).

4 Each of the processed `TokenStreams` (one per requested field type) is stacked/merged back into one `TokenStream` in **`mergeToSingleTokenStream()`** ❼. This method uses the position increments from each `Token` to determine where each `Token` is stacked in the final stream. This merged `TokenStream` is saved as an instance variable and then used to process each `Token` internally after each subsequent call to the `incrementToken` method.

With those steps, `MultiTextFieldTokenizer` is able to dynamically change its analysis chain to that of one or more other text fields. This chapter is specifically using this capability to request one or more language-specific fields, but it should be noted that this capability does not have to be limited to language variations; it can enable you to swap out and/or combine any text analysis configurations on the fly for a field as you see fit. This is a powerful capability, but it also is also quite advanced and could lead to unexpected search results if the same (dynamic) analysis is not requested on content at both index and query time.

With these capabilities now in place, the following listing demonstrates how to use this `MultiTextField` implementation to enable multilingual indexing and searching within a single field by using the analyzers defined for other language-specific field types.

> **Listing 14.9   Indexing and querying multiple languages within the same field**

Schema.xml
```
...
<field name="content" type="multiText" indexed="true" stored="true"/>
...
<fieldType name="multiText"
           class="sia.ch14.MultiTextField" sortMissingLast="true"
           defaultFieldType="text_general"
           fieldMappings="en:text_english,
                          es:text_spanish,
                          fr:text_french"/>
...
```

Document
```
<doc>
  <field name="id">1</field>
  <field name="title">Proverbs</field>
```

```
  <field name="content">
    en,fr,es|No la abandones y ella velará sobre ti, ámala y ella te
    protegerá. Voici le début de la sagesse: acquiers la sagesse. Though
    it cost all you have, get understanding.
  <field>
</doc>
```

Add document

```
cd $SOLR_IN_ACTION/example-docs/
java -Durl=http://localhost:8983/solr/multi-language-field/update
    -jar post.jar ch14/documents/multi-language-field.xml
```

Query

```
http://localhost:8983/solr/multi-language-field/select?
  fl=title&
  df=content&
  q=en,fr,es|abandon AND en,fr,es|understanding AND en,fr,es|sagess
```

Results

```
{
   "responseHeader":{
     "status":0,
     "QTime":1},
   "response":{"numFound":1,"start":0,"docs":[
       {
         "title":["Proverbs"]}]
}}
```

As you can see, the query successfully matched abandon, understand, and sagess, even though the document contained abandones (Spanish), understanding (English), and sagesse (French). Because a field mapping for each of the languages was requested both at index time and at query time (through the use of the en,fr,es| prefix), any variation in any of these languages should match as it would if you used separate fields or separate Solr cores per language.

If you would like to further experiment with the MultiTextField, playing with Solr's Analysis page in the Solr Admin UI can provide a good sense of how everything works under the covers. Figure 14.7 demonstrates how Solr would process a query using an English text field and a Spanish text field separately, and how the Multi-TextField would combine the output for the same text.

Figure 14.7 demonstrates that the final output from a MultiTextField mapped to an English field type and a Spanish field type is a combined token stream of both of those field types merged together. In this case, the input text was the schools, las escualas. The English field type's analyzer transforms this text into three tokens: school, la, and escuela. The Spanish field type's analyzer transforms this text into three different tokens: the, schools, and escuel. These language-specific analyzers understandably do a poor job of handling the words in the other language. When the languages are combined using the MultiTextField, you can see that all of the variations from each language are present in the final TokenStream: the,

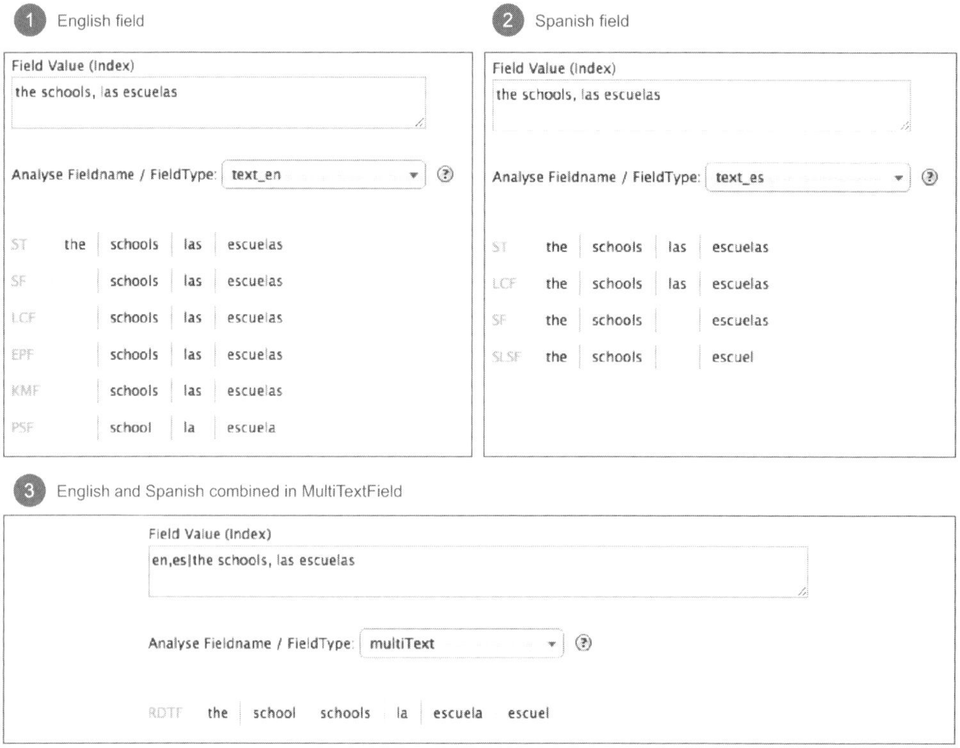

① English field

Field Value (Index)

the schools, las escuelas

Analyse Fieldname / FieldType: text_en ▾ ⑦

ST		the	schools	las	escuelas
SF			schools	las	escuelas
LCF			schools	las	escuelas
EPF			schools	las	escuelas
KMF			schools	las	escuelas
PSF			school	la	escuela

② Spanish field

Field Value (Index)

the schools, las escuelas

Analyse Fieldname / FieldType: text_es ▾ ⑦

ST		the	schools	las	escuelas
LCF		the	schools	las	escuelas
SF		the	schools		escuelas
SLSF		the	schools		escuel

③ English and Spanish combined in MultiTextField

Field Value (Index)

en,es|the schools, las escuelas

Analyse Fieldname / FieldType: multiText ▾ ⑦

| RDTF | the | school | schools | la | escuela | escuel |

Figure 14.7   Example of combining output from an English analyzer and a Spanish analyzer into a `MultiTextField` using Solr's Analysis page. The first box represents an English field type, the second a Spanish field type, and the third a `MultiTextField` which is using the English and Spanish field types to analyze its text.

`school`, `schools`, `la`, `escuela`, `escuel`. These tokens are not merely appended in the token stream, however; they are stacked in such a way that you could perform cross-language phrase searching by using position offsets from each independent analyzer (in this case, the English and Spanish analyzers). If you were to turn on verbose mode for the previous query, the output of the Analysis page would look like figure 14.8.

You can see from figure 14.8 that the terms `school` and `schools` are both located at position 2, the terms `escuela` and `escuel` are both located at position 4. It may be easier to comprehend this token stream by seeing a more stacked representation:

[Position 1]	[Position 2]	[Position 3]	[Position 4]
the	school	la	escuela
	schools		escuel

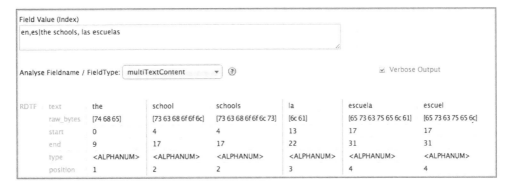

Figure 14.8 The same Analysis page output from figure 14.7, but with verbose output turned on. You can see that the positions for the terms "school" and "schools" are the same, as well as the positions for "escuala" and "escuel".

This stacking of multiple languages within the same token stream is a unique benefit of combining multiple languages in a single field: although it may not be a particularly common use case, if you have mixed language content such as in this example, you can perform a phrase or proximity search such as `"the school la escuela"` or `"school escuelas"~2`, and you will be able to find mixed-language matches, unlike in the field-per-language or core-per-language approaches to multilingual search.

Because of the ease with which you can swap out languages at both index time and query time, you do need to be careful to ensure you're choosing the right languages. Because user queries often contain so little text, it's sometimes impossible to guess which language is being used for the query unless you know something about the user. Many websites are able to make use of a user's profile, the requested language from the user's web browser, or the user's location from their IP address, or search to determine the most likely language for their query. If you only support a few languages, you can specify them all, but this will incur the performance cost of the extra processing for each language. If all else fails, you could require the user to select their language at query time.

In addition to determining the language at query time, it's arguably even more important to select the correct language of your documents at index time. This can be done before content is passed to Solr, as in listing 14.9, but Solr also has built-in support for language detection of your documents. The next section will demonstrate how to make use of it.

14.7 *Language identification*

One of the challenges inherent in supporting multilingual content is being able to determine the language(s) present in each of your documents. In many applications, you may know the language up front because you ask your users to identify the language of the content or because you have language-specific websites or channels through which your content arrives. Unfortunately, in many cases all you have is a bunch of untagged documents spanning many languages. Thankfully, Solr has built-in language identification libraries, which can help with this problem.

Before jumping into an example, it's important to point out that the accuracy of language identification algorithms almost always increases as the amount of text available for analysis increases. Consider a document containing the phrase "Lucene/Solr." In which language is this document? Well, if the full document content is "Estoy aprendiendo Lucene/Solr" then the answer would be Spanish, whereas if the content is "I am learning Lucene/Solr" then the document would be in English. The short phrase is not enough to determine the language of the document, but when additional words are added, you (and language identification algorithms) are better able to discern the language.

Because of the need for chunks of text in order to identify a language, it's typically much easier to identify languages at index time, when full documents are present, than at query time. We do not recommend using language identification algorithms to determine the language(s) of user queries, as user queries in most search applications are often short and do not provide enough meaningful context to accurately discern the language. Given that many applications, particularly web-based ones, are able to determine the language of the user through other means (such as through the country of the website they are hitting or their personal location based upon user profile or IP address), the lack of reliable query-time language identification based upon the user's query is often not a problem.

14.7.1 *Update processors for language identification*

To support language identification of documents, Solr provides two specific `Update-Processors`: `TikaLanguageIdentifierUpdateProcessor` and `LangDetectLanguage-IdentifierUpdateProcessor`. The first uses the language identification libraries in Apache Tika; the second makes use of the open source Language Detection Library for Java, which has benchmarked high Precision rates (over 99% for many languages). The next listing demonstrates how you would configure language identification to identify the language of a document.

Listing 14.10 Update processor configuration for basic language identification

solrconfig.xml

```
...
<updateRequestProcessorChain name="langid">
  <processor class="org.apache.solr.update.processor.
    LangDetectLanguageIdentifierUpdateProcessorFactory">
    <lst name="invariants">
      <str name="langid.fl">content,content_lang1,content_lang2,
        content_lang3</str>
      <str name="langid.langField">language</str>
      <str name="langid.langsField">languages</str>
      ...
    </lst>
  </processor>
</updateRequestProcessorChain>
```

```
   ...
</updateRequestProcessorChain>
...

<requestHandler name="/update" class="solr.UpdateRequestHandler">
  <lst name="invariants">
    <str name="update.chain">langid</str>
  </lst>
</requestHandler>
...
```

schema.xml
```
...
<field name="language"  type="string"  indexed="true"  stored="true" />
<field name="languages" type="string"  indexed="true"  stored="true"
    multiValued="true"/>
...
```

There are three important things going on in the listing. First, an update processor named `langid` has been defined and an invariant has been added to the `/update` request handler to ensure the `langid` update processor is run on every update. You do not have to define the invariant in the `/update` handler, but if you do not you will not be guaranteed that it runs for every document. For example, you could have alternatively defined the `update.chain` as a default, which could optionally be overridden on any given query:

```
<requestHandler name="/update" class="solr.UpdateRequestHandler">
  <lst name="defaults">
    <str name="update.chain">langid</str>
  </lst>
</requestHandler>
```

Otherwise, the `update.chain` can be passed in on every request as a query string variable:

```
http://localhost:8983/solr/langid/update?update.chain=langid
```

Second, two separate language field parameters are defined: `langid.langField` and `langid.langsField`. The primary detected language of the document will be written to the field defined in `langid.langField`, and every uniquely detected language—one per field—will be mapped into the `langid.langsField`. As such, although it's fine for the `langid.langField` to be a single-valued field, the `langid.langsField` will not work unless its `multiValued` property is set to `true` in the *schema.xml* file.

The final important takeaway is that, as mentioned earlier, two different language identifier implementations exist in Solr. Listing 14.10 demonstrates use of the Language Detection Library for Java implementation (`LangDetectLanguageIdentifierUpdateProcessorFactory`), but you can easily substitute the Tika implementation by using the `TikaLanguageIdentifierUpdateProcessorFactory` class from the same package. We'll be making use of the Language Detection Library for Java throughout the rest of this chapter.

With the language identification `UpdateProcessor` defined, let's submit a few documents to Solr. We'll reuse the documents from listing 14.3, but with the field names redefined so as to no longer use language-specific fields. These modified documents are presented in the next listing.

Listing 14.11   Documents for language identification

```
<doc>
  <field name="id">1</field>
  <field name="title">The Adventures of Huckleberry Finn</field>
  <field name="content">YOU don't know about me without you have read
      a book by the name of The Adventures of Tom Sawyer; but that ain't no
      atter. That book was made by Mr. Mark Twain, and he told the truth,
      mainly. There was things which he stretched, but mainly he told the
      truth.
  <field>
</doc>
<doc>
  <field name="id">2</field>
  <field name="title">Les Misérables</field>
  <field name="content">Nul n'aurait pu le dire; tout ce qu'on savait,
      c'est que, lorsqu'il revint d'Italie, il était prêtre.
  </field>
</doc>
<doc>
  <field name="id">3</field>
  <field name="title">Don Quixote</field>
  <field name="content">Demasiada cordura puede ser la peor de las locuras,
      ver la vida como es y no como debería de ser.
  </field>
</doc>
<doc>
  <field name="id">4</field>
  <field name="title">Proverbs</field>
  <field name="content_lang1"> No la abandones y ella velará sobre ti,
      ámala y ella te protegerá. Lo principal es la sabiduría; adquiere
      sabiduría, y con todo lo que obtengas adquiere inteligencia
  </field>
  <field name="content_lang2">
      Do not forsake wisdom, and she will protect you; love her, and she
      will watch over you. Wisdom is supreme; therefore get wisdom. Though
      it cost all you have, get understanding
  </field>
  <field name="content_lang3">
      N'abandonne pas la sagesse, et elle te gardera, aime-la, et elle te
      protégera. Voici le début de la sagesse: acquiers la sagesse,
      procure-toi le discernement au prix de tout ce que tu possèdes.
  <field>
</doc>
```

Notice that out of the four documents in the listing, one is English only, one is Spanish only, one is French only, and one contains all three languages. The next listing shows what happens if we send these documents to Solr.

Listing 14.12 Language identification in action

Sending documents
```
cd $SOLR_IN_ACTION/example-docs/
java -Durl=http://localhost:8983/solr/langid/update
    ➥ -jar post.jar ch14/documents/langid.xml
```

Query
```
http://localhost:8983/solr/langid/select?
  q=*:*&
  fl=title,language,languages
```

Result
```
{
   "responseHeader":{
     "status":0,
     "QTime":0},
   "response":{"numFound":4,"start":0,"docs":[
       {
         "title":"The Adventures of Huckelberry Finn",
         "language":"en",              ◁——┐
         "languages":["en"]},                │
       {                                      │
         "title":"Les Misérables",            │
         "language":"fr",              ◁──    │  The language field
         "languages":["fr"]},                 │  contains the primary
       {                                      │  detected language of
         "title":"Don Quoxite",               │  the document.
         "language":"es",              ◁──    │
         "languages":["es"]},                 │
       {                                      │
         "title":"Proverbs",                  │
         "language":"fr",              ◁──────┘
         "languages":["fr",     │  The languages field can
           "en",                │  contain multiple detected
           "es"]}]              │  languages per document.
}}
```

As one would expect, *Les Misérables* is identified as a French document, *Don Quixote* is identified as a Spanish document, and *The Adventures of Huckleberry Finn* is identified as an English document in both the primary `language` field and the (multivalued) `languages` field. For *Proverbs*, which contained translations in each of these three languages, the `languages` field correctly lists en (English), es (Spanish), and fr (French) as the identified languages. The single-valued `language` field only lists one language code, in this case fr, as its best guess for the primary language of this document.

DYNAMICALLY MAPPING CONTENT TO LANGUAGE-SPECIFIC FIELDS

Although it's interesting to add a language field to a document, which may be useful for faceting on language or limiting results to a particular language, it would be much more useful for multilingual searching if you could use this language identification to map content to different analyzers.

For a field-per-language setup, this capability is available out of the box with either of the language identifier update processors, as are several other useful extended features. Table 14.4 demonstrates additional language-identification options available in the language-identification update processors, several of which will be useful for mapping content to different fields based upon the language(s) identified.

Table 14.4   Available parameters for Solr's language-identification update processors

Parameter	Description	Type	Default
`langid`	Enables/disables language detection.	Boolean	`true`
`langid.fl`	*Required*: A comma- or space-delimited list of fields to be used in language identification.	String	–
`langid.langField`	*Required*: Specifies a field into which the primary identified language is mapped.	String	–
`langid.langsField`	Specifies a field into which all of the identified language codes with a threshold greater than `langid.threshold` will be mapped.	String	–
`langid.overwrite`	Specifies whether the content of the `langField` and `langsField` fields will be overwritten if they already contain values. If `false`, any preexisting value in `langField` will be copied to `langsField` if whitelisted (`langid.whitelist`).	Boolean	`false`
`langid.threshold`	Specifies a threshold value between `0` and `1` that the language identification score must reach before being accepted. With longer text fields, a high threshold such as `0.8` will yield better results. For shorter text fields, you may need to lower the threshold.	Float	`0.5`
`langid.whitelist`	Specifies a list of allowed language identification codes. If you specify `langid.map`, you can use the whitelist to ensure that you only index documents into fields that exist in your schema.	String	–
`langid.map`	Enables field name mapping. If `true`, Solr will map the content for each field specified in `langid.fl` to a new language-specific field. The new field will be in the format `fieldname_xx`, where xx is the identified language code.	Boolean	`false`
`langid.map.fl`	A comma-separated list of fields for `langid.map` to be used instead of all fields in the `langid.fl`.	String	–

Table 14.4 Available parameters for Solr's language-identification update processors *(continued)*

Parameter	Description	Type	Default
`langid.map.keepOrig`	If `true`, Solr will leave a copy of the content in the original field in addition to the version moved to the language-specific field.	Boolean	`false`
`langid.map .individual`	If `true`, Solr will detect and map languages for each field individually. Set this if you have different languages per field and want to use those instead of the global document language(s).	Boolean	`false`
`langid.map .individual.fl`	A comma-separated list of fields for use with `langid.map.individual` that's different than the fields specified in `langid.fl`. If set, only fields in this list will be mapped based upon their individual languages, and the remaining fields from `langid.fl` will be mapped using the global document language(s).	String	
`langid .fallbackFields`	Specifies one or more fields to check (in order) for a fallback language value in case no language is detected that meets the `langid.threshold` score, or the detected language is not in the `langid.whitelist`. If no appropriate fallback languages are found, Solr will use the language code specified in `langid.fallback`.	String	–
`langid.fallback`	Specifies a language code to use if no language is detected or if no language is found in `langid.fallbackFields`. If no fallback is defined, the final language code will be an empty string, which could cause unexpected behavior.	String	–
`langid.map.lcmap`	Allows you to map language codes to your own chosen field prefixes. The format is `ja:cjk zh:cjk ko:cjk`. This example maps Japanese, Chinese, and Korean to a field in the format `<fieldname>_cjk`.	String	–
`langid.map.pattern &` `langid.map.replace`	Allows you to override the default field name format for mapping to language-specific fields. By default, fields are mapped to `<fieldname>_<language>`. `Pattern` is a Java Regex Pattern, and `replace` is a Java Regex Replace. The `<language>` value will be replaced with the mapped extension for the identified language.	Java Regular Expression/ Replace	–

Table 14.4   Available parameters for Solr's language-identification update processors *(continued)*

Parameter	Description	Type	Default
langid .enforceSchema	If `false`, the update processor does not vali- date field names against your schema. This may be useful if you're creating temporary fields and plan to rename or delete them later.	Boolean	true

You have seen how to perform basic language identification (listing 14.12), and table 14.4 demonstrates the additional capabilities and flexibility that Solr's language-identification update processors provide. If you're trying to implement multilingual search using the separate-field-per-language approach described in section 14.6.1, automatically mapping your content into language-specific fields is easy to pull off without any coding required. The next listing demonstrates how to configure several options from table 14.4 to have Solr automatically map incoming content to identified language-specific fields.

Listing 14.13   Automatic mapping of content into language-specific fields

SolrConfig.xml

```
...
<updateRequestProcessorChain name="langid">
  <processor class="org.apache.solr.update.processor.
    LangDetectLanguageIdentifierUpdateProcessorFactory">
    <lst name="invariants">
      <str name="langid.fl">content</str>
      <str name="langid.langField">language</str>
      <str name="langid.map">true</str>
      <str name="langid.map.fl">content</str>
      <str name="langid.whitelist">en,es,fr</str>
      <str name="langid.map.lcmap">en:english es:spanish fr:french</str>
      <str name="langid.fallback">en</str>
    </lst>
  </processor>
  ...
</updateRequestProcessorChain>
...
<requestHandler name="/update" class="solr.UpdateRequestHandler">
  <lst name="invariants">
    <str name="update.chain">langid</str>
  </lst>
</requestHandler>
...
```

Schema.xml

```
...
<field name="language" type="string" indexed="true" stored="true" />
...
<dynamicField name="*_english" type="text_english" indexed="true"
    stored="true" multiValued="true"/>
<dynamicField name="*_spanish" type="text_spanish" indexed="true"
    stored="true" multiValued="true"/>
```

```
<dynamicField name="*_french" type="text_french" indexed="true"
    stored="true" multiValued="true"/>
```

...

This listing indicates that both the `title` and the `content` fields should be used to identify the language for the document, but that only the `content` field should be mapped to a language-specific field. A whitelist was also specified to include only three languages: `fr`, `en`, and `es`.

For demonstration purposes, dynamic fields were created such that content for these languages would be mapped to the `content_french`, `content_english`, or `content_spanish` field, depending upon which language is identified. If you stick with the default dynamic field extensions for these languages found in Solr's example *schema.xml*, you would not have to provide the custom `langid.map.lcmap` parameter to explicitly map the field extensions for these languages. The next listing shows this language detection configuration in action.

> **Listing 14.14 Language detection mapping content to language-specific fields**

Sending documents

```
cd $SOLR_IN_ACTION/example-docs/
java -Durl=http://localhost:8983/solr/langid2/update
    -jar post.jar ch14/documents/langid.xml
```

The original content maps to one language-specific field per document.

Query

```
http://localhost:8983/solr/langid2/select?
  q=id:[1 TO 3]&
  fl=title,language,content_english,content_spanish,content_french&
  defType=edismax&
  qf=content_english content_spanish content_french
```

Use the eDisMax query parser for any real keyword queries.

Results

```
{
  "responseHeader":{
    "status":0,
    "QTime":0},
  "response":{"numFound":3,"start":0,"docs":[
      {
        "title":"The Adventures of Huckleberry Finn",
        "language":"en",
        "content_english":["YOU don't know about me without..."]},
      {
        "title":"Les Misérables",
        "language":"fr",
        "content_french":["Nul n'aurait pu le dire; tout ce..."]},
      {
        "title":"Don Quixote",
        "language":"es",
        "content_spanish":["Demasiada cordura puede ser la peor..."]}]
    }}
```

The original content maps to one language-specific field per document.

As you can see, Solr's language-identifier update processor chains provide great support for automatically identifying languages for a field-per-language multilingual

approach. In this case, each of the documents matching our example query was originally indexed with a content field, but once its language was identified for each
document, the content was moved to a language-specific field. By using the eDisMax
query parser to search across each of the fields as discussed in section 14.6.1, you can
completely delegate the complexity of detecting and searching across multiple languages to Solr in a field-per-language configuration. If you're considering one of the
other two approaches to multilingual search mentioned in this chapter, redirecting
content to a separate Solr core for a language-per-core setup would unfortunately be
extremely difficult, because content would either have to be sent to every core and discarded in the cores in which it doesn't belong or would have to be forwarded from
one Solr core to another after language detection—something there is no direct support for today. What about supporting the multiple-languages-per-field approach?
This can be pulled off fairly easily with a little bit of extra code.

14.7.2 *Dynamically assigning detected language analyzers within a field*

There's not much fundamentally different between identifying languages and mapping them to different fields versus identifying languages and mapping them (as
prefixes) to the same field. This can be accomplished by extending LangDetect-
LanguageIdentifierUpdateProcessor and making some fairly simple changes. This
listing demonstrates an extended update processor made for this purpose.

Listing 14.15   LanguageIdentifierUpdateProcessor for MultiTextField

```
public class MultiTextLanguageIdentifierUpdateProcessor
    extends LangDetectLanguageIdentifierUpdateProcessor {

  private static String MULTI_TEXT_FIELD_LANGID = "mtf-langid";
  private static String PREPEND_GRANULARITY =
      MULTI_TEXT_FIELD_LANGID + ".prependGranularity";
  private final static String HIDE_PREPENDED_LANGS =
      MULTI_TEXT_FIELD_LANGID + ".hidePrependedLangs";

  private enum PrependGranularities { document, field, fieldValue }

  private static String PREPEND_FIELDS =
      MULTI_TEXT_FIELD_LANGID + ".prependFields";

  protected IndexSchema indexSchema;
  protected Collection<String> prependFields = new LinkedHashSet<String>();
  private PrependGranularities prependGranularity =
      PrependGranularities.document;
  private Boolean hidePrependedLangs = true;

  public MultiTextFieldLanguageIdentifierUpdateProcessor(SolrQueryRequest req,
      SolrQueryResponse rsp, UpdateRequestProcessor next) {
    super(req, rsp, next);
    indexSchema = req.getSchema();
    initParams(req.getParams());
  }
```

```
        private void initParams(SolrParams params) {
          //Default parameter initialization ... accompanying source code
        }

        @Override
        protected SolrInputDocument process(SolrInputDocument doc) {

          SolrInputDocument outputDocument = super.process(doc);

          Collection<String> fieldNames = new ArrayList<String>();
          for (String nextFieldName : outputDocument.getFieldNames()) {
            fieldNames.add(nextFieldName);
          }

          List<DetectedLanguage> documentLangs =
              this.detectLanguage(this.concatFields(doc, this.inputFields));

          for (String nextFieldName : this.prependFields) {
            if (indexSchema.getFieldOrNull(nextFieldName) != null) {
              if (indexSchema.getField(nextFieldName).getType()
                  instanceof MultiTextField) {
                outputDocument = detectAndPrependLanguages(
                    outputDocument, nextFieldName, documentLangs);
              } ...
            }
          }

          return outputDocument;
        }

        protected SolrInputDocument detectAndPrependLanguages(
            SolrInputDocument doc,
            String multiTextFieldName,
            List<DetectedLanguage> documentLangs){

          MultiTextField mtf = (MultiTextField) indexSchema
              .getFieldType(multiTextFieldName);
          MultiTextFieldAnalyzer mtfAnalyzer = (MultiTextFieldAnalyzer) mtf
              .getAnalyzer();

          List<DetectedLanguage> fieldLangs = null;
          if (this.prependGranularity == PrependGranularities.field
              || this.prependGranularity == PrependGranularities.fieldValue) {

            fieldLangs = this.detectLanguage(
                this.concatFields(doc, new String[] { multiTextFieldName }));
          }

          if (fieldLangs == null || fieldLangs.size() == 0) {
            fieldLangs = documentLangs;
          }

          SolrInputField inputField = doc.getField(multiTextFieldName);
          SolrInputField outputField = new SolrInputField(inputField.getName());
          if (inputField.getValues() != null) {
            for (final Object inputValue : inputField.getValues()) {
              Object outputValue = inputValue;
```

Process all fields marked for prepending languages.

Detect languages at a document level.

Detect languages at a field level if requested.

```
                List<DetectedLanguage> fieldValueLangs = null;
                if (this.prependGranularity == PrependGranularities.fieldValue) {
                  if (inputValue instanceof String) {
                    fieldValueLangs = this.detectLanguage(inputValue.toString());
                  }
                }

                if (fieldValueLangs == null || fieldValueLangs.size() == 0) {
                  fieldValueLangs = fieldLangs;
                }

                LinkedHashSet<String> langsToPrepend = new LinkedHashSet<String>();
                for (DetectedLanguage lang : fieldValueLangs) {
                  langsToPrepend.add(lang.getLangCode());
                }

                StringBuilder fieldLangsPrefix = new StringBuilder();
                for (String lang : langsToPrepend) {
                  if (mtfAnalyzer.Settings.ignoreMissingMappings
                      || mtfAnalyzer.Settings.fieldMappings.containsKey(lang)
                      || indexSchema.getFieldOrNull(lang) != null) {

                    if (fieldLangsPrefix.length() > 0) {
                      fieldLangsPrefix.append(
                          mtfAnalyzer.Settings.multiKeyDelimiter);
                    }

                    fieldLangsPrefix.append(lang);
                  }
                }

                if (fieldLangsPrefix.length() > 0) {
                  fieldLangsPrefix.append(
                      mtfAnalyzer.Settings.keyFromTextDelimiter);
                }

                if (this.hidePrependedLangs) {
                  fieldLangsPrefix.insert(0, '[');
                  fieldLangsPrefix.append(']');
                }

                outputValue = fieldLangsPrefix + (String) outputValue;
                outputField.addValue(outputValue, 1.0F);
              }
            }
            outputField.setBoost(inputField.getBoost());
            doc.removeField(multiTextFieldName);
            doc.put(multiTextFieldName, outputField);
            return doc;
          }
```

Detect languages for each field value (in multivalued field).

Build the (detected) languages prefix to prepend.

Special syntax to not store prepended languages.

New field containing languages prefix replaces original field.

The `MultiTextFieldLanguageIdentifierUpdateProcessor` extends the `LangDetect-LanguageIdentifierUpdateProcessor` and adds the language prefixes into the content of the fields for which it's detecting languages. The following listing shows how you would configure this update processor using the accompanying `MultiTextField-LanguageIdentifierUpdateProcessorFactory` (not shown, but in the downloadable chapter code).

Listing 14.16   Configuring the `MultiText` language identifier in *solrconfig.xml*

```
<requestHandler name="/update" class="solr.UpdateRequestHandler">
  <lst name="invariants">
    <str name="update.chain">multi-langid</str>
  </lst>
</requestHandler>

<updateRequestProcessorChain name="multi-langid">
  <processor class=
      "sia.ch14.MultiTextFieldLanguageIdentifierUpdateProcessorFactory">
    <lst name="invariants">
      <str name="langid.fl">title,content</str>
      <str name="langid.langField">language</str>
      <str name="langid.whitelist">en,es,fr</str>
      <str name="langid.fallback">en</str>
    </lst>
    <lst name="defaults">
      <str name="mtf-langid.prependFields">content</str>
      <str name="mtf-langid.prependGranularity">fieldValue</str>
      <str name="mtf-langid.hidePrependedLangs">false</str>
    </lst>
  </processor>
  <processor class="solr.LogUpdateProcessorFactory" />
  <processor class="solr.RunUpdateProcessorFactory" />
</updateRequestProcessorChain>
```

The new supported settings include the ability to specify the list of fields which should have detected languages prepended automatically (`mtf-langid.prependFields`); the ability to specify whether language detection should happen per document, per field, or per field value (for multivalued fields) by setting the `mtf-langid.prepend-Granularity` equal to `document`, `field`, or `fieldValue`; and the ability to prevent the prepended languages from appearing in the stored version of your field. The following listing demonstrates how you would index example documents into Solr using the configuration from listing 14.16.

Listing 14.17   Indexing documents with the `MultiText` language identifier

Sending documents
```
cd $SOLR_IN_ACTION/example-docs/
java -Durl=http://localhost:8983/solr/multi-langid/update
  ➥ -jar post.jar ch14/documents/multi-langid.xml
```

Query
```
http://localhost:8983/solr/multi-langid/select?
  q=*:*&
  df=content&
  fl=title,content,language
```

Results
```
{
  "responseHeader":{
    "status":0,
```

```
  "QTime":0},
"response":{"numFound":4,"start":0,"docs":[
  {
    "title":"The Adventures of Huckleberry Finn",
    "language":"en",
    "content":["en|YOU don't know about me without..."]},
  {
    "title":"Les Misérables",
    "language":"fr",
    "content":["fr|Nul n'aurait pu le dire; tout ce..."]},
  {
    "title":"Don Quixote",
    "language":"es",
    "content":["es|Demasiada cordura puede ser la peor..."]},
  {
    "title":"Proverbs",
    "language":"es",
    "content":[
      "es|No la abandones y ella velará sobre ti...",
      "en|Do not forsake wisdom, and she will protect you...",
      "fr|N'abandonne pas la sagesse, et elle te gardera... "]}]
}}
```

Each field's value is prefixed with the identified languages.

Languages are identified for each entry in the field (prependGranularity =fieldValue).

As you can see, the `content` field for each document was prepended with the detected language of its text. This occurred because the `content` field is defined as a `MultiText` field and because listing 14.16 specified that the `content` field should have languages prepended (`mtf-langid.prependFields`). Additionally, you'll notice that languages were identified for each entry in the last document. Because the prepend granularity requested was per `fieldValue` and the `content` field is a multivalued field, this caused each separate entry for the field to have its language identified separately. The executed query was a wide-open search, but you could execute any query using the syntax demonstrated in listing 14.17 for the `MultiTextField`.

One parameter we did not make use of in our example configuration in listing 14.16 is `mtf-langid.hidePrependedLangs`. This parameter enables you to separate out the stored value from the value to be indexed in your `MultiTextFields`. By setting this value to `true`, the `content` field will continue to have the language codes prepended to the indexed version of the field (for the `MultiTextField` to process), but it will not add the language codes to the stored version of the field. The following listing demonstrates sending the same document to Solr with the `mtf-langid.hidePrependedLangs` value set to `true`.

Listing 14.18   Prepending detected languages without modifying stored values

Sending documents
```
cd $SOLR_IN_ACTION/example-docs/
java -Durl=http://localhost:8983/solr/multi-langid/update
  ➥?mtf-langid.hidePrependedLangs=true
  ➥ -jar post.jar ch14/documents/multi-langid.xml
```

Override the default of false to turn on hiding of prepended languages.

Query

```
http://localhost:8983/solr/multi-langid/select?
  q=en,es,fr|abandon&
  df=content&
  fl=title,content,language
```

The language prefixes are not stored, but stemming is still working as expected in each language.

Results

```
{
  "responseHeader":{
    "status":0,
    "QTime":0},
  "response":{"numFound":4,"start":0,"docs":[
      {
        "title":"Proverbs",
        "language":"es",
        "content":[
          "No la abandones y ella velará sobre ti...",
          "Do not forsake wisdom, and she will protect you...",
          "N'abandonne pas la sagesse, et elle te gardera... "]}]
  }}
```

The language prefixes are not stored, but stemming is still working as expected in each language.

You can see that even though the language prefixes are not stored, stemming is nevertheless working as expected, with the terms abandones (Spanish) and abandonne (French) both stemming down to the term abandon in the index. (You could add the parameters facet=true&facet.field=content to your query to inspect each of the indexed stems.) This can provide the best of both worlds: multilingual text analysis based upon dynamically detected languages without requiring the incoming content to be modified in any way for the stored value (returned in results and used in highlighting). The details of how it's possible to store a different value than the value being indexed are fairly involved and are not important within the context of this chapter. (You can explore the code yourself if you're curious.) What is useful to understand is that the way this feature is exposed in the MultiTextField is through wrapping the language prefix in square brackets. For example, instead of passing in es|no la abandones… (which would both index and store the language prefix), if we pass in [es|]no la abandones… then this will instruct the MultiTextField to only index but not store the language prefix. If you refer to the code in listing 14.15, you will see where this special square bracket syntax is being inserted when mtf-langid.hidePrependedLanguages is set to true. If you're not using automatic language detection, feel free to still pass in this special square bracket syntax yourself to accomplish the same effect.

There are many ways to combine the built-in language handling and analysis capabilities in Solr, and hopefully this chapter has provided a good overview of what is available in Solr and how you can easily extend it to fit your needs.

14.8 Summary

The ability to handle full-text searching across content in many languages is one area in which Solr shines. Whether you use the built-in Lucene stemmers or find some other open source or commercial lemmatization libraries, the ability to find shortened forms of words in a language-specific way can greatly improve the Recall of your search application. This chapter covered common techniques for handling language variations, including many language-specific `Tokenizer` and `TokenFilter` configurations. It also demonstrated three techniques for handling multilingual content: field-per-language, core-per-language, and multiple-languages-per-field. Although the field-per-language approach is the most supported out of the box with Solr, it can lead to slower queries as the number of fields searched per query grows, and it effectively forces you to use a version of the DisMax query parser for all of your queries. The core-per-language approach allows for better query speed as you scale out to handle multiple languages, but it presents a fair amount of server management overhead due to managing multiple Solr cores, and it does not integrate well with automatic language identification inside of Solr.

The chapter also demonstrated creating a custom `FieldType`, `Analyzer`, and `Tokenizer` that are able to dynamically handle multiple languages per field. This is the most flexible of the three options and scales well, but the implementation is complex, and the query syntax can be cumbersome because it requires prefixing each term with the list of languages in which it should be processed. The chapter wrapped up with a demonstration of language identification of documents, including automatic mapping of content to language-specific fields and code to integrate language identification with the multiple-languages-per-field approach. At this point, you should have a large number of tools at your fingertips to implement a great multilingual search experience.

Complex query operations

This chapter covers

- Using and creating your own function queries
- Geospatial searching
- Multilevel pivot faceting
- Referencing external data sources in queries
- Utilizing Solr for big data analytics

Although Solr serves as a powerful text search engine, finding and returning documents based upon keywords is far from its only common use. You have seen many of Solr's core document search capabilities—such as rich text analysis, hit highlighting, and results grouping—that enhance the relevancy and usefulness of the list of results returned for a query. Although presenting the specific documents that best match a query is important for many search applications, another common use case for Solr is reporting aggregate results for data analytics capabilities. Pivot faceting, Solr's ability to return multiple levels of hierarchical facet results, enables the computation of an arbitrary number of aggregate breakdowns in a single Solr request, making Solr efficient for use in data analytics reporting.

Another of Solr's key features is its ability to execute functions upon data at query time, the results of which can be used to filter out documents, enhance relevancy calculations, sort results, and append dynamically generated content to the fields returned for each document. Solr also has robust geospatial searching capabilities, which enable polygon searching over points and shapes, enabling features like geographic radius searching on latitude/longitude coordinates and boosting relevancy or sorting based upon proximity to some location.

At times, it may also be useful or necessary to reference content external to the set of documents as part of a query. Solr includes the ability to include fields in documents that reference external files; it also includes the ability to perform basic join operations on foreign key fields of documents in any Solr core located in the same Solr instance. Each of these complex data operations will be demonstrated in this chapter, highlighting Solr's strengths (and a few weaknesses) as a data analytics engine suitable for building far more than a traditional text search and retrieval application.

15.1   Function queries

Functions in Solr allow you to dynamically compute values for each document instead of only dealing with the static values set for a field at index time. *Function queries* are special queries that can be added like keywords to a query, but which match all documents and return their function calculation as the score, just as a traditional keyword would yield a relevancy score. By using function queries, the results of a function calculation can be used to modify the relevancy score calculation and/or to sort the search results. The computed function calculation can also be returned on each document as a dynamically added field for use in your application layer. Functions can also be *nested*, meaning that the output of one function can be used as one of the inputs of another function, enabling functions to be nested arbitrarily deeply.

15.1.1   Function syntax

The standard function syntax in Solr specifies a function's name, followed by an opening parenthesis, zero or more comma-separated input parameters, and a closing parenthesis:

```
functionName()
functionName(input1)
functionName(input1, input2)
functionName(input1, input2, ... inputN)
```

The inputs to a function can be any of the following:

- *A constant* (a numeric or string literal)
  Syntax: `100`, `1.45`, `"hello world"`
- *A field*
  Syntax: `fieldName`, `field(fieldName)`
- *Another function*
  Syntax: `functionName(...)`
- *A parameter substitution*
  Syntax: `q={!func}min($f1,$f2)&f1=sqrt(popularity)&f2=1`

Although perhaps confusing at first, the Solr documentation defines each of these input parameter types as functions themselves. Most functions follow standard function syntax, but the constant function, field function, and parameter substitution are special cases that support a simplified syntax. The syntax for a constant function is the value itself; the syntax for a field function is the name of the field, optionally wrapped in a function named `field`; and the syntax for a substituted parameter is `$parameter`, where `parameter` references a query string parameter from the request URL. All other functions use the standard function syntax.

Because all inputs to a function are considered functions themselves (even if the input is a constant function), the standard function syntax could be simplified conceptually to `functionName(function1, ... functionN)`. Assuming the `fieldContaining-Number` field on a document contains the value -99, consider the following functions:

```
max(2, fieldContainingNumber)                        Result: 2
max(fieldContainingNumber, 2)                        Result: 2
max(2, -99)                                          Result: 2
max(-99, 2)                                          Result: 2
max(2, field(fieldContainingNumber))                Result: 2
max(field(fieldContainingNumber), add(1,1))         Result: 2
```

Notice that each function is able to easily swap out the field function for a constant function or even another standard function. Although the order and means of calculating the input parameters is different for each example, they all ultimately find the maximum value between -99 and 2. One of the key benefits to treating every function input as another function is that it allows arbitrarily complex computations by combining functions in interesting ways.

Not all functions accept the same types of input parameters. Some expect the constant value input to be a string; others expect an integer or floating-point value. Take the following examples, assuming `fieldContainingString` holds the value "hallo":

```
strdist("hello", fieldContainingString, edit)     Result: 0.8
strdist("hello", "hallo", "edit")                 Result: 0.8
```

The `strdist` function calculates a similarity of two strings, based upon a specific algorithm (defined by the third parameter, in this case the constant function with a string literal value of "edit" or just edit). What happens if you pass the wrong type into the previous function?

```
strdist("hello", 1000, edit)                      Result: 0
strdist(1000, "1000", edit)                       Result: 1
strdist("1001", 1000, edit)                       Result: 0.75
```

Although you might expect this function to throw an exception, you will see that it instead marshals the constant values into the appropriate types, in this case converting the numeric constant of 1000 into a string of "1000". In many cases, this kind of marshaling is not possible (for example, how do you safely convert a string into a numeric type?). In these cases, you will generally receive an exception back from Solr, so it's important to be mindful that even though the function-nesting syntax is generic, not all functions can be successfully combined.

> ### Firing up this chapter's preconfigured examples
>
> As in the previous chapter, the configuration files for this chapter's examples have been preconfigured in separate Solr cores to allow you to start up Solr one time and easily navigate through all of the chapter's examples. To get Solr immediately up and running with all of the chapter's examples available, execute the following:
>
> ```
> cd $SOLR_INSTALL/example/
> cp -r $SOLR_IN_ACTION/example-docs/ch15/cores/ solr/
> cp $SOLR_IN_ACTION/solr-in-action.jar solr/lib/
> java -jar start.jar
> ```
>
> The *solr-in-action.jar* file contains most of the dependencies needed for this chapter's examples. There is one additional external dependency (on the Java Topology Suite) that will require extra setup, but we will cover this later in the chapter when discussing Solr's geospatial capabilities.

Solr's generic implementation of functions enables them to be used across a wide variety of key Solr features. Functions can affect relevancy, can be used to filter results, can be sorted upon, can have their values returned on documents, and can even be faceted upon. The next few sections will dive into these use cases.

15.1.2 *Searching on functions*

When you perform a typical keyword search in Solr, each keyword is looked up in the inverted index, and a relevancy score is calculated to determine how relevant each document is in matching that keyword. (See chapter 3 for an overview of this process.) A query is not limited to searching on terms only, though; you can insert a function query into your query and have it behave as another keyword. To demonstrate this, let's index sample documents to a news Solr core:

```
cd $SOLR_IN_ACTION/example-docs/
java -Durl=http://localhost:8983/solr/news/update
    ➥ -jar post.jar ch15/documents/news.xml
```

With the documents indexed, we can now demonstrate the inclusion of a function along with keywords in the main user query:

```
http://localhost:8983/solr/news/select?
  q="United States" AND France AND President AND
    _val_:"recip(ord(date),1,100,100)"
```

This query runs a Boolean search for the keywords "United States", France, and President, and a function that returns a value between 1 and 100 based upon how old a matching document is (the newer the document, the higher the value). There are three important things to note about this query:

1. The syntax _val_:"value" is used to inject a function query (utilizing nested recip and ord functions, which will be described in section 15.1.5) as a term in the main user query.

2 A function query, by default, matches *all* documents. In the previous example, the query will be limited to all documents containing the terms `"United States"`, `France`, and `President`, but the additional term (the function query) will not change the total number of results that the query matches.

3 The relevancy score of a query is the sum of the scores for each term in a query. The terms `"United States"`, `France`, and `President` will have scores calculated based upon their tf-idf similarity calculation (see chapter 3 [section 3.2]), but the score for the function query is the calculated value of the function itself.

Based upon these three points, you can see that the example function query serves the purpose of boosting the relevancy score higher for newer documents. Internally, the newest document will have 100 added to its relevancy score, the oldest will have a value of 1 added to its relevancy score, and the rest of the documents will fall somewhere in between. Note that the final score for each document is normalized, which means you will not see 100 added to the final score of each document; what you will see is more recent documents showing up higher relative to where they did before. If you remove the function from our example query, you will be able to see this in the ordering of results returned from Solr.

You can imagine applying similar relevancy boosts based upon geographical distance, popularity, or some other calculation. Chapter 16 will cover a few of these relevancy boosting use cases in more detail.

Hooking a function into a query

Functions are pervasive in Solr. They can be used to boost the relevancy of the user query (`q` parameter), used in specialized boost parameters in different query parsers (such as the `bf` parameter in the eDisMax query parser), used as part of an applied filter, used to sort documents, and used to return dynamically calculated values with documents. These will all be covered in this (or the next) chapter, but it's useful to understand how a function query is invoked inside a query.

In this section, you've seen the `_val_:"functionName(…)"` syntax, which can be inserted anywhere inside the query as if it were a keyword. You may remember from chapter 7 that Solr includes a function query parser, which can be invoked using local params: `{!func}functionName(…)`. Both options are valid and should have the same effect: adding the value of the function as a term in the query whose score is the value of the function. As such, all of the following are equivalent:

- *Value hook:*
  `q=solr AND _val_:"add(1, boostField)"`

- *Query parser hook (explicit nested query):*
  `q=solr AND _query_:"{!func}add(1, boostField)"`

- *Query parser hook (implicit nested query):*
  `q=solr AND {!func v="add(1, boostField)"}`

(continued)

Each form yields the same end result, but the variations are listed here so that you will not be confused when you see them throughout this (and the next) chapter and in Solr examples and documentation elsewhere.

Although adding a function to a query seems useful for modifying the relevancy scores of documents matching a query, the fact that a function query by default matches all documents makes it somewhat less useful if your intention is to filter out results which do not fall within the range of suitable results from a function calculation. Thankfully, Solr provides a special Function Range query parser that enables such a use case.

FRANGE QUERY PARSER

If you need to filter results down to only documents that yield specific values for a function calculation, the *Function Range query parser* (frange for short) is likely your solution. A frange filter works by executing a specified function query, then filtering out documents whose value for the function do not fall between a requested lower and upper limit. To demonstrate this capability, we'll use a function to calculate sales tax on a product, so we'll first need to add documents to our salestax Solr core:

```
java -Durl=http://localhost:8983/solr/salestax/update
    -jar post.jar ch15/documents/salestax.xml
```

To see a frange filter in action, look at the following query:

```
http://localhost:8983/solr/salestax/select?q=*:*&
    fq={!frange l=10 u=15}product(basePrice, sum(1, $userSalesTax))&
    userSalesTax=0.07
```

This query calculates the total price of an item on the fly by accepting a userSalesTax parameter and adding the sales tax to the base price of a product defined in the base-Price field. The frange query parser filters out all documents whose total calculated price is not between the lower bound of 10 and upper bound of 15, defined by the l (lower) and u (upper) local parameters. The lower and upper bounds are inclusive by default, which means that if you want to only match documents containing a specific value, you can set the same value for the l and u parameters. The lower and upper bounds are also optional; you do not have to limit values in both directions. If necessary, you can also set the incll (include lower) and inclu (include upper) local parameters to false for a frange query, which will make the filtered results exclusive of the lower and upper limits.

As you can probably tell, the ability to limit result sets to only documents which match your own arbitrarily complex functions provides an incredibly flexible tool for query customization. Section 15.1.6 will demonstrate how to write code to add your own custom function to Solr, providing the ultimate extension point for manipulating your data inside of Solr. Now that you know how to search on functions and understand how function scores are calculated, it's time to dive into how the dynamically calculated function scores can be used in place of static field values.

15.1.3 *Returning functions like fields*

In section 15.1.1, you saw that all function inputs—constants and fields, among them—are ultimately themselves considered functions for the purpose of the function query syntax. This being the case, it seems it should also be possible to substitute functions in place of fields in other places in Solr, because functions and fields both ultimately return a value.

Indeed, not only can you calculate a value per document for each function, you can also return that calculated value with your documents as a *pseudo-field* that looks like any other field. Referring back to the sales tax example from section 15.1.2, let's craft a request that will calculate the total price of the item in each document and return it along with the other fields:

```
http://localhost:8983/solr/salestax/select?q=*:*&
  userSalesTax=0.07&
  fl=id,basePrice,product(basePrice, sum(1, $userSalesTax))
```

What will the results of this request look like? For a document containing only an `id` and a `basePrice` field, the results will look as follows:

```
{
    "id":"1",
    "basePrice":10.0,
    "product(basePrice, sum(1, $userSalesTax)":10.700001
}
```

As you can see, by adding a function to the list of fields requested, a new field has been added to the document. This isn't a real field stored in the index, but it's nevertheless returned on the document like any of the stored fields would be.

One suboptimal characteristic of the last example is that the name of the pseudo-field being returned on the document is the function syntax used to calculate the value. Parsing this and mapping it back to a useful name can be painful in whatever application is calling Solr. Thankfully, Solr allows aliasing the pseudo-field name for the returned value to any name of your choosing, as shown in the next listing.

Listing 15.1 Returning function calculations in a pseudo-field

Query
```
http://localhost:8983/solr/salestax/select?q=*:*&
  userSalesTax=0.07&
  fl=id,basePrice,totalPrice:product(basePrice, sum(1, $userSalesTax))   ◁─┐
```

> Requests a pseudo-field which will calculate base price + sales tax.

Response
```
{
    {
      "id":"1",
      "basePrice":10.0,
      "totalPrice":10.700001      ◁─┐
    }
}
```

> The new "totalPrice" field is populated on returned documents.

The name of the dynamically added pseudo-field, `totalPrice`, is defined based upon the syntax `totalPrice:product(basePrice, sum(1, $userSalesTax))`, where the pseudo-field name precedes the colon, and the function to calculate the pseudo-field value comes after the colon. This makes it easy to return a function calculation as if it were a real field in your documents. In fact, it's even possible to override a real field with a dynamically calculated field if you so choose. You can imagine a use case where you want to return different values from Solr for the same field under different use cases; for example, blanking out a field based upon user access privileges or modifying a value if you need to provide different translations of content for different markets. Through the use of functions, you have the ability to manipulate the values of any field before it's returned in your search results. Not only can you modify the fields in the documents returned based upon functions, it's also possible to modify the order of documents returned through sorting on functions.

15.1.4 *Sorting on functions*

In the previous section, you saw that calculated results of functions can be added to documents as fields to be returned in search results. This is possible because a `Value-Source` (your function query) is generating `DocValues` (a map of each document to its value) holding the calculated values for each document. You have already seen how to use calculated function values to filter your result set, modify the relevancy of documents, and add or modify the fields and values returned for a search request. Next, we will cover how to sort your search results based upon calculated function values.

The syntax for sorting on a function is no different than sorting on a field, except that the full function syntax (or dereferenced parameters containing the full function syntax) stands in place of a field name:

```
http://localhost:8983/solr/salestax/select?q=*:*&
   userSalesTax=0.07&
   sort=product(basePrice, sum(1, $userSalesTax)) asc, score desc
```

This request sorts by the earlier described total price calculation (lowest price to highest), and then from highest score to lowest for documents of the same price. You can certainly combine all of the methods we've described into a more complex query:

```
http://localhost:8983/solr/salestax/select?
   q=_query_:"{!func}recip(ord(date),1,100,100)"&
   userSalesTax=0.07&
   totalPriceFunc=product(basePrice, sum(1, $userSalesTax))&
   fq={!frange l=10 u=15 v=$totalPriceFunc}&
   fl=*,totalPrice:$totalPriceFunc&
   sort=$totalPriceFunc asc, score desc
```

This request uses a dereferenced (pulled out as a separate variable) `userSalesTax` parameter, passes it to a dereferenced `totalPriceFunc` parameter, and reuses the `total-PriceFunc` parameter in a filter (using the `frange` query parser), in the returned field list, and as the first sort in ascending order. Because a separate function was defined in the query to boost more recent documents, the second part of the sort (score desc) will result in all documents with the same price ordered by most recent first.

At this point, you have all of the important tools necessary to intelligently use functions in your search application. What we still need to cover, however, is the large collection of functions available in Solr.

15.1.5 *Available functions in Solr*

Up to this point, you have seen how to make use of functions, with a few specific examples of the kinds of functions available in Solr. Because the full list of available Solr functions is long and constantly growing, we will not cover the syntax of all of them in this chapter, but you can refer to the most up-to-date list on the Solr Wiki at http://wiki.apache.org/solr/FunctionQuery. We will cover the overall types of functions, which should give you a good high-level overview of what is available. There are a few major categories of functions in Solr: data transformation, math, relevancy, and Boolean.

DATA-TRANSFORMATION FUNCTIONS

Many of the commonly used functions in Solr serve to transform data from one format into another. The function map(x, min, max, target), for example, enables you to replace the value of x with the value of target if x falls between min and max. If a field named price is supposed to only contain values greater than 10.00, then you could map all values between 0 and 10.00 to the minimum price of 10.00 using the function map(price, 0, 10, 10). Table 15.1 demonstrates several other useful data-transformation functions.

Table 15.1 Available data-transformation functions in Solr

Function syntax	Description
def(x, y)	Returns the value of x if x exists, otherwise returns the value of y.
field(fieldName)	Returns the field value of an indexed field with a maximum of one value per document for the field.
map(x, min, max, target) map(x, min, max, target, else)	Returns target if x falls between min and max exclusive. If specified (optional), else will be returned otherwise.
ms(time2, time1) ms(time1) ms()	Returns time2 - time1. If time2 is not specified, it's NOW. If time1 is not specified, it's the Unix Epoch of 1/1/1970.
ord(fieldName)	Returns the position of the term in the search index (one term per field per document), from 1 to the number of unique terms in the index.
rord(fieldName)	Returns the reverse ordering of the ord function.

Table 15.1   Available data-transformation functions in Solr *(continued)*

Function syntax	Description
scale(x, number1, number2)	Scales the values of x in each document between number1 and number2 based upon the min and max value of x across all documents.
top(x)	Forces the calculated values to be derived from the top-level IndexReader instead of per-segment IndexReaders. Useful for functions that need to consider values from other documents (such as the ord and rord functions, which implicitly use the top function).

MATH FUNCTIONS

Some of the most common data analysis operations in Solr involve mathematical functions. Although the basics (addition, subtraction, multiplication, and division) are among the most commonly used, Solr supports a full range of operations, even including trigonometric functions. Table 15.2 demonstrates available mathematical functions in Solr.

Table 15.2   Available mathematical functions in Solr

Function syntax	Description
abs(x)	Absolute value of x.
acos(x)	Arc cosine of x.
asin(x)	Arc sine of x.
atan(x)	Arc tangent of x.
atan2(x,y)	Returns the angle resulting from the conversion of the rectangular coordinates x, y to polar coordinates.
cbrt(x)	Cubed root of x.
ceil(x)	Rounds the number x up to the next integer.
cos(x)	Cosine of angle x.
cosh(x)	Hyperbolic cosine of x.
deg(x)	Converts x radians to degrees.
div(x,y)	Divides x by y.
e()	Returns an approximation to Euler's number, the base of the natural logarithm.
exp(x)	Euler's number raised to the power of x.
floor(x)	Rounds the number x down to the last integer.
hypo(x,y)	Returns the hypotenuse of a right angle: $sqrt(x^2+y^2)$.
linear(m,x,b)	Returns the value of a linear function in the form f(x) = m*x + b.

Table 15.2 Available mathematical functions in Solr *(continued)*

Function syntax	Description
`ln(x)`	Natural log of `x`.
`log(x)`	base10 log of `x`.
`pi()`	Returns an approximation of `pi`, the ratio of the circumference of a circle to its diameter.
`pow(x,y)`	Raises `x` to the power of `y`.
`product(x,...n)` `mul (x,...n)`	Multiplies all inputs together.
`rad(x)`	Converts `x` degrees to radians.
`recip(x,m,a,b)`	A reciprocal function implementing `a/(m*x+b)`.
`rint(x)`	Rounds the number `x` to the nearest integer.
`sin(x)`	Trigonometric sine of angle `x` in radians.
`sinh(x)`	Hyperbolic sine of `x`.
`sqrt(x)`	Square root of `x`.
`sub(x,y)`	Subtracts `y` from `x`.
`sum(x,...n)` `add (x,...n)`	Adds all inputs together.
`tan(x)`	Tangent of angle `x`.
`tanh(x)`	Hyperbolic tangent of `x`.

RELEVANCY FUNCTIONS

Solr's relevancy score, by default, is calculated based upon the `DefaultSimilarity` class, the inner workings of which are described in detail in section 3.2. This class makes use of many statistics from the search index (and query terms) in order to determine which documents best match any query. Although these relevancy statistics are typically only used to calculate a composite relevancy score per document, the individual statistics can be used or returned through the use of available relevancy functions in Solr. All of the core relevancy statistics, such as tf-idf, are included. Table 15.3 contains the available relevancy functions in Solr.

Table 15.3 Available relevancy functions in Solr

Function syntax	Description
`docfreq(fieldName, term)`	The number of documents containing the term in the field named `fieldName`.
`idf(fieldName, value)`	The idf calculation for the value in the field named `fieldName`.

Table 15.3   Available relevancy functions in Solr *(continued)*

Function syntax	Description
maxdoc()	The number of documents in the index, including deleted documents not yet purged.
norm(fieldName)	The norm stored in the index for the field named fieldName.
numdocs()	The number of documents in the index, excluding deleted documents not yet purged.
query(subquery, defaultScore)	The score of the subquery for all documents matching the subquery, and the defaultScore for documents not matching the subquery.
sumtotaltermfreq(field) sttf(field)	The number of indexed tokens in the field across the index.
termfreq(fieldName, term)	The number of times the term appears in the field in the document.
tf(fieldName, term)	The tf factor for the term in the field using that field's similarity.
totaltermfreq(fieldName, term) ttf(fieldName, term)	The number of times the term appears in the entire index.

You can see from the list of relevancy functions in table 15.3 that it would be possible to rewrite the relevancy calculation used to score documents for a query by substituting a function in place of a query. Consider the following Solr request:

```
/select?
  fq={!cache=false}content:"microsoft office"&
  q={!func}sum(
            product(
              tf(content, "microsoft"),
              idf(content, "microsoft")
            ),
            product(
              tf(content, "office"),
              idf(content, "office")
            )
          )
```

This query would filter on the phrase "microsoft office" and proceed to look up and multiply the tf-idf factors from the Solr index for each of the two terms ("Microsoft" and "office"). Because the function is being called in the main query, the function calculation is returned as the score for the query. Although this example does not represent the entire default relevancy calculation, you can see how easy it would be to reuse the elements of the relevancy calculation in any number of ways to effectively create your own relevancy calculations at query time. By providing these relevancy functions, Solr has completely opened up the scoring model for your own experimentation.

DISTANCE FUNCTIONS

At times, it can be useful to measure the distance between two values. This could be the geographical distance between two points on the globe, it could be the geometric distance between two points or vectors, or it could even be the distance of characters in two strings from each other. Table 15.4 demonstrates the available distance functions in Solr.

Table 15.4 Available distance functions in Solr

Function syntax	Description
`dist(power, x1, ... n1, x2 ... n2)`	Calculates the distance between 2 vectors/points in n-dimensional space based upon the specified distance measure defined by `power`. The most common values for `power` are `0`—Sparseness calculation `1`—Manhattan (taxicab) distance `2`—Euclidean distance `Infinity`—Infinite norm (maximum value in the vector)
`sqedist(x1, ... n1, x2 ... n2)`	Returns the square of the Euclidean distance from the `dist(2, ...)` function, which is more efficient (it eliminates a square root calculation) if you only need relative ordering of values (for sorting or relevancy boosting) and not exact distance calculations.
`hsin(radiusInKM, isDegrees, x1, y1, x2, y2)`	Calculates the Haversine, or greater circle, distance, the distance between two points when traveling along a sphere.
`geohash(lat, lon)`	Returns a `geohash` value for two points. A geohash is a special string encoding for locations on the Earth. This function is useful for creating an input parameter for the `ghhsin` function.
`ghhsin(radiusInKM, geohash1, geohash2)`	Runs the Haversine function on two geohash values instead of degrees or radians. The `geohash1` and `geohash2` fields can be either geohash fields (of type `GeoHashField`) or results from the `geohash` function.
`strdist(s1, s2, distType)` `strdist(s1, s2, "ngram", ngramSize)`	Calculates the similarity, or distance apart, of characters within two strings ranging between 0 (not similar) and 1 (exactly the same). The valid values for `distType` are `jw`—Jaro-Winkler `edit`—The edit distance (Levenshtein distance) `ngram`—The NGramDistance Additionally, the fully qualified name of any class which implements the `StringDistance` interface can be specified (useful if you write your own plugin).

`geodist(sfield, lat, lon)`
`geodist(sfield, pt)`
`geodist()`
	Returns the distance between two points on Earth, one specified by a spatial field (`sfield`), and the other by coordinate.

As you can see from the table, Solr supports a wide range of distance functions. The `dist` function allows you to specify the 0-norm (sparseness calculation), 1-norm (Manhattan distance), 2-norm (Euclidean distance), or infinite norm (max value in the vector) to be used for the distance calculation, along with two vectors/points in an n-dimensional space. The number of coordinates must be even, with the first half defining the first point and the second half defining the second point. For example, the Euclidean distance between 2-dimensional points would be `dist(2, x1, y1, x2, y2)`, and the Manhattan distance between 3-dimensional points would be `dist(1, x1, y1, z1, x2, y2, z2)`.

The `sqedist` function is a less expensive form of the Euclidean distance function (the 2-norm for the `dist` function) that returns the square of the Euclidean distance. The squared Euclidean distance calculates the c^2 portion of the Pythagorean theorem ($a^2 + b^2 = c^2$) for a set of 2-dimensional points. Because the Euclidean distance calculation must additionally take the square root of c^2 to calculate the precise value of c, it's more efficient to use the `sqedist` function if you only need relative ordering of documents (for sorting or relevancy, for example) and do not need the distance to be returned.

The `hsin` function calculates the distance between two points when traveling across a sphere (including, but not limited to, the Earth). The `radiusInKm` parameter for the `hsin` function should be the radius of the sphere. If you want to calculate the distance between points on the Earth (probably the most common use case), a good approximation for the Earth's radius is `6371.01` (the radius at the equator), though the accuracy can vary by up to 0.5% depending upon the location because the Earth is not a perfect sphere. The `isDegrees` parameter should be set to `true` if latitude/longitude degrees are specified, and `false` if radians are specified for the points. The `x1,y1` values define the first point, and the `x2,y2` values define the second point.

The `ghhsin` function is a version of the `hsin` function that can accept `geohash` values instead of degrees or radians, and the `geohash` function is able to take in a latitude and longitude and convert them to a geohash-encoded value for use as an input into the `ghhsin` function. You'd likely want to make use of these functions if you were using a field in your search index that stored geohash-encoded values.

The `strdist` function compares character differences to determine how far away two strings are from each other, which is useful for doing fuzzy matching on similar terms. If you think of a string as a vector of multiple characters, the `strdist` function is calculating the distance between two strings (character vectors). The resulting similarity calculation will fall into the range of `0` (not at all similar) to `1` (exactly the same). The string inputs for the `strdist` function are represented by `s1` and `s2`, and the `distType` parameter is used to specify the distance measure used to measure the similarity between the strings. If the `"ngram"` `distType` is specified, it defaults to using two characters to compare the distance, but you can override this by passing in the optional `ngramSize` parameter.

The `geodist` function returns the distance between two points on Earth. The `sfield` (spatial field) should be a `LatLonType` field, and the returned distance will be the number of kilometers between the point in the `sfield` and the comma-separated `lat` and `lon` that make up the `pt` (point). If you leave off the `sfield` and `pt` parameters when calling the `geodist()` function, the function will use the `sfield` and `pt` parameters specified on the request. The `geodist` function uses the `HaversineFunction` (`hsin`) under the covers, which assumes the radius of the Earth and enables the use of a `LatLonType` field instead of storing each value separately, providing for a simpler syntax. The `geodist` function is probably the most commonly used distance function in Solr, and it will be covered in greater depth in section 15.2 on geospatial search.

BOOLEAN FUNCTIONS

Boolean operations are not limited to keyword queries; they can also be used and combined to create arbitrarily complex function queries. Through combining the `if`, `and`, `or`, `not`, `xor`, and `exists` functions, you can check the values of fields and other calculated functions within your documents and return values conditionally based upon those checks. Table 15.5 describes Solr's Boolean functions.

Table 15.5 Available Boolean functions in Solr

Function syntax	Description
`and(x, y)`	Returns `true` if both x and y are true.
`exists(x)`	Returns `true` if a value exists for x.
`if(x, trueValue, falseValue)`	Returns `trueValue` if x is `true` and `falseValue` if x is `false`.
`not(x)`	Returns `false` if x is `true`. Returns `true` if x is `false`.
`or(x, y)`	Returns `true` if x is `true`, if y is `true`, or if both x and y are `true`. Returns `false` otherwise.
`xor(x, y)`	Returns `true` if either x or y is `true`, but `false` if both x and y are `true`.

With such a rich selection of data-transformation, math, relevancy, and Boolean functions available out of the box (and with more being added all the time), most people are able to handle any additional document-level calculations required for their search application with Solr. As with many other features in Solr, however, it's also easy to extend Solr's function support by writing a plugin to implement your own custom functions. The next section will demonstrate how easy it is to create your own pluggable function.

15.1.6 *Implementing a custom function*

At times, you may want to perform data manipulations which are not covered by any of Solr's built-in functions. Thankfully, Solr makes it easy to implement your own custom functions. Code is run inside the function, which means you can technically do anything from simple in-memory calculations, to reaching out to external files or data sources to pull in more information, to running any arbitrary code. The only real constraint on what you can implement in your function is how long you can wait on the function's value calculation to complete. Because the code in your function will be run for each matching document, it needs to run quickly in order to return a search response in a reasonable amount of time.

In this section, we will demonstrate the creation of a basic function that concatenates the values of multiple fields into a string. In order to use your own function in a plugin for Solr, you will need to complete three steps:

1   Write a class to represent your function. This class should inherit from the Value-Source class, which is able to return a calculated value for each document in your search index.

2   Write a ValueSourceParser class, which is able to understand the syntax for your function and parse it into the variables needed for the custom Value-Source you created to represent your function in step 1.

3   Add an XML element into your *solrconfig.xml* defining the name of your function and the location of your ValueSourceParser. When the function is invoked using the name you defined, your ValueSourceParser class (from step 2) will handle parsing the inputs into the ValueSource (from step 1).

IMPLEMENTING A CUSTOM FUNCTION BY EXTENDING VALUESOURCE

The concatenation function we will implement will extend the ValueSource class in Solr. A ValueSource implements a getValues method that returns a FunctionValues object. The FunctionValues object is able to return the calculated value for your function for any document in the Solr index. The next listing demonstrates how to create the ConcatenateFunction class.

Listing 15.2   **Writing a custom function to concatenate two values**

```
public class ConcatenateFunction extends ValueSource {
    protected final ValueSource valueSource1;
    protected final ValueSource valueSource2;
    protected final String delimiter;

    public ConcatenateFunction(ValueSource valueSource1,
                               ValueSource valueSource2,
                               String delimiter) {

      if (valueSource1 == null || valueSource2 == null){
        throw new SolrException(
          SolrException.ErrorCode.BAD_REQUEST,
          "One or more inputs missing for concatenate function"
        );
      }

      this.valueSource1 = valueSource1;
      this.valueSource2 = valueSource2;
```

❶ Requires two ValueSource inputs (fields, functions, values).

❷ An optional string delimiter.

```java
        if (delimiter != null){
            this.delimiter = delimiter;
        }
        else{
            this.delimiter = "";
        }
    }

    @Override
    public FunctionValues getValues(Map context,
            AtomicReaderContext readerContext) throws IOException {
        final FunctionValues firstValues = valueSource1.getValues(
                                        context, readerContext);
        final FunctionValues secondValues = valueSource2.getValues(
                                        context, readerContext);

        return new StrDocValues(this) {

            @Override
            public String strVal(int doc) {
                return firstValues.strVal(doc)
                                .concat(delimiter)
                                .concat(secondValues.strVal(doc));
            }
            @Override
            public String toString(int doc) {
                StringBuilder sb = new StringBuilder();
                sb.append("concatenate(");
                sb.append("\"" + firstValues.toString(doc) + "\"")
                    .append(',')
                    .append("\"" + secondValues.toString(doc) + "\"")
                    .append(',')
                    .append("\"" + delimiter + "\"");
                sb.append(')');
                return sb.toString();
            }
        };
    }

    @Override
    public boolean equals(Object o) {
        if (this.getClass() != o.getClass()) return false;
        ConcatenateFunction other = (ConcatenateFunction) o;
        return this.valueSource1.equals(other.valueSource1)
                    && this.valueSource2.equals(other.valueSource2)
                    && this.delimiter == other.delimiter;
    }

    @Override
    public int hashCode() {
        long combinedHashes;
        combinedHashes = (this.valueSource1.hashCode()
                        + this.valueSource2.hashCode()
                        + this.delimiter.hashCode());
        return (int) (combinedHashes ^ (combinedHashes >>> 32));
    }
```

3 The function returns a FunctionValues object from this method.

4 A special FunctionValues object for string outputs.

5 For any document ID, return the calculated function value.

```
    @Override
    public String description() {
        return
          "Concatenates two values together with an optional delimiter";
    }

}
```

The most important things to note about the ConcatenateFunction class are its input parameters and what is returned by its getValues function. In terms of the input parameters, the ConcatenateFunction class takes in two ValueSource objects ❶ and a string representing a delimiter ❷. Recall from section 15.1.1, the input parameters to a function are other functions. By defining the two inputs to be concatenated as ValueSource objects as opposed to strings or fields, your function will be able to accept any of these inputs and use the values contained within them. Although defining all input parameters as ValueSource objects provides the most flexibility, you will notice that the third parameter in the ConcatenateFunction constructor, the delimiter, was defined as a string. This input parameter could have also been defined as a ValueSource, in which case it could have pulled its value from another field or another function calculation. In this case, however, we are assuming that the delimiter is something that will be explicitly passed in on the request (otherwise, the user could call the concatenate function multiple times if they wanted to use another field or function calculation to dynamically find a delimiter).

To understand the output of the ConcatenateFunction class, we need to look at its getValues method ❸. Notice that this method returns a FunctionValues object. The getValues method must return a FunctionValues object, but because the output of our concatenation operation is a string, we are internally using the StrDocValues class ❹. The StrDocValues class is a specific implementation of FunctionValues that returns strings as opposed to integers, Booleans, or other types. There are many subclasses of FunctionValues, including ones with specific caching implications that may allow you to trade off memory usage for speed, so you may want to check them out further in the Solr codebase if your use case warrants such optimizations.

The StrDocValues object ❺ contains a strVal(docid) method which is called once per document for each document in the document set under consideration at the time the function is invoked. This method performs the calculation of the function's return value, and for expensive queries it can be called once for every document in your search index, so it's generally important to ensure that the calculations performed in this method run as quickly as possible.

PARSING FUNCTION INPUTS WITH A VALUESOURCEPARSER

Now that we have seen how the return value for a function is calculated, the next step is to understand how the request input gets parsed into our Concatenate-Function object. The next listing demonstrates the parsing of input parameters into our function.

Listing 15.3 Mapping the input parameters from the request to the function

```
public class ConcatenateFunctionParser extends ValueSourceParser {

  public ValueSource parse(FunctionQParser fqp) throws SyntaxError{
    ValueSource value1 = fqp.parseValueSource();
    ValueSource value2 = fqp.parseValueSource();
    String delimiter = null;

    if (fqp.hasMoreArguments()){
      delimiter = fqp.parseArg();
    }

    return new ConcatenateFunction(value1, value2, delimiter);
  }
}
```

Parse inputs as **ValueSources**, which can also represent other nested functions.

Parse delimiter as an explicit **String** value.

The listing demonstrates the fairly straightforward step of parsing input values into our custom function using our FunctionQParser object. The FunctionQParser parses the standard function syntax of functionName(input1,input2,…), finding the appropriate ValueSourceParser based upon the name of the function requested. Internally, the FunctionQParser holds the inputs for our function, and by calling one of its many parse methods—such as parseValueSource(), parseArg(), or parseFloat()—we can grab the expected inputs for our function.

In the case of the ConcatenateFunctionParser, it's expecting two ValueSource inputs (a field, user-inputted string, or any other function) and an optional string delimiter. After reading these inputs from the request, it creates a ConcatenateFunction object and populates the inputs.

INVOKING THE CUSTOM FUNCTION

With both of the necessary classes created to implement our custom concatenation function, all that's left is to let Solr know about the new function by adding the following entry to *solrconfig.xml*:

```
<valueSourceParser name="concat"
    class="sia.ch15.ConcatenateFunctionParser" />
```

The name you choose here is up to you, but it will be the name expected in the function syntax when the function query is requested. To make use of this function in your query, you can invoke it as you would any of the examples listed in table 15.6.

Table 15.6 Sample outputs for the custom `Concatenate` function

Function syntax	Value of 1st parameter	Value of 2nd parameter	Value of 3rd parameter	Output
concat(field1, field2, "-")	"hello"	"world"	"-"	"hello-world"
concat(field1, "Trey", ", ")	"hello"	"Trey"	", "	"hello, Trey"

Table 15.6   Sample outputs for the custom `Concatenate` function *(continued)*

Function syntax	Value of 1st parameter	Value of 2nd parameter	Value of 3rd parameter	Output
`concat(123, field3, ".")`	123	456	`"."`	`"123.456"`
`concat("no", "delimiter")`	`"no"`	`"delimiter"`	null	`"nodelimiter"`
`concat(field1, field2, field1)`	`"hello"`	`"world"`	`"field1"`	`"hellofield1world"`

As you can see from the last example in the table, the choice of using a `ValueSource` type for the first two inputs and a string type for the last input makes a difference in how the inputs are interpreted, as the first and last inputs are syntactically the same but are interpreted differently. In the last row of table 15.6, for example, you will see that the input `field1` is interpreted differently when it's the third parameter as opposed to the first parameter. To make your functions as reusable as possible, it's likely a good idea to make use of a `ValueSource` in as many places as possible for your input parameters, as you can always pass constants in explicitly if that's your intention.

If you want to test the concatenation function yourself, we've included a fully configured Solr core named `customfunction` for this purpose. To add a sample document, execute the following command:

```
java -Durl=http://localhost:8983/solr/customfunction/update
    -jar post.jar ch15/documents/customfunction.xml
```

With the `customfunction` core available and a sample document indexed (containing `field1=hello` and `field2=world`), you can now easily experiment with the custom concatenation function. To create a pseudo-field within this document named `introduction` with a value of `"hello, world!"`, for example, you can issue a request like the following.

Request
```
http://localhost:8983/solr/customfunction/select?q=*:*&
    fl=introduction:concat(concat(field1,field2,", "),"!")
```

Response
```
{
  ...
  "response":{"numFound":1,"start":0,"docs":[
      {
        "introduction":"hello, world!"}]
  }}
```

At this point, you should have a solid understanding of how function queries work in Solr, including how to easily create and use your own function through Solr's powerful plugin capabilities. The next section will introduce Solr's geospatial abilities (which also happen to make use of functions), demonstrating how to calculate distances and search for shapes based upon a coordinate system (such as latitude and longitude values around the globe).

15.2 Geospatial search

One popular feature available in Solr is its ability to do location-based searching. This is most commonly implemented by indexing a field in each document containing a geographical point (a latitude and longitude), and then asking Solr at query time to filter out documents that do not fall within a specified radius of some other point.

Solr contains two primary geospatial search implementations. The older is simpler and supports radius searching based upon a single latitude/longitude pair and also sorting by and returning the distance away from the searched point for each document. The newer geospatial implementation is much more sophisticated, enabling filtering not only on a single point, but also on shapes, including arbitrarily complex polygons. The simple implementation works by calculating distances between points in documents at query time and filtering out values that are too far apart. The advanced implementation works by indexing shapes as a series of grid coordinate boxes and then forming a query across those indexed grid boxes to quickly search through a large number of documents without having to calculate distances. The simple version can be faster on small indexes and does not require indexing extra data, whereas the advanced version is generally faster with a large number of documents and is more flexible with the kinds of shapes that can be searched.

15.2.1 Searching near a single point

Solr's simple geospatial implementation enables searching based upon a single point, usually a latitude and longitude. This implementation supports a simple syntax for filtering based upon either a true circular radius or based upon a square (which is faster to calculate) with sides equal to the diameter of the true circular radius.

DEFINING THE LOCATION FIELDS

The first step in performing a radius search is to create a field type in your *schema.xml* to contain your geographical location:

```
<fieldType name="location"
    class="solr.LatLonType"
    subFieldSuffix="_coordinate" />
```

The `LatLonType` class, used for this location field definition, works by accepting a latitude/longitude pair in the form `latitude,longitude` and ultimately splitting the two coordinates and mapping them into separate fields. In order to map the latitude and longitude into two separate fields under the covers, those two fields will also need to exist in the *schema.xml*. This is accomplished by adding a dynamic field that ends with the `subFieldSuffix` specified in the `fieldType` definition (in this case, the pattern is "`_coordinate`"):

```
<dynamicField name="*_coordinate"
    type="tdouble"
    indexed="true"
    stored="false" />
```

With the `location` field defined and with a dynamic field put in place for the `location` field to map the latitude and longitude coordinates into separately, all that's left is to send documents into the search engine, such as those in this listing.

Listing 15.4   Indexing locations for geospatial searching

```
<add>
    <doc>
        <field name="id">1</field>
        <field name="location">33.748,-84.391</field>
        <field name="city">Atlanta, GA</field>
    </doc>
    <doc>
        <field name="id">2</field>
        <field name="location">40.715,-74.007</field>
        <field name="city">New York, NY</field>
    </doc>
    <doc>
        <field name="id">3</field>
        <field name="location">37.775,-122.419</field>
        <field name="city">San Francisco, CA</field>
    </doc>
    <doc>
        <field name="id">4</field>
        <field name="location">37.445,-122.161</field>
        <field name="city">Palo Alto, CA</field>
    </doc>
</add>
```

These documents can be found in the accompanying source code, so you can easily send them to Solr by running these commands:

```
cd $SOLR_IN_ACTION/example-docs/
java -Durl=http://localhost:8983/solr/geospatial/update
    ➥ -jar post.jar  ch15/documents/geospatial.xml
```

Once your documents are indexed in Solr, it's then possible to search upon the locations in various ways. You could search upon the text version of the location with a query such as `city:"San Francisco, CA"`. The problem with this approach is that it won't be able to find documents that are nearby, but potentially outside of the borders of the city for which you're searching.

GEOGRAPHY AND BOUNDING BOX FILTERS

Another approach to geographical searching is to query for all documents within a specific distance of a given location. Solr contains a special query parser named `geofilt` that takes in a latitude/longitude coordinate, a location field, and a maximum

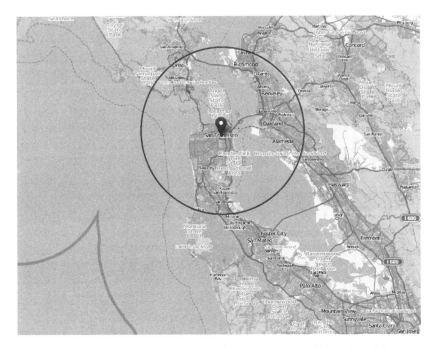

Figure 15.1 The geographical area from which documents would be returned from a `geofilt` query requesting a distance of d=20 km from the center of San Francisco, CA. (© OpenStreetMap.org contributors)

distance (in km) and matches only documents falling within the geographical area specified. The syntax for such a query searching for a 20 km radius from San Francisco, CA, would be as follows:

```
http://localhost:8983/solr/geospatial/select?q=*:*&
  fq={!geofilt sfield=location pt=37.775,-122.419 d=20}
```

The `sfield` (spatial field) parameter defines which field in the *schema.xml* contains the `LatLonType` field to be used for the query. The `pt` (point) parameter defines the latitude/longitude coordinate to base the radius search upon. The `d` (distance) parameter defines the radius inside of which documents should be considered matches for the `geofilt` filter. Figure 15.1 demonstrates the area inside of which documents would be returned from the previous query for a 20 km radius.

The `geofilt` query demonstrated in figure 15.1 works under the covers using a two-pass filtering mechanism. The first pass creates a *bounding box*: a square with sides equal in length to the diameter of the radius being searched. Once the document set has been filtered down by the relatively quick bounding box filter, the distance is then calculated for all documents remaining so that documents inside the bounding box but outside the circular radius can be filtered out. Figure 15.2 demonstrates a bounding box for a 20 km search around San Francisco, CA, as well as the circular radius that would be calculated inside that bounding box.

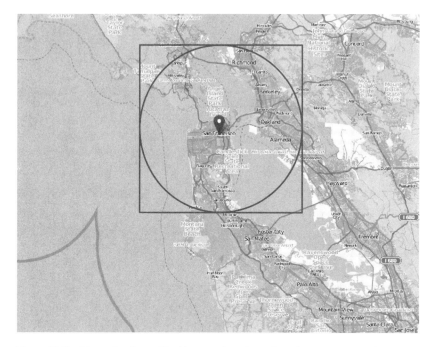

Figure 15.2   A bounding box with sides equal to the radius of the geography filter. The area inside the box is guaranteed to contain all documents within a 20 km radius of the center of the box, though it may also contain documents a greater distance away. The radius circle is calculated after the bounding box filter is applied in order to remove documents near the four corners of the bounding box. (© OpenStreetMap.org contributors)

Although the second part of the geofilt query—the calculation of the distance—enables accurate location resolution (often within a few meters), it can be expensive to calculate the exact distance of many documents if you have a large document set. In some cases, it's good enough to include all the matching documents within the bounding box and forego incurring the cost of the more precise circular radius filter. Solr contains another query parser, the bbox (bounding box) query parser, which can do that.

The bbox query parser makes use of the same syntax as the geofilt query parser, making it easy to substitute the two within any geography filter:

```
http://localhost:8983/solr/geospatial/select?q=*:*&
  fq={!bbox sfield=location pt=37.775,-122.419 d=20}
```

Up to this point, you have seen how to perform a fast bounding box (bbox) filter to find geographically close locations and how to apply a more accurate geofilt filter that will calculate distances for each document inside a bounding box and filter out any documents which fall outside the requested radius. Because Solr is already calculating the distance of each matching document from the point specified in the query (for the geofilt, not the bbox filter), it could be useful for Solr to use those distances in other ways. In particular, it would be great if Solr could allow documents to be sorted by distance away or for the calculated distance to be returned with the rest of the fields in the field list. It probably comes as no surprise that Solr already contains built-in support for both of these use cases.

RETURNING CALCULATED DISTANCES IN SEARCH RESULTS

In addition to filtering on distance from a point, Solr is able to return the calculated distance for each document in the search results through the use of the `geodist` function. You saw how to return the calculated results of functions as pseudo-fields in section 15.1.3, and returning the calculation from the `geodist` function follows this same model.

The syntax for the `geodist` function is `geodist(sfield, latitude, longitude)`. Using this function, you can return the calculated distance of each document from any latitude and longitude and return it as a dynamically calculated pseudo-field. The following listing demonstrates calculating the distance of each document from a point in San Francisco (37.77493, -122.41942) and returning it as a pseudo-field.

> **Listing 15.5 Returning the calculated distance as a pseudo-field**

Query
```
http://localhost:8983/solr/geospatial/select?q=*:*&
    fl=id,city,distance:geodist(location,37.77493, -122.41942)
```
The geodist function's calculation will be assigned to a pseudo-field called distance.

Results
```
{
...
    "response":{"numFound":4,"start":0,"docs":[
        {
          "id":"1",
          "city":"Atlanta, GA",
          "distance":3436.669993915123
        },
        {
          "id":"2",
          "city":"New York, NY",
          "distance":4128.9603389283575
        },
        {
          "id":"3",
          "city":"San Francisco, CA",
          "distance":0.03772596784117343
        },
        {
          "id":"4",
          "city":"Palo Alto, CA",
          "distance":43.17493506307893
        }]
    }}
```
Each document now contains a dynamically calculated "distance" field.

Notice that each document in the result set now contains a new field named `distance`. As with any other function query, it's easy to return the calculated `geodist` function as a pseudo-field like this. Do keep in mind, however, that calculating the geospatial distance between two points involves some nontrivial math, so you may find it to be a slow operation across millions of documents. As such, you will often be better off applying a `geofilt` filter to limit your result set first.

SORTING ON DISTANCE

As you saw in section 15.1.4, it's not only possible to return the calculated values of functions, but also to sort on them. The `geodist` function is no different than any other function in this regard. To order documents from closest to furthest away, you can add the `geodist` function to your `sort` parameter, as shown in this listing.

Listing 15.6   Sorting on geographical distance

Query

```
http://localhost:8983/solr/geospatial/select?q=*:*&
   fl=id,city,distance:geodist(location,37.77493, -122.41942)&
   sort=geodist(location,37.77493, -122.41942) asc, score desc
```

Results will be sorted first by the geodist function.

Results

```
{
...
   "response":{"numFound":4,"start":0,"docs":[
      {
        "id":"3",
        "city":"San Francisco, CA",
        "distance":0.03772596784117343
      },
      {
        "id":"4",
        "city":"Palo Alto, CA",
        "distance":43.17493506307893
      },
      {
        "id":"1",
        "city":"Atlanta, GA",
        "distance":3436.669993915123
      },
      {
        "id":"2",
        "city":"New York, NY",
        "distance":4128.9603389283575
      }]
   }}
```

Each result is farther away than the last.

This request will sort all documents from smallest distance to largest, and then by score from highest to lowest (if there is a meaningful relevancy score, unlike in this example). You could flip the order of the sorts if you prefer to show the most relevant jobs first and then sort on distance away as a secondary sort. Through combining multiple function queries, you could also combine the keyword relevancy score and a geographical proximity as separate factors in a composite relevancy score for each document. Chapter 16 will demonstrate some more advanced function-based relevancy techniques like this.

Each of the examples so far (filtering, returning pseudo-fields, and sorting) has been demonstrated independently. If you wanted to make use of all of these in a single request, it would be reasonable to combine them all as presented into a request like the following:

```
http://localhost:8983/solr/geospatial/select?q=*:*&
  fq={!geofilt sfield=location pt=37.775,-122.419 d=20}&
  fl=*,distance:geodist(location, 37.775,-122.419)&
  sort=geodist(location, 37.775,-122.419) asc, score desc
```

Such a request is wasteful, however, as it requires you to repeat the same input parameters multiple times. Thankfully, the `geofilt`, `bbox`, and `geodist` implementations are all able to pull their parameters from dereferenced query string values on the request. As such, you can simplify the previous query to the following:

```
http://localhost:8983/solr/geospatial/select?q=*:*&
  fq={!geofilt}&
  fl=*,distance:geodist()&
  sort=geodist() asc, score desc&
  sfield=location&pt=37.775,-122.419&d=20
```

Using this simplified syntax, you can still override the default `sfield`, `pt`, and `d` parameters from the request by explicitly specifying them as local params for any of the geospatial components, but for basic use cases this will likely not be necessary, because they often use the same point for filtering, sorting, and returning a calculated distance.

15.2.2 Advanced geospatial search

In addition to the simple single-point geospatial search implementation described in section 15.2.1, Solr supports a newer, more advanced implementation that supports indexing much more than a single point per document. This advanced geospatial support enables indexing fields containing arbitrary polygons (as opposed to just points), and it supports indexing multiple points or shapes per field.

How would such capabilities be useful? In terms of supporting multiple location values per document, imagine if your search index contained restaurants, and that some of the restaurants were chains with multiple locations around the world. Instead of having to create separate documents for each restaurant location, you could index a single document with multiple latitude/longitude coordinates. At query time, any query that intersects one or more of the restaurant locations within the document would return the document.

In terms of supporting shapes (circles, squares, or any arbitrary polygons), it could certainly be useful to represent documents as not being mapped to a single point. For example, what if your documents modeled government officials, and the locations indexed were for the geographical regions containing the citizens they represented? Likewise, what if you wanted documents to represent landmarks such as the Great Wall of China or to represent cities, states, or even countries? Although you could certainly try to represent such places as points around which you draw a radius, they would be much better represented as polygons representing their geographical area. This way, if someone runs a search for documents within 100 km, they will find all documents whose indexed locations overlap at any point with the radius in the query, not only objects whose central point overlaps with the geospatial query.

UNDERSTANDING GRID-BASED LOCATION SEARCHING

To efficiently index and search on one or more arbitrary shapes, Solr makes use of a special field type—invoked through the `SpatialRecursivePrefixTreeFieldType` class—that's able to divide the world into a grid. At the most zoomed out level, the world could be divided into a grid with some number of sections; we will use four quadrants as an example. Each quadrant could then be further divided into a smaller grid with four more quadrants, and this division can be applied recursively many levels deep. Figure 15.3 demonstrates how such division into quadrants would work going three levels deep.

You can see from figure 15.3 that every box in the grid contains a unique identifier with an additional level of precision at each tier. By modeling the world in this way, it can be efficient to search for locations based upon indexed terms instead of calculated distances. In figure 15.3, Miami, FL, would be located within box 0, box 03, and box 032, so all three of these tiers (plus as many additional tiers as necessary to achieve the desired level of precision) would be saved into the Solr index. This enables powerful query capabilities. Do you want to search for documents in the Western Hemisphere? This internally becomes a search for the terms "0" OR "2" in the location field in the Solr index. Such a search on indexed grid locations is generally much faster than calculating the distance for every document and filtering out documents that fall outside of a radius around that calculated distance. Do you want to

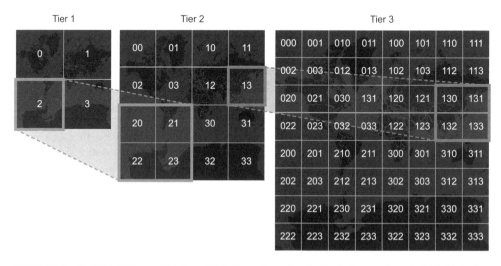

Figure 15.3   Division of the world into multiple tiers of quadrants. Each tier can be subdivided into four quadrants as many levels deep as necessary to achieve a desired level of geographical accuracy at the final level.

search for documents in Australia? This internally becomes a query for box `"310"` OR `"311"`. Using the three tiers of specificity from figure 15.3, you clearly will not be able to find locations with any realistic level of precision, which is why many grid tiers are stored (the number is configurable) to ensure your geospatial queries can be as accurate as your application requires. Figure 15.4 provides a more concrete example for how a search for documents near San Francisco, CA, might be constructed.

You can see from figure 15.4 that if the world is broken up into multilevel grids, querying for something in the "shape" of the San Francisco area is a matter of finding the best combination of larger and smaller grid boxes which wholly contain San Francisco without accidentally including other areas. Because every necessary box will become part of the query, the best combination ultimately means finding the smallest number of terms (boxes) from any combination of tiers that can be combined in the query to meet the accuracy requirements of the application. Thankfully, Solr makes this optimized selection of which grid boxes to search for you, so this is not a problem you have to personally worry about. Although it's technically not even necessary for you to understand how this grid-based system works to make use of Solr's advanced geospatial capabilities, having a basic understanding should help you make better trade-offs when choosing configuration options for how precise you need your locations to be at index and query time.

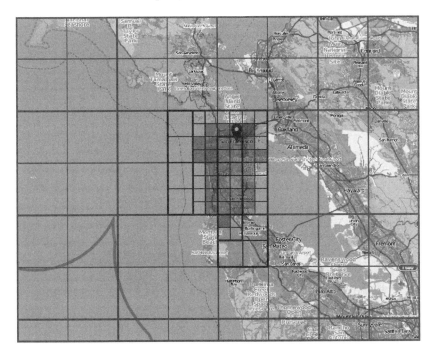

Figure 15.4   The San Francisco, CA, area, as modeled into grid levels. The central parts of the area are wholly contained within more granular levels (larger boxes), whereas the edges may require using more precise levels to closely approximate the shape's edges. (© OpenStreetMap.org contributors)

PrefixTree implementations: GeoHash and Quad

The grid-based location system we've described makes use of the concept of *prefix trees*—representations of places as a series of prefixes (such as 31102...) ranging from more general to more specific. `SpatialRecursivePrefixTreeFieldType` provides an abstract representation of prefix trees that allows for different implementations of a multilevel grid system to be used for indexing and searching spatial data. The examples so far have described a simple quad grid implementation that defines four quadrants at each level. Another prefix tree implementation exists based upon a well-known industry standard called *Geohash*, which divides the earth into 32 boxes at each level instead of four. Geohash is specifically designed to model the earth's geography, and is therefore the implementation used if you specify `geo=true` when defining your `SpatialRecursivePrefixTreeFieldType` in your schema. The Geohash standard is well documented elsewhere, and the specifics of the standard are not important for understanding this chapter, because it functions conceptually similarly to the quad grid implementation already discussed. To learn more about Geohash, check out the Wikipedia entry at http://en.wikipedia.org/wiki/Geohash.

This basic understanding of a grid-based searching system should be more than sufficient for you to understand how to effectively use Solr's advanced geospatial capabilities. Thankfully, all of the complexities of mapping locations (points and shapes) into grid coordinates at both index and query time are handled within the `SpatialRecursive-PrefixTreeFieldType` class and the classes upon which it depends. All you have to do is add a field type into your *schema.xml*, as demonstrated in the next listing.

> **Listing 15.7   Defining a `location` field to support advanced geospatial searching**

The maximum acceptable distance error—this determines how many grid levels will be calculated.

```
<fieldType name="location_rpt"
    class="solr.SpatialRecursivePrefixTreeFieldType"
    spatialContextFactory=
      "com.spatial4j.core.context.jts.JtsSpatialContextFactory"
    distErrPct="0.025"
    maxDistErr="0.000009"
    autoIndex="true"
    units="degrees" />

<field name="location_rpt"
    type="location_rpt"
    indexed="true"
    stored="true"
    multiValued="true" />
```

Adds a dependency only necessary for polygons other than points, circles, and rectangles.

Precision level between 0.0 (fully precise) and 0.5 (imprecise) for shapes.

Allows multiple points/shapes to be supported per field.

With the field defined, we can now index example shapes and points into the field.

POINT

A point can be defined using a traditional comma-separated, `latitude,longitude` format or by omitting the comma, as `longitude latitude`. The following two examples are therefore identical:

```
<field name="location_rpt">43.17614,-90.57341</field>
<field name="location_rpt">-90.57341 43.17614</field>
```

RECTANGLE

A rectangle is indexed with four points to represent the corners. These points should be represented in `MinX, MinY, MaxX, MaxY` order:

```
<field name="location_rpt">-74.093 41.042 -69.347 44.558</field>
```

CIRCLE

A circle is defined based upon a centroid and distance radius. In order to identify it as a more complex shape, the input parameters are wrapped in a special syntax to identify the shape:

```
<field name="location_rpt">Circle(37.775,-122.419 d=20)</field>
```

The centroid (center point) of the circle is also defined using the point syntax in either `latitude,longitude` or `longitude latitude` format. The radius of the circle is specified by the `d` parameter, which stands for *distance* (not to be confused with diameter) in degrees.

OTHER SHAPES

In order to support arbitrarily complex shapes, Solr has support for defining polygons utilizing the WKT (well-known text) standard. Although the most commonly used shapes in Solr—point, circle, and rectangle—are natively supported through Solr's use of the Apache 2.0 Licensed Spatial4J library, utilizing WKT-defined polygons requires adding an otherwise-optional dependency on JTS (the Java Topology Suite).

> ### Open source licenses and legal implications of using JTS
>
> Apache Solr is open source and licensed under the Apache 2.0 License, which grants you the right to use the code and software in any system, including proprietary systems, without any legal responsibility to share your code or pay any license fees.
>
> The decision was made to allow "integration with" JTS, which is licensed under a much less permissive LGPL (lesser general public license). The JTS library (JAR file) is *not* included in the Solr distribution along with Spatial4j, leaving JTS as an optional dependency not required to use basic shapes (point, rectangle, and circle) in Solr. If you want to make use of JTS in Solr, you'll have to add the dependency yourself.
>
> As long as you do not make changes to the code in JTS, it's generally considered safe to reference the JTS libraries without subjecting your application to exposure to the LGPL license (which would require you to open source your application if it's a derivative work). Referencing any LGPL library is a legal decision, however, which should be made in consultation with your company's policies and/or legal counsel. If you only need support for points, circles, and squares, you should leave out the optional JTS `spatialContextFactory` attribute when defining your geography field type.

To enable the optional WKT support described in this section, you'll need to add the JTS JAR to your *solr.war* file so that your servlet container can load the JTS dependency when Solr first starts up. Because JTS does not ship with Solr (due to license concerns), this requires adding the JTS JAR file (*"jts.jar"*) to the *WEB-INF/lib/* folder inside of your *solr.war* file. You can do this with the following commands:

```
cd $SOLR_INSTALL/example/webapps/
cp -r $SOLR_IN_ACTION/example-docs/ch15/jts/ ./
jar -uf solr.war WEB-INF/lib/jts.jar
rm -rf WEB-INF/
```

Once you've updated your *solr.war* file to include the JTS dependency, you can then reference the JTS library in your *schema.xml*, as shown previously in listing 15.7. You should now stop Solr (if it's running), and then run the following commands to update your schema and restart Solr.

```
cd $SOLR_INSTALL/example/
cp solr/geospatial/conf/jts_schema.xml solr/geospatial/conf/schema.xml
java -jar start.jar
```

With Solr up and running with JTS support, we can demonstrate some powerful spatial capabilities for indexing and querying shapes.

The WKT format enables defining arbitrary polygons using the following format:

```
<field name="location_rpt">
    POLYGON((-10 30, -40 40, -10 -20, 40 20, 0 0, -10 30))
</field>
```

Please note the following characteristics of using this syntax to define arbitrary polygons:

- Each point is separated by a comma from the next point.
- Each point is in `longitude latitude` format.
- The first and last point defined are the same, effectively closing the shape.
- WKT points are mapped into valid latitude (+/-90°) and longitude (+/-180°) ranges.
- Dateline wrapping is supported, but only circles support pole wrapping.

Through enabling the indexing of arbitrary polygons, Solr provides support for complex location-based searching. Searching upon these shapes, however, is where the real power of Solr's spatial capabilities is unlocked.

QUERYING FOR SHAPES

You saw in section 15.2.1 how to perform radius and bounding box searches using a `LatLonType` field and Solr's simple, single-point geospatial implementation. It's possible to perform this same type of searching upon `SpatialRecursivePrefixTreeFieldType` fields through the use of the `geofilt` and `bbox` query parsers discussed in section 15.2.1:

```
http://localhost:8983/solr/geospatial/select?q=*:*&
  fq={!geofilt pt=37.775,-122.419 sfield=location_rpt d=5}
```

```
http://localhost:8983/solr/geospatial/select?q=*:*&
  fq={!bbox pt=37.775,-122.419 sfield=location_rpt d=5}
```

In addition to drawing circular radiuses and bounding boxes, it's possible to query using the same kinds of shapes that can be indexed using the more advanced grid-based prefix system that `SpatialRecursivePrefixTreeFieldType` provides. The syntax for performing these kinds of queries is as follows:

```
http://localhost:8983/solr/geospatial/select?q=*:*&
  fq=location_rpt:"Intersects(-90 -90 90 90)"
```

This request searches for a rectangle and will return all documents containing shapes in the `location_rpt` field that intersect somewhere with the rectangle in the query.

In addition to the `Intersects` operation, queries against a `SpatialRecursive-PrefixTreeFieldType` field support the `IsWithin`, `Contains`, and `IsDisjointTo` operations, which are defined in table 15.7.

Table 15.7   Operations for advanced shape queries

Shape operation	Description
Intersects	Matches all documents with one or more shapes which overlap the shape in the query
IsWithin	Matches all documents with one or more shapes fully contained within the shape in the query
Contains	Matches all documents with one or more shapes which fully contain the shape in the query
IsDisjointTo	Returns all documents containing no shapes which intersect with the shape in the query

Using the operations from table 15.7, you could craft a query to find all shapes which are fully contained within a specified polygon:

```
http://localhost:8983/solr/geospatial/select?q=*:*&
  fl=id,location_rpt,city&
  fq=location_rpt:"IsWithin(
    POLYGON((
      -85.4997 34.7442,
      -84.9723 30.6134,
      -81.2809 30.5255,
      -80.9294 32.0196,
      -83.3024 34.8321,
      -85.4997 34.7442))
  ) distErrPct=0"
```

This specific query searches for all documents within a polygon roughly the size of the U.S. state of Georgia (GA). Figure 15.5 demonstrates visually the area being searched by the defined polygon.

When you run the query, as expected, you find only the one document located in Atlanta, GA:

```
{
    ...
    "response":{"numFound":1,"start":0,"docs":[
        {
          "id":"1",
          "location_rpt":["33.748,-84.391"],
          "city":"Atlanta, GA"}]
    }}
```

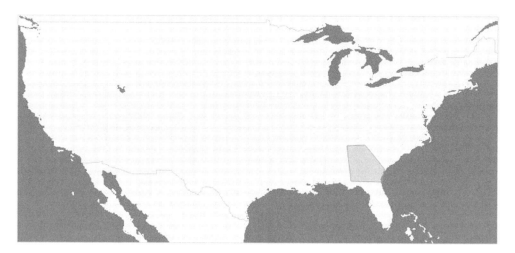

Figure 15.5   The area searched by the polygon in the shape of the U.S. state of Georgia.

You can combine such shape queries using standard Boolean logic to create complex query operations based upon your spatial data. Not only can you find documents matching your shape queries, but you can also use the distance of the indexed shapes from the shapes in your query to affect the relevancy of your query. Chapter 16 will go into more depth about using geographical distance to influence the relevancy score within your main query (q parameter), but it will be useful to see here how to return the score from the geofilt operation.

SORTING ON DISTANCE WITH SPATIALRECURSIVEPREFIXTREEFIELDTYPE

As of Solr 4.5, the geodist() function works with the SpatialRecursivePrefix-TreeFieldType (in addition to the LatLonType, which was already supported). Unfortunately, because shapes are indexed with some loss of precision when using a prefix tree implementation, the distances calculated can be off slightly. Generally this isn't a problem, as long as your distErrPct is set sufficiently high, but it can look somewhat strange when searching for the exact point that was indexed and getting a distance of something like 5.8165506E-6 back from Solr instead of only 0.0. In versions of Solr prior to 4.5, however, the geodist() function was not yet able to work with Spatial-RecursivePrefixTreeFieldType fields. A workaround for this exists which can prove to be more performant in many cases—using the score of a geofilt query.

SORTING ON DISTANCE WITH GEOFILT

It's possible to simulate the geodist() calculation by having the distance returned from an applied geofilt operation. If you recall from figure 15.2, the geofilt query parser contains a performance optimization in that it first applies a bounding box filter and then calculates the distance for the remaining points inside that box. Because the geofilt query parser calculates the distance between the point in the query and every document under consideration, it's possible to have that distance returned as the score for a document:

```
http://localhost:8983/solr/geospatial/select?
  sort=score asc&
  q={!geofilt pt=37.775,-122.419 sfield=location d=5 score=distance}
```

The `score=distance` parameter in the `geofilt` operation causes `geofilt` to internally return the distance between the point in the query and the (closest) point in the geo field for each document. Because this `geofilt` is part of the main query (q parameter), the score for the document will be equal to the distance calculated for the document. In addition to `score=distance`, you can also request `score=recipdistance`, which will return the reciprocal of the distance such that closer documents rank higher. If you do not pass in a `score` parameter, the distance is not necessarily calculated (for `SpatialRecursivePrefixTreeFieldType` fields), so every document receives the same constant score for the requested `geofilt`.

If you want the score calculated for all documents (even those falling outside of the `geofilt`), you can also turn filtering off for the `geofilt` query parser:

```
http://localhost:8983/solr/geospatial/select?
  sort=score asc&
  q={!geofilt pt=37.775,-122.419 sfield=location_rpt d=5
      score=distance filter=false}
```

By turning filtering off on the `geofilt` (yes, that does sound bizarre, but it works), you can effectively cause `geofilt` to behave similarly to the `geodist` function, in that it returns the distance calculation, but does not apply a filter. Unfortunately, because the `geofilt` is not a function query, if you want to use it in a function for purposes of sorting separately from the score of the main query, you will have to wrap the `geofilt` query in a `query` function as follows:

```
http://localhost:8983/solr/geospatial/select?
  sort=$distance asc&
  fl=id,distance:$distance&
  q=*:*&
  distance=query($distFilter)&
  distFilter={!geofilt pt=37.775,-122.419 sfield=location_rpt d=5
      score=distance filter=true}
```

This request passes the `geofilt` into the `query` function, which ultimately returns the score of the `distFilter` operation (in this case, the shortest distance from the point specified in the `geofilt`). This dereferenced distance parameter can then be passed to the `sort` and `fl` parameters and used as the `geodist()` function would be when using a `LatLongType`. As you can see, there are many options for calculating the distance of the value(s) in a field from a given point.

FACETING ON DISTANCE

You learned in chapter 8 how to facet upon arbitrary queries. By combining this ability with one or more geospatial filters, you can easily generate interesting data analytics capabilities based upon geographical distance. To make this section more interesting, we're going to generate a large number of documents—over 100,000—in order to see faceting upon more than a few data points. To generate these documents to send to

Solr, run the following commands (the `file` parameter is optional and will default to the value shown):

```
cd $SOLR_IN_ACTION/example-docs/
java -jar ../solr-in-action.jar ch15.DistanceFacetDocGenerator
  ➥ -file ch15/documents/distancefacet.xml
```

Once you've generated these documents (they take up about 15 MB on disk), you can send them to Solr by executing the following commands from the same directory:

```
java -Durl=http://localhost:8983/solr/distancefacet/update
  ➥ -jar post.jar ch15/documents/distancefacet.xml
```

You'll see the documents in your console window as they're created. Each document contains the latitude and longitude of a location, along with the city name. With that information, we can create facets that show the overall distance away of documents from any given point. You could, for example, generate query facets for all documents within 10 km, 20 km, 50 km, 100 km, and so on.

To show a more complicated example, imagine running a facet for your top 10 cities within a 50 km radius, and then running a second query to get facet counts for documents within 20 km of those top 10 cities. Sound complicated? The following listing demonstrates how this could be implemented.

Listing 15.8   Running a radius search for the top 10 cities matching a query

Request 1
```
http://localhost:8983/solr/distancefacet/select?q=*:*&rows=0&
  fq={!geofilt sfield=location pt=37.777,-122.420 d=80}&
  facet=true&
  facet.field=city&                    ❶ Only get top 10 cities
  facet.limit=10                          within large radius...
```

Response 1
```
facet_fields":{
  "city":[
    "San Francisco, CA",11713,          ◁┐ First city: San
    "San Jose, CA",3071,                   │  Francisco, CA.
    "Oakland, CA",1482,
    "Palo Alto, CA",1318,
    "Santa Clara, CA",1212,
    "Mountain View, ca",1045,
    "Sunnyvale, CA",1004,
    "Fremont, CA",726,
    "Redwood City, CA",633,             ┐ Tenth city:
    "Berkeley, CA",599]                 ◁┘ Berkeley, CA.
}
```
Second city: San Jose, CA. (annotation pointing to "San Jose, CA",3071,)

❷ ...get only docs within smaller radius for the top 10 cities.

Request 2
```
http://localhost:8983/solr/distancefacet/select?q=*:*&rows=0&
  facet=true&
  fq=(
      _query_:"{!geofilt sfield=location      ◁ First city: San
                  pt=37.777,-122.420 d=20}"   ◁   Francisco, CA.
```

```
      OR _query_:"{!geofilt sfield=location
                           pt=37.338,-121.886 d=20}"
      ...
      OR _query_:"{!geofilt sfield=location
                           pt=37.870,-122.271 d=20}"
    )&
    facet.query={!geofilt key="san francisco, ca"
                         sfield=location
                         pt=37.7770,-122.4200 d=20}&
    facet.query={!geofilt key="san jose, ca"
                         sfield=location
                         pt=37.338,-121.886 d=20}&
    ...
    facet.query={!geofilt key="berkeley, ca"
                         sfield=location pt=37.870,-122.271 d=20}
```

Second city: San Jose, CA.

Tenth city: Berkeley, CA.

...get facet counts for docs near the ❸ top 10 cities.

First city: San Francisco, CA.

Tenth city: Berkeley, CA.

As you can see, an initial query is run to find the top 10 cities (by counts) ❶ within a 50 km radius of the latitude/longitude of San Francisco. Based upon these results, you could plot the latitude/longitude coordinates for those cities on a map, draw a 20 km radius around each, and call it a day. By running the second query, you can provide counts of all documents within 20 km of each of those cities ❷ (even if they fall outside of your first query), enabling you to display those results to your users or to apply a darker shade to cities with a greater number of documents within 20 km ❸.

Notice in figure 15.6, because two searches were run to generate the results, locations from the second search are able to stretch beyond the constraints of the radius from the first query. In this way, the first query was used to discover candidate cities

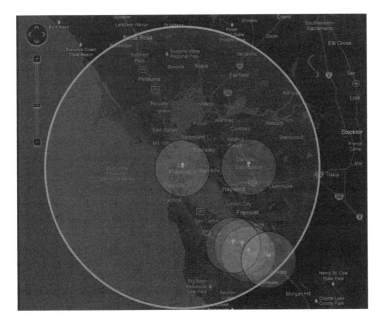

Figure 15.6 A visual representation of facets based upon geographical distances

upon which the second real faceting queries could be generated. You could probably think of hundreds of other ways to generate interesting faceting combinations like this to enable complex geospatial analytics for your application.

At this point, you should have all the tools you need to be able to create Solr queries for some fantastic geospatial-based user experiences. The next section will move beyond geospatial capabilities and focus upon some of the more interesting kinds of data analytics capabilities you can make use of in Solr.

15.3 Pivot faceting

In chapter 8, you learned all about faceting in Solr, and how it can be used to power interesting data analytics and subsequent data visualizations. All of the examples demonstrated in chapter 8—field faceting, range faceting, and query faceting— were based upon the idea of returning aggregate counts for values based upon a single field or query. In many cases, however, it can be useful to provide nested facets: facets which return aggregate calculations that can pivot on values from multiple fields (functioning similarly to pivot tables in modern spreadsheet applications). Solr supports an advanced form of faceting called *pivot faceting* (or sometimes *decision-tree faceting*) that can provide contingent facet counts based upon values from multiple fields.

Say your Solr index contains restaurant documents with three fields: `state`, `city`, and `rating`. The `rating` field, in this case, represents a rating between 1 and 5 stars. If you wanted to see how many 4- and 5-star restaurants exist in the top 3 cities in the top 3 states, you could easily accomplish this through the pivot facet request in this listing.

Listing 15.9   Pivot facet on three fields

Send documents to Solr
```
cd $SOLR_IN_ACTION/example-docs/
java -Durl=http://localhost:8983/solr/pivotfaceting/update
    -jar post.jar ch15/documents/pivotfaceting.xml
```

Query
```
http://localhost:8983/solr/pivotfaceting/select?q=*:*&
  fq=rating:[4 TO 5]&
  facet=true&
  facet.limit=3&
  facet.pivot.mincount=1&
  facet.pivot=state,city,rating
```

1 Requests a pivot facet on three fields.

Results
```
{
...
  "facet_counts":{
    ...
    "facet_pivot":{
      "state,city,rating":[{
```

```
                    "field":"state",
                    "value":"GA",
                    "count":4,
                    "pivot":[{
                        "field":"city",
                        "value":"Atlanta",
                        "count":4,
                        "pivot":[{
                            "field":"rating",
                            "value":4,
                            "count":2},
                          {
                            "field":"rating",
                            "value":5,
                            "count":2}]}]},
                {
                    "field":"state",
                    "value":"IL",
                    "count":3,
                    "pivot":[{
                        "field":"city",
                        "value":"Chicago",
                        "count":3,
                        "pivot":[{
                            "field":"rating",
                            "value":4,
                            "count":2},
                          {
                            "field":"rating",
                            "value":5,
                            "count":1}]}]},
                {
                    "field":"state",
                    "value":"NY",
                    "count":3,
                    "pivot":[{
                        "field":"city",
                        "value":"New York City",
                        "count":3,
                        "pivot":[{
                            "field":"rating",
                            "value":5,
                            "count":2},
                          {
                            "field":"rating",
                            "value":4,
                            "count":1}]}]}
    ]}}}
```

Counts are smaller as you further subdivide a facet. ❸

❷ The pivot facet shows hierarchical counts for state, city, and rating.

The listing demonstrates a three-level pivot facet, as defined by the facet.pivot parameter ❶, which contains a comma-separated list of three fields. Unlike the traditional faceting methods introduced in chapter 8, which only showed counts for values within a single field, pivot faceting lets you further subdivide each facet value by the values within another field, which can then be subdivided by yet another field (and so on). This allows for interesting analytics capabilities in a single query without requiring you to loop through all of the values from the first query and execute separate queries to subdivide the facets by another field. In the example, data was broken down ❷ by state, city, and then a rating field. You can see that as facets are subdivided by more specific values ❸, the counts for the facet are further restricted. In a search index of social networking profiles, you might instead break documents down by categories like gender, school, degree, or even a company or job title. By being able to pivot on each of these different kinds of information, you can uncover a wealth of knowledge through exploring the aggregate relationships between your documents.

PIVOT-FACETING LIMITATIONS

Pivot faceting also has practical performance constraints. Because a pivot facet request is subdividing an original facet by another facet, there is an additional upfront performance (speed) cost for calculating each additional level of facets, as if you had requested each facet individually. Generally of greater concern is the cost of returning large amounts of data in your pivot facet results. For example, listing 15.9 requested the top 3 ratings for the top 3 cities, for the top 3 states, which will return 27 unique values (3 x 3 x 3). If you had merely requested the number of facets at each level from 3 to 7 you would be requesting 1000 unique facet values back.

Considering that the pivot-faceting response format is already more verbose than traditional faceting, it would be easy to return responses many megabytes in size if you're not selective about how many values you return at each level, which could wreak havoc on your Java heap, slow down your queries, and potentially bog down your application stack, which must read and parse the response. For these reasons, you need to be mindful when choosing both the number of values per field to return and the number of fields to pivot upon.

Another limitation of pivot faceting in Solr is that it's currently only enabled for field facets on a single Solr core. Pivot faceting also does not yet support range or query facets. These last two limitations are more a reflection on the maturity of the pivot faceting feature than of technical challenges. Distributed pivot faceting does have an available patch (https://issues.apache.org/jira/browse/SOLR-2894) which is likely to make it into an official release of Solr soon, and future versions of Solr will no doubt also expand the types of facets that can be used in pivot faceting.

FUTURE IMPROVEMENTS TO PIVOT FACETING

As Solr continues to become a more popular tool for real-time data analytics, it's likely that faceting will mature along many additional dimensions. For example, there is some exciting work currently being undertaken to implement statistics within pivot facet breakdowns—such as sums, averages, and percentiles—on the numerical values within a field at each pivot level (https://issues.apache.org/jira/browse/SOLR-3583). There is also a new "analytics component" under active development that supports a wide variety of statisticial analysis upon search results (https://issues.apache.org/jira/browse/SOLR-5302). In addition, there are discussions about whether pivot faceting should even exist separately from traditional faceting, or whether all facets should be pivot facets.

After all, other than the response format differences, a traditional facet can be thought of as just a 1-dimensional pivot facet.

A final change that could provide the ultimate in flexibility would be the ability to pivot on multiple types of facets at different levels. In this scenario, it would be possible to facet on a `state` field, then break that facet down by query facets for documents within 10, 25, and 50+ km, and then further subdivide those values by a range facet across a final numeric or date field. Although not available yet, this kind of faceting implementation has received a reasonable amount of support and is the general direction pivot faceting is likely to head in the future. At the moment, however, pivot faceting is limited to only working with field facets, unless you can find and apply a patch for some of this work in progress to experiment with some of these promising future capabilities. Nevertheless, even in its current form, pivot faceting provides a powerful analytics capability for requesting many nested/conditional aggregate counts within a single request to Solr.

Beyond nested pivot faceting, Solr also provides the ability to both nest queries (make one query/filter conditional upon the results of another) and reference external data within a query, all of which will be covered in the following section.

15.4   *Referencing external data*

Three primary mechanisms exist for using data external to a Solr index at query time. The first is implementing code inside a custom function query that reaches out to an external data source. Although not specifically demonstrated, now that you know how to write a custom function (see section 15.1.6), it should be fairly straightforward to insert code into your own custom function that references data outside of your Solr index.

If the data you need to reference is for purposes of determining relationships between documents, a second method for referencing data outside of your Solr core is to use cross-document joins with another Solr core residing on the same server. For example, if you wanted to limit your result set to documents viewed by particular users that day, you could keep a separate Solr core of documents mapping users to documents they have viewed (instead of having to modify the original documents with information about every user who views them). With this setup, you can perform a join between Solr cores to limit the documents returned in the main query to those not found in a subquery on the second Solr core. Section 15.5 will provide an overview of how to perform these kinds of cross-document and cross-core joins.

A third mechanism for utilizing data from outside the Solr index at query time is the use of a special field type—the `ExternalFileField`—that can load values from an external file.

USING SOLR'S EXTERNALFILEFIELD

The `ExternalFileField` is designed to enable you to update a specifically defined field in your documents independently from the Solr indexing process. This is accomplished by specifying a text file on the Solr server containing a mapping of each document ID to its value for the special external field. This can be particularly useful if you want to batch update a field across all your documents without having to rein-dex your documents.

An external file field is defined like any other field in your *schema.xml*, but with a few extra parameters:

```
<fieldType name="popularity" keyField="id" defVal="0"
    stored="false" indexed="false" class="solr.ExternalFileField"
    valType="pfloat"/>
```

The defined popularity field pulls in its value for each document from an external file that you must place on the Solr server (as opposed to pulling the value from the Solr index, as with other fields). The external file should be located in the Solr index direc-tory defined for your Solr core (by default, this *data/*). The name of the file must be *external_{field}* or *external_{field}.**, where *{field}* is the name of the ExternalFileField defined in your schema. For our defined field, the file can therefore be named *external_popularity*, *external_popularity.txt*, or even *external_polularity.2013_11_03_09_00*. If multiple files exist for a field, then the last one in lexicographically sorted order is used. This can be handy when updating files, because you may want to keep the old version around for some time or may not be able to overwrite the previous file while it's still in use.

An example *external_popularity* file looks like the following:

```
doc123=22
doc456=15.7
doc789=19.4
```

In this example, any reference to the popularity field for doc123 would return the value of 22 as pulled in from the external file. The ExternalFileField has a few prop-erties worth noting.

First, the values for the field cannot be searched upon directly; they can only be used in the return field list (fl parameter) or used in function queries. Technically you could filter on a value or range of values through the use of a frange filter (see section 15.1.2), but this will be slower than a direct index lookup.

Second, not all keys in the external file have to map to real values in your index, and not all keys in your index have to map to values in your external file. If there is no entry matching the key for a document, the value in the ExternalFileField for that document will be the default value specified for the field in the *schema.xml*.

Third, the ExternalFileField only currently supports float values (using any of Solr's float types for the valType), as support for other types was never implemented. As such, this significantly limits what you can do with the ExternalFileField. For all practical purposes, the ExternalFileField could be easily replaced with a custom function that pulls in values from an external file. After reading section 15.1.6, you can probably figure out how to pull this off with minimal effort if you do need to sup-port external values that are not floats in a similar fashion to the ExternalFileField.

Fourth, the values from the ExternalFileField are loaded into memory upon the first use of the field from the external file, and they're not automatically reloaded when the file is updated or when a commit occurs. If you want to prevent the first query utilizing your `ExternalFileField` from being slow or would like for the file to be reloaded upon each commit, you should add an event listener to the `first-Searcher` and/or `newSearcher` events respectively. To do this, you would add the following entries to your *solrconfig.xml*:

```
<listener event="newSearcher"
    class="org.apache.solr.schema.ExternalFileFieldReloader"/>
<listener event="firstSearcher"
    class="org.apache.solr.schema.ExternalFileFieldReloader"/>
```

Although the `ExternalFileField` (and alternatively using a custom function query) can be useful for adding information to your documents from an external data source, it can also be useful to limit the results of one query to only documents found by running a subquery against another field or set of documents. The next section will cover how to run pseudo-join queries to enable subqueries between documents or even across separate Solr cores.

15.5 Cross-document and cross-index joins

In section 3.4.1, we made the point that Solr documents are *not* relational and that content should generally be denormalized within each of your documents. Denormalization, if you remember, means that each document must contain fields for all of the information necessary for queries against that document, even if that information ends up duplicated across many documents.

Although this denormalized document approach represents the recommended best practice for designing your search index, there are times when it's impractical to do this. For these edge cases, Solr provides a basic join capability that allows you to find documents containing a field with values matching a field in results from a separate query.

CROSS-DOCUMENT JOINS

Solr's join capability is equivalent to an SQL nested query, in which the results of a primary query are limited by a separate subquery. The Solr syntax for such a join query is

```
/select?
  fl=RETURN_FIELD_1, RETURN_FIELD_2&
  q={!join from=FROM_FIELD
        to=TO_FIELD}CONSTRAINT_FIELD:CONSTRAINT_VALUE
```

For comparison, the equivalent SQL expression for this query would be

```
Select RETURN_FIELD_1, RETURN_FIELD_2 FROM join-data
WHERE TO_FIELD IN (
  SELECT FROM_FIELD from join-data
  WHERE CONSTRAINT_FIELD = 'CONSTRAINT_VALUE'
)
```

This kind of Solr join query is not a true join in the traditional SQL sense, because data from the subquery cannot be returned with the results of the main query. Instead, only the documents from the primary query are returned; the subquery is only used to limit the results of the main query. Nevertheless, such an ability to constrain the results of one Solr query based upon the results of a subquery against different documents can be quite useful.

Under what circumstances would you want to make use of this Solr join feature? If you had primary documents (say restaurants) and needed to keep track of which restaurants had been acted upon (clicked upon, reviewed, or visited) by particular users, it might be painful to update every restaurant document with a user actions field every time a user performed an action. It would also be challenging to keep track of separate kinds of actions per user and per restaurant in such a model unless you created separate user action documents to model the behavior. Using Solr's join functionality, you could create separate sets of documents in order to model this behavior: one set for user actions and one set for restaurants.

In the last join query example, you probably noticed that both sets of documents resided in the same Solr core (called `join-data`). Because running a subquery requires taking into consideration a large amount of data, Solr requires that all of the documents considered in a join query reside together on the same server. Thankfully, this does not mean that you have to cram all of your documents into the same Solr core. As long as all of your Solr cores containing data to be joined reside within the same Solr instance, Solr will also allow you to perform cross-core joins.

CROSS-CORE JOINS

Going back to the example of restaurant documents and documents for user actions on those restaurants, you would possibly want to separate your restaurant and user action documents into separate Solr cores so that they can be more easily queried upon and updated separately without impacting the index of the other set of documents. Solr's join query parser supports additional `fromIndex` and `toIndex` parameters that enable cross-core joins. Let's assume the following schema for the restaurants and user action documents:

Restaurant core's *schema.xml*

```
<field name="id" indexed="true" stored="true" />
<field name="restaurantname" indexed="true" stored="true" />
<field name="description" indexed="true" stored="false" />
```

User actions core's *schema.xml*

```
<field name="id" type="string" indexed="true" stored="true" />
<field name="userid" type="string" indexed="true" stored="true" />
<field name="restaurantid" type="string" indexed="true" stored="true" />
<field name="actiontype" type="string" indexed="true" stored="false" />
<field name="actiondate" indexed="true" stored="false" />
```

In order to test out a cross-core join, let's index some example documents into both our `join_restaurants` and `join_useractions` cores:

```
cd $SOLR_IN_ACTION/example-docs/
java -Durl=http://localhost:8983/solr/join_restaurants/update
    ➥ -jar post.jar ch15/documents/join_restaurants.xml
```

```
java -Durl=http://localhost:8983/solr/join_useractions/update
    -jar post.jar ch15/documents/join_useractions.xml
```

With example documents indexed, we can now demonstrate a join across both cores. Here's the syntax for a cross-core join to return the name of all the Indian restaurants a particular user has reviewed within the last two weeks:

```
http://localhost:8983/solr/join_restaurants/select?
  fl=restaurantname,text&
  q="Indian"&
  fq={!join fromIndex=join_useractions
           toIndex=join_restaurants
           from=restaurantid
           to=id}userid:user123 AND actiontype:clicked
               AND actiondate:[NOW-14DAYS TO *]
```

This query is running a subquery for an action criteria (user123 clicked within the last 14 days) in the join_useractions core, and is then restricting the documents in the join_restaurants core to only documents with the term "Indian" in the default field and which have an ID that matches a restaurantid from the subquery on the join_useractions index. As you can see, it's possible to maintain two separate sets of documents, linked by a foreign key, and issue a subquery against one set of documents to limit the other. Because the join subquery is implemented as a query parser, it's possible to invoke multiple joins in a single request by applying multiple filters (fq parameters), each containing a separate join operation. Additionally, if you decided to use nested queries (covered in chapter 7) for each of your join queries, you could also combine multiple join queries using arbitrarily complex Boolean logic, because each query parser in a nested query is invoked independently as if it were a search term being evaluated in the main query.

Although the inability to pull back fields from the set of documents from which you're joining is certainly a limitation, Solr's join functionality still provides the useful ability to limit the results of one query based upon the values found for other documents in a separate query. You should still strive to denormalize your documents as opposed to frequently relying on Solr's join functionality for the reasons discussed in section 3.4, but the ability to join can certainly come in handy for use cases in which it's computationally unreasonable to update otherwise normalized values across many documents. Join queries are yet another tool in your toolbox of complex query operations made possible with Solr.

In addition to the join query parser, there are also several advanced query parsers used for joins, the block join children query parser ({!child of=…}) and the block join parent query parser ({!parent of=…}). These allow for much faster joins across your data, at the expense of having to define parent-child relationships between documents at index time so that they can be collocated in the search index. We won't cover the semantics of using these query parsers here, but if you find the performance of the standard join query parser to be too slow, you may want to investigate block joins as a more complicated yet faster replacement.

15.6   *Big data analytics with Solr*

Although it started as a full-text search engine for matching and ranking documents, Solr has evolved in recent years to handle much more. Organizations are now using Solr as a NoSQL database, as a caching layer, as a classification engine, and even as a recommendation engine. One of the other growing uses of Solr is in the area of big data analytics. Many organizations use Hadoop to perform analytics across massive amounts of data. This approach works great for offline processing, but it does not allow customers to drill into the data in real-time in any ways which were not accounted for in a preprocessing stage. Hadoop generally does not run quickly enough to maintain a user's attention in a real-time scenario (on a website, for example), and it therefore does not serve as a good delivery mechanism to users for real-time analytical results on ad hoc queries.

With Solr, customers can search for any arbitrary keyword or other value in any indexed field and see aggregate counts of documents matching the query in tens or hundreds of milliseconds across millions or even billions of documents. As you saw in chapter 8, aggregate counts in the form of facets can be returned almost instantly due to the nature of Solr's inverted index. When you consider that Solr enables you to facet on fields, ranges, or any arbitrary query (including all of the functions in this chapter or any you write yourself), you will quickly realize that the range of real-time analytics calculations you can perform with Solr is vast. When you add pivot facets into the mix, realize you can join queries across multiple sets of indexes, and consider that it's also possible to facet on collapsed (grouped) results, it's easy to see how Solr makes an excellent real-time analytics engine.

What kinds of use cases exist for utilizing Solr as a data analytics engine? As an example, a website may send its server logs or visitor behavior information to Solr so that it can query on specific dates, keywords, or users and graph the aggregate number of data points (page views) that match an arbitrary query on that data. A job search website may be able to plot the growth in jobs or resumes posted, the growth trends for particular skills, or the compensation levels associated with any combination of skills, locations, education levels, or years of experience. An e-commerce site could plot the growth in purchases for particular products or categories over time, digging instantly into attributes such as price sensitivity and regional interest.

Because of Solr's ability to quickly handle arbitrarily complex Boolean queries across many fields and to scale horizontally to handle billions of data points, many organizations are choosing Solr as the delivery mechanism for their real-time big data analytics products. This puts the power in the customer's hands to slice and dice the data how they see fit to discover meaningful insights. By utilizing the complex query operations covered in this chapter and your knowledge of faceting from chapter 8, you should have no problem implementing your own analytics engine using Solr to help quickly derive intelligence from your data.

15.7 *Summary*

This chapter presented many of the more complex data operations in Solr. You learned the power of function queries, even learning how to easily plug in your own custom functions. You also saw the powerful geospatial search capabilities in Solr, enabling basic radius searching based upon latitude and longitude, as well as indexing and searching of arbitrarily complex shapes.

This chapter also demonstrated pivot faceting, the ability to see multiple levels of nested facets, with each level representing the counts that would be returned if the constraints at each higher level were applied. This functionality and the ability to facet on arbitrary functions highlight the rich data analytics capabilities available in Solr.

In addition to learning how to build your own custom functions, you also saw two ways to integrate external data into your documents at query time: `ExternalFile-Fields` and join queries. `ExternalFileFields` enable you to define fields whose data is contained outside the Solr index for use in function queries and return fields, and joins enable you to match documents based upon values found in other documents matching a different query: either from documents in the same Solr index or from documents in a Solr core running under the same Solr instance. All of the capabilities in this chapter enable you to perform complex query and analytics operations far beyond the traditional keyword matching and relevancy ranking for which Solr is best known. There are also many ways to take traditional matching and relevancy ranking much further, which we will focus on in the next chapter.

Mastering relevancy

16

This chapter covers

- Debugging relevancy scores
- Boosting relevancy based upon fields, terms, and payloads
- Crafting function queries to improve relevancy scores
- Using Solr for personalized search and recommendations
- Running and measuring relevancy experiments

The overview of Solr's default relevancy scoring algorithm in chapter 3 introduced how Solr calculates the similarity score (by default) between a query and its matching documents. Since then, most of this book has focused upon using additional search features to scale Solr, improving the user experience, and configuring text and query analysis in order to find the right set of documents which match any given query.

Once that right set of documents is found, it's usually just as important to order those documents based upon relevancy to ensure your application's users find the best matches at the very top of their search results. Although Solr's default similarity calculation works well on generic text, you can usually significantly improve the relevancy of your search results by passing along additional information to Solr about your content.

If you can tell Solr which fields in your document (such as a `title` field) are more important, for example, Solr can weight them higher when calculating relevancy scores. Additionally, if you have user behavior—such as clicks or purchases—on each document, you could pass this information along to Solr so that it can better understand which documents are related to each other based upon which ones similar users acted upon together. This is the basis of how many recommendation engines work, and you can build your own personalized search experience (or a Solr-based recommendation engine) using these same techniques.

This chapter will cover many tips and tricks, including swapping in alternative similarity calculations inside Solr, boosting relevancy based upon functions, making use of user behavior to increase/decrease document relevancy, and testing the results of your relevancy experiments. Although Solr provides decent relevancy scoring out of the box, improving the relevancy of your search results will enable your users to find the right content as quickly as possible, which can result in far happier customers from whom your company can derive more value. Although it's a challenging problem, most mature search-based companies end up spending years tuning and tweaking relevancy because of the measurable impact that it has on any business. This chapter should get you started down the path of delivering much more relevant results from your search system and delivering the most value from your Solr implementation.

16.1 *The impact of relevancy tuning*

Relevancy of query results is one of the most important differentiators between search engines and most other data stores. Databases may be able to query billions of documents and retrieve them very quickly, but returning enormous amounts of data without highlighting the most relevant documents will provide a very frustrating user experience. Because Solr provides a decent relevancy algorithm out of the box for keyword search (see section 3.2 for a thorough overview of the algorithm), one may ask how much additional benefit can be achieved by "tuning" and otherwise experimenting with the relevancy of Solr searches.

The answer to this question is very much dependent upon what you mean by "relevancy." In chapter 3, the ideas of Precision and Recall were introduced. If you remember, Precision answers the question, "Were the documents that were returned supposed to be returned?" and Recall answers the question, "Were all of the documents returned that were supposed to be returned?" Although achieving both Precision and Recall is possible, there is a natural tension between the two ideals, which most search applications must balance.

If your only goal is to always return every correct result, you can achieve 100% Recall by always returning every result, but this likely will not impress your users very much. Likewise, if your only goal is to always be correct, you can achieve near 100% Precision by only ever returning the best matching result (you will be wrong sometimes, but hopefully not often). Again, if users only ever see your top result, they will likely not be overly impressed if they are trying to search through multiple potentially related documents.

If a user is searching for restaurants with the keyword `hamburger`, and multiple Burger King locations take up the entire first page of search results, are these relevant search results? In some sense, yes: all Burger King locations are equally relevant for the keyword `hamburger`. From the user's standpoint, however, they may consider something geographically closer more relevant, or they may expect a diversity of results from different restaurants, as opposed to multiple documents from the same restaurant.

With all of these variables in play, it's clear that keyword relevancy is only one of the many factors that influence the perception of relevancy for your end user. For some search applications, like generic web search engines, the *perception* of relevancy by end users may be the only measurement that matters. For other applications, such as e-commerce websites, revenue resulting from searches may be a more important metric. For job search engines, the total number of job applications resulting from job searches may be the primary goal, and for an online dating site, the number of matches resulting in dates (or better yet, the number of customers who make it to a second date) may be the golden metric. For some of these search applications, it's important to find the one best answer to each query, whereas in others, it's important to spread out the results evenly across users. (You would not want everyone applying for the same job on a job search site or going on a date with the same person on a dating site.)

It is important to understand the domain into which your search application falls in order to best improve the relevancy of your application. There is no question that if you can optimize the relevancy of your search application, you can dramatically improve the success—however you choose to measure it—of your search application.

This chapter will demonstrate many approaches to improving relevancy, from the core similarity algorithms traditionally used to score keyword relevancy, to boosting relevancy by geographical proximity, content freshness, and document popularity, to using the wisdom of the crowds to boost related items based upon user behavior. You will learn how to implement and measure relevancy improvements to your search application to dramatically improve the relevancy of your search application. To begin, we will cover how to debug relevancy calculations in Solr and how to implement basic adjustments for problematic queries based upon what you uncover.

16.2   *Debugging the relevancy calculation*

Before we jump into the methods of improving Solr's relevancy scoring, it will be useful to become familiar with a built-in tool for debugging the relevancy scores of the documents matching your query. Although you're used to seeing the final score for each document in the search results, and although you may feel like chapter 3 provided you with a good conceptual grasp of how the score is being calculated, nothing beats being able to see the computation line by line to debug it.

All you need to do to pull this information back from Solr is to turn on query debugging by setting the `debug=results` or `debug=true` parameter on your Solr request. The `debug` parameter enables debugging information to be returned in a separate section at the end of your Solr response.

Before we can debug a relevancy calculation, we first need to set up our chapter examples and send some documents to Solr. To get Solr up and running, as in previous chapters, let's copy our example core configurations in place and start Solr:

```
cd $SOLR_INSTALL/example/
cp -r $SOLR_IN_ACTION/example-docs/ch16/cores/ solr/
java -jar start.jar
```

With Solr running, let's now send a few example documents:

```
cd $SOLR_IN_ACTION/example-docs/
java -Durl=http://localhost:8983/solr/no-title-boost/update
    -jar post.jar  ch16/documents/no-title-boost.xml
```

The documents we just sent to Solr look as follows:

```
<add>
  <doc>
    <field name="id">1</field>
    <field name="restaurant_name">Red Lobster</field>
    <field name="description">
      We deliver the freshest caught seafood every day.
    </field>
  </doc>
  <doc>
    <field name="id">2</field>
    <field name="restaurant_name">Joe's Crab Shack</field>
    <field name="description">
      We serve delicious red crabs, large lobsters, and other delicious
      seafood. Our lobsters are our specialty.
    </field>
  </doc>
</add>
```

To demonstrate how to debug Solr's relevancy calculation, we are going to send a query to Solr for terms that appear in some form in both documents: `red lobster`. This listing shows an example `debug=true` output for this query.

Listing 16.1   Example debug output for search results' relevancy explanations

Request
```
http://localhost:8983/solr/no-title-boost/select?
  defType=edismax&
  q=red lobster&
  qf=restaurant_name description&
  debug=true&
```

Response
```
{
...
```

```
"response":{"numFound":2,"start":0,"docs":[
    {
      "id":"2",
      "restaurant_name":"Joe's Crab Shack",
      "description":"We serve delicious red crabs, large lobsters, and
  other delicious seafood. Our lobsters are our specialty."},
    {
      "id":"1",
      "restaurant_name":"Red Lobster",
      "description":"We deliver the freshest caught seafood every day."}]
  },
  "debug":{
    "rawquerystring":"red lobster",
    "querystring":"red lobster",
    "parsedquery":"(+(DisjunctionMaxQuery((description:red |
    restaurant_name:red)) DisjunctionMaxQuery((description:lobster |
    restaurant_name:lobster))))/no_coord",
    "parsedquery_toString":"+((description:red | restaurant_name:red)
    (description:lobster | restaurant_name:lobster))",
    "explain":{
      "2":"
1.7071067 = (MATCH) sum of:
  0.70710677 = (MATCH) max of:
    0.70710677 = (MATCH) weight(description:red in 1) [DefaultSimilarity],
    result of:
      0.70710677 = score(doc=1,freq=1.0 = termFreq=1.0
), product of:
        0.70710677 = queryWeight, product of:
          1.0 = idf(docFreq=1, maxDocs=2)
          0.70710677 = queryNorm
        1.0 = fieldWeight in 1, product of:
          1.0 = tf(freq=1.0), with freq of:
            1.0 = termFreq=1.0
          1.0 = idf(docFreq=1, maxDocs=2)
          1.0 = fieldNorm(doc=1)
  0.99999994 = (MATCH) max of:
    0.99999994 = (MATCH) weight(description:lobster in 1)
    [DefaultSimilarity], result of:
      0.99999994 = score(doc=1,freq=2.0 = termFreq=2.0
), product of:
        0.70710677 = queryWeight, product of:
          1.0 = idf(docFreq=1, maxDocs=2)
          0.70710677 = queryNorm
        1.4142135 = fieldWeight in 1, product of:
          1.4142135 = tf(freq=2.0), with freq of:
            2.0 = termFreq=2.0
          1.0 = idf(docFreq=1, maxDocs=2)
          1.0 = fieldNorm(doc=1),
  "1":"
0.8838835 = (MATCH) sum of:
  0.44194174 = (MATCH) max of:
    0.44194174 = (MATCH) weight(restaurant_name:red in 0)
    [DefaultSimilarity], result of:
      0.44194174 = score(doc=0,freq=1.0 = termFreq=1.0
), product of:
```

```
          0.70710677 = queryWeight, product of:
            1.0 = idf(docFreq=1, maxDocs=2)
            0.70710677 = queryNorm
          0.625 = fieldWeight in 0, product of:
            1.0 = tf(freq=1.0), with freq of:
              1.0 = termFreq=1.0
            1.0 = idf(docFreq=1, maxDocs=2)
            0.625 = fieldNorm(doc=0)
  0.44194174 = (MATCH) max of:
    0.44194174 = (MATCH) weight(restaurant_name:lobster in 0)
    [DefaultSimilarity], result of:
      0.44194174 = score(doc=0,freq=1.0 = termFreq=1.0
), product of:
          0.70710677 = queryWeight, product of:
            1.0 = idf(docFreq=1, maxDocs=2)
            0.70710677 = queryNorm
          0.625 = fieldWeight in 0, product of:
            1.0 = tf(freq=1.0), with freq of:
              1.0 = termFreq=1.0
            1.0 = idf(docFreq=1, maxDocs=2)
            0.625 = fieldNorm(doc=0)"},
  ...
  "timing":{
      "time":4.0,
      "prepare":{
        "time":0.0,
        "query":{
          "time":0.0},
        "facet":{
          "time":0.0},
  ...
      "process":{
        "time":3.0,
        "query":{
          "time":0.0},
        "facet":{
          "time":0.0},
    ... }
}}
```

As you can see, a full debug block was returned, including information about the parsed query, the time taken for each search component, and an "explain" section that provides the full relevancy calculation for each document that matched the query. Each section can be incredibly helpful for debugging search performance. If all you want to see is the explanation of the relevancy-scoring calculation, you can use the debug=results (instead of debug=true) parameter to exclude the other debug sections. Alternatively, if you would prefer to see the explanation returned inline as a field in each document, you can also request the relevancy explanation back through the field list (fl) parameter as shown in this listing.

Listing 16.2   Returning the relevancy explanation as a field for each document

---

Request

```
http://localhost:8983/solr/no-title-boost/select?
  defType=edismax&
  q=red lobster&
  qf=restaurant_name description&
  fl=id,restaurant_name,description,[explain]
```

◁── **Requests the relevancy explanation as a field within each document.**

Response

```
{
...
"response":{"numFound":2,"start":0,"docs":[
        {
          "id":"2",
          "restaurant_name":"Joe's Crab Shack",
          "description":"We serve delicious red crabs, large lobsters, and
      other delicious seafood. Our lobsters are our specialty.",
          "[explain]":"
1.7071067 = (MATCH) sum of:
  0.70710677 = (MATCH) max of:
    0.70710677 = (MATCH) weight(description:red in 1) [DefaultSimilarity],
      result of:                                        ◁─
      0.70710677 = score(doc=1,freq=1.0 = termFreq=1.0
), product of:
        0.70710677 = queryWeight, product of:
          1.0 = idf(docFreq=1, maxDocs=2)
          0.70710677 = queryNorm
        1.0 = fieldWeight in 1, product of:
          1.0 = tf(freq=1.0), with freq of:
            1.0 = termFreq=1.0                          ◁─
          1.0 = idf(docFreq=1, maxDocs=2)
          1.0 = fieldNorm(doc=1)
  0.99999994 = (MATCH) max of:
    0.99999994 = (MATCH) weight(description:lobster in 1)
      [DefaultSimilarity], result of:
      0.99999994 = score(doc=1,freq=2.0 = termFreq=2.0   ◁─
), product of:
        0.70710677 = queryWeight, product of:
          1.0 = idf(docFreq=1, maxDocs=2)
          0.70710677 = queryNorm
        1.4142135 = fieldWeight in 1, product of:
          1.4142135 = tf(freq=2.0), with freq of:
            2.0 = termFreq=2.0                          ◁─
          1.0 = idf(docFreq=1, maxDocs=2)
          1.0 = fieldNorm(doc=1)"
        },
        {
          "id":"1",
          "restaurant_name":"Red Lobster",
          "description":"We deliver the freshest caught seafood every day."},
          "[explain]":"
0.8838835 = (MATCH) sum of:
  0.44194174 = (MATCH) max of:
```

Calculates the score for the term red in the description field of document 2.

In document 2, red occurs one time in the description field (termFreq = 1.0).

Calculates the score for the term lobster in the description field of document 2.

In document 2, lobster occurs two times in the description field (termFreq = 2.0).

```
    0.44194174 = (MATCH) weight(restaurant_name:red in 0)
      [DefaultSimilarity], result of:
      0.44194174 = score(doc=0,freq=1.0 = termFreq=1.0
), product of:
        0.70710677 = queryWeight, product of:
          1.0 = idf(docFreq=1, maxDocs=2)
          0.70710677 = queryNorm
        0.625 = fieldWeight in 0, product of:
          1.0 = tf(freq=1.0), with freq of:
            1.0 = termFreq=1.0
          1.0 = idf(docFreq=1, maxDocs=2)
          0.625 = fieldNorm(doc=0)
  0.44194174 = (MATCH) max of:
    0.44194174 = (MATCH) weight(restaurant_name:lobster in 0)
      [DefaultSimilarity], result of:
      0.44194174 = score(doc=0,freq=1.0 = termFreq=1.0
), product of:
        0.70710677 = queryWeight, product of:
          1.0 = idf(docFreq=1, maxDocs=2)
          0.70710677 = queryNorm
        0.625 = fieldWeight in 0, product of:
          1.0 = tf(freq=1.0), with freq of:
            1.0 = termFreq=1.0
          1.0 = idf(docFreq=1, maxDocs=2)
          0.625 = fieldNorm(doc=0)"
]}}
```

Calculates the score for the term red in the restaurant_name field of document 1.

In document 1, red occurs one time in the restaurant_name field (termFreq = 1.0).

Calculates the score for the term lobster in the restaurant_name field of document 1.

In document 1, lobster occurs one time in the restaurant_name field (termFreq = 1.0).

The idf is 1.0 for each term, so it doesn't affect the score in this case.

For this chapter, we will ignore all of the additional debug information from listing 16.1, and focus upon the "explain" section that is laid out inline with each document in listing 16.2. You may be overwhelmed by the amount of information being reported in the relevancy calculation, but the calculation is a line-by-line description of the default relevancy calculation discussed in detail in section 3.2. You can see references to tf (termFreq), idf, and most other relevancy variables discussed in chapter 3. It may take you some time to mentally parse each line, but a review of section 3.2 and a little bit of invested time should enable you to make sense of relevancy explanations like these when debugging your Solr-based search application.

In the example from listing 16.2, one disturbing problem your application's users may notice is that in a search for red lobster, the restaurant named Joe's Crab Shack is showing higher in the search results than the restaurant actually named Red Lobster. Referring to the relevancy explanation in listing 16.2, we can see that the total relevancy score for Joe's Crab Shack was 1.7071067, which was the sum of the score for the terms red (score=0.70710677) and lobster (score=0.99999994). Meanwhile, the relevancy score for the restaurant named Red Lobster was 0.8838835, which was the sum of the score for the terms red (score=0.44194174) and lobster (score=0.44194174). The idf for every term is 1.0 in this example, so it's not impacting the results in this simple example.

Why is there such a discrepancy between these two scores? From analyzing the relevancy explanation, it appears there are two primary factors in play.

- The term `lobster` appears twice in the document for Joe's Crab Shack, giving it twice the score for the tf (`termFreq`) variable.
- We've turned the `omitNorms=true` option on for the `description` field; `omitNorms=false` is set for the `restaurant_name` field. This has the effect of penalizing the `restaurant_name` field relative to the `description` field, because it naturally has less content and the relative content length is being ignored.

Knowing both of these variables, you can make certain kinds of changes in order to ensure that the document for Red Lobster shows up higher in the results when it's searched for by name. Because it's unlikely that you will want to change the content itself, you might consider turning norms on for the `description` field so the longer text is penalized the same as in the `restaurant_name` field. Because you know that the `restaurant_name` field should almost always be considered more relevant than the `description` field, however, you may also consider adding a boost to the `restaurant_name` field. The next section will discuss different kinds of boosting that you can use to influence the relevancy of your content.

16.3 Relevancy boosting

The previous section showed you how to debug Solr's relevancy score, but what do you do when you find a problem with the way the relevancy score is calculated? Thankfully, Solr provides many ways to modify the relevancy calculation, allowing you to easily modify the weight applied to terms, fields, and even entire documents. Many of these adjustments can be applied either at index or query time, and document reordering can even be applied selectively on a per-query basis. This section will demonstrate how to apply these kinds of modifications based upon your understanding of the important features within your content.

16.3.1 Per-field boosting

In most documents, certain fields could be considered more relevant than others. If your fields represent a product, a `product_name` field is likely more relevant than a `description` field, because customers are most likely to search for the names of products, and if there is an exact match in the product name, you would likely want to return the exact match first. Similarly, if your documents represent social networking profiles, you likely want to make the `person_name` field the most important (as opposed to a field containing a list of friends), because an exact match on the person's name should probably show up at the top of the search results.

INDEX-TIME FIELD BOOSTS

Solr enables you to specify that certain fields are more important than others in a few ways. If you know at index time that a field is more important (and the importance of the field is unlikely to change), you can apply a field-level boost when you send the document to Solr. Let's apply such a boost to the documents from section 16.2:

```
<add>
  <doc>
    <field name="id">1</field>
    <field name="restaurant_name" boost="10.0">Red Lobster</field>
    <field name="description">
      We deliver the freshest caught seafood every day.
    </field>
  </doc>
  <doc>
    <field name="id">2</field>
    <field name="restaurant_name" boost="10.0">Joe's Crab Shack</field>
    <field name="description">
      We serve delicious red crabs, large lobsters, and other delicious
      seafood. Our lobsters are our specialty.
    </field>
  </doc>
</add>
```

You can send these documents to Solr from the *Solr in Action* source code with the following commands:

```
cd $SOLR_IN_ACTION/example-docs/
java -Durl=http://localhost:8983/solr/title-boost/update
    ➥ -jar post.jar ch16/documents/title-boost.xml
```

In this example, you can see that both documents contain an added boost=10.0 attribute on the restaurant_name field, which indicates that the field should be considered ten times as important as other fields for a search across multiple fields. Boosting
the restaurant_name field by a factor of 10.0 ensures that keywords in the description of a restaurant like Joe's Crab Shack will not be able to easily overtake the same
keywords in the restaurant_name field of another restaurant (as we saw occur previously with the query for red lobster).

With these documents indexed into Solr with a boost on the restaurant_name
field, let's rerun our query from earlier for red lobster. The following listing shows
the query and results for this query.

Listing 16.3   Improved results after an index-time boost to an important field

Request
```
http://localhost:8983/solr/title-boost/select?
  defType=edismax&
  q=red lobster&
  qf=restaurant_name description&
  fl=id,restaurant_name,description
```

Response
```
{
  ...
  "response":{"numFound":2,"start":0,"docs":[          Red Lobster now shows up
    {                                                  higher due to the index-time
      "id":"1",                                        restaurant_name field boost.
      "restaurant_name":"Red Lobster",
      "description":"We deliver the freshest caught seafood every day."},
```

```
{
    "id":"2",
    "restaurant_name":"Joe's Crab Shack",
    "description":"We serve delicious red crabs, large lobsters, and
        other delicious seafood. Our lobsters are our specialty."}
]}
}
```

The description field isn't weighted as high, so this document now scores lower.

Just like that, the document for the Red Lobster restaurant now appears higher in the search results for the query `red lobster`. If you add `debug=results` back to the URL for this query, you can examine how the relevancy calculation changed to incorporate the index-time boost compared with listing 16.2. Additionally, because it's likely that you would almost always want matches on the name of a restaurant to be considered more relevant than matches on the `description` field, this will likely solve the same problem for many future documents in your search index.

Although the index-time field boost works, it does present a few problems. What happens if you want to change the boost of a particular field to experiment with how it affects your search relevancy? With index-time boosts, you will have to reindex all of your documents to pull this off. Additionally, index-time field boosts are stored internally in the `fieldNorm` (covered in section 3.2.5), which compresses the boost into a byte along with a document boost and field length normalization. Because of this, index-time boosts require that `omitNorms=false` is set on your field (otherwise the boost will not be stored), and the boost amount may not be exact because it's compressed into a byte with other values. Due to these limitations, applying the intended field boosts at query time will, in most cases, be a better option.

QUERY-TIME FIELD BOOSTS

Although index-time field boosts make conceptual sense, they can also be unnecessarily limiting. A simpler strategy, which was introduced in section 3.2.4, is to boost your fields at query time. This accomplishes the same goal as the index-time boosts, but it allows you the flexibility to modify the field boost factors on the fly:

Manual query
```
http://localhost:8983/solr/no-title-boost/select?
  q=restaurant_name:(red lobster)^10 OR description:(red lobster)
```

eDisMax
```
http://localhost:8983/solr/no-title-boost/select?
  defType=edismax&
  q=red lobster&
  qf=restaurant_name^10 description
```

In this example, the `restaurant_name` field is again given a boost of ten times the amount of the `description` field, and the need to apply an index-time boost is eliminated. There is also no longer a requirement to leave `omitNorms=false` in the field configuration of the *schema.xml* to store the index-time field boost, and the loss of fidelity in the boost by indexing it into a byte for index-time storage is now gone. In general, unless you need different documents to have different boosts for the same field, you should probably opt for query-time field boosts over index-time field boosts.

16.3.2 *Per-term boosting*

At times it may be more useful to boost individual terms in a query than to boost all of the terms in a field by the same factor. This was covered in section 3.2.4, and it uses the same query-boosting syntax as the query-time field boost, but with the boosts applied directly to the individual terms:

```
http://localhost:8983/solr/no-title-boost/select?
  q=restaurant_name:(red^2 lobster^8)
    OR description:(red^2 lobster^8)
```

In this query, you can see separate boosts were applied to the terms red and lobster, based upon some information you're passing into Solr about the relative importance of each of those terms within your query. It is also possible to combine query-time term-level boosts with query-time field-level boosts as follows:

Manual query
```
http://localhost:8983/solr/no-title-boost/select?
  q=restaurant_name:(red^2 lobster^8)^10
    OR description:(red^2 lobster^8)
```

eDisMax
```
http://localhost:8983/solr/no-title-boost/select?
  defType=edismax&
  q=red^2 lobster^8&
  qf=restaurant_name^10 description
```

In the preceding example, both the field (restaurant_name) and the terms (red and lobster) are boosted. The natural question, then, becomes this: How are the boosts combined when a boosted term matches within a boosted field? In Solr, the answer to the combined boosts question is simple: they are multiplied together. If the terms red and lobster match in the restaurant_name field of the last example, the term red will get a boost of $(2 \times 10) = 20$, and the term lobster will get a boost of $(8 \times 10) = 80$, prior to any other scoring that will take place. This rule applies for all types of boosting in Solr; if multiple boosts come into play, they will be multiplied together.

16.3.3 *Payload boosting*

Up to this point, we've discussed boosting fields within documents (both at index and query time) as well as boosting terms within a query, but what about boosting individual terms within a field? What if you built a parts-of-speech detector into your system, and you wanted to boost all terms that are nouns higher than other terms in the document? One way to do this would be to create a separate field for the important parts of speech, and give that field a higher boost. This approach may work well if you have a limited number of boosts you want to apply, but what if your application needs to supply a unique boost for each term within a field?

The best way to implement this kind of per-term boost within a document would be through a feature in Solr called *payloads*. When Solr puts each term from a document in the search index, it can optionally store an array of bytes along with that term containing additional information that may be useful at query time. This array of bytes is called a payload, and it can be used when scoring documents in order to affect the relevancy score of any terms in the document that have a payload stored.

Although indexing payloads is officially supported in Solr through objects like `DelimitedPayloadFilterFactory`, using payloads in your query to affect relevancy is not currently supported out of the box in Solr. An open ticket does exist to implement this functionality in Solr (https://issues.apache.org/jira/browse/SOLR-1485), and several organizations have implemented custom query parsers and similarity objects to make use of payloads in their relevancy scoring, but this is an advanced feature that you will have do a bit of work to support. It's at least worth knowing that this option exists, however, in case you need to go down this path.

16.3.4   *Function boosting*

In chapter 15 you were introduced to functions in Solr. In this section, we will demonstrate how to use function calculations as part of your relevancy scoring model. First, let's add sample documents to a few cores for the examples:

```
cd $SOLR_IN_ACTION/example-docs/
java -Durl=http://localhost:8983/solr/distance-relevancy/update
    ➥ -jar post.jar ch16/documents/distance-relevancy.xml
java -Durl=http://localhost:8983/solr/news-relevancy/update
    ➥ -jar post.jar ch16/documents/news-relevancy.xml
```

When placed inside a query, functions are treated as terms which match all documents and which generate a relevancy score equal to the numerical value returned from the function. This means that by injecting functions into your queries, you can manipulate Solr's relevancy algorithm (or replace it) in order to reengineer the relevancy scoring to meet your search application's needs. Consider the following query:

```
http://localhost:8983/solr/distance-relevancy/select?
  q=restaurant_name:(Burger King) AND
    _query_:"{!func}recip(geodist(location,37.765,-122.43),1,10,1)"
```

This request will find all documents containing the terms `Burger` and `King` in the document, and will then calculate a similarity score for each document roughly equal to `score("Burger") + score("King") + LocationProximityBoost`.

This provides the benefit that documents closer to the geographical location specified in the query will receive an additive relevancy boost of up to `10`, which will make locations which are closer appear higher in the search results than they would for just the keyword query. You can play around with the inputs to the `recip` function to control the slope of the curve and maximum value for the distance relevancy boost. If you happen to know where your users are located or where they are interested in searching for documents, you can also easily apply a geospatial filter on their requests. In some cases, however, you may only want to boost documents located closer to a point of interest rather than filtering out other documents that don't fall within a nearby radius. Applying a location proximity boost like this can help bubble up documents to the top of the search results that are both relevant and nearby.

   In addition to providing a location-based boost, many search applications have custom relevancy needs related to the freshness or popularity of content. Consider an online news website that is constantly posting news articles. On such a website, the relevancy of an article is probably some combination of keyword relevancy, the geographical location of the article's topic, how recently the article was posted, and how popular the article is. If you considered only location and keyword relevancy, you would be likely to show old articles (which is generally not desirable for a news website), and if you only sorted by the news article publication date, you might find obscure matches to user keywords instead of the best matches. By augmenting these factors within a popularity boost, you could elevate articles based upon how they are trending in terms of views by other website visitors. What might such a request to Solr look like?

```
http://localhost:8983/solr/news-relevancy/select?
  fq={!cache=false v=$keywords}&
  q=_query_:"{!func}scale(query($keywords),0,100)"
    AND _query_:"{!func}div(100,map(geodist(location,$pt),0,1,1))"
    AND _query_:"{!func}recip(rord(publicationDate),1,100,1)"
    AND _query_:"{!func}scale(popularity,0,100)"&
  keywords="street festival"&
  pt=33.748,-84.391
```

The filter (`fq` parameter) will limit results to those matching `keywords`, which is a query for the phrase `"street festival"`. The query (`q` parameter) will then calculate a value between `0` and `100` for each of the following: (1) the keyword relevancy score, (2) the geographical proximity score, (3) the age of the document, and (4) the popularity of the document. Although the `recip` function and the `div` functions independently enable you to limit each of their maximum scores to `100` (the `map` inside the `div` function is ensuring `100` cannot be divided by a value of less than 1), the `query` function and the `popularity` value (unless you ensure it's set between `0` and `100` in the indexed documents) are a bit harder to control. As such, we've made use of the `scale` function in several cases, which finds the minimum and maximum value across all documents and scales all values to between our range of `0` to `100`.

   While the scaling of the keyword relevancy score, the calculation of the geographical closeness, and the scaling of the popularity are probably reasonably clear based upon previous examples in the book, the approach we took to boost more recent documents may be less obvious here. Because we are dealing with a news website, we made the assumption that the newer an article the better, regardless of how old the last article is. As such, we chose to utilize the order of the documents in the index (using the `rord` function) to boost the most recent documents higher and penalize all older documents, even if they are from only hours or minutes prior. In most search applications that utilize a date boost, you will likely want to apply a different strategy, boosting based upon the time since a document was published instead of upon how many newer documents have been subsequently posted. To do this and still keep the scores between `0` and `100`, you could fall back on the `scale` function again: `scale(ms(publicationDate),0,100)`. The difference between the two approaches here is that using the `scale(ms(…))` combination will supply a large boost to all recent documents based upon time, whereas the `recip(rord(…))` combination provides a larger boost when a smaller total number of newer documents exist. These are just a few of the many ways that you can utilize functions on the dates and other values within your documents to influence relevancy.

By combining functions like `scale`, `div`, and `recip`, each with a resulting value between `0` and `100`, we would expect the highest possible score in the last query to be `400` for a document that has the most relevant keywords, is the closest geographically, is the newest, and is the most popular. The final scores will be normalized lower before they are returned from Solr, but the scaled scores will be visible if you turn `debug` on and assess the relevancy explanations. Although we've evenly weighted each of these four specific variables, you should choose your own relevancy variables wisely and should supply your own set of weights based upon the needs of your search application. You will also need to be mindful of the performance impact upon your searches as you increase the complexity of your queries by adding functions. Some functions, such as `scale`, require significant extra processing in order to take into account the values of every document. You will need to carefully balance the speed of your queries against the added value of these more complex relevancy calculations.

16.3.5 *Term-proximity boosting*

If you discover that documents matching the phrase your users are searching for are routinely showing up below documents containing the user's individual search terms distributed across the document, you may consider adding a term-proximity boost to your request to improve upon your relevancy calculation.

When running a search, Solr (out of the box) combines two information-retrieval models: Boolean matching and a vector-space relevancy calculation for each term using the relevancy model discussed in section 3.2. Because the relevancy score of the vector is based upon the sum of the scores for each term, information related to the proximity of terms in the query is not taken into account by default. This means that if you run a search for `content:(statue of liberty)`, any documents containing all of the three terms `statue`, `of`, and `liberty` will match, but documents containing the exact phrase `"statue of liberty"` will score no higher than documents which contain the words separately throughout the document.

In most search applications, it can be useful to boost the relevancy of documents that contain matching terms in closer proximity than other documents. This is generally accomplished in two primary ways in Solr: one using the eDisMax query parser and one using the default Lucene query parser.

TERM PROXIMITY BOOSTS WITH THE EDISMAX QUERY PARSER

If you're using the eDisMax query parser (covered in chapter 7), there are special parameters you can pass in to enable phrase-based relevancy boosts. The chief among these is the `pf` (phrase fields) parameter, which enables you to supply extra boosts to terms found more closely together within a field. The syntax for the `pf` parameter is field~slop^boost, so if you were searching for the terms big, data, and analytics in the content field of a Solr core and wanted to boost the relevancy when those terms appeared within three positions of each other, your query to Solr would look like the following:

```
/select?
  defType=edismax&
  q=big data analytics&
  qf=content&
  pf=content~3^10
```

In addition to the pf parameter, the eDisMax query parser supports additional fields for defining phrase fields that use bigrams (the pf2 parameter) and trigrams (the pf3 parameter). If the previous query had specified a parameter of pf2=content, it would have applied a boost if either the phrase "big data" or the phrase "data analytics" appeared within the content field. To specify how precisely the bigram phrases must match, a corresponding parameter of ps2 (which stands for phrase slop for 2-grams) can be supplied with a double value. The eDisMax query parser also supports another parameter for trigrams (the pf3 parameter specifying a field, with a corresponding ps3 parameter specifying the accompanying phrase slop), which allows boosts if three adjacent terms appear together—"big data analytics" in this case. See section 7.5.4 for a refresher on how to use these phrase field and phrase slop parameters. By playing around with these parameters, you can find ways to greatly improve the relevancy of documents containing your search terms within close proximity to each other.

TERM-PROXIMITY BOOSTS WITH THE EDISMAX QUERY PARSER

If you're using the traditional Lucene query parser instead of the eDisMax query parser, you'll need to follow a slightly different approach. Instead of using a different request parameter, you can add your proximity boost as an additional term in your query (q) parameter. The Lucene syntax for this is "term1 term2 … termN"~slop^boost. As an example, a query for "customer service"~2^10 would match all documents containing the words customer or service within two positions of each other and would boost that match by a factor of 10. In many cases, you might want to match all documents containing the terms customer and service, but boost documents higher that contained both terms in close proximity. The following example queries would achieve this goal:

1 q=+customer +service OR "customer service"

2 q=+customer +service OR "customer service"~2^10

3 q=customer OR service +{some other terms}
       +(*:* OR "customer service"^100)

4 q=+customer +service +representative
       OR "customer service representative"~10000^10

In the first example query, any document containing both customer and service anywhere in the document will match, but if the terms are found together as a phrase, then it will count as an additional match and will therefore receive essentially twice the relevancy boost (because there were two matches on each term). In this example, the exact phrase query for "customer service" has an implicit boost of 1, so it's equivalent to specifying "customer service"^1, or even "customer service"~0^1.

In the second example, "customer service"~2 will match and apply a relevancy boost to any documents with the terms customer and service within two positions. As such, this will match "customer needs service" (one position away), "service customer" (two positions away), and "customer needs some service" (two positions away), but not "customer really needs some service" (three positions away) or "service the customer" (three positions away). You will also see a relevancy boost in this example of ^10, indicating that the relevancy of this proximity query should be boosted by a factor of 10.

The third example demonstrates how you can apply a proximity boost to only specific terms in the query. Because we don't want the proximity boost to expand or limit our results in this case, we are making the entire proximity-boost part of the query optional by requiring it, but making it match all documents. This allows it to provide the expected relevancy boost, while having no effect on the number of results returned.

The fourth example demonstrates two important features. First, notice that more than two terms can be added to the proximity query. The position offset calculation will take into consideration each of the terms, so the more terms you have, the higher you will probably want to set the slop variable. Second, notice that there is an extremely large slop of 10,000 applied to this proximity query. Although this may seem silly, as it's essentially no different than a search for +customer +service +representative (because the terms can appear up to 10000 positions apart, which is likely larger than your document), it does serve a purpose. The score calculated for a proximity query is higher when the terms are found closer together than when they are further apart, so adding a proximity query such as this with a large slop factor will serve the purpose of boosting essentially all documents with a weight based upon how close the terms appear. Because the default relevancy algorithm in Solr does not apply any such proximity boost, adding a proximity query such as this to your queries may improve the relevancy of your search application. It does take additional time to process the proximity boost, so you'll want to weigh carefully the improved relevancy versus the query speed impact.

16.3.6 *Elevating the relevancy of important documents*

There are three primary ways to increase the relevancy of documents which are considered more important than other documents within your search application. The simplest method is to apply an *index-time document boost*. This functions the same as the index-time field-level boost discussed in section 16.3.1, but it's applied to the entire document instead of just a single field:

```
<add>
  <doc boost="10.0">
    <field name="id">1</field>
```

```
   <field name="restaurant_name">Red Lobster</field>
   <field name="description">We deliver the freshest caught
      seafood every day.</field>
 </doc>
</add>
```

Internally, a document-level boost like this is implemented as an index-time field-level boost across all fields in the document. What does this mean? It means that applying an index-time document-level boost is just a convenience method for applying an index-time field-level boost to all fields within your document. It also means that the boost will not be applied for searches on fields that have omitNorms set to true. The same benefits and drawbacks discussed previously related to index-time field-level boosts apply.

Because we previously (in section 16.3.1) recommended replacing index-time field-level boosts with query-time field boosts, you may be wondering if there is a corresponding query-time replacement for document-level boosts. Indeed there is, and we've already briefly introduced it.

BOOSTING DOCUMENT RELEVANCY WITH A POPULARITY FIELD

To get around the limitations of index-time document-level boosting, a more flexible method of boosting documents is to index a popularity field and to perform a function query across that field to boost the popularity of each document. We introduced this concept in section 16.3.4 when trying to boost news articles by an indexed popularity field. Technically an index-time boost is distributed (multiplied) into each term's relevancy, which is somewhat different than using a function query against a popularity field, which is added to the overall score. Although it's possible to construct your function queries in such a way as to mimic the index-time boost, in practice the additive boost will likely accomplish your desired outcome, so too much focus on this detail is likely a premature optimization until you discover a problem with this approach.

Both the index-time document boost and the boosting of a document by a function on a popularity field are focused upon globally boosting a document's relevancy versus all other documents. This might make sense for an e-commerce application in which certain products tend to sell better overall or for a news website where certain popular articles are trending. In many applications, however, you may want to only boost documents based upon particular queries, as opposed to supplying a universal boost for all queries.

If you recall the Red Lobster versus Joe's Crab Shack example from listing 16.1, the problem was not that the Red Lobster document needed to be universally more relevant than the Joe's Crab Shack document; the problem was that for the particular query for red lobster, Joe's Crab Shack was showing up higher when we would expect Red Lobster to show up first.

Solr contains a search component designed to move specific documents to the top of the search results (or exclude some documents) for particular queries. This component, called the *query elevation component*, is useful for spot-fixing problematic queries for which the default similarity calculation just does not return quite what your users are expecting.

SPOT-FIXING RELEVANCY WITH THE QUERY ELEVATION COMPONENT

In order to use the query elevation component, you will need to enable it in your *solrconfig.xml* by adding the following section:

```
<searchComponent name="elevation"
    class="solr.QueryElevationComponent" >
  <str name="queryFieldType">text</str>
  <str name="config-file">elevate.xml</str>
</searchComponent>
```

Note that the `queryFieldType` should be defined based upon how you want the user's query parsed for lookup in the `config-file` (*elevate.xml*). For example, if you want to only match the exact text the user typed in, you may consider using a `string` field type. If you want the user's query tokenized and want to match any of the user's keywords, then you would want to use a `text` field type as we've done in the example configuration. Once you have the query elevation component defined, you have to perform one additional step to make use of it. Although the most common search components are configured by default (`query`, `facet`, `mlt`, `highlight`, `stats`, `debug`), the elevation component is not turned on by default, so you will have to add it to your request handler. For our example, we'll create our own request handler mapping:

```
<requestHandler name="/elevate" class="solr.SearchHandler" >
    ...
    <arr name="last-components">
      <str>elevation</str>
    </arr>
</requestHandler>
```

With the query elevation component properly configured, the last remaining step is to define some queries and the corresponding documents that should return at the top (or not return at all) given that query. The *elevate.xml* file, which should be placed in your Solr core's *conf/* directory, should look something like the next listing.

Listing 16.4   Sample elevate.xml for the query elevation component

```
<elevate>
 <query text="red lobster">
   <doc id="1" />
   <doc id="2" exclude="true" />
 </query>
<query text="some other query">
  <doc id="2" />
  <doc id="3" />
  <doc id="1" />
 </query>
</elevate>
```

Always put this document first for this query.

Never show this document.

Multiple prioritized documents can be defined per query.

Once you have enabled your query elevation component and defined your elevation queries, you can rest assured that you have overridden Solr's relevancy algorithm for those queries. We have included the /elevate handler configuration in the Solr core in which we originally noticed the problem of Joe's Crab Shack appearing at the top for the query `"red lobster"`. You can now go back to the Solr core and compare the difference between the original query and the same query using the elevation component:

Original query

```
http://localhost:8983/solr/no-title-boost/select?defType=edismax&
  q=red lobster&qf=restaurant_name description&fl=id,restaurant_name
```

Original results

```
...
"docs":[{
      "id":"2",
      "restaurant_name":"Joe's Crab Shack"},
    {
      "id":"1",
      "restaurant_name":"Red Lobster"}]
```

Elevation query

```
http://localhost:8983/solr/no-title-boost/elevate?defType=edismax&
  q=red lobster&qf=restaurant_name description&fl=id,restaurant_name
```

Elevation results

```
...
"docs":[{
      "id":"1",
      "restaurant_name":"Red Lobster"}]
```

Manually defining the results of your queries is very labor intensive, so this approach is generally recommended only to spot-fix your top queries. You could also build a precompiled results list for your top queries based upon externally available information (for example, the top purchases for any given query in an e-commerce application), which may help you squeeze out additional value from your users.

Now that you know how to significantly influence the relevancy of your search application—either by document, by term, by payload, by term proximity, or by function—the next section will introduce you to an even more involved approach: completely replacing Solr's core relevancy algorithm.

16.4 *Pluggable Similarity class implementations*

Since chapter 3, we've discussed relevancy in Solr in terms of the implementation in the `DefaultSimilarity` class. For years, this tf-idf vector-space cosine similarity calculation was hardcoded into the fabric of how Lucene and Solr dealt with relevancy.

In recent years, multiple alternative `Similarity` classes have been introduced, and Solr now has explicit support for substituting in other `Similarity` classes not only on a per-schema basis, but also on a per-field basis. These `Similarity` classes are not restricted to manipulating the traditional relevancy statistics such as tf, idf, and norms; they can store their own unique relevancy statistics in the Solr index for later use.

In order to change the `Similarity` class used to score the documents matching your queries, you can either change the global similarity specified in your *schema.xml* or you can define a custom similarity on a per-field basis. To change the similarity globally, you would add an entry such as the following to the main configuration section of your *schema.xml*:

```
<similarity class="solr.DFRSimilarityFactory">
    <str name="basicModel">I(F)</str>
    <str name="afterEffect">B</str>
    <str name="normalization">H2</str>
</similarity>
```

In this example, the global similarity factory has been redefined from the Default-SimilarityFactory to the DFRSimilarityFactory class (described in table 16.1), with specific input parameters necessary for the class (basicModel, afterEffect, and normalization) specified inside the XML block. If you created your own Similarity class that required no input parameters, it would look like this:

```
<similarity class="my.package.MyCustomSimilarity" />
```

If you don't need to redefine the Similarity class globally (because Default-Similarity works well out of the box for most use cases), you can also choose to redefine the Similarity class only for specific fields by placing the Similarity definition inside the configuration for those fields:

```
<fieldType name="text_custom_similarity" class="solr.TextField">
    <analyzer>
    . . .
    </analyzer>
    <similarity class="my.package.MyCustomSimilarity" />
</fieldType>
```

Although you can certainly implement your own custom Similarity class to suit your needs, this is an expert-level change that could significantly impact the perceived quality of your search application. Solr provides several alternative Similarity classes out of the box that are based upon industry research in the field of information retrieval, so if you're performing full-text search, you may want to consider trying one of these implementations if the DefaultSimilarity class is not suiting your needs. The technical implementations of each Similarity class are too involved to cover in detail here, but table 16.1 provides a high-level overview of each of the available algorithms.

Table 16.1   Available Similarity implementations in Solr

Similarity class	Description
DefaultSimilarity	The default Similarity class in Solr explained in detail in chapter 3 (section 3.2). Uses a vector-space cosine similarity model based upon tf-idf plus several normalization factors.
BM25Similarity	An alternative tf-idf relevancy implementation based upon a probabilistic model. Academic research points to the BM25 algorithms outperforming DefaultSimilarity for many document sets.

Table 16.1 Available `Similarity` **implementations in Solr** *(continued)*

Similarity class	Description
`DFRSimilarity`	The DFR (divergence from randomness) scoring formula considers the relative distribution of term frequencies within each document relative to other documents to determine the relative importance of the terms for that document.
`IBSimilarity`	The IB (information-based) scoring formula is a newer algorithm similar to the `DFRSimilarity`, but with simpler inputs.
`LMDirichletSimilarity`	Uses a language model that provides a Bayesian smoothing of term weightings from the corpus of terms.
`LMJelinekMercerSimilarity`	Also uses a language model, but with a simpler scoring implementation than the `LMDirichletSimilarity`.
`SweetSpotSimilarityFactory`	An extension of the `DefaultSimilarity` class that provides tuning options for determining the "sweet spot" for the optimal tf and `lengthNorm` stats. Allows for sane limits to be put in place, beyond which additional terms will not further increase (for tf) or decrease (for `lengthNorm`) the relevancy score.

As you can see, you have many options to experiment with if you want to test out different core relevancy algorithms in Solr. Most of the similarity implementations in the table contain a lengthy list of input parameters, a solid understanding of which would require you digging deep into the Solr code and likely reading the research papers upon which the algorithms are based. Although you should feel free to dive deep into the academic research, there are often easier methods for improving your search relevancy that are much less theoretical. Providing more information at query time based on domain knowledge, your users' behaviors, and the preferences of your users generally serves as the quickest and most impactful way to improve relevancy within your search application. The remainder of this chapter will focus upon ways to integrate this information and measure the overall impact upon the relevancy of your searches.

16.5 *Personalized search and recommendations*

As search technology has become commoditized through the growth of open source technologies like Solr, organizations have been able to move beyond investing time in basic keyword matching to solving much harder problems within their search applications. One of these problems is how to move beyond a transactional search experience, in which a user is forced to type a keyword and browse through results, often filtering down to specific documents with the use of facets and providing an initial inspection of the content through the use of hit highlighting. One way organizations have tried to enhance this traditional search experience is by building profiles of their users in order to be able to provide more personalized search results to them based upon locations, categories, or other interests known about the users.

Meanwhile, many organizations have also discovered that the art of keeping users engaged (particularly for web-based businesses) often requires pushing information to users, as opposed to requiring them to explicitly interact with a search application. This shifts the paradigm completely, because it requires software systems to be intelligent enough to recommend information to users as opposed to having them explicitly search for it. Although organizations such as Netflix and Amazon are well known for their recommender systems and have spent millions of dollars developing them, it's both possible and easy to develop such systems yourself—particularly on top of Solr—to drastically improve the relevancy of your application.

16.5.1 *Search vs. recommendations*

When one thinks of a search engine, the vision of a keyword box (and sometimes a separate location box) typically comes to mind. Likewise, when one thinks of a recommendation engine, the vision of a magical algorithm which automatically suggests information based upon past behavior and preferences likely comes to mind. In reality, both search and recommendations are just related forms of matching, with search engines generally matching keywords and locations in a query to keywords and locations in a document, and recommendation engines typically matching behavior of users to documents for which other users exhibited similar behaviors or matching content of one document to the content of another document.

At a base level, both search engines and recommendation engines generally function the same way: by building up sparse matrices of links between documents and searching through this information for the best matches, using some kind of similarity measure. These matrices can be composed of terms mapped to documents (a typical inverted index for keyword search) or preferences mapped to documents (an inverted index of behaviors useful for a recommendation technique known as collaborative filtering).

At the end of the day, the real difference between search and recommendations is that search is typically a manual task requiring user input, and recommendations are typically provided automatically based upon what is already known about the user. One can view recommendations as nothing more than an automated search for what you believe would be relevant to a user.

Instead of thinking of Solr as a text search engine, it can be mentally freeing to think of Solr as a "matching engine that happens to be able to match on parsed text." Whether the search is manual or automated is of no consequence to Solr. In fact, several organizations have successfully built recommender systems directly on top of Solr using this thinking. The following sections will cover how to build your own Solr-powered recommendation engine and ultimately how to merge the concepts of a user-driven search experience and an automated recommendation system to provide a powerful, personalized search experience.

In particular, we will discuss several content-based recommendation approaches including attribute-based matching, hierarchical-classification-based matching, matching based upon extracted interesting terms (More Like This), concept-based matching, and geographical matching. We will also discuss using a technique called collaborative filtering, which can provide recommendations based on user interactions with your content, allowing Solr to learn from your users' behaviors and reflect that intelligence back in the form of more relevant results. Finally, we will discuss combining these approaches into recommendation queries that can also serve as the basis for a more personalized search experience.

16.5.2 *Attribute-based matching*

In the same way that Solr is able to parse text into tokens to be indexed into an inverted index, so too can it index interesting structured information about documents (such as categories, locations, or other attributes). In order to build a recommendation engine based upon attributes, you will need to ensure that both your users and documents are tagged with the same kinds of attributes. If you're building a search application to search across job openings, your jobs may be tagged with locations, salaries, and job titles. If you have users applying for those jobs, you're likely able to collect similar information from them through their resume, user profiles, or search behaviors.

To demonstrate several of the upcoming chapter concepts, we've created a Solr core configured for this job-searching use case. To get started, let's send some documents to our preconfigured job-search Solr core:

```
java -Durl=http://localhost:8983/solr/jobs/update/csv
  ➡ -Dtype=text/csv -jar post.jar ch16/documents/jobs.csv
```

With our job-search engine in place, let's now consider how we might be able to use a user's profile to generate an automated search query to provide job recommendations. For example, consider this profile that you might build up in your application for a user named Jane:

```
Profile:{
  Name: "Jane Doe",
  Industry: "healthcare",
  Locations: "Boston, MA",
  JobTitle: "Nurse Educator",
  Salary:{
    min:40000,
    max:60000
  },
}
```

Given Jane's profile, and without Jane having to explicitly search for anything, you could easily provide recommendations to her by automating a search for her on your job search index. The following listing demonstrates what such a recommendation query might look like.

Find the desired title, with an exact match weighted higher.

Score jobs higher that fall within Jane's desired salary range.

Listing 16.5   Attribute-based recommendations query from a user profile

Query
```
http://localhost:8983/solr/jobs/select?
   fl=jobtitle,city,state,salary&
   q=(jobtitle:"nurse educator"^25 OR jobtitle:(nurse educator)^10)
     AND ((city:"Boston" AND state:"MA")^15
          OR state:"MA")
     AND _val_:"map(salary, 40000,60000,10,0)"
```

Find jobs within Jane's exact location…

…but also include jobs in the same state with a lower weight.

Results
```
{
    ...
    "response":{"numFound":22,"start":0,"docs":[
        {
            "jobtitle":"Clinical Educator (New England/ Boston)",
            "city":"Boston",
            "state":"MA",
            "salary":41503},
        {
            "jobtitle":"Nurse Educator",
            "city":"Braintree",
            "state":"MA",
            "salary":56183},
        {
            "jobtitle":"Nurse Educator",
            "city":"Brighton",
            "state":"MA",
            "salary":71359},
        ...
]}}
```

A relevant job in Boston shows up first (as expected).

Relevant jobs in other cities in MA show up next.

Salaries outside of the boosted range still return, but with a lower weight.

First, notice that many of the attributes on the user's profile match up quite nicely with the content being searched. This will be the case in many search applications, but certainly not all. Second, notice that the job title clause and location clause were both required in the search, but that they allowed for both exact matches (with higher relevancy weights) and fuzzier matches. This is a domain-specific choice, because a job seeker is likely to be sensitive to both the location and title of a job, but it favors being less restrictive about how well the query matches each of these. In this case, the query matches any location within the same state and does not require results to contain both the terms nurse and educator within the same phrase.

Third, notice that although matching Jane's salary range will provide a boost, it's only a boost and not a filter. This may be because not all jobs contain a salary range, or it could be because the salary may not be that important. (Would you want to exclude jobs containing a higher salary, for example?) Fourth, notice that the industry from Jane's profile is not included in the query. Although it may have added additional value to the query (if our jobs were tagged by industry), it was left off to demonstrate that it's not necessary or always prudent to make use of every piece of information in your recommendation queries.

Finally, why is the location clause searching upon the exact name of the city and state instead of using a radius filter? There is no good reason for this, other than to keep the example simple; you're ultimately responsible for figuring out both the most appropriate way to construct your queries and which data to use in them to optimize the relevancy of your search application. It may be more appropriate here, for example, to use a radius filter based upon a calculated geographical distance (as demonstrated in chapter 15). The example using Jane's profile is only intended as a demonstration of how easy it can be to create an automated search to provide recommendations.

16.5.3 *Hierarchical matching*

In discussing attribute-based matching in the last section, we made a point to show that not all attributes are created the same, and sometimes you need to make specific attributes optional, although weighting them higher if they do match. The idea behind *hierarchical matching* is the same. Assuming that you have the ability to classify your users and content into some kind of hierarchy, from more general to more specific categories, you can then query this hierarchy and apply a stronger relevancy weight to more specific matches, although still matching at all levels of the hierarchy.

Going back to our example, let's increase the scope of Jane's profile by assigning her to a few categories we think will be interesting to her:

```
Janes_Profile:{
  MostLikelyCategory:"healthcare.nursing.oncology",
  2ndMostLikelyCategory:"healthcare.nursing.transplant",
  3rdMostLikelyCategory:"educator.postsecondary.nursing",
  …
}
```

In Jane's profile and in the job search index, we are assuming that each entry contains a three-level classification, in which each level of specificity is separated by a period (and the field's analyzer is splitting tokens on the period, as well). The next listing contains an example query you could construct that would return matching documents based upon a fuzzy combination of these hierarchical classifications.

Listing 16.6 Matching based upon hierarchical classifications

```
http://localhost:8983/solr/jobs/select?
  df=classification&
  q=(
      (
        "healthcare.nursing.oncology"^40          ◁⎯  This is the "Most
          OR                                           Likely" category
        "healthcare.nursing"^20              ◁⎯      hierarchy from
          OR                                         Jane's profile.
        "healthcare"^10                    ◁⎯
      )
    OR
      (
```

```
    "healthcare.nursing.transplant"^20
      OR
    "healthcare.nursing"^10
      OR
    "healthcare"^5
  )
OR
  (
    "education.postsecondary.nursing"^10
      OR
    "education.postsecondary"^5
      OR
    "education"
  )
)
```

The "Second Most Likely" category hierarchy.

The "Third Most Likely" category hierarchy.

You may notice several things about the structure of the query. First, each category from Jane's profile is broken into three terms in the query, with each term corresponding to a level of specificity of the classification (`healthcare.nursing.oncology` vs. `healthcare.nursing` vs. `healthcare`). Second, each term is assigned a different query weight, with higher weights assigned to more specific terms. This serves the purpose of boosting the more specific (and presumably better) matches higher in the search results. Third, there are three distinct sets of queries corresponding to the three potential classifications listed on Jane's profile (`healthcare.nursing.oncology`, `healthcare.nursing.transplant`, `educator.postsecondary.nursing`).

Because it's possible that our "Most Likely" category is incorrect or that all categories add some value, the alternate categories are also being included in the query, with a lower weight. The end result is that by using query weights on terms which combine a measure of their probability (most to least likely) and also their specificity (most to least descriptive), a fuzzy query can be constructed to match documents that match any of the criteria, while boosting documents to the top of the search results that match the best combinations of those attributes within this hierarchy.

16.5.4 *More Like This*

Although the attribute-based and hierarchy-based recommendation approaches so far have assumed that you have a profile built up on your users containing structured information that can be readily turned into automated queries against your content, there are also ways to make use of unstructured content to build automated recommendations. If you have a particular document the user has shown interest in or—better yet—a document describing your user's interests (such as a user profile or resume), it's not necessary for you to extract structured information out of that document to provide recommendations based upon it.

Solr comes out of the box with both a configurable request handler and a search component that are designed to provide content-based recommendations based upon a document as opposed to user-entered keywords. The More Like This Handler in Solr is able to take in any document (by indexed document ID or by passing in the text of the document), extract the interesting terms from the document, and automatically use those terms as a keyword search to find similar documents. It internally extracts the interesting terms from a document by treating the document as a term vector and extracting the highest matching terms based upon a tf-idf similarity calculation. It can then use those top-ranking terms as a query for other similar documents.

In order to use the More Like This Handler, you first need to enable it in your *solrconfig.xml*:

```
<requestHandler name="/mlt" class="solr.MoreLikeThisHandler" />
```

With the More Like This Handler enabled, you can now find similar documents. To demonstrate, let's issue a query against the job-search core we populated in section 16.5.2:

```
http://localhost:8983/solr/jobs/mlt/?
  df=jobdescription&
  q=J2EE&
  mlt.fl=jobtitle,jobdescription
```

This query will run a search for documents containing the keyword J2EE, find the top matching document, and then perform statistical analysis on the text in the jobtitle and jobdescription fields. It is important to note that the More Like This functionality requires that any fields used for statistical analysis (specified in the mlt.fl parameter) either have termVectors="true" or stored="true" set in the *schema.xml*. Enabling term vectors is faster, as the More Like This implementation will otherwise have to process the stored content to get term vectors at query time. The next listing demonstrates the example recommendations that will be returned for this query, with an additional parameter of mlt.interestingTerms=details set to bring back information about which terms were used for the recommendations query.

Listing 16.7   More Like This results for a query for "J2EE"

Query
```
http://localhost:8983/solr/jobs/mlt?                ❶ Original query
  df=jobdescription&                                    for J2EE.
  fl=id,jobtitle&
  rows=5&                                             ❷ The fields in which to look
  q=J2EE&                                                for interesting terms.
  mlt.fl=jobtitle,jobdescription&
  mlt.interestingTerms=details                          Requests interesting
                                                        terms to be returned
                                                     ❸ along with documents.
```

Results
```
{
    "match":{"numFound":122,"start":0,"docs":[
        {
          "id":"fc57931d42a7ccce3552c04f3db40af8dabc99dc",     Top document matching
          "jobtitle":"Senior Java / J2EE Developer"}]          the query and used to
    },                                                         find interesting terms.
    "response":{"numFound":2225,"start":0,"docs":[             List of recommended
        {                                                      documents.
          "id":"0e953179408d710679e5ddbd15ab0dfae52ffa6c",
          "jobtitle":"Sr Core Java Developer"},
```

```
    {
      "id":"5ce796c758ee30ed1b3da1fc52b0595c023de2db",
      "jobtitle":"Applications Developer"},
    {
      "id":"1e46dd6be1750fc50c18578b7791ad2378b90bdd",
      "jobtitle":"Java Architect/ Lead Java Developer -
                     WJAV Java -    Java in Pittsburgh PA"},
    {
      "id":"4735d1f62503c330c74e470d2d0a26fa855a4257",
      "jobtitle":"Java Developer / Software Developer ( 5 - 7 + Openings)"},
    {
      "id":"2d27ee49cba8189035367f0e048bae07e0faae30",
      "jobtitle":"Java Developer"}]
  },
  "interestingTerms":[
    "jobdescription:j2ee",1.0,
    "jobdescription:java",1.0,
    "jobdescription:senior",1.0,
    "jobtitle:developer",1.0,
    "jobdescription:source",1.0,
    "jobdescription:code",1.0,
    "jobdescription:is",1.0,
    "jobdescription:client",1.0,
    "jobdescription:our",1.0,
    "jobdescription:for",1.0,
    "jobdescription:a",1.0,
    "jobdescription:to",1.0,
    "jobdescription:and",1.0]}
```

List of interesting terms found in the top document used for recommendations. ④

There is a lot going on in the More Like This request in listing 16.7. The first step is specifying a query ❶, the top result of which the recommendations will be based upon. In many cases, you may have a particular document in mind for which you want recommendations, in which case it's probably best to search for that document explicitly with a query such as q=id:fc57931d42a7ccce3552c04f3db40af8dabc99dc. Your request should also specify ❷ which fields to inspect for interesting terms. The More Like This Handler will examine each term in the top document matching your query to determine potential significance based upon a tf-idf score comparison for each term, and the most interesting terms will then be turned into a large OR query that will ❹ bring back the list of recommended documents.

If you want more insight into which terms are being used in the query, you can add the mlt.interestingTerms=details parameter ❸ to the query to return the list of interesting terms that are used for the recommendation query. Although listing 16.7 shows a score of 1.0 for each term, indicating that they all receive equal weight in the recommendation query, it's also possible to use the tf-idf calculation to represent per-term boosts by specifying the mlt.boost=true parameter, as shown in this listing.

Listing 16.8   Boosted interesting terms for a More Like This request

Query
```
http://localhost:8983/solr/jobs/mlt?
  df=jobdescription&
```

```
q=id:fc57931d42a7ccce3552c04f3db40af8dabc99dc &
mlt.fl=jobtitle,jobdescription&
mlt.interestingTerms=details&
mlt.boost=true                              ⟵──┤ Request interesting
                                                 terms to be boosted
                                                 with their tf-idf score.
```

Results
```
{
   ...
  "response":{"numFound":301764,"start":0,"docs":[
    {
      "id":"0e953179408d710679e5ddbd15ab0dfae52ffa6c",
      "jobtitle":"Sr Core Java Developer"},          ❶  Notice a different
    {                                                    results ordering
      "id":"1e46dd6be1750fc50c18578b7791ad2378b90bdd",  with interesting
      "jobtitle":"Java Architect/ Lead Java Developer - ⟵ term boosting on.
                  WJAV Java -  Java in Pittsburgh PA"},
   ...

    ]},

  "interestingTerms":[                       ⟵── The tf-idf boosts
    "jobdescription:j2ee",1.0,                      for each term are
    "jobdescription:java",0.68131137,      ❷  now returned.
    "jobdescription:senior",0.52161527,
    "jobtitle:developer",0.44706684,
    "jobdescription:source",0.2417754,
    "jobdescription:code",0.17976432,
    "jobdescription:is",0.17765637,
    "jobdescription:client",0.17331646,
    "jobdescription:our",0.11985878,
    "jobdescription:for",0.07928475,
    "jobdescription:a",0.07875194,
    "jobdescription:to",0.07741922,
    "jobdescription:and",0.07479082]}
```

By pulling back the interesting terms from the document specified, along with their tf-idf weights, it's possible to make use of these even in your application stack. You may notice that the recommended results look slightly different than in listing 16.7; in particular, the second result ❶ is now for a document for a "Java Architect…" instead of an "Applications Developer". This is because each of the interesting terms used in the recommendation query is now boosted based upon the tf-idf calculation for the term, so terms such as j2ee and java are now weighted higher than when every term had the same weight of 1.0. You can see ❷ the relative weights of each of the terms in the interestingTerms section of the Solr response for the More Like This Handler.

MORE LIKE THIS FOR EXTERNAL DOCUMENTS

The process described so far of passing in a query to find the top document works well for finding related recommendations for documents already in the search engine, but this can be limiting if the content you want to match does not already exist in your search index. Thankfully, the More Like This Handler also supports passing in a content stream containing the full text of an external document for which to provide recommendations. In order to make use of this capability, you need to do an HTTP POST to the More Like This request handler, with the content of the document you want recommendations for contained in the body of the POST. If the document size is not too large for an HTTP GET request, you can also make use of the stream.body parameter, which essentially simulates passing in a content stream to Solr. The next listing demonstrates passing in a document this way (note that you can also do this with other request handlers, such as the /update handler, when passing in documents).

Listing 16.9   Getting More Like This recommendations for an external document

Query

```
http://localhost:8983/solr/jobs/mlt?
  df=jobdescription&
  mlt.fl=jobtitle,jobdescription&
  mlt.interestingTerms=details&
  mlt.boost=true&
  stream.body=Solr is an open source enterprise search platform from the
    Apache Lucene project. Its major features include full-text search, hit
    highlighting, faceted search, dynamic clustering, database integration,
    and rich document (e.g., Word, PDF) handling. Providing distributed
    search and index replication, Solr is highly scalable. Solr is the most
    popular enterprise search engine. Solr 4 adds NoSQL features.
```

The text of the external document to match.

Results

```
{
    "response":{"numFound":2211,"start":0,"docs":[
        {
          "id":"eff5ac098d056a7ea6b1306986c3ae511f2d0d89",
          "jobtitle":"Enterprise Search Architect - Plymouth, MN; Hartford,
                  CT; Cypress, CA; Salt Lake City, UT or Telecommute"},
        {
          "id":"37abb52b6fe63d601e5457641d2cf5ae83fdc799",
          "jobtitle":"Sr. Java Developer"},
        {
          "id":"349091293478dfd3319472e920cf65657276bda4",
          "jobtitle":"Java Lucene Software Engineer"},
        {
          "id":"8139a347d87ab24ffe6895de800d31d338b216ea",
          "jobtitle":"Websphere Java Lead"},
        {
          "id":"f10a09ac5a30ec7743c67198a3cec50a0aafdef6",
          "jobtitle":"Sr. Java Engineer with Search / Algorithm experience"}]
    },
    "interestingTerms":[
      "jobdescription:search",1.0,
      "jobdescription:solr",0.9155779,
      "jobdescription:features",0.36472517,
      "jobdescription:enterprise",0.30173126,
      "jobdescription:is",0.17626463,
      "jobdescription:the",0.102924034,
      "jobdescription:and",0.098939896]}
```

You can see that any arbitrary document can be passed into the More Like This Handler for analysis. The More Like This Handler will analyze the incoming text based upon the analyzers on the fields specified in the `mlt.fl` parameter. It will then treat the analyzed text as it would for a document already inside the Solr index.

> ## Opportunities for improving More Like This results
>
> Although the More Like This Handler is fairly flexible, there are two important points to note. First, you may have noticed that although many of the terms in the interesting terms list are descriptive of the source documents (such as `solr` and `search` in listing 16.9), there are also many noisy terms such as `and`, `is`, and `the`. You can often overcome some of this noise by putting good stop word lists in place. An alternative approach might be to build an analyzer that does part-of-speech analysis and only makes use of nouns from within your text. Because the "good" terms often outweigh the "bad" terms, your recommendation results will likely still look good even with the useless terms, but anything you can do to reduce noise should further improve the overall quality of the results.

Although this section has covered the main features of the More Like This Handler, there are many additional options you can tweak to improve the results. It is also possible to make use of the More Like This functionality as a search component along with a typical search query, as opposed to hitting a separate request handler. For more information about these extended capabilities, you can check out the Wiki page for Solr's More Like This functionality at http://wiki.apache.org/solr/MoreLikeThis.

You have seen how to recommend documents based upon a large amount of text by having Solr extract interesting terms from source documents. What happens, however, when you don't have a large amount of text (full documents) to describe the interests of your users? The next section will cover how to start with a minimal piece of information—even a keyword or two—and find related concepts that can be used to provide useful recommendations.

16.5.5 *Concept-based matching*

Solr is most commonly used to search for documents using keywords entered by a user. As you saw in the last two sections, it's also possible to search using attributes such as category classifications or even entire documents. In both of these cases, however, the terms used in the search come directly from the query; even in the More Like This Handler, the "interesting terms" used are extracted from the document used in the query.

It may not always be ideal for recommendations to be quite so restrictive, however; the ability to find related but different content can be a valuable tool. This section will introduce Solr's *clustering component*, which can enable you to find similarities between documents that can ultimately be used to find related concepts not necessarily present in your initial query or document.

The clustering component is a search component that can be added to any request using `SearchHandler`. It works by taking the results of a query and looking for similar terms or phrases found within the search results. To explain the general concept behind search results clustering, let's examine the results for the query `.Net Jobs` in a

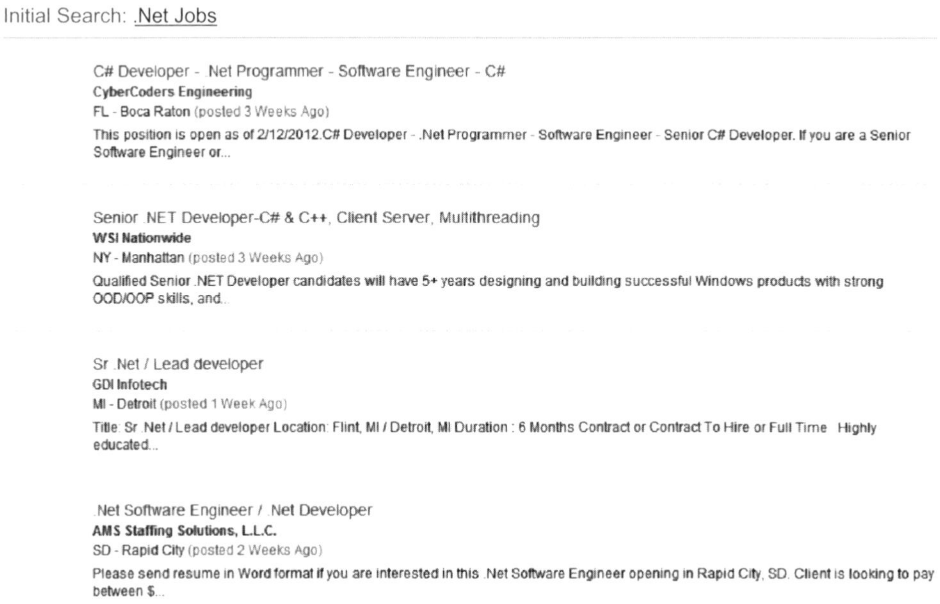

Initial Search: .Net Jobs

C# Developer - .Net Programmer - Software Engineer - C#
CyberCoders Engineering
FL - Boca Raton (posted 3 Weeks Ago)
This position is open as of 2/12/2012.C# Developer - .Net Programmer - Software Engineer - Senior C# Developer. If you are a Senior
Software Engineer or...

Senior .NET Developer-C# & C++, Client Server, Multithreading
WSI Nationwide
NY - Manhattan (posted 3 Weeks Ago)
Qualified Senior .NET Developer candidates will have 5+ years designing and building successful Windows products with strong
OOD/OOP skills, and...

Sr .Net / Lead developer
GDI Infotech
MI - Detroit (posted 1 Week Ago)
Title: Sr .Net / Lead developer Location: Flint, MI / Detroit, MI Duration : 6 Months Contract or Contract To Hire or Full Time   Highly
educated...

.Net Software Engineer / .Net Developer
AMS Staffing Solutions, L.L.C.
SD - Rapid City (posted 2 Weeks Ago)
Please send resume in Word format if you are interested in this .Net Software Engineer opening in Rapid City, SD. Client is looking to pay
between $...

Figure 16.1   Search results for the query `.Net Jobs` **in a typical job search engine**

public job search engine, shown in figure 16.1. Note that figure 16.1 is not based upon
our example chapter data, though you should find similar results if you want to try
this out on the `jobs` index we've been using in the last few sections.

If the initial search is for a fairly specific keyword, as in figure 16.1, the results of
the query are likely to be related not only by that specific keyword, but also by similar
concepts to that keyword. If we examine the results of our search for `.Net Jobs`, we
will notice that other keywords and phrases related to our search, such as `software
engineer`, `developer`, `c#`, and `.net developer` seem to show up frequently in the text
of the results. Figure 16.2 highlights these related terms and phrases.

As you can see from figure 16.2, by clustering the keywords in the top-returned
documents (ordered by relevancy score), it's possible to infer other concepts that are
related to the original query. Using this approach, we could then expand our query
from q=`.Net Jobs` to something like the following:

```
q=.Net Jobs OR ("software engineer" OR "c#"
            OR ".net developer" OR "developer")^0.25
```

This query would effectively expand your search results to include the other related
concepts, while applying a lower weight to these related concepts than to the original
search terms. If you already have too many results being returned and want to boost
the results that seem more conceptually related to the original search query of `.Net
Jobs`, you could modify the query to something like the following:

```
q=.Net Jobs AND (*:* OR "software engineer" OR "c#"
            OR ".net developer" OR "developer")
```

Initial Search: .Net Jobs

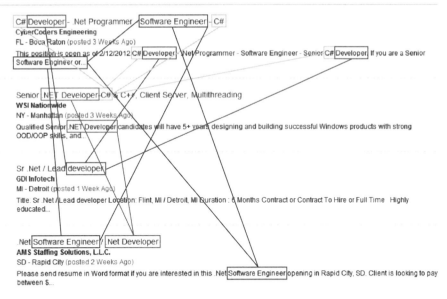

Figure 16.2 Discovery of related concepts through clustering similar words/phrases in the search results of a specific keyword query

This query will not modify the number of results returned from the original query, but it will reorder them such that documents matching the related concepts show up higher in the search results. If you're receiving too many search results and many of them are not good matches because they only match the specific keyword but are not conceptually related, you could apply the concepts as a required part of the query, effectively eliminating any documents that don't match both the original query and at least one of the related concepts:

```
q=.Net Jobs AND ("software engineer" OR "c#"
               OR ".net developer" OR "developer")
```

There are an unlimited number of ways you can restructure your query to improve Precision (by requiring a high level of conceptually related terms) or Recall (by pulling back documents which may be conceptually related but don't specifically match) of your search results based upon the needs of your matching system. Thankfully, it's easy to enable the clustering component in Solr to give you back labeled clusters from your search results that you can use for conceptual matching.

ENABLING SEARCH RESULTS CLUSTERING

To enable search results clustering in Solr, you need to add the `ClusteringComponent` class to the list of search components in your search handler configuration in *solrconfig.xml*. The next listing demonstrates setting up a new `SearchHandler` specifically for enabling clustering.

Listing 16.10   Enabling the clustering component in *solrconfig.xml*

```
<searchComponent name="clustering" enable="true"
    class="solr.clustering.ClusteringComponent">
  <lst name="engine">
    <str name="name">default</str>
    <str name="carrot.algorithm">
      org.carrot2.clustering.lingo.LingoClusteringAlgorithm
    </str>
    <str name="carrot.resourcesDir">clustering/carrot2</str>
  </lst>
</searchComponent>

<requestHandler name="/clustering" enable="true"
    class="solr.SearchHandler">
  <lst name="defaults">
    <bool name="clustering">true</bool>
    <str name="clustering.engine">default</str>
    <bool name="clustering.results">true</bool>
    <str name="fl">*,score</str>
  </lst>
  <arr name="last-components">
    <str>clustering</str>
  </arr>
</requestHandler>
```

Step 1: Define the clustering search component.

Defines a clustering "engine"— an algorithm plus its settings.

Lingo is the default Carrot2 clustering algorithm and works best for most datasets.

Uses the clustering "engine" defined earlier.

Step 2: Enable the clustering search component in the SearchHandler definition.

With the clustering component defined and added to your search handler, you can now retrieve labeled clusters on any search request. In listing 16.10, we defined a new request handler (/clustering) to use specifically for clustering searches, but you can also add it to your main (/select) request handler if you prefer. In order to retrieve clustered search results, we now need to issue a query requesting that results be clustered:

```
http://localhost:8983/solr/jobs/clustering?
  q=content:(solr OR lucene)&
  rows=100&
  carrot.title=jobtitle&
  carrot.snippet=jobtitle&
  LingoClusteringAlgorithm.desiredClusterCountBase=25
```

This request specifies a few parameters, all of which can alternatively be specified in the default configuration for the request handler if you prefer. The rows parameter indicates how many search results will be returned, which is the same as the number of documents the clustering component will use to cluster the text. The clustering component uses a title field, specified with the carrot.title parameter, and a snippet field, specified by the carrot.snippet parameter. These make use of the fact that titles of documents are often shorter and more descriptive of the document, but content sections can also be important in the clustering operation. For the sake of this example, we are pointing both the title and snippet to the same field.

The LingoClusteringAlgorithm.desiredClusterCountBase parameter allows you to define the ideal number of clusters you would like to be returned. There is no guarantee that this exact number of clusters will be found, but it provides the algorithm a target so that it can choose to search for clusters on a spectrum from general (a few clusters) to specific (many clusters). Several different clustering algorithms can be used, each with its own specific configuration settings. You can find more information about clustering on the Solr Wiki at http://wiki.apache.org/solr/ClusteringComponent. Let's now examine the results of our query, shown in the following listing.

Listing 16.11 Clustering documents

Query
```
http://localhost:8983/solr/jobs/clustering?
  q=content:(solr OR lucene)&
  fl=id,jobtitle&
  rows=100&
  carrot.title=jobtitle&
  carrot.snippet=jobtitle&
  LingoClusteringAlgorithm.desiredClusterCountBase=25
```

Results
```
{
   "responseHeader":{
     "status":0,
     "QTime":46},
   "response":{"numFound":62,"start":0,"docs":[
       {
         "id":"349091293478dfd3319472e920cf65657276bda4",
         "jobtitle":"Java Lucene Software Engineer"},
       {
         "id":"bea2d65c7786f6fccea1cdc134f1f743f20b10a1",
         "jobtitle":"Java Developer"},
       ...
   ]},
   "clusters":[{
     "labels":["Software Engineer"],
     "score":15.47007225959035,
     "docs":["349091293478dfd3319472e920cf65657276bda4",
       "c6e08b25102353da348334c8cbd0018fa8912559",
       "76ab5e51d759a93613d056d1930845a211aabee6",
       "b5bdbf64ce704b927992060e5eb02fcefa99a0cf",
       ...
       "c643b258bc1fae773b3059abe0b3acc0befd5f34"]},
   {
     "labels":["Java Developer"],
     "score":12.731272597053874,
     "docs":[...]},
   ...
   {
     "labels":["Software Developer"], ...
   },
   ...
   {
     "labels":["Systems Engineer"], ...
   },
```

The original documents must contain the field(s) specified for clustering.

Clusters include the IDs of the documents within them.

Labeled clusters are derived from the carrot.title and carrot.snippet fields.

Labeled clusters are derived from the carrot.title and carrot.snippet fields.

```
{
  "labels":["Web Developer"], ...              ◄─┐
{
  "labels":["Search"], ...                     ◄─┤
}
{                                                │    Labeled clusters
  "labels":["Senior Java Developer"], ...       ◄─┤    are derived from
}                                                │    the carrot.title and
{                                                │    carrot.snippet
  "labels":["Data Architect"], ...              ◄─┤    fields.
}                                                │
{                                                │
  "labels":["Data Developer"], ...              ◄─┘
}
...
{
  "labels":["Other Topics"],                   ◄─┐   Documents which
  "score":0.0,                                   │   can't be clustered fall
  "other-topics":true,                           │   into "Other Topics".
  "docs":["34fe10d760d2d7b34588acc0c25b90599859ed84",
    "7fb1c9039228cb9649b0c403cd4bbb2a321a0c98",
    "0b5dcc61b81cbf6d3773a5d45d746d0b3b55d587",
    "e921ee1f92fb317f8d11877b81ee71548b153341",
    ...
    "c6c92acd461d997ae9471cf46f30698f93d198d7"]}]}}
```

You will notice that the clustering component attempts to find similar clusters based upon the text of the top documents matching the query. The clustering response includes both a list of document IDs that were clustered together and a label based upon the most descriptive term or phrase found in common between the documents in the cluster. This can be useful as a sort of dynamically generated facet to display to users, or you can make use of the cluster labels as similar concepts that can then be used to expand the original query.

By treating the cluster labels as related concepts, it's possible to expand a user's search to other similar concepts. Turning the results from listing 16.11 into a keyword query would yield results similar to those in the next listing.

> **Listing 16.12   Recommendations based upon related/clustered concepts**

Query
```
http://localhost:8983/solr/jobs/select?
  df=jobdescription&
  fl=id,jobtitle&
  q=(solr OR lucene) OR "Java Engineer" OR "Software Developer"   ◄─┐
```

Results   The top-few cluster labels are
```                                            added to expand the query.
{
  ...
  "response":{"numFound":196,"start":0,"docs":[   ◄─┐  More results are
    {                                                │  returned once
      "id":"f10a09ac5a30ec7743c67198a3cec50a0aafdef6",  related clusters are
      "jobtitle":"Sr. Java Engineer with Search / Algorithm │ added to query.
               experience"},
```

```
{
  "id":"1612550afd8e536c7db7e75b90cbb5fe29a5ed48",
  "jobtitle":"Senior Java Engineer"},
{
  "id":"349091293478dfd3319472e920cf65657276bda4",
  "jobtitle":"Java Lucene Software Engineer"},
  . . .
```

```
}}
```

As you can see, after running a search for the cluster labels found in listing 16.11, many similar documents are returned based upon the concepts found in the original search for (solr OR lucene). This approach works great when you have a limited amount of data—such as only keyword searches previously run by a user—and you want to be able to automatically suggest conceptually similar content to the original keyword search(es).

You have so far seen several content-based approaches to enhancing search results, including searching for attributes and hierarchical classifications, recommending similar documents by using a document as a query through Solr's More Like This functionality, and even discovering related concepts for a query using Solr's clustering component. The content of your documents is not the only important feature that users may consider relevant in their recommendations, however. The next section will discuss the role that geographical proximity may play in your relevancy optimization.

16.5.6 *Geographical matching*

When providing content-based recommendations, it's important to consider the sensitivity of your users to geographical location. For some search applications, such as a restaurant guide, an internet job board, or an online dating website, understanding the location of your user (or where they are interested in being) will be of critical importance if you're going to automatically recommend content to them. There is no faster way to anger your customers and make them think your application is completely irrelevant than to routinely recommend they travel somewhere that is thousands of miles away for a casual outing.

Likewise, if you're operating an e-commerce website, a streaming music or movie website, or an online bookstore, your customers will likely be fairly insensitive to location because your products can be easily shipped or streamed to them.

If your users care about location, you should consider carefully whether to apply a strict filter on desired location for highly sensitive users (as demonstrated in section 15.2) or to apply a small relevancy boost to documents that are geographically closer (as demonstrated in section 16.3.4). The approach you should take to geographical matching is highly dependent upon your application domain, but it's important to get the decision right in order to provide the most relevant results to your users.

Each of the approaches discussed so far for recommending similar documents is based upon information derived from the content of your documents. In the next section, we will explore the idea of using user behavior—how your users interact with your documents—to create an automatic feedback mechanism based upon crowd-sourced intelligence that can greatly improve the relevancy of your search system.

16.5.7 *Collaborative filtering*

Collaborative filtering is one of the most commonly used and best performing recommendation algorithms in the machine-learning world. It deviates from the other recommendation approaches described so far in that it isn't based upon content similarity, but is instead based upon the behavior of your users as they interact with your documents.

You have likely seen collaborative filtering in action many times. When you purchase items from e-commerce sites such as www.amazon.com, you have likely seen product recommendations indicating that users who purchased that item also purchased certain other items. In a nutshell, collaborative filtering assumes that similar users will interact with related content in similar ways. If someone purchases a DVD of Season 1 of the television show *The Big Bang Theory*, then there is a reasonable likelihood that they may also purchase Season 2. If enough users purchase Season 1 and Season 2 together, then a correlation has been formed that can enable a collaborative-filtering algorithm to suggest Season 2 of *The Big Bang Theory* to users who have purchased (or are considering purchasing) Season 1. Figure 16.3 demonstrates this phenomenon.

It so happens that so many people purchase Seasons 1, 2, and 3 of *The Big Bang Theory* together that Season 2 and Season 3 are probably always recommended to anyone who purchases Season 1. In this particular case, any good content-based recommendation system would probably also recommend something similar, because the recommendations are for the same kind of products with the same characteristics and keywords. Where collaborative filtering becomes interesting is in its ability to recommend correlated products that are different from the product under consideration. Figure 16.4 demonstrates such a scenario.

In figure 16.4, the user is about to purchase a Blu-ray player and is seeing recommendations for different items such as HDMI cables and an equipment protection plan. These types of recommendations are excellent on a checkout page, as users are unlikely to purchase two related Blu-ray players together, but they might be likely

Figure 16.3 Demonstration of collaborative filtering. Items purchased together by multiple users indicate a correlation that can be harnessed to recommend those items to users in the future.

Figure 16.4 Collaborative filtering can be good at recommending complementary items—those that are related to but different (content-wise) than the original item.

to purchase these other products, which complement the Blu-ray player they are purchasing. This example shows where collaborative-filtering algorithms are able to outshine content-based recommendation algorithms: in suggesting complementary documents which are likely interesting to users even though their content may not seem at first to be a good match. Similarly, a recommendation based upon collaborative filtering may recommend pacifiers and diapers to someone purchasing a baby stroller, or M&Ms and other snack foods to someone purchasing a pregnancy test. Each of these recommendation decisions, whether correct or incorrect, is based upon the aggregate correlation of groups of items to other items.

Collaborative filtering makes use of collective intelligence, or the wisdom of the crowd, to enable your users to effectively tune the algorithm themselves based upon their behavior. In practice, the algorithm is outsourcing the similarity ranking of documents to your users, allowing their actions to adjust the relevancy weighting on a per-item basis. Because of this, collaborative filtering algorithms have been demonstrated to handily beat content-based recommendations across many industry implementations.

IMPLEMENTING COLLABORATIVE FILTERING

How would one go about implementing collaborative filtering in a search application? In the same way as Solr is able to build a sparse matrix of terms mapped to documents in the Solr index, so too can it map user behavior to those documents. If you remember from chapter 3, when Solr receives documents with fields, it parses the content from the fields into tokens in an inverted index. If we wanted to build a behavior-based search for an e-commerce application, we could model the user behaviors (purchases, for example) as fields on the documents for the purchased products, as indicated in figure 16.5.

By mapping the purchasing behavior of users to documents in an e-commerce application, you're effectively creating links in the Solr index between documents. If

What you SEND to Lucene/Solr:

Document	"Users who bought this product" field
doc1	user1, user4, user5
doc2	user2, user3
doc3	user4
doc4	user4, user5
doc5	user4, user1
. . .	. . .

How the content is INDEXED into Lucene/Solr (conceptually):

Term	Documents
user1	doc1, doc5
user2	doc2
user3	doc2
user4	doc1, doc3, doc4, doc5
user5	doc1, doc4
. . .	. . .

Figure 16.5   Mapping user preferences for documents as fields on the documents

we make the assumption that similar users purchase similar products, this means that documents mapped to similar users are likely related. In order to make use of these relationships to recommend items to a new user, all we need to do is find other similar users and recommend other items they purchased. As an example, let's consider a current user who has added two documents to his shopping cart corresponding to doc1 and doc4. Figure 16.6 demonstrates the first step of the recommendation process, looking up other similar users who have purchased the items in the current user's shopping cart.

As you can see, finding similar users based upon one or more items is as simple as doing a lookup on document ID. In fact, you don't even need to use Solr for this lookup if you have the document-to-user mappings stored in another key/value store. You probably want to find the users who are the most similar, so you would need to implement the ability to weight users higher who appeared in more of the documents. In this case, for example, user4 and user5 appear in both doc1 and doc4, whereas

Step 1: Find similar users who like the same documents

q=id:("doc1" OR "doc4")

Document	"Users who bought this product" field
doc1	user1, user4, user5
doc2	user2, user3
doc3	user4
doc4	user4, user5
doc5	user4, user1
. . .	. . .

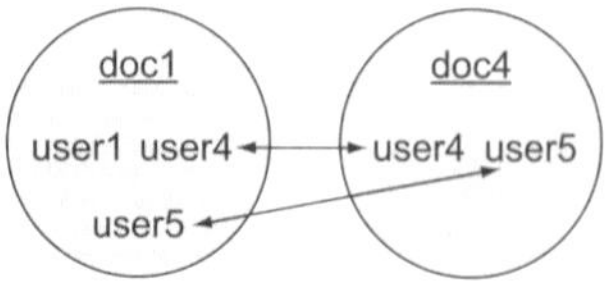

Top-scoring results (most similar users):

1 user4 (2 shared likes)

2 user5 (2 shared likes)

3 user1 (1 shared like)

Figure 16.6   Looking up similar users based upon the items in which a new user is expressing interest

Step 2: Search for docs "liked" by those similar users

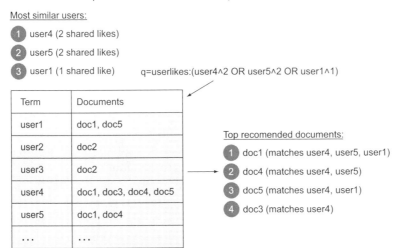

Most similar users:

1 user4 (2 shared likes)

2 user5 (2 shared likes)

3 user1 (1 shared like)   q=userlikes:(user4^2 OR user5^2 OR user1^1)

Term	Documents
user1	doc1, doc5
user2	doc2
user3	doc2
user4	doc1, doc3, doc4, doc5
user5	doc1, doc4
...	...

Top recomended documents:

1 doc1 (matches user4, user5, user1)

2 doc4 (matches user4, user5)

3 doc5 (matches user4, user1)

4 doc3 (matches user4)

Figure 16.7   Searching for documents "liked" by similar users

user1 is probably less relevant because he only appears in doc1. If you did want to pull the users back with weights based upon how many documents they appear in, you could facet on the user field (&facet=true&facet.field=user&facet.mincount=1). Either way, the goal is to get the top users mapped to the documents for which you want recommendations. Once you have a list of similar users, the next step is to find the other documents those similar users purchased, as demonstrated in figure 16.7.

In the second step of the collaborative filtering process, we take the similar users from step 1 and turn them into a query. Because some users appeared in multiple documents we were considering, those users are receiving a higher weight in the query. The more documents you have available to consider up front, the more similar users you will find, and the more important it will be to weight overlapping users with a higher boost and potentially even exclude some less important users if the number becomes too large for the query to execute efficiently. If you only have a few users then you should include them all in the query, but you will reach diminishing returns at some point, after which it no longer helps to include additional users to link the documents.

Once you execute the query from figure 16.7 for the users who "liked" the same documents (who were identified in figure 16.6), you will receive a relevancy-sorted list of search results matching the query. In the case of our e-commerce example, the "likes" were purchases, but they don't have to be. If your search application has limited users or traffic, you may consider using clicks on search results as "likes" until you have a better mechanism for expressing user interest. Because it's much easier for a user to click a search result than to purchase the associated product, using clicks will introduce extra noise in the relevancy calculation, so you will usually find more relevant results by using the best signal from your users available to model an expression of interest.

Another useful feature to note is that the second query, the one running the search for documents with similar users, makes use of Solr's default tf-idf relevancy algorithm. Although your tf will generally be `1.0` for all documents (unless you mark a document with the same user twice, though you could alternatively handle this with a boost on the user instead), the idf will model how many other documents the user preferred. This can be incredibly helpful in scenarios in which your application has some users who are spammy and indiscriminately express an interest in many different documents. Because of the idf calculation, the more different the documents are that a user expresses an interest in, the less each expression of interest from that user counts. Therefore, discriminating users linking a few documents are considered more valuable than users who indiscriminately link many documents.

One final characteristic of collaborative filtering worth mentioning is that it's not at all limited to finding similar items based upon previous items. The item-to-item recommendation in our example served to demonstrate the concept of collaborative filtering, but it's not the only way to implement it. It is also possible to recommend users to users by flipping the model on its head and using documents to link the users. For example, instead of indexing documents, you could index users, with a field for each user showing which documents the user liked. Then you can find users similar to any other user by demonstrating that "documents liked by this user were also liked by these other users." This can be useful if you need to find potential purchasers for a new product based upon their past purchasing behavior or otherwise need to group users together.

The beauty of collaborative filtering, regardless of the implementation, is that it's able to work without any knowledge about the content of your documents. Therefore, you could build a recommendation engine based upon Solr with documents containing nothing more than document IDs and users, and you should still see quality recommendations as long as you have enough users linking your documents together. If you don't put any text content, attributes, or classifications into Solr, then it means you will not be able to make use of those additional techniques at all. The next section will discuss why you may want to consider combining multiple techniques to achieve optimal relevancy in your recommendation system.

16.5.8 *Hybrid approaches*

Throughout this chapter, you have seen multiple different recommendation approaches, each with its own strengths and weaknesses. In the real world, it can often be beneficial to combine these approaches to improve relevancy. Because each of these recommendation types results in a query, it's trivial to mix and match the elements of those queries. What are the strengths and weaknesses of each of the approaches?

Approaches using Solr's More Like This Handler or the clustering component to find related concepts are good at finding specific keyword-based similarities between documents, but they also often result in many false positives by being overly inclusive of (bad) potentially interesting terms to use for matching. You can counter this by combining a classification-based filter (or boost) that will limit top results to a known good general classification with boosting documents to the top that also match specific features of the documents. This also helps overcome the limitations of classification-based approaches, which only match broad categories when used alone.

Collaborative filtering is excellent at finding relationships between documents based upon user behavior only, but sometimes specific characteristics of a user are overlooked when only recommending based upon other users' interests. By combining attribute-based filters in addition to the collaborative filtering clause in your queries, you may be able to more specifically target related documents (that your other users agree upon) to the current user for whom you're actually recommending. Adding a geography clause can help any of these approaches if your users are at all location-sensitive. Although you will need to be mindful of the performance (speed) impacts of combining too many approaches in a single query, most industry research has found that combining multiple approaches tends to yield better results than following a single model. It's up to you to experiment to find the right balance for your search application. If you're looking for a good place to start and you have the data, collaborative filtering tends to beat content-based approaches in most real-world applications. If you start there, you can always add on other approaches over time to arrive at an improved recommendations experience for your users.

16.6 *Creating a personalized search experience*

The previous section detailed how you can build a recommendation engine—a system for running automated searches for similar content—based upon Solr. This included making use of behavioral information to weight the relevancy of similar documents, as well as matching content of documents based upon known similarities between a user and the content for which they would likely search.

Although search engines and recommendation engines are often thought of as separate entities, often even running on entirely separate technology stacks in many companies, many possibilities for relevancy enhancements can be opened up by treating searches and recommendations as complementary approaches to matching.

Throughout the course of this book, you have seen many ways to improve the quality of your user's search experiences. Based upon information collected about users— documents upon which they express interest, keywords and locations of searches they have run, and registration/profile information you may be able to collect containing their interests—you have seen how you might build a behavioral profile of your users to enable an automated recommendation system.

Once you have reached this point, why not combine the best of both worlds and enable your behavioral profile to affect traditional search results? Likewise, why not let users apply their own filters and further refine their recommendation queries in real time? If a user comes to your search application and runs a keyword search without specifying a location, you could easily add a "distance boost" as described in section 16.5.6 to elevate documents closer to the user. Likewise, if a user searches for documents near a specific location (such as in a restaurant search, job search, or concert search), why not boost documents in the search results containing content matching the user's interests from their profile? Additionally, if you have the user's IP address, why not look up the location of their IP address and automatically boost documents that are nearby? It's worth mentioning that, depending upon what data you use and how you present it, a personalized search experience may come across as creepy to some of your users, particularly if you use their personal information without their tacit consent. Privacy may be a real concern for your users, so you will want to think carefully about how you approach personalization in your search application to enhance your user's experiences.

By combining the traditional search experience with personalized relevancy boosts based upon collected or learned information about your users, you can enable your users to more quickly find information relevant to their specific interests. This will not work for every kind of search application, but many large web search engines are moving in the direction of personalized search, with tremendous results for their businesses. If an important goal of your search application is providing relevant content to your users, adding user-specific information to augment their search experience is both possible and simple using the capabilities built into Solr and the techniques covered so far in this chapter.

Not every idea you try to improve relevancy is going to be a home run. You will probably need to try many techniques with various settings before you reach your desired relevancy level. In fact, many organizations pursue relevancy tuning as a never-ending endeavor, constantly experimenting to make additional improvements. The next section will provide guidance on how you can run these kinds of experiments yourself.

16.7 *Running relevancy experiments*

This chapter has focused upon ways to enhance the relevancy of your Solr-based search application. It would be conceptually easy to spend years attempting all of the techniques proposed in this chapter and hope that they improve the quality of your users' search experiences, but how would you actually measure the impact?

If you have a concrete business metric for your search application, measuring that metric is certainly a great place to start. If you have an e-commerce application, this may be the total number or value of items sold. If you have a web search engine, this may be a metric such as the mean reciprocal rank (http://en.wikipedia.org/wiki/Mean_reciprocal_rank), which measures how close the ideal search result was to the top of the results list, or the average number of links a user clicks on before settling on a search result. If you have a job search engine, the metric might be how quickly a job seeker applies for a job, or how many additional job applications an algorithm produces. When using a business-defined metric, you're essentially defining relevancy as that which optimizes the particular purpose of the search engine, even if your end user may not explicitly agree on that metric. From a business standpoint, however, you have achieved the desired outcome (assuming you have selected the right metric).

The best way to experiment with different relevancy parameters in such a situation is to run *A/B experiments* that randomly divide users into groups over the same time period, with each group seeing a different algorithm. Assuming that you wanted to test out two new algorithms with 10% of your users per algorithm, you would place 10% of your users into a control group that represents your current status quo algorithm, 10% of your users into a test group for algorithm 1, and 10% of your users into a test group for algorithm 2. This allows you to measure your metric for each of the three groups independently to determine which group performed best. Unless you're using a good open source or commercial framework to set up and measure the results of your experiments, you will want to be sure to have a solid grasp of basic statistics to ensure that your results are statistically valid.

Beyond A/B testing, which requires exposing changes to a subset of production users to collect results, there is another common method for measuring the relative performance of algorithms using often already available log data: creating a Precision versus Recall graph. In this approach, you can take previously saved user behavior data from log files and test how good each of your candidate algorithms is at predicting the results previously acted upon by the users. In the case of an e-commerce platform, you can take the list of search results (let's say that five were requested per search) for every search or recommendation run for the user, and you can plot them in aggregate on a Precision versus Recall graph showing whether the algorithm made the right prediction, based upon your user's historical behavior. In an e-commerce platform, for example, the right prediction might be defined in terms of which products a user purchased, so any query model that resulted in higher Precision and Recall for those products would be considered a better algorithm. Table 16.2 demonstrates what this kind of Precision and Recall data might look like.

Table 16.2   A Precision and Recall table based upon an aggregate of many searches benchmarked against historical user data

Result #	Current algorithm		Algorithm 1		Algorithm 2	
	Precision	Recall	Precision	Recall	Precision	Recall
1	0.8	0.3	0.65	0.25	0.84	0.31
2	0.56	0.41	0.51	0.35	0.65	0.38
3	0.45	0.5	0.43	0.43	0.51	0.49
4	0.35	0.63	0.33	0.55	0.41	0.62
5	0.28	0.8	0.26	0.76	0.3	0.79

The data in table 16.2 represents aggregate Precision and Recall calculations based upon historical user information. The assumption is that the correct matches correspond with documents the user previously acted upon. If you remember from chapter 3 (section 3.3), Precision is calculated as # Correct Matches / # Total Results

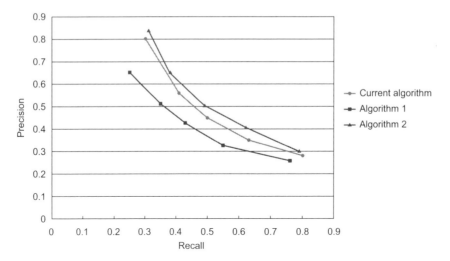

Figure 16.8   A Precision versus Recall graph showing the relative performance of different relevancy algorithms when benchmarked against historical data showing the content users actually preferred

`Returned`, and Recall is calculated as `# Correct Matches / (# Correct Matches + # Missed Matches)`. Although Precision and Recall are not perfectly negatively correlated, there is a natural tension between the two such that improvements in one often lead to declines in the other. The data from table 16.2 can be easily turned into a graph, as in figure 16.8.

As you can see from figure 16.8, algorithm 2 seems to have a higher Precision versus Recall curve, indicating that it appears to be outperforming both the current algorithm and algorithm 1. The beautiful thing about running this kind of analysis is that the results are generated entirely based upon historical benchmark data, which means the tests can be run offline without impacting production systems. Other measures exist, such as the F-measure (http://en.wikipedia.org/wiki/Precision_and_recall#F-measure), which enables calculating an absolute score for an algorithm that strives for a good balance between Precision and Recall.

Whether you track a single number like the F-measure or you track Precision and Recall separately and analyze a curve as in figure 16.8, having the ability to perform offline relevancy testing to sanity check your algorithms can reduce the amount of time you must spend A/B testing in a production system, minimizing unexpected problems caused by bugs that may not have been noticed until your algorithms were tested against real user expectations. With both A/B production testing and offline Precision and Recall testing, you should ensure that you follow appropriate statistical guidelines for accuracy. You should only test your algorithms with a subset of your historical data when tuning your algorithms, for example, so that you don't fit your parameters to your aggregate historical data. Likewise, you should perform tests for statistical significance, as it's possible that your results can be inconclusive even if one algorithm appears to be outperforming another, if there are large variances in your users' responses to your algorithms. At the end of the day, you have an enormous number of features you can enable, data you can use, and variables you can tune to improve the relevancy of your search application. With a solid understanding of Solr and some practice running relevancy experiments, you should be able to create a highly relevant search experience.

16.8 Summary

Congratulations. You have just finished the final chapter of *Solr in Action*! Not only have you learned how to configure and run Solr like an expert, but you have also encountered many examples that have helped demonstrate why and how you can best make use of most of Solr's key features. From configuring your text analysis to grouping, faceting, and performing complex data operations on your content, Solr enables you to deliver real-time, relevant results to your customers in a horizontally scalable and high-throughput search server. Whether you need to handle complex multilingual documents, implement an autosuggest or spelling-correction system, or simply squeeze every bit of relevancy out of your search application, your journey through *Solr in Action* should leave you feeling equipped to tackle some very challenging search problems.

We hope that you have learned a tremendous amount from the conceptual discussions and examples throughout this book, and we wish you the best as you go on to build something fantastic with Solr that will redefine what's possible and have a lasting impact upon your career and the world.

appendix A
Working with
the Solr codebase

A new version of Solr (along with Lucene) is officially released several times per year, but because it is completely open source, the most recent trunk version of Solr is available to be pulled and built at any time. The Lucene and Solr codebases are combined, meaning that even though Lucene can be used without Solr, Solr's development proceeds in lockstep with Lucene, and the codebases are built and officially released together. The trunk version of Lucene/Solr contains all committed changes, though any functionality in trunk could still be subject to change because it has not yet made it into an official release.

In addition to newly committed changes, there is a large collection of patches available on Solr's JIRA page (https://issues.apache.org/jira/browse/SOLR) that have been contributed by developers all around the world. Many of these patches will eventually be committed to the trunk version of Lucene/Solr once a Solr committer agrees to review and approve the changes contributed in the patch. Since all of this code is publicly available and free to use, you can create your own custom Solr distribution if you need features or bug fixes not available in an official release. This section will demonstrate the process of developing and deploying your own Solr distribution.

A.1   *Pulling the right version of Solr*

The first step to developing your own Solr distribution is to pull down the version of Lucene/Solr against which you want to develop. You can either download the full source code and binaries from the Solr homepage (http://lucene.apache.org/solr/), as discussed in chapter 2, or you can pull it by using either SVN or Git with one of the following commands:

```
svn checkout http://svn.apache.org/repos/asf/lucene/dev/trunk
➥ lucene-solr
```

or

```
git clone https://github.com/apache/lucene-solr.git lucene-solr
```

The SVN repository is the official Lucene/Solr codebase, and the GitHub repository is a (slightly delayed) mirror for those who prefer to use Git as their version control system. For the SVN version, you must indicate the specific version of Solr you want to pull when checking the code out. The trunk branch is where active new development takes place and is considered both the most up-to-date version and still experimental. If you want to pull code other than the current trunk version, you can replace "trunk" in the SVN URL with the tag or branch of the version you want. Official releases are tagged as *tags/lucene_solr_x_y_z* (where *x_y_z* is the released version number), so you could you pull the official release of Solr 4.7.0 using this command:

```
svn checkout
➥ http://svn.apache.org/repos/asf/lucene/dev/tags/lucene_solr_4_7_0
➥ lucene-solr
```

Likewise, if you want to pull a current development branch of Solr (not necessarily a tagged release), you can specify the branch you want by replacing "tags" with "branches" in the URL, and specifying the name of the branch you want to pull:

```
svn checkout
➥ http://svn.apache.org/repos/asf/lucene/dev/branches/lucene_solr_4_7
➥ lucene-solr
```

If you are using Git, you can pull the entire Solr repository (containing all versions) using the previous Git clone command, and then switch to the version you are looking for with the following command (for Solr 4.7.0):

```
cd lucene-solr
git checkout tags/lucene_solr_4_7_0
```

If you would prefer to see the active development branch of the current minor release (Solr 4.7.x as of the printing of this book), you can issue the following command to pull the branch:

```
git checkout lucene_solr_4_7
```

In the preceding two Git examples, the first example switches to the official Lucene/Solr 4.7.0 tagged release, whereas the second example pulls the 4.7.x development branch. If you want to browse the available branches and tagged releases, you can browse the list of tags on GitHub (https://github.com/apache/lucene-solr) or by using the official Apache Software Foundation SVN web interface, linked from the version control page on Solr's official website (http://lucene.apache.org/solr/version-control.html).

A.2   *Setting up Solr in your IDE*

In order to do serious Solr development, you will need to set up Lucene/Solr in your IDE (Integrated Development Environment) of choice. Depending upon which version of Solr you pull, there may be a different minimum Java version required, but this tutorial assumes that you have a Java 1.7 JDK installed (search Google for Java installation instructions for your OS if you need them). This section will cover how to set up Solr in Eclipse and IntelliJ IDEA, two of the most common freely available IDEs used for Solr development.

Once you have pulled (or downloaded and unzipped) the code into the *lucene-solr/* folder, getting it set up in your favorite IDE should only take a few steps. If you look in the *lucene-solr/* folder you've created, you'll see (among other things) three important items: the *lucene/* folder (containing all of the Lucene source code), the *solr/* folder (containing all of the Solr source code), and the *build.xml* file (containing all of the Ant build system targets).

Ant, Ivy, and external dependencies

The combined Lucene and Solr codebase uses Apache Ant, a Java-based command-line tool, as its build system. A global *build.xml* file exists for the project as a whole in the main directory of the codebase. Lucene and Solr also contain their own separate *build.xml* files in the *lucene/* and *solr/* directories off of the main directory.

Because Lucene and Solr contain many external dependencies that may also be used by other projects developers are working on, it can be inconvenient for developers to have to pull down all of those dependencies when they initially pull down Solr. To get around this, the Lucene and Solr codebase makes use of *Apache Ivy* for dependency management. When you build Lucene and Solr, Ivy will check for library dependencies and, if they have not previously been pulled, will reach out and download them from publicly trusted sources.

If you use Ant but have never installed Ivy, it is possible you could get exceptions when building Solr about Ivy not being available. If this happens, you should run the following command from the main directory of the Lucene/Solr codebase:

```
ant ivy-bootstrap
```

This command will automatically install Ivy, ensuring you are able to automatically pull in any external dependencies needed to successfully build Solr. If you are planning to set up Solr in an IDE, you'll want to make sure that you have Ivy installed and that you first build Lucene/Solr at least once (dependencies are pulled automatically when you build) to prevent "missing dependency" problems in your IDE. To build Solr, execute the following commands from the root *lucene-solr/* directory:

```
cd solr/
ant dist
```

Although the Lucene and Solr codebase is IDE-agnostic, it does contain convenience commands to create configuration files for two of the most popular IDEs for Lucene/Solr development: Eclipse and IntelliJ IDEA.

IMPORTING LUCENE/SOLR INTO ECLIPSE

In order to enable a seamless import into Eclipse, run the following command from the main directory of the Lucene/Solr codebase:

```
ant eclipse
```

With the configuration files now in place, all you have to do is open Eclipse and import the main Lucene/Solr project directory (which we previously called *lucene-solr/* when we pulled it in section A.1) as a project. These instructions were created while using the Kepler release of Eclipse, but they should work with few to no changes for any recent Eclipse release. After opening Eclipse, go to the File menu, click Import, and then select General > Existing Projects into Workspace > Next. With the Select root directory option selected, enter the path (or browse) to your *lucene-solr/* directory, and hit the Finish button. Now you have the Lucene/Solr project successfully imported, and you're ready to begin developing!

IMPORTING LUCENE/SOLR INTO INTELLIJ IDEA

If you want to use IntelliJ IDEA to develop or debug Solr code, the steps are similar to the Eclipse import process. These instructions were specifically created using IntelliJ IDEA 12 Community Edition, but they should work with only minor changes for other recent editions. To initially create the necessary configuration files for IntelliJ IDEA, you would run the equivalent command from your *lucene-solr/* folder:

```
ant idea
```

With the necessary IntelliJ IDEA configuration files now in place, you can open the IDE, go to the File menu, click Import, and then navigate to your *lucene-solr/* directory and click Next. Make sure the Create Project from Existing Sources option is selected and click Next again. Several more screens will provide options to rearrange how the projects look, select a Java JDK, and select libraries and dependencies. In general, you can use the defaults provided for each of these options and can keep hitting Next until setup is complete.

Congratulations! You now have the Lucene/Solr project successfully imported, and you are ready to begin developing within IntelliJ IDEA. As you begin developing, it will be important for you to be able to debug any changes you make, which will be covered in the next section.

A.3   *Debugging Solr code*

The easiest way to step through the Solr codebase (along with any changes you make to Solr) is to enable the JVM's remote debugging capabilities when you start up the example Solr application. This method works with all major IDEs, and it allows you to debug Solr from a remote server. In order to build the most recent version of the example after you modify the Solr code (or add your own plugins), run the following commands from the root *lucene-solr/* directory you created/pulled in the last section:

```
cd solr/
ant example
```

After this command finishes rebuilding Solr and the example web application, you can then pass in parameters to enable remote debugging when you start up Solr:

```
cd example/
java
➥ -agentlib:jdwp=transport=dt_socket,server=y,suspend=y,address=8984
➥ -jar start.jar
```

The `agentlib:jdwp` parameter starts up the JVM to run in remote debugging mode. The `address` you specify for the remote debugging port is arbitrary; we chose one close to the default Solr port. The `suspend=y` option tells the JVM not to begin execution of the *start.jar* code until after a debugger has been attached. If you want Solr to start as usual and you plan on attaching a debugger at some point in the future, you can set `suspend=n`. If you need to debug Solr startup logic, you will want to set `suspend=y`, but otherwise it may be easier to wait and attach your debugger later, sometime before you send a request to Solr that you want to debug.

Running Solr from inside Eclipse

If you're using Eclipse and don't have a need to remotely debug Solr, you can alternatively set up Eclipse to run Jetty (through Solr's included *start.jar*) directly. This will send the Solr output to Eclipse's console and keep the running of Solr self-contained within Eclipse.

To set up such a debug configuration, go to Run > Debug Configurations > Java Application and set the following:

Main Class ("Main" tab): `org.eclipse.jetty.start.Main`
Working Directory ("Arguments" tab): `${workspace_loc:lucene-solr/solr/example}`

Then add Solr's *start.jar* file to the classpath so that Eclipse can find and run Jetty's `Main` class. From the Classpath tab, click

Classpath > User Entries > Add JARs > *lucene-solr/solr/example/start.jar*

That's all there is to it. You can now save and run this configuration as many times as you want to debug Solr inside Eclipse. You should also be able to create a similar configuration in most other IDEs. Otherwise, you can also use the remote debug configuration described previously if you prefer to run Solr externally to your IDE; the next section will demonstrate how to debug that configuration.

ATTACHING YOUR IDE TO A RUNNING SOLR INSTANCE

Once Solr is started in remote debug mode, you can attach your IDE to the running Solr instance. In Eclipse, you would do this by going to the menu bar and clicking Run > Debug Configurations > Remote Java Application, selecting `lucene-solr` as the project, `localhost` as the host, `8984` as the port, and then clicking Debug.

If you previously set `suspend=y`, you'll see Solr start up (from the terminal in which you previously launched it in debug mode), and you'll now be able to set breakpoints inside of Eclipse and step through the code as it's executed within Solr.

If you are using IntelliJ IDEA, you'll follow similar steps. From the menu bar, go to Run > Edit Configurations, then click the + (Add) button, and select Remote as the new kind of configuration you want to add. Next, give the configuration a name (such as `lucene-solr`), set the host to `localhost`, set the port to `8984`, and click OK. With your debug configuration defined, you can now go back to the menu bar, select Run > Debug, and select `lucene-solr` (or the name of the debug configuration you provided) to begin debugging.

> ### Remotely debugging Solr's code
> It's worth noting that, although we're using this technique to debug Solr locally, this remote debugging capability works across networked computers. This means that if you have a production Solr server and start it up with remote debugging enabled, you will be able to attach your IDE to the remote server and debug any code issues you are encountering. All you need do is change the name of the server in your IDE's debug configuration from `localhost` to the server's address on the network, and ensure you select a remote debugging port that is not blocked on your network. Keep in mind that you're halting execution of the code when you hit breakpoints, so you'll want to ensure that no users are hitting the server before you begin debugging.

Now that you know how to set up Solr in your IDE for development and how to debug the Solr code, the next logical step is to attempt to improve your Solr distribution by applying code patches to Solr to add additional functionality or fix known bugs.

A.4 Downloading and applying Solr patches

It's possible that from time to time you may uncover a bug in Solr or may have a need for a feature that is not yet available in Solr. Because Solr is an open source project with a large community of developers, it can often be the case that other developers have the same need and may have even started developing code to tackle the problem. Solr has a publicly accessible ticket tracker available at https://issues.apache.org/jira/browse/SOLR.

This ticket tracker, referred to subsequently as the Solr JIRA, is used to both submit feature requests and upload changes to the Solr codebase in the form of patch files. This means you may be able to find already working (though perhaps unfinished) code that can solve your problem.

In order to apply the patch, you should find the most recent patch file available, keeping in mind that if the patch file does not correspond with your current version of Solr, you may get an error when applying the patch due to a code mismatch.

The Solr community uses standard patch files created by either the `svn diff` or the `git format-patch` command (or an equivalent diff format from another version control system). To test a patch, you need to run the following commands from your *lucene-solr/* directory for a patch created with the `svn diff` command:

```
wget <URL to the patch> -O - | patch -p0 --dry-run
```

Likewise, if you have a patch created with the `git format-patch` command, you will need to pass in the `-p1` option instead of the `-p0` option to account for the different patch format:

```
wget <URL to the patch> -O - | patch -p1 --dry-run
```

Both examples assume you want to pull a publicly posted patch from a URL on the Solr JIRA without downloading it manually to your computer, but it's also possible to test the patch from a local patch file. If you already have a local copy of the patch file, copy it to the root of your Lucene/Solr project (the *lucene-solr/* folder you pulled previously) and run the following command for an SVN-style patch:

```
patch -p0 -i <patchfile> --dry-run
```

If you have trouble applying the patch, try the following command, which handles patches formatted in the default Git patch style:

```
patch -p1 -i <patchfile> --dry-run
```

Those patch commands include the `--dry-run` flag, which tests whether the patch would apply cleanly without actually applying the patch. It's best practice to always test a patch before applying it, so that you do not end up with a broken codebase due to only certain parts of a patch applying cleanly. To apply a patch after successfully passing a dry run, all you need to do is remove the `--dry-run` parameter from your command.

If you make a mistake applying the patch or want to revert, you can revert the repository (using `svn revert -R ./` if using SVN or `git reset --hard HEAD` if using Git). There are many tricks (beyond the scope of this book) for working effectively with your source control system to support moving back and forth between local branches to easily test changes without destroying your local repository, but these patching options should provide what you need to be able to make use of community-contributed patches.

Once you begin testing patches, it's likely that you'll want to contribute improvements you've made. The following section demonstrates how to create and submit a Solr patch.

A.5   *Contributing patches*

If you decide to fix a bug with Solr, add a feature, or work to improve an existing patch, you can contribute it for others to use by uploading it to the Solr JIRA. To do this, you'll need to create an account for the Solr JIRA, and create a tracking ticket if one does not already exist for the feature you are contributing.

If you think you need to submit a new Solr JIRA ticket, it's best to first send an email to the Solr users' mailing list to make sure the feature does not already exist or the Solr development mailing list to ensure you're on the right track with the solution you're implementing. Information on how to sign up for these mailing lists is available at http://lucene.apache.org/solr/discussion.html.

Once you've determined that a patch is necessary and have written code to handle your use case, there are a few items for consideration. First, Solr maintains a list of coding guidelines (http://wiki.apache.org/solr/HowToContribute#Making_Changes) that should be followed for any submitted patches. One of the most important requirements for a new patch is that it does not break any existing unit tests in Solr or Lucene. Before you begin creating your patch, you should run the full suite of unit tests from the root *lucene-solr/* directory:

```
ant clean test
```

If the output of the test run is a `BUILD SUCCESSFUL` message, you can proceed with creating your patch, but otherwise you need to check into why tests are failing and get any problems corrected first. In order to ensure that other basic mistakes are avoided in patches, you should next run the `precommit` Ant task before trying to create your patch file:

```
ant precommit
```

If all `precommit` checks pass, you're now ready to create your patch. If you're using SVN, you need to find all of your modified files:

```
svn stat
```

Next, you'll need to add any new files listed from the `svn stat` command:

```
svn add path/to/newfile1
svn add path/to/newfile2
...
```

Solr and Lucene both maintain a *CHANGES.txt* file in their project root directories (*solr/* and *lucene/*). Before contributing your patch, you should add an entry into the Solr *CHANGES.txt* (and/or the Lucene file if you've made changes there) including the JIRA ticket number for the change and a brief explanation of what the change does. Once the changes are documented, the last step is to create the patch file by running the `svn diff` command:

```
svn diff > SOLR-XXXX.patch
```

This command will create a patch file corresponding with the ticket number of the patch that can then be uploaded to the Solr JIRA. The patch filename should follow this exact format, and any future patches should be uploaded with the same filename to indicate to the Solr JIRA that they are newer versions of the same patch.

If you're using Git instead of SVN, you can alternatively create a patch using the following related Git commands:

```
git status
git add path/to/file1
git add path/to/file2
...
git commit -m"Description of your commit"
git format-patch --stdout -p --no-prefix -1 > SOLR-XXXX.patch
```

Note two things about the `git format-patch` command. First the `-1` argument indicates that the patch should be created based upon a diff of the latest commit with the previous commit. If you are trying to create a patch including multiple commits, you will do best to replace the -1 with the last commit ID prior to your changes. You can use the git log command to see the recent commit history and find the appropriate commit ID.

The second thing to note about the git format-patch command is the --no-prefix argument, which causes the patch file to be generated in the patch –p0 format (SVN style) as opposed to the patch –p1 format (default Git style), as discussed in the previous section about applying Solr patches.

Because the Solr community uses both SVN and Git, providing patches in the former (patch –p0) format provides a helpful standard which enables easy collaboration across both environments.

Once you have created your patch, you may want to consider reverting your local repository and applying the patch using the steps in section A.4 to make sure the patch is not missing any of your changes. If everything passes, the last step is to upload the patch to the Solr JIRA for the ticket that you created or upon which you are collaborating. If all goes well and a Solr committer agrees with your changes, you'll see them in an official release of Solr soon! Once you have all of your patches finished and applied to the Lucene/Solr codebase, you'll likely be ready to build Solr and deploy it. Please refer to chapter 12 for steps on how to build Solr and deploy it in a production environment.

appendix B
Language-specific field
type configurations

Because of the wide variations between languages, there is not a single, consistent model to follow when defining a field in Solr to properly handle a language. Some languages require their own stemming filters, others require multiple filters to handle different language characteristics (such as normalization of characters, removal of accents, and even custom lowercasing functionality), and some languages even require their own tokenizers due to the complexity of parsing the language. The following table provides good out-of-the-box configurations for many of the languages Solr supports. These are by no means the only way to configure a language, but they will serve as a good starting point.

Because many of the analysis components are shared across many languages, all language-specific components and configurations are highlighted in bold.

Language	Example analyzer chain	
Arabic	StandardTokenizerFactory	
	LowerCaseFilterFactory	
	StopFilterFactory	[words="lang/**stopwords_ar.txt**"]
	ArabicNormalizationFilterFactory	
	ArabicStemFilterFactory	
Armenian	StandardTokenizerFactory	
	LowerCaseFilterFactory	
	StopFilterFactory	[words="lang/**stopwords_hy.txt**"]
	SnowballPorterFilterFactory	[language="**Armenian**"]

Language	Example analyzer chain
Basque	StandardTokenizerFactory LowerCaseFilterFactory StopFilterFactory [words="lang/**stopwords_eu.txt**"] SnowballPorterFilterFactory [language="**Basque**"]
Bulgarian	StandardTokenizerFactory LowerCaseFilterFactory StopFilterFactory [words="lang/**stopwords_bg.txt**"] **BulgarianStemFilterFactory**
Catalan	StandardTokenizerFactory ElisionFilterFactory [articles="lang/**contractions_ca.txt**"] LowerCaseFilterFactory StopFilterFactory [words="lang/**stopwords_ca.txt**"] SnowballPorterFilterFactory [language="**Catalan**"]
Chinese	SmartChineseSentenceTokenizerFactory* SmartChineseWordTokenFilterFactory* LowerCaseFilterFactory PositionFilterFactory *Note: Requires additional dependencies. See solr/contrib/analysis-extras/README.txt for details.*
CJK (Chinese, Japanese, Korean bigrams)	StandardTokenizerFactory **CJKWidthFilterFactory** LowerCaseFilterFactory **CJKBigramFilterFactory**
Czech	StandardTokenizerFactory LowerCaseFilterFactory StopFilterFactory [words="lang/**stopwords_cz.txt**"] **CzechStemFilterFactory**
Danish	StandardTokenizerFactory LowerCaseFilterFactory StopFilterFactory [words="lang/**stopwords_da.txt**"] SnowballPorterFilterFactory [language="**Danish**"]
Dutch	StandardTokenizerFactory LowerCaseFilterFactory StopFilterFactory [words="lang/**stopwords_nl.txt**"] StemmerOverrideFilterFactory [dictionary="lang/**stemdict_nl.txt**"] SnowballPorterFilterFactory [language="**Dutch**"]
English	StandardTokenizerFactory StopFilterFactory [words="lang/**stopwords_en.txt**"] LowerCaseFilterFactory **EnglishPossessiveFilterFactory** **(EnglishMinimalStemFilterFactory** OR **KStemFilterFactory** OR **PorterStemFilterFactory** OR SnowballPorterFilterFactory) [language="**English**"]

Language	Example analyzer chain
Finnish	StandardTokenizerFactory LowerCaseFilterFactory StopFilterFactory　　　　　　　　　　　　[words="lang/**stopwords_fi.txt**"] (**FinnishLightStemFilterFactory** 　OR SnowballPorterFilterFactory)　　　　　　　[language="**Finnish**"]
French	StandardTokenizerFactory ElisionFilterFactory　　　　[articles="lang/**contractions_fr.txt**"] LowerCaseFilterFactory StopFilterFactory　　　　　　　　　　　[words="lang/**stopwords_fr.txt**"] (**FrenchLightStemFilterFactory** 　OR **FrenchMinimalStemFilterFactory** 　OR SnowballPorterFilterFactory)　　　　　　　[language="**French**"]
Galician	StandardTokenizerFactory LowerCaseFilterFactory StopFilterFactory　　　　　　　　　　　[words="lang/**stopwords_gl.txt**"] (**GalicianStemFilterFactory** 　OR **GalicianMinimalStemFilterFactory**)
German	StandardTokenizerFactory LowerCaseFilterFactory StopFilterFactory　　　　　　　　　　　[words="lang/**stopwords_de.txt**"] **GermanNormalizationFilterFactory** (**GermanLightStemFilterFactory** 　OR **GermanMinimalStemFilterFactory** 　OR SnowballPorterFilterFactory)　　　　　　　[language="**German**"]
Greek	StandardTokenizerFactory GreekLowerCaseFilterFactory StopFilterFactory　　　　　　　　　　　[words="lang/**stopwords_el.txt**"] **GreekStemFilterFactory**
Hindi	StandardTokenizerFactory LowerCaseFilterFactory **IndicNormalizationFilterFactory** **HindiNormalizationFilterFactory** StopFilterFactory　　　　　　　　　　　[words="lang/**stopwords_hi.txt**"] **HindiStemFilterFactory**
Hungarian	StandardTokenizerFactory LowerCaseFilterFactory StopFilterFactory　　　　　　　　　　　[words="lang/**stopwords_hu.txt**"] (**HungarianLightStemFilterFactory** 　OR SnowballPorterFilterFactory)　　　　　　[language="**Hungarian**"]

Language	Example analyzer chain
Indonesian	StandardTokenizerFactory LowerCaseFilterFactory StopFilterFactory [words="lang/**stopwords_id.txt**"] **IndonesianStemFilterFactory**
Irish	StandardTokenizerFactory ElisionFilterFactory [articles="lang/**contractions_ga.txt**"] StopFilterFactory [words="lang/**hyphenations_ga.txt**"] **IrishLowerCaseFilterFactory** StopFilterFactory [words="lang/**stopwords_ga.txt**"] SnowballPorterFilterFactory [language="**Irish**"]
Italian	StandardTokenizerFactory ElisionFilterFactory [articles="lang/**contractions_it.txt**"] LowerCaseFilterFactory StopFilterFactory [words="lang/**stopwords_it.txt**"] (**ItalianLightStemFilterFactory** OR SnowballPorterFilterFactory) [language="**Italian**"]
Japanese	**JapaneseTokenizerFactory** [userDictionary="lang/**userdict_ja.txt**"] **JapaneseBaseFormFilterFactory** **JapanesePartOfSpeechStopFilterFactory** [tags="lang/**stoptags_ja.txt**"] **CJKWidthFilterFactory** StopFilterFactory [words="lang/**stopwords_ja.txt**"] **JapaneseKatakanaStemFilterFactory** LowerCaseFilterFactory
Latvian	StandardTokenizerFactory LowerCaseFilterFactory StopFilterFactory [words="lang/**stopwords_lv.txt**"] **LatvianStemFilterFactory**

Norwegian	StandardTokenizerFactory
	LowerCaseFilterFactory
	StopFilterFactory [words="lang/**stopwords_no.txt**"]
	(**NorwegianLightStemFilterFactory**
	   OR
	NorwegianMinimalStemFilterFactory
	   OR
	SnowballPorterFilterFactory) [language="**Norwegian**"]

Persian	**PersianCharFilterFactory** StandardTokenizerFactory LowerCaseFilterFactory **ArabicNormalizationFilterFactory** **PersianNormalizationFilterFactory** StopFilterFactory [words="lang/**stopwords_fa.txt**"]

Language	Example analyzer chain

Portuguese	StandardTokenizerFactory
	LowerCaseFilterFactory
	StopFilterFactory [words="lang/**stopwords_pt.txt**"]
	(**PortugueseLightStemFilterFactory**
	  OR
	PortugueseMinimalStemFilterFactory
	  OR
	PortugueseStemFilterFactory
	  OR
	SnowballPorterFilterFactory) [language="**Portuguese**"]

Romanian	StandardTokenizerFactory LowerCaseFilterFactory StopFilterFactory [words="lang/**stopwords_ro.txt**"] SnowballPorterFilterFactory [language="**Romanian**"]
Russian	StandardTokenizerFactory LowerCaseFilterFactory StopFilterFactory [words="lang/**stopwords_ru.txt**"] (**RussianLightStemFilterFactory** OR SnowballPorterFilterFactory) [language="**Russian**"]
Spanish	StandardTokenizerFactory LowerCaseFilterFactory StopFilterFactory [words="lang/**stopwords_es.txt**"] (**SpanishLightStemFilterFactory** OR SnowballPorterFilterFactory) [language="**Spanish**"]
Swedish	StandardTokenizerFactory LowerCaseFilterFactory StopFilterFactory [words="lang/**stopwords_sv.txt**"] (**SwedishLightStemFilterFactory** OR SnowballPorterFilterFactory) [language="**Swedish**"]
Thai	StandardTokenizerFactory LowerCaseFilterFactory **ThaiWordFilterFactory** StopFilterFactory [words="lang/**stopwords_th.txt**"]
Turkish	StandardTokenizerFactory **TurkishLowerCaseFilterFactory** StopFilterFactory [words="lang/**stopwords_tr.txt**"] SnowballPorterFilterFactory [language="**Turkish**"]

appendix C
Useful data import
configurations

As discussed in chapter 12, the Data Import Handler provides the ability for Solr to pull in datasets from many kinds of external sources. In chapter 10, we used the DIH to transform Wikipedia pages from a partial Wikipedia data dump file into Solr documents and index them. This appendix will provide more detail into how the DIH was configured to enable this import, and we'll demonstrate how to import both the full Wikipedia dataset and also another large dataset useful for experimentation: a data dump from Stack Exchange.

C.1 Indexing Wikipedia

In chapter 12, we imported a subset of articles from Wikipedia into a preconfigured Solr core named `solrpedia`. In order to enable the DIH, several steps were necessary.

First, we had to obtain a copy of a Wikipedia dataset. In chapter 10, we used a small subset of Wikipedia articles (13,000) we pulled from Wikipedia's main enwiki dataset and included with this book's code. If you want to experiment with the full dataset, you can obtain the most recent data dump of any Wikipedia dataset from http://dumps.wikimedia.org/. Note that a downloaded data dump containing only the most recent version of each article can take up more than 45 GB of disk space when uncompressed, not to mention the originally downloaded compressed file (over 10 GB) and any Solr indexes you create based upon that data. For the purposes of this appendix, feel free to use the sample dataset in *$SOLR_IN_ACTION/example-docs/ch10/documents/solrpedia.xml*.

Once you have your dataset available, make three important configuration changes to use the DIH utility. First, in *solrconfig.xml*, add the `<lib>` directive to load the JAR files for the DIH and its dependencies.

```
<lib dir="../../../contrib/dataimporthandler/lib" regex=".*\.jar" />
<lib dir="../../../dist/" regex="solr-dataimporthandler-.*\.jar" />
```

Second, you also need to define the /dataimport request handler as in *solrconfig.xml*:

```
<requestHandler name="/dataimport"
      class="org.apache.solr.handler.dataimport.DataImportHandler">
   <lst name="defaults">
     <str name="config">data-config.xml</str>
   </lst>
</requestHandler>
```

Notice that the DataImportHandler class pulls its configuration from the *data-config.xml* file. Setting up the *data-config.xml* is the third and final configuration change we need to make to make use of the DIH. The next listing shows the configuration elements in the *data-config.xml* file needed to import Wikipedia XML articles.

Listing C.1   Data import configuration to import Wikipedia articles

```
<dataConfig>
  <dataSource type="FileDataSource" encoding="UTF-8" />     ◁——┐ Pull data from
  <document>                                                      a local file.
    <entity name="page"                                    ◁—— Each page element will be
            processor="XPathEntityProcessor"                    a document in the index.
            stream="true"
            forEach="/mediawiki/page/"                      ┌── Local file from which
            url="solrpedia.xml"                            ◁—┘ to load XML data.
            transformer="RegexTransformer,DateFormatTransformer">
      <field column="id"        xpath="/mediawiki/page/id"/>
      <field column="title"     xpath="/mediawiki/page/title"/>
      <field column="revision"  xpath="/mediawiki/page/revision/id"/>
      <field column="user"
             xpath="/mediawiki/page/revision/contributor/username"/>
      <field column="userId"
             xpath="/mediawiki/page/revision/contributor/id"/>
      <field column="text"      xpath="/mediawiki/page/revision/text"/>
      <field column="timestamp"
             xpath="/mediawiki/page/revision/timestamp"
             dateTimeFormat="yyyy-MM-dd'T'hh:mm:ss'Z'"/>
      <field column="$skipDoc"  regex="^#REDIRECT .*"       ◁──┐ Documents
             replaceWith="true" sourceColName="text"/>           matching the
    </entity>                                                     specified regex
  </document>                                                     are skipped.
</dataConfig>
```

(Field mappings for indexed documents.)

In a nutshell, the configuration in listing C.1 sets up the DIH to parse <page> elements from the *solrpedia.xml* file to create documents in our index. Consequently, you need to copy the *$SOLR_IN_ACTION/example-docs/ch10/documents/solrpedia.xml* file to *$SOLR_INSTALL/example/* so that the DIH can locate the XML file to import. You can open the *solrpedia.xml* file in any text editor if you're curious what the data looks like before it's imported. In chapter 10, we added the solrpedia core to your Solr instance at runtime, making use of the Core Admin page's ability to create Solr cores at runtime from preconfigured configuration files on disk. If your Solr instance is

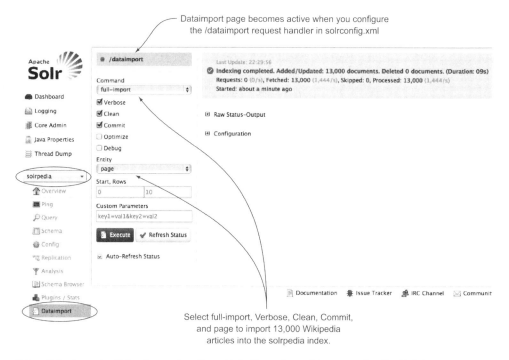

Dataimport page becomes active when you configure the /dataimport request handler in solrconfig.xml

Select full-import, Verbose, Clean, Commit, and page to import 13,000 Wikipedia articles into the solrpedia index.

Figure C.1   Import articles from *solrpedia.xml* into the `solrpedia` core using the Dataimport page.

already running, you can also restart Solr once your configuration files are in place with your DIH settings.

With your Solr core running and configured to use the Data Import Handler, let's run the data import process to build our index. Reload the administration colsole and select the Dataimport page under the `solrpedia` core. Fill out the form and click Execute as shown in figure C.1.

You have several available options, including whether to do a full import or incremental import, whether to clean out previous documents before indexing, and whether to commit or optimize when finished. There is also an Auto-Refresh Status option that will cause the page to continuously update as the import is occurring to keep you informed of the current status of the import. If all goes well, you should see the number of documents being added continually climb until the entire contents of your Wikipedia data dump are fully indexed within your Solr core.

C.2   *Indexing Stack Exchange*

In addition to Wikipedia articles, another publicly available body of content that can be a useful sample dataset is the information available in Stack Exchange data dumps. While Wikipedia provides rich, descriptive articles focussed (mostly) on important entities, Stack Exchange information is in the form of questions and answers focused upon many different categories of topics. To create a Stack Exchange Solr index, first download one of the monthly data dumps (using a torrent client) available from http://www.clearbits.net/creators/146-stack-exchange-data-dump.

Once you've downloaded a data dump, you will see many compressed files, each corresponding to different subcommunities within the Stack Exchange ecosystem. For example, there are question-and-answer communities specifically devoted to sci-fi, gaming, cooking, and even SharePoint and WordPress, among many other topics. As with the Wikipedia data dumps, the Stack Exchange data dumps require a lot of disk space. The initial compressed download can take nearly 20 GB of disk space before the internal files are decompressed, and the largest community archive (the main Stack Exchange community) can take over 50 GB of space to further decompress. You'll want to make sure you have plenty of space on your server before starting the download process.

Once your download is complete, you will need to decompress one of the *.7z* files in order to access the content for that community, after which you will find several files:

- *Badges.xml*—Badges received by users for participation in the community
- *Comments.xml*—Comments on posts
- *Posts.xml*—Questions and answers to questions (posts)
- *PostHistory.xml*—The edit history of posts
- *Users.xml*—General information about users in the community
- *Votes.xml*—Information about votes on posts

The *Posts.xml* file contains all of the questions and answers for each community and is therefore the most useful content for setting up a general text search index. We'll skip the other XML files, but you should be able to follow the same template we'll use for the *Posts.xml* file to easily generate your own *data-config.xml* for the other Stack Exchange XML files.

The first few steps to importing the posts are exactly the same as setting up a Solr core to index Wikipedia documents. First, import the Data Import Handler JAR files; second, add a request handler (/dataimport) to enable the DIH in your *solrconfig.xml*. See section C.1 for instructions on how to do this.

Once your /dataimport request handler is configured, create your *data-config.xml* file, which can be used to parse Stack Exchange posts format. This listing demonstrates a sample *data-config.xml* file that can import a *Posts.xml* file.

Listing C.2 Data import configuration to import Stack Exchange posts

```
<dataConfig>
    <dataSource type="FileDataSource" encoding="UTF-8" />
    <document>
        <entity name="post"
            processor="XPathEntityProcessor"
            stream="true"
            forEach="/posts/row/"
            url="solrexchange.xml"
            transformer="RegexTransformer,
                    DateFormatTransformer,HTMLStripTransformer">
```

```
            <field column="id" xpath="/posts/row/@Id" />
            <field column="postTypeId" xpath="/posts/row/@PostTypeId" />
            <field column="acceptedAnswerId"
                xpath="/posts/row/@AcceptedAnswerId" />
            <field column="creationDate" xpath="/posts/row/@CreationDate"
                dateTimeFormat="yyyy-MM-dd'T'hh:mm:ss.SSS" />
            <field column="postScore" xpath="/posts/row/@Score" />
            <field column="viewCount" xpath="/posts/row/@ViewCount" />
            <field column="body" xpath="/posts/row/@Body"
                stripHTML="true" />
            <field column="ownerUserId" xpath="/posts/row/@OwnerUserId" />
            <field column="lastEditorUserId"
                xpath="/posts/row/@LastEditorUserId" />
            <field column="lastEditorDisplayName"
                xpath="/posts/row/@LastEditorDisplayName" />
            <field column="lastActivityDate"
                xpath="/posts/row/@LastActivityDate"
                dateTimeFormat="yyyy-MM-dd'T'hh:mm:ss.SSS" />
            <field column="title"  xpath="/posts/row/@Title" />
            <field column="trimmedTags" xpath="/posts/row/@Tags"
                regex="&lt;(.*)&gt;" />
            <field column="tags" sourceColName="trimmedTags"
                splitBy="&gt;&lt;" />
            <field column="answerCount" xpath="/posts/row/@AnswerCount" />
            <field column="commentCount"
                xpath="/posts/row/@CommentCount" />
            <field column="favoriteCount"
                xpath="/posts/row/@FavoriteCount" />
            <field column="communityOwnedDate"
                xpath="/posts/row/@CommunityOwnedDate"
                dateTimeFormat="yyyy-MM-dd'T'hh:mm:ss.SSS" />
        </entity>
    </document>
</dataConfig>
```

You must also make sure that you have fields defined in your *schema.xml* that correspond to the column attribute for each field in the *data-config.xml*. As with the `solrpedia` core in chapter 10, we've created a preconfigured Solr core (called `solrexchange`) for you to test out importing Stack Exchange documents. The necessary *schema.xml* field configurations are located inside this core's *conf/* folder. In order to set up this example solrexchange core, execute the following commands:

```
cd $SOLR_IN_ACTION/example-docs/appendixC
cp -r cores/ $SOLR_INSTALL/example/solr/
cp documents/solrexchange.xml $SOLR_INSTALL/example/
cd $SOLR_INSTALL/example/
java -jar start.jar
```

The *$SOLR_IN_ACTION/example-docs/appendixC/documents/solrexchange.xml* file contains a subset of the *Posts.xml* file from the main Stack Exchange website. Specifically, it contains only posts about Solr or related technologies. We've included this *solrexchange.xml* file with the book's source code to allow you to test this configuration without having to download the entire Stack Exchange data dump. If you decide to download a full Stack Exchange data dump, replace *solrexchange.xml* with the *Post.xml* file that you can extract from one of the community *.7z files.

With Solr running, you can now navigate to the Data Import page in Solr Admin (as shown in figure C.1) and start the import of your Stack Exchange documents as you would have done previously for the Wikipedia documents.

The DIH can import much more than XML documents; it can also reach out to websites, databases, and other external data sources. For more information about the DIH's capabilities, please refer to chapter 12.

index